Lecture Notes in Computer Science 2423

Edited by G. Goos, J. Hartmanis, and J. van Leeuwen

T0140083

Lecture Notes in Computer Science 2423

Springer
Berlin
Heidelberg
New York
Barcelona
Hong Kong
London
Milan
Paris
Tokyo

Daniel Lopresti   Jianying Hu
Ramanujan Kashi (Eds.)

Document
Analysis Systems V

5th International Workshop, DAS 2002
Princeton, NJ, USA, August 19-21, 2002
Proceedings

 Springer

Series Editors

Gerhard Goos, Karlsruhe University, Germany
Juris Hartmanis, Cornell University, NY, USA
Jan van Leeuwen, Utrecht University, The Netherlands

Volume Editors

Daniel Lopresti
Bell Labs, Lucent Technologies
600 Mountain Avenue, Murray Hill, NJ 07974, USA
E-mail: dpl@research.bell-labs.com
Jianying Hu
Ramanujan Kashi
Avaya Labs Research
233 Mount Airy Road, Basking Ridge, NJ 07920, USA
E-mail:{jianhu/ramanuja}@research.avayalabs.com

Cataloging-in-Publication Data applied for

Die Deutsche Bibliothek - CIP-Einheitsaufnahme

Document analysis systems V : 5th international workshop ; proceedings /
DAS 2002, Princeton, NJ, USA, August 19 - 21, 2002. Daniel Lopresti ... (ed.).
[IAPR]. - Berlin ; Heidelberg ; New York ; Barcelona ; Hong Kong ; London ;
Milan ; Paris ; Tokyo : Springer, 2002
     (Lecture notes in computer science ; Vol. 2423)
     ISBN 3-540-44068-2

CR Subject Classification (1998): I.5, H.3, I.4, I.7, J.1, J.2

ISSN 0302-9743
ISBN 3-540-44068-2 Springer-Verlag Berlin Heidelberg New York

Springer-Verlag Berlin Heidelberg New York
a member of BertelsmannSpringer Science+Business Media GmbH

http://www.springer.de

© Springer-Verlag Berlin Heidelberg 2002
Printed in Germany

Typesetting: Camera-ready by author, data conversion by PTP-Berlin, Stefan Sossna e. K.
Printed on acid-free paper   SPIN 10873837   06/3142   5 4 3 2 1 0

Preface

This volume contains papers selected for presentation at the *5th IAPR Workshop on Document Analysis Systems (DAS 2002)* in Princeton, NJ on August 19–21, 2002. As such, it represents the contributions of an international community of academic, industrial, and government researchers and reflects the state of the art in such diverse domains as character recognition and classifier design, text segmentation, table understanding, page layout analysis, and document engineering, indexing, and retrieval, along with emerging application areas including the World-Wide Web, where algorithms developed for "traditional" paper documents take their place alongside completely new techniques.

DAS 2002 continues in the fine tradition of past workshops held in Kaiserslautern, Germany (1994), Malvern, PA (1996), Nagano, Japan (1998), and Rio de Janeiro, Brazil (2000). DAS is distinguished from other gatherings of document analysis researchers by its emphasis on systems. To extract useful information from a noisy page image is a complex process requiring multiple stages, each of which is a research topic in its own right. The integration of such components introduces additional complications. Hence, building and testing document analysis systems is a challenging task for which no definitive solution yet exists. You will find that the papers in this volume carry with them a "flavor" that is unique to DAS.

The 44 regular and 14 short papers that appear herein derive from 15 different countries, highlighting the international make-up of our discipline. Regular papers were subjected to rigorous review by members of the Program Committee as well as other noted researchers. Short papers were chosen by the Co-Chairs for their relevance to the themes of the workshop.

We would like to thank the reviewers for their diligence, the members of the Program Committee and past DAS chairs for their support, and Larry Spitz, in particular, for his encouragement. We also wish to acknowledge the generous financial assistance of Avaya Labs, as well as that of Yasuaki Nakano, Co-Chair of DAS 1998. Lastly, we offer our gratitude to Princeton University for making its first-rate facilities available to DAS 2002.

June 2002   Daniel Lopresti
                                                                             Jianying Hu
                                                                             Ramanujan Kashi

Organization

Workshop Co-chairs

Daniel Lopresti   Bell Labs, Lucent Technologies, USA
Jianying Hu   Avaya Labs Research, USA
Ramanujan Kashi   Avaya Labs Research, USA

Program Committee

Apostolos Antonacopoulos	Univ. of Liverpool, UK
Henry Baird	Palo Alto Research Center, USA
Mohamed Cheriet	ETS, Canada
Andreas Dengel	DFKI, Germany
David Doermann	Univ. of Maryland, USA
Dov Dori	Technion, Israel and MIT, USA
Andrew Downton	Univ. of Essex, UK
Floriana Esposito	Univ. of Bari, Italy
Hiromichi Fujisawa	Hitachi CRL, Japan
Robert M. Haralick	City Univ. of New York, USA
Tin Kam Ho	Bell Labs, Lucent Technologies, USA
Jonathan Hull	Ricoh CRC, USA
Matthew Hurst	WhizBang! Labs, USA
Sebastiano Impedovo	Univ. of Bari, Italy
Rolf Ingold	Univ. of Fribourg, Switzerland
Junichi Kanai	Panasonic Technologies, USA
Seong-Whan Lee	Korea Univ., Korea
Nabeel Murshed	Univ. of Parana, Brazil
Masaki Nakagawa	Tokyo Univ. of Agri. and Tech., Japan
Lambert Schomaker	Rijksuniversiteit Groningen, The Netherlands
Larry Spitz	Document Recognition Technologies, USA
Sargur Srihari	State Univ. of New York at Buffalo, USA
George Thoma	National Library of Medicine, USA
Karl Tombre	LORIA-INPL, France
Luc Vincent	LizardTech, USA

Additional Referees

Stephan Baumann

Yeongwoo Choi

Markus Ebbecke

Stefano Ferilli

Katherine Guo

Hee-Jong Kang

Thomas Kieninger

Bertin Klein

Stefan Klink

Wenyin Liu

Maria Grazia Lucchese

Matthew Ma

Donato Malerba

Raffaele Modugno

Pasquale Lops

Anna Salzo

Lucia Sarcinella

Sponsoring Institution

Avaya Inc., Basking Ridge, NJ, USA

Table of Contents

OCR Features and Systems

Handwriting Recognition

Classifiers and Leaning

Layout Analysis

Tables and Forms

Text Extraction

Indexing and Retrieval

Document Engineering

New Applications

Relating Statistical Image Differences and Degradation Features

Elisa Barney Smith[1] and Xiaohui Qiu[2]

[1] Boise State University, Boise, Idaho 83725, USA,
EBarneySmith@boisestate.edu,
http://coen.boisestate.edu/EBarneySmith
[2] Nanjing University of Post and Telecommunication, China

Abstract. Document images are degraded through bilevel processes such as scanning, printing, and photocopying. The resulting image degradations can be categorized based either on observable degradation features or on degradation model parameters. The degradation features can be related mathematically to model parameters. In this paper we statistically compare pairs of populations of degraded character images created with different model parameters. The changes in the probability that the characters are from different populations when the model parameters vary correlate with the relationship between observable degradation features and the model parameters. The paper also shows which features have the largest impact on the image.

1 Introduction

Document images can be degraded through processes such as scanning, printing and photocopying. This paper discusses bilevel degradations in the context of the scanning process. For the bilevel processes, two observable image degradations were described in [3]–[7]. These degradations are the amount an edge is displaced from its original location and the amount of erosion in a black or white corner. The variables that cause these image degradations can be related to the functional form of the degradation model: the PSF, the associated PSF width, and the binarization threshold.

From a calibrated model, one can predict how a document image will look after being subjected to the appropriate printing and scanning processes and, therefore, predict system performance. Large training sets of synthetic characters can be created using the model when the model parameters are matched to the source document. This can increase recognition accuracy. Models of the degradation process, along with estimates of the parameters for these models, can be combined to make a decision on whether a given document should be entered by hand or sent to an OCR routine [8,13,14]. A model will allow researchers to conduct controlled experiments to improve OCR and DIA performance. Knowledge of the system model parameters can also be used to determine which documents originated from the same source and, when the model includes multiple

D. Lopresti, J. Hu, and R. Kashi (Eds.): DAS 2002, LNCS 2423, pp. 1–12, 2002.
© Springer-Verlag Berlin Heidelberg 2002

printing/scanning steps, which document was the original and which was a later generation copy.

The degradation model used for this research is convolution followed by thresholding [1]. The two most significant parameters affecting degradations of bilevel images are the point spread function (PSF) width and the binarization threshold [9]. Each pair of these values will affect an image differently. However, several combinations of these parameters will affect images in a similar fashion. The PSF accounts for the blurring caused by the optics of the scanner. Its functional form is not constrained, but needs to be specified. A form that is circularly symmetric is usually chosen so its width is determined by one parameter. The size is in units of pixels, which allows the model to be used for scanning at any optical resolution. The threshold converts the image to a bilevel image. This is often done in software, and a global threshold is assumed. The units for the threshold are absorptance. The variations in the resulting bilevel bitmaps come largely from phase effects [12].

Several methods have been proposed to calibrate this model from bilevel images [2,4,6,7]. The resulting parameter estimates will never be error-free. However, not all errors are equally bad. Some will produce characters that have similar appearances and that are more likely to have the same response from an OCR system. This type of estimation error can be treated differently than estimation errors that result in a larger change in the character appearance. This paper explores the amount that characters made with different model parameters will differ as the true model parameters change.

Kanungo et al. [10] proposed a method of validating degradation models. This was achieved through a nonparametric two-sample permutation test. It decided whether two images are close enough to each other to have originated from the same source, having passed through the same sequence of systems. The application he proposed was to decide whether a model of a character degradation produced characters that were "close" to a set of "real" characters generated by physical printing and scanning. This testing could validate the degradation model and the choice of model parameters. The underlying statistical method is not restricted to comparing real and synthetic characters. Consequently, the two images could also be two real images, or two synthetic images. This statistical testing procedure can also be used to determine which parameters of the degradation model created the sample of characters. Another statistical device, the power function, was used to choose between algorithm variables.

Kanungo et al. demonstrated their method using a bit flipping and morphological degradation model. Their approach of statistically comparing character populations is applied in this paper to the convolution and thresholding degradation model shown in Figure 1. The parameters in this model are the point spread function (PSF) width, w, and the binarization threshold, Θ. Both populations of character images were synthetically generated to see by how much the characters created with different model parameters will vary over the regions of the parameter space.

This paper starts by describing two image degradations and how they relate quantitatively to the degradation model parameters. It then describes the experiment conducted using Kanungo's non-parametric permutation test to mathematically illustrate the size of the difference between two sets of degraded characters created using our model with different parameters. We then describe how the difference between characters relates to the degradations.

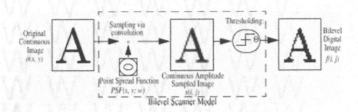

Fig. 1. Scanner model used to determine the value of the pixel (i, j) centered on each sensor element.

2   Image Degradations

Each model parameter set will produce a different character image. Examples of the characters that are produced for 600 dpi 12-point sans-serif font 'W' over a range of PSF widths and binarization thresholds are shown in Figure 2. Some of the degradations that are introduced are common to multiple characters, such as the final thickness of the character strokes, but each character is slightly different. Two primary image degradations associated with bilevel processes were defined in [4,5,6]. These are the edge displacement and the erosion of a black or white corner. All these degradations are functions of the degradation model parameters, w and Θ.

During scanning, the profile of an edge changes from a step to an edge spread function, ESF, through convolution with the PSF. This is then thresholded to reform a step edge, Figure 3. The amount an edge was displaced after scanning, δ_c, was shown in [3,4] to be related to w and Θ by

$$\delta_c = -w ESF^{-1}(\Theta). \tag{1}$$

The edge spread determines the change in a stroke width after scanning. An infinite number of (w, Θ) values could produce any one δ_c value. Equation (1) holds when edges are considered in isolation, for example when the edges are separated by a distance greater than the support of the PSF. Figure 4 shows how the values of (w, Θ) vary for 5 different constant δ_c values for each of four PSF shapes. A positive threshold value will produce a negative edge displacement. The curves for δ_c and $-\delta_c$ are symmetric around the $\Theta=1/2$ line. If $\Theta=1/2$, then $\delta_c=0$ for all values of w.

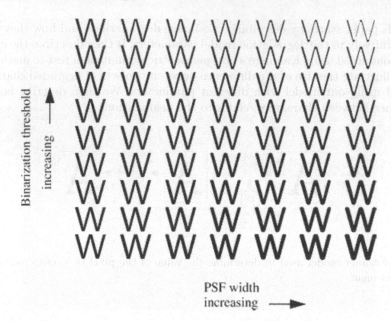

Fig. 2. Characters after blurring and thresholding over a range of PSF widths, w, and binarization thresholds, Θ. A broad range of character appearances can be seen, but some characters have general similarities.

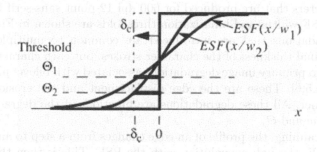

Fig. 3. Edge after blurring with a generic PSF of two widths, w. Two thresholds that produce the same edge shift δ_c are shown.

The other pair of bilevel image degradations are the amount of erosion seen in a black or a white corner after scanning [4,6]. This degradation is caused by the interaction of the two edges, but also includes the displacement of the individual edges. The erosion of a corner can occur in any of the three forms shown in Figure 5. Point p_0 is the apex of the original corner. Point p_2 is the point along the angle bisector of the new rounded corner where the blurred corner equals the threshold value. Point p_1 is the point where the new corner edges would intersect if extrapolated. The distance

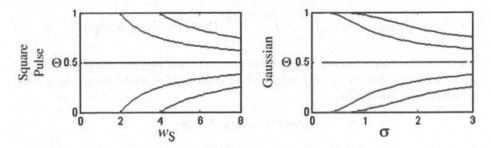

Fig. 4. Contours showing constant edge spread of δ_c =[-2 -1 0 1 2] (from top to bottom) for two PSF functions.

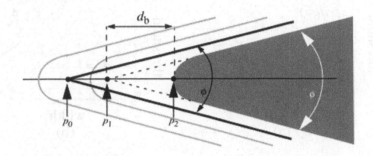

Fig. 5. The blurred corner (grey area and lines) may be displaced from the original corner position (black line) in three different ways. The visible erosion, d_b, is calculated the same for all three.

$$d_b = \overline{p_1p_2} \tag{2}$$

is not the erosion from the original corner location, but it does represent the degradation actually seen on the corner, and this quantity can be measured from bilevel document images. The corner erosion distance, d_b, depends on the threshold, the PSF width, and the functional form similar to the edge displacement above.

The corner erosion distance is a combination of the distance from the original corner to the extrapolated corner, $\overline{p_1p_0}$, which is based on the edge spread δ_c, and the distance along the angle bisector from the original corner to where the amplitude of the blurred corner equals the threshold, $\overline{p_1p_2}$. Thus

$$d_b = \overline{p_1p_2} = \overline{p_1p_0} + \overline{p_0p_2} \tag{3}$$
$$= \frac{-wESF^{-1}(\Theta)}{sin(\phi/2)} + f_b^{-1}(\Theta; w, \phi)$$

where

$$f_b(d_{ob}; w, \phi) = \int_{x=0}^{x=\infty} \int_{y=-x\tan\frac{\phi}{2}}^{y=x\tan\frac{\phi}{2}} PSF(x - d_{ob}, y; w) dy dx. \tag{4}$$

As with edge displacement, a given amount of corner erosion can also occur for an infinite number of (w, Θ) values. The erosion of a white corner is defined similarly and results in

$$d_w(w, \Theta) = d_b(w, 1 - \Theta). \tag{5}$$

Samples of constant d_b and d_w are shown in Figure 6.

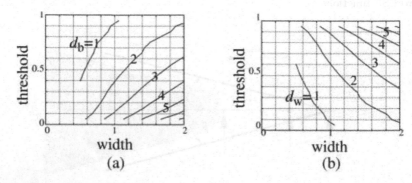

Fig. 6. Observable erosion contours for constant erosion on (a) a black corner, d_b, and (b) on a white corner, d_w. Loci are for a Gaussian PSF and $\phi = \pi/4$.

3   Experiment

Experiments were run to statistically compare characters in pairs of populations each made with different parameters based on the method proposed by Kanungo et al. [10]. In the experiments presented in this paper, the two populations, X and Y, are both composed of synthetically generated characters created by the blurring and thresholding model with varying phase offsets [12]. The characters in population X were created with PSF width and binarization threshold parameters (w_0, Θ_0), and those in population Y with (w_1, Θ_1). The null hypothesis that these sets of characters have been drawn from populations with a common set of parameters was compared to the alternate hypothesis that they have been drawn from populations with different parameters:

$$H_N : (w_0, \Theta_0) = (w_1, \Theta_1) \tag{6}$$

$$H_A : (w_0, \Theta_0) \neq (w_1, \Theta_1). \tag{7}$$

Each experiment consisted of the following steps:

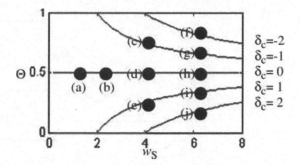

Fig. 7. Set of (w_0, Θ_0) values used as null hypotheses in the sequence of experiments.

1. Create a set of synthesized characters $X = \{x_1, x_2, ..., x_{2M}\}$ with the model parameters of $\{w_0, \Theta_0, PSF\}$.
2. Using the permutation test method, calculate the null distribution of the population and choose a threshold, d_0, to make the misdetection rate or significance level, ε, about 5%.
3. Create a set of synthesized degraded characters $Y = \{y_1, y_2, ..., y_{2M}\}$ of the same character class, using parameters $\{w_1, \Theta_1, PSF\}$.
4. Randomly permute the sets X and Y and select M characters from each.
5. Compute the distance D_k between the sets of $\{x_{k1}, x_{k2}, ...x_{kM}\}$ and $\{y_{kM+1}, y_{kM+2}, ..., y_{k2M}\}$.
6. Repeat steps (4) and (5) K times and get K distances $D_1, D_2, ..., D_K$.
7. Compute the probability of $P\{D_k > d_0\} = \#\{k|D_k \geq d_0\}/K$.

The Hamming distance was used to calculate the distance between individual characters, and the distance between sets of characters was calculated using the truncated mean nearest-neighbor distance. K was set to 1000. Steps (3)-(7) were repeated for several parameter sets (w_1, Θ_1) in the vicinity of (w_0, Θ_0) to generate a two-dimensional power function. This will show how likely it is that a change in system parameters will cause the characters to differ.

Experiments were conducted around several initial parameter combinations (w_0, Θ_0) to see how the location in the (w, Θ) space affects the results. The combinations of initial points (w_0, Θ_0) that were used are shown in Figure 7. These points were chosen to give a range of edge displacements $\delta_c = \{-2, -1, 0, 1, 2\}$ for the initial characters and to fill the (w, Θ) space. The initial character image used was a 600-dpi 12-point sans-serif 'W'. The PSF form was a square pillbox with a base width w_s.

The two-dimensional power functions for several (w_0, Θ_0) are shown as contour images in Figure 8. These contours show the place where the probability of rejecting the null hypothesis is constant over a range of alternate parameters (w_1, Θ_1). The probability of rejecting the null hypothesis is less than 0.1 in the shaded region. It is 1 in the area outside of the contour lines. The blockiness in

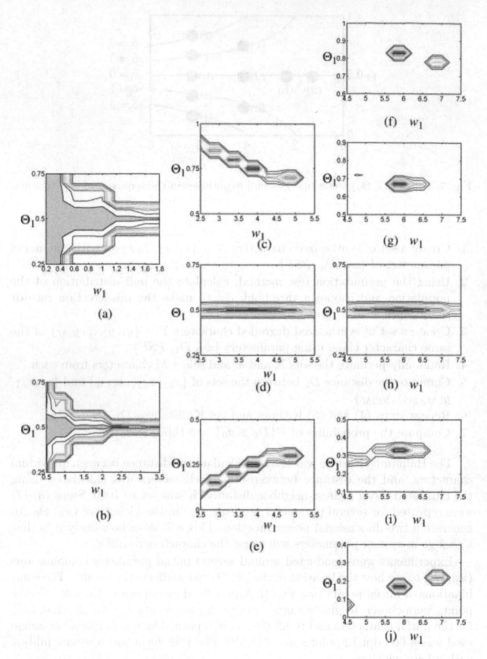

Fig. 8. Probability of rejecting null hypotheses with the letter 'W' (a) $(w_0, \Theta_0) = (1.0, 0.5)$, (b) $(2.0, 0.5)$ (c) $(4.0, 0.75)$, (d) $(4.0, 0.5)$, (e) $(4.0, 0.25)$, (f) $(6.0, 0.83)$, (g) $(6.0, 0.67)$, (h) $(6.0, 0.5)$, (i) $(6.0, 0.33)$, (j) $(6.0, 0.17)$. The shaded region has a probability of less than 0.1.

the contour shapes is caused by the quantization in the range of (w_1, Θ_1) values used in the experiments and the Matlab interpretation of the contour.

The constant reject probabilities have a shape similar to the constant edge spread contours shown in Figure 4. This is more easily seen in Figure 9, where the hypothesis reject probability contours have been superimposed on the δ_c contours. The edge spread degradation has the predominant effect on the appearance of a character visually [5] and, from these results, also statistically.

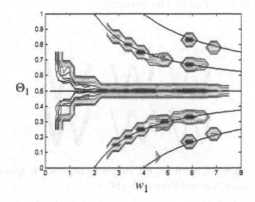

Fig. 9. Composite showing results from Figure 8 superimposed over constant δ_c lines.

To show the sensitivity of this procedure, consider the corresponding sets of characters in the right and left columns of Figure 10 which are created with parameters that are very close. These appear similar, however, the null hypothesis that the populations from which these characters came were generated with the same parameters was rejected with probability equal to 1. In [5] it was proposed that characters with a common δ_c value would appear most similar to humans, while other degradation features, such as d_b and d_w, change the character's appearance less. This similarity is now quantified through statistical testing.

(a)   (b)

Fig. 10. Synthetic characters created at two (w, Θ) combinations with varying phase offsets. (a) $(w, \Theta) = (0.4, 0.50)$, (b) $(w, \Theta) = (0.4, 0.55)$. The characters in the two sets look the same but are decided to be from different parameter sets with probability of 1.

Maintaining a constant δ_c increases the probability of the characters appearing similar, but they are only similar within a small range of (w, Θ) values. Figure 11 shows sample characters with pairs having a common δ_c. The first column shows $\delta_c < 0$, the middle $\delta_c = 0$, the right $\delta_c > 0$. For characters with a positive δ_c (low threshold), the characters have thicker strokes, whereas with negative δ_c, the characters have thinner strokes. The pairs of characters in Figure 11 look similar, but the differences can be easily seen because the model parameters used to create them are very different. The places where the characters with common δ_c differ is at the corners.

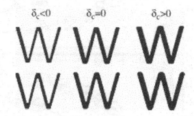

Fig. 11. Characters degraded with (w, Θ) values to produce negative, zero and positive δ_c values. Each character has a different (w, Θ) .

While the δ_c value has remained the same, the corner erosion and thus the character appearance is different. For $\delta_c > 0$, $(\Theta < 1/2)$ the d_b isolines are almost perpendicular to the δ_c isolines, and for $\delta_c < 0$ $(\Theta > 1/2)$ the d_w isolines are almost perpendicular to the δ_c isolines. When w and $|\Theta - 1/2|$ are large, a small change in (w, Θ) will produce a larger change in the d_b and d_w values (see Figure 6). This causes the size of the region of low probability of rejecting the null hypothesis in Figure 8f,g,i and j to be smaller than the corresponding regions in Figure 8c and e.

A similar set of experiments was run using a 12-point sans-serif 'O' over a subset of the cases used for the letter 'W'. This character has approximately the same stroke width for the whole character but contains no corners. The resulting power function contours are shown in Figure 12. When the plots are compared to the plots for the corresponding null hypothesis for the 'W' shown in Figure 8a,c,e,g,h and i, the appearance of the same general shape can be seen. What is different, particularly for $(w_0, \Theta_0) = (6, 0.67)$ and $(6, 0.33)$, is the probability of rejecting the null hypothesis being less than 1 extends for a larger range of values for the letter 'O'. This is due to the absence of corners. The degradation seen in the characters is only due to the edge spread for a large range of (w, Θ) values. With an absence of corners, no corner erosion is present. However, the edge spread was defined for edges that are isolated from each other, and when the PSF width is large enough, this premise is no longer valid [11]. The edges will interfere, and an effect similar to the corner erosion will occur degrading the character images. The corner erosion is a special case of two edges spreading with interference, where the overlap occurs at any PSF support width because the distance between the edges at the corners is zero.

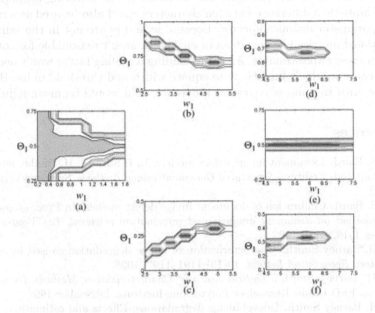

Fig. 12. Probability of rejecting null hypotheses with the letter 'O' (a) $(w_0, \Theta_0) = (1.0, 0.5)$, (b) $(4.0, 0.75)$, (c) $(4.0, 0.25)$, (d) $(6.0, 0.67)$, (e) $(6.0, 0.5)$, (f) $(6.0, 0.33)$. The shaded region has a probability less than 0.1.

4   Conclusion

A statistical test was conducted to compare the similarity between groups of characters synthetically generated with parameters (w, Θ) varying over the parameter space. The amount of variation in the characters correlated highly with the change in the edge spread degradation. This change can be quantified in terms of the degradation system model parameters. When estimating the degradation model parameters, errors along the δ_c isolines will not produce as large a difference in the characters generated with the model as would an error perpendicular to these isolines.

The effects of an estimation error will be less for characters with fewer corners. Characters with many corners, thin strokes, or variable width strokes will remain similar over a smaller range of (w, Θ) values. This can be used to decide how much of an effect an error in estimating the system parameters will have when using those parameters to generate synthetic characters for choosing an OCR structure, training OCR systems, or predicting OCR performance. This can also be used to decide how to distribute model parameters if we want to experiment with characters with small differences, or larger differences that are evenly distributed. These experiments have also given more insight on how the shape of a character will influence the variation in the resulting bitmap.

The statistical difference between characters could also be used as a metric of model parameter estimation error. Because w and Θ are not in the same units, conventional metrics like euclidean or city block aren't reasonable for combining errors in these two estimates. Also, just adding a scaling factor won't necessarily help because we don't know how to equate width and threshold units. But if we measure error in units of character difference, that would be meaningful.

References

1. H. S. Baird. Document image defect models. In H.S.Baird, H. Bunke, and K. Yamamoto(eds), editors, *Structured Document Image Analysis*. Springer-Verlag, June 1992.
2. H. S. Baird. Calibration of document image defect models. In *Proc. of 2nd annual symposium on document analysis and information retrieval, Las Vegas, Nevada*, pages 1–16, April 1993.
3. E. H. Barney Smith. Characterization of image degradation caused by scanning. *Pattern Recognition Letters*, 19(13):1191–1197, 1998.
4. E. H. Barney Smith. *Optical Scanner Characterization Methods Using Bilevel Scans*. PhD thesis, Rensselaer Polytechnic Institute, December 1998.
5. E. H. Barney Smith. Bilevel image degradations: Effects and estimation. In *Proc. 2001 Symposium on Document Image Understanding Technology*, pages 49–55, Columbia, MD, 2001.
6. E. H. Barney Smith. Estimating scanning characteristics from corners in bilevel images. In *Proc. SPIE Document Recognition and Retrieval VIII*, volume 4307, pages 176–183, San Jose, CA, 2001.
7. E. H. Barney Smith. Scanner parameter estimation using bilevel scans of star charts. In *Proc. International Conference on Document Analysis and Recognition 2001*, pages 1164–1168, Seattle, WA, 2001.
8. L. R. Blando, J. Kanai, and T. A. Nartker. Prediction of OCR accuracy using simple features. In *Proc. of the Third International Conference on Document Analysis and Recognition*, pages 319–322, Montreal, Quebec, Canada, 1995.
9. T. K. Ho and H. S. Baird. Large-scale simulation studies in image pattern recognition. *IEEE PAMI*, 19(10):1067–1079, 1997.
10. T. Kanungo, R. M. Haralick, H. S. Baird, and D. M. Werner Stuezle. A statistical, nonparametric methodology for document degradation model validation. *IEEE PAMI*, 22(11):1209–1223, 2000.
11. T. Pavlidis, M. Chen, and E. Joseph. Sampling and quantization of bilevel signals. *Pattern Recognition Letters*, 14:559–562, 1993.
12. P. Sarkar, G. Nagy, J. Zhou, and D. Lopresti. Spatial sampling of printed patterns. *IEEE PAMI*, 20(3):344–351, 1998.
13. T. Sziriáinyi and Á. Böröczki. Overall picture degradation error for scanned images and the efficiency of character recognition. *Optical Engineering*, 30(12):1878–1884, 1991.
14. W. R. Throssell and P. R. Fryer. The measurement of print quality for optical character recognition systems. *Pattern Recognition*, 6:141–147, 1974.

Script Identification in Printed Bilingual Documents

D. Dhanya and A.G. Ramakrishnan

Department of Electrical Engineering,
Indian Institute of Science,
Bangalore 560 012, India
ramkiag@ee.iisc.ernet.in

Abstract. Identification of script in multi-lingual documents is essential for many language dependent applications such as machine translation and optical character recognition. Techniques for script identification generally require large areas for operation so that sufficient information is available. Such assumption is nullified in Indian context, as there is an interspersion of words of two different scripts in most documents. In this paper, techniques to identify the script of a word are discussed. Two different approaches have been proposed and tested. The first method structures words into 3 distinct spatial zones and utilizes the information on the spatial spread of a word in upper and lower zones, together with the character density, in order to identify the script. The second technique analyzes the directional energy distribution of a word using Gabor filters with suitable frequencies and orientations. Words with various font styles and sizes have been used for the testing of the proposed algorithms and the results obtained are quite encouraging.

1 Introduction

Multi-script documents are inevitable in countries housing a national language different from English. This effect is no less felt in India, where as many as 18 regional languages coexist. Many official documents, magazines and reports are bilingual in nature containing both regional language and English. Knowledge of the script is essential in many language dependent processes such as machine translation and OCR. The complexity of the problem of script identification depends on the disposition of the input documents. Recognition can be done on a block of text such as a paragraph, a line or a word. The features are to be selected depending on the size of input text blocks, to bring out the characteristics of the script. It is not advisable to work on individual characters, because one loses the whole advantage of script recognition, which is meant to reduce the search space for the OCR. Algorithms that work on text blocks of large size may or may not retain their performance when applied on a smaller block of text. The foremost deciding parameter for the algorithm to be used then is the size of the largest contiguous text block of any one of the scripts that one is always assured of being available in the given document. As shown in Fig. 1, in the Indian

D. Lopresti, J. Hu, and R. Kashi (Eds.): DAS 2002, LNCS 2423, pp. 13–24, 2002.

context, the bilingual documents contain single words of English interspersed in an otherwise Indian language text. The document 1 (a) is taken from a college application form; (b) from a weekly magazine and (c) from an International conference proceedings [1]. In order to be of general applicability then, script recognition needs to be performed at the word level.

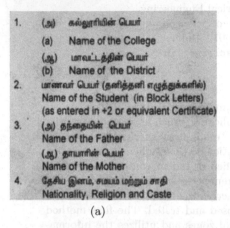

(a)   (b)

(c)

Fig. 1. Typical bilingual documents (a) Official document (b) Magazine (c) Technical report

Among the work done in this area, Spitz et al. [2,3,4] have worked on textual paragraphs for recognizing Roman and Asian scripts. They have used spatial relationship of structural features of characters for differentiating Han and Latin based scripts. Asian scripts (Japanese, Korean and Chinese) are distinguished from Roman by a uniform vertical distribution of upward concavities. In the case of the above Asian scripts, the measure of optical density i.e. the number of ON-pixels per unit area is employed to distinguish one from the other. Hochberg et al. [5] use cluster-based templates for script identification. They consider 13 different scripts including Devanagari, an Indian script. Their technique involves clustering of textual symbols (connected components) and creating a representative symbol or a template for each cluster. Identification is through the comparison of textual symbols of the test documents with the templates. This method necessitates a local approach in the sense that each connected component needs to be extracted for identifying the script. Wood et al. suggest a method based on Hough transform, morphological filtering and analysis of projection profile [6]. Though their work involves the global characteristics of the text, the results obtained are not encouraging.

Tan [7] has attempted a texture based approach to identify six different scripts - Roman, Persian, Chinese, Malayalam, Greek and Russian. The inputs for script recognition are textual blocks of size 128 x128 pixels, which, for the scanning resolution used by him, cover several lines of text. This method requires such image blocks containing text of single script. These blocks are filtered by 16 channel Gabor filters with an angular spacing of 11.25°. The method has been tested for single fonts assuming font invariance within the same block. A recognition accuracy greater than 90% has been reported. However, the efficiency is reported to go down to 72% when multiple fonts are incorporated.

Tan et al. [8] have worked on three scripts - Latin, Chinese and Tamil. These scripts are used by the four official languages of Singapore. Their work is based on attributes like aspect ratio and distribution of upward concavities. The use of such primitive features necessitates long passages of input text for good performance. They report recognition accuracies above 94%.

Pal and Chaudhuri [9] have proposed a decision tree based method for recognizing the script of a line of text. They consider Roman, Bengali and Devanagari scripts. They have used projection profile besides statistical, topological and stroke based features. Initially, the Roman script is isolated from the rest by examining the presence of the headline , which connects the characters in a word. Devanagari is differentiated from Bangla by identifying the principal strokes [9]. In [10], they have extended their work to identification of the script from a given triplet. Here, they have dealt with many of the Indian scripts. Besides the headline, they have used some script dependent structural properties such as distribution of ascenders and descenders, position of vertical line in a text block, and the number of horizontal runs. Chaudhuri and Seth [11] have used the horizontal projection profile, Gabor transform and aspect ratio of connected components. They have handled Roman, Hindi, Telugu and Malayalam scripts. Their work involves identifying the connected components and convolving them with a six channel Gabor filter bank. The output is full-wave rectified and its standard deviation calculated. Their results vary from 85% for Hindi to 51% for Malayalam. Most of these works require large textual regions to achieve good performance. However, this necessity cannot be satisfied by most Indian documents, in which the script changes at the level of a word. Here, bilingual script recognition has been attempted to work at the word level. Each word is assumed to contain at least four patterns. Though quite a few number of English words

16   D. Dhanya and A.G. Ramakrishnan

do not meet this requirement, our assumption is justified by the fact that the probability of finding such words, in a bilingual Tamil document, is quite low. In such a context, the above assumption guarantees high recognition accuracy.

2   Language Description

The spatial spread of the words formed by the scripts, as well as the orientation of the structural elements of the characters play a major role in our approach. A clear understanding of the properties of the associated scripts is essential for the design of an identifier system.

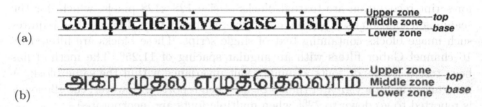

(a)

(b)

Fig. 2. Three distinct zones of (a) Roman script and (b) Tamil script

The various properties as analyzed are:

(1) Both Tamil and Roman characters (words) are structured into three distinct zones, viz. Upper, Middle and Lower, based on their occupancy in the vertical direction (2). For our discussion, we define the following terms: top line, base line, descenders and ascenders. We call the boundary that separates the upper and middle zones as the top line and the one that separates the middle and lower zones as the base line. The structures that extend into the lower and upper zones are called descenders and ascenders, respectively.
(2) Roman script has very few descenders (only in 'g', 'j', 'p', 'q' and 'y'), as compared to Tamil. The probability of lower zone occupancy is therefore less in Roman script. For example, in an analysis of 1000 words each of both scripts, it has been observed that 908 words of Tamil script (90%), and only 632 words (63%) of English have descenders.
(3) Roman alphabet contains more slant and vertical strokes as compared to Tamil, which has a dominance of horizontal and vertical strokes.
(4) The number of characters per unit area is generally less in Tamil.

3   Feature Extraction

Feature extraction aims at selecting features that maximize the distinction between the patterns. For the task at hand, those features that highlight the characteristic properties of the scripts have been chosen. As explained in Sec.2, the relative distribution of ascenders and descenders in a word as well as the directional distribution of stroke elements of the alphabets differ for Tamil and Roman scripts. The spatial distribution of ascenders and descenders in a word can be quantified through the analysis of the projection profile of the word. The directional distribution of strokes can be extracted by looking at the energy distribution of the word in various directions.

3.1 Spatial Spread Features: Character Density and Zonal Pixel Concentration

It has been observed that the number of characters present per unit area of any Tamil word is generally less than that in English. Based on this observation, we define a feature, character density, as,

$$characterdensity = \frac{No.\ of\ Characters\ in\ a\ word}{Area\ of\ the\ bounding\ box} . \tag{1}$$

The analysis of the horizontal projection profile in the three zones of the words suggests use of zonal pixel concentration (ratio of number of ON-pixels in each zone to the total number of ON- pixels) as a feature for script recognition. Considering the top left most index as the origin, and denoting the horizontal profile (the row sum of the image) by P, the zone boundaries are defined as,

$$top = arg(max(P(y) - P(y-1))) \qquad \forall 0 <= y < H/2 . \tag{2}$$

$$base = arg(min(P(y) - P(y-1))) \qquad \forall H/2 >= y < H . \tag{3}$$

where H is the height of the word or line. Figs. 3(a) and 3(b) show the projection profiles of single English and Tamil words, respectively. The profiles show very sharp transitions at the zone boundaries, which are identified from the first difference of the profile as given by equations 2 and 3. If U, M and L represent the upper, middle and lower zones respectively, then

$$U = \{(x,y)|y < top\} . \tag{4}$$

$$M = \{(x,y)|top \le y \le base\} . \tag{5}$$

$$L = \{(x,y)|y > base\} . \tag{6}$$

where (x,y) are the image coordinates. Let $f(x,y)$ be the binary image, whose value is '1' for foreground pixels, and '0' for background pixels. Zonal pixel concentration is defined as,

$$PC_k = \frac{\sum_{(x,y)\epsilon k} f(x,y)}{\sum_{(x,y)} f(x,y)} . \tag{7}$$

where k is U, L.

The formation of the feature vector is as follows. The pixel concentrations in U and L zones are calculated and these form the first two elements of the feature

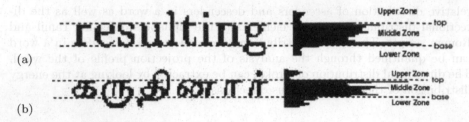

(a)

(b)

Fig. 3. The three distinct zones of (a) English and (b) Tamil words and their corresponding projection profiles.

vector. The character density forms the third dimension of the feature vector. Since only relative densities are used, there is no need for size normalization.

Figure 4 shows the scatter plot of the feature vectors for a typical bilingual Tamil and Roman document. There is clear distinction between the feature vectors of the two scripts. However, it can be seen that some vectors belonging to Tamil script fall near the cluster of English feature vectors. These are attributed to those sample words formed by characters having less downward extensions.

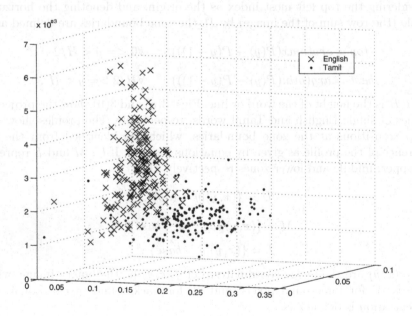

Fig. 4. Scatter plot of the spatial features : Upper zone pixel concentration Vs Lower zone concentration Vs No. of components per unit area

3.2   Directional Features: Gabor Filter Responses

The motivation for using directional features arose from the observation of the nature of strokes. The stroke information is effectively and inherently captured by the Human Visual System (HVS), the best-known pattern recognizer that identifies distinctive patterns through their orientation, repetition and complexity. Repetition is indicative of the frequency selectivity; orientation, of the directional sensitivity and complexity, of the type of pattern. Hence we attempted to have a feature extractor, which performs the same functions as HVS. Studies indicate that cells in primary visual cortex of human brain are tuned to specific frequencies with a bandwidth of one octave and orientations with an approximate bandwidth of 30° each [12,13]. This type of organization in the brain, leading to a multi-resolution analysis, motivated us to use Gabor filters, which have been known to best model the HVS. These directional filters, with proper design parameters, are used to effectively capture the directional energy distribution of words.

A Gabor function is a Gaussian modulated sinusoid. A complex 2-D Gabor function with orientation θ and center frequency F is given by:

$$h(x,y) = \frac{1}{2\pi\sigma_x\sigma_y} \, exp\left\{-\frac{1}{2}\left[\frac{x^2}{\sigma_x^2} + \frac{y^2}{\sigma_y^2}\right]\right\} exp\{j2\pi F[xcos\theta + ysin\theta]\} \, . \quad (8)$$

The spatial spreads σ_x and σ_y of the Gaussian are given by:

$$\sigma_x = \frac{\sqrt{ln2}(2^{\Omega_F}+1)}{\sqrt{2}\pi F(2^{\Omega_F}-1)} \, . \quad (9)$$

$$\sigma_y = \frac{\sqrt{ln2}}{\sqrt{2}\pi F \tan(\Omega_\theta/2)} \, . \quad (10)$$

where Ω_F and Ω_θ are the frequency and angular bandwidths, respectively. Change of frequency and scaling of Gabor functions provide the parameters necessary to model the HVS. A filter bank, with both angular bandwidth and spacing set to 30°, and the frequency spacing to one octave, closely models the HVS. With a circular Gaussian ($\sigma_x = \sigma_y$), we can obtain a variable spread (scale) that helps to capture information at various scales and orientations.

Figure 5 shows the filter bank designed to suit the purpose. Frequency spacing of one octave with two frequencies (0.25 and 0.50 cpi) is considered. For the formation of the feature vector, the word is thinned and filtered by the filter bank. Initially, two frequencies are specified and all possible directions with an angular bandwidth of 30°, have been used. This leads to twelve feature coefficients. These are normalized by the norm of the feature vector. However, the analysis of the efficiency of individual feature element proved that not all coefficients are effective discriminators. Hence only a subset of these coefficients have been used as features.

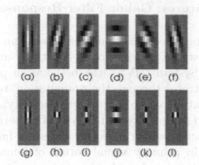

Fig. 5. Gabor filters: (a)-(f) F = 0.25 cpi and $\theta = 0°$ to $150°$ with angular spacing of $30°$; (g)-(l) F = 0.5 cpi and $\theta = 0°$ to $150°$ with angular spacing of $30°$

Feature selection for Directional Energy Coefficients. It is well known in Pattern Recognition literature that features should have small intraclass variance and a large interclass scatter. Several criterion functions have also been proposed in order to examine the clustering ability of the features. One such standard criterion function is the Fisher's ratio. This ratio is normally used in order to arrive at the transformation matrix for dimension reduction procedure. However, the same ratio can also be used for the purpose of feature selection.

For a two class problem, Fisher's ratio is as follows:

$$FR = \frac{var(X_1) + var(X_2)}{det(cov(X1, X2))} .$$ (11)

where X_i represents the feature vectors belonging to class i and $cov(.)$ represents the covariance. Figure 6 shows the ratio for all the 12 dimensions. It is apparent that features with small ratios are better discriminators. This is verified by comparing the performance of the complete 12-dimensional Gabor features with that of a subset of only 8 elements corresponding to lower ratio values.

4   Experiments and Results

The feature extraction techniques have been tested on a variety of documents obtained from various reports and magazines. The text-only input document is a gray scale image scanned with a resolution of 300 dpi. This is binarized using a two-stage process and deskewed to avoid errors due to tilt in text lines [14], [15]. Text lines and words are identified using the valleys in the profile in the corresponding direction. Segmented words are thinned and feature extraction is then performed on them. Thinning aids in a concise concentration of energy along particular directions.

The extracted features are classified using Support Vector Machines (SVM) [16], Nearest Neighbor (NN) and k-Nearest Neighbor (k-NN) classifiers. Euclidean metric is assumed. The value of k in the case of k-NN classifier is set at

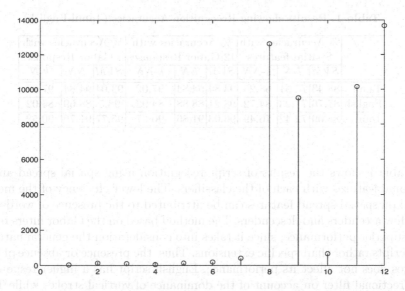

Fig. 6. Ratio for the twelve feature coefficients

30. We have used Gaussian kernel for the SVM classifier. The variance σ^2 for the Gaussian kernel is set to that of the reference data set. The results are tabulated in Table 1. The training and test patterns have 1008 samples each, consisting of equal number of Tamil and English words. Figure 7 shows some of the samples of various fonts used in the experiment.

Fig. 7. Sample words of various fonts used in the experiment.

Table 1. Results showing Recognition Accuracies (Tamil-English)

	% Accuracies with Spatial features			% Accuracies with 12 Gabor Responses			% Accuracies with 8 Gabor Responses		
	SVM	*NN*	*k-NN*	*SVM*	*NN*	*k-NN*	*SVM*	*NN*	*k-N*
Tamil	88.43	73.61	68.25	93.84	94.84	97.02	93.04	94.84	97.02
English	87.76	71.23	84.72	98.21	88.88	84.92	98.5	88.69	84.02
Total	88.09	72.42	76.49	96.03	91.86	90.97	95.77	91.76	90.52

Table 1 shows the results of script recognition using spatial spread and directional features with each of the classifiers. The lower efficiency of the method based on spatial spread features can be attributed to the presence of words with very few ascenders and descenders. The method based on the Gabor filters results in a superior performance, since it takes into consideration the general nature of the scripts rather than specific extensions. Thus, the presence or absence of a few strokes does not affect its performance. English script has a higher response to $0°$ directional filter on account of the dominance of vertical strokes while Tamil script has a higher response to $90°$ filter due to dominance of horizontal strokes. It is observed that the reduced set of Gabor features performs as well as the original set.

Among the works reported in the literature, Tan's approach [8] also uses Gabor filters. However, his work is based on large blocks of text. A recognition accuracy greater than 90% has been obtained using text containing a single font only. However, the efficiency has been reported to go down to 72% when multiple fonts are incorporated. Further, the reported results are based on a small test set of 10 samples each, for each script. On the other hand, our proposed approach works well with multiple fonts, achieving a good accuracy of above 90% and has been tested thoroughly on a set of 1008 samples each, for each script.

Pal and Chaudhuri [10] have used structural features, (principal strokes) and distribution of ascenders and descenders. Their work has given a good recognition accuracy of 97.7% for distinguishing among Tamil, Devanagari and Roman text lines. Chaudhury and Sheth's work [11], though uses Gabor filter based features, gives an accuracy of around 64% only. Better results are obtained (around 88%) using projection profile and height to width ratio. However, these methods operate at the line or paragraph level.

Our method works under the assumption that any word contains a minimum number of four connected components. The assumption is justified by the fact that the probability of occurrence of words with very few components is low. This assumption also eliminates symbols such as bullets and numerals. Difficulty is encountered while classifying Hindu-Arabic numerals since they are shared by both the scripts. Since most of the mono-script OCRs incorporate numerals also, this problem can be easily circumvented. Thus, irrespective of the script the numbers are classified into, they are taken care of by the respective OCRs.

The proposed method can be extended to other South Indian Dravidian languages as they too are quite distinct from Roman script. The algorithm was

Fig. 8. Three distinct zones of Kannada and the corresponding projection profile

tested to isolate Kannada from Roman script. Figure 8 shows a typical word of Kannada script which also is structured into three zones. Also shown is its projection profile. The algorithms were tested on Kannada-Roman bilingual texts and the results are tabulated in Table 2. Kannada words have a uniform response to Gabor filters on account of their circular nature.

Table 2. Results showing Recognition Accuracies (Kannada-English)

	% Accuracies with Spatial features			% Accuracies with 12 Gabor Responses			% Accuracies with 8 Gabor Responses		
	SVM	*NN*	*k-NN*	*SVM*	*NN*	*k-NN*	*SVM*	*NN*	*k-NN*
Kannada	86.99	74.38	69.41	94.63	93.84	97.02	94.44	91.6	96.826
English	88.71	68.07	68.83	95.02	92.04	91.85	94.65	91.48	93.46
Total	87.85	71.22	69.12	94.83	92.94	94.44	94.53	94.43	92.84

5   Conclusion

Two different sets of features have been employed successfully for discriminating Tamil and English words. The first method uses the pixel concentration in the different zones and the average number of connected components per unit area in a word as features. Directional features, obtained as the responses of Gabor filters, are employed in the second approach. These features are observed to possess better discriminating capabilities than the spatial spread features. Experiments are conducted with documents covering a wide range of fonts. Accuracies as high as 96% have been obtained with SVM classifiers using directional energy features.

References

1. Proceedings of Tamil Internet (2000) 22-24 July, Singapore.
2. Spitz, A.L.: Determination of Script and Language Content of Document Images. IEEE Transactions on Pattern Analysis and Machine Intelligence **19** (1997) 235–245
3. Sibun, P., Spitz, A.L.: Natural Language Processing from Scanned Document Images. In: Proceedings of the Applied Natural Language Processing, Stuttgart (1994) 115–121

4. Nakayama, T., Spitz, A.L.: European Language Determination from Image. In: Proceedings of the International Conference on Document Analysis and Recognition, Japan (1993) 159–162
5. Hochberg, J., et al.: Automatic Script Identification from Images Using Cluster-Based Templates. IEEE Transactions on Pattern Analysis and Machine Intelligence **19** (1997) 176–181
6. Dang, L., et al.: Language Identification for Printed Text Independent of Segmentation. In: Proceedings of the International Conference on Image Processing. (1995) 428–431
7. Tan, C.L., et al.: Language Identification in Multi-lingual Documents. IEEE Transactions on Pattern Analysis and Machine Intelligence **20** (1998) 751–756
8. Tan, T.N.: Rotation Invariant Texture Features and their Use in Automatic Script Identification. IEEE Transactions on Pattern Analysis and Machine Intelligence **20** (1998) 751–756
9. Chaudhuri, B.B., Pal, U.: A complete Printed *bangla* OCR System. Pattern Recognition **31** (1998) 531–549
10. Chaudhuri, B.B., Pal, U.: Automatic Separation of Words in Multi-lingual Multi-script Indian Documents. In: Proceedings of the International Conference on Document Analysis and Recognition, Germany (1997) 576–579
11. Chaudhury, S., Sheth, R.: Trainable Script Identification Strategies for Indian languages. In: Proceedings of the International Conference on Document Analysis and Recognition, India (1999) 657–660
12. Hubel, D.H., Wiesel, T.N.: Receptive Fields and Functional Architecture in Two Non-striate Visual Areas 18 and 19 of the Cat. Journal of Neurophysiology **28** (1965) 229–289
13. Campbell, F.W., Kulikowski, J.J.: Orientational Selectivity of Human Visual System. Journal of Physiology **187** (1966) 437–445
14. Chen, Y.K., et al.: Skew Detection and Reconstruction Based on Maximization of Variance of Transition-Counts. Pattern Recognition **33** (2000) 195–208
15. Dhanya, D.: Bilingual OCR for Tamil and Roman Scripts. Master's thesis, Department of Electrical Engineering, Indian Institute of Science (2001)
16. Burges, C.J.C.: A Tutorial on Support Vector Machines for Pattern Recognition. Data Mining and Knowledge Discovery **2** (1998) 955–974

Optimal Feature Extraction for Bilingual OCR

D. Dhanya and A.G. Ramakrishnan

Department of Electrical Engineering,
Indian Institute of Science,
Bangalore, India
ramkiag@ee.iisc.ernet.in

Abstract. Feature extraction in bilingual OCR is handicapped by the increase in the number of classes or characters to be handled. This is evident in the case of Indian languages whose alphabet set is large. It is expected that the complexity of the feature extraction process increases with the number of classes. Though the determination of the best set of features that could be used cannot be ascertained through any quantitative measures, the characteristics of the scripts can help decide on the feature extraction procedure. This paper describes a hierarchical feature extraction scheme for recognition of printed bilingual (Tamil and Roman) text. The scheme divides the combined alphabet set of both the scripts into subsets by the extraction of certain spatial and structural features. Three features *viz* geometric moments, DCT based features and Wavelet transform based features are extracted from the grouped symbols and a linear transformation is performed on them for the purpose of efficient representation in the feature space. The transformation is obtained by the maximization of certain criterion functions. Three techniques : Principal component analysis, maximization of Fisher's ratio and maximization of divergence measure have been employed to estimate the transformation matrix. It has been observed that the proposed hierarchical scheme allows for easier handling of the alphabets and there is an appreciable rise in the recognition accuracy as a result of the transformations.

1 Introduction

Development of English as the universal language has resulted in the evolution of multi-script documents in many nations hosting a national language different from English. Borrowed words are usually followed by explanations in the language native to the reader. In a country like India, housing 18 official languages, the use of English along with the regional language in many official documents, reports and magazines has become a necessity. Conversion of such printed texts into editable format cannot be achieved through the use of a single monolingual OCR.

The problem of bilingual OCR can be viewed as an extension of the basic character set to include those of the second script. However, the increase in the number of symbols to be identified poses several problems such as the requirement of a large number of features for discrimination among all symbols.

D. Lopresti, J. Hu, and R. Kashi (Eds.): DAS 2002, LNCS 2423, pp. 25–36, 2002.

This in turn calls for large number of training samples in order to overcome the 'peaking' phenomenon. Mixture of symbols from two different scripts might also result in the patterns having multi-modal distributions which cannot be efficiently represented by a single set of features. Hence it is prudential to resort to a hierarchical scheme having multiple stages of feature extraction. Such a scheme not only reduces the number of classes at each level, but also allows for independent handling of groups of patterns. One such hierarchical scheme for classification of Tamil and Roman scripts is described in this paper. Section II describes the characteristics of the scripts that have been made use of for classification purposes. Section III describes the hierarchical scheme along with its different stages and section IV describes the experiments conducted and the results obtained.

2   Characteristics of Tamil and Roman Scripts

Tamil language belongs to the group of Dravidian languages and is the official state language of Tamil Nadu, a southern state of India, a national language in Singapore and a major language in Malaysia and Sri Lanka. Tamil script belongs to the group of Southern Indic scripts and is derived form Grantha script, a descendant of ancient Brahmi script. A brief description of the script follows:

1. Tamil alphabet set has 12 vowels, 18 native consonants and 5 borrowed consonants.
2. The twelve vowels combine with the consonants to form compound characters. These characters are modifications of the basic characters. A modification appears in the form of a matra or diacritic (consonant modifier) that either gets connected to the basic character or remains disjoint from it.
3. The diacritics get added to the right, left, top or bottom of the consonants. Those added to the right and left are disconnected from the consonant they modify, whereas those added at the top and bottom are connected and change the shape of the consonant.
4. Consonant clusters, which are series of consonants without any intervening vowel, are represented in Tamil script by suppressing the inherent vowels except the last one in the series. The vowel suppresser is called as *pulli*; it appears as a dot placed as a superscript above the basic consonant.
5. While all consonant-vowel combinations are derived as modifications of the basic set in Tamil script, no such concept exists in Roman script. This makes the Roman script easier to handle.
6. Both Tamil and Roman characters (words) are structured into three distinct zones, *viz.* Upper, Middle and Lower, based on the occupancy of the characters in the vertical direction [1].
7. Though Tamil has native numerals, they are hardly used in contemporary texts; only the Hindu-Arabic numeral set is being used.

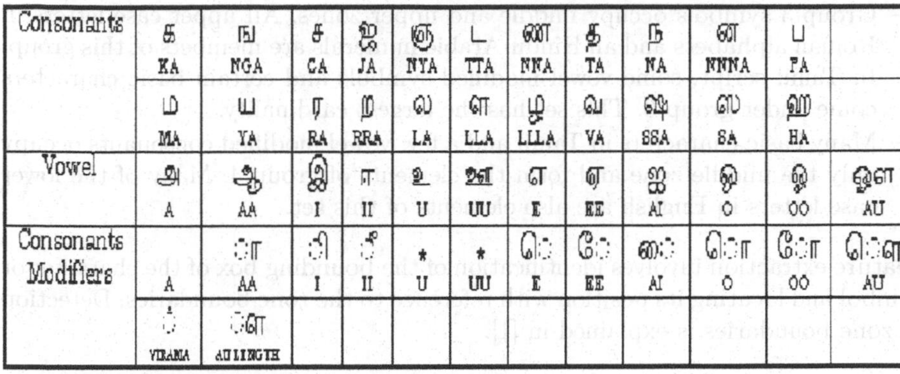

Consonants												
	KA	NGA	CA	JA	NYA	TTA	NNA	TA	NA	NNNA	PA	
	MA	YA	RA	RRA	LA	LLA	LLLA	VA	SSA	SA	HA	
Vowel	A	AA	I	II	U	UU	E	EE	AI	O	OO	AU
Consonants Modifiers	A	AA	I	II	U	UU	E	EE	AI	O	OO	AU
	VIRAMA	AU LENGTH										

Fig. 1. Basic alphabet set of Tamil script with corresponding diacritics

Figure 1 shows the basic alphabet set of Tamil characters along with the modifiers or matras. One can see that some of the vowel modifiers appear as separate symbols and these are dealt as separate patterns for identification. The * in the figure indicates that those matras change the entire shape of the characters differently for different consonants. In such cases, each modified consonant is considered a separate class for identification. In the rest of the discussion, the term "symbol" is used to denote any pattern taken for classification: a character, a disjoint matra or a numeral.

3   Three-Level Hierarchical Scheme

The primary factors to be considered in a hierarchical scheme are the features to be used at each level and the corresponding decision rule. In the proposed scheme the symbols are grouped initially into different subsets depending on the spatial distribution of symbols and presence or absence of a loop. Features such as geometric moments, discrete cosine transform coefficients and wavelet coefficients are then extracted and each of them transformed into a subspace of reduced dimension for optimum representation.

3.1   Primary Grouping

In the first level of classification, the zonal occupancy of the characters is used to divide the observation space into four major groups as follows.

- Group 1 contains symbols that occupy all three zones. This group consists solely of Tamil characters, since Roman script does not have any alphabet that occupies all three zones.
- Group 2 symbols occupy middle and lower zones. It has a majority of Tamil symbols consisting both basic characters and modified ones; only a few alphabets from Roman, namely, p, q, y, j and g come under this group.

- Group 3 symbols occupy middle and upper zones. All upper case letters in Roman alphabets and all Hindu-Arabic numerals are members of this group. In Tamil script, some vowel modified symbols and certain basic characters come under group 3. This set has the largest cardinality.
- Many basic characters in Tamil and a few vowel modified consonants occupy only the middle zone and form the elements of group 4. Many of the lower case letters in English are also elements of this set.

Feature extraction involves identification of the bounding box of the character or symbol and locating its position with reference to the zone boundaries. Detection of zone boundaries is explained in [1].

3.2   Sub-grouping

Traditionally, structural features have been exploited for the purpose of character recognition. Structural features need to be consistent across different fonts and their variations. Features such as presence or absence of loops, strokes and their distributions have been explored. For handwritten digits, presence of loops is a very important feature [2]. In the proposed scheme, this feature is used for the purpose of sub-grouping. A loop is a closed curve or a hole and its presence is detected on a thinned contour by means of a contour tracing algorithm. Sub-grouping is performed on Groups 3 & 4 thereby dividing them into two subsets: one consisting of symbols with loops and other without them. However, the presence of noise often distorts certain symbols which have a very small hole in them. On such characters, grouping is not performed at all.

3.3   Tertiary Features

An efficient representation can be described as the ability of the features to form disjoint clusters in the feature space such that their intra-class variance is small while the inter-class variance is large. Though there is no quantitative measure to determine the suitability of a particular feature, some insight can be obtained from the characteristics of the alphabet set. Though the direct application of the 'suitable' features can ensure fair performance, performance improvement could be obtained by transforming these features into a different space where symbols are better represented. The transformation can also help reduce the dimension of the feature vectors thereby reducing the 'curse of dimensionality problem'. The extraction of an optimal set of features with minimum dimension is the essential part of any pattern recognition problem. In this paper, three features have been studied with respect to their ability for compact representation in the feature space: geometric moments, Discrete Cosine Transform (DCT) based features and Discrete Wavelet Transform (DWT) based features. Considerable improvement in the performance in terms of reduced dimension and increased efficiency has been obtained through linear transformations of these features.

Geometric Moments. The use of moments as a tool for character recognition has been widely explored [3], [4] and [5]. Such features capture the shape information of the character. Moments such as geometric moments, Zernike moments and Legendre moments are some of the important features used for character recognition. Moments are projections of the symbol onto different polynomials. Their representation efficiency is described in terms of their susceptibility to noise and affine transforms. The simplest of them is the geometric moment (GM), in which the polynomial of order $p + q$, onto which the pattern $f(x, y)$ of dimension $M \times N$ with coordinates x and y is projected, is given by $x^p y^q$. GM of order $p + q$ is defined by

$$M_{pq} = \sum_{x=0}^{M-1} \sum_{y=0}^{N-1} x^p y^q f(x, y) \, . \tag{1}$$

The main disadvantage of geometric moments is the non-orthogonal nature of the monomials which leads to redundancy in representation. The parameters to be chosen in using geometric moments as features are (i) the order of moments (ii) area of operation on the image. Though it is well known that these moments represent the global properties of the image, little is known about what the higher order moments indicate. As the order of moments increases, the features become sensitive to each image pixel. Very low order features provide a fair description of the pattern, but are not powerful discriminators when the number of classes is quite high. Operating on the whole pattern results in loss of details while having a very small area makes the features too sensitive to small perturbations. Thus, selection of the area of operation on the input pattern involves a trade-off between discrimination capability and noise sensitivity.

In our work, up to third order moments have been considered for classification. Localization is better achieved by dividing the symbol image into blocks of size 12×12 pixels and extracting features from each of the blocks.

Discrete Cosine Transform. Transform based features have found widespread use because they are easy to compute and have good reconstruction properties. DCT is a very efficient transform with regard to decorrelation and energy compaction properties. It is asymptotically equivalent to the Karhunen-Loeve transform (KLT) which is the optimal transform. The DCT of an image f of dimension $M \times N$ is given by

$$F^{II}(u, v) = \alpha(u)\alpha(v) \sum_{y=0}^{N-1} \sum_{x=0}^{M-1} f(x, y) \cos\left(\frac{(2x+1)u\Pi}{2M}\right) \cos\left(\frac{(2y+1)v\Pi}{2N}\right) . \tag{2}$$

where

$$\alpha(u) = \begin{cases} \frac{1}{P} & u = 0 \\ \frac{2}{P} & u > 0 \, . \end{cases} \tag{3}$$

and P is the size of the image in the corresponding spatial direction. The subscript II denotes that the DCT is of type-II. In this work, each size-normalized symbol is divided into four sub-blocks and DCT is taken on each sub-block. DCT being a separable transform, the above operation is executed via one-dimensional DCT. Owing to the nature of the input patterns, most of the signal energy (information) is concentrated in few low frequency coefficients. Thus, only the low frequency coefficients of DCT are considered for recognition. In our work, we have considered only $H/6 \times W/6$ low frequency coefficients where H and W are the dimensions of the sub-blocks.

Wavelet Based Features. The lack of localization property in most of the transform based techniques including DCT leads to ambiguous results for all pairs of similar looking characters or symbols. In the recent times, a lot of research work has been done on wavelet transforms and their localization properties. Some of the properties of wavelet transforms, which are responsible for their popularity are:

(i) Time-frequency localization
(ii) Efficient representation in the case of orthogonal basis functions.

In general, if $\Psi_{s,n}$ represents the wavelet basis with a dilation scale parameter s and translation parameter n, then the wavelet transform of a signal f at scale s and position n is given by,

$$Wf(s,n) = f * \Psi_{s,n} .$$
(4)

where $*$ denotes the convolution operation. Discrete wavelet transform (DWT) is implemented through a filter bank as shown in Fig. 2. Decomposition is performed by low and high pass filters operating in parallel and decimation of the filtered signal. Binary images are efficiently represented using Haar wavelets. For Haar wavelet transform, the low and high pass filters h and g are given by

$$h = \frac{1}{\sqrt{2}} \left(\delta(n) + \delta(n+1) \right) .$$
(5)

$$g = \frac{1}{\sqrt{2}} \left(\delta(n) - \delta(n+1) \right) .$$
(6)

A two level decomposition is performed using the above filters. Since Haar wavelet has a separable kernel, the transform is implemented by operating on the rows first, followed by columns. The coefficients corresponding to the low pass filtered image in the second level are used to form the feature vector.

3.4   Feature Transformation

In general, as the dimension of the feature vector increases, the efficiency increases initially and then starts to decrease. This phenomenon called 'peaking phenomenon' is a major handicap in feature extraction process. Also, as the dimension of a feature vector increases, the number of training samples required

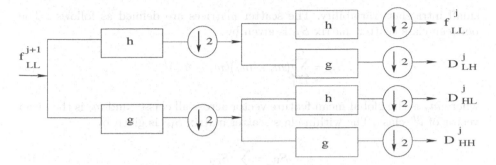

Fig. 2. Filter bank implementation of wavelet transform

also increases. Hence, dimensionality reduction is essential. Linear transformations are used to project the feature vector in a higher d-dimensional space onto a lower m-dimensional space such that they are better represented in the transformed space. Thus if x represents a feature vector in the original domain and y represents the transformed vector, the transformation is defined by,

$$y = W^T x . \tag{7}$$

where W is the transformation matrix. The aim is to find the matrix W which produces a better representation in the transformed domain. This is brought about by maximizing certain criterion functions. Three transformation techniques have been employed for the purpose : *principal component analysis* (PCA), maximization of *Fisher's ratio* and maximization of *divergence measure*. In order to have a common platform for comparing the efficiency of these methods, m is always set to the number of symbols in each group irrespective of the transformation used.

Principal Component Analysis (PCA). PCA demands that the projection vectors in W decorrelate the input data. These projection vectors are the eigenvectors corresponding to m largest eigenvalues of the covariance matrix, S, of the original feature set.

$$S = \frac{1}{n-1} \sum_{i=1}^{n} (x - m_x)(x - m_x)^T . \tag{8}$$

where x is the feature vector, n the sample size and m_x is the global mean of all feature vectors. The transformation matrix W is formed by m eigenvectors corresponding to m largest eigenvalues where m is the required dimension.

Fisher's Ratio. Fisher's ratio is one of the important criterion functions and is defined as the ratio of total between-class scatter to within-class scatter. Maximization of this criterion function ensures maximum inter-class variability and small intra-class variability. The scatter matrices are defined as follows : The between-class scatter matrix S_B is given by

$$S_B = \sum_{i=1}^{C} (m_i - m_x)(m_i - m_x)^T .$$ (9)

where m_x is the global mean feature vector across all classes and m_i is the mean vector of ith class. The within-class scatter matrix S_W is given by

$$S_W = \sum_{i=1}^{C} S_i .$$ (10)

where S_i is the within class scatter matrix for i^{th} class given by,

$$S_i = \sum_{x} (x - m_i)(x - m_i)^T .$$ (11)

with the summation taken over all feature vectors x belonging to class i. If J represents the criterion function, (Fisher's ratio), then

$$J(W) = \frac{|W^T S_B W|}{|W^T S_W W|} .$$ (12)

The required transformation matrix W is the one that maximizes the above criterion function. W is solved as a generalized eigenvalue problem

$$S_B w_i = \lambda_i S_W w_i .$$ (13)

where λ_i is an eigenvalue and w_i is the eigenvector.

Divergence Measure. In [6], a criterion function that uses a weighted average divergence measure is proposed for the purpose of speech identification. This method takes into account the difficulty associated with certain pairs of characters. The criterion function is the divergence measure and using the same notation as above, the criterion function that is maximized is given by

$$J = tr \left[\left(W^T S_W W \right)^{-1} \left(W^T M W \right) \right] .$$ (14)

where M is given by

$$M = \sum_{i=1}^{C} \sum_{j=1}^{C} P_i P_j (m_i - m_j)(m_i - m_j)^T .$$ (15)

and P_i is the priori probability of class i. The transformation matrix W that maximizes the above function is found by solving the generalized eigenvalue problem:

$$M w_i = \lambda_i S_W w_i .$$ (16)

Using the above three methods, the transformation matrix is found

3.5   Results and Discussion

In order to analyse the performance of each of the features, the algorithms have been tested on samples collected from various magazines, reports and books. Documents are scanned at 300dpi and binarized using the two stage method described in [7]. The skew introduced during the process of scanning is estimated and corrected. Textual lines and words are segmented by determining the valley points in the projection profiles and symbols are isolated using connected component analysis.

The primary and secondary levels of classification are based on spatial occupancy and presence of structural features and do not require training samples. Initially, samples are grouped depending on the zone they occupy. To accommodate for varying thickness of the symbol on account of font differences, a 2 pixel margin is kept while detecting zone boundaries. However, it is assumed that all symbols within a line are of the same font size.

Symbols are then passed through the hierarchical feature extractor. Each symbol is normalized in size and thinned. The normalization size is dependent on the group to which the symbol belongs. Symbols belonging to groups 1, 2 and 3 are normalized to size 48×48 while those belonging to group 4 are normalized to 36×36. Further grouping is done on these thinned characters depending on the presence or absence of a loop structure. Final level features such as, geometric moments, DCT and wavelet coefficients are then extracted from these sets of samples.

The training file contains 150 to 200 samples of each of the frequent prototypes. The infrequent symbols are represented by the bootstrapped samples [8]. The transformation matrix is computed for each of the feature sets, and dimensionality reduction is performed for the entire training set. For testing purposes, samples are similarly collected from various books, magazines, reports *etc* with a large font variability. Test set consists of 6000 symbols containing samples from all of the 183 classes. These samples are obtained from as many as 20 scanned pages, each containing a minimum of 300 characters. Many of the frequently occurring characters are represented by as many as 40 samples, while some of the infrequent characters are represented by 20 samples or less. In order to compare the performance of each of the feature extraction methods, the algorithms have been tested on the same set of test samples that are pre-grouped, normalized and thinned. The recognition accuracy of each of the sets S1 to S6 has been found using the nearest neighbor classifier. The overall efficiency, which is the percentage of symbols correctly classified in all the sets, is calculated. The flow diagram of the procedure is explained in Fig. 3.

The results are tabulated in tables 1, 2 and 3. From the tables, the following can be observed :

Geometric Moments

1. Geometric moments achieve an overall recognition rate of 94% without any dimensionality reduction.

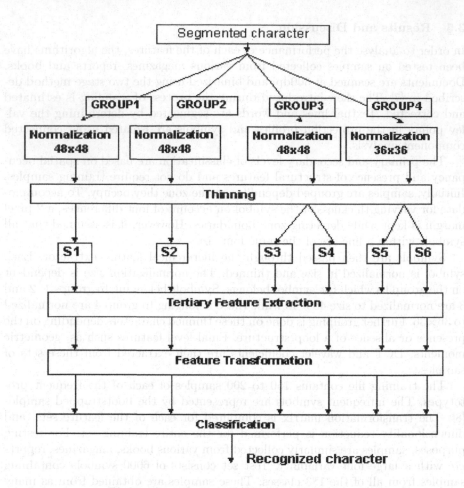

Fig. 3. Flow diagram of the recognition scheme

2. The overall accuracy increases when the dimension of the features is reduced using Fisher's ratio and divergence measure, while PCA retains the performance. These results reiterate the fact that there exists some amount of correlation and redundancy in the GM based features.

3. A good recognition rate of 95 to 97% is obtained for the individual sets S5 and S6 and the minimum rate is obtained for set S1. Since S5 contains a large number of commonly occurring classes, this result is encouraging. Also, S1 contains many symbols of low occurrence probability. Hence, the performance in general, for a scanned document, will not be much affected because of the low efficiency of S1.

4. For certain sets, the method based on divergence maximization gives a better performance. Since this method tries to optimize the separation between each pair of classes, the performance improves to some extent where the number of similar patterns is more.

Table 1. Recognition Accuracies with Geometric Moments (PCA: Principal Component Analysis; FR: Fischer's Ratio; DM: Divergence Measure)

Class	S1	S2	S3	S4	S5	S6	S7
3rd Order Moments	93.27	92.98	93.69	92.98	96.06	96.09	94
PCA	89.58	92.98	93.37	93.18	95.30	95.35	93.64
FR	95.01	96.22	94.32	94.36	96.21	97.39	95
DM	88.5	95.91	94.84	95.28	97.27	95.16	94.5

Table 2. Recognition Accuracies With DCT Based Features

Class	S1	S2	S3	S4	S5	S6	S7
DCT	95.69	96.00	92.58	95.84	96.96	94.42	95
PCA	97.05	97.69	93.11	95.84	96.66	95.53	96.29
FR	98.41	97.92	95.48	96.49	97.27	94.79	96.73
DM	98.41	97.77	95.37	96.75	97.72	94.79	96.80

DCT Based Features

1. They give a good performance of above 95% without dimensionality reduction.
2. All methods of dimension reduction give good performance improvement.
3. For individual sets, DCT shows a good performance. The performance for sets S3 and S6 is lower compared to the others. However, the recognition rates for all the other sets are higher than those of the GM features and in general outperform the corresponding results of geometric moments.

DWT Based Features

1. Wavelet based features show a fair performance with an overall performance rate of approximately 94%.
2. Among the feature dimension reduction methods, PCA gives results comparable to that of the original set without apparent increase in the efficiency. Fisher's method gives an improved performance of 95%. Similarly, the method based on divergence measure gives a performance comparable to those of the original and PCA based methods.

Table 3. Recognition Accuracies with DWT Based Features

Class	S1	S2	S3	S4	S5	S6	S7
DWT	96.29	93.86	92.75	92.60	94.36	92.75	94
PCA	96.73	94.7	92.22	92.73	94.65	94.6	94.33
FR	97.16	96.85	95.31	93.77	92.91	92.75	95
DM	94.98	94.16	94.78	92.09	95.08	91.63	93.79

3. One of the reasons for ineffective performance of the dimension reduction techniques could be the following. The features in wavelet domain still retain the apparent shape of the character, with the values being real. There is no clustering of the coefficients, which is very much needed for dimensionality reduction. Hence, there is some loss of information when the dimension is reduced.
4. The overall efficiency for wavelet based features is comparable to that of GM features and is less than that of DCT.

3.6   Conclusions

Effective representation is an important aspect in feature extraction as evidenced by the results. The hierarchical approach taken has reduced the number of classes to be handled into manageable limits. Of the three features extracted, DCT gives a very good performance and further improvement has been obtained by the transformation of the extracted features into a different space. Of the transformation methods, Fisher's method performs consistently well. Principal component analysis, though in some cases does not improve the efficiency appreciably, does not degrade it. Hence, the advantage of dimensionality reduction still remains. The method based on maximization of divergence measure, also does improve the performance and these methods when incorporated in combination with DCT would certainly ensure good performance of the OCR system.

References

1. Dhanya, D., Ramakrishnan, A.G.: Script identification in printed bilingual documents. Published in the same (2002).
2. A. Sinha: Improved recognition module for the identification of handwritten digits. Master's thesis, Department of Electrical Engineering and Computer Science, Massachuset (1999)
3. Teh, C.H., Chin, R.T.: On image analysis by method of moments. IEEE Transaction on Pattern Analysis and Machine Intelligence 10 (1993) 496–513
4. Khotanzad, A., Hong, Y.H.: Rotation invariant image representation using features selected via a systematic method. Pattern Recognition 23 (1990) 1089–1101
5. Bailey, R.R.: Orthogonal moment features for use with parametric and nonparametric classifiers. IEEE Transaction on Pattern Analysis and Machine Intelligence 18 (1996) 389–399
6. P.C. Loizou, Spanias, A.: Improved speech recognition using a subspace projection approach. IEEE Transaction on Speech and Audio Processing 7 (1999)
7. Dhanya, D.: Bilingual ocr for tamil and roman scripts. Master's thesis, Department of Electrical Engineering, Indian Institute of Science (2001)
8. Hamamoto, Y., et al.: A bootstrap technique for nearest neighbour classifier design. IEEE Transaction on Pattern Analysis and Machine Intelligence 19 (1993) 73–79

Machine Recognition of Printed Kannada Text

B. Vijay Kumar and A.G. Ramakrishnan

Department of Electrical Engineering,
Indian Institute of Science, Bangalore 560012, India
{vijaykb,ramkiag}@ee.iisc.ernet.in

Abstract. This paper presents the design of a full fledged OCR system for printed Kannada text. The machine recognition of Kannada characters is difficult due to similarity in the shapes of different characters, script complexity and non-uniqueness in the representation of diacritics. The document image is subject to line segmentation, word segmentation and zone detection. From the zonal information, base characters, vowel modifiers and consonant conjucts are separated. Knowledge based approach is employed for recognizing the base characters. Various features are employed for recognising the characters. These include the coefficients of the Discrete Cosine Transform, Discrete Wavelet Transform and Karhunen-Louve Transform. These features are fed to different classifiers. Structural features are used in the subsequent levels to discriminate confused characters. Use of structural features, increases recognition rate from 93% to 98%. Apart from the *classical* pattern classification technique of nearest neighbour, Artificial Neural Network (ANN) based classifiers like Back Propogation and Radial Basis Function (RBF) Networks have also been studied. The ANN classifiers are trained in supervised mode using the transform features. Highest recognition rate of 99% is obtained with RBF using second level approximation coefficients of Haar wavelets as the features on presegmented base characters.

1 Introduction

Kannada, the official language of the south Indian state of Karnataka, is spoken by about 48 million people. The basic structure of Kannada script is distinctly different from Roman script. Unlike many North Indian languages, Kannada characters don't have shirorekha (a line that connects all the characters of any word) and hence all the characters in a word are isolated. This creates a difficulty in word segmentation. Kannada script is more complicated than English due to the presence of compound characters. However, the concept of upper/lower case characters is absent in this script.

Modern Kannada has 48 base characters, called as *varnamale*. There are 14 vowels (Table 1) and 34 consonants. Consonants are further divided into grouped consonants (Table 2) and ungrouped consonants (Table 3). Consonants take modified shapes when added with vowels. Vowel modifiers can appear to the right, on the top or at the bottom of the base consonant. Table 4 shows the shapes of the consonant 'ರ' when modified by vowels. Such consonant-vowel

D. Lopresti, J. Hu, and R. Kashi (Eds.): DAS 2002, LNCS 2423, pp. 37–48, 2002.

combinations are called modified characters. Same consonants combine to form consonant conjucts (Table 5). In addition, two, three or four characters can generate a new complex shape called a compound character.

Table 1. Vowels and their ASCII representations

ಅ	ಆ	ಇ	ಈ	ಉ	ಊ	ಋ
a	aa	e	ee	u	oo	Ru
ಋೂ	ಎ	ಏ	ಐ	ಒ	ಓ	ಔ
Roo	ae	aee	i	o	O	au

Table 2. Grouped consonants and their ASCII representations

ಕ	ಖ	ಗ	ಘ	ಙ
ka	kha	ga	gha	Gnya
ಚ	ಛ	ಜ	ಝ	ಞ
ca	cha	ja	jha	Jnya
ಟ	ಠ	ಡ	ಢ	ಣ
ta	Ta	Da	Dha	Na
ತ	ಥ	ದ	ಧ	ನ
tha	Tha	da	dha	na
ಪ	ಫ	ಬ	ಭ	ಮ
pa	pha	ba	bha	ma

Table 3. Ungrouped consonants and their ASCII representations

ಯ	ರ	ಲ	ವ	ಶ	ಷ	ಸ	ಹ	ಳ
ya	ra	la	va	Sa	Sha	sa	Ha	La

Table 4. Modification of base consonant by vowels

Vowel	Vowel Modifiers	When attached to consonat(ರ)
ಅ	್	ರ
ಆ	ಾ	ರಾ
ಇ	ಿ	ರಿ
ಈ	ೀ	ರೀ
ಉ	ು	ರು
ಊ	ೂ	ರೂ
ಋ	ೃ	ರೃ
ಋೂ	ೄ	ರೄ
ಎ	ೆ	ರೆ
ಏ	ೇ	ರೇ
ಐ	ೈ	ರೈ
ಒ	ೊ	ರೊ
ಓ	ೋ	ರೋ
ಔ	ೌ	ರೌ

Table 5. Consonant conjuncts

1.1 Line Segmentation

To segment the lines, the horizontal projection profile (HPP) of the document is obtained. HPP is the histogram of the number of ON pixels accumulated horizontally along every pixel row of the image. This profile has valleys of zero height between the lines, which serve as the separators of the text lines as depicted in Fig. 1. In the case of Kannada script, sometimes the bottom conjuncts of a line overlap with the top-matras of the following text line in the projection profile. This results in non-zero valleys in the HPP as shown in Fig. 2. These lines are called *kerned* [2] text lines. To segment such lines, the statistics of the heights of

the lines are found out from the HPP. Then the threshold is fixed at 1.6 times
the average line height. This threshold is chosen based on experimentation of
our segmentation algorithm on a large number of Kannada documents. Non-
zero valleys below the threshold indicate the locations of the text line and those
above the threshold correspond to the location of *kerned* text lines. The mid
point of a non-zero valley of a *kerned* text line is the separator of the line.

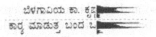 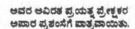

Fig. 1. The dotted lines indicate the obtained line boundaries.	**Fig. 2.** Kerned text lines. The horizontal projection profile does not have zero valleys in between the text lines.

Fig. 3. Word segmentation: A. Input text line, B. Text line image after dilation. C.
Vertical projection of image in B. The zero valleys in the projection separate the words.

1.2 Word Segmentation

Kannada words do not have *shirorekha*, all the characters in a word are isolated.
Further, the character spacing is non-uniform due to the presence of consonant
conjuncts. In fact, whenever the latter are present, the spacing between the base
characters in the middle zone becomes comparable to word spacing. This could
affect the accuracy of word segmentation. Hence, morphological dilation [3] is
used to connect all the characters in a word, before performing word segmentation. Each ON pixel in the original image is dilated with a structuring element.
Based on experimentation, we found that, for a scanning resolution of 400 DPI,
a structuring element of size 2x6 with all 1's (foreground) is adequate to connect
all the characters in a word. Then, the vertical projection profile (VPP) of the
dilated image is determined. This is the histogram of column-wise sum of ON
pixels. The zero-valued valleys in the profile of the dilated image separate the
words in the original image. This is illustrated in Fig. 3.

1.3   Zone Detection

Based on the HPP, each word is partitioned into three zones as depicted in Fig. 4. The imaginary horizontal line passing through the index corresponding to the maximum in the top half of the profile is the headline (starting of the ascenders) and the baseline corresponds to the maximum in the bottom half of the profile (starting of the descenders). The top zone denotes the portion above the headline, where top matras or ascenders occur. The gap between headline and baseline is the middle zone, which covers base and compound characters. Portion below the baseline is bottom zone in which bottom matras or descenders of aspirated characters occur. Also, the consonant conjuncts (see Table 5) occur in this zone.

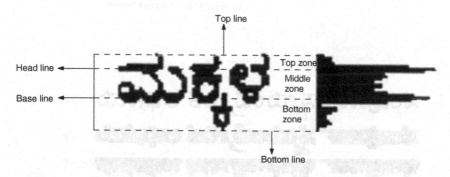

Fig. 4. Different zones of a Kannada word

1.4   Character Segmentation

Zone detection helps in character segmentation. Adjacent characters in a Kannada word sometimes overlap in the VPP due to the presence of consonant conjuncts as shown in Fig. 5(b). These are called *kerned* characters. Such characters cannot be segmented using zero-valued valleys in the projection profile. Using the baseline information, the text region in the *middle* and *top* zones of a word is extracted and its VPP is obtained. Zero-valued valleys of this profile are the separators of the characters (see Fig. 5(d)). Sometimes, the part of a consonant conjunct in the middle zone is segmented as a separate symbol. Such things are eliminated in the recognition phase, based on the total number of ON pixels in the symbol. The total number of Kannada characters, including base characters, characters formed with consonant-vowel combination, consonants with conjuncts and compound characters, are 34*34*14 + 14. This results in a huge number of classes for recognition, which is difficult to handle. So, we split the segmented character into a *base character* and a *vowel modifier* (top or right matra). The consonant conjuncts are segmented separately based on connected component analysis (CCA).

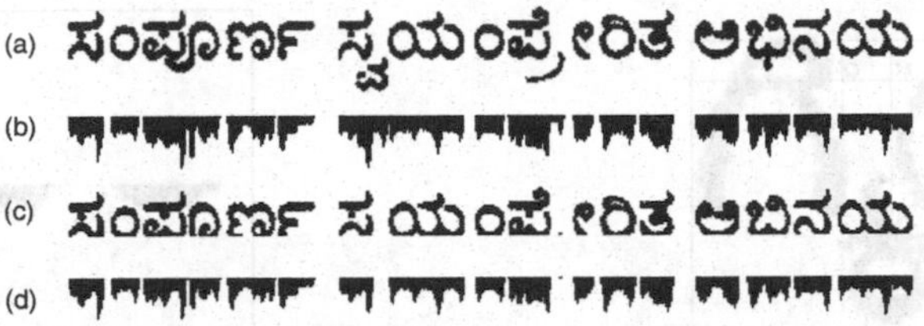

(a) ಸಂಪೂರ್ಣ ಸ್ವಯಂಪ್ರೇರಿತ ಅಭಿನಯ

(b) ┳┓┳┳┳┓┳┳┳ ┳┓┳┓┳┳┳┳┳ ┳┓┳┓┳┳┳

(c) ಸಂಪೂರ್ಣ ಸ ಯಂಪೆ.ೇರಿತ ಅಬಿನಯ

(d) ┳┓┳┳┳┳┳ ┳┓┳┳┳┳┳ ┳┳┳ ┳┓┳┳┳┳┳

Fig. 5. Character segmentation. (a) Input text image. (b) Its vertical projection. (c) The text part of the image (a) in middle and top zone above the baseline. (d) Vertical projection of image in (c). The zero valleys in this profile separate the characters.

Consonant Conjunct Segmentation. *Knowledge* based approach is used to separate the consonant conjuncts. The spacing to the next character in the middle zone is more for characters having consonant conjuncts than it is for others. To detect the presence of conjuncts, a block of image in the *bottom zone* corresponding to the gap between adjacent characters in the *middle zone* is considered as shown in Fig. 6. We call this image block as *partial image*. If the number of ON pixels in the partial image exceeds a threshold (set 15 pixels), a consonant conjunct is detected. Sometimes a part of the conjunct enters the middle zone between the adjacent characters. Such parts will be lost if the conjunct is segmented only in the bottom zone. Thus, in order to extract the entire conjunct, we use CCA. However, in some cases, the conjunct is connected to the character in the middle zone, causing difficulty in using CCA for segmenting only the conjunct. To address this problem, the character in the middle zone is removed before applying CCA. For example, in Fig. 6, CCA is applied on the image PQRS, after setting all the pixels in the part PMNO to zero. This results in the image shown in Fig. 7, which leads to the detection of three distinct connected components. The component with the maximum number of ON pixels is the conjunct.

Vowel Modifier Segmentation. This is divided into segmentation of *top* and *right* matras. The part of the character above the headline in the top zone is the *top matra*. Since the headline and baseline of each character are known and if the aspect ratio of the segmented character in the combined top and middle zones is more than 0.95, then it is checked for the presence of the right matra.

For *right matra* segmentation, three subimages of the character are considered as shown in Fig. 8: the whole character, head and tail images. The head image is the segment containing five rows of pixels starting from the headline downwards. Similarly, the tail image contains 5 rows downwards from the baseline. VPP for each of these images is determined. Let the index corresponding to the maximum of the profile of the character image be P. Let b1 and b2 be the indices corresponding to the first zero-values immediately after the index P, in the profiles of head and tail images, respectively. The break point is selected

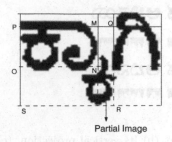

Fig. 6. Segmentation of consonant conjuncts

Fig. 7. Image used for connected component analysis, after setting the PMNO part of PQRS of Fig. 6 to background.

as the smaller of b1 and b2. The characters are normalized before feature extraction to avoid the effects of variations on the character image such as size and displacement. A separate normalization size is used for the base character and the vowel modifiers. The base characters are normalized to 32X32, while modifiers and consonant conjuncts are resized to a size of 16X16 using bilinear interpolation.

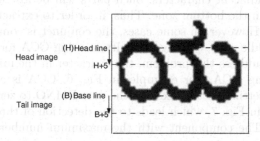

Fig. 8. Different subimages of a character considered for vowel modifier segmentation

2   Results

Fig. 9 gives the flow chart of the total Kannada OCR system. The software is implemented on a Sun-Ultra Sparc workstation using C language and *MATLAB* package under Unix platform. The data samples are collected by scanning various Kannada magazines with a resolution of 400 DPI. More than 40,000 characters are collected from these images. The results presented are based on presegmented characters. The training set for the base characters contains 1110 samples corresponding to 37 classes and each category has 30 patterns. In order to make the system more robust, some noisy characters are also included in the training

set. The performance of various features and classifiers have been evaluated on
a test set containing 1453 randomly selected characters with different font styles
and sizes. The results corresponding to different techniques employed for feature
extraction and classification are presented in the subsequent sections and these
results are based on presegmented characters. The vowels in Kannada script occur only at the beginning of a word. This information, if used while testing, not
only improves recognition accuracy but also helps in fast classification. Since this
knowledge is used in our work, each pattern in the test set also contains the information about its position in the word. The training sets for the modifiers and
the consonant conjuncts contain 180 and 540 patterns, corresponding to 9 and
27 classes, respectively. Various transform based features are used to evaluate
the performance of nearest neighbour (NN) and Neural network based classifiers.
The employed features include, the coefficients of the Discrete Cosine Transform
(DCT), Discrete Wavelet Transform (DWT) and Karhunen-Louve Transform
(KLT). The transforms are applied on the complete pattern image, rather than
on the subblocks. Due to energy compaction property of DCT, only the significant coefficients are considered for recognition. However, in case of DWT, the
approximate coefficients in the second level of decomposition are considered for
recognition. The KLT transformation matrix is obtained from the training samples. Using the eigen vectors corresponding to different numbers of significant
eigen values, results are obtained. Table 6 shows the recognition accuracy of NN
classifier for base characters using the various features.

Table 6. Recognition accuracy of NN Classifier on various features

Feature block size	Recognition rate (%) without structural features	Recognition time (min)	Recognition rate (%) with structural features	Recognition time (min)
Discrete cosine transform				
4x4	91.81	0.48	93.80	0.60
8x8	93.54	1.03	98.70	1.23
12x12	92.63	2.00	98.27	2.11
Karhunen-Louve transform				
40	92.56	0.78	98.70	0.92
50	92.70	0.93	98.55	1.13
60	92.84	1.18	98.77	1.32
Discrete wavelet transform				
Haar (8x8)	92.42	1.83	98.83	2.65
db2 (10x10)	92.36	2.25	98.55	3.53

Table 7 lists the pairs of confused characters using the NN classifier on DCT
features. DWT and KLT also gave almost the same confusion character pairs as
DCT using the NN classifier. The recognition rate is improves by around 6%, on
using the structural features in the second and third level to resolve the confused
characters. The structural features, such as aspect ratio, orientation of particular

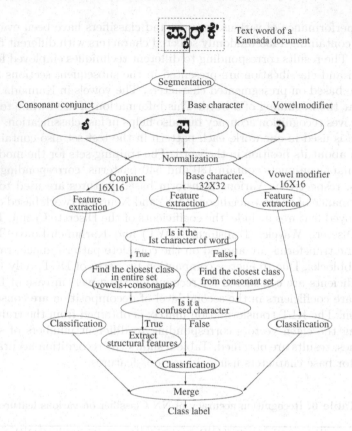

Fig. 9. Flow chart of the complete Kannada recognition system.

Table 7. Confused base character pairs using NN classifier on DCT features

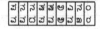

strokes, width of the middle zone and height of the segment in the top zone are extracted from the subimages of the character. Table 8 lists a group of confused characters and the structural features used to resolve them.

2.1 Performance Evaluation of Back Propagation Network (BPN) and Radial Basis Function (RBF) Network on Base Characters

The features found to be best in the previous sections are used to evaluate the performance of BPN and RBF networks [4]. The BPN was trained in batch mode using supervised learning employing logsigmoidal activation function. In order to obtain good generalization with the network, the weights and biases of the network are set to small random values. Because of the form of the activation function, the input is normalized to a range of 0 to 1 before training.

Table 8. Resolving confused characters using structural features

Confusion character set	ಚ ಜ ಜ ಜ
ಚ	The number of ON pixels more than 40 in the orientation 40-70 degrees in the lower right quarter image
ಜ	The length of maximum in the bottom half of image less than the 75% of the width of the character
ಜ	The number of ON pixels more than 35 in the orientation 20-50 degrees in the upper middle region of the image
ಜ	If all the above conditions are not satisfied

Also, the presentation of the training samples to the network is randomized. The RBF network employing Gaussian kernel as the activation function was trained in supervised mode of learning. The radial basis functions are centered on each training pattern and the layer biases are all kept constant depending on the spread of the Gaussian. The recognition performance studied for different values of the variance of the gaussian. In both the cases (BPN and RBF), structural features have been used in further levels of classification to discriminate between similar characters from different classes. The results corresponding to BPN and RBF are listed in the Tables 9 and 10, respectively. RBF performed

Table 9. Recognition accuracy using BPN with Haar (db1) wavelet features. [L1 and L2 are the number of nodes in the first and second hidden layers, respectively.]

Number of hidden layers	Number of hidden neurons	Recognition rate (%)	Recognition time (min)
Using 8x8 Haar features			
1	20	96.14	1.78
1	25	96.28	1.78
2	L1=35,L2=25	97.04	1.87
Using 8x8 DCT features			
1	20	95.87	1.81
1	25	95.73	1.64
2	L1=40,L2=25	94.15	0.98

better than the NN classifier and BPN with the same set of features. However, the highest recognition rate of around 99 % is achieved with Haar wavelets. On the other hand, DCT and KLT gave recognition accuracies of 98.8 % and 98.6 %, respectively with a spread of 11. As before, the performance using Haar features is consistently better. Advantage of the RBF network over the BPN is that, training time is very less.

Table 10. Recognition accuracy using RBF network with various features

Spread of Gaussian	Haar		DCT		KLT	
	Rec rate (%)	Rec time (min)	Rec rate (%)	Rec time (min)	Rec rate (%)	Rec time (min)
4	69.23	3.71	52.92	2.94	29.86	1.70
8	98.07	2.65	97.66	2.58	98.48	1.79
10	98.83	2.65	98.83	2.50	98.62	1.74
11	99.03	2.59	98.89	2.55	98.62	1.91

2.2   Recognition of Top and Right Matras

The training set for top and right matras, contains 9 classes with 20 samples
in each class and the test set contains 345 patterns. NN and RBF network are
compared for their performance. The spread of RBF is set based on the previous
experimental results. The results are listed in Table 11. RBF performed better
than NN classifier with the same set of features. However, the NN classifier
classifies faster than RBF.

2.3   Recognition of Consonant Conjuncts

The training set contains 27 classes with 20 samples in each class and the test
has 531 patterns. All the tests are performed with the 64-dimensional feature
vector, which is found to be best in the previous sections. The BPN and RBF are
trained in supervised mode of learning. In the case of wavelets, the approximation
coefficients of the first level of decomposition are used as features. Results are
shown in Table 12. Recognition performance of the NN classifier is better than
those of RBF and BPN networks, employing the best features. The recognition
time using db1 is always more than the time using DCT features. RBF and BPN
might perform better than NN classifier if the various parameters of the network
are properly tuned.

Table 11. Performance of NN classifier and RBF network on matras

Feature	Size of feature vector	NN Classifier		RBF, Spread=10	
		Recognition rate (%)	Recognition time (min)	Recognition rate (%)	Recognition time (min)
Haar (db1)	64	94.20	0.56	96.81	0.66
DCT	64	93.04	0.43	96.81	0.55

Table 12. Recognition of consonant conjuncts by various classifiers with Haar and DCT as features

Classifier	Size of feature vector	db1 (Haar) Recognition rate (%)	db1 (Haar) Recognition time (min)	DCT Recognition rate (%)	DCT Recognition time (min)
NN	64	96.61	0.37	96.79	0.21
BPN (50)	64	95.10	0.40	93.78	0.24
RBF (S=10)	64	95.66	0.48	95.48	0.31

2.4 Final Recognition Results

The classifier outputs the labels corresponding to the recognized base character, vowel modifier and consonant conjunct in the middle, top/middle and bottom zones, respectively. The recognized modifier and consonant labels are then appropriately attached to the recognized base character label to produce the final character label. These labels are then mapped to customized codes and stored in a file. This file can be viewed using any compatible Kannada type-setting software. KanTex is [5] is one such software which is compatible with LaTeX type-setting tools. Fig. 10 shows a test document (top part of the image) with a large number of noisy characters and the corresponding recognized output (bottom) is also shown in Fig. 10. The symbol '*' indicates rejected characters.

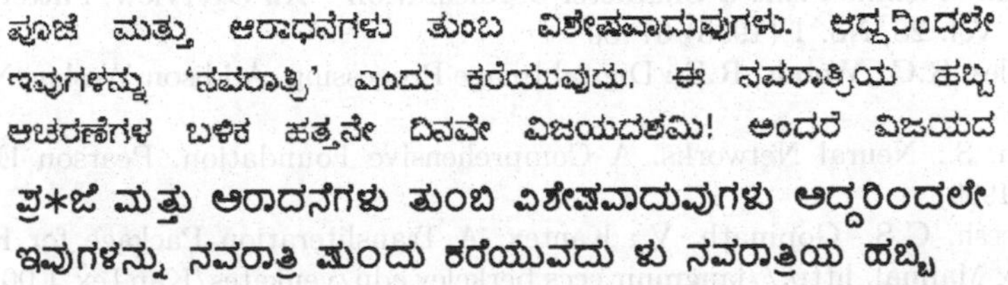

ಪೂಜೆ ಮತ್ತು ಆರಾಧನೆಗಳು ತುಂಬ ವಿಶೇಷವಾದುವುಗಳು. ಆದ್ದರಿಂದಲೇ ಇವುಗಳನ್ನು 'ನವರಾತ್ರಿ' ಎಂದು ಕರೆಯುವುದು. ಈ ನವರಾತ್ರಿಯ ಹಬ್ಬ ಆಚರಣೆಗಳ ಬಳಿಕ ಹತ್ತನೇ ದಿನವೇ ವಿಜಯದಶಮಿ! ಅಂದರೆ ವಿಜಯದ

ಪ್ರೈ*ಜ ಮತ್ತು ಆರಾದನೆಗಳು ತುಂಬಿ ವಿಶೇಷವಾದುವುಗಳು ಆದ್ದರಿಂದಲೇ ಇವುಗಳನ್ನು ನವರಾತ್ರಿ ಮಂದು ಕರೆಯುವದು ಳು ನವರಾತ್ರಿಯ ಹಬ್ಬಿ ಆಚರಣಗಳ ಬಿಳಿಕ ಹತ್ತನೆ* ದಿನವೇ ವಿಜಯದಶಮಿ ಅಂದರೆ ಎಜಯದ

Fig. 10. Input test document (top) and recognized output

3   Conclusions

The present work addresses the issues involved in designing a full fledged OCR system for printed Kannada text. Recognition of Kannada characters is more difficult than many other Indian scripts due to higher similarity in character shapes, a larger set of symbols and higher variability across fonts in the characters belonging to the same class. The performance evaluation of the various classifiers using transform based features has been presented. Experimental results show that employing structural features in the second stage of classification improves the recognition accuracy. This kind of hierarchical classification makes a high recognition rate possible with a small dimensional set of features. In the case of base characters, the performance of the RBF networks using Haar wavelet features followed by the structural features resulted in the highest recognition rate of around 99.03 %. On the other hand, NN classifier and BPN using the same input features achieved recognition rates of 98.83 % and 97.04 %, respectively. However, the recognition time of NN classifier was less than those of RBF and BPN.

In the case of consonant conjuncts, NN classifier performs better than RBF and BP networks. The recognition rate using NN classifier is 96.79 % with a recognition time of 0.21 minute by selecting the best of the features. On the other hand, RBF and BPN achieved recognition rates of 95.66 % and 95.10 % with recognition times of 0.25 min and 0.31 min, respectively.

For the recognition of the top and right matras, two different classifiers are applied on the test set containing 345 characters with 64-dimensional best feature vector. The recognition performance of RBF is 96.8 % and that of NN classifier is 94.2 % employing as features the approximation coefficients of the Haar wavelets in the first level of decomposition.

References

1. Chaudhuri, B.B., Pal, U.: A Complete Printed Bangla OCR System. Pattern Recognition, Vol. 31, No. 5 (1998) 531–549
2. Lu, Y.I.: Machine Printed Character Segmentation – An Overview. Pattern Recognition, Vol. 28, No. 1 (1995) 67–80
3. Gonzalez, R.C., Woods, R.E.: Digital Image Processing. Addison Wesley, New York (1993)
4. Haykin, S.: Neural Networks. A Comprehensive Foundation. Pearson Education Asia (1999)
5. Jagadeesh, G.S., Gopinath, V.: Kantex, A Transliteration Package for Kannada. Kantex Manual. http://langmuir.eecs.berkeley.edu/venkates/KanTex_1.00.html

An Integrated System for the Analysis and the Recognition of Characters in Ancient Documents

Stefano Vezzosi, Luigi Bedini, and Anna Tonazzini

Istituto di Elaborazione della Informazione - CNR
Via G. Moruzzi, 1, I-56124 PISA, Italy
{vezzosi, bedini, tonazzini}@iei.pi.cnr.it

Abstract. This paper describes an integrated system for processing and analyzing highly degraded ancient printed documents. For each page, the system reduces noise by wavelet-based filtering, extracts and segments the text lines into characters by a fast adaptive thresholding, and performs OCR by a feed-forward back-propagation multilayer neural network. The probability recognition is used as a discriminant parameter for determining the automatic activation of a feed-back process, leading back to a block for refining segmentation. This block acts only on the small portions of the text where the recognition was not trustable, and makes use of blind deconvolution and MRF-based segmentation techniques. The experimental results highlight the good performance of the whole system in the analysis of even strongly degraded texts.

1 Introduction

Standard Optical Character Recognition (OCR) systems, based on preliminary character segmentation, fail when applied to ancient printed texts, where aging of paper and diffusion of ink caused non-uniform contrast reduction of the images, presence of broken and touching characters, and background noise. Also Intelligent Character Recognition (ICR) systems, based on neural networks, though more robust against degradation, require correctly segmented characters. Often, the degradation can be modeled as an unknown space-variant blur plus additive noise, so that blind deconvolution is appropriate to enhance/restore the image. This highly underdetermined problem requires the adoption of a priori information and regularization strategies. Markov Random Fields (MRF) are efficient and flexible in modeling images, and allow for performing blind restoration and character segmentation jointly. To reduce the high computational complexity of these techniques, we use them for refining segmentation only on those zones of the document where the recognition fails. We thus define an integrated system that first applies a neural network classifier to a document page, preprocessed by simple and fast image enhancement and character segmentation techniques, and then, based on the recognition probability, automatically re-processes those small image areas where broken or touching characters were not correctly recognized. For small areas, blind restoration coupled with MRF segmentation is relatively cheap, allows for managing space-variant degradations, and is very effective in producing properly segmented, and then recognizable, characters.

D. Lopresti, J. Hu, and R. Kashi (Eds.): DAS 2002, LNCS 2423, pp. 49–52, 2002.

2 From the Document to the Characters

We assume that the degraded image $\mathbf{g}$ of a document page can be modeled as $\mathbf{g} = H(d)\mathbf{f} + \mathbf{n}$, where $\mathbf{f}$ is the ideal image, d is the blur mask, $H(d)$ is the matrix performing $2D$ convolution, and $\mathbf{n}$ is a white Gaussian noise.

The integrated system for the analysis of the document is constituted of various processing blocks that interact with each other as shown in Fig. 1. The first

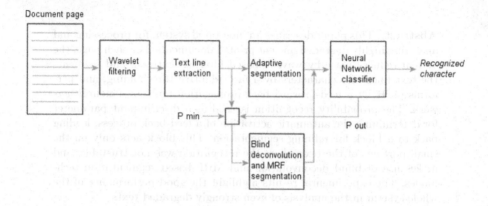

Fig. 1. Integrated system for document analysis and character recognition

block is designed to perform denoising through wavelet-based filtering. Neglecting the blur, the degraded image is decomposed by using the discrete wavelet transform (DWT), with the *symlet* function as the mother wavelet. In order to remove noise, the high frequency terms of the decomposition that are lower than the noise power are discarded via *soft thresholding* [1], and the others are used to reconstruct the image. This allows for preserving the character boundaries, usually mapped by frequency terms higher than the noise power.

The second step is devoted to the the extraction of the text lines. Since the lines are repeated in the page with an approximately fixed vertical distance, the projection of the page on the vertical axis is a periodic signal. The peak of the amplitude of the Fourier transform of this signal gives the repetition frequency of the text lines. Thus, once known the position of the first, all the lines can be extracted in sequence.

In the next step, each text line is segmented into blobs corresponding to the characters. The line is first converted into a two-level image, where the two levels, $a < b$, are the peaks of the bimodal hystogram, and correspond to the characters and the background, respectively. All pixels with value below a suitable threshold th are assigned with a and the others with b. The blobs are then segmented by extracting the connected components at value a. Since the quality of the image greatly varies across the page, the threshold is adaptively computed on small portions of the text line, as the one that minimizes the distance between the gray level image and the corresponding binarized image.

In the fourth block of the system, the blobs of each line are individually and sequentially processed by a neural network classifier. We used a multilayer feed-forward network, with a hidden layer, trained with an adaptive back-propagation algorithm, that uses the batch gradient descent with momentum and variable learning rate, to avoid local minima [2]. The training set was constituted of characters selected from a page of the document, and previously binarized and segmented with the techniques described above. We found that when the recognition percentage is above 90%, the recognition is correct and the corresponding segmentation is accurate. Below this value, both the recognition and the segmentation are usually wrong. In these cases, the corresponding sub-image is re-processed by taking the degradation into account. The new segmented blobs are given again as input to the network. If the percentage is now higher than 90%, the recognition is accepted, otherwise the blob is classified as unrecognizable.

3   Segmentation Refining Procedure

The refining of the segmentation is performed by the fifth processing block. When two adjacent blobs, recognized with low probabilities, are both smaller than a minimum size, they are joined into a single blob. When the recognition probability is low and the blob is large it likely corresponds to two or more joined characters. To split the characters we perform blind deconvolution [3] coupled with MRF image models [4], designed to produce a binarized solution. We define an energy function constituted of a data coherence term, plus a term related to the MRF model chosen. It is:

$$E(\mathbf{f}, d) = \|\mathbf{g} - H(d)\mathbf{f}\|^2 + \lambda U(\mathbf{f}) \qquad (1)$$

where $U(\mathbf{f})$ is the prior MRF energy, and λ is the regularization parameter. $U(\mathbf{f})$ describes constraints on the geometry of local configurations of the pixels. We adopted an extension of the Ising model to enforce smoothness on pairs of adjacent pixels [4], and to describe peculiar configurations of text pixels [5]. Since $E(\mathbf{f}, d)$ is non-convex, and has mixed, continuous and discrete, variables, we minimize it via the following iterative alternate scheme [6]:

$$d^k = argmin_d \|\mathbf{g} - H(d)\mathbf{f}^k\|^2 \qquad (2)$$

$$\mathbf{f}^{(k+1)} = argmin_\mathbf{f} \|\mathbf{g} - H(d^{(k)})\mathbf{f}\|^2 + \lambda U(\mathbf{f}) \qquad (3)$$

Within a simulated annealing (SA) scheme governed by a decreasing temperature parameter [7], (2) is solved via least mean squares, and a Metropolis algorithm [7] is used to update $\mathbf{f}$ in (3). This approach is very efficient for refining segmentation, thus improving recognition as well. Its high computational complexity does not significantly affect the cost of the overall system, since it is applied to a few, small areas of the page. Moreover, the back-forward loop is governed by simple parameters, i.e. the minimum probability for accepting the recognition of a character, and the minimum and maximum extent allowed for the blobs.

52   S. Vezzosi, L. Bedini, and A. Tonazzini

4 Discussion of the Experimental Results

The integrated system has been tested on some pages of the Opera Omnia by
Girolamo Cardano. Here we provide the results of the analysis of one of the
text lines. Fig. 2 shows the line segmented into blobs through the adaptive
thresholding algorithm. Though satisfactory, the segmentation presents some

principales Robur virium,Morbi exiften-

Fig. 2. Segmentation superposed to the filtered gray level image

errors: the two "n" are both broken into two separated blobs, and the adjacent
"o" and "b" are joined into a single blob. These errors are detected by the
neural network, that gives a recognition probability lower than 90% for the blobs.
These are back-forwarded to the segmentation refining procedure. For the "n",
the two small blobs were connected into a single one. For the large blob "ob",
we employed 15 iterations of scheme (2-3), obtaining a correct separation (Fig.
3). The final recognition resulted in the string "principales (t)obur virium(l)

principales Robur virium,Morbi exiften-

Fig. 3. Refined segmentation superposed to the filtered gray level image.

(si)orbi existen -", where only three blobs, over a total of 34, are recognized with
a probability lower than 90%. We highlight that the recognition errors are due
to the presence, in the training set, of only a few samples of characters R, M
and comma.

References

1. Donoho, D.L.: IEEE Trans. Information Theory. **41** (1995) 613–627.
2. Vogl, T.P. et al.: Biological Cybernetics. **59** (1988) 256–264.
3. Kundur, D., Hatzinakos, D.: IEEE Sig. Proc. Mag. (1996) 43–62.
4. Li, S.Z.: Markov Random Field Modeling in Computer Vision. (1995) Springer-Verlag Tokyo.
5. Tonazzini, A., Bedini, L.: Proc. 10th ICIAP. (1999) 836–841.
6. Ayers, G.R., Dainty, J.G.: Opt. Lett. **13** (1988) 547–549.
7. Aarts, E., Korst , J.: Simulated Annealing and Boltzmann Machines. (1989) Wiley.

A Complete Tamil Optical Character Recognition System

K.G. Aparna and A.G. Ramakrishnan

Biomedical Laboratory, Department of Electrical Engineering
Indian Institute of Science, Bangalore – 560 012
{prjocr,ramkiag}@ee.iisc.ernet.in

1 Introduction

Document Image processing and Optical Character Recognition (OCR) have been a frontline research area in the field of human-machine interface for the last few decades. Recognition of Indian language characters has been a topic of interest for quite some time. The earlier contributions were reported in [1] and [2]. A more recent work is reported in [3] and [9]. The need for efficient and robust algorithms and systems for recognition is being felt in India, especially in the post and telegraph department where OCR can assist the staff in sorting mail. Character recognition can also form a part in applications like intelligent scanning machines, text to speech converters, and automatic language-to-language translators.

Tamil is the official language of the southern state of Tamil Nadu in India, and also of Singapore, and is a major language in Sri Lanka, Malaysia and Mauritius. It is spoken by over 65 million people worldwide. The assumptions made in our work are that the document contains only printed text with no images and are uni-lingual.

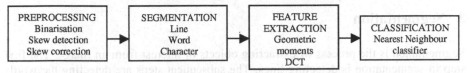

Fig. 1. Block diagram of our OCR System

2 Preprocessing

The block diagram of our OCR System is shown in Fig. 1. Preprocessing is the first step in OCR, which involves binarisation, skew detection [5] and skew correction. Binarisation is the process of converting the input gray scale image scanned with a resolution of 300 dpi into a binary image with foreground as white and background as black.

The skew introduced during the process of scanning is detected using the algorithm proposed by Kaushik et al [4], which is based on Hough transform and principal component analysis. An estimate of the skew angle is found to an accuracy of $\pm\ 0.06^{0}$. Such a high skew accuracy is needed as the first level of classification is based on the spatial occupancy of the characters as shown in Fig. 5. If skew is not properly detected, then characters will get misclassified in the first level itself.

While the skew detection is performed on the binarised document, correction, which involves rotating the image in the appropriate direction, is performed on a gray

D. Lopresti, J. Hu, and R. Kashi (Eds.): DAS 2002, LNCS 2423, pp. 53–57, 2002.
© Springer-Verlag Berlin Heidelberg 2002

scale image to lessen the quantization effects [7], which is caused when a binary image is rotated. Bilinear interpolation is employed for this purpose. The output of skew correction is shown in Fig 2.

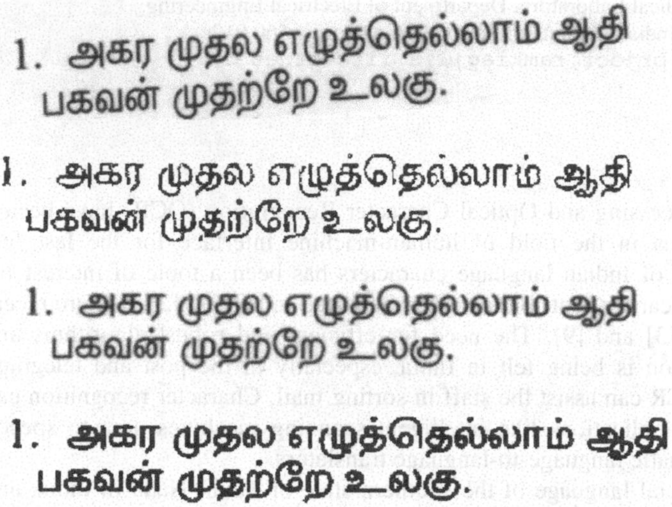

1. அகர முதல எழுத்தெல்லாம் ஆதி பகவன் முதற்றே உலகு.

Fig. 2a. Original skewed image

1. அகர முதல எழுத்தெல்லாம் ஆதி பகவன் முதற்றே உலகு.

Fig. 2b. Skew correction performed on binary image

1. அகர முதல எழுத்தெல்லாம் ஆதி பகவன் முதற்றே உலகு.

Fig. 2c. Skew corrected gray scale image

1. அகர முதல எழுத்தெல்லாம் ஆதி பகவன் முதற்றே உலகு.

Fig. 2d. Skew corrected binarised image

Fig. 2. Skew correction performed on Binary and Grayscale image

3 Segmentation

Segmentation is the process of extracting objects of interest from an image. The first step in segmentation is detecting lines. The subsequent steps are detecting the words in each line and the individual characters in each word, respectively.

Horizontal and vertical projection profiles are employed for line and word detection, respectively. Connected component analysis [6] is performed to extract the individual characters. The segmented characters are normalised to a predefined size and thinned before the recognition phase. Figures 3 and 4 show, respectively, the horizontal and vertical projections of a Tamil sentence.

கற்றதனால் ஆய பயனென்கொல் வாலறிவன் நற்றாள் தொழா அர் எனின்.

Fig. 3. Text lines with corresponding horizontal projection profiles

3. மலர்மிசை ஏகினான் மாணடி சேர்ந்தார்

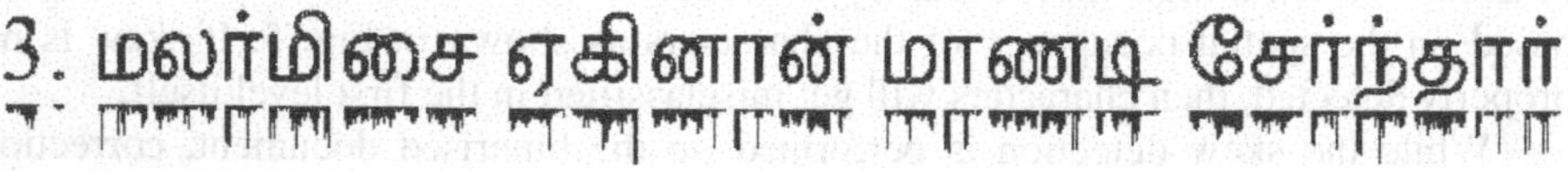

Fig. 4. Text lines with corresponding vertical projection profiles

4 Symbol Recognition

Tamil alphabet set contains 154 different symbols. This increases the recognition time and the complexity of the classifier, if single level classification is used. Hence, it is desirable to divide the characters into some clusters, so that the search space is reduced during recognition, which in turn results in lesser recognition time. Classification is based on spatial occupancy and on matras/extensions and recognition is based on orthonormal transform features.

5 Feature Extraction and Classification

5.1 Classification Based on Spatial Occupancy

This is the first level of clustering. The text lines of any Tamil text have three different segments as shown in Fig. 5. Depending upon the occupancy of these segments, the symbols are divided into one of the four different classes, defined as follows: Class 0 for symbols occupying segment 2, Class 1 for symbols occupying segments 1 & 2, Class 2 for symbols occupying 2 & 3 and Class 3 for symbols occupying all 3 segments.

Fig. 5. The three distinct vertical segments of Tamil script.

5.2 Classification Based on Matras/Extensions

This level of classification is applied only to symbols of classes 1 and 2, which have upward matras and downward extensions. The classes are further divided into Groups, depending on the type of ascenders and descenders present in the character. This level of classification is feature based i.e. the feature vectors of the test symbol are compared with the feature vectors of the normalised training set. The features [10] used in this level are *second order geometric moments* and the classifier employed is the nearest neighbour classifier.

5.3 Recognition Based on Orthonormal Transform Features

In the third level, feature-based recognition is performed. For each of the groups, the symbol normalisation scheme is different. The dimensions of the feature vector are different for different groups, as their normalisation sizes are different. Truncated Discrete cosine transform (DCT) coefficients are used as features at this level of classification. DCT [6] is the most compact frequency-domain description. It is possible to reconstruct the image with a high degree of accuracy, even with very few coefficients. This motivated us to use DCT of the image as a feature vector. Nearest neighbour classifier is used for the classification of the symbols.

6 Training Set

In order to obtain good recognition accuracy, a vast database of training data exceeding 4000 samples was created. Each character has around 50 samples collected from various magazines, novels, etc. The database includes bold and italic characters along with few special symbols and numerals. Font sizes from 14 to 20 were handled while testing the system.

The training feature set contains the features obtained from normalised and thinned symbols and a label to identify the character. The features of the unknown symbol are compared with the features of the known symbols in the training set. The label of the training sample that closely matches with the test character is assigned to the latter. A symbol is declared unknown if its nearest neighbour is beyond a certain threshold distance.

7 Classification Results

The System is being tested on files taken from tamil magazines and novels which are scanned at 300 dpi (dots per inch).. Results on a set of 100 chosen samples are discussed below. About 40% of the samples were taken from the Training Set. These resulted in an accuracy of over 99%. The remaining samples (disjoint from the Training Set) resulted in an recognition accuracy of around 98%. Hence the average recognition accuracy stands at an appreciable 98%. The result obtained with one of the test documents is shown in Fig. 6. For this sample the total number of input samples were 351. There was one rejection (~ symbol) and two symbols were misclassified.

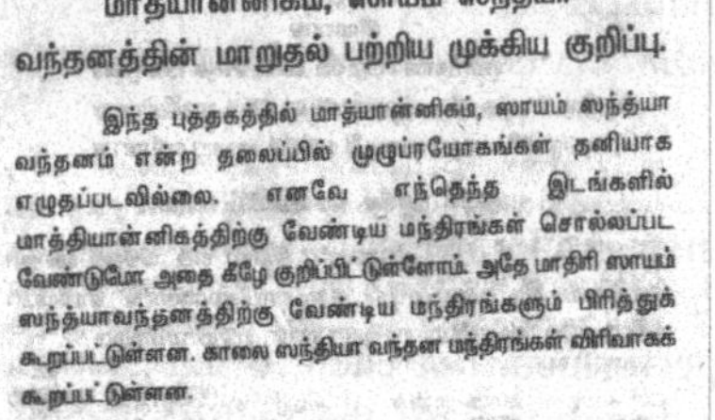
மாத்யான்னிகம், ஸாயம் ஸந்த்யா
வந்தனத்தின் மாறுதல் பற்றிய முக்கிய குறிப்பு.
இந்த புத்தகத்தில் மாத்யான்னிகம், ஸாயம் ஸந்த்யா
வந்தனம் என்ற தலைப்பில் முழுப்ரயோகங்கள் தனியாக
எழுதப்படவில்லை. எனவே எந்தெந்த இடங்களில்
மாத்தியான்னிகத்திற்கு வேண்டிய மந்திரங்கள் சொல்லப்பட
வேண்டுமோ அதை கீழே குறிப்பிட்டுள்ளோம். அதே மாதிரி ஸாயம்
ஸந்த்யாவந்தனத்திற்கு வேண்டிய மந்திரங்களும் பிரித்துக்
கூறப்பட்டுள்ளன. காலை ஸந்தியா வந்தன மந்திரங்கள் விரிவாகக்
கூறப்பட்டுள்ளன.

Fig. 6a. Original document

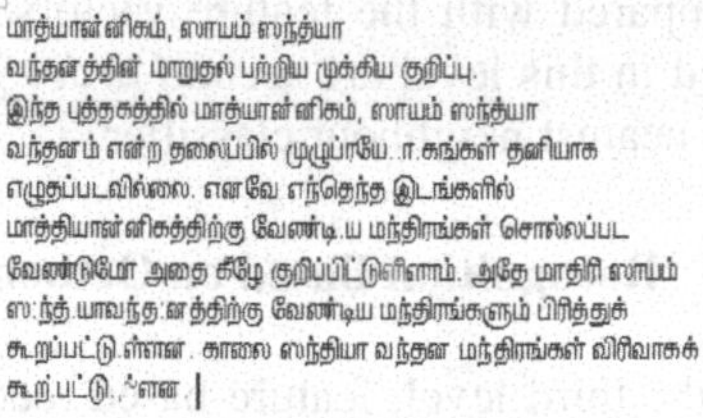
மாத்யான்னிகம், ஸாயம் ஸந்த்யா
வந்தனத்தின் மாறுதல் பற்றிய முக்கிய குறிப்பு.
இந்த புத்தகத்தில் மாத்யான்னிகம், ஸாயம் ஸந்த்யா
வந்தனம் என்ற தலைப்பில் முழுப்ரயே..ா.கங்கள் தனியாக
எழுதப்படவில்லை. எனவே எந்தெந்த இடங்களில்
மாத்தியான்னிகத்திற்கு வேண்டி.ய மந்திரங்கள் சொல்லப்பட
வேண்டுமோ அதை கீழே குறிப்பிட்டுள்ளோம். அதே மாதிரி ஸாயம்
ஸ:ந்த்.யாவந்த:னத்திற்கு வேண்டிய மந்திரங்களும் பிரித்துக்
கூறப்பட்டு.ள்ளன . காலை ஸந்தியா வந்தன மந்திரங்கள் விரிவாகக் ;
கூற்.பட்டு.,ʼளன . |

Fig. 6b. Recognised document

References

[1] Siromoney, G., Chandrashekaran, R., Chandrashekaran, M.: Computer recognition of printed Tamil characters, Vol. 10. Pattern Recognition, (1978) 243-247

[2] Sinha, R.M.K., Mahabala, H.: Computer recognition of printed Devnagari scripts, Vol. 9. IEEE trans. on Systems Man and Cybernetics, (1979) 435–441

[3] Pal, U., Choudhuri, B.B.: A Complete Printed Bangla OCR System, Vol. 31. Pattern Recognition, (1998)

[4] Kaushik Mahata, Ramakrishnan, A.G.: Precision Skew Detection through Principal Axis, Proc, Intern. Conf. on Multimedia Processing and Systems, Chennai, (2000)

[5] Chen, M., Ding, X.: A robust skew detection algorithm for grayscale document image, ICDAR, (1999) 617–620

[6] Gonzalez, R.C., Woods, R.E.: Digital Image Processing, Addison – Wesley Press, New York (1999)

[7] Dhanya, D., Ramakrishnan, A.G., Peeta Basa Pati.: Script Recognition in Bilingual Documents, Sadhana, (2002)

[8] Duda, R.O., Hart, P.E.: Pattern Classification and Scene Analysis, John Wiley and Sons, New York (1973)

[9] Govindan, V.K., Shivaprasad, A.P.: Character recognition – a review, Pattern Recognition (1990) 671-683

[10] Trier, O., Jain, A.K., Taxt, T.: Feature extraction methods for character recognition – a survey, Vol. 29. Pattern Recognition, (1996) 641–662

Distinguishing between Handwritten and Machine Printed Text in Bank Cheque Images

José Eduardo Bastos Dos Santos[1,2], Bernard Dubuisson[1], and Flávio Bortolozzi[2]

Heudiasyc – Université de Technologie de Compiègne(UTC)
BP 20529 – 60205 Compiegne cedex France
Tel. 33 3 44 23 44 23 – Fax. 33 3 44 23 44 77
{jose-eduardo.santos,bernard.dubuisson}@hds.utc.fr

[2]LUCIA –Pontifícia Universidade Católica do Paraná (PUCPR)
Rua Imaculada Conceição, 1155
80.215-901 Curitiba – Brasil
Tel. 55 41 330-1543 – Fax. 55 41 330-1392
{jesantos,fborto}@ppgia.pucpr.br

Abstract. In the current literature about textual element identification in bank cheque images, many strategies put forward are strongly dependent on document layout. This means searching and employing contextual information as a pointer to a search region on the image. However human handwriting, as well as machine printed characters, are not dependent on the document in which they are inserted. Components of handwritten and machine printed behavior can be maintained in a generic and independent way. Based on these observations this paper presents a new approach to identifying textual elements from a set of local features enabling the category of a textual element to be established, without needing to observe its environment. The use of local features might allow a more generic and reach classificatory process, enabling it in some cases to be used over different sorts of documents. Based on this assumption, in our tests we used bank cheque images from Brazil, USA, Canada and France. The preliminary results show the efficiency and the potential of this approach.

1 Introduction

The automatic treatment of bank cheques is a task that has been receiving increasing attention from scientists over past years. It remains a complex and challenging task where automatic detection of filled-in information is one of the main causes of difficulties. Up until to now, different solutions have been proposed to resolve these technical problems. Many of these are based on assumptions such as the spatial position of the information sought after on the image, the location of baselines or other kinds of contextual information. In this paper we present a new vision of how to treat the handwritten text identification of bank cheque images based on some local features. The main idea of this methodology centres on the fact that both machine printed and handwritten texts retain some characteristic features irrespective of the environment in which they are printed, i.e. independent of the document type. This allows us to look at these elements in such a way as to design a model able to characterize them without needing to look at other elements on the image besides

D. Lopresti, J. Hu, and R. Kashi (Eds.): DAS 2002, LNCS 2423, pp. 58–61, 2002.

textual objects. This means that we believe it is possible to determine a set of features devoted to textual elements identification and discrimination, with a strong degree of independence of the documents involved. Once we have defined this set, a classification process based on this feature group, can be applied in a generic way over an wide variety of documents.

This paper describes our experiences of obtaining a condensed yet sufficient group of features applied to handwritten text extraction. The documents used to test the selected features are bank cheque images presenting a great variety of different backgrounds, fonts and handwritten styles.

Preliminary results show the efficiency of our approach since cheque images from different banks and different countries were tested, allowing a more extensive view of features performance.

2 How to Observe Local Features

As mentioned in the previous section we observe some features locally in textual elements. These elements are isolated from the background by a morphological tophat that aims to suppress slow trends while enhancing the contrast of some elements on the image.

In order to observe selected features we have to divide the image into small portions containing only individual parts of textual elements. Firstly the entire image is equally shared between small frames of 11 x 11 pixels each. This can cause some bad apportionment since frames containing minute portions of elements or more than one object can be obtained. In this latter case we can isolate each of the elements on the frame image and treat them as individual elements. Where the portions of an element in a single frame are too small, we carry out an aggregation phase responsible for re-organizing portion sub-division. This gives a better representation of isolated objects. These small images would normally contain a portion of a handwritten or pre-printed character, since having portions of two different objects in the same frame can cause problems during the classification phase, since this is also based on some geometrical features. A well-divided image avoids the need for an eventual verification of some parts that have been poorly classified due to an inadequate representation on the frame (too few pixels).

Since we have an image that is well divided up into small elements, we will extract from these, some features representing their shape and their contents. Statistical features normally provide enough information about content, which due to different printing processes for handwritten and machine printed text, should provide a reliable and important discrimination factor. Mean and standard deviation are classical examples of content representation, since the ink distribution changes from printed to handwritten characters.

Even if we are not considering the characters on the image in its integrality, shape is another source of information that should not be forgotten when characterizing the two different types of text. Eccentricity and symmetry (related to the convex area) are examples of shape descriptors extracted from the objects.

In order to evaluate the pertinence of the features set chosen, we used a multi-layer perceptron based classifier. The input data set was composed of selected features extracted from the sample images. Different configurations were tested and the results proved not to be very dependent on network architecture. The diversity of the database needs to be underlined, since it was composed of cheques from more than 30 different banks based in four different countries. The features employed were selected using a neural network based method which considers how the algorithm and the training sets interact. Nine mainly geometrical and statistical features make up the resulting features sub-set.

Results obtained point to a significant improvement with regard to previous experiments, where frames were considered since their initial division and features arrangements were not taken into account. The images are represented by 256 gray levels and a 300 dpi resolution. More than 6800 sample images, equally divided between handwritten and machine printed text, were used in the classification process. The input data are reduced and centred on the mean after being used. The goal is to distinguish between handwritten or machine printed objects. A tax of nearly 90% of well-classified images was achieved in the test phase. The misclassified group of sample images is well composed of the two represented classes. Ambiguous samples were mainly composed of printed elements. A great diversity of writing styles were tested since the whole database contains more than 700 images from several different banks.

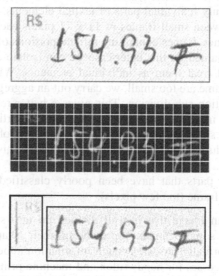

Fig. 1. Extract of a Brazilian bank cheque, its inital partition and final classification result.

Ambiguous samples were treated in order to increase the number of well-classified images. In this case, observing its neighbourhood gave us the probability of each ambiguous sample belonging to the handwritten or the machine printed class. The results were improved. One such example is shown in image 1.

3   Concluding Remarks

In this paper we presented a local feature based textual classification process. The idea of using local features is linked to the assumption that handwritten and machine printed text preserve their general typographical features independent of the context in which they are inserted. Defining an adequate set of features related to textual elements' shape and content allows the identification of these elements in a more generic and context free way.

Our main objective in this paper is to demonstrate the effectiveness of handwriting identification when performed through modelling textual elements. This modelling is carried out by observing some local features in a way that is totally independent of context and which can allow for the use of the current methodology with similar tasks for different kinds of documents.

Using content and shape as discriminative elements for the two kinds of text analyzed, we assume that is possible to verify directly the behaviour of a textual element - handwritten or not - over its component pixels, without needing to observe the environment in which it is inserted. This assumption can be easily verified for example when writing one's name on a form or on another document type. Most people tend to do this in the same manner for every kind of document.

Initial results prove that this methodology contributes a new perspective to the textual element identification of documents which is broad reaching and generic.

We are currently working to improve our features set in order to ameliorate our results. The use of other faster classifiers is also under study.

References

1. John D. Hobby. Using shape and layout information to find signatures, text and graphics. *Computer Vision and Image Understanding*, 80(1): 88–110, October, 2000.
2. J. E. B. Santos, B. Dubuisson and F. Bortolozzi. *Handwritten Text Extraction from Bank Cheque Images by a Multivariate Classification Process*. 6th World Multi Conference on Systemics, Cybernetics and Informatics – SCI'02, Orlando – USA, 2002.
3. Nikolay Gorski, Valery Anisimov, Emmanuel Augustin, Olivier Baret, Sergey Maximov. *Industrial bank check processing: the a2ia check reader*. International Journal on Document Analysis and Recognition, 3(4) :196–206, May, 2001.
4. P. Clark and M. Mirhehdi. *Combining statistical measures to find image text regions*. In ICPR'00, pages 450 – 453, Barcelona – España, 2000.
5. Xiangyun Ye, Mohamed Cheriet and Ching Y. Suen. *A generic system to extract and clean handwritten data from business forms*. In Seventh International Workshop on Frontiers in Handwriting Recognition, pages 63–72, Amsterdam, 2000.

Multi-expert Seal Imprint Verification System for Bankcheck Processing

Katsuhiko Ueda and Ken'ichi Matsuo

Department of Information Engineering, Nara National College of Technology
Yamatokoriyama, Nara 639-1080, Japan
ueda@info.nara-k.ac.jp

Abstract. A difficult problem encountered in automatic seal imprint verification is that the system is required an extremely low error rate despite of the variety of seal imprint quality. To conquer this problem, we propose a multi-expert seal imprint verification system, which combines two different verification algorithms. The first verification algorithm is based on a method using local and global features of seal imprint. The second one uses a special correlation method based on a global approach. The two algorithms are combined by a voting strategy. Experimental results showed that the combination of the two algorithms improves significantly the verification performance both on "false-acceptance error rate" and "false-rejection error rate".

1 Introduction

Automatic bankcheck processing is an active topic in the field of document analysis and processing. Validity confirmation of bankchecks is one of the important problems in automatic bankcheck processing. In Japan and some oriental countries, seal imprints have been widely used for validating bankchecks.

Many researches on this problem have been made. However the design of seal imprint verification system for validating bankchecks still remains a difficult problem because of some specific characteristics: (1) forged seal imprints with very similar pattern to a registered one may appear in practical applications. (2) seal imprints may have a lot of variations, even if they are all produced from a single seal. As for (1), Ueda[1] proposed a verification algorithm using local and global features of seal imprints (called "feature-based algorithm" in this paper). As for (2), Horiuchi[3] proposed an algorithm using a special correlation method (called "correlation-based algorithm" in this paper). However it is difficult to adapt to all of the above specific characteristics by only individual verification algorithms.

In this paper, we propose a new multi-expert seal imprint verification system, which combines two different verification algorithms mentioned above. Through the verification experiments, we will also present that the combination of the two verification algorithms allows a significant improvement in the verification performance.

D. Lopresti, J. Hu, and R. Kashi (Eds.): DAS 2002, LNCS 2423, pp. 62–65, 2002.

2   Verification Scheme

The seal imprint verification system presented in this paper is shown in Fig.1. The seal imprint is first extracted from a bankcheck image by a color clustering technique[2]. Successively, the extracted seal imprint is positioned over the corresponding registered seal imprint[1]. Each verification module verifies the seal imprint with the corresponding registered one. The system provides the response on the authenticity of bankcheck by combining the outputs of both verification modules.

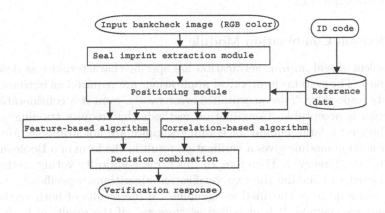

Fig. 1. Multi-expert seal imprint verification system.

2.1   Feature-Based Algorithm[1],[2]

This module verifies seal imprints using their local and global features. The dissimilarity measure for verifying seal imprints is computed by using the features. Let $\{D_i(i = 1, 2, ..., n)\}$ be the obtained dissimilarities between the registered seal imprint and its n genuine samples for training. Moreover, let D_{av} and σ_I be the mean value and the standard deviation of $\{D_i\}$ respectively. The dissimilarity limit (threshold) D_T of the genuine seal imprints for each registered one is defined as the following equation.

$$D_T = D_{av} + a\sigma_I \qquad (1)$$

where "a" is a certain constant value.

After the dissimilarity D_u of an examined seal imprint is computed, two types of decision can be made as follows:

1. If $D_u \leq D_T$, the input seal imprint is classified as a genuine.
2. If $D_u > D_T$, the input seal imprint is classified as a forgery.

2.2   Correlation-Based Algorithm[3]

The dissimilarity measure between an examined and a registered seal imprints is defined as follows:

$$D = 1 - \frac{\sum_{x,y} f(x,y)g(x,y)}{\sum_{x,y} f(x,y)} \tag{2}$$

where, $f(x,y), g(x,y)$ denote an examined and a registered seal imprint image respectively. Both images are binary. Equation (2) means that this correlation algorithm evaluates only the excess of pixels of an examined seal imprint. The methods of a threshold definition and a decision are the same as those described in the above subsection.

2.3   Decision Combination Module

The problem of seal imprint verification has specific characteristics as described in Section 1. The systems in practical applications are required an extremely low error rate (especially "false acceptance error rate"), even if a considerable rate of rejection is acceptable. Combination methods that require training are not useful, because a large number of training samples are not available. Moreover each verification module gives a verification result in the form of a Boolean value ("genuine" or "forgery"). Therefore, in this work, a majority voting method has been adopted to combine the two verification algorithms. Specifically, the examined seal imprint is classified as "genuine", if the results of both verification algorithms are genuine. It is classified as "forgery", if the results of both verification algorithms are forgery. Otherwise it is rejected as "ambiguous".

3   Experimental Results

We used five genuine seals with various shapes and three forged seals for each genuine one. The example of seal imprints generated from each seal is shown in Fig.2. 100 imprints for each genuine seal and 50 imprints for each forged seal were stamped on real bankchecks. Therefore, 500 genuine seal imprints and 750 forged seal imprints were used for the performance evaluation of this system.

The performance of this system were measured by verification experiment. The verification performance of the combination system as well as the performance of individual algorithms is compiled in Table 1. In this Table, FAR and FRR mean "false-acceptance error rate" and "false-rejection error rate" respectively. Rejection rate means "ambiguous rate" caused by rejection due to discrepancy between two verification results from individual verification algorithms. This result shows the different behavior of two verification algorithms, i.e., the feature-based algorithm performs better for detecting forgeries, while the correlation-based algorithm performs better for accepting genuine seal imprints. The proposed combination system allows a significant improvement in the verification performance. In fact, this system was able to achieve FAR=0.4%, FRR=1.2%, with Rejection rate of 17.1%.

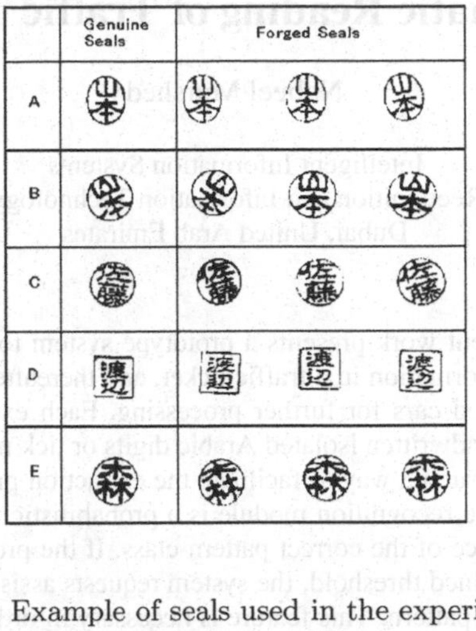

Fig. 2. Example of seals used in the experiments.

Table 1. Performance of the proposed system and individual verifiers.

	Feature-based Algorithm	Correlation-based Algorithm	Proposed system
FAR(%)	2.9	9.3	0.4
FRR(%)	11.4	5.6	1.2
Rejection Rate(%)	—	—	17.1

4 Conclusions

In this paper, we proposed a multi-expert seal imprint verification system, which combines two different verification algorithms. The experimental results showed that the combination of the two different verification algorithms improves significantly the verification performance. This system might be feasible for practical applications.

Acknowledgement. This work was supported in part by Grant-in-Aid for Scientific Research under Grant No. 13680500 sponsored by Japan Society for the Promotion of Science.

References

1. K. Ueda, "Automatic seal imprint verification system with imprint quality assessment function", IEICE Trans. Inf. & Syst., E77-D, 8, pp.885–894 (1994).
2. K. Ueda, T. Mutoh and K. Matsuo, "Automatic verification system for seal imprints on Japanese bankchecks", Proc. of ICPR'98, pp.629–632 (1998).
3. T. Horiuchi, "Automatic seal verification by Evaluating Positive Cost", Proc. of ICDAR'01 (2001).

Automatic Reading of Traffic Tickets

Nabeel Murshed

Intelligent Information Systems
A Pattern Recognition and Information Technology Company
Dubai, United Arab Emirates

Abstract. The present work presents a prototype system to extract and recognize handwritten information in a traffic ticket, and thereafter feeds them into a database of registered cars for further processing. Each extracted information consists either of handwritten isolated Arabic digits or tick mark "x". The ticket form is designed in such a way to facilitate the extraction process. For each input, the output of the recognition module is a probabilistic value that indicates the system confidence of the correct pattern class. If the probabilistic output is less than the determined threshold, the system requests assistance from the user to identify the input pattern. This feature is necessary in order to avoid feeding in wrong information to the database, such as associating the traffic ticket with the wrong registered car.

1. Introduction

Automatic reading of documents has become an interesting application area of Document Analysis Systems. Many systems have been developed for a wide range of applications. The reader is referred to the proceedings of the IAPR Workshops on Document Analysis Systems [1–4]. Most systems have been targeted towards Latin, Germanic, and Far Eastern languages. The present work is aimed at extracting and recognizing Arabic handwritten numerals for police application. To our knowledge, no system have been developed so far for such application.

Independent of the language, most automatic reading systems share two principle requirements: high recognition rate and short processing time, which are directly related to each other. In almost all cases, achieving high recognition rates could yield a relatively long processing time. One may argue that with the high speed of personal computers, one could obtain acceptable recognition results with acceptable processing time. A third important requirement is the degree of human interaction to increase the recognition rate, particularly in critical applications.

The objective of the proposed system is to extract and recognize six pieces of handwritten information from a traffic violation ticket. The information represent the following: date and time of violation, number and color of the number plate, violation type, and the policeman's ID number. All of those information are handwritten numerals except the color and violation type which are tick mark "x". The recognized information are put into a record associated with the number plate. Figure 1, in page 4, shows an example of the traffic violation form designed for the application at hand.

The paper is organized as follow. Section 2 and 3 describes, respectively, system architecture and experimental results. Comments and conclusion are given in section 3.

D. Lopresti, J. Hu, and R. Kashi (Eds.): DAS 2002, LNCS 2423, pp. 66–69, 2002.
© Springer-Verlag Berlin Heidelberg 2002

2. System Description

The proposed system is composed of three modules: Preprocessing, extraction of handwritten information, and recognition. Input image is scanned at 300 dpi. The output of the scanning process is a black and white image. The preprocessing module uses de-skewing algorithm to correct image inclination and, thereafter, applies thinning process [5] to reduce the image to a one-pixel wide image. Hull [6] described the performance of various image skew detection algorithms. We have evaluated all of the algorithms mentioned in that reference and found the method of Bessho et al [7] is sufficient for our purpose.

As seen in figure 1 the image contains six fields of information, each of which is composed of specific number of squares. The size of all squares are equal (28x28 pixels. For the sake of discussion, we will use the term "*infobits*" to refer to the information contained in each square. From the point of view of image processing, an infobits is a set of connected black pixels. The marks "– ", localized at specific points, on the right-hand side of the image is included to aid the extraction process. To extract each infobits, we have employed a modified architecture of the Discrete Neural Networks (DNN) proposed by Murshed [8]. The DNN detects one-pixel-wide line segments, and it is composed of slabs whereby each slab is composed of layers of neurons. The size of the slab equals the size of the input image. The modified network consists of one slab only, the size of which equals the size of the square, i.e., 28x28 pixels. Its purpose is to detect the existence of a square and an infobits. Parallel programming was used to process each neuron simultaneously. A square is detected if 80% of the boundary pixels are black. This number was determined empirically using database of 4000 images. From the analysis of those images, we have noticed the existence of line discontinuity (number of white pixels in a sequence of adjacent black pixels) due to the scanning and thinning processes. In all cases the magnitude of the discontinuity did not exceed 10 pixels. The extraction network provides two signals, each of which indicates, respectively, the existence of a boundary and an infobits. If the value of each signal is '1', then the recognition module is triggered and the detected infobits is centralized inside a 28x28 square, and then passed to the recognition network.

The recognition module is composed of a Probabilistic Fuzzy ART neural network, which is a modified version of the original network introduced by Carpenter and Grossberg [9]. Its internal mechanism is modified such that its output is a probabilistic value that indicates how confidence the network is with respect to the pattern class. The confidence level is set internally. If the network confidence is lower than the preset value, the system requests the user to identify the input pattern. Such user interaction reduces the overall system error to zero. This feature is crucial when dealing with automatic reading of traffic tickets, because a single error means a wrong number plate is ticketed which in turn causes annoyance to its owner.

3. Experimentation and Results

The prototype system was evaluated with a database of 8000 images. The database was split into two sets d_{6000} and d_{2000}, each of which was used for training/testing and evaluation, respectively. The subscript indicates the magnitude of the data set. The magnitude of the training set is 0.8 | d_{6000}| and that of the test set is 0.2 | d_{6000}|. Training and testing were repeated 33 times using the same magnitude of the corresponding data set but different images. It should be noted that the images were selected randomly. The following algorithm describes the experimental setup.

```
Start;
    for i = 1 to 33;
        select randomly the training set from d_6000;
        train the network;
        test the network;
        calculate the error;
        shuffle the data set d_6000;
    end for;
    evaluate the network with the evaluation set d_2000;
end.
```

The average correct recognition rate, on the test set, calculated over 33 trials was 93%. The lowest and highest were, respectively, 87% and 97%. The recognition rate on the evaluation set was 90%, and the lowest rate was 89%. Note that when applying the confidence criterion and user interaction, the recognition rates increased to 100%.

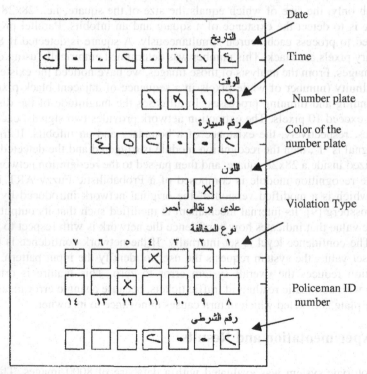

Fig. 1. An image of the traffic ticket form. For legal reasons some information were not shown. Moreover, the number plate and the policeman ID number are fictitious.

4. Comments and Conclusion

In this paper we have presented a prototype system for reading the traffic tickets. The system presented satisfactory results and the application of the confidence criterion helped increasing the recognition rates to 100%. Currently we are working towards improving the recognition rate, which will require fewer interactions from the user, and reducing the processing time, which is currently 10 seconds per form. We will also modify the experimental setup to select the optimum skew detection and thinning algorithms in terms of processing time and recognition rate.

Besides the Fuzzy Art network, we have also tested the Back-propagation NN, Probabilistic NN, and SOM NN. The Fuzzy ART presented better results. The front end of the system was implemented with Visual basic, and all the processing algorithms in Visual C++.

References

1. Proceedings of the First IAPR Workshop on Document Analysis Systems. Eds. A. Lawrence Spitz and Andreas Dengel. World Scientific Press. 1995.
2. Document Analysis Systems II , Proceedings of the Second IAPR Workshop on Document Analysis Systems. Eds. Jonathan Hull and Suzanne Taylor. World Scientific Press. 1998.
3. Proceedings of the Third IAPR Workshop on Document Analysis Systems. 1998.
4. Proceedings of the Fourth IAPR Workshop on Document Analysis Systems. Eds. Nabeel Murshed and Adnan Amin. 2000.
5. G. Dimauro, S. Impedovo and G. Pirilo, "A new Thinning Algorithm Based on Controlled Detection of Edge Region," Thinning Methodologies for Pattern Recognition, C. Y. Suen and P. S. P. Wang, World Scientific Press, 1994, 969–986.
6. Jonathan Hull, "Document Image Skew Detection: Survey and Annotation Bibliography," Document Analysis Systems II, Second IAPR Workshop on Document Analysis Systems. Eds. Jonathan Hull and Suzanne Taylor. World Scientific Press. 1998, 40–64.
7. G. Bessho, K. Ejiri and J. F. Cullen, "Fast and accurate skew detection algorithm for a text or a document with straight lines," Proceedings of the SPIE – The International Society for Optical Engineering, Conference on Document Recognition 2181 (February 9–10, 1994), 133–140.
8. Nabeel Murshed, "A Discrete Neural Network for Detection of Line Segments," Proceedings of the Fourth IAPR Workshop on Document Analysis Systems. Eds. Nabeel Murshed and Adnan Amin. 2000.
9. Gail Carpenter and Steven Grossberg, "Fuzzy ART: Fast stable learning and categorization of analog patterns by an adaptive resonance system," Neural Networks, 4, 759–771.

A Stochastic Model Combining Discrete Symbols and Continuous Attributes and Its Application to Handwriting Recognition

Hanhong Xue and Venu Govindaraju

CEDAR, Department of Computer Science and Engineering
SUNY at Buffalo, Buffalo, NY 14260, USA
{hxue, govind}@cedar.buffalo.edu

Abstract. This paper introduces a new stochastic framework of modeling sequences of features that are combinations of discrete symbols and continuous attributes. Unlike traditional hidden Markov models, the new model emits observations on transitions instead of states. In this framework, a feature is first labeled with a symbol and then a set of feature-dependent continuous attributes is associated to give more details of the feature. This two-level hierarchy is modeled by symbol observation probabilities which are discrete and attribute observation probabilities which are continuous. The model is rigorously defined and the algorithms for its training and decoding are presented. This framework has been applied to off-line handwritten word recognition using high-level structural features and proves its effectiveness in experiments.

1 Introduction

Stochastic models, especially hidden Markov models (HMMs), have been successfully applied to the field of off-line handwriting recognition in recent years. These models can generally be categorized as being either discrete or continuous, depending on their observation types.

Bunke *et al.* [1] model an edge in the skeleton of a word image by its spatial location, degree, curvature and other details, and derived 28 symbols by vector quantization for discrete HMMs. Chen *et al.* [2] use 35 continuous features including momental, geometrical, topological and zonal feature in building continuous density and variable duration HMMs. Mohammed and Gader [3] incorporate locations of vertical background-foreground transitions in their continuous density HMMs. Senior and Robinson [4] describe a discrete HMM system modeling features extracted from a grid. The features include information such as the quantized angle that a stroke enters from one cell to another and the presence of dots, junctions, endpoints, turning points and loops in a cell. El-Yacoubi *et al.* [5] adopt two sets of discrete features, one being global features (loops, ascenders, descenders, etc.) and the other being bidimensional dominant transition numbers, in their HMMs.

As can be seen, most of the previous studied stochastic models focus on modeling low-level statistical features and fall into being either discrete or continuous.

D. Lopresti, J. Hu, and R. Kashi (Eds.): DAS 2002, LNCS 2423, pp. 70–81, 2002.
© Springer-Verlag Berlin Heidelberg 2002

In studying handwriting recognition using high-level structural features, such as loops, crosses, cusps and arcs shown in Figure 1(a), we find it more accurate to associate these features, which are discrete symbols, with some continuous attributes. These attributes include position, orientation, and angle between strokes as shown in Figure 1(b) and they are important to recognition tasks because more details are given regarding the feature. For example, vertical position is critical in distinguishing an 'e' and an 'l' when both of them are written in loops. Since the vertical position can be anywhere in the writing zone, it takes continuous values.

Therefore, this paper tries to explore a new approach of modeling sequences consisting of discrete symbols and their continuous attributes for off-line handwriting recognition.

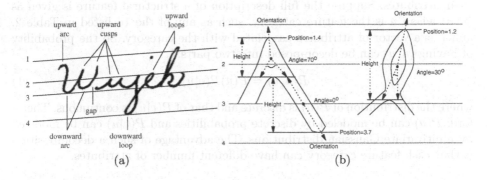

(a) (b)

Fig. 1. High-level structural features and their possible continuous attributes

Table 1. Example of structural features and their attributes, extracted from Figure 1(a)

character	symbol	position	orientation	angle
W	upward arc	1.2		126°
	downward arc	3.1		143°
	upward cusp	1.6	74°	
	downward arc	2.9		153°
	upward cusp	1.4	82°	
	gap	0.2		
...	...			
k	downward cusp	3.0	-90°	
	upward loop	1.0		
	downward arc	3.0		149°
	upward cusp	2.0	80°	

2   Structural Features

Table 2 lists the structural features that are used to model handwriting in this paper. In these features, long cusps and short cusps are separated by threshold-ing their vertical length. Left-terminated arcs are arcs whose stroke ends at its left side; right-terminated arcs are arcs whose stroke ends at its right side. All other features can be easily understood. For each feature, there is a set of con-tinuous attributes associated with it. (Refer to Figure 1 for the meaning of the attributes.) Position is relative to reference lines. Orientation and angle are in radius (shown in degrees in Figure 1 to be better understood). Width is relative to average character width. All the features and their attributes are obtained by the skeletal graph approach described in [6].

To model the distribution of structural features, we need to also consider their attributes. Suppose the full description of a structural feature is given as (u, v) where u is the feature category, such as any of the 16 listed in Table 2, and v is a vector of attributes associated with the category. So the probability of having (u, v) can be decomposed into two parts:

$$P(u, v) = P(u)P(v|u), \tag{1}$$

where the distribution of $P(u)$ is discrete and that of $P(v|u)$ is continuous. There-fore, $P(u)$ can be modeled by discrete probabilities and $P(v|u)$ can be modeled by multivariate Gaussian distributions. The advantage of such a decomposition is that each feature category can have different number of attributes.

Table 2. Structural features and their attributes. 16 features in total. Attributes as-sociated with a feature are marked.

structural feature	position	orientation	angle	width
upward loop	X			
upward long cusp	X	X		
upward short cusp	X	X		
upward arc	X			X
upward left-terminated arc	X			X
upward right-terminated arc	X			X
circle	X			
downward loop	X			
downward long cusp	X	X		
downward short cusp	X	X		
downward arc	X			X
downward left-terminated arc	X			X
downward right-terminated arc	X			X
cross	X			
bar	X			
gap				X

3   Model Definition

To model sequences of structural features with continuous attributes, we define stochastic finite-state automaton $\lambda = < S, L, A >$ as follows.

- $S = \{s_1, s_2, ..., s_N\}$ is a set of states, assuming single starting state s_1 and single accepting state s_N.
- $L = \{l_1, l_2, ..., l_M\}$ is a set of discrete symbols corresponding to feature categories. For each symbol, there is a set of continuous attributes to describe its details. So an observation is represented as $o = (u, v)$ where $u \in L$ is a symbol and v a vector of continuous values. A special symbol, the null symbol ϵ, has no attributes and does not appear in the input.
- $A = \{a_{ij}(o)\}$, the *observation probability*, is a set of probability density functions (pdfs), where $a_{ij}(o)$ is the pdf of features observed while transitioning from state i to state j. The sum of outgoing probabilities from a state must be 1, *i.e.*

$$\sum_j [a_{ij}(\epsilon) + \sum_u \int_v a_{ij}(u, v) dv] = 1 \tag{2}$$

for all state i.

Given a non-null observation $o = (u, v) = (l_k, v)$, the observation probability is decomposed into two parts:

$$a_{ij}(o) = P(l_k, v | i, j) = P(l_k | i, j) P(v | l_k, i, j) = f_{ij}(l_k) g_{ijk}(v). \tag{3}$$

The first part is called the *symbol observation probability*, which is the probability of observing a symbol l_k regardless its attributes. The second part is called the *attribute observation probability*, which is defined by a probability density function on the attributes that the symbol l_k has. The null symbol does not have any attribute, so its observation probability is denoted as

$$a_{ij}(\epsilon) = f_{ij}(\epsilon), \tag{4}$$

where only the symbol observation probability presents. Unlike in HMMs, here we do not have pure transition probabilities since observations are actually emitted by transitions instead of states.

We model attribute observation probabilities by multivariate Gaussian distributions

$$g_{ijk}(v) = \frac{1}{\sqrt{(2\pi)^{d_k} |\sigma_{ijk}|}} e^{-\frac{1}{2}[(v - \mu_{ijk})' \sigma_{ijk}^{-1} (v - \mu_{ijk})]}, \tag{5}$$

where μ_{ijk} is the average of attributes of symbol l_k on the transition from state i to state j, σ_{ijk} is the covariance matrix of these attributes, and d_k is the number of attributes symbol l_k has. In practice, we assume the covariance matrix is diagonal for simplicity and for the fact that attributes involved are strongly independent to each other. It should be noticed that symbols are not required to have the same number of attributes. As the number of attributes increases, observation probabilities decrease exponentially. Therefore, they are actually normalized by taking their d_k-th root to make them comparable.

The input to a model is an observation sequence $O = (o_1, o_2, ..., o_T)$ where $o_t = (u_t, v_t)$, $u_t \in L$ and v_t is a vector of continuous values. For example, $u_1 =$ "upward arc", $v_1 = (1.2, 126°)$ and $u_6 =$ "gap", $v_6 = (0.2)$ in Table 1.

We define the predicate $Q(t, i)$ to mean that the model is in state i at time t. Given the input, a state sequence $Q(t_0, q_0), Q(t_1, q_1), ..., Q(t_W, q_W)$ describes how the model interprets the input by transitioning from the starting state at time 0 to the accepting state at time T. So it is required that $t_0 = 0$, $q_0 = 1$, $t_W = T$ and $q_W = N$.

In this stochastic model, the general problem is to decide observation probabilities which also imply the model topology. At the training phase, the Forward-Backward algorithm can be used to decide observation probabilities given a set of sample observation sequences; while at the decoding phase, the Viterbi algorithm gives a good approximation to the probability of having some input given the model. Details will be given in later sections.

4 Training

The training is done by the Forward-Backward or Baum-Welch algorithm [7], with a little modification. This algorithm is a subcase of the Expectation-Maximization algorithm, which guarantees to converge to a local extremum.

4.1 Forward and Backward Probabilities

The forward probability $\alpha_j(t) = P(o_1, o_2, ...o_t, Q(t, j)|\lambda)$ is defined as the probability of being in state j after the first t observations given the model. It can be recursively calculated by the following equation.

$$\alpha_j(t) = \begin{cases} 1 & , j = 1, t = 0 \\ \sum_i (\alpha_i(t)a_{ij}(\epsilon) + \alpha_i(t-1)a_{ij}(o_t)) & , \text{otherwise} \end{cases} \tag{6}$$

The first term in the sum accounts for observing the null symbol, which does not consume any input observation, and the second term accounts for observing some non-null symbol in the input.

The backward probability $\beta_i(t) = P(o_{t+1}, o_{t+2}, ...o_T, Q(t, i)|\lambda)$ is defined as the probability of being in state i before the last $T - t$ observations given the model. It can be calculated recursively as follows.

$$\beta_i(t) = \begin{cases} 1 & , i = N, t = T \\ \sum_j (a_{ij}(\epsilon)\beta_j(t) + a_{ij}(o_t)\beta_j(t+1))s & , \text{otherwise} \end{cases} \tag{7}$$

Similarly, the two terms in the sum account for the null symbol and some non-null symbol in the input, respectively.

Finally, $\alpha_N(T) = \beta_1(0) = P(O|\lambda)$ is the overall probability of having the input given the model.

4.2   Re-estimation

Define $\omega_{ij}(t) = P(Q(t,i), Q(t,j)|O, \lambda)$ as the probability of observing ϵ while transitioning from state i to state j at time t, and $\tau_{ij}(t) = P(Q(t-1,i), Q(t,j)|O, \lambda)$ as the probability of observing a non-null symbol while transitioning from state i at time $t-1$ to state j at time t. $\omega_{ij}(t)$ and $\tau_{ij}(t)$ can be computed by the following equations.

$$
\begin{aligned}
\omega_{ij}(t) &= P(Q(t,i), Q(t,j)|O, \lambda) \\
&= \frac{P(Q(t,i), Q(t,j), O|\lambda)}{P(O|\lambda)} \\
&= \frac{P(o_1, o_2, \ldots o_t, Q(t,i)|\lambda) a_{ij}(\epsilon) P(Q(t,j), o_{t+1}, o_{t+2}, \ldots o_T|\lambda)}{P(O|\lambda)} \\
&= \frac{\alpha_i(t) a_{ij}(\epsilon) \beta_j(t)}{\alpha_N(T)}
\end{aligned}
\tag{8}
$$

$$
\begin{aligned}
\tau_{ij}(t) &= P(Q(t-1,i), Q(t,j)|O, \lambda) \\
&= \frac{P(Q(t-1,i), Q(t,j), O|\lambda)}{P(O|\lambda)} \\
&= \frac{P(o_1, o_2, \ldots o_{t-1}, Q(t-1,i)|\lambda) a_{ij}(o_t) P(Q(t,j), o_{t+1}, o_{t+2}, \ldots o_T|\lambda)}{P(O|\lambda)} \\
&= \frac{\alpha_i(t-1) a_{ij}(o_t) \beta_j(t)}{\alpha_N(T)}
\end{aligned}
\tag{9}
$$

The symbol observation probability $f_{ij}(u)$ is re-estimated as the expected number of transitions from state i to state j seeing symbol u divided by the expected number of transitions out from state i.

$$
\hat{f}_{ij}(u) = \begin{cases} \dfrac{\sum_t \omega_{ij}(t)}{\sum_j \sum_t (\omega_{ij}(t) + \tau_{ij}(t))} & , u = \epsilon \\[3ex] \dfrac{\sum_{t, u_t = u} \tau_{ij}(t)}{\sum_j \sum_t (\omega_{ij}(t) + \tau_{ij}(t))} & , u \neq \epsilon \end{cases}
\tag{10}
$$

This estimation directly conforms to the constraint that the sum of outgoing probabilities from a state must be 1.

Since the null symbol does not have any attribute, re-estimation of attribute observation probability is only necessary for non-null symbols. The definition of attribute observation probability has two parameters. The average of attributes of symbol l_k on the transition from state i to state j is re-estimated as

$$
\hat{\mu}_{ijk} = \frac{\sum_{t, u_t = l_k} \tau_{ij}(t) v_t}{\sum_{t, u_t = l_k} \tau_{ij}(t)}
\tag{11}
$$

and the covariance of these attributes is similarly re-estimated as

$$
\hat{\sigma}_{ijk} = \frac{\sum_{t, u_t = l_k} \tau_{ij}(t) (v_t - \mu_{ijk})'(v_t - \mu_{ijk})}{\sum_{t, u_t = l_k} \tau_{ij}(t)}.
\tag{12}
$$

Notice that the denominators in the above two equations are the same as the numerator of the $u \neq \epsilon$ case in Equation 10.

4.3   Parameter Tying

Sometimes model parameters cannot be reliably re-estimated due to large variations or the lack of sufficient samples. For example, self-transitions absorb extra
features that are more likely to have all kinds of attributes, so their parameters
tend to be less reliable. In this case, parameters for all self-transitions in a model
can be tied in re-estimation and shared in decoding.

We tie the attribute observation probabilities for all self-transitions in a
model. Let μ_k and σ_k be the mean and the variance of the attributes of l_k on all
self-transitions, respectively. They are re-estimated by the following equations.

$$\hat{\mu}_k = \frac{\sum_i \sum_{t,u_t=l_k} \tau_{ii}(t)v_t}{\sum_i \sum_{t,u_t=l_k} \tau_{ii}(t)}, \tag{13}$$

$$\hat{\sigma}_k = \frac{\sum_i \sum_{t,u_t=l_k} \tau_{ii}(t)(v_t - \mu_k)'(v_t - \mu_k)}{\sum_i \sum_{t,u_t=l_k} \tau_{ii}(t)}. \tag{14}$$

5   Decoding

The decoding is done by the Viterbi algorithm, which produces the most probable
state sequence for a given input O. Define $\gamma_i(t)$, the Viterbi probability, as the
highest probability of being in state i at time t produced by one state sequence,
then it can be recursively calculated as follows.

$$\gamma_j(t) = \begin{cases} 1 & ,j=1,t=0 \\ \max(\max_i\ \gamma_i(t)a_{ij}(\epsilon),\ \max_i\ \gamma_i(t-1)a_{ij}(o_t)) & ,\text{otherwise} \end{cases} \tag{15}$$

Finally, $\gamma_N(T)$ is the Viterbi probability of observing the entire sequence O given
the model.

6   Modeling Words

Word models are obtained by concatenating character models. However, word
modeling is different for training and decoding, as shown in Figure 2. During
training, image truths are provided with the case (uppercase or lowercase) of
all letters determined, so linear concatenation is sufficient. In decoding, since
the image truth is unknown, the model of a candidate word must allow all
possible combinations of cases. Therefore, bi-gram case probabilities, which are
the probabilities of having the case of a character given the case of its previous
character, are applied to modeling the case change between neighboring letters.

We obtain the bi-gram case probabilities from training data and give them
in Table 3. According to this table, it is much more probable to have uppercase
letters as the first letter of a word than have lowercase letters. This is because
our training set is made of postal words that are usually capitalized. It also
can be seen, a letter is likely to have the same case as its previous letter, with
exceptions for vowels that are more likely to be in lowercase than in uppercase.

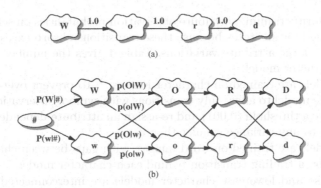

Fig. 2. Connecting character models to build word models for (a) training, and (b) decoding.

Table 3. Probabilities of the case of a character given the case of its previous character. If a character begins a word, then its previous character is #.

	a	A	b	B	c	C	d	D	e	E	f	F	g	G
#	0.308	0.692	0.002	0.998	0.022	0.978	0.015	0.985	0.011	0.989	0.029	0.971	0.073	0.927
lowercase	0.982	0.018	0.982	0.018	0.989	0.011	0.992	0.008	0.993	0.007	0.987	0.013	0.998	0.002
uppercase	0.644	0.356	0.065	0.935	0.145	0.855	0.290	0.710	0.660	0.340	0.339	0.661	0.267	0.733

	h	H	i	I	j	J	k	K	l	L	m	M	n	N
#	0.010	0.990	0.021	0.979	0.047	0.953	0.008	0.992	0.015	0.985	0.065	0.935	0.103	0.897
lowercase	0.992	0.008	0.997	0.003	0.500	0.500	0.966	0.034	0.997	0.003	0.989	0.011	0.981	0.019
uppercase	0.675	0.325	0.748	0.252	0.500	0.500	0.172	0.828	0.489	0.511	0.588	0.412	0.228	0.772

	o	O	p	P	q	Q	r	R	s	S	t	T	u	U
#	0.046	0.954	0.029	0.971	0.333	0.667	0.006	0.994	0.029	0.971	0.022	0.978	0.111	0.889
lowercase	0.998	0.002	0.972	0.028	0.947	0.053	0.982	0.018	0.984	0.016	0.993	0.007	0.998	0.002
uppercase	0.666	0.334	0.451	0.549	0.200	0.800	0.517	0.483	0.176	0.824	0.324	0.676	0.839	0.161

	v	V	w	W	x	X	y	Y	z	Z				
#	0.018	0.982	0.025	0.975	0.500	0.500	0.099	0.901	0.500	0.500				
lowercase	0.993	0.007	0.993	0.007	0.958	0.042	0.987	0.013	0.950	0.050				
uppercase	0.178	0.822	0.076	0.924	0.250	0.750	0.436	0.564	0.500	0.500				

7   Experimental Results

We implement the above-described stochastic models for handwritten word recognition. Figure 3 pictures the control flow of the system. Details of the entire training-decoding process are given as follows.

1. Feature sequences of training characters, training words and testing words are extracted.
2. Character models, including both uppercase and lowercase, are built from training feature sequences extracted on character images. The number of states in a model is simply decided according to the average length of the training sequences and a state i is connected to a state j if (a) $j = i$, or, (b) $j > i$ and $j - i \equiv 1 \bmod 2$. Therefore, the models are guaranteed to be acyclic in topology (except for self transitions) and the connections are not fully

dense. During training, attribute observation probabilities on self transitions will be tied for all states because these transitions absorb excessive features that have large attribute variations. Table 4 gives the number of states for each character model.

3. The models are trained on character images. [1] To prevent over-training, we prune the model to allow only transitions with symbol observation probabilities above a threshold (0.001) and re-assign an attribute-dependent minimum variance to any variance smaller than it.

4. The models are trained on word images, with gaps between characters considered by a trailing transition behind each character model.

5. Uppercase and lowercase character models are interconnected by bi-gram probabilities to get word models for matching against an input feature sequence.

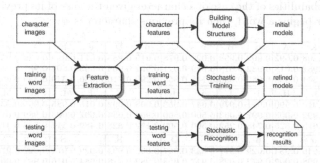

Fig. 3. Control flow of the word recognition system, including both training and decoding(recognition)

Table 4. Numbers of states in character models. (8.0 on average for uppercase and 8.4 on average for lowercase)

character	A	B	C	D	E	F	G	H	I	J	K	L	M	N	O	P	Q	R	S	T	U	V	W	X	Y	Z
# states	8	8	7	7	8	8	9	8	7	8	8	8	11	9	7	7	7	8	7	8	8	8	10	7	9	8

character	a	b	c	d	e	f	g	h	i	j	k	l	m	n	o	p	q	r	s	t	u	v	w	x	y	z
# states	8	9	8	8	8	8	8	9	8	8	8	8	11	9	7	8	9	8	7	8	9	9	11	8	9	8

In order to test the effectiveness of associating continuous attributes with discrete symbols, we start without any attributes and add in them one by one. The first attribute added is the width of gaps and the position of all other

---

[1] It is possible to skip this step and train the models directly on word images. However, this step gives a chance to reach a better local extremum for the next step according to our experimental experiences.

structures. The second attribute added is the orientation of cusps and the angle of arcs. It should be noticed that some features, such as gaps and loops, do not have more than one attribute, so eventually we are modeling features with different numbers of attributes. Table 5 shows accuracy rates obtained on a set of 3,000 US postal images (CEDAR BHA testing set) with lexicons of different sizes. This testing set is considered as relatively difficult because some words that are very similar to the truth have been inserted in the lexicon to confuse recognizers. It can be seen that the addition of continuous attributes significantly improves the recognizer's performance, especially when the lexicon size is large.

Table 5. Recognition results using different number of continuous attributes, on lexicon of size 10, 100, 1000 and 20000.

Lexicon size	10			100			1000			20000		
max # attr.	0	1	2	0	1	2	0	1	2	0	1	2
Top 1	94.46	95.66	96.56	80.14	85.15	89.12	62.56	69.97	75.38	38.35	50.40	58.14
Top 2	97.96	98.19	98.77	88.28	91.56	94.06	74.87	82.68	86.29	48.10	49.15	66.49
Top 10				96.90	97.93	98.19	88.19	92.29	94.39	66.76	75.63	81.31
Top 20							91.99	94.59	96.50	73.60	80.41	85.71
Top 100										86.45	89.79	93.39

Table 6 compares the stochastic recognizers against other recognizers tested on the same data set. The first one is a recognizer modeling image segments by continuous density variable duration HMMs [8]. The second one is an approach of over-segmentation followed by dynamic programming on segment combinations [9]. The third one is a recently improved version of the second one by incorporating Gaussian mixtures to model character clusters [10]. To compare, the stochastic recognizer is better than [8] and [9] but worse than [10]. This is largely due to the inconsistency in the feature extraction procedure where many different heuristics are used to identify structural features and to arrange them approximately in the same order as they are written. For some images, the procedure produces unexpected feature sequences, such as features in reversed order, which are not familiar to the trained models and cause recognition errors.

8   Conclusions and Future Work

This paper presents a stochastic framework of modeling features that consist of discrete symbols associated with continuous attributes, aiming at its applications to off-line handwritten word recognition using high-level structural features. In this framework, different sets of attributes can be associated with different discrete symbols, providing variety and flexibility in modeling details. As supported by experiments, the addition of continuous attributes to discrete symbols does improve the overall recognition accuracy significantly.

Now we are investigating some possible ways of improving the recognizer. The first one is to expand the feature set to capture more detailed handwriting

Table 6. Performance comparison against other three word recognizers on the same testing set.

Lex size		[8]	[9]	[10]	This paper
10	Top 1	93.2	96.80	96.86	96.56
	Top 2		98.63	98.80	98.77
100	Top 1	80.6	88.23	91.36	89.12
	Top 2		93.36	95.30	94.06
	Top 3	90.2			
	Top 20		98.93	99.07	99.10
1000	Top 1	63.0	73.80	79.58	75.38
	Top 2		83.20	88.29	86.29
	Top 3	79.3			
	Top 5	83.9		93.29	91.69
	Top 50		98.70	98.00	98.40
20000	Top 1			62.43	58.14
	Top 2			71.07	66.49
	Top 10			83.62	81.31
	Top 20			87.49	85.71
	Top 100			93.59	93.39

styles, which means more symbols and more attributes. The second one is to make feature extraction more robust to writing styles and image quality. The third one is to optimize the model topology by learning from training examples. All these remain challenging tasks for the future.

References

1. H. Bunke, M. Roth, and E. Schukat-Talamazzini, "Off-line cursive handwriting recognition using hidden Markov models," *Pattern Recognition*, vol. 28, no. 9, pp. 1399–1413, 1995.
2. M. Chen, A. Kundu, and S. Srihari, "Variable duration hidden Markov model and morphological segmentation for handwritten word recognition," *IEEE Transactions on Image Processing*, vol. 4, pp. 1675–1688, December 1995.
3. M. Mohammed and P. Gader, "Handwritten word recognition using segmentation-free hidden Markov modeling and segmentation-based dynamic programming techniques," *IEEE Transactions on Pattern Analysis and Machine Intelligence*, vol. 18, pp. 548–554, May 1996.
4. A. Senior and A. Robinson, "An off-line cursive handwriting recognition system," *IEEE Transactions on Pattern Analysis and Machine Intelligence*, vol. 20, no. 3, pp. 309–321, 1998.
5. A. El-Yacoubi, M. Gilloux, R. Sabourin, and C. Y. Suen, "An HMM-based approach for off-line unconstrained handwritten word modeling and recognition," *IEEE Transactions on Pattern Analysis and Machine Intelligence*, vol. 21, pp. 752–760, August 1999.
6. H. Xue and V. Govindaraju, "Building skeletal graphs for structural feature extraction on handwriting images," in *International Conference on Document Analysis and Recognition*, (Seattle, Washington), pp. 96–100, September 2001.

7. L. Baum, "An inequality and associated maximization technique in statistical estimation for probabilistic functions of Markov processes," *Inequalities*, vol. 3, pp. 1–8, 1972.
8. M. Chen, *Handwritten Word Recognition Using Hidden Markov Models*. PhD thesis, State University of New York at Buffalo, September 1993.
9. G. Kim and V. Govindaraju, "A lexicon driven approach to handwritten word recognition for real-time applications," *IEEE Transactions on Pattern Analysis and Machine Intelligence*, vol. 19, pp. 366–379, April 1997.
10. S. Tulyakov and V. Govindaraju, "Probabilistic model for segmentation based word recognition with lexicon," in *Proceedings of Sixth International Conference on Document Analysis and Recognition*, (Seattle), pp. 164–167, September 2001.

Top-Down Likelihood Word Image Generation Model for Holistic Word Recognition

Eiki Ishidera[1], Simon M. Lucas[2], and Andrew C. Downton[3]

[1] Multimedia Research Labs. NEC Corporation
4-1-1, Miyazaki, Miyamae-ku, Kawasaki, 216-8555, Japan
`ishide@ccm.cl.nec.co.jp`
[2] Dept. of Computer Science
University of Essex, Colchester CO4 3SQ, UK
`sml@essex.ac.uk`
[3] Dept. of Electronic Systems Engineering
University of Essex, Colchester CO4 3SQ, UK
`acd@essex.ac.uk`

Abstract. This paper describes a new top-down word image generation model for word recognition. This model can generate a word image with a likelihood based on linguistic knowledge, segmentation and character image. In the recognition process, first, the model generates the word image which approximates an input image best for each of a dictionary of possible words. Next, the model calculates the distance value between the input image and each generated word image. Thus, the proposed method is a type of holistic word recognition method. The effectiveness of the proposed method was evaluated in an experiment using type-written museum archive card images. The difference between a non-holistic method and the proposed method is shown by the evaluation. The small errors accumulate in non-holistic methods during the process carried out, because the non-holistic methods can't cover the whole word image but only part images extracted by segmentation, and the non-holistic method can't eliminate the black pixels intruding in the recognition window from neighboring characters. In the proposed method, we can expect that no such errors will accumulate. Results show that a recognition rate of 99.8% was obtained, compared with only 89.4% for a recently published comparator algorithm.

1 Introduction

Converting old documents, such as museum archive cards, into electronic data is one of the most important applications of OCR techniques [1]. Such archives are typically recorded using poor quality typewriting that dates from the early 20th Century. Depending on such factors as the age of the archive card, and the state of typewriter and its ribbon, archives contain faded or broken characters, or over-heavy touching characters. These make segmentation difficult.

Several methods have been proposed to avoid the segmentation difficulties in poor quality machine-printed documents. Sawaki [2] proposed a method of

D. Lopresti, J. Hu, and R. Kashi (Eds.): DAS 2002, LNCS 2423, pp. 82–94, 2002.

segmenting and recognizing characters in a newspaper by using displacement matching and a complementary similarity measure. Lucas [3] proposed a method with a sliding OCR window and an efficient graph search algorithm. In the case of handwriting, the method employed by Ozdil [4] can extract each individual character from cursive script. Since these methods do not involve any prior segmentation, they are robust to problems such as broken and touching characters. We classify these methods as the "comprehensive OCR approach". They assume that the region in which the best recognition score is obtained constitutes the best segmentation. However, it is difficult to know how to treat a good recognition score from an area which does not represent the correct single character(s), thus we should not overlook the potential correctness of the segmentation.

There are also other segmentation-free approaches such as the holistic approach[5][6][7] and HMM approaches [8][9][10]. Holistic word matching treats the word as a single, indivisible entity and attempts to recognize it using features of the word as a whole[5][6]. The method employed by Lu [7] generates the word template from individual character templates and then compares the word template to the image to be recognized. This method is not very robust to the case of including partly faded or broken characters because it eliminates all of the space between the adjacent characters in both the template image and the word image. Such an elimination seriously deforms the shape of the image with included faded or broken characters.

In the HMM method, the potential correctness of the segmentation is not used explicitly[8], so the HMM method involves the same problem as the comprehensive OCR approach. Lethelier[9] and Gilloux[10] proposed a probabilistic model based on HMMs by which the potential correctness of the segmentation is represented. However, the method proposed by Lethelier[9] generates some segmentation hypotheses, so this method is not a segmentation-free approach. In the method employed by Gilloux[10], the potential correctness of the segmentation is estimated through the Baum-Welch re-estimation algorithm. All these approaches are however based on bottom-up models.

In this paper we describe a new top-down likelihood word image generation model for word recognition. Since the model proposed in this paper contains three kinds of explicit likelihoods (linguistic knowledge, segmentation and character image), it can generate each word image with a likelihood value of itself. In the recognition process, first, the model generates the word image which approximates an input best over all search parameters. Next, the model calculates the distance value between the input image and the generated word image. The effectiveness of the proposed method was evaluated in an experiment using type-written museum archive card images. Results show that a recognition rate of 99.8% was obtained.

2   Word Image Generation Model

In this section, we define the word image generation model. Let us consider the case of a human writing down a given word on a piece of paper by hand.

First, the word to be written down is generated from a word generator. Next, the style of writing (cursive script or block style) is chosen[11][12] and the position of the writer's hand and the paper roughly gives a location of each individual character. Then the writer can draw each character's pattern on the paper. We can also consider the case that the person types a given word on paper with a typewriter. In this case, the status of the typewriter gives the style (font type) and the location of each character. We can consider that each individual character's pattern appears individually and independently.

The word image generation model proposed here consists of four parts. The first is a word generator, the second a style generator, the third a character locator and the fourth a character image generator (fig 1).

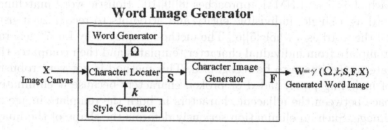

Fig. 1. Word Image Generator

The word generator generates the word $\Omega = \{\omega_1, \omega_2, \cdots, \omega_n\}$ to be written. The word Ω consists of n characters, and ω_i indicates the i-th character's category. Since we are considering the case that the word Ω is given, we can assume that Ω is independent of any other information and thus, the probability of Ω is set as a constant.

$$P(\Omega) = Const.$$

The style of writing is also specified. In the case of typewriting, for example, the style gives the type of typewriter (font type, the size of the font and the pitch of individual characters), status of the ink ribbon, the strength of typing (heavy or light). We assume that the style is independent of any other information, so the probability of the style "k" can be set as constant.

$$P(k) = Const.$$

Next, let X be an image canvas consisting of width and height. When the word Ω, the style k and the image canvas X is obtained, the character locater gives the location and the size of each character as $S = \{s_1, s_2, \cdots, s_n\}$. Here, $s_i = \{w_i, h_i, x_i, y_i\}$ is the i-th segment which is represented by the size and coordinate parameters. A segment s_i gives the position and size of the character image corresponding to the i-th character's category ω_i. Here, w_i and h_i are the width and the height, and (x_i, y_i) is the center of the segment s_i respectively.

We assume that the size and the location of the character depends only on the category of the character, and the category, size and location of the previous character. Thus, we assume a bi-gram for the character locator, that the i-th segment s_i is correlated only to the (i-1)-th segment s_{i-1}, the i-th character's category ω_i and the (i-1)-th character's category ω_{i-1}. We also assume that the size of the image canvas X roughly gives the size of the word image to be generated. Then, we can write the probability of S as follows.

$$P(S \mid \Omega, k, X) = P(s_1 \mid \Omega, k, X) P(s_2 \mid s_1, \Omega, k, X) \cdots P(s_n \mid s_{n-1}, \Omega, k, X)$$
$$= P(s_1 \mid \omega_1, k, X) \prod_{i=2}^{n} P(s_i \mid s_{i-1}, \omega_{i-1}, \omega_i, k, X)$$

In the last step, the character image generator fills each segment of the postulated word by corresponding character images (normalized in size) according to the style k. When we consider the case of typewriting, we can assume that the character's image is generated independently and individually only according to the law of a probability density function. Thus, we can write the probability of $F = \{f_1, f_2, \cdots, f_n\}$ as follows.

$$P(F \mid \Omega, k, S, X) = \prod_{i=1}^{n} P(f_i \mid \omega_i, k)$$

Here, f_i is the i-th character's image, corresponding to ω_i and s_i.

Then we can obtain the probability of a generated word image W as follows;

$$P(W \mid X) = P(\Omega, k, S, F \mid X)$$
$$= P(\Omega)P(k)P(s_1 \mid \omega_1, k, X)P(f_1 \mid \omega_1, k)$$
$$\prod_{i=2}^{n} P(f_i \mid \omega_i, k)P(s_i \mid s_{i-1}, \omega_{i-1}, \omega_i, k, X) \qquad (1)$$

Figure 2 shows an example of the case where the word $\Omega=\{A,l,b,a,n,y\}$ and the image canvas X are given. In this figure, the first character's category ω_1="A", the first segment s_1 and the first character's image f_1 are shown.

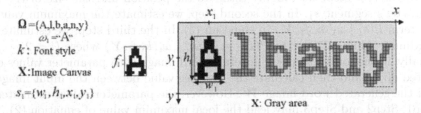

$\Omega = \{A,l,b,a,n,y\}$
ω_1 ="A"
k: Font style
X: Image Canvas
$s_1 = \{w_1, h_1, x_1, y_1\}$

X: Gray area

Fig. 2. Example X, Ω, S and F

3   Word Recognition Algorithm

In this section, we discuss how to recognize the input image Y with the proposed word image generation model. A recognition process can be carried out by searching for the generated word image $\hat{W}$ as shown below.

$$P(\hat{W} \mid Y) = \max_{W} \frac{P(Y \mid W)P(W)}{P(Y)}$$

To maximize the equation above, we can negrect the term of $P(Y)$, we obtain the equation below.

$$\max_{W} P(Y \mid W)P(W) = \max_{\Omega,k,S,F} P(Y \mid \gamma(\Omega,k,S,F,X))P(\gamma(\Omega,k,S,F,X))$$

$$(2)$$

Here, we set $W = \gamma(\Omega, k, S, F, X)$. Since the generated word image $\hat{W}$ is generated from the parameter values of Ω, k, S and F, the recognition process will be carried out by searching for parameter values that give the maximum value of the equation (2). To do this, we can generate all possible word images, trying all possible parameter values, and then compare each generated word image to the input image Y. However, this is computationally very expensive.

Generating the word images that are obviously different from the input image makes no sense, because such images generated may be useless most of the time and they may not give a maximum value of the equation (2). In this paper, we at first search parameter values which maximize the equation below instead of equation (2), and then generate word image with estimated parameter values.

$$P(W \mid Y) = P(\Omega)P(k)P(f_1 \mid \omega_1, k)P(s_1 \mid \omega_1, k, f_1, Y)$$
$$\prod_{i=2}^{n} P(f_i \mid \omega_i, k)P(s_i \mid s_{i-1}, \omega_{i-1}, \omega_i, k, f_i, Y) \qquad (3)$$

The word recognition algorithm consists of four steps. Since we are considering the case of typewriting, the size of the segment (w_i, h_i) is set as constant.

In the first step, we roughly estimate the position and the size of the first character's segment s_1. In the second step, we estimate the maximum value of the term $P(s_1 \mid \omega_1, k, f_1, Y)$ in equation (3). In the third step, we estimate the maximum value of the term $P(s_i \mid s_{i-1}, \omega_{i-1}, \omega_i, k, f_i, Y)$ where $(i = 2, \cdots, n)$. Finally, in the fourth step, we generate word image with parameter values estimated above and then calculate the distance value between the input image Y and the generated word image W. However, the parameter values estimated in Step1, Step2 and Step3 may lead the local maximim value of equation (2).

Since the states of Ω and k are independent of any other information, this procedure is carried out for all possible words in the dictionary and all defined font styles. Then we can choose the best candidate as the recognition result.

3.1   Step 1

In step 1, we find the left side edge (x_{min}) of the input image Y, and the upper edge (y_{min}) within the fixed area as shown in figure 3. Here, the fixed area means a standard character area that approximates the standard width of character (w_s).

We can roughly estimate the position of the first character from the position (x_{min}, y_{min}) with standard width and height of the character. This step allow us to roughly estimate the location s_1.

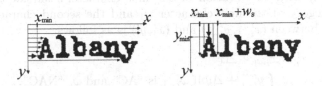

Fig. 3. Finding initial location

3.2   Step 2

In step 2, we find the best location of the first character ω_1. After the initial location s_1 is obtained in step 1 (Figure 3), we optimise this location by moving the template of ω_1 within a fixed area to find the location which gives the best matching (city block distance) between the template and the part image of Y extracted by s_1.

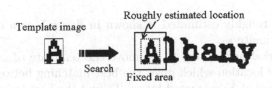

Fig. 4. Example searching area

Figure 4 shows the case where we try to recognize the input "Albany" image as the word "Albany". In figure 4, the dashed box is the location roughly estimated in Step1 and the larger box surrounding it shows the fixed area within which the template is moved. To find the best location means that we estimate s_1 which gives the maximum value $P(s_1 \mid \omega_1, k, f_1, Y)$ in equation (3).

The size of the s_i (w_i and h_i) is fixed for each joint event of ω_i and k. The area to be searched is set as ± 3 pixels horizontally and ± 4 pixels vertically from the initial position, but these values are variable parameters. In the section on evaluation, we will evaluate various parameter values.

3.3   Step 3

In step 3, first, we roughly assume the location of the second character (s_2) from the location of the first character (s_1) calculated in Step2. The character's category ω_1 and ω_2 is also used for estimating s_2. We can roughly classify the font metrics of characters into two classes. One is the "ascender class" (AC) and the other "non-ascender class" (NAC). The capital characters are classified as ascender class. The lower case characters of "b,d,f,h,i,j,k,l,t" are also classified as ascender class. The non-ascender class includes "a,c,e,g,m,n,o,p,q,r,s,u,v,w,x,y,z".

We can roughly predict the location of the second character's leftside-upper corner (x'_i, y'_i) with the location of the first character's leftside-upper corner and the category of the first character ω_1 and the second character ω_2. The relationship between (x'_{i-1}, y'_{i-1}) and (x'_i, y'_i) is as follows;

$$x'_i = x'_{i-1} + \Delta x$$

$$y'_i = \begin{cases} y'_{i-1} + \Delta y \text{ If } \omega_{i-1} \text{ is "AC" and } \omega_i \text{ "NAC".} \\ y'_{i-1} - \Delta y \text{ If } \omega_{i-1} \text{ is "NAC" and } \omega_i \text{ "AC".} \\ y'_{i-1} \qquad \text{else.} \end{cases}$$

Here, we set the value of Δx at 12, and the value of Δy at 5.

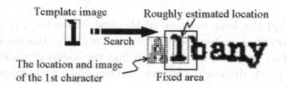

Fig. 5. Example searching area

The location roughly estimated is shown in figure 5 as a dashed box, and gives a rough estimate s_2.

Then, as carried out in step 2, we move the template of ω_2 within a fixed area and find the location which gives the best matching between the template and the part image of $\boldsymbol{Y}$ extracted by s_2. To find the best location of s_2 means that we estimate the value of s_2 which gives the maximum value of the term $P(s_i \mid s_{i-1}, \omega_{i-1}, \omega_i, k, f_i, \boldsymbol{Y})$, here ($i = 2$). This process then continues until the end of the word ($i = n$).

3.4   Step 4

After we have estimated the parameter values of $\boldsymbol{S}$ and $\boldsymbol{F}$ from Step 1 to Step 3 for each dictionary word Ω in each style k, we generate word image $\boldsymbol{W}$ with the estimated parameters and calculate the city block distance value between the input image $\boldsymbol{Y}$ and the generated image $\boldsymbol{W}$. Finally, we choose the word image with minimum distance value as the recognition result.

3.5   Making Character Templates

In this section, we describe how to make template images. Since the image to be recognized is a binary image in this paper, training data are also binary images. To make a template of each category in each font, first, we make gray scale images by summing all the training data for each category in each font. Then, we make two different binary images by binarizing the summed image with two different thresholds. We set three types of font and two types of binarization level for each font. Thus, these templates allow us to estimate the six types of style k for the input image.

Figure 6 shows examples for the template. The first pattern shows the summed image in three types of typewriter, the second pattern shows the binarized image with a high threshold value and the third with a low threshold value.

When we make summed images, the centre of gravity for each training data ample is located at the same position. Each threshold value is calculated with the maximum pixel value of the summed image (p_{max}). The high threshold value is calculated as $0.7 \times p_{max}$, and the low as $0.3 \times p_{max}$.

The number of images for each category in each font is not the same. For example, the number of "a" image is about 100, but in the case of "q" only about 20.

Typewriter 1	Typewriter 2	Typewriter 3
aaa	aaa	aaa

Fig. 6. Example templates

4   Evaluation

We evaluated the effectiveness of the proposed method using a word dictionary that consists of about 28,000 genus and species names and includes all the words in the test images. The number of images evaluated was 4468. The recognition rates with the proposed method and with a method proposed by Lucas (evaluated on the same database)[3] are shown in table 1 below. We evaluated with three types of parameter sets where the area to be searched in step2 and step3 is ± 2 pixels horizontally and ± 2 vertically as set1, ± 2 pixels horizontally and ± 4 pixels vertically as set2 and ± 3 horizontally and ± 4 vertically as set3.

Table 1. Recognition Rate

	Conventional	Set1($\pm 2 \times \pm 2$)	Set2($\pm 2 \times \pm 4$)	Set3($\pm 3 \times \pm 4$)
1st	89.4%	99.5%	99.7%	99.8%
10-best	94.6%	99.8%	99.9%	99.9%

Example images that are correctly recognized by the proposed method (Set3) are shown in Figure 7.

As may be seen in Figure 7, this method can correctly recognize word images including partly faded or heavily touching characters. The proposed method can also adapt to the images such as "approximata" in which characters are not arranged in a straight line.

Example images that are not correctly recognized by the proposed method are shown in Figure 8.

In the "ACHROIA" and "unicolor" case, the local minimum in step2 and step3 causes the error. In the "demotellus" case, the second character "e" is heavily touched by the next character "m", so it is difficult to recognize correctly. In the "lutulentalis" case, the noise causes the error.

We also evaluated the non-holistic method where step 4 is not used for the recognition process. The score of the word C is calculated by using the equation below.

$$C = \sum_{i=1}^{n} \{S(Y, s_i, f_i) - B\} \qquad (4)$$

Original Image	Generated Word Image	Recognition Result
cypholoma	cypholoma	cypholoma
angulata	angulata	angulata
DOHERTYA	DOHERTYA	DOHERTYA
quinquelineata	quinquelineata	quinquelineata
SICULODES	SICULODES	SICULODES
CHEVALIERELLA	CHEVALIERELLA	CHEVALIERELLA
approximata	approximata	approximata
nummulalis	nummulalis	nummulalis

Fig. 7. Example images (correctly recognized)

Here, $S(Y, s_i, f_i)$ is the city block distance value between a template f_i and a part image extracted from the input image Y by s_i , and B a bonus. We evaluated the recognition rate with various values of B. The relationship between the recognition rate and the values of B is shown in figure 9.

Results show that the recognition rate is maximum when the value of B is set at 50 in Set2. The recognition rate is 98.8%. In the case of Set3, the recognition rate is maximum (99.0%) when the value of B is set at 40. The recognition rate of the non-holistic method is lower than the proposed method, but still higher than the conventional method. The results show the importance of segmentation. In the conventional method, the arrangement of characters is assumed as all capital case characters. On the other hand, both in the non-holistic method and the

Original Image	Generated Word Image (1st rank)	Generated Word Image (Correct Script)	Correct Script	Recognition Result
ACHROIA	SIFEIUIA	ACHROIA	ACHROIA	SUFETULA
unicolor	tricolor	unicolor	unicolor	tricolor
demotellus	damotellus	demotellus	demotellus	damotellus
lutulentalis	discodontalis	Lutulentalis	lutulentalis	discodontalis

Fig. 8. Example images (erroneously recognized)

proposed method, the arrangement of the characters is not fixed. This causes the difference in the recognition rate between the conventional method and the non-holistic method.

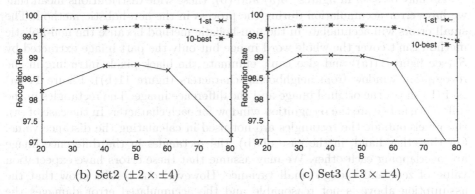

(b) Set2 (±2 × ±4)   (c) Set3 (±3 × ±4)

Fig. 9. Recognition Rate of non-holistic method on various value of B

When the individual character images are drawn on the input image arranged with enough gap between neighboring characters, the word score C calculated without bonus will be the same distance value as the proposed method. That is to say, the bonus means the approximated distance value that is calculated from the part of the input image that has no corresponding template. For example, when the input image consists of three characters but the word generated by the model consists of two characters, the last character's part should be calculated as a distance value. So the bonus B can be considered as a prefixed distance value corresponding to the third character's images.

We compared the distance value of the correct script obtained by the proposed method and the non-holistic method. Here, the distance value with the non-holistic method is the word score C calculated without bonus. Figures 10(a) and (b) show the distribution of the distance value of the correct script obtained by the non-holistic method where each value is divided by the distance value of the correct script obtained by the proposed method. Figure 10(a) is the results for Set2 and (b) for Set3.

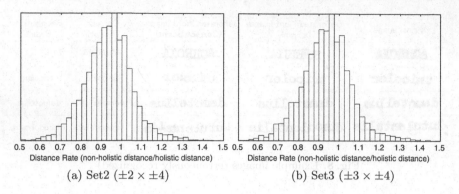

(a) Set2 (±2 × ±4)   (b) Set3 (±3 × ±4)

Fig. 10. Distribution of the distance value of correct script obtained by non-holistic method

As may be seen in figures 10(a) and (b), these wide distributions mean that we have error accumulation during the process in the non-holistic method. The small errors will accumulate in the non-holistic method because the non-holistic method can't cover the whole word image but only the part image extracted by S (see figure 11(a)) and also can't eliminate the black pixels intruding in the recognition window from neighboring characters (figure 11(b)). Figure 11 (a) and (b) shows the original image and the difference image. The rectangles in the difference image are the recognition window for each character. In the case of (a), the pixels outside the rectangles are not used in calculating the distance value. On the other hand, in the case of (b), the rectangles in the difference image are overlapping each other. We may assume that these errors have expectation value of zero and enough small variance. However, our results show that the assumption above is not reasonable and the accumulated error damages the recognition rate in the non-holistic method. In the proposed method, we can expect that no such errors will accumulate.

(a)   (b)

Fig. 11. Example Images

Next, we compared the distance value of the correct script (Dc) and the minimum distance value of the erroneous script (De). For example, when the first recognition candidate is correct, the distance value of the second candidate is the minimum value of erroneous script. To calculate the De and Dc with the non-holistic method, first, we calculate the word score C with equation (4), and then add $B \times N_c$ to each word score. Here, N_c is the number of characters in the correct script[1]. Figures 12(a) and (b) show the distribution of the erroneous script on De/Dc. Figure 12(a) is the results of Set2 with the value of $B = 50$ and (b) Set3 with $B = 40$.

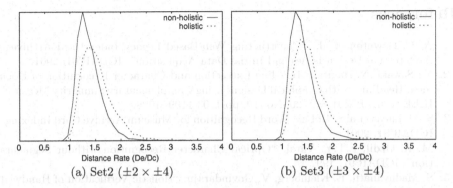

(a) Set2 ($\pm 2 \times \pm 4$)   (b) Set3 ($\pm 3 \times \pm 4$)

Fig. 12. Distribution of the distance value of erroneous script

As in figure 12(a) and (b), the proposed method can separate the correct candidate from erroneous candidates better than the non-holistic method.

These results show that the difference between the conventional method and the non-holistic method is caused by the difference of segmentation, and the difference between the non-holistic method and the proposed method is caused by the difference of the error accumulation.

5   Conclusion

We have proposed a new top-down likelihood word image generation model for word recognition. We have defined a word image generation model and word recognition problem with the model proposed here. The word recognition algorithm is defined as a parameterised search problem.

The difference between a non-holistic method and the proposed method is shown by the evaluation. The small errors accumulate in non-holistic methods during the process carried out. We confirmed that such an accumulated error seriously damages the recognition rate in the non-holistic method. Results show that a recognition rate of 99.8% was obtained in the proposed method.

Future work aims to extend this model for non dictionary applications using a character's bi-gram, where it is very important to estimate a likelihood value for each term accurately.

---

[1] We add $B \times N_c$ even in the case that the number of the characters in the erroneous script is different to the number in correct script. This process doesn't change the rank order in the recognition results obtained by the non-holistic method, but just shifts all the word score. This process roughly normalizes the word score C of the correct script. Then it will be easy to compare the separation of the correct candidate from erroneous candidate between the two.

Acknowledgements. We are grateful to the UK Natural History Museum for kindly providing the archive card database under an EPSRC/BBSRC Bioinformatics research contract 84/BIO11933.

References

1. A. C. Downton et al.: "Constructing Web-Based Legacy Index Card Archives – Architectual Design Issues and Initial Data Acquisition", ICDAR'01, 2001.
2. M. Sawaki, N. Hagita: "Text-line Extraction and Character Recognition of Document Headlines with Graphical Designs using Complementary Similarity Measure", IEEE trans. PAMI, vol. 20, No. 10, pp 1103-1109, 1998.
3. S. M. Lucas et al.: "Robust Word Recognition for Museum Archive Card Indexing", ICDAR'01, 2001.
4. M. A. Ozdil, F.T.Y. Vural: "Optical Character Recognition without Segmentation", ICDAR'97, 1997
5. S. Madhvanath, E. Kleinberg, V. Govindaraju: "Holistic Verification of Handwritten Phrases", IEEE trans. PAMI, vol. 21, No. 12, pp 1344-1356, 1999.
6. S. Madhvanath, V. Govindaraju: "The Role of Holistic Paradigms in Handwritten Word Recognition", IEEE trans. PAMI, vol. 23, No. 2, pp. 149-164, 2001.
7. Y. Lu, C.L. Tan, W.Huang, L.Fan: "An Approach to Word Image Matching Based on Weighted Hausdorff Distance", ICDAR'01, 2001.
8. R. Plamondon, S.N. Srihari: "On-Line and Off-Line Handwriting Recognition: A Comprehensive Survey", IEEE trans. PAMI, vol. 22, No. 1, pp 63-84, 2000.
9. E. Lethelier, M. Leroux, M. Gilloux: "An Automatic Reading System for Handwritten Numeral Amounts on French Checks", ICDAR'95, 1995
10. M. Gilloux, B.Lemaré, M. Leroux: "A Hybrid Radial Basis Function Network/Hidden Markov Model Handwritten Recognition System", ICDAR'95, 1995
11. I. Bazzi, C. LaPre, J. Makhoul, C. Raphael, R. Schwartz: " Omnifont and Unlimited-Vocabulary OCR for English and Arabic",ICDAR'97,1997.
12. P. Sarkar, G. Nagy: "Style-consistency in isogenous patterns", ICDAR'01, 2001.

The Segmentation and Identification of Handwriting in Noisy Document Images

Yefeng Zheng, Huiping Li, and David Doermann

Laboratory for Language and Media Processing
Institute for Advanced Computer Studies
University of Maryland, College Park, MD 20742
{zhengyf, huiping, doermann}@cfar.umd.edu

Abstract. In this paper we present an approach to the problem of segmenting and identifying handwritten annotations in noisy document images. In many types of documents such as correspondence, it is not uncommon for handwritten annotations to be added as part of a note, correction, clarification, or instruction, or a signature to appear as an authentication mark. It is important to be able to segment and identify such handwriting so we can 1) locate, interpret and retrieve them efficiently in large document databases, and 2) use different algorithms for printed/handwritten text recognition and signature verification. Our approach consists of two processes: 1) a segmentation process, which divides the text into regions at an appropriate level (character, word, or zone), and 2) a classification process which identifies the segmented regions as handwritten. To determine the approximate region size where classification can be reliably performed, we conducted experiments at the character, word and zone level. We found that the reliable results can be achieved at the word level with a classification accuracy of 97.3%. The identified handwritten text is further grouped into zones and verified to reduce false alarms. Experiments show our approach is promising and robust.

1 Introduction

The ability to segment a document into functionally different parts has been an ongoing goal of document analysis research. In the case where the content is presented differently (in a different font, or as handwritten as opposed to machine printed), different analysis algorithms may be required for interpretation. In the case of handwritten annotations, such marks often indicate corrections, additions or other supplemental information that should be treated differently from the main or body content. We have found annotations of particular interest in the processing of correspondence and related business documents.

Previous work related to this problem has focused on distinguishing handwritten from machine-printed text with the assumption that the text region is available and/or segmented. The identification is typically performed at the text line [1, 2, 3, 4], word [5] or character level [6, 7]. At the line level, the printed text lines are typically arranged regularly, while the handwritten text lines are irregular. This characteristic is exploited by several researchers. Srihari et al. implemented a text line based approach and achieved the identification accuracy of 95% [1]. One advantage of the approach is

D. Lopresti, J. Hu, and R. Kashi (Eds.): DAS 2002, LNCS 2423, pp. 95–105, 2002.

it can be used in different scripts (Chinese, English etc.) with little or no modification. However, this feature is not available at the word level. Guo et al. proposed an approach based on the vertical projection profile of the word [5]. They used a Hidden Markov Model (HMM) as the classifier and achieved the identification accuracy of 97.2%. Although at the character level less information is available, humans can still identify the handwritten and printed characters easily, inspiring researchers to pursue classification at the character level. Kuhnke proposed a neural network-based approach with straightness and symmetry as features, and achieved an identification accuracy of 96.8% and 78.5% for the training and test sets respectively [7]. Zheng used a run-length histograms as features to identify handwritten and printed Chinese characters [6]. About 75% of the strokes are either horizontally or vertically straight in printed Chinese characters, but curved in handwritten characters. This distinctive characteristic is used to identify handwritten and printed Chinese characters. Based on the run-length histogram features, Zheng achieved the identification accuracy of 98%. However, the method cannot be extended to Latin character because the strokes of most Latin characters are curved.

Most of the previous research is focused on the identification problem with the assumption that the regions to be identified is already segmented or available. In practice, however, handwritten annotations are often mixed with printed text. The handwritten regions must be separated from the printed text first. Previous page segmentation algorithms can be classified into three categories: bottom-up, top-down and hybrid[8]. In a typical bottom-up approach[9], connected components are extracted then merged into words, lines and zones based on the spatial proximity. A top-down approach starts from the whole document and then splits it recursively into columns, zones, lines, words and characters[10]. No matter what segmentation method is used, the special consideration must be given to the size of the region being segmented. If the region is too small, the information contained in it may be not be sufficient for identification; if the region is too large the handwritten text may mix with the printed text in the same region. Figure 1 shows the relation between the accuracy of segmentation and the amount of information contained for identification at different region sizes. The experimental results presented later show the identification process is robust and reliable at the word level.

The diagram of our system is shown in Figure 2. After filtering the noise, we extract the connected components and merge them into words based on the spatial proximity. A trained Fisher classifier is then used to identify the handwritten and printed words. Finally, the identified handwritten words are merged into zones.

The rest of the paper is organized as follows: In Section 2 we present our segmentation and identification method. Section 3 describes the experimental results. Discussions and future work are provided in Section 4.

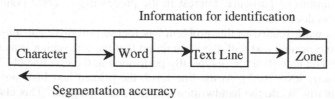

Fig. 1. The relation between the accuracy of segmentation and the amount of information contained for identification at different region sizes.

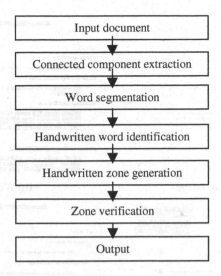

Fig. 2. The diagram of our system

2 The Approach

In this section we will present our method for the segmentation and identification of handwritten annotations.

2.1 Word Segmentation

We use a bottom-up approach to segment the text into words. After the connected components are extracted from the document image, we estimate the average character size using a histogram of component heights [9]. We then group the neighboring connected components into words if they are spatially close in the horizontal direction. Sometimes handwritten annotations come in contact with or are very close to the printed text. When they are grouped into the same word due to the spatial proximity, we enforce the following rules: Two neighboring components $C1$ and $C2$ are merged only when they satisfy $\max(h_1, h_2) < 2 \times \min(h_1, h_2)$, where h_1 and h_2 are the heights of $C1$ and $C2$ respectively.

Currently we assume the document has been de-skewed and the primary direction of the text line is horizontal. Figure 3 shows an example of the segmentation. Figure 3a is the original document with handwritten annotations and Figure 3b shows the segmentation result. We observe that sometimes spurious handwritten marks are not grouped into words due to the variability of the gap between characters. However, this will not affect the classification result significantly. After words are segmented, we perform the classification described in next section.

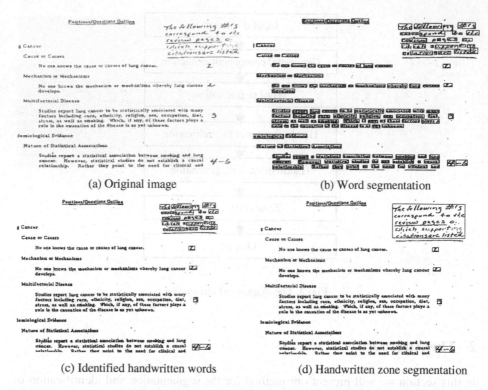

(a) Original image   (b) Word segmentation

(c) Identified handwritten words   (d) Handwritten zone segmentation

Fig. 3. Procedures of handwritten zone segmentation and identification

2.2 Handwritten Annotation Identification

In this section we present details of our handwritten/machine-printed text identification approach. After extracting structural and texture features, we use a Fisher classifier to map the extracted features to a value used to classify handwritten/printed text.

2.2.1 Feature Extraction

Structural Features

We use two groups of structural features. The first group is related to the physical size of the regions, including the width and height of the normalized region, the aspect ratio of the region and the density of the black pixels. The variance of the size distribution of the handwritten words is often larger than that of the printed words. We use a histogram technique to estimate the dominant font size, and then use the dominant font size to normalize the width and height of the region respectively. The aspect ratio of the region and the black pixel density are also used as features.

The second group contains features consisting of the average width and height of the connected components in the word, the aspect ratio of the connected components, the overlap rate of the connected components, and the variance of the projection profile. In a handwritten region, the bounding boxes of the connected components tend to overlap with each other, resulting in a larger overlap area. The overlap areas are normalized by the total area of the region. In a machine-printed text region, the characters tend not to touch each other and therefore, the vertical projection profile has obvious valleys and peaks. The variance of the vertical projection is used to represent this characteristic.

Bi-level Co-occurrence

A co-occurrence histogram is the number of times a given pair of pixels occurs at a fixed distance and orientation. In the case of binary images, the possible occurrences are white-white, black-white, white-black and black-black at each distance and orientation. In our case, we are concerned primarily with the foreground. Since the white background region often accounts up to 80% of a document page, the occurrence frequency of white-white or white-black pixel pairs would always be much higher than that of black-black pairs. The statistics of black-black pairs carry most of the information. To eliminate the redundancy and reduce the effects of over-emphasizing the background, only black-black pairs are considered. Four different orientations (horizontal, vertical, major diagonal and minor diagonal) and four distance levels (1, 2, 4, 8 pixels) are used for identification (altogether 16 features). The details can be found in[11].

Bi-level 2×2-grams

The N×M-gram was introduced by Soffer in the context of image classification and retrieval [13]. We are using bi-level 2×2-grams at a hierarchy of distance from the origin. As described above, we first remove the dominant background (all the white background grams). We then scale each entry by multiplying the number of occurrence by a coefficient proportional to the number of black pixels in the 2×2-gram. The more black pixels, the larger the coefficient. In this work, we used $p^b(1-p)^{4-b}$, where p is the density of the image block, and b is the number of 1's in the 2×2-gram. We then normalize the entire vector of occurrences by dividing them by the sum of all occurrences. Four distances (1, 2, 4, 8 pixels) are used for identification (altogether 60 features). The details can be found in [11].

Pseudo Run Lengths

True run length counts are expensive to compute. We proposed a much faster method for computing pseudo run length statistics as features. The basic idea is we first downsample the image to effectively preserve the low frequency components; the larger the down-sampling rate, the lower the frequency of the preserved components. By comparing the original signal with the down-sampled one, we can estimate the high frequency components that are present in the original signal. Down-sampling can be implemented efficiently using a look-up table. We do 1/2 down-sampling twice and get 16 features. The details can be found in [11].

Gabor Filters

Gabor filters can represent signals in both the frequency and time domains with minimum uncertainty [14] and have been widely used for texture analysis and segmentation [12]. Researchers found that it matches the mammal's visual system very well, which provides further evidence that we can use it in our segmentation tasks.

In spatial and frequent space, the two dimensional Gabor filter is defined as:

$$g(x, y) = \exp\left\{-\pi\left(\frac{x'^2}{\sigma_x^2} + \frac{y'^2}{\sigma_y^2}\right)\right\} \times \cos\{2\pi(u_0 x + v_0 y)\} \tag{1}$$

$$G(u,v) = 2\pi\sigma_x\sigma_y\left(\exp\left\{-\pi\left[(u'-u_0')^2\sigma_x^2 + (v'-v_0')^2\sigma_y^2\right]\right\} + \exp\left\{-\pi\left[(u'+u_0')^2\sigma_x^2 + (v'+v_0')^2\sigma_y^2\right]\right\}\right) \tag{2}$$

where $x' = -x\sin\theta + y\cos\vartheta$, $y' = -x\cos\theta - y\sin\theta$, $u' = u\sin\theta - v\cos\theta$,

$v' = -u\cos\theta - v\sin\theta$, $u_0' = -u_0\sin\theta + v_0\cos\theta$, $v_0' = -u_0\cos\theta - v_0\sin\theta$, $u_0 = f\cos\theta$,

$v_0 = f\sin\theta$. Here f and θ are two parameters, indicating the central frequency and orientation.

Suppose an original image is $I(x,y)$, then the filtered image $I'(x,y)$ can be described as:

$$I'(x, y) = I(x, y) * g(x, y) \tag{3}$$

$$I'(u,v) = I(u,v)G(u,v) \tag{4}$$

It is very expensive, however, to calculate the filter in the spatial domain defined in Equation 3. Instead, we use an FFT to calculate it in the frequent domain. Let $I(u,v)$ be the FFT of the original image and $G_k(u,v)$ be the frequency response of the kth Gabor filter. Then the frequency spectrum of filtered image $I_k'(u,v)$ equals to the product of $I(u,v)$ and $G_k(u,v)$. The filtered image can be achieved by calculating the inverse FFT of $I_k'(u,v)$. For Gabor filters with different parameters, $G_k(u,v)$ is calculated and pre-stored. $I(u,v)$ is calculated only once and shared among different Gabor filters. This can reduce the computation significantly. However, it is still expensive to calculate FFT when image regions are big. To reduce the computation further, we divide the whole region into several small blocks. Suppose the variance of the filtered small block using the kth filter is σ_i^k, then the feature of the filtered image is calculated as the weighted sum of the variance of each small block as described in Equation 5:

$$g_k = \frac{\sum_{i=1}^{N} w_i \sigma_i^k}{\sum_{i=1}^{N} w_i} \qquad k = 1,2,...16 \tag{5}$$

Where the weight w_i is the number of black pixels in the block.

For each orientation θ we can get a different filtered images and calculate the weighted variance (Equation 5) as a feature. In our experiments we let $\theta_k = k * \frac{180}{N}$, k = 1, 2, ... N, with N = 16. Altogether there are 16 features.

2.2.2 Classification

We use Fisher classifier for classification. For a feature vector X, the Fisher classifier projects X onto one dimension Y in the direction W:

$$Y = W^T X \tag{6}$$

The Fisher criterion finds the optimal projection direction W_o by maximizing the ratio of the between-class scatter to the within-class scatter, which benefits the classification. Let S_w and S_b be within- and between-class scatter matrix respectively,

$$S_w = \sum_{k=1}^{K} \sum_{x \in class\, k} [(x - u_k)(x - u_k)^T] \tag{7}$$

$$S_b = \sum_{k=1}^{K} (u_k - u_0)(u_k - u_0)^T \tag{8}$$

$$u_0 = \frac{1}{K} \sum_{k=1}^{K} u_k \tag{9}$$

where u_k is the mean vector of the kth class, u_0 is the global mean vector and K is the number of the classes. The optimal projection direction is then the eigenvector of $S_w^{-1} S_b$, corresponding to the largest eigenvalue [15]. For two-class classification problems, we do not need to calculate the eigenvector of $S_w^{-1} S_b$. It is shown that the optimal projection direction is:

$$W_o = S_w^{-1}(u_1 - u_2) \tag{10}$$

Let y_1 and y_2 be the projection of two classes and $E[y_1]$ and $E[y_2]$ be the *mean* of y_1 and y_2. Suppose $E[y_1] > E[y_2]$, then the decision can be made as:

$$C(x) = \begin{cases} class\,1 & \text{If } y > (E[y1] + E[y2])/2 \\ class\,2 & \text{Otherwise} \end{cases} \tag{11}$$

It is shown that if the feature vector X is jointly Gaussian distributed, the Fisher classifier achieves optimal classification in a minimum classification error sense [15]. Figure 3c shows the result after the identification. Only the identified handwritten words are marked with rectangle boxes.

2.3 Handwritten Zone Generation

After identifying the handwritten words, we merge them into zones using the following rules:
1) Select the largest unmerged handwritten word as a seed.
2) Find the candidate word with the minimum distance to the seed.

3) If the minimum distance is smaller than a threshold (we choose four times of character width in the experiment), then group it with the seed.
4) Repeat Step 2 and 3 until no words can be grouped with the seed. The grouped region is marked as a handwritten zone.
5) Repeat Step 1 to 4 to generate all handwritten zones.

To reduce the false alarm, we run the identification process on the merged zones to verify further. Those zones with small confidence   Figure 3d shows the extracted handwritten zone after merging words.

3   Experiments

3.1   Data Collection

We collected 318 documents containing handwritten annotations provided by the tobacco industry. Each handwritten zone and word is ground truthed for the evaluation purposes. However, the ground truth at the character level is expensive to achieve. Instead, we extract connected components inside the specified handwritten word as characters. Sometimes the handwritten characters touch each other so a connected component may contain several characters. It does not, however, affect the overall result significantly. All together we have 641 zones, 1504 words and 5177 characters in the specified handwritten zones. Since machine-printed characters outnumber handwritten characters, we randomly select roughly the same number of machine-printed characters, words and zones for experiments.

3.2   Identification of Handwritten/Machine-Printed Text

For the purpose of comparison, the experiment of handwritten/printed text identification is conducted at the character, word and zone levels. We use a N-fold cross validation technique to estimate the identification accuracy [15]. First, we divide the data into 10 groups. We then use one group as the test set and the remaining nine groups as the training set to conduct classification. This process is repeated ten times with a different group selected as the test set at each iteration. The average and variance of accuracy are shown in Table 1.

Table 1. Handwritten/printed text identification at different levels (in percentage)

	Structural features	Bi-level co-occurrence	Bi-level 2×2-grams	Pseudo run lengths	Gabor filter	All features
Character	84.4±1.0	83.4±0.5	87.6±1.1	84.4±0.8	86.6±0.8	93.0±0.6
Word	95.7±0.5	87.5±1.5	94.3±1.2	89.8±1.5	95.0±1.3	97.3±0.5
Zone	89.7±2.4	88.1±2.8	94.0±2.7	91.0±1.8	94.9±1.9	96.8±1.6

From Table 1, we can see the identification achieves the best result at the word level with an accuracy of 97.3%, which provides further evidence that it is appropriate for us to segment the document at the word level. For all three levels, it shows the classification with all features achieves better result than with a single group of features.

ARTHUR J. STEVENS
SENIOR VICE PRESIDENT-GENERAL COUNSEL
(212) 841-8708

troversy over ~~Barclay~~'s tar and

, J. Reynolds have claimed the

how a ~~Barclay~~ is smoked by

(a). A printed zone is falsely identified as a handwritten zone due to the font

(b) Two handwritten zones are falsely identified as printed

Fig. 4. Identification errors

It may be surprising that the identification accuracy at the zone level is not as good as at the word level. We observed most identification errors at the zone level occur in the small zones containing only one or two words. Therefore, actually no more information can be used at the zone level than at the word level. Large zones containing more words can be identified more reliably, but the small zones containing fewer words are more error-prone. It is more reasonable to evaluate the zone level identification accuracy by considering the number of words in the zone as weights.

Figure 4a shows an identification error where a printed text zone is identified as a handwritten one because the font is so similar to handwriting. Figure 4b shows an example that two handwritten zones are falsely identified as printed.

3.3   Experiments on Handwriting Segmentation and Identification

We tested our algorithm on 318 documents. Figures 5 and 6 show some examples of segmented results. The identification error rate at the word level is between 2-3%. For a typical document, there are about 200 printed words. Therefore between 4 and 6 printed text zones will be identified as handwritten zones. Another type of error is that some noise is segmented and identified as handwritten zones. The problem occurs when the document is extremely noisy. Figure 7 shows the segmentation and identification result for an extremely noisy document image. Although our system identifies all the handwritten text, other regions (logo, noise, etc) are also identified as handwritten text. We are actively investigating more features and classifiers to improve the result.

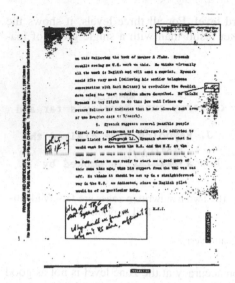

Fig. 5. One example of handwritten zone segmentation and identification

Fig. 6. Another example of handwritten zone segmentation and identification

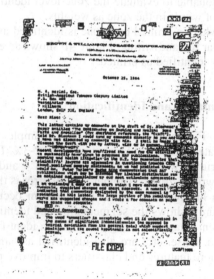
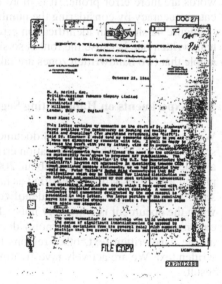

(a) Handwritten word identification result

(b) Handwritten zone segmentation result

Fig. 7. A challenge case on an extremely noisy document image. Although all of the handwritten are correctly identified, some of the noise regions are incorrectly segmented as handwritten

4 Conclusions and Future Work

We have presented an algorithm to segment and identify handwritten/printed text in document images. Our approach consists of two processes: 1) a segmentation process, which segments the text into regions at the word level, and 2) a classification process which identifies the segmented handwritten regions. The experimental results show our method is promising.

We are actively extending this work in three directions. First, our current method filters the noise by the size, which is not robust enough when document is extremely noisy. We need to explore more robust features and classifier to identify handwritten/printed text and noise well. Second, we are developing a scheme to use contextual information to further increase identification accuracy. And at last we will quantitatively evaluate the final segmentation and identification result.

References

1. S. N. Srihari, Y. C. Shim and V. Ramanaprasad. A system to read names and address on tax forms. *Technical Report CEDAR-TR-94-2*, CEDAR, SUNY, Buffalo, 1994
2. K. C. Fan, L. S. Wang and Y. T. Tu. Classification of machine-printed and handwritten texts using character block layout variance. *Pattern Recognition, 31(9)*, pages 1275–1284, 1998
3. V. Pal and B. B. Chaudhuri. Machine-printed and handwritten text lines identification. *Pattern Recognition Letters*, 22, pages 431–441, 2001
4. J. Fanke and M. Oberlander. Writing style detection by statistical combination of classifier in form reader applications. In *Proc. of the 2nd Inter. Conf. On Document Analysis & Recognition*, pages 581–584, 1993
5. J. K. Guo and M. Y. Ma. Separating handwritten material from machine printed text using hidden Markov models. In *Proc. of the 6th Inter. Conf. On Document Analysis & Recognition*, pages 439–443, 2001
6. Y. Zheng, C. Liu and X. Ding. Single character type identification. In *Proc. of SPIE Vol. 4670, Document Recognition & Retrieval IX*, pages 49–56, 2001
7. K. Kuhnke, L. Simoncini and Zs. M. Kovacs-V. A system for machine-written and handwritten character distinction. In *Proc. of the 3rd Inter. Conf. On Document Analysis & Recognition*, pages 811–814, 1995
8. S. Mao and T. Kanungo. Empirical performance evaluation methodology and its application to page segmentation algorithms. *IEEE Trans. on Pattern Analysis and Machine Intelligence*, 23(3), pages 242–256, 2001
9. L. O'Gorman. The document spectrum for page layout analysis. *IEEE Trans. on Pattern Analysis & Machine Intelligence*, 15(11), pages 1162–1173, 1993
10. G. Nagy, S. Seth and S. Stoddard. Document analysis with an expert system. *Pattern Recognition in Practice II*, Elsevier Science, pages 149–155, 1984
11. D. Doermann and J. Liang. Binary document image using similarity multiple texture features. In *Proc. of Symposium on Document Image Understanding Technology*, pages 181–193, 2001
12. A. K. Jain and S. Bhattacharjee. Text segmentation using Gabor filters for automatic document processing. *Machine Vision Application*, 5, pages 169–184, 1992
13. A. Soffer. Image categorization using texture features. In *Proc. of the 4th Inter. Conf. on Document Analysis & Recognition*, pages 233–237, 1997
14. D. Gabor. Theory of communication. *J. Inst. Elect. Engr.* 93, pages 429–459, 1946
15. K. Fukunaga. Introduction to statistical pattern recognition. Second edition, Academic Press Inc. 1990

The Impact of Large Training Sets on the Recognition Rate of Off-line Japanese Kanji Character Classifiers

Ondrej Velek and Masaki Nakagawa

Tokyo University of Agr. & Tech. 2-24-16 Naka-cho, Koganei-shi, Tokyo 184-8588, Japan
velek@hands.ei.tuat.ac.jp

Abstract. Though it is commonly agreed that increasing the training set size leads to improved recognition rates, the deficit of publicly available Japanese character pattern databases prevents us from verifying this assumption empirically for large data sets. Whereas the typical number of training samples has usually been between 100-200 patterns per category until now, newly collected databases and increased computing power allows us to experiment with a much higher number of samples per category. In this paper, we experiment with off-line classifiers trained with up to 1550 patterns for 3036 categories respectively. We show that this bigger training set size indeed leads to improved recognition rates compared to the smaller training sets normally used.

1 Introduction

It is a well-known fact that having enough training data is a basic condition for getting good recognition rate. The same as a small child can read only neatly written characters similar to characters in his textbook, the recognizer can correctly recognize only characters which are similar to characters used for training. For western languages it is easier to collect training sets with hundreds or thousands of character samples per category because the number of different categories is low. This is different for far-east languages, such as Japanese and Chinese, where a much higher number of different categories must be taken into account. Because collecting large numbers of Japanese and Chinese character patterns is an extremely time and money-consuming process, until now, only small Kanji character pattern databases have been made publicly available. The ETL-9 database, collected ten years ago in the Electrotechnical Laboratory; the Japanese Technical Committee for Optical Character Recognition, has been the number one database for developing and testing new algorithms in off-line character recognition for many years. During the recent years, nevertheless, new on-line databases were introduced and made publicly available, so that there is sufficient benchmark data available today.

We have used these new databases for training and testing off-line classifiers. In this paper, we will investigate if these training set sizes several times bigger than usually available will significantly increase the recognition rate. Section 2 will first introduce these new databases. Section 3 describes the two off-line classifiers used in our experiments followed by Section 4 presenting our experimental results. Finally, Section 5 contains our general conclusion.

D. Lopresti, J. Hu, and R. Kashi (Eds.): DAS 2002, LNCS 2423, pp. 106–110, 2002.

2 Japanese Character Databases

We use four handwritten Japanese character databases in our experiments: the ETL-9 database, and three new databases: JEITA-HP, Kuchibue and Nakayosi.

The new JEITA-HP database collected in Hewlett-Packard Laboratories Japan consists of two datasets: Dataset A (480 writers) and Dataset B (100 writers). Dataset A and B were collected under different conditions. Generally speaking, Dataset B is written more neatly than Dataset A. The entire database consists of 3,214 character classes (2,965 kanji, 82 hiragana, 10 numerals, 157 other characters /English alphabet, katakana and symbols/). The most frequent hiragana and numerals are twice in each file. Each character pattern has resolution 64x64 pixels, which are encoded into 512Bytes. In [1] authors of JEITA-HP shortly introduce new database.

Two large, originally on-line characters databases were collected in recent years in Nakagawa Laboratory of Tokyo University of Agriculture & Technology [2][3][4]. They are now publicly available to the on-line character recognition community. The two databases are called "Kuchibue" and "Nakayosi" respectively. In total, there are over 3 million patterns in both databases, which are written by 120 writers (Kuchibue) and 163 writers (Nakayosi) respectively, with the set of writers being different for both databases. Both on-line databases have the advantage that they account better for the variability in practice because the characters were written fluently; in sentences without any style restrictions and their character shapes are more natural compared to most off-line databases, such as ETL9B. However, on-line databases cannot be directly used for an off-line recognizer. We will generate bitmaps using our newly developed method for generating highly realistic off-line images from on-line patterns.

From the pen trajectory of an on-line pattern, our method generates images of various stroke shapes using several painting modes. Particularly, the calligraphic modes combine the pen trajectory with real stroke-shape images so that the generated images resemble the characters produced with brush pen or any other writing tool. In the calligraphic painting mode based on primitive stroke identification (PSI) [5], the strokes of on-line patterns are classified into different classes and each class of strokes is painted with the corresponding stroke shape template; while in the calligraphic painting mode based on stroke component classification (SCC) [6], each stroke is decomposed into ending, bending and connecting parts, and each part is painted with a stroke shape template. The sample of generated images can be seen in Figure 1.

We generated from each on-line pattern five off-line images, always using different painting modes. The size of the generated images is 96x96 pixels.

The last database used in our experiment is ETL-9. ETL-9 includes 3,036categories with 200 sample patterns for each category. The image size 64x63 pixels encoded into 504B.

In, Table 1, we compare the characteristics of all the databases. However, in our following experiments we use only Kanji and hiragana characters (3036 categories), which form the intersection of all the databases.

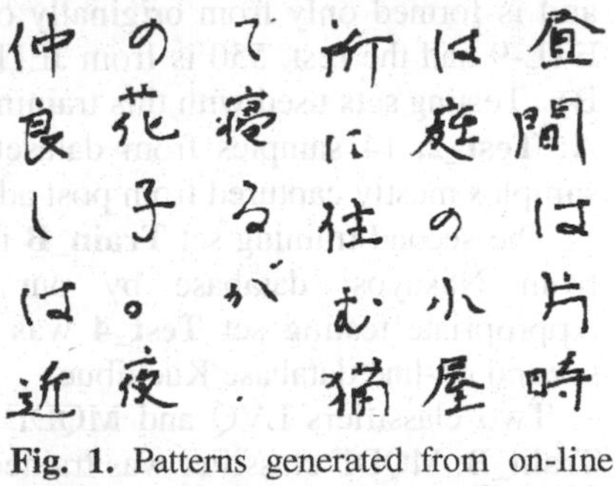

Fig. 1. Patterns generated from on-line database Nakayosi by calligraphic painting mode.

Table 1. Statistics of Kanji character pattern databases.

Database	Format	#Categories	#Writers	#Pattern		
				Per category	Per writer	Total
Kuchibue	vector	3356	120	120-47760	11962	1435440
Nakayosi	vector	4438	163	163-45314	10403	1695689
Etl9B	bitmap	3036	4000	200	N/A	607200
JEITA-HP	bitmap	3214	580	580-1160	3306	1917480

3   Classifiers Used in Our Experiments

We use two off-line recognition schemes in our experiments. The first recognizer represents each character as a 256-dimensional feature vector. It scales every input pattern to a 64x64 grid by non-linear normalization and smoothes it by a connectivity-preserving procedure. Then, it decomposes the normalized image into 4 contour sub-patterns, one for each main orientation. Finally, it extracts a 64-dimensional feature vector for each contour pattern from their convolution with a blurring mask (Gaussian)

For our first classifier [MQDF] a pre-classification step precedes the actual final recognition. Pre-classification selects the 100 candidate categories with the shortest Euclidian distances between their mean vectors and the test pattern. The final classification uses a modified quadratic discriminant function (MQDF2) developed by Kimura from traditional QDF. Our second classifier [LVQ] uses only 196-dimensional feature vectors; i.e., 49 features for each orientation. It is based on the MCE training method (minimum classification error) proposed by Juang and Katagiri, which is a well-known LVQ algorithm.

4   Training Off-line Recognizers with Large-Size Training Sets

From four databases described in Table 1, we will create two large training sets and several sets for testing.

The first training set **Train_A** includes 750 samples per each of 3,036 categories and is formed only from originally off-line samples. The first 200 samples are from ETL-9 and the rest, 550 is from JEITA-HP (464 from dataset A and 86 from dataset B). Testing sets used with this training file are these: **Test_1**, 16 samples from dataset A; **Test_2,** 14 samples from dataset B of JEITA-HP. **Test_3** is from independent samples mostly captured from post addresses.

The second training set **Train_B** includes 800 samples per category and is created from Nakayosi database by our methods for generating hi-realistic images. Appropriate testing set **Test_4** was generated by the same methods, but from the second on-line database Kuchibue.

Two classifiers LVQ and MQDF from section 3 were trained with Train_A and Train_B. MQDF classifier was trained also with merged {Train_A ∪ Train_B} set, so that the maximum number of training sample achieved 1,550 patterns for each of 3,036 categories.

Table 2. LVQ classifier. Train_A set: 50-750 training samples.

[LVQ]	50	100	200	400	750
Test_1	85.01	87.16	88.71	91.36	92.98
Test_2	90.58	92.35	93.49	95.42	96.19
Test_3	85.4	87.1	88.71	91.21	91.99

Table 4. MQDF classifier Train_A $\cup$ Train_B set: 50-1550 training samples.

mqdf	50	100	200	400	750	1550
Test_1	88.34	90.29	91.46	93.02	93.87	94.41
Test_2	93.31	95.07	95.84	97.07	97.45	97.53
Test_3	89.74	91.49	92.67	94.04	94.31	94.52

Table 3. LVQ classifier Train_B set: 50-800 training samples.

[LVQ]	50	100	200	400	800
Test_4	81.86	84.65	86.63	88.05	89.31

Table 5. MQDF classifier Train_B $\cup$ Train_A set: 50-1550 training samples.

mqdf	50	100	200	400	800	1550
Test_4	84.84	88.32	90.4	91.01	92.28	93.88

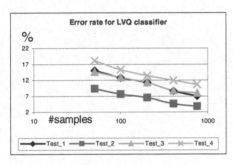

Graph 1. Error rate for LVQ classifier

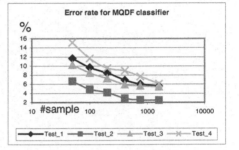

Graph 2. Error rate for MQDF classifier

5   Conclusion

In this paper, we have demonstrated the effect of large training sets on Japanese Kanji character classifiers. The collection of training sets of up to 1,550 samples for each of 3,036 categories was only possible thanks to several newly collected Kanji character databases and our new method for generating highly realistic images from on-line patterns, which allows us to employ also on-line databases in off-line recognition. We have proved that increasing the training set beyond the size typically used still significantly increases recognition rate for Japanese character recognition.

References

[1]   T. Kawatani, H. Shimizu; Handwritten Kanji Recognition with the LDA Method, Proc. 14th ICPR, Brisbane, 1998, Vol.II, pp.1031-1035
[2]   M. Nakagawa, et al., On-line character pattern database sampled in a sequence of sentences without any writing instructions, Proc. 4th ICDAR, 1997, pp.376-380.

[3] S. Jaeger, M. Nakagawa, Two on-line Japanese character databases in Unipen format, Proc. 6th ICDAR, Seattle, 2001, pp.566-570.

[4] K. Matsumoto, T. Fukushima, M. Nakagawa, Collection and analysis of on-line handwritten Japanese character patterns, Proc. 6th ICDAR, Seattle, 2001, pp.496-500.

[5] O. Velek, Ch.Liu, M. Nakagawa, Generating Realistic Kanji Character Images from On-line Patterns, *Proc. 6th ICDAR*, pp.556-560, 2001

[6] O. Velek, Ch.Liu , S.Jaeger, M.Nakagawa, An Improved Approach to Generating Realistic Kanji Character Images and its Effect to Improve Off-line Recognition Performance, accepted for ICPR 2002.

Automatic Completion of Korean Words for Open Vocabulary Pen Interface

Sungho Ryu and Jin-Hyung Kim

AI Lab., CS Div., KAIST, Kusung-Dong, Yusung-Gu, Taejon, Korea,
shryu@ai.kaist.ac.kr, jkim@ai.kaist.ac.kr

Abstract. An automatic completion method of general Korean words is proposed. A word model that describes the frequency of usage is used for generation of word candidates from a given prefix. In experiments, several different models for Korean words were tested for prediction performance. The results show that the best model can reduce the number of writing characters about 38% with 5 candidates.

1 Introduction

The automatic completion of a word is predicting the entire word from a prefix. If the accuracy of prediction is high, the overall input efficiency can be greatly improved. However, because the natural language is not a mathematically well-defined entity, the prediction of word is very complicated.

The prediction of word is highly dependent on the modeling of words itself. From a practical point of view, the most important issues in modeling natural language are the size of lexicons and the reliability of estimated likelihood of each lexical entry. The desirable word model should be able to generate reliable estimate of the likelihood for any word, even if it was not observed in the training. In this paper, the automatic completion methods for Korean are tested using various word models.

2 Prediction of Korean Words

A Korean word is usually composed of several morphemes. However, the high irregularity in inflections and derivations makes it difficult to perform morpheme-based prediction. Therefore, the word is chosen as a basic unit of prediction instead of the morpheme in this paper.

The basic rule of prediction is choosing the most probable string based on a given clue. In a pen-based interface, the clue is a partially complete prefix of the word.

The probability of a word can be modeled using the frequency of usage of words. The probability of a prefix is the sum of all probabilities of words that can be derived from the prefix (1).

D. Lopresti, J. Hu, and R. Kashi (Eds.): DAS 2002, LNCS 2423, pp. 111–114, 2002.
© Springer-Verlag Berlin Heidelberg 2002

$$p_S(s) = \sum_{\forall w \text{ that has } s \text{ as a prefix}} p(w) \tag{1}$$

Then, the prediction can be regarded as selecting a longer prefix based on the like-lihood.

$$s' = \arg\max_{s'} \frac{p_S(s')}{p_S(s)} \tag{2}$$

where s' is longer string that has s as its prefix.

Therefore, the prediction is primarily dependent on the choice of the word probability model, $p(W)$.

In dictionary-based model, the probability of each word is explicitly specified using the trie. The probabilities of words are directly calculated from the occurrences of each word in a large raw text corpus. In order to estimate probability of unseen words, the probabilities are smoothed using Lidstone's method.

In character n-gram based models, a word is represented as a sequence of characters. The probability of the word is the joint probability of the character sequence. To make the computation tractable, the joint probability is usually approximated using n-th order Makov assumption. For example, in trigram-based model (character n-gram with length 3), the probability of a word can be calculated as follows.

$$p(w) = p(c_1)p(c_2 \mid c_1)p(c_3 \mid c_1, c_2) \cdots p(c_n \mid c_{n-2}, c_{n-1}) \tag{3}$$

In n-gram based models, the equation for prediction becomes much simpler. By ruling out common terms, eq. (2) can be reduced to a conditional probability mass function (4).

$$s' = c_1, \ldots c_p c_{next}$$

where $c_1, c_2, \ldots c_p$ is the given prefix, $\tag{4}$

$$\text{and } c_{next} = \arg\max_C p(C \mid c_{l-n+1} \cdots c_{l-1})$$

Probabilities of character n-grams are calculated from raw text corpus using Katz's back-off method.

3   Prediction Interface

For fair comparison between different models, a pen-based interface with word prediction is used. In this interface, the basic unit of recognition is a character. When each character is recognized, the word model generates candidates from the current prefix. Users can either select a word from candidates to complete the whole word, or write subsequent characters by themselves if it does not exist.

The proposed interface has three primitive operations:

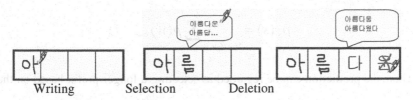

Fig. 1. The primitive operations

- Writing
  Writing an individual character.

- Selection
  Selecting one of the candidates generated by the prediction interface.

- Deletion
  Deleting characters after a certain position. Used to trigger a new prediction at a specific position within the string.

The total cost of input is defined as a weighted sum of the ratio of primitive operations.

$$Cost\ of\ input = \frac{\alpha_{writing}n(Writing) + \alpha_{selection}n(Selection) + \alpha_{Deletion}n(Deletion)}{n(Total\ Chars)} \qquad (5)$$

The weights represent the easiness and robustness of each operation. In general, it can be assumed that the weight of writing is much greater than the weights of selection or deletion.

4 Experiments

For training word models, '97 KAIST raw text corpus was used. It has about 1,200,000 distinct words and 15,500,000 words in total. The prediction performance of each model was tested using '96 KAIST raw text corpus. It has about 1,300,000 distinct words and 15,800,000 words in total. The number of total characters used for testing was about 45,600,000.

The table below shows the number of primitive operations for each model. In all models, 5 candidates were generated for the selection.

Primitive Operations	Models			
	Word-trie	bigram	trigram	4gram
n(Writing)/ n(Total char)	0.66	0.72	0.62	0.62
n(Selection)/ n(Total char)	0.32	0.27	0.34	0.34
n(Deletion)/ n(Total char)	0.02	0.005	0.01	0.01

$$p_S(s) = \sum_{\forall w \text{ that has } s \text{ as a prefix}} p(w) \tag{1}$$

Then, the prediction can be regarded as selecting a longer prefix based on the like-lihood.

$$s' = \arg\max_{s'} \frac{p_S(s')}{p_S(s)} \tag{2}$$

where s' is longer string that has s as its prefix.

Therefore, the prediction is primarily dependent on the choice of the word prob-ability model, $p(W)$.

In dictionary-based model, the probability of each word is explicitly specified us-ing the trie. The probabilities of words are directly calculated from the occurrences of each word in a large raw text corpus. In order to estimate probability of unseen words, the probabilities are smoothed using Lidstone's method.

In character n-gram based models, a word is represented as a sequence of charac-ters. The probability of the word is the joint probability of the character sequence. To make the computation tractable, the joint probability is usually approximated using n-th order Makov assumption. For example, in trigram-based model (character n-gram with length 3), the probability of a word can be calculated as follows.

$$p(w) = p(c_1)p(c_2 \mid c_1)p(c_3 \mid c_1, c_2) \cdots p(c_n \mid c_{n-2}, c_{n-1}) \tag{3}$$

In n-gram based models, the equation for prediction becomes much simpler. By ruling out common terms, eq. (2) can be reduced to a conditional probability mass function (4).

$$s' = c_p \dots c_p c_{next}$$
where $c_1, c_2 \dots c_p$ is the given prefix, $\tag{4}$

$$and \quad c_{next} = \arg\max_C p(C \mid c_{l-n+1} \cdots c_{l-1})$$

Probabilities of character n-grams are calculated from raw text corpus using Katz's back-off method.

3   Prediction Interface

For fair comparison between different models, a pen-based interface with word pre-diction is used. In this interface, the basic unit of recognition is a character. When each character is recognized, the word model generates candidates from the current prefix. Users can either select a word from candidates to complete the whole word, or write subsequent characters by themselves if it does not exist.

The proposed interface has three primitive operations:

Using Stroke-Number-Characteristics for Improving Efficiency of Combined Online and Offline Japanese Character Classifiers

Ondrej Velek and Masaki Nakagawa

Tokyo University of Agr. & Tech. 2-24-16 Naka-cho, Koganei-shi, Tokyo 184-8588, Japan
velek@hands.ei.tuat.ac.jp

Abstract. We propose a new technique for normalizing likelihood of multiple classifiers prior to their combination. During a combination process we utilize the information about their efficiency correctly recognize a character with a given stroke number. In the beginning, we show that this recognizer's efficiency based on a stroke number is different for a common on-line and off-line recognizer. Later, we demonstrate on elementary combination rules, such as sum-rule and max-rule that using this information increases a recognition rate.

1 Introduction

Combining different classifiers for the same classification problems has become very popular during the last years [1]. The bigger difference among classifiers promises better improvement of a recognition rate, which can be achieved by their combination. To take an advantage of the difference between on-line and off-line classifiers seems be a good idea: on-line recognition can use valuable information of writing order and has no problem with segmentation of overlapped strokes, complementary to it, off-line recognition guarantees robustness against stroke order and stroke number variations, which is usually the main disadvantage of on-line systems.

However, combination of two independent off/on-line classifiers brings the problem, how to decide which result of which classifier is correct. Our approach is based on well-known fact that a specialization is good way to achieve improvement. Let's suppose that an off-line recognizer is better for recognizing some characters than an on-line recognizer. We try to find an identifiable characteristic of characters, which can divide unknown input character patterns to several groups. We will investigate which recognizer is more efficient for correct classifying to each of these classes and in a combination scheme we will utilize this additive information. In this paper, we investigate a characteristic of on-line and off-line Japanese character classifiers in dependency on number of strokes.

2 Characteristic of Classifiers According to Stroke Number

Number of stroke is the basic feature of each Chinese or Japanese character. The right stroke number can be found in a dictionary and varied from 1 to about 30. However, for fluently and quickly written characters, number of strokes is often lower, because

D. Lopresti, J. Hu, and R. Kashi (Eds.): DAS 2002, LNCS 2423, pp. 115–118, 2002.
© Springer-Verlag Berlin Heidelberg 2002

some strokes are connected. In some cases number of strokes can be higher than should be. An interesting characteristic of a variation in stroke numbers is in [2].

Let's see a recognition rate according to a stroke number for one on-line and two off-line recognizers Graph 1. Even from a brief view, we see the big difference between on-line and off-line classifiers. Both off-line recognizers are weaker in recognizing characters written by a low number of strokes. The recognition rate simultaneously grows with increasing complexity of patterns. It's in accordance to well-known fact that for off-line classifier it's more difficult to recognize simple characters like kana than difficult kanji. On the contrary, on-line recognizer is hi-efficient for patterns written by one stroke. We see that although an average rate of the on-line recognizer is about 5% worst than that of the off-line recognizer, for characters written by one, two and three strokes a recognition rate is better, or at least similar. In the rest of this paper we will try to utilize this feature in a combination scheme.

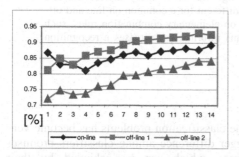

Graph 1. Recognition rate according to a stroke number for three recognizers.

3 Combining Classifiers

A typical output of each recognizer is several candidates and for each candidate also his likelihood, which can merely be approximations of the correct a-posteriori probabilities. In [3] we have introduced a new warping technique for normalizing likelihood of multiple classifiers, so that likelihood can be easily compared. Our technique takes classifier-specific likelihood character-istics into account and maps them to a common, ideal characteristic allowing fair combination. For each classifier we create an accumulated characteristic function, which express an a-posteriori probability $P(<0,a_i>)$ that for each interval $<0,a_i>$, a_i is an output value of a recognizer, an input pattern was recognized correctly. An accumulated recognition rate is a continuous, monotone growing function over a classifier's output.

We normalize the output of each single recognizer so that the accumulated probability function $P(<0,a>)$ becomes a linear function proportional to the classifier output. Accordingly, we normalize each classifier output by adding an adjustment: $a'_i = a_i + charf(a_i)$ with

$$charf(a_i) = a_{max} * R_i - a_i = a_{max} * \frac{\sum_{k=0}^{i} n_{correct}(k)}{N} - a_i$$

where a_{max} is the maximum possible output of a classifier ($a_{max} = 1,000$ in our experiments), N is the number of overall patterns, and R_i stands for the partially accumulated recognition rate. We call this classifier-specific adjustment the characteristic function [$charf_i$] of a classifier. In our previous work, we calculated one characteristic function for each classifier. Now we will create not one, but many different characteristic functions, one for characters written by the same number of strokes. In this paper we have 14 functions, where the last one is for patterns written by fourteen or more strokes. In Graph 2 we see characteristic function [*charf₁*] for our on-line recognizer and in Graph 3 for an off-line recognizer.

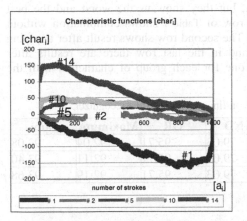

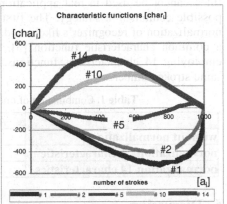

Graph 2. Characteristic function for on-line recognizer.

Graph 3. Characteristic function for off-line_1 recognizer.

4 Classifiers and Database Used in Experiments

Off-line_1 recognizer is based on MQDF, while **off-line_2** recognizer on LVQ. More information about these two off-line recognizers and also about our **On-line** recognizer is written in our previous paper [3].

We use NTT-AT database, which contains data written by elderly people with an average age of 70.5 years; with the oldest writer being 86 years old. The patterns contained in NTT-AT are casually written, very often with an untypical stroke order. We have chosen this database because it is difficult to recognize for many recognizers. We also consider it a very good test bed for underpinning our conjecture saying that combining on-line classifiers with stroke-order independent off-line classifiers leads to better overall recognition rates. From this database we generate a dual off-line version using our method for generating realistic Kanji character images from on-line patterns [4]. This method combines on-line patters with a calligraphic stroke shape library, which contains genuine off-line patterns written with different writing tools. Since the artificially generated off-line images are combinations of actual on-line and off-line patterns they look very natural and realistic. Thanks to this duality, an on-line database can be used by off-line as well as an on-line classifier.

5 Experimental Results

We used two different combination strategies for combining our on-line and off-line recognizer: max-rule and sum-rule. The max-rule takes the class with the maximum output value among each classifier, while the sum-rule sums up the output for each class and selects the one with the highest sum. These rules are motivated by a paper by Kittler et al. [5], which gives a theoretical explanation for the frequently observed superiority of the sum-rule. We have added also AND and OR rules, which means that pattern was recognized by both recognizers, or respectively at least by one. These rules cannot be used in real application, but they show us the worst and the best possible combination strategy. The first row of Table 1 shows combination without normalization of recognizer's likelihood. The second row shows result after applying a common characteristic function [3], and in the last row there are results after employing 14 characteristics functions, one for each group of characters with the same stroke number.

Table 1. Combination of one on-line and one off-line recognizer

	AND	OR	Maximum	Sum
without normalization	79.03	95.71	92.04	92.08
normalization 1 characteristic	79.03	95.71	92.11	93.40
normalization 14 characteristics	79.03	95.71	92.19	93.68

6 Discussion

We have demonstrated a new method for combining different classifiers with a various range of output likelihood. Unlike our previous method [3], where only one characteristic is for a recognizer, in our new approach we study recognizer's characteristic in more details and we make 14 different characteristic functions in dependency on number of strokes. By applying this, we have got further improvement of recognition rate. Advantage of this method is that the realization doesn't consume additive time during the recognition process and only minimal additive space for saving more characteristic functions. Making characteristic function is done only once, after training recognizer. From [3] we know, that our normalization method is more beneficial, if more classifiers are combined, so next time we want to employ more than two classifiers. We are also experimenting with another characteristics, not only these based on different number of strokes. If we find another characteristic, for which the difference between on-line and off-line classifier is bigger, we can more utilize advantage of each single classifier.

References

[1] H. Tanaka, K. Nakajima, K. Ishigaki, K. Akiyama, M. Nakagawa, Hybrid Pen-Input Character Recognition System Based on Integration of On-Line – Off-Line Recognition, 5th ICDAR (1999) 209-212
[2] K. Matsumoto, T. Fukushima, M. Nakagawa, Collection and analysis of on-line handwritten Japanese character patterns, Proc. 6th ICDAR, Seattle, 2001, pp.496-500.
[3] O. Velek, S. Jaeger, M. Nakagawa, A warping technique for normalizing likelihood of multiple classi-fiers and its effectiveness in combined on-line/off-line Jap. char.recognition, accepted for IWFHR 2002
[4] O. Velek, Ch. Liu, M. Nakagawa, Generating Realistic Kanji Character Images from On-line Patterns, Proc. 6th ICDAR (2001) 556-560
[5] J.Kittler, M.Hatef, R.Duin, J.Matas, On Combining Classifiers, IEEE PAMI 20(3) (1998) 222-239

Closing Gaps of Discontinuous Lines: A New Criterion for Choosing the Best Prolongation

Eugene Bodansky and Alexander Gribov

Environmental System Research Institute (ESRI), Inc.
380 New York St., Redlands, CA, 92373-8100, USA
{ebodansky,agribov}@esri.com

Abstract. Polylines that are or should be continuous can have gaps in them, either because of scanning or digital processing or because they are depicted with discontinuous symbology like dots or dashes. This paper presents a new criterion for finding the most likely prolongation of discontinuous polylines .

1 Introduction

Correctly recognizing discontinuous lines is an important part of raster-to-vector conversion or vectorization. Discontinuous lines can appear on raster representations of linear drawings because complex kinds of line were used (for example, dashed lines and dash-dotted lines) and because of scanning, binarization, and vectorization of source documents. For finding the most probable prolongation of the polyline, several parameters and thresholds have been used: the maximum value of gaps, the fan angle, and the range of line components for regular (for example, dashed) line symbology. Paper [1] presents a detection technique that uses a sequential stepwise recovery of components that meet certain continuity conditions. In [1], the maximum allowed length of a gap and the deviation angle between the gap of the new component and the previously detected component is used for choosing the next component of the discontinuous curve.

Let L be the maximum allowed length of a gap and T the maximum allowed deviation angle or fan angle. In compliance with [1] if $G_i < L$, $AG_i * AS_i > 0$, $|AG_i| < T$, and $|AS_i| < T$, then the candidate segment S_i is considered as the next component or a prolongation of the discontinuous curve (see Figure 1). These criteria have two disadvantages.

In the example shown in figure 2, the component "c" will be selected as the prolongation for the line "a" because for "c" $AG_1 * AS_1 > 0$ and for "b" $AG_2 * AS_2 < 0$. We think that the component "b" is the more logical prolongation.

The criteria also do not allow selecting a prolongation from several candidates that all satisfy stated constraints.

D. Lopresti, J. Hu, and R. Kashi (Eds.): DAS 2002, LNCS 2423, pp. 119–122, 2002.

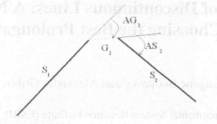

Fig. 1. Two components of a discontinuous line

S_i - *a continuous segment,* G_i - *a gap,* AS_i *and* AG_i - *deviation angles*

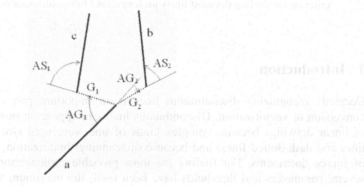

Fig. 2. Two candidate components (*b* and *c*) for the line *a*

2   New Criterion for Choosing the Best Prolongation

We suggest the new method for selecting the linear component that is the best prolongation for a discontinuous curve. The method based on the mechanical analogy. Let a curve be the path of a particle moving at a constant speed. It is possible to calculate what job is needed to continue from the line to a candidate segment. A transfer from the line to the candidate segment will be defined as the segment connecting the closest ends of the centerline and the candidate segment. To compensate for the influence of noise, a part of a new virtual centerline containing the connecting segment will be smoothed with the local continuous smoothing algorithm described in article [2]. The derivatives of a transfer path will be continuous and so the radius of a curve at each point of the transfer path can be defined. The radius of smoothed curve can be calculated using the smoothing algorithm.

The job used for the transfer of the particle from the line to the candidate segment can be calculated as P1 + P2, where $P1 = \int k_1 \dfrac{1}{R(l)} dl$ is a job for the direction changing, $P2 = \int k_2 dl = k_2 L$ provides a constant speed. $R(l)$ is a local radius of the curve, L is the length of the transfer path, k_1 and k_2 are constants. If $P_i = $ k* $P1_i$ + (1-k)* $P2_i$ is a penalty where k is a constant, satisfying the restriction 0 < k < 1, and i = 1, ..., n, n is the number of candidates for the prolongation of the line, then the candidate with the minimum value for the penalty will be chosen for the prolongation of the line. For large values of k, the criteria gives preference to more smooth result lines, for small values of k to lines with short transfer paths. Figure 3 shows the lines obtained with the gap closing technique with different values for k.

3   Tracing and Batch Mode

A sequential stepwise recovery technique can be used for semi automatic tracing with the operator control, but it could be not good for batch mode because closing gaps depends on the orientation of the document. In Figure 4, we show the result of closing gaps for source lines obtained by flipping the source lines shown in Figure 3.

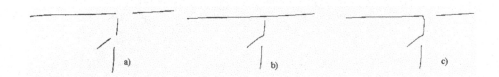

Fig. 3. The source lines and the result of closing gaps. a) source lines, b) k = 1, c) k = 0

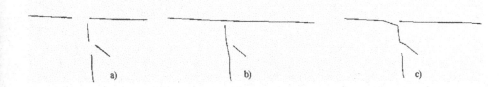

Fig. 4. Flipped source lines and the result of closing gaps. a) flipped source lines, b) k = 1, c) k = 0

4 Conclusions

Recognition of discontinuous polylines is difficult in documents that contain a lot of noise (speckles) and many different layers (for example, lines, letters, digits, and symbols). To increase the probability of making the correct solution, the recognition algorithm is needed that can be tuned with the operator. Sometimes it is necessary to find straight lines, sometimes smooth curves, sometimes polylines consisted of straight components, and so on. The suggested criterion of choosing prolongations of discontinuous polylines makes this possible.

References

1. Dori, D., Wenyin, L., Peleg, M.: How to Win a Dashed Line Detection Contest. In: Kasturi, R., Tombre, K. (eds): Methods and Applications. Lecture Notes in Computer Science, Vol. 1072, First International Workshop, Springer-Verlag, Berlin Heidelberg New York (1997) 286–300
2. Bodansky, E., Gribov, A., Pilouk, M.: Post-processing of lines obtained by raster-to-vector conversion. In: Vision (machine Vision Association of SME), Vol. 18, #1 (www.sme.org/mva), First Quarter, 2002.

Classifier Adaptation with Non-representative Training Data

Sriharsha Veeramachaneni and George Nagy

Rensselaer Polytechnic Institute, Troy, NY 12180, USA,
veeras@rpi.edu

Abstract. We propose an adaptive methodology to tune the decision boundaries of a classifier trained on non-representative data to the statistics of the test data to improve accuracy. Specifically, for machine printed and handprinted digit recognition we demonstrate that adapting the class means alone can provide considerable gains in recognition. On machine-printed digits we adapt to the typeface, on hand-print to the writer. We recognize the digits with a Gaussian quadratic classifier when the style of the test set is represented by a subset of the training set, and also when it is not represented in the training set. We compare unsupervised adaptation and style-constrained classification on isogenous test sets of five machine-printed and two hand-printed NIST data sets. Both estimating mean and imposing style constraints reduce the error-rate in almost every case, and neither ever results in significant loss. They are comparable under the first scenario (specialization), but adaptation is better under the second (new style). Adaptation is beneficial when the test is large enough (even if only ten samples of each class by one writer in a 100-dimensional feature space), but style conscious classification is the only option with fields of only two or three digits.

1 Introduction

The design objective of document recognition systems is to yield high accuracy on a large variety of fonts, typefaces and handwriting styles. The most obvious approach, which is also the most popular amongst design engineers, is to collect patterns from all possible styles to train the classifier. Another approach is to design features that obscure differences between various styles. Due to the proliferation of fonts and typefaces with the advent of digital font design and the decreasing emphasis on neat handwriting, new styles encountered in the field often render these methods ineffective. Typically, OCR systems are overhauled periodically and retrained with patterns from newly encountered styles.

Statistical training of OCR engines is based on the assumption that the training set is representative of the statistics of the *test set*, i.e, the text that is encountered in the field. The only departure from this assumption has been the study of small-sample estimation problems, i.e., the *variance* of the classifier due to different draws from the population.

Although there are an immense variety of glyphs that correspond to each class, within a given document we expect to see a certain consistency owing to

D. Lopresti, J. Hu, and R. Kashi (Eds.): DAS 2002, LNCS 2423, pp. 123–133, 2002.

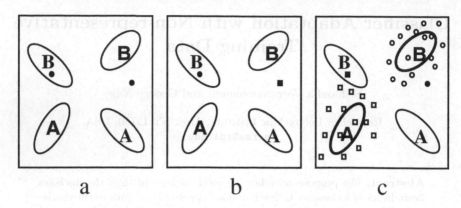

Fig. 1. Illustrative example. The equi-probability contours of the class-conditional feature distributions, for two typefaces and two classes {A, B}, estimated from the training data, are shown. The squares represent patterns classified as A's and the circles represent patterns classified as B's by each of the methods. The same two input patterns are shown filled in all three subfigures. (a) The conventional singlet classifier assigns the label (B, B) to these two patterns independently, oblivious to any style-consistency. (b) The style-conscious classifier assumes that both patterns are from the same typeface and assigns the label (B, A) to the left and right patterns respectively. (c) The existence of a large test set drawn from a single typeface causes an adaptive classifier to assign the label (A, B).

the common source. We call this consistency *style* or *spatial context*. The commonality denoted by style may arise from the processes of printing, scanning or copying as well as consistency of writer or typeface. Even documents composed with multiple scripts and fonts contain only a negligible fraction of all existing glyphs. In such scenarios, even if the style in which the current document is rendered is represented in the training data, the classification accuracy suffers from the relatively small weight given to the particular style by the classifier (which was trained on patterns drawn from a large number of styles). It is therefore appealing to consider the possibility of adapting the classifier parameters to the test set. Figure 1 illustrates the concepts of style-conscious classification and adaptive parameter estimation using a simple example.

Although little use of adaptive methods has been reported for OCR, there has been considerable work done in the field of communications, adaptive control and more recently in speech recognition [1]. Castelli and Cover explore the relative value of labeled and unlabeled samples for pattern classification [2]. Nagy and Shelton proposed a heuristic self-corrective character recognition algorithm that adapts to the typeface of the document to improve accuracy [3], which was later extended by Baird and Nagy to a hundred-font classifier [4]. Sarkar exploits style consistency in short documents (fields) to improve accuracy, under the assumption that all styles are represented in the training set, by estimating style-and-class-conditional feature distributions using the EM algorithm [5] [6]. We have proposed a style-conscious quadratic discriminant classifier that improves accuracy on short fields under essentially the same assumptions [7].

Mathis and Breuel propose a hierarchical Bayesian approach very similar to our method to utilize the test data to improve accuracy [8]. They recursively apply EM estimation by combining the training and test data. We believe that this method introduces an avoidable classifier bias, especially if the size of the training data is commensurate with the size of the document being classified.

In the following sections we define the problem formally and describe a partial solution. We then present an experimental comparision of style-constrained classification and adaptation under different scenarios, and discuss the implications of the results.

2   Classifier Parameter Adaptation

We consider the problem of classifying the patterns in a large test set $T = \{x_1, \ldots, x_t\}$ where each x_i is a d-dimensional feature vector, into one of N classes $\{\omega_1, \ldots, \omega_N\}$. The test set T is drawn according to the class-conditional feature distributions $p(x|\omega_i) = f_i(x) \sim \mathcal{N}(\mu_i, \Sigma_i)$, $i = 1, \ldots, N$ and a priori class probabilities $p(\omega_i) = p_i$, $i = 1, \ldots, N$.

We postulate the existence of a training set for estimating the class-conditional feature distributions given by $f_i^{(0)}(x) \sim \mathcal{N}(\mu_i^{(0)}, \Sigma_i^{(0)})$, $i = 1, \ldots, N$ and

$p^{(0)}(\omega_i) = p_i^{(0)}$, $i = 1, \ldots, N$.

T is classified using a quadratic discriminant function classifier constructed with the estimated parameters. Clearly, the expected error-rate of the classifier on T is higher than the Bayes error-rate due to the discrepancies between the estimated parameters and the true parameters. We wish to adapt the classifier to the true parameters of the test set T.

We will assume that only the class-conditional feature means are misrepresented in the training set. That is, $\mu_i^{(0)} \neq \mu_i$ for some i, but $p_i^{(0)} = p_i$ and $\Sigma_i^{(0)} = \Sigma_i$ for all $i = 1, \ldots, N$. We adapt the estimate of the mean according to the following EM update formula

$$\mu_i^{(k+1)} = \frac{\sum_{x \in T} x p^{(k)}(\omega_i | x)}{\sum_{x \in T} p^{(k)}(\omega_i | x)}, \ i = 1, \ldots, N$$

$$\text{where } p^{(k)}(\omega_i | x) = \frac{p_i f_i^{(k)}(x)}{\sum_{i=1}^{N} p_i f_i^{(k)}(x)}, \ f_i^{(k)}(x) \sim \mathcal{N}(\mu_i^{(k)}, \Sigma_i)$$

Although convergence to the means of the test distribution is not guaranteed with arbitrary initialization, it appears that the true mean is a fixed point of the algorithm with good covariance estimates.

3   Experimental Results on Machine-Printed Data

A database of multi-font machine-printed numerals was generated as follows [6]. Five pages, containing the ten digits 0-9 spaced evenly and replicated 50 times, were prepared using Microsoft Word 6.0. Each page was rendered in a different 6 pt typeface, namely Avant Garde (A), Bookman Old Style (B), Helvetica (H), Times New Roman (T), and Verdana (V), and printed on a 600 dpi Apple LaserWriterSelect. Each page was scanned 10 times at 200 dpi into 10 bilevel bitmaps using an HP flatbed scanner. This yielded a total of 25,000 samples (5000 samples per typeface). A few of the samples are shown in Figure 2. The resulting scanned images were segmented and for each digit sample 64 blurred directional (chaincode) features were extracted and stored [9]. We used only the top 8 principal component features for experimentation so that the gains in accuracy are significant. For each typeface, 2500 samples were included in the training set, while the remaining 2500 samples were used for testing. That is, the number of errors in each cell of the tables below are based on 2500 test patterns.

Avant Garde 0 1 2 3 4 6 6 7 8 9
Bookman Old Style 0 1 2 3 4 5 6 7 8 9
Helvetica 0 1 2 3 4 5 6 7 8 9
Times New Roman 0 1 2 3 4 5 6 7 8 9
Verdana 0 1 2 3 4 5 6 7 8 9

Fig. 2. Samples of the machine-printed digits, reproduced at approximately actual size.

Figure 3 shows the scatter plot of the top two principal component features of the test samples from typefaces Helvetica and Verdana. For clarity only some of the classes are shown.

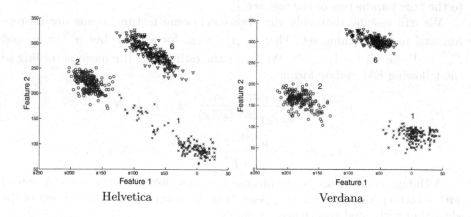

Helvetica   Verdana

Fig. 3. Scatter plot of the top two principal component features for test samples from classes '1', '2' and '6'.

3.1   Multiple-Style Training, Test Style Represented

Here we consider the case when the classifier is trained on patterns from multiple typefaces including the typeface of the test set. We use the training data from all typefaces to train the classifier and adapt to each typeface separately. The recognition results for iterated adaptation of the mean are presented in Table 1.

Table 1. Error counts on different typefaces for successive EM iterations, 2,500 samples per typeface for testing (All-typefaces training)

	Test typeface				
Iterations	A	B	H	T	V
0	17	3	34	1	33
1	7	2	37	1	3
5	6	2	39	1	3
10	6	2	39	1	3

We now compare the results in Table 1 with our style-conscious quadratic classification [7]. The error-rates for various field lengths are presented in Table 2.

Table 2. Error counts using style-conscious field classification, 2,500 samples per typeface for testing (All-typefaces training)

	Test typeface				
Field length	A	B	H	T	V
1	17	3	34	1	33
2	6	4	35	0	7
3	1	4	33	0	2

We observe from Tables 1 and 2 that even when the test style is represented in the training set, utilizing the information that the entire test set is drawn from the same style can lead to improved accuracy. The style-conscious quadratic classifier outperforms the adaptive scheme. We attribute this anomaly to the violation of our assumption that the estimates of the covariance matrices from the training data are representative. Actually, the estimated feature variances are 'larger' than the typical single-typeface variance due to the variation in means across typefaces. We have tried using the average typeface-specific covariance matrix estimated from the training set. The error rates after adaptation were higher due to the higher initial error rate (the covariance matrix including the variance of the means is more representative of all the typefaces than the average typeface-specific covariance matrix). Also because of the high degree of consistency in machine-printed numerals, a few test patterns (i.e., short fields) are sufficient to specialize to the test style. The best that we can hope to achieve with either the style-conscious classifier or the adaptive classifier is accuracy equaling typeface-specific singlet classification (diagonal entries in Table 5).

3.2 Multiple-Style Training, Test Style Not Represented

Here the classifier is trained on patterns from multiple typefaces, but excluding the typeface of the test data. We trained the classifier five times, each time excluding the training data from the typeface of the test data. The recognition results for the mean adaptation are presented in Table 3.

Table 3. Error counts on different typefaces (Leave-one-typeface-out training)

	Test typeface				
Iterations	A	B	H	T	V
0	102	113	146	33	141
1	7	14	76	5	6
5	5	2	44	4	4
10	5	2	43	4	4

Table 4 shows the error counts of the style-conscious quadratic field classifier when the test style is not represented in the training set.

Table 4. Error counts with style-conscious field classification (Leave-one-typeface-out training)

	Test typeface				
Field length	A	B	H	T	V
1	102	113	146	33	141
2	109	115	160	34	115
3	97	119	166	29	98

The potential of the adaptive scheme is more evident when the test style is *not* represented in the training data. Table 3 indicates that the classifier converges after only a few iterations and yields startling improvement in accuracy. As expected, the style-conscious classifier is impotent here, performing poorly even when classifying triples (Table 4).

3.3 Single-Style Training

This is a more challenging task for the adaptive algorithm. We train on only one typeface and classify the test sets of each typeface. The recognition results are presented in Table 5 for 0, 1 and 5 iterations of the mean adaptation algorithm.

The experimental results presented in Table 5 explore the most extreme case of non-representative training data. We observe that the adaptive classifier

Table 5. Error counts with cross-training (Each row is for the same training set, each column is for the same test set)

	Iter	A	B	H	T	V
		Test typeface				
A	0	**0**	520	440	276	486
	1	**0**	326	305	133	230
	5	**0**	40	179	2	0
B	0	145	**1**	111	54	92
	1	15	**1**	36	1	3
	5	8	**2**	51	0	1
H	0	17	154	**13**	164	555
	1	5	8	**13**	2	73
	5	5	8	**13**	1	0
T	0	163	324	433	**0**	3
	1	73	290	404	**0**	0
	5	0	162	402	**0**	0
V	0	251	481	517	34	**0**
	1	98	289	401	4	**0**
	5	4	321	408	3	**0**

improves for every pairing of training and test sets, although not uniformly. For finite sized test set the maximum likelihood estimates do not necessarily yield the minimum error. In Table 3 there are cases where the accuracy after 5 iterations is lower that after one iteration. The gains obtained from adaptation are not symmetric because the convergence properties of the EM algorithm depend upon the initial estimates of the parameters. Figure 4 shows the loci of the class-conditional feature means of the top two principal component features for five iterations. The adaptative estimation of the means is much less effective when Verdana is used for training and Helvetica for testing than vice-versa because of convergence to a local minimum.

In Table 5 the error counts along the diagonal (in boldface) represent the lower bounds attainable with same-typeface training. They are, as expected, stable under EM iteration.

4   Experimental Results on Handwritten Data

We used the databases SD3 and SD7, which are contained in the NIST Special Database SD19 [10]. The database contains handwritten numeral samples labeled by writer and class (but not of course by style). SD3 was the training data released for the First Census OCR Systems Conference and SD7 was used as the test data. We constructed four datasets, two from each of SD3 and SD7, as shown in Table 6. Each writer has approximately 10 samples per class.

We extracted 100 blurred directional (chaincode) features from each sample [9]. We then computed the principal components of the SD3-Train+SD7-

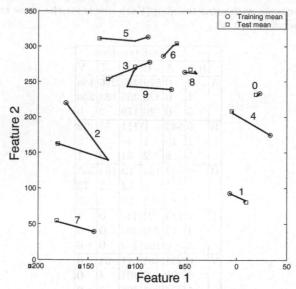

Training on Helvetica, Testing on Verdana

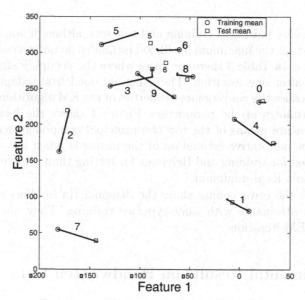

Training on Verdana, Testing on Helvetica

Fig. 4. Loci of the class-conditional feature means, during adaptation, of the top 2 principal component features. The circles represent the class means of the training data and the squares represent the class means of the test data. The dots represent the means after each iteration.

Table 6. Handwritten numeral datasets

	Writers	Number of samples
SD3-Train	0-399 (395)	42698
SD7-Train	2100-2199 (99)	11495
SD3-Test	400-799 (399)	42821
SD7-Test	2200-2299 (100)	11660

Train data onto which the features of all samples were projected to obtain 100 principal-component features for each sample.

Since the writers were arbitrarily chosen to form the training and test sets we did not expect any significant improvement in accuracy with mean adaptation when the *entire* test data was assumed to be from the same style. Our belief was confirmed by the recognition rates obtained.

Table 7. Error-rates in % with mean adaptation on handwritten data (Each row is for the same training set, each column is for the same test set)

	Iter	Test set	
		SD3-Test	SD7-Test
SD3-Train	0	2.2	8.0
	1	2.0	7.0
	5	1.9	6.5
SD7-Train	0	3.7	3.6
	1	2.8	3.2
	5	2.6	3.0
SD3-Train	0	1.7	4.7
+SD7-Train	1	1.5	4.0
	5	1.5	3.7

When the test data is known to be from a single writer, we do expect a good adaptive scheme to specialize the decision regions to the said writer. Table 7 shows the recognition rates for various iterations of the mean adaptation algorithm when samples of the test set are adaptively classified, operating on one writer at a time. For each writer in the test set the means are initialized before adaptation to those of the entire training set.

The recognition results on handwritten data (Table 7) indicate that even when the test data is small (approximately 10 samples per class) adapting the mean improves accuracy. The adaptive classifier that averages over the approximately 10 samples per digit available from each writer is better than the style-conscious classifier operating on fields of only two digits owing to the large variation in handwriting styles. The style-conscious classifier cannot fully exploit style consistency with such short fields.

Table 8. Error-rates on handwritten data before and after adaptation (5 iterations), showing the percentage of test writers that improved or worsened with adaptation.

		Error-rate (%)		% writers	
		Before	After	Accuracy	Accuracy
Training set	Test set	Adaptation	Mean Adaptation	increased	decreased
SD3-Train	SD3-Test	2.2	1.9	19.5	1.3
	SD7-Test	8.0	6.5	54.0	2.0
SD7-Train	SD3-Test	3.7	2.6	43.9	1.3
	SD7-Test	3.6	3.0	39.0	4.0
SD3-Train	SD3-Test	1.7	1.5	15.8	2.0
+SD7-Train	SD7-Test	4.7	3.7	54.0	2.0

Table 8 shows the percentage of writers in the test set on which the accuracy increased and decreased with adaptive classification (after 5 iterations). The maximum improvement for any particular writer was approximately 10% while the maximum decrease in accuracy was about 2%.

5   Discussion and Future Work

The above results confirm the value of adaptive classification in the presence of a large volume of style-consistent test data. It is possible to design OCR systems that improve with use. For machine-printed data, when the style of the test data is represented in the training set, but the size of the test data is small, it is advantageous to use a style-conscious classifier over an adaptive methodology. Either method can, of course, be combined with language context.

We intend to extend the adaptive methodology to recursively estimating the covariance matrices as well. We believe that when only a moderate sized test data is available, the EM algorithm is unstable if used to estimate the covariances, and therefore intend to explore methods that exploit the configuration of the class-conditional densities in the feature space. We also intend to explore the possibility of using adaptation as a substitute for covariance matrix regularization in small training sample scenarios. Another important problem is to identify, at run-time, situations when the adaptive classifier degrades accuracy. This problem is related to the convergence properties of the EM algorithm and depends on the initialization strategy. Although we currently intialize the EM algorithm to the parameters estimated from the training set, we intend to explore other intialization methods. We also plan to study the conditions under which the adaptation can be guarateed to improve accuracy.

Acknowledgements. We thank Dr Hiromichi Fujisawa, Dr. Cheng-Lin Liu and Dr. Prateek Sarkar for the informative discussions we had over the years.

References

1. C. J. Leggetter and P. C. Woodland. Maximum likelihood linear regression for speaker adaptation of continuous density hidden Markov models. *Computer Speech and Language*, 9(2):171–185, April 1995.
2. V. Castelli and T. M. Cover. The relative value of labeled and unlabeled samples in pattern recognition with an unknown mixing parameter. *IEEE Transactions on Information Theory*, 42:2102–2117, November 1996.
3. G. Nagy and G. L. Shelton Jr. Self-corrective character recognition system. *IEEE Transactions on Information Theory*, IT-12(2):215–222, April 1966.
4. H. S. Baird and G. Nagy. A self-correcting 100-font classifier. In L. Vincent and T. Pavlidis, editors, *Document Recognition, Proceedings of the SPIE*, volume 2181, pages 106–115, 1994.
5. P. Sarkar. *Style consistency in pattern fields*. PhD thesis, Rensselaer Polytechnic Institute, Troy, NY, 2000.
6. P. Sarkar and G. Nagy. Style consistency in isogenous patterns. In *Proceedings of the Sixth International Conference on Document Analysis and Recognition*, pages 1169–1174, 2001.
7. S. Veeramachaneni, H. Fujisawa, C.-L. Liu, and G. Nagy. Style-conscious quadratic field classifier. In *Proceedings of the Sixteenth International Conference on Pattern Recognition*, 2002. (Accepted).
8. C. Mathis and T. Breuel. Classification using a Hierarchical Bayesian Approach. Submitted for publication.
9. C.L. Liu, H. Sako, and H. Fujisawa. Performance evaluation of pattern classifiers for handwritten character recognition. *International Journal on Document Analysis and Recognition*, 4(3):191–204, 2002.
10. P. Grother. Handprinted forms and character database, NIST special database 19, March 1995. Technical Report and CDROM.

A Learning Pseudo Bayes Discriminant Method Based on Difference Distribution of Feature Vectors

Hiroaki Takebe, Koji Kurokawa, Yutaka Katsuyama, and Satoshi Naoi

FUJITSU LABORATORIES LTD.
4-1-1, Kamikodanaka Nakahara-ku, Kawasaki, 211-8588, Japan
{takebe.hiroaki, cross, katsuyama,
naoi.satoshi}@jp.fujitsu.com

Abstract. We developed a learning pseudo Bayes discriminant method, that dynamically adapts a pseudo Bayes discriminant function to a font and image degradation condition present in a text. In this method, the characteristics of character pattern deformations are expressed as a statistic of a difference distribution, and information represented by the difference distribution is integrated into the pseudo Bayes discriminant function. The formulation of integrating the difference distribution into the pseudo Bayes discriminant function results in that a covariance matrix of each category is adjusted based on the difference distribution. We evaluated the proposed method on multi-font texts and degraded texts such as compressed color images and faxed copies. We found that the recognition accuracy of our method for the evaluated texts was much higher than that of conventional methods.

1 Introduction

It is often difficult to recognize characters in deformed fonts compared with Mincho and Gothic, which are the most popular fonts for Japanese characters, and in texts degraded significantly depending on the input/output conditions. There have been a number of attempts to solve these problems. Nagy and Xu, for example, proposed a method in which character prototypes are extracted directly from a given text and recognition is performed based on template matching by using the prototypes [2]. Moreover, Ho proposed an adaptive text recognition method that does not depend on ground truth; it is used to first recognize the most frequently occurring words, and then obtain character prototypes from these words [3]. In these methods, the classifier can be "trained" only for the font and degradation condition of a given text, so that it could more accurately recognize the text. However, it is difficult to use these methods for Japanese OCR, because there are more than 3000 categories in Japanese. Thus, to solve the above problems with Japanese OCR, a discriminant function needs to be adapted dynamically to a given font and degradation condition. Omachi proposed methods that detect blurred regions in a character image, and modify a discriminant function based on the detected regions [4][5]. In these methods, eigenvalues and eigenvectors of the covariance matrix of each category are transformed into new values and vectors based on the blurred regions. Blurred regions are detected by

D. Lopresti, J. Hu, and R. Kashi (Eds.): DAS 2002, LNCS 2423, pp. 134–144, 2002.
© Springer-Verlag Berlin Heidelberg 2002

repeatedly "eroding" the character image. The detected blurred regions determine the vector operation in the feature vector space, which is performed for eigenvalues and eigenvectors of each category. However, this method is limited to blurred text images and cannot be used with font variations and the other image degradations. In this paper, we propose a method, that dynamically adapts pseudo Bayes discriminant function to any font and any image degradation condition. In this method, the characteristics of character pattern deformations due to font variations and image degradation are expressed as a statistic of a difference distribution, and information represented by the difference distribution is integrated into the pseudo Bayes discriminant function. The difference distribution represents autocorrelation of character pattern deformations, and the formulation of integration results in adjusting a covariance matrix of each category based on the difference distribution.

The difference distribution is defined and its integration into the pseudo Bayes discriminant function is formulated in Chapter 2. Chapter 2 also presents our experimental results of character recognition, which demonstrate the effectiveness of our method. In Chapter 3, we describe how this method can be used for text recognition and explain how the process of calculation can be made efficient. We also present our experimental results of text recognition, which demonstrate the effectiveness of the method.

2 Learning Pseudo Bayes Discriminant Method

2.1 Difference Distribution

The shapes of different character patterns in one font have common properties. For example, their strokes may be thin/thick or rounded/angular, and so on. The shapes of character patterns input/output by using the same process also have common properties. For example, their strokes in a particular direction may be blurred, and so on. These properties are reflected in the statistic of the difference distribution generated by difference vectors of the character patterns. A difference vector can be defined as follows. Let a feature vector of a character pattern of category C be $\mathbf{x}$ and the average vector of category C be $\mathbf{m}_C$. Then a difference vector is defined as $\mathbf{d} = \mathbf{x} - \mathbf{m}_C$. Next, a difference distribution is defined as follows. Let a character pattern set be $P = \{\mathbf{x}_i \mid i = 1, 2, \ldots, n\}$ and let the category of each pattern be known. Then we can obtain a set of difference vectors of P and let it be $\{\mathbf{d}_i \mid i = 1, 2, \ldots, n\}$ and the autocorrelation matrix be $S_P = \frac{1}{n} \sum_{i=1}^{n} \mathbf{d}_i \mathbf{d}_i^t$. Then we define the difference distribution of pattern set P as a normal distribution with autocorrelation matrix S_P given as a covariance matrix. Autocorrelation matrix S_P represents the average autocorrelation of pattern deformations of P. If there are a sufficient number of categories in P, S_P approximates the matrix generated by averaging the covariance matrices of all categories. This matrix may be used for pre-classification by multiple discriminant analysis (canonical discriminant method) [1].

2.2 Formulation of Integration

The pseudo Bayes discriminant function (a modified quadric discriminant function) can be used to accurately recognize greatly deformed character patterns such as handwritten ones [7][8]. Integrating information represented by the difference distribution into the pseudo Bayes discriminant function will result in more accurate recognition of characters in deformed fonts or in degraded texts. We formulate the integration as follows. First, we integrate the difference distribution into a quadric discriminant function. Let character pattern set P_0 be given and the category of each pattern of $P = \{x_i \mid i = 1, 2, \ldots, n\} \subset P_0$ be known. Let the difference distribution of P be D_P. Then we define a new discriminant function for each category as follows. A new discriminant function of a specific category C for a feature vector x of an unknown pattern is an expected value of the quadric discriminant function of C obtained using difference distribution D_P as a probability density function. The discriminant function defined above is calculated by using the following equation (Appendix A)

$$\Phi_c(x) = (x - m_c)^t (\Sigma + \Sigma_c)^{-1} (x - m_c) + \log|\Sigma + \Sigma_c|, \qquad (1)$$

where m_c is an average vector of category C, Σ_c is a covariance matrix of category C, and Σ is a covariance matrix of difference distribution D_P. This function equals a discriminant function obtained by replacing Σ_c with $\Sigma + \Sigma_c$ in the quadric discriminant function. This means that we can adjust the covariance matrix of a category by using the difference distribution. If the unknown pattern has the same deformation characteristics as those of the pattern set with the difference distribution, the recognition accuracy for the unknown pattern can be improved. This is illustrated in Fig.1. Recall that the formula for replacing Σ_c with $\Sigma + \Sigma_c$ is in common with the RDA method, which reduces the estimation error of eigenvalues of a covariance matrix generated by small samples [6]. Next, we shift Φ_c to a pseudo Bayes discriminant function. The pseudo Bayes discriminant function is obtained by equalizing small eigenvalues in the quadric discriminant function [7]. The computational and memory costs can be reduced by the approximation. Kimura approximated an optimal discriminant function where unknown parameters of a covariance matrix are estimated by using Bayes approach [8]. Here, in the same way as in the shift from a quadric discriminant function to a pseudo Bayes discriminant function [7], the following new discriminant function is defined by

$$\Psi_c(\mathbf{x}) = \frac{1}{\gamma_c^{l+1}} \left\{ \|\mathbf{x} - \mathbf{m}_c\|^2 - \sum_{i=1}^{l} \left(1 - \frac{\gamma_c^{l+1}}{\gamma_c^i}\right)\left((\mathbf{x} - \mathbf{m}_c) \cdot \mathbf{z}_c^i\right)^2 \right\} + \log\left(\prod_{i=1}^{l} \gamma_c^i \cdot \prod_{i=l+1}^{n} \gamma_c^{l+1}\right), \tag{2}$$

where γ_c^i is the i-th eigenvalue of $\Sigma + \Sigma_c$, $\mathbf{z}_c^i$ is an eigenvector corresponding to γ_c^i, and l is an integer smaller than the dimension of the feature vector space n. Let pattern set P_0 be given and a category of each pattern of $P = \{\mathbf{x}_i \mid i = 1, 2, \dots, n\} \subset P_0$ be known. We call it a learning pseudo Bayes discriminant method, to calculate the difference distribution of P and to recognize unknown pattern of P_0 based on the value of discriminant function $\Psi_c(\mathbf{x})$.

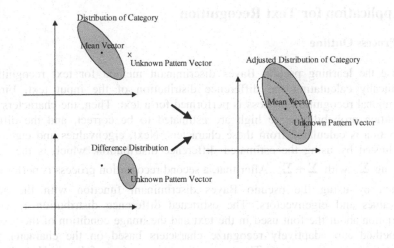

Fig. 1. Adjusting covariance matrix of category by using difference distribution.

2.3 Experimental Results

We used a chain code direction feature. A character image is divided into some sub-windows in the three different directions: horizontally, vertically and diagonally. The total number of sub-windows is 72. So, the dimension of the feature vector is 288. We evaluated the proposed method on about 50 thousand kanji characters in 17 fonts including Mincho, Gothic, Square, Gona, and Nar. For each font, 600 character patterns corresponding to 1/5 of all was supposed to be known, and a difference distribution was generated from the 600 character patterns. We applied the proposed discriminant function to the remaining unknown 2400 character patterns corresponding to 4/5 of all. The recognition accuracy of the proposed method for a total of 40 thousand character patterns was 97.3%, which was 6.8% better than that of the city block distance function and 1.1% better than that of the pseudo Bayes discriminant function.

Table 1. Character recognition accuracy.

City block	Pseudo bayes	Proposed method
90,4%	96,2%	97,3%

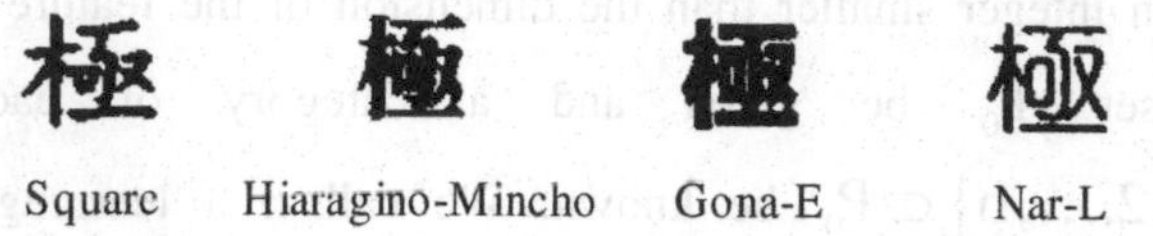

極　　極　　極　　極

Square　　Hiaragino-Mincho　　Gona-E　　Nar-L

Fig. 2. Examples of fonts used in experiment.

3 Application for Text Recognition

3.1 Process Outline

We use the learning pseudo Bayes discriminant method for text recognition by dynamically calculating the difference distribution of the input text. First, the conventional recognition process is performed for a text. Then, the characters whose recognition probabilities are high are estimated to be correct, and the difference distribution is calculated from these characters. Next, eigenvalues and eigenvectors are adjusted by using the estimated difference distribution, which is the same as replacing Σ_c with $\Sigma + \Sigma_c$. After that, a second recognition process is performed for the text by using the pseudo Bayes discriminant function with the adjusted eigenvalues and eigenvectors. The estimated difference distribution reflects the information about the font used in the text and the image condition of the text. Thus our method can adaptively recognize characters based on the character pattern deformations in a given text. The recognition process is as follows. Here, we use a conventional pseudo Bayes discriminant function in the first recognition process. We use recognition probability to estimate correctly recognized characters, which is explained in Section 3.2. We use a high-speed approximation method using only principal eigenvalues and eigenvectors to adjust the eigenvalues and eigenvectors of each category, which is explained in Section 3.3.

3.2 Recognition Probability

We use recognition probability proposed in [9]. A recognition probability is obtained as follows. Let the discriminant function value of a character pattern for an i-th candidate character be d_i, and the reciprocal of d_i be $r_i = \dfrac{1}{d_i}$. If the difference between r_1 and another r_i is large, the first candidate is certain to be correct. Then

$r = \dfrac{r_1}{r_1 + r_2 + r_3 + \cdots}$ is defined as the certainty of recognition. We use $r = \dfrac{r_1}{r_1 + r_2}$ here. Next, the certainty of recognition r is transformed into the recognition probability based on a table $p(r)$, generated as follows. A discriminant function was performed for a large number of character patterns for the evaluation. Let the number of patterns whose certainty of recognition was r be $N(r)$, and let the number of patterns whose certainty of recognition was r and whose 1st candidates were correct be $N_{OK}(r)$. Then the recognition probability for r was defined as

$$p(r) = \frac{N_{OK}(r)}{N(r)}.$$

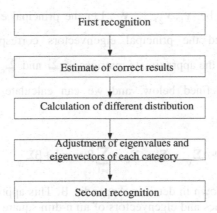

First recognition

Estimate of correct results

Calculation of different distribution

Adjustment of eigenvalues and eigenvectors of each category

Second recognition

Fig. 3. Recognition process

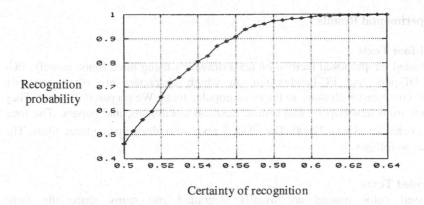

Recognition probability

Certainty of recognition

Fig. 4. Relation between certainty of recognition and recognition probability.

3.3 Adjusting Eigenvalues and Eigenvectors

Let the covariance matrix of category C be Σ_c, and the covariance matrix of the difference distribution be Σ. Then we need to calculate the eigenvalues and eigenvectors of $\Sigma + \Sigma_c$. However, calculating the eigenvalues and eigenvectors of all categories will take a very long time. Therefore we calculate the approximate values of the eigenvalues and eigenvectors of $\Sigma + \Sigma_c$ by using the principal eigenvalues and eigenvectors of Σ and Σ_c. The principal eigenvalues of a matrix are those in the higher ranks in the descending order of eigenvalues, and the principal eigenvectors are those corresponding to the principal eigenvalues. Let the principal eigenvalues of Σ be $\alpha_1 \geq \alpha_2 \geq \cdots \geq \alpha_s$, and the principal eigenvectors corresponding to those be $v_1, v_2, \ldots, v_s$. Let the principal eigenvalues of Σ_c be $\beta_1 \geq \beta_2 \geq \cdots \geq \beta_t$, and the principal eigenvectors corresponding to those be $w_1, w_2, \ldots, w_t$. Then the approximate matrices of Σ and Σ_c are, respectively, $\tilde{\Sigma}$ and $\tilde{\Sigma}_c$ which are defined below, and we can calculate the eigenvalues and eigenvectors of $\tilde{\Sigma} + \tilde{\Sigma}_c$.

$$\Sigma \approx \tilde{\Sigma} = \sum_{i=1}^{s} \alpha_i v_i v_i^t + \alpha \Sigma_{v^\perp}, \; \Sigma_c \approx \tilde{\Sigma}_c = \sum_{i=1}^{t} \beta_i w_i w_i^t + \beta \Sigma_{w^\perp} \tag{3}$$

The calculation is shown in detail in Appendix B. This approximation enables the calculation of eigenvalues and eigenvectors of an n-dim square matrix to be replaced with the calculation of eigenvalues and eigenvectors of, at most, an s+t-dim square matrix.

3.4 Experimental Results

1) Multi-font Texts
We evaluated the proposed method on texts drawn by using three fonts, namely, FC-square, DF-pop, and FC-handwritten, in which characters are often seriously deformed compared with those in the most popular fonts. We prepared 20 texts. They were texts from newspapers, magazines, business documents, and papers. The total number of characters was 22600. The 20×3 texts were drawn using three fonts. The result was as follows.

2) Degraded Texts
Compressed color images are usually degraded and many share the same characteristics. Thus we evaluated the proposed method on compressed color texts. Twenty-two color images of texts from magazines were prepared in the BMP format,

Table 2. Character recognition accuracy for multi-font texts.

	City block	Pseudo bayes	Proposed method
FC-square	65,8%	78,0%	84,3%
DF-pop	84,4%	91,4%	94,2%
FC-handwritten	85,7%	93,9%	95,8%

外部発表の受付状況について（送付）　*Internet*

FC-square

外部発表の受付状況について（送付）　**Internet**

DF-pop

外部発表の受付状況について（送付）　*Internet*

FC-handwritten

Fig. 5. Examples used in experiment.

and they were compressed by 75% into the JPEG format. Then, they were transformed into binary images through binarization. We used the proposed method for the binary images. The total number of characters was about 13000. We also evaluated the proposed method on degraded faxed copies. Twenty texts from newspapers, magazines, and papers were prepared, and sent by fax and the faxed copies were then scanned. The total number of characters was about 22000. The result was as follows.

Table 3. Character recognition accuracy for degraded texts.

	City block	Pseudo bayes	Proposed method
Compressed images	93,8%	95,0%	95,9%
FAX images	96,5%	96,7%	97,4%

報告書　→　報告書

400dpi image　　　　　Faxed copy image

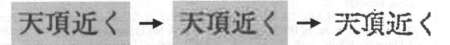

BMP　　　　　　JPEG　　　　　　Binary image

Fig. 6. Examples of texts used in experiment.

3) Processing Time

In the adjustment process of the eigenvalues and eigenvectors, those of $\Sigma + \Sigma_c$ are calculated for each category. The method of calculating directly them of $\Sigma + \Sigma_c$ took about 20 minutes by using a PC with a 1-GHz CPU. However, the method of calculating the approximate values of these eigenvalues and eigenvectors reduced the processing time to about 20 seconds. Moreover dimensionality reduction by feature selection enabled the processing time to be reduced from about 20 to about 4.2 seconds.

4 Conclusion

We developed a learning pseudo Bayes discriminant method, in which a pseudo Bayes discriminant function is dynamically adapted to the font and degradation condition present in a given text. In this paper, we first defined the difference distribution of a character pattern set, which represents the characteristics of character pattern deformations of the set, and then formulated the integration of the difference distribution into the pseudo Bayes discriminant function. This formulation results in that a covariance matrix of each category is adjusted based on the difference distribution. Next we used this method for text recognition. First, a recognition process is performed for an input text, and correct characters are estimated based on the recognition probability. A difference distribution is generated from the estimated correct characters. Then, the eigenvalues and eigenvectors of each category are dynamically adjusted by the estimated difference distribution, and the recognition process by using pseudo Bayes discriminant function is performed for the text once again. We evaluated the proposed method for multi-font texts and degraded texts such as compressed color images and faxed copies. The recognition accuracy of our method was much higher than that of conventional methods.

References

1.   R.O.Duda and P.E.Hart, "Pattern Classification and Scene Analysis", pp.118–121, John Wiley & Sons, Inc., New York, 1973.
2.   G.Nagy and Y.Xu, "Automatic Prototype Extraction for Adaptive OCR", Proceedings of Fourth International Conference on Document Analysis and Recognition, Ulm, Germany, August, pp.18-20 1997, 278–282.
3.   T.K.Ho, "Bootstrapping Text Recognition from Stop Words", Proceedings of Fourteenth International Conference on Pattern Recognition, Brisbane, Australia, August, pp.17–20, 1998, 605-609.
4.   S.Omachi and H.Aso, "A Qualitative Adaptation of Subspace Method for Character Recognition", Trans. of IEICE(D-II), vol. J82-D-II, No.11, pp.1930–1939, Nov., 1999.
5.   S.Omachi, F.Sun, and H.Aso, "A Noise-Adaptive Discriminant Function and Its Application to Blurred Machine Printed Kanji Recognition", PAMI-22, 3, pp314–319, March 2000.

6. J.H.Friedman, "Regularized Discriminant Analysis", Journal of American Statistical Association, 84, No.405, pp.165–175, 1989.
7. S.Tsuruoka, M.Kurita, T.Harada, F.Kimura, and K.Miyake, "Handwritten "KANJI"and "HIRAGANA" Character Recognition Using Weighted Direction Index Histogram Method", Trans. of IEICE (D), vol.J70-D, No.7 pp.1390–1397 July, 1987.
8. F.Kimura, K.Takashina, S.Tsuruoka, and Y.Miyake, "Modified quadratic discriminant functions and the application to Chinese character recognition", IEEE Trans. PAMI, vol.9, no.1, pp.149–153, 1987.
9. K.Fujimoto and H.Kamada, "Fast and Precise Character Recognition by Estimating Recognition Probability", Proceeding of the 1996 Information and Systems Society Conference of IEICE, D-361, Sep. 1996.

Appendix A: Formulation of Discriminant Function

Function $q(\mathbf{m}_1, \mathbf{m}_2, \Sigma_1, \Sigma_2)$ obtained by summing up a normal distribution of average $\mathbf{m}_1$ and covariance matrix Σ_1 weighted with a normal distribution of average $\mathbf{m}_2$ and covariance matrix Σ_2, is calculated based on the following equation.

$$q(\mathbf{m}_1, \mathbf{m}_2, \Sigma_1, \Sigma_2)$$

$$= \int_{R^d} \frac{1}{(2\pi)^{\frac{d}{2}}|\Sigma_1|^{\frac{1}{2}}} \exp\left\{-\frac{1}{2}(\mathbf{x}-\mathbf{m}_1)^t \Sigma_1^{-1}(\mathbf{x}-\mathbf{m}_1)\right\} \cdot \frac{1}{(2\pi)^{\frac{d}{2}}|\Sigma_2|^{\frac{1}{2}}} \exp\left\{-\frac{1}{2}(\mathbf{x}-\mathbf{m}_2)^t \Sigma_2^{-1}(\mathbf{x}-\mathbf{m}_2)\right\} d\mathbf{x}$$

$$= \frac{1}{(2\pi)^{\frac{d}{2}}|\Sigma_1 + \Sigma_2|^{\frac{1}{2}}} \exp\left\{-\frac{1}{2}(\mathbf{m}_1-\mathbf{m}_2)^t (\Sigma_1+\Sigma_2)^{-1}(\mathbf{m}_1-\mathbf{m}_2)\right\}$$

A new discriminant function of specific category C for feature vector $\mathbf{x}$ of an unknown pattern is defined by $\varphi_c(\mathbf{x}) = -2\log q(\mathbf{x}, \mathbf{m}_c, \Sigma, \Sigma_c)$, where $\mathbf{x}$ is a n-dimensional feature vector of an input image, $\mathbf{m}_c$ is an average vector of category C, Σ_c is a covariance matrix of category C, and Σ is a covariance matrix of the difference distribution of pattern set P. By removing the constant terms from this equation, we obtain the following discriminant function.

$$\Phi_c(\mathbf{x}) = (\mathbf{x}-\mathbf{m}_c)^t (\Sigma+\Sigma_c)^{-1}(\mathbf{x}-\mathbf{m}_c) + \log|\Sigma+\Sigma_c|$$

Appendix B: Calculation of Eigenvalues and Eigenvectors

We assume that a vector subspace covered by $\mathbf{v}_1, \mathbf{v}_2, \ldots, \mathbf{v}_s$ and a vector subspace covered by $\mathbf{w}_1, \mathbf{w}_2, \ldots, \mathbf{w}_t$ are V and W, respectively, and that a minimal vector subspace including V and W is U. Then, both $\mathbf{w}'_1, \mathbf{w}'_2, \ldots, \mathbf{w}'_u$ and $\mathbf{v}'_1, \mathbf{v}'_2, \ldots, \mathbf{v}'_t$ that satisfy the following equation are calculated by Gram-Schmidt orthogonalization.

$$\mathbf{U} = \mathbf{V} + \mathbf{W} = \left\{ \mathbf{v}_1, \mathbf{v}_2, \ldots, \mathbf{v}_s, \mathbf{w}_1', \mathbf{w}_2', \ldots, \mathbf{w}_u' \right\} = \left\{ \mathbf{v}_1', \mathbf{v}_2', \ldots, \mathbf{v}_v', \mathbf{w}_1, \mathbf{w}_2, \ldots, \mathbf{w}_t \right\}$$

And matrices $\mathbf{V_W}, \mathbf{W_V}, \mathbf{P}, \mathbf{A}$ and $\mathbf{B}$ are defined as

$$\mathbf{V_W} = \begin{pmatrix} \mathbf{v}_1 & \mathbf{v}_2 & \cdots & \mathbf{v}_s & \mathbf{w}_1' & \mathbf{w}_2' & \cdots & \mathbf{w}_u' \end{pmatrix},$$

$$\mathbf{W_V} = \begin{pmatrix} \mathbf{w}_1 & \mathbf{w}_2 & \cdots & \mathbf{w}_t & \mathbf{v}_1' & \mathbf{v}_2' & \cdots & \mathbf{v}_v' \end{pmatrix},$$

$$\mathbf{P} = \mathbf{V_W^t} \mathbf{W_V}, \quad \mathbf{A} = \begin{pmatrix} \alpha_1 & & & & & \\ & \ddots & & & & \\ & & \alpha_s & & & \\ & & & \alpha & & \\ & & & & \ddots & \\ & & & & & \alpha \end{pmatrix}, \quad \text{and} \quad \mathbf{B} = \begin{pmatrix} \beta_1 & & & & \\ & \ddots & & & \\ & & \beta_t & & \\ & & & \beta & \\ & & & & \ddots \\ & & & & \beta \end{pmatrix}.$$

Then we can show that

$$\tilde{\Sigma} + \tilde{\Sigma}_c = \mathbf{V_W} \left(\mathbf{A} + \mathbf{PBP}^t \right) \mathbf{V_W^t} + (\alpha + \beta) \Sigma_{\mathbf{U}^\perp}.$$

Thus matrix $\mathbf{A} + \mathbf{PBP}^t$ is diagonalized as $\mathbf{A} + \mathbf{PBP}^t = \mathbf{X\Gamma X}^t$,

where $\mathbf{X} = \begin{pmatrix} \mathbf{x}_1 & \mathbf{x}_2 & \cdots & \mathbf{x}_{s+u} \end{pmatrix}$ and $\Gamma = \begin{pmatrix} \gamma_1 & & & \\ & \gamma_2 & & \\ & & \ddots & \\ & & & \gamma_{s+u} \end{pmatrix}.$

Then the obtained diagonal components equal $\gamma_1, \gamma_2, \ldots, \gamma_1$, and $\mathbf{z}_1, \mathbf{z}_2, \ldots, \mathbf{z}_1$ are calculated according to the following equation $\begin{pmatrix} \mathbf{z}_1 & \mathbf{z}_2 & \cdots & \mathbf{z}_{s+u} \end{pmatrix} = \mathbf{V_W X}.$

Increasing the Number of Classifiers in Multi-classifier Systems: A Complementarity-Based Analysis

L. Bovino[2], G. Dimauro[1], S. Impedovo[1], G. Pirlo[1], and A. Salzo[2]

[1] Dipartimento di Informatica, Università degli Studi di Bari
Via Orabona 4, 70126 Bari-Italy
impedovo@di.uniba.it
[2] Consorzio Interuniversitario Nazionale per l'Informatica (CINI),
Via G.Petroni 15/F.1, 70124 Bari– Italy

Abstract. Complementarity among classifiers is a crucial aspect in classifier combination. A combined classifier is significantly superior to the individual classifiers only if they strongly complement each other. In this paper a complementarity-based analysis of sets of classifier is proposed for investigating the behaviour of multi-classifier systems, as new classifiers are added to the set. The experimental results confirm the theoretical evidence and allow the prediction of the performance of a multi-classifier system, as the number of classifiers increases.

1 Introduction

Complementarity among classifiers is crucial in classifier combination. In fact, classifier combination significantly outperforms individual classifiers only if they are largely complementary each other. Complementarity among classifiers can be achieved by using different feature sets and classification strategies [1,2]. Alternatively, complementarity is also expected when different training sets and resampling strategies are used [3,4,5,6].

In this paper a complementarity-based analysis of sets of classifier is used for investigating the behaviour of multi-classifier systems, as new classifiers are added to the set. The result allows the prediction of the effect of increasing the number of classifiers on the performance of multi-classifier systems. The experimental tests, which have been carried out in the field of hand-written numeral recognition, confirm the expected performance of the combination method and validate the proposed approach.

The paper is organised as follows: Section 2 introduces an estimator of complementarity for *abstract-level* classifiers. Section 3 shows the complementarity of a set of classifiers, as the number of classifiers increases. Section 4 presents the methodology used for the analysis of combination methods. The experimental results are discussed in Section 5.

D. Lopresti, J. Hu, and R. Kashi (Eds.): DAS 2002, LNCS 2423, pp. 145–156, 2002.

2   Complementarity among Classifiers

In order to measure the degree of complementarity among *abstract-level* classifiers, the *Similarity Index* has been recently introduced [7]. Let $A=\{A_1, A_2\}$ a set of two classifiers and $P = \{P_t \mid t=1,2,...,N\}$ a set of patterns and let $A_i(P_t)$ be the class label produced by A_i for the input pattern P_t. The *Similarity Index* ρ_A for the set $\{A_1,A_2\}$ is defined as:

$$\rho_{\{A_1,A_2\}} = \frac{1}{N} \sum_{t=1}^{N} Q\left(A_1(P_t), A_2(P_t)\right) \tag{1}$$

and

$$Q(A_1(P_t),A_2(P_t))=\begin{cases} 1 & \text{if } A_1(P_t)=A_2(P_t) \\ 0 & \text{otherwise} \end{cases} \tag{2}$$

Of course, $\rho_A \in [0,1]$: when ρ_A is close to 0, classifiers are strongly complementary; when ρ_A is close to 1, classifiers are weakly complementary. Figure 1 shows the outputs of two classifiers A_1, A_2 for N=10 input patterns $P_1,P_2,...,P_{10}$. Recognitions are indicated by R, substitutions by the labels S1, S2,S3 (with Si≠Sj, ∀ i≠j). In this case the recognition rates for A_1 and A_2 are $R_1=0.7$ and $R_2=0.6$, respectively. The degree of complementarity between A_1 and A_2 is $\rho_{A_1,A_2}= 0.6$. In fact:

- P_1,P_2,P_3,P_6,P_7 are recognised by both classifiers ($Q(A_1(P_t),A_2(P_t))=1$, t=1,2,3,6,7);
- P_4 is substituted by both classifiers which provide different responses: $A_1(P_4)=$S1, $A_2(P_4)=$S3 ($Q(A_1(P_4),A_2(P_4))=0$);
- P_5 is substituted by both classifiers which provide the same response: $A_1(P_5)=A_2(P_5)=$S2 ($Q(A_1(P_5),A_2(P_5))=1$);
- P_8 and P_{10} are recognized by A_1 and substituted by A_2: $A_1(P_8)=$R and $A_2(P_8)=$S2, $A_1(P_{10})=$R and $A_2(P_{10})=$S1 ($Q(A_1(P_t),A_2(P_t))=0$, t=8,10);
- P_9 is substituted by A_1 and recognised by A_2: $A_1(P_9)=$S3, $A_2(P_9)=$R ($Q(A_1(P_9),A_2(P_9))=0$).

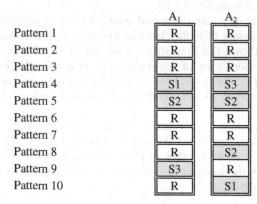

	A_1	A_2
Pattern 1	R	R
Pattern 2	R	R
Pattern 3	R	R
Pattern 4	S1	S3
Pattern 5	S2	S2
Pattern 6	R	R
Pattern 7	R	R
Pattern 8	R	S2
Pattern 9	S3	R
Pattern 10	R	S1

Fig. 1. List of output of two classifiers

In general, let $A = \{A_i \mid i=1,2,...,K\}$ be a set of classifiers, $P = \{P_t \mid t=1,2,...,N\}$ a set of patterns the *Similarity Index* ρ_A for the set A is defined as [7]:

$$\rho_A = \frac{\displaystyle\sum_{\substack{i,j=1,...K \\ i<j}} P\{A_i, A_j\}}{\dbinom{K}{2}}. \tag{3}$$

3   Increasing the Number of Classifiers: Analysis of Complementarity

Let $A = \{A_i \mid i=1,2,...,K\}$ be a set of classifiers with *Similarity Index* equal to ρ_A, and suppose that a new classifier A_{K+1} is added to the set. The *Similarity Index* of $A \cup \{A_{K+1}\}$ is (see eq. (3)):

$$\rho_{A \cup \{A_{K+1}\}} = \frac{\displaystyle\sum_{\substack{i,j=1,...K+1 \\ i<j}} \rho_{A_i, A_j}}{\dbinom{K+1}{2}} = \frac{\displaystyle\sum_{\substack{i,j=1,...K \\ i<j}} \rho_{A_i, A_j} + \sum_{i=1,...K} \rho_{A_i, A_{K+1}}}{\dbinom{K+1}{2}}$$

$$= \frac{\displaystyle\sum_{\substack{i,j=1,...K \\ i<j}} \rho_{A_i, A_j}}{\dbinom{K+1}{2}} + \frac{\displaystyle\sum_{i=1,...K} \rho_{A_i, A_{K+1}}}{\dbinom{K+1}{2}} = \frac{\displaystyle\sum_{\substack{i,j=1,...K \\ i<j}} \rho_{A_i, A_j}}{\dfrac{(K+1)}{(K-1)}\dbinom{K}{2}} + \frac{\displaystyle\sum_{i=1,...K} \rho_{A_i, A_{K+1}}}{\dbinom{K+1}{2}}$$

$$= \frac{(K-1)}{(K+1)} \frac{\displaystyle\sum_{\substack{i,j=1,...K \\ i<j}} \rho_{A_i, A_j}}{\dbinom{K}{2}} + \frac{\displaystyle\sum_{i=1,...K} \rho_{A_i, A_{K+1}}}{\dfrac{(K+1)K}{2}}.$$

Hence:

$$\rho_{A \cup \{A_{K+1}\}} = \frac{K-1}{K+1}\rho_A + \frac{2}{K(K+1)} \sum_{i=1,...,K} \rho_{A_i, A_{K+1}} \tag{4}$$

Of course, the variability of $\rho_{A \cup \{A_{K+1}\}}$ depends on

$$\sum_{i=1,...,K} \rho_{A_i, A_{K+1}} \tag{5}$$

In order to estimate to what extent the quantity (5) can vary, the relationships between $\rho_{A_i A_j}$ (A_i, $A_j \in A$) and $\rho_{A_i A_{K+1}}$, $\rho_{A_j A_{K+1}}$ (due to the extra classifier A_{K+1}) are determined in the following. For this purpose, from now on we suppose that all classifiers have similar performance, i.e. all of them have recognition rate equal to R.

3.1 Analysis of the Complementarity between A_i and A_j.

Let A_i and A_j be two classifiers of A with *Similarity Index* equal to ρ_{A_i,A_j} (Figure 2).
The analysis of the outputs of A_i and A_j leads to the following cases:

[A] $A_i(t)=Si$, $A_j(t)=Sj$ (Si =Sj);
[B] $A_i(t)=Si$, $A_j(t)= Sj$ (Si ≠Sj);
[C] $A_i(t)= Si$, $A_j(t)= R$;
[D] $A_i(t)=R$, $A_j(t)= R$;
[E] $A_i(t)= R$, $A_j(t)= Sj$.

Now, let P_A, P_B, P_C, P_D, P_E be the percentage of patterns corresponding to the cases A,B,C,D,E respectively, the following equations hold:

❖ $P_A+P_B+P_C+P_D+P_E=1$;   (6)
❖ $P_C+P_D=R$ and $P_D+P_E=R$ (7)
❖ $P_A+P_D= \rho_{Ai,Aj}$ (the quantity $\rho_{Ai,Aj}$ concerns all the cases in which the decisions of A_i
    and A_j agree, i.e. cases (A) and (D)).   (8)

From eq. (8) it follows that:

$$P_A=\delta$$ (9)
$$P_D=\rho_{Ai,Aj} -\delta$$ (10)

where δ is a positive quantity ($\delta<\rho_{Ai,Aj}$).
Moreover, from (7), (9) and (10), it results:

$$P_C=P_E=R-P_D=R-(\rho_{Ai,Aj}-\delta),$$ (11)

while from (6),(9),(10) and (11):

$$P_B=1-P_A-P_C-P_D-P_E=1-\delta-(R-(\rho_{Ai,Aj}-\delta))-(\rho_{Ai,Aj}-\delta)-(R-(\rho_{Ai,Aj}-\delta))=1-2R+\rho_{Ai,Aj}-2\delta .$$ (12)

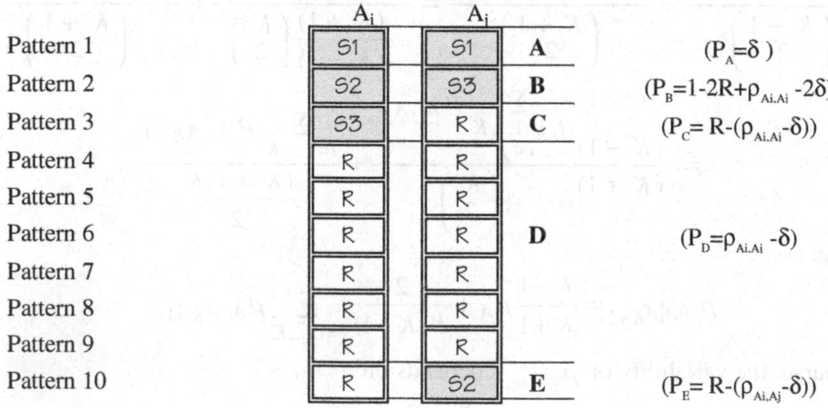

	A_i	A_j		
Pattern 1	S1	S1	A	($P_A=\delta$)
Pattern 2	S2	S3	B	($P_B=1-2R+\rho_{Ai,Ai}-2\delta$)
Pattern 3	S3	R	C	($P_C= R-(\rho_{Ai,Ai}-\delta)$)
Pattern 4	R	R		
Pattern 5	R	R		
Pattern 6	R	R	D	($P_D=\rho_{Ai,Ai} -\delta$)
Pattern 7	R	R		
Pattern 8	R	R		
Pattern 9	R	R		
Pattern 10	R	S2	E	($P_E= R-(\rho_{Ai,Aj}-\delta)$)

Fig. 2. Analysis of complementarity between the classifiers A_i and A_j

3.2 Analysis of the Complementarity between A_{K+1} and A_i , A_j.

When the new classifier A_{K+1} is considered, two cases must be examined concerning respectively the minimum (Case (a)) and the maximum (Case (b)) value of the quantity (5):

Case (a). In this case the outputs of A_{K+1} must be as complementary as possible to those of A_i and A_j. Hence, the recognitions of A_{K+1} must occur according to the following priorities (see Fig. 3):

a.1) both A_i and A_j substitute the patterns (cases A and B). For this case, the contribution of A_{K+1} to the *Similarity Index* is null since A_{K+1} disagrees both with A_i and A_j. The percentage of patterns concerning (a.1) is P_A+P_B at the best.

a.2) A_i or A_j substitute the patterns (cases C and E). In this case A_{K+1} agrees with A_i or A_j. Therefore the contribution due to each pattern recognized by A_{K+1} is weighted by 1. The percentage of patterns concerning (a.2) is P_C+P_E at the best.

a.3) both A_i and A_j recognise the patterns (case D). In this case A_{K+1} agrees both with A_i and A_j. Therefore the contribution due to each pattern recognized by A_{K+1} is weighted by 2. The percentage of patterns concerning (a.3) is P_{D_2} at the best, where $P_{D_2}=R-P_A-P_B-P_C-P_E$ (if we assume the common condition: $R>P_A-P_B-P_C-P_E$).

Concerning substitutions, it must be assumed that A_{K+1} always provides substitutions as different as possible from those of A_i and A_j. Hence it results (see figure 3):

$$\rho_{A_i,A_{K+1}} + \rho_{A_j,A_{K+1}}=0\cdot(P_A+P_B)+1\cdot(P_C+P_E)+2\cdot P_{D_2} = P_C+P_E+2\cdot P_{D_2} \quad (13)$$

where
P_c is due to patterns recognised by A_{K+1} and A_j, and substituted by A_i;
P_{D_2} is due to patterns recognised by A_{K+1} , A_i and A_j;
P_E is due to patterns recognised by A_{K+1} and A_i, and substituted by and A_j.

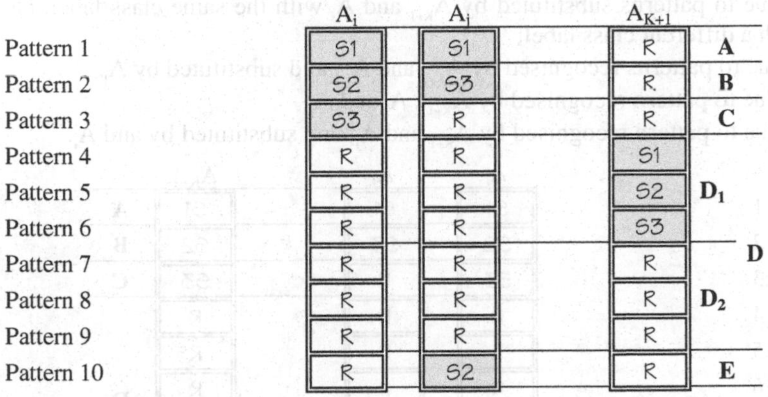

	A_i	A_j	A_{K+1}	
Pattern 1	S1	S1	R	A
Pattern 2	S2	S3	R	B
Pattern 3	S3	R	R	C
Pattern 4	R	R	S1	
Pattern 5	R	R	S2	D_1
Pattern 6	R	R	S3	
Pattern 7	R	R	R	D
Pattern 8	R	R	R	D_2
Pattern 9	R	R	R	
Pattern 10	R	S2	R	E

Fig. 3. Analysis of complementarity among A_{K+1} and A_i , A_j- Case (a)

Substituting eqs. (9),(10),(11) and (12) in (13) it results:

$$\rho_{A_i,A_{K+1}}+\rho_{A_j,A_{K+1}}=2(R-(\rho_{Ai,Aj}-\delta))+2[R-\delta-(1-2R+\rho_{Ai,Aj}-2\delta)-2(R-(\rho_{Ai,Aj}-\delta))]=2(2R-1) \quad (14)$$

Case (b). In this case the outputs of A_{K+1} must be as similar as possible to those of A_i and A_j.Hence,the recognitions of A_{K+1} must occur according to the following priorities (see Fig. 4):

b.1) both A_i and A_j recognise the patterns (case D). For this case the contribution of A_{K+1} to the *Similarity Index* is weighted by 2, since A_{K+1} agrees both with A_i and A_j. The percentage of patterns concerning (b.1) is P_D at the best.

b.2) A_i or A_j substitute the patterns (cases C and E). In this case A_{K+1} agrees with A_i or A_j. Therefore the contribution due to each pattern recognized by A_{K+1} is weighted by 1. The percentage of patterns concerning (b.2) is P_C+P_E at the best.

b.3) both A_i and A_j substitute the patterns (cases A and B). For these cases the contribution of A_{K+1} to the *Similarity Index* is null since A_{K+1} disagrees both with A_i and A_j. The percentage of patterns concerning (b.1) is P_A+P_B at the best.

Concerning substitutions, A_{K+1} must provides substitutions as similar as possible to those of A_i and A_j. Precisely:

b'.1) if $A_i(t)=A_j(t)=Si$ then it must results that $A_{K+1}(t)=Si$. For this case the contribution to the *Similarity Index* due to each pattern recognized by A_{K+1} is weighted by 2 since A_{K+1} agree both with A_i and A_j. The percentage of patterns concerning (b'.1) is P_A at the best.

b'.2) if $A_i(t)=Si$ and $A_j(t)=Sj$ then it must results that $A_{K+1}(t)=Si$ (or equivalently $A_{K+1}=Sj$). For this case the contribution to the *Similarity Index* due to each pattern recognized by A_{K+1} is weighted by 1 since A_{K+1} agrees with A_i (or A_j). The percentage of patterns concerning (b'.2) is P_B at the best (or equivalently P_E).

In this case we obtain (see figure 4):

$$\rho_{A_i,A_{K+1}} + \rho_{A_j,A_{K+1}}=2\cdot P_D+1\cdot(P_C+P_E)+2\cdot P_A+1\cdot P_B=2\cdot P_A+P_B+P_C+2\cdot P_D+P_E \quad (15)$$

where:

- P_A is due to patterns substituted by A_{K+1}, A_i and A_j with the same class label;
- P_B is due to patterns substituted by A_{K+1} and A_i with the same class label, and by A_j with a different class label;
- P_C is due to patterns recognised by A_{K+1} and A_i, and substituted by A_j;
- P_D is due to pattern recognised by A_{K+1}, A_i and A_j;
- P_E is due to pattern recognised by A_{K+1} and A_j, and substituted by and A_i.

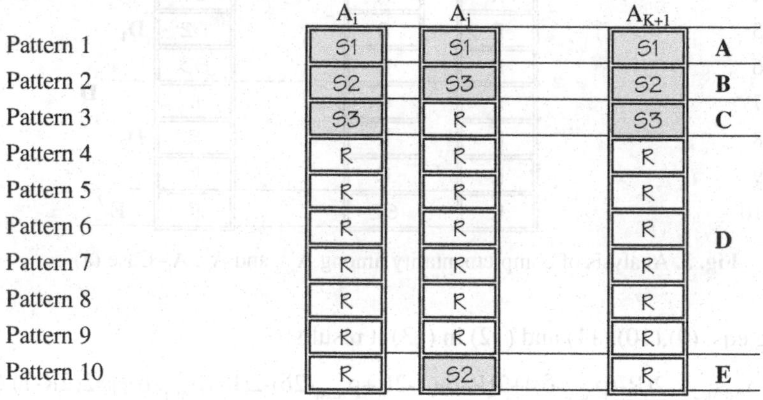

	A_i	A_j		A_{K+1}	
Pattern 1	S1	S1		S1	A
Pattern 2	S2	S3		S2	B
Pattern 3	S3	R		S3	C
Pattern 4	R	R		R	
Pattern 5	R	R		R	
Pattern 6	R	R		R	D
Pattern 7	R	R		R	
Pattern 8	R	R		R	
Pattern 9	R	R		R	
Pattern 10	R	S2		R	E

Fig. 4. Analysis of complementarity among A_{K+1} and A_i, A_j- Case (b)

Substituting eqs. (9),(10),(11) and (12) in (15) it results:

$$\rho_{A_i,A_{K+1}}+\rho_{A_j,A_{K+1}}=2(\rho_{Ai,Aj}-\delta)+2\delta+(R-(\rho_{Ai,Aj}-\delta))+(1-2R+\rho_{Ai,Aj}-2\delta)=1+\rho_{Ai,Aj} \quad (16)$$

3.3 Analysis of the Complementarity of $A \cup \{A_{K+1}\}$.

From eqs. (14) and (16) it follows that, $\forall i,j = 1,2,\ldots,N$:

$$2(2R-1) \le \rho_{A_i,A_{K+1}} + \rho_{A_j,A_{K+1}} \le 1 + \rho_{A_i,A_j}. \tag{17}$$

Adding the inequalities (17), for $i,j=1,2,\ldots,N$, $i<j$, it results:

$$\sum_{\substack{i,j=1 \\ i<j}}^{K} 2(2R-1) \le \sum_{\substack{i,j=1 \\ i<j}}^{K} (\rho_{A_i,A_{K+1}} + \rho_{A_j,A_{K+1}}) \le \sum_{\substack{i,j=1 \\ i<j}}^{K} (1 + \rho_{A_i,A_j})$$

$$\binom{K}{2} 2(2R-1) \le (K-1)\sum_{i=1}^{K} \rho_{A_i,A_{K+1}} \le \binom{K}{2} + \sum_{\substack{i,j=1 \\ i<j}}^{K} \rho_{A_i,A_j}$$

$$\binom{K}{2} 2(2R-1) \le (K-1)\sum_{i=1}^{K} \rho_{A_i,A_{K+1}} \le \binom{K}{2} + \binom{K}{2}\rho_A$$

$$\frac{K(K-1)}{2} 2(2R-1) \le (K-1)\sum_{i=1}^{K} \rho_{A_i,A_{K+1}} \le \frac{K(K-1)}{2}(1+\rho_A)$$

$$(2R-1)K \le \sum_{i=1}^{K} \rho_{A_i,A_{K+1}} \le \frac{K}{2}(1+\rho_A) \tag{18}$$

Substituting expression (18) in (4) we obtain that the range of variability of the *Similarity Index,* when a new classifier is added to the set A, is given by:

$$\rho_{A \cup \{A_{K+1}\}} \in [\text{Min } \rho_{A \cup \{A_{K+1}\}}, \text{ Max } \rho_{A \cup \{A_{K+1}\}}] ,$$

where:

✓ $\text{Min } \rho_{A \cup \{A_{K+1}\}} = \dfrac{K-1}{K+1}\rho_A + \dfrac{2}{K(K+1)}(2R-1)K = \dfrac{K-1}{K+1}\rho_A + 2\dfrac{2R-1}{(K+1)};$ (19)

✓ $\text{Max } \rho_{A \cup \{A_{K+1}\}} = \dfrac{K-1}{K+1}\rho_A + \dfrac{2}{K(K+1)}\dfrac{K}{2}(1+\rho_A) = \dfrac{K}{K+1}\rho_A + \dfrac{1}{(K+1)}.$ (20)

4   Analysis of Combination Methods

Although classifier combination is widely applied in many fields, theoretical analysis of combination schemes can be very difficult. The net result is that only simple combination have been explained up to now from a theoretical point of view [8]. In many cases the performance of a combination method cannot be estimated theoretically and it can be evaluated on experimental basis in specific working conditions (a specific set of classifiers, training data and sessions, etc.). In this case the result depends on the specific conditions of the test and no information can be derived on the performance of the combination method if the working conditions change. A different approach to estimate systematically the performance of a combination method **C** for abstract-level classifiers is based on the simulation of various sets of classifiers which are used to test the method under different conditions

[9]. In this case, performance of **C**, which combines K abstract-level classifiers, is evaluated as a function of the recognition rate of the classifiers (R) and the degree of complementarity among them (ρ):

$$\mathbf{C}\,(K,R,\rho) \rightarrow (R_\mathbf{C}\,, L_\mathbf{C}) \tag{21}$$

where $R_\mathbf{C}$ and $L_\mathbf{C}$ are respectively the recognition rate and the reliability rate of **C** [1]. More precisely, since *abstract-level* classifiers are combined, each individual classifier is considered as a discrete random variable whose outputs are N class labels if N patterns are supposed to be input: N·R recognitions (labels equal to R) and N·(1-R) substitutions (labels equal to S1,S2,S3,…). Of course, for any 3-tuple (K,R,ρ), several sets (50 in out tests) of classifiers are simulated and used to test the combination method **C**, in order to estimate its mean performance in terms of R_C and L_C.

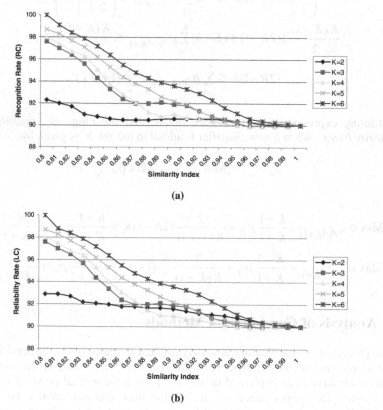

(a)

(b)

Fig. 5. Performance of DS as a function of ρ in combining K classifiers (R=90%)

In this work, the behaviour of the Dempster-Shafer (DS) combination method is analysed [10]. Specifically, we use the DS combination scheme and the decision rule proposed respectively in Section VI.C and Section VI.D (eq. [50], α=0) of ref. [1]. The performance of DS is reported in Figure 5 as a function of ρ, when sets of K classifiers are combined (K=2,3,4,5,6), each one with a recognition rate equal to R=90% (see ref. [11] for more details).

5   Experimental Results

This Section shows the analysis of complementarity of a set of classifiers, as the number of classifiers increases. Based on this result, the performance of the Dempster-Shafer (DS) method in combining classifiers is investigated. Two cases are discussed hereafter.

Case (a). In this case four initial sets of classifiers A ={A$_i$ |i=1,2,...,K}, for K=2,3,4,5, are given. The recognition rate of the classifiers is R=90% and the degree of complementarity of each set is ρ_A=0.85.

Table 1. DS Performance as the number of classifier increases: Case (a)

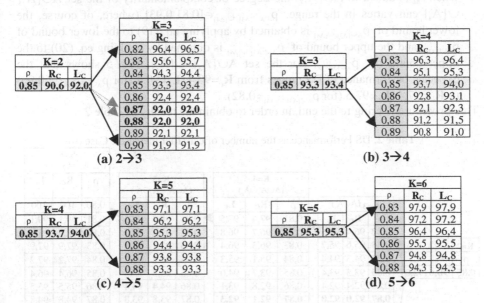

K=2

ρ	R$_C$	L$_C$
0,85	90,6	92,0

K=3

ρ	R$_C$	L$_C$
0,82	96,4	96,5
0,83	95,6	95,7
0,84	94,3	94,4
0,85	93,3	93,4
0,86	92,4	92,4
0,87	92,0	92,0
0,88	92,0	92,0
0,89	92,1	92,1
0,90	91,9	91,9

(a) 2→3

K=3

ρ	R$_C$	L$_C$
0,85	93,3	93,4

K=4

ρ	R$_C$	L$_C$
0,83	96,3	96,4
0,84	95,1	95,3
0,85	93,7	94,0
0,86	92,8	93,1
0,87	92,1	92,3
0,88	91,2	91,5
0,89	90,8	91,0

(b) 3→4

K=4

ρ	R$_C$	L$_C$
0,85	93,7	94,0

K=5

ρ	R$_C$	L$_C$
0,83	97,1	97,1
0,84	96,2	96,2
0,85	95,3	95,3
0,86	94,4	94,4
0,87	93,8	93,8
0,88	93,3	93,3

(c) 4→5

K=5

ρ	R$_C$	L$_C$
0,85	95,3	95,3

K=6

ρ	R$_C$	L$_C$
0,83	97,9	97,9
0,84	97,2	97,2
0,85	96,4	96,4
0,86	95,5	95,5
0,87	94,8	94,8
0,88	94,3	94,3

(d) 5→6

Table 1 reports the effect of adding one extra classifier to each set. Eqs. (19) and (20) are used to determine the range of variability of the degree of complementarity , while the results in Fig.5 allows the prediction of the performance of the DS method:

❖ for K=2 (Table 1a), DS performance is equal to R$_c$= 90.6, L$_c$= 92.0 (Fig. 5). If an extra classifier A$_{K+1}$ is added to A, the complementarity of A∪{A$_{K+1}$} is in the range [0.82, 0.90] (eqs.(19),(20)). Hence it results that the expected performance for A∪{A$_{K+1}$} ranges from R$_c$=91.9, L$_c$=91.9 (Fig.5, for $\rho_{A \cup \{A_{K+1}\}}$=0.90) to R$_c$= 96.4, L$_c$=96.5 (Fig.5, for $\rho_{A \cup \{A_{K+1}\}}$=0.82).

❖ for K=3 (Table 1b), DS performance is equal to R$_c$= 93.3, L$_c$= 93.4 (Fig. 5). If an extra classifier A$_{K+1}$ is added to A, the complementarity of A∪{A$_{K+1}$} is in the range [0.83, 0.89] (eqs.(19),(20)) and from Fig. 5 it results that the expected performance for $A\cup\{A_{K+1}\}$ ranges from R_c=90.8, L_c=91.0 (Fig. 5, for $\rho_{A\cup\{A_{K+1}\}}$=0.89) to R_c=96.3, L_c=96.4 (Fig. 5, for $\rho_{A\cup\{A_{K+1}\}}$=0.83). Similar considerations lead to the results in Table 1c,d.

Case (b). In this case the initial set of K=2 classifiers A ={A_1 , A_2 } is given, with R=90% and ρ_A=0.85, and four extra classifiers A_3, A_4, A_5 and A_6 are added to the set A, one after the other (es. 2→3→4→5→6). In this case eqs (19) and (20) must be applied by an iterative scheme, in order to predict the range of variability of the enlarged sets of classifiers;

❖ when A_3 is added to the set A, the degree of complementarity $\rho_{A\cup\{A3\}}$ can varies in the range $\rho_{A\cup\{A3\}}\in[0.82,0.90]$ (eqs. (19),(20)) and from Fig.5 the performance of DS ranges from R_c=91.9, L_c=91.9 (for $\rho_{A\cup\{A_{K+1}\}}$=0.90) to R_c= 96.4, L_c=96.5 (for $\rho_{A\cup\{A_{K+1}\}}$=0.82).

❖ when A_4 is added to $A\cup\{A_3\}$, the degree of complementarity of the set $A\cup\{A_3\}$ $\cup\{A_4\}$ can varies in the range $\rho_{A\cup\{A3\}\cup\{A4\}}\in[0.81,0.93]$ (where, of course, the lower bound of $\rho_{A\cup\{A3\}\cup\{A4\}}$ is obtained by applying eq. (19) to the lower bound of $\rho_{A\cup\{A3\}}$, and the upper bound of $\rho_{A\cup\{A3\}\cup\{A4\}}$ is obtained by applying eq. (20) to the upper bound of $\rho_{A\cup\{A3\}}$). For the set $A\cup\{A_3\}$ $\cup\{A_4\}$, Fig. 5 shows that the expected performance of DS ranges from R_c=90.4, L_c=90.4 (for $\rho_{A\cup\{A3\}\cup\{A4\}}$=0.93) to R_c= 97.4, L_c=97.5 (for $\rho_{A\cup\{A3\}\cup\{A4\}}$=0.82).

This procedure is bring to the end, in order to obtain the results in Table 2.

Table 2. DS Performance as the number of classifier increases: Case (b).

K=2 (A={A_1,A_2})			K=3 (A∪A$_3$)			K=4 (A∪A$_4$∪A$_4$)			K=5 (A∪A$_4$∪A$_4$∪A$_5$)			K=6 (A∪A$_3$∪A$_4$∪A$_5$∪A$_6$)		
ρ	R_C	L_C	ρ	R_C	L_C	ρ	R_C	L_C	ρ	R_C	L_C	ρ	R_C	L_C
												0,80	100	100
						0,81	97,4	97,5	0,81	98,3	98,3	0,81	99,1	99,1
			0,82	96,4	96,5	0,82	96,7	96,8	0,82	97,7	97,7	0,82	98,4	98,4
			0,83	95,6	95,7	0,83	96,3	96,4	0,83	97,1	97,1	0,83	97,9	97,9
			0,84	94,3	94,4	0,84	95,1	95,3	0,84	96,2	96,2	0,84	97,2	97,2
0,85	90,6	92,0	0,85	93,3	93,4	0,85	93,7	94,0	0,85	95,3	95,3	0,85	96,4	96,4
			0,86	92,4	92,4	0,86	92,8	93,1	0,86	94,4	94,4	0,86	95,5	95,5
			0,87	92,0	92,0	0,87	92,1	92,3	0,87	93,8	93,8	0,87	94,8	94,8
			0,88	92,0	92,0	0,88	91,2	91,5	0,88	93,3	93,3	0,88	94,3	94,3
			0,89	92,1	92,1	0,89	90,8	91,0	0,89	92,6	92,7	0,89	93,9	93,9
			0,90	91,9	91,9	0,90	91,0	91,0	0,90	92,2	92,2	0,90	93,6	93,6
						0,91	90,7	90,7	0,91	91,9	91,9	0,91	93,3	93,3
						0,92	90,6	90,6	0,92	91,3	91,3	0,92	92,9	92,9
						0,93	90,4	90,4	0,93	90,8	90,8	0,93	92,3	92,3
									0,94	90,6	90,6	0,94	91,6	91,7
												0,95	91,1	91,1

Finally, a multi-classifier system for hand-written numeral recognition has been considered. The system combines by DS up to six classifiers trained on 12.000 digits extracted from courtesy amounts on bank-checks [12]: A_1-Region, A_2-Crossing, A_3-Contour Slope, A_4-Enhanced Loci, A_5-Histogram, A_6-Local Contour. Each classifiers outputs a single class label and no rejection is allowed at the level of individual classifiers. Moreover the recognition rate of each classifier is about 90% (differences are less than 0.4%). Table 3 reports the values of ρ for each subset (K=2,3,4,5,6) of classifiers. It is easy to verify from Tables 1 and 2 that the complementarity measured on real sets of classifiers, as the number of classifiers increases, is consistent with the results determined in eqs. (19), (20) (for instance, the particular case of adding new classifiers to the set $\{A_4, A_6\}$, for which ρ_A =0.85, is reported in bold type in Table 3 and in Tables 1,2). Finally, the effect of increasing the number of classifier on the performance of the multi-classifier system has been evaluated. It results that the differences between predicted and real recognition rate is less than 1.0%, while it is less than 1.3% in terms of reliability rate.

Table 3. Degree of Complementarity of sets of classifiers

K=2 A	ρ_A	K=3 A	ρ_A	K=4 A	ρ_A	K=5 A	ρ_A	K=6 A	ρ_A
A_4,A_6	**0,85**	A_1,A_2,A_6	0,87	A_2,A_3,A_4,A_6	**0,87**	A_1,A_2,A_3,A_4,A_6	**0,88**	A_1,A_2,A_3,A_4,A_5,A_6	**0,89**
A_1,A_6	0,86	A_2,A_3,A_6	0,87	A_1,A_2,A_4,A_6	**0,88**	A_1,A_2,A_3,A_5,A_6	0,89		
A_2,A_6	0,87	A_3,A_4,A_6	**0,87**	A_1,A_3,A_4,A_6	**0,88**	A_1,A_2,A_4,A_5,A_6	0,89		
A_3,A_6	0,87	A_2,A_4,A_6	**0,87**	A_2,A_4,A_5,A_6	**0,88**	A_1,A_3,A_4,A_5,A_6	0,89		
A_1,A_2	0,88	A_2,A_3,A_4	0,88	A_1,A_2,A_3,A_4	0,89	A_2,A_3,A_4,A_5,A_6	0,89		
A_2,A_3	0,88	A_4,A_5,A_6	**0,88**	A_1,A_2,A_3,A_6	0,89	A_1,A_2,A_3,A_4,A_5	0,90		
A_2,A_4	0,88	A_1,A_3,A_6	0,88	A_1,A_2,A_5,A_6	0,89				
A_5,A_6	0,88	A_1,A_4,A_6	**0,88**	A_1,A_3,A_5,A_6	0,89				
A_3,A_4	0,89	A_1,A_5,A_6	0,88	A_1,A_4,A_5,A_6	**0,89**				
A_1,A_3	0,90	A_1,A_2,A_3	0,89	A_2,A_3,A_5,A_6	0,89				
A_4,A_5	0,90	A_1,A_2,A_4	0,89	A_3,A_4,A_5,A_6	**0,89**				
A_1,A_5	0,91	A_2,A_5,A_6	0,89	A_1,A_2,A_4,A_5	0,90				
A_1,A_4	0,92	A_1,A_3,A_4	0,90	A_2,A_3,A_4,A_5	0,90				
A_2,A_5	0,92	A_2,A_4,A_5	0,90	A_1,A_2,A_3,A_5	0,91				
A_3,A_5	0,95	A_3,A_5,A_6	0,90	A_1,A_3,A_4,A_5	0,91				
		A_1,A_2,A_5	0,91						
		A_2,A_3,A_5	0,91						
		A_3,A_4,A_5	0,91						
		A_1,A_4,A_5	0,91						
		A_1,A_3,A_5	0,92						

6   Conclusion

This paper presents a complementarity-based analysis of sets of abstract-level classifiers and uses the results to investigate the performance of multi-classifier systems, as the number of classifiers increases. This work clarifies important aspects of the collective behaviour of multiple classifiers systems, based on the analysis of complementarity among them.

Acknowledgements. This paper has been supported by the Italian Ministry "Ministero dell'Istruzione, dell'Università e della Ricerca ", MIUR under law 488, Project "Rete Puglia" CINI-BA - D.M. n.600, 11-11-1999.

References

1.   Ley Xu, Adam Krzyzak, Ching Y-Suen, "Methods of Combining Multiple Classifiers and Their Applications to Handwriting Recognition", *IEEE Transaction on Systems, Man and Cybernetics*, Vol. 22, N. 3, 1992, pp. 418–435.

2. L. Lam, Y.-S. Huang, C.Y. Suen, "Combination of Multiple Classifier Decision for Optical Character Recognition", in *Handbook of Character Recognition and Document Image Analysis*, Eds. H. Bunke and P.S.P.Wang, World Scient. Publ., Singapore,1997,pp.79-101.
3. D. Wolpert, "Stacked Generalization", *Neural Networks*, Vol. 5, pp. 241–259, 1992.
4. T.K.Ho, "Random Decision Forests", *Proc.ICDAR '95*,Montreal,Canada,1995, pp.278-282.
5. L. Breiman, "Bagging Predictors", *Machine Learning*, Vol. 24, no. 2, pp. 123–140, 1996.
6. R.E.Schapire,"The strength of weak Learnability", *Mach. Learning*,Vol.5,pp.197–227, 1990.
7. G. Dimauro, S. Impedovo, G. Pirlo, A. Salzo, "Multiple Classifiers: a new methodology for the evaluation of the combination processes", *Progress in Handwriting Recognition*, A.C.Downton and S. Impedovo (eds.), World Scientific, Singapore, pp. 329–335, 1995.
8. J. Kittler, M. Hatef, R.P.W. Duin and J. Matias, "On combining classifiers", *IEEE T-PAMI*, vol. 20, no. 3, pp. 226–239, 1998.
9. V.Di Lecce, G.Dimauro, A.Guerriero, S.Impedovo, G.Pirlo, A.Salzo, "Classifier Combination: The role of a-priori knowledge", IWFHR VII, eds. L.R.B. Schomaker et al., 2000, Nijmegen: International Unipen Foundation Publishing, pp. 143–152.
10. E. Mandler and J. Schuermann, "Combining the Classification Results of independent classifiers based on the Dempster/Shafer theory of evidence", in *Pattern Recognition and Artificial Intelligence*, eds. E.S.Gelsema et al., North Holland,Amsterdam,1988,pp.381–393.
11. S. Impedovo and A. Salzo, "A new methodology for expert combination in multi-expert system designing". In Lecture Notes in Computer Science, (vol. 1857), J. Kittler and F.Roli Eds., MCS2000, Cagliari, Italy, pp.230–239.
12. G.Dimauro, S.Impedovo, G.Pirlo, A.Salzo, "Automatic Bankchecks Processing: A New Engineered System", *Int. Journal of Pattern Recognition and Artificial Intelligence*, Vol.11, N.4, World Scientific Publ.,Singapore, 1997, pp.1–38.

Discovering Rules for Dynamic Configuration of Multi-classifier Systems

G. Dimauro[1], S. Impedovo[1], M.G. Lucchese[2], G. Pirlo[1], and A. Salzo[2]

[1] Dipartimento di Informatica, Università degli Studi di Bari
Via Orabona 4, 70126 Bari-Italy
impedovo@di.uniba.it
[2] Consorzio Interuniversitario Nazionale per l'Informatica (CINI),
Via G.Petroni 15/F.1, 70124 Bari– Italy

Abstract. This paper addresses the problem of dynamic configuration of multi-classifier systems. For this purpose, the performance of combination methods for abstract-level classifiers is predicted, under different working conditions, and sets of rules are discovered and used for dynamic configuration of multi-classifier systems. The experimental tests have been carried out in the field of hand-written numeral recognition. The result demonstrates the validity of the proposed approach.

1   Introduction

The combination of classifiers is a diffuse strategy to design high-performance classification systems. In fact it is common experience that the complexity of the classification problem and pattern variability do not allow the development of classifiers as good as required for many practical applications [1].

Up to now, several methods have been proposed to combine different classifiers [2,3,4]. This notwithstanding, the problem of multi-classifier system design is still open [5]. For instance, in the field of hand-written numeral recognition, several decades of research activity have lead to develop thousands of different algorithms that can be combined in a multi-classifier system. A lot of different features have been considered (based on mathematical transforms, structural decomposition, geometrical and topological characteristics, etc.), and many different classification strategies (based on pattern-matching, structural-analysis, etc.) have been used. Similarly, many combination methods are also available. Hence, the prediction of the performance of a multi-classifier system is difficult, since it depends on both the classifiers and the method considered [6]. Moreover, in many cases, the working conditions can change dynamically. For instance, this is the case of neural network classifiers whose characteristics can change significantly, depending on the learning conditions.

D. Lopresti, J. Hu, and R. Kashi (Eds.): DAS 2002, LNCS 2423, pp. 157–166, 2002.
© Springer-Verlag Berlin Heidelberg 2002

Another case of change of the working conditions can be due to modification in the characteristics of the input data (different types of writing styles, or input data from different sources, which require different pre-processing algorithms, etc.). Therefore, the development of advanced strategies is required for the design of multi-classifier systems able to change dynamically their configurations, depending on the modifications of the working conditions.

This paper presents a first attempt to solve the problem. In particular, the most effective combination method of a multi-classifier system is dynamically selected, on the basis of the estimation of the degree of complementarity among the individual classifiers. For this purpose, a simulation procedure is used to determine systematically different working conditions in which the performance of various combination methods for abstract-level classifiers is evaluated a-priori. This information is used to determine sets of rules which are used, during the run-time, for the dynamic selection of the optimal combination method. Two combination methods for abstract-level classifiers are used for the experimental tests. The Dempster-Shafer (DS) method and the Behavioural Knowledge Space (BKS) method. In Section 2 the combination methods are briefly described. Section 3 describes the methodology for the evaluation of combination methods. Section 4 presents the new approach for dynamic selection of combination method. Section 5 reports the experimental results that have been obtained in the field of hand-written numeral recognition, using the data from the CEDAR database. The conclusion of this work is presented in Section 6.

2   Analysis of Combination Methods

In a multi-classifier parallel system, the input pattern x_t is fed to K individual classifiers in parallel. Each classifier A_i provides its response $A_i(x_t)$, i=1,2.,..K. The responses obtained by all the classifiers are then combined to obtain the final results $E(x_t)$ according to a suitable combination strategy $E(A_1(x_t), A_2(x_t)....A_K(x_t)) \rightarrow E(x_t)$[1].

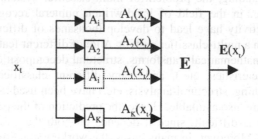

Fig. 1. A Multi-classifier Parallel System

The effectiveness of a multi-classifier system depends not only on the performance of the individual classifiers but also on the collective behavior of the entire set of classifier as well as on the capability of the combination method to integrate the results. On the basis of this consideration, a methodology for the evaluation of a combination process has been recently proposed [6]. It uses a Similarity Index which provides a measure of the degree of complementarity among the decisions of a set of classifiers. Precisely, let A_1 , A_2 be two classifiers and $A_1(x_t)$ and $A_2(x_t)$ respectively the top-candidates provided for the pattern x_t, for x_t belonging to a database $T=\{x_1,x_2,x_3,\ldots,x_N\}$ and let be

$$E\,(A_1\,(x_t),\,A_2\,(x_t)\,)=\begin{cases}1 & \text{if } A_1\,(x_t)=A_2(x_t)\\ 0 & \text{otherwise}\end{cases} \tag{1}$$

The Similarity Index between A_1 , A_2 is defined as:

$$\rho_{A_1,A_2}=\frac{1}{\text{Card}(T)}\sum_{x_t\in T}C(A_1(x_t),\,A_2(x_t)) \,. \tag{2}$$

Figure 2a shows the decisions of two classifiers A_1 and A_2 , for 10 input patterns belonging to the set of the ten digits. The recognition rate of both classifiers is 70%. Moreover it is easy to verify that A_1 and A_2 always provide the same response. Thus, we have $\rho=1$ (fig. 2a). Also the recognition rate of both classifiers in Figure 2b is 70%. However, in this case $\rho=0.4$.

Pattern n.	A_1	A_2		Pattern n.	A_1	A_2
$x_1\in$ '4'	4	4		$x_1\in$ '4'	2	4
$x_2\in$ '0'	8	8		$x_2\in$ '0'	8	0
$x_3\in$ '8'	8	8		$x_3\in$ '8'	8	8
$x_4\in$ '2'	2	2		$x_4\in$ '2'	2	2
$x_5\in$ '0'	0	0		$x_5\in$ '0'	0	8
$x_6\in$ '1'	7	7		$x_6\in$ '1'	1	7
$x_7\in$ '9'	9	9		$x_7\in$ '9'	9	9
$x_8\in$ '3'	3	3		$x_8\in$ '3'	8	3
$x_9\in$ '8'	0	0		$x_9\in$ '8'	8	0
$x_{10}\in$ '7'	7	7		$x_{10}\in$ '7'	7	7
(a) $\rho=1$				(b) $\rho=0.4$		

Fig. 2. Variability range for the Similarity Index

In general, for a set of K classifiers $A=\{A_i\,|\,i=1,2,\ldots,K\}$, the Similarity Index is [6]:

$$\rho_A=\frac{\displaystyle\sum_{\substack{i,\,j=1,\ldots K\\i<j}}\rho_{A_i,A_j}}{\dbinom{K}{2}} \tag{3}$$

The performance of a method E for classifier combination is then considered as a function $P_E(K,\underline{R},\ \rho)$, where K is the number of individual classifiers that are combined; $\underline{R}=(R_1,R_2,\ldots,R_K)$ is the vector of the recognition rates of the classifiers (for the sake of simplicity in this paper we suppose that all classifiers have the same recognition rate - i.e. $R=R_i$, i=1,2,…,K); ρ is the Similarity Index of the set of classifiers. Hence, in order to evaluate the performance of a classifier combination method in different working conditions, several sets of classifiers are simulated and grouped into different categories each one characterized by: the number of classifiers (K), the recognition rate (R), the similarity index (ρ). Hence, each value $P_E(K,R,\ \rho)$ is obtained as the average performance of the method E, when the sets of the category (K,R, ρ) are considered [6].

3   Dynamic Selection of the Combination Method

The analysis on the performance of combination methods, carried out by simulated data, can be useful to select dynamically the combination method for a multi-classifier system. For this purpose let us consider the advanced multi-classifier system in figure 3. It works as a traditional multi-classifier system (see fig. 1) even if it contains a control module for the run-time monitoring of the Similarity Index ρ of the set of classifiers. Depending on the value of ρ (computed by the analysis of the agreements among the outputs of the classifiers) and taking into consideration the performance of the combination methods $E_{BKS}(K,R,\rho)$ and $E_{DS}(K,R,\rho)$, the control module selects dynamically the most profitable method.

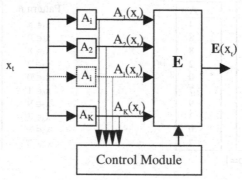

Fig. 3. Dynamic Selection of the Combination Method

4   The Combination Methods

In this paper two combination methods for abstract-level classifiers are considered: the Dempster-Shafer (DS) [5] and the Behaviour Knowledge Space (BKS) [4].

(a) Dempster-Shafer Method (DS)

The Dempster-Shafer method combines different classifiers using their recognition and substitution rates as a priori knowledge [4]. For a given input pattern x, all classifiers having the same output are collected into a group E_k, k=1,...,K', (where K' is the number of different outputs). $E_1, E_2,...,E_{k'}$ are then considered as new classifiers and for each of them the recognition and substitution rates are estimated. Successively, $E_1, E_2,...,E_{k'}$ are combined in order to calculate the belief of the correct output $Bel(A_j)$ and the belief of a misrecognition output $Bel(\neg A_j)$ [4]. The result of the combined classifier E is defined by the following decision rule:

$$E(x) = \begin{cases} j, & \text{if } Bel(A_j) = \max\{Bel(A_i)\,|\,Bel(\neg A_i)\} \leq \alpha, i = 0,1,...,9\} \\ \text{Reject,} & \text{otherwise} \end{cases} \quad (4)$$

where α is a suitable threshold value.

(b) Behaviour-Knowledge Space Method (BKS)

The Behaviour Knowledge Space method is based on two processing phases: the "learning" phase and the "operation" phase [3].

•   In the "learning" phase the set of learning pattern is fed to K classifiers. The result is used to fill a discrete K-dimensional space in which each dimension corresponds to the decision of a specific classifier. So, the K-tuple of decisions provided by the K classifiers defines a unit in the space generally called "Focal Unit". When a "Focal Unit" is addressed by the vector of recognition responses, the index corresponding to the class of the input pattern is incremented. This index counts the number of times in which a pattern belonging to that class generates the specific K-tuple of decisions.

•   In the "operation" phase, the K-tuple of decisions provided by the classifiers is used to address a "Focal Unit". From the analysis of the data in the "Focal Unit" the result of the combined classifier E is obtained by the following rule:

$$E(x) = \begin{cases} j_{FU(x)} & \text{if } T_{FU(x)} > 0 \text{ and } \dfrac{\text{Card}(j_{FU(x)})}{T_{FU(x)}} > a \\ \\ \text{Reject} & \text{otherwise} \end{cases} \quad (5)$$

where:

♦ $FU(x)$ is the Focal Unit selected by the input pattern x;

♦ $j_{FU(x)}$ is the best representative class;

♦ $T_{FU(x)}$ is the total number of samples in the Focal Unit;

♦   a is a suitable threshold value.

5   Experimental Results

The performance of each method has been evaluated by considering sets of 3 and 4 classifiers each one with an individual recognition rate of 60%, 70%, 80% and 90%.

For instance, figures 4 and 5 show the recognition rate of the BKS and DS, respectively, as a function of the Similarity Index of the set of individual classifiers [8].

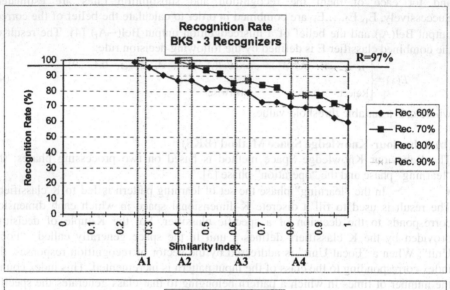

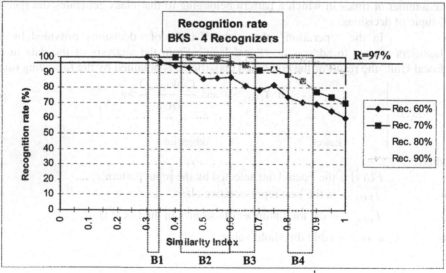

Fig. 4. Recognition Rate of the BKS method.

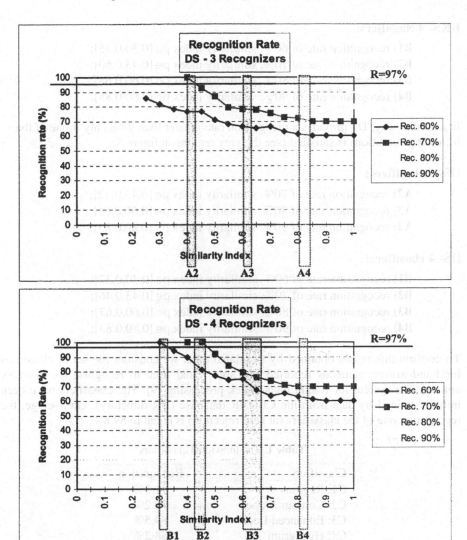

Fig. 5. Recognition Rate of the DS method.

These results first allow the determination of the expected performance of the combination methods. For example, if the target requirement is the recognition rate greater than 97%, we have that, when BKS is used, one of the following conditions must be satisfied (see the regions delimited in figure 4):

BKS- 3 classifiers:

        A1) recognition rate of 60%, similarity index ρ∈ [0.26,0.28];
        A2) recognition rate of 70%. similarity index ρ∈ [0.43,0.45];
        A3) recognition rate of 80%. similarity index ρ∈ [.60,0.65];
        A4) recognition rate of 90%. similarity index ρ∈ [0.80,0.86];

BKS- 4 classifiers:

> **B1)** recognition rate of 60%. similarity index $\rho \in [0.30, 0.35]$;
> **B2)** recognition rate of 70%. similarity index $\rho \in [0.43, 0.60]$;
> **B3)** recognition rate of 80%. similarity index $\rho \in [0.60, 0.68]$;
> **B4)** recognition rate of 90%. similarity index $\rho \in [0.80, 0.88]$;

In a similar way, DS provides a recognition rate greater than 97% only if one of the following conditions is satisfied (see the grey regions in figure 5):

DS- 3 classifiers:

> **A2)** recognition rate of 70%. similarity index $\rho \in [0.43, 0.42]$;
> **A3)** recognition rate of 80%. similarity index $\rho \in [0.60, 0.62]$;
> **A4)** recognition rate of 90%. similarity index $\rho \in [0.80, 0.83]$;

DS- 4 classifiers:

> **B1)** recognition rate of 60%. similarity index $\rho \in [0.30, 0.32]$;
> **B2)** recognition rate of 70%. similarity index $\rho \in [0.43, 0.46]$;
> **B3)** recognition rate of 80%. similarity index $\rho \in [0.60, 0.67]$;
> **B4)** recognition rate of 90%. similarity index $\rho \in [0.80, 0.83]$;

To confirm this result, obtained by simulated data, we consider the set of classifiers for hand-written numerals reported in Table 1 and used to recognise the courtesy amount in a system for Italian bank-check processing [9]. The classifiers have been initially trained by data from the CEDAR database (BR directory). On average, the recognition rate of the classifiers (at zero rejection) is equal to 89,8%.

Table 1. The individual classifiers

Classifiers	Recognition
C1: Regions	91.3%
C2: Contour Slope	90.2%
C3: Enhanced Loci	89.5%
C4: Histogram	88.2%

When combined by BKS and DS, the classification performance is reported in Table 2 (tested on the CEDAR database – BS directory). Table 2 confirms the previous results obtained by simulated data. For instance, if the recognition rate must be greater than 97%, we have: if BKS is used (Fig. 4), the set of classifiers 1,2 and 3 (condition A4) and also 5 (condition B4) must be selected; when the DS is used (Fig.5), the set of classifiers 1 and 2 (condition A3) must be selected.

This analysis also provides information useful for the dynamic selection of the combination method. In our tests, the classifiers of Table 1 have been trained with additional sets of hand-written numerals. Three learning levels are considered: at the

Table 2. Performance of the combination methods

Set	ρ	Classifiers	BKS		DS	
			Recognition	Reliability	Recognition	Reliability
1	0.82	C1-C2-C3	98.0% (A4)	99.2%	97.8% (A3)	98.7%
2	0.83	C1-C3-C4	97.1% (A4)	98.3%	97.2% (A3)	98.4%
3	0.85	C2-C3-C4	97.3% (A4)	98.4%	95.6%	97.1%
4	0.87	C1-C2-C4	95.6%	96.8%	95.1%	96.9%
5	0.87	C1-C2-C3-C4	97.5% (B4)	99.0%	96.9%	98.7%

first level (L1) a first set of 1000 patterns is provided to each individual classifier for learning, at the second level (L2) another set of 1000 patterns is added to the first set, at the third level (L3) an additional set of 1000 patterns is added to the first two sets. Table 3 reports the characteristics of the set of experts at the three learning levels and the performance of their combination by BKS and DS. The dynamic selection procedure, based on the a-priori information obtained by simulated data (Figs. 4,5), allows the selection of the best combination method (indicated with a grey background in Table 3), depending on the degree of correlation among the four classifiers. At the first level (ρ=0,84) the DS achieves the best result (R=95,3%). At the second and third learning levels (ρ=0,85 and ρ=0,87 respectively), BKS is the best (R=94,4% and R=93.3%, respectively).

Table 3. Dynamic Selection of Combination Method

Learning Level	ρ	Average Recognition Rate	Recognition Rate	
			DS	BKS
L1	0,84	89,5	95,3	94,5
L2	0,85	89,7	93,7	94,4
L3	0,87	89,8	92,5	93,3

6   Conclusion

This paper presents a new approach for the dynamic configuration of multi-classifier systems. Rules are discovered by the a-priori analysis of the combination methods and used, during the run time, to select dynamically the most effective combination method, depending on the degree of complementarity among the individual classifiers. The experimental results are promising and lead to continue researches in this direction.

Acknowledgements. This paper has been supported by the Italian Ministry "Ministero dell'Istruzione, dell'Università e della Ricerca ", MIUR under law 488, Project "Rete Puglia" CINI-BA - D.M. n.600, 11-11-1999.

References

1. Ley Xu, Adam Krzyzak, Ching Y-Suen, "Methods of Combining Multiple Classifiers and Their Applications to Handwriting Recognition" , IEEE Transaction on Systems, Man and Cybernetics- Vol. 22, N. 3, 1992, pp. 418–435.
2. T. Matsui, I. Yamashita, T. Wakahara, "Results of Second IPTP Character Recognition Competition and Studies on Multi-Expert Handwritten Numeral Recognition", Proc. of IWFHR-4, 1994, pp.338–346.
3. Huang, C.Y. Suen, "An Optimal Method of Combining Multiple Classifiers for Unconstrained Handwritten Numeral Recognition", Proc. of IWFHR-3, Buffalo, NY, 1993, pp. 11–20.
4. Y. Lu, F. Yamaoka, "Integration of Handwritten Digit Recognition results using Evidential Reasoning", Proc. of IWFHR-4, 1994, pp. 456–463.
5. J. Kittler, M. Hatef, R.P.W. Duin, J. Matias, "On combining classifiers", *IEEE Trans. on Pattern Analysis Machine Intelligence*, Vol.20, no.3, pp.226–239, 1998.
6. G.Dimauro, S.Impedovo, G.Pirlo, "Multiple Experts:A New Methodology for the Evaluation of the Combination Processes", IWFHR-5, Colchester,Uk,1996,pp.131–136.
7. V. Di Lecce, G.Dimauro, A. Guerriero, S.Impedovo, G.Pirlo, A. Salzo, "Classifier Combination: the role of a-priori knowledge", *Proc. of IWFHR-7*, Sept. 2000, Amsterdam, The Netherlands, pp. 143–152.
8. S. Impedovo and A. Salzo, "A new methodology for expert combination in multi-expert system designing". In Lecture Notes in Computer Science, (vol. 1857), J. Kittler and F.Roli Eds., MCS2000, Cagliari, Italy, pp.230–239.
9. G. Dimauro, S. Impedovo, G. Pirlo, A. Salzo, "Automatic Bankchecks Processing: A New Engineered System", *International Journal of Pattern Recognition and Artificial Intelligence*, Vol.11, N.4, World Scientific Publ., Singapore, 1997, pp.1–38.

Multiple Classifier Combination for Character Recognition: Revisiting the Majority Voting System and Its Variations

A.F.R. Rahman[1], H. Alam[1], and M.C. Fairhurst[2]

[1] Document Analysis and Recognition Team (DART)
BCL Technologies Inc.
Santa Clara, CA 95050, USA, Tel: +1 408 557 5279, Fax: +1 408 249 4046
fuad@bcltechnologies.com
[2] Department of Electronics
University of Kent, Kent, CT2 7NT, UK
Tel: +44 1227 823389, Fax: +44 1227 456084
M.C.Fairhurst@ukc.ac.uk

Abstract. In recent years, strategies based on combination of multiple classifiers have created great interest in the character recognition research community. A huge number of complex and sophisticated decision combination strategies have been explored by researchers. However, it has been realized recently that the comparatively simple Majority Voting System and its variations can achieve very robust and often comparable, if not better, performance than many of these complex systems. In this paper, a review of various Majority Voting Systems and their variations are discussed, and a comparative study of some of these methods is presented for a typical character recognition task.

Keywords: Multiple classifier combination, majority voting, character recognition.

1 Introduction

Combination of multiple classifiers is now accepted as a very important method in achieving robustness and accuracy in many recognition tasks, especially in character recognition problems (Ho et al.[1], Huang et al.[2], Rahman and Fairhur-st [3,4,5], Lam et al.[6], Kittler et al.[7] etc.). Despite huge advances, the recognition of handwritten characters is still an unsolved problem. With the advent of new computer technologies and the explosion in Internet-based on-line data manipulation applications, automatic conversion of written and spoken information into computer readable forms is becoming increasingly important. Against this backdrop, researchers are exploring various ways of combining decisions from multiple classifiers as a viable way of delivering very accurate and robust performance over a wide range of applications. This has resulted in the design of

D. Lopresti, J. Hu, and R. Kashi (Eds.): DAS 2002, LNCS 2423, pp. 167–178, 2002.

many decision combination algorithms. In recent years, attention has been refocused on using more simple techniques, e.g. Majority Voting Systems, precisely because of their simplicity and very high level of accuracy and robustness which can be achieved in appropriate circumstances (Lam and Suen[8,9]. In this paper, a review of various multiple classifier approaches exploiting the principle of majority voting is presented. In addition, a comparative study of some of these methods on a typical handwritten character recognition task is also reported.

2   Majority Voting and Its Variations

Majority Voting Systems have quite a number of variations in terms of application and methodology, although the underlying principle is the same. A basic issue to be addressed here concerns two potentially conflicting strategies for achieving decision combination, which may be broadly identified as:

- Should the decision agreed by the majority of the experts (in some fashion) be accepted without giving due credit to the competence of each expert? or,
- should the decision delivered by the most competent expert be accepted, without giving any importance to the majority consensus?

This ultimately amounts to a choice between selecting either the "consensus decision" or the "decision delivered by the most competent expert", yet both strategies could contribute overall to a successful decision, and ideally require careful integration within the decision making process. Moreover, by their very nature, these two considerations are often contradictory and hence most multiple expert decision combination algorithms emphasize either one or other of the strategies. This section presents some of the principal techniques based on Majority Voting System.

2.1   Simple Majority Voting

If there are n independent experts having the same probability of being correct, and each of these experts produces a unique decision regarding the identity of the unknown sample, then the sample is assigned to the class for which there is a consensus, i.e. when at least k of the experts agree, where k can be defined as:

$$k = \begin{cases} \frac{n}{2} + 1 & \text{if n is even,} \\ \frac{n+1}{2} & \text{if n is odd.} \end{cases} \tag{1}$$

Assuming each expert makes a decision on an individual basis, without being influenced by any other expert in the decision-making process, the probabilities of various different final decisions, when $x + y$ experts are trying to a reach a decision, are given by the different terms of the expansion of $(P_c + P_e)^{x+y}$, where, P_c is the probability of each expert making a correct decision, P_e is the probability of each expert making a wrong decision, with $P_c + P_e = 1$. Bernoulli[10] is credited with first realizing this group decision distribution. The probability that x experts would arrive at the correct decision is $\frac{(x+y)!}{x!y!}(P_c)^x(P_e)^y$ and the probability that they arrive at the wrong decision is $\frac{(x+y)!}{x!y!}(P_c)^y(P_e)^x$. So in general, the precondition of correctness (Condorcet[11]) of the combined decision for $x > y$ can be conveniently expressed as:

$$\kappa = \frac{(P_c)^x(P_e)^y}{(P_c)^x(P_e)^y + (P_c)^y(P_e)^x} \tag{2}$$

Reordering Eq 2 and assuming the fraction of the experts arriving at the correct decision to be fixed, (e.g. x and y to be constant), it is possible to show that,

$$\frac{\delta\kappa}{\delta P_c} = \kappa^2(x-y)\frac{(P_e)^{x-y-1}}{(P_c)^{x-y-1}}(P_c + P_e) \tag{3}$$

Since $(x - y - 1 \geq 0)$, $\frac{\delta\kappa}{\delta P_c}$ is always positive. Thus when x and y are given, as P_c increases κ increases continuously from zero to unity. This demonstrates that the success of the Majority Voting Scheme (like most decision combination schemes) directly depends on the reliability of the decision confidences delivered by the participating experts. It is also clear that as the confidences of the delivered decisions increase, the quality of the combined decision increases.

Recently, it has been demonstrated that although majority vote is by far the simplest of the variety of strategies used to combine multiple experts, properly applied it can also be very effective. Suen et al.[12] presented a method for decision combination incorporating different types of classifiers based on a straightforward voting scheme. A detailed study of the working of the majority voting scheme has been presented by Lam and Suen[8]. Ng and Singh[13], have discussed the applicability of majority voting techniques and have proposed a support function to be used in the combination of votes. Researchers have also used various types of classifiers in these majority voting schemes. Stajniak et al.[14] presented a system having three voting nonlinear classifiers: two of them based on the multilayer perceptron (MLP), and one using the moments method. Belaid and Anigbogu[15] reported a character recognition system using six classifiers built around first and second order hidden Markov models (HMM) as well as nearest neighbor considerations. Parker[16] has reported voting methods for multiple autonomous agents. Ji and Ma[17] have reported a learning method to combine weak classifiers, where weak classifiers are linear classifiers (perceptrons) which can do little better than making random guesses. The authors have demonstrated, both theoretically and experimentally, that if the weak classifiers are properly chosen, their combinations can achieve a good generalization performance with polynomial space- and time-complexity.

2.2   Weighted Majority Voting

A simple enhancement to the simple majority systems can be made if the decisions of each classifier are multiplied by a weight to reflect the individual confidences of these decisions. In this case, Weighting Factors, ω_k, expressing the comparative competence of the cooperating experts, are expressed as a list of fractions, with $1 \leq k \leq n$, $\sum_{k=1}^{n} \omega_k = 1$, n being the number of participating experts. The higher the competence, the higher is the value of ω. So if the decision by the kth expert to assign the unknown to the ith class is denoted by d_{ik} with $1 \leq i \leq m$, m being the number of classes, then the final combined decision d_i^{com} supporting assignment to the ith class takes the form of: $d_i^{com} = \sum_{k=1,2,\ldots,n} \omega_k * d_{ik}$. The final decision d^{com} is therefore: $d^{com} = \max_{i=1,2,\ldots,m} d_i^{com}$.

Lam and Suen[9] have studied the performance of combination methods including a Bayesian formulation and a weighted majority vote with weights obtained through a genetic algorithm. Alpaydin[18] has employed a weighted majority voting scheme by adopting a Bayesian framework where 'weights' in voting may be interpreted as plausibilities of the participating classifiers. Additional discussion of the weighted majority voting technique may be found in Kittler et al.[19] and Lam et al.[6].

2.3   Class-Wise Weighted Majority Voting Scheme

The Class Confidence Index, $\beta_{i,j}$, $1 \leq i \leq n$, $1 \leq j \leq m$, where n is the number of decisions and m is the number of classes under consideration, denotes the ranking of the different decisions on a class by class basis. The higher the class recognition rate, the higher the ranking. These class-wise confidences can then be conveniently converted to suitable weight values ω_k^i, expressing the comparative competence of the decisions on a class-wise basis, are expressed as a list of fractions, with, $1 \leq k \leq n$, $\sum_{k=1}^{n} \omega_k^i = 1$, n again being the number of the decisions being combined. So if the kth decision to assign the unknown pattern to the ith class is denoted by d_{ik} with $1 \leq i \leq m$, m being the number of classes, then the final combined decision d_i^{com} supporting assignment to the ith class takes the form of: $d_i^{com} = \sum_{k=1,2,\ldots,n} \omega_k^i * d_{ik}$. The final decision d^{com} is therefore: $d^{com} = \max_{i=1,2,\ldots,m} d_i^{com}$.

2.4   Restricted Majority Voting

Sometimes it is important to shift the emphasis of decision combination in selecting the best appropriate classifier from an array of classifiers. The Overall Confidence values, γ_k, expressing the comparative competence of the classifiers, are expressed as a ranking list, with $1 \leq k \leq n$, and n being the number of experts. The higher the recognition rate, the higher the ranking. It is straightforward to convert this ranking to a set of weighting factors. These weighting factors, ω_k, expressing the comparative competence of the cooperating classifiers, are expressed as list of fractions, with $1 \leq k \leq n$, $\sum_{k=1}^{n} \omega_k = 1$, n again being the number of classifiers. The best representative expert for a particular problem domain can then be noted by finding the maximum weighting factor ω_m, so that, $\omega_m = max(\omega_k)$. The final decision by this method is then expressed by, $d_{Best} = d_m$.

Gang *et al.*[20] have described such a modularized neuroclassifier. This classifier combines four modularized classifiers using MLP modules. The same idea of identifying the best classifier in a voting scheme can be further extended in a more generalized framework (Rahman and Fairhurst[21]). Defining γ_k, $1 \leq k \leq n$, as Overall Confidence Indices, representing the ranking of the experts ($\gamma_k = 1, 2, ..., n$), β_{ij}, ($1 \leq i \leq n, 1 \leq j \leq m$, where m is the number of classes under consideration), as Class Confidence Indices, denoting the ranking of the different experts ($\beta_{ij} = 1, 2, ..., n$) on a class by class basis, and finally α_{ijk}, as Sample Confidence Indices, denoting the confidence value assigned by the ith expert to the kth sample of the jth class in the test set, this generalized decision combination framework selects the best final combined decision by the following logical structure: The decision associated with the highest sample confidence index is accepted as the final decision, provided the sample confidence index is greater than or equal to a threshold value from the nearest confidence value assigned by a competing expert, so that, $|\alpha_{uwt} - \alpha_{vwt}| \geq \psi_c$, where u and v denote the top two competing experts, w is the class under consideration, t is the sample in question and ψ_c is the threshold. In circumstances where this criteria is not met, a decision combination is attempted based on $|\beta_{sw} - \beta_{tw}| \geq \theta_c$, where s and t denote the top two competing experts, w is the class under consideration by that particular expert and $\theta_c > 0$. The motivation behind using this criterion is to give due preference to the strengths of particular experts in recognizing a particular class of characters. In the unlikely event of a failure to draw a final decision at this stage, the criterion $|\gamma_s - \gamma_w| \geq \phi_c$ can be applied, where s and w are the top two competing experts and $\phi_c > 0$. If no decision can be achieved at this stage, this denotes a classifier redundancy and an arbitrary decision of accepting the decision of the first expert in the array is taken. The characters which are rejected by one or more of the experts are channelled to the re-evaluating expert. If a sample is rejected, then the expert rejecting the character is excluded from the decision making process. Hence, if a sample is rejected by u experts out of a total of n experts, then the decision combination problem is reduced to a simpler problem of combining n-u decisions according to the decision-making algorithm of the decision fusion expert. In the extreme case, where the test sample is rejected by all the experts, no decision can be taken and the sample is finally rejected (Rahman and Fairhurst[22]).

2.5   Class-Wise Best Decision Selection

The Class Confidence Index, $\beta_{i,j}$, $1 \leq i \leq n$, $1 \leq j \leq m$, where n is the number of decisions and m is the number of classes under consideration, denotes the ranking of the different decisions $\beta_{i,j} = 1, 2, ..., n$ on a class by class basis. The higher the class recognition rate, the higher the ranking. These class-wise confidences can then be conveniently converted to suitable weight values ω_k^i, expressing the comparative competence of the decisions being combined on a class-wise basis, are expressed as a list of fractions, with $1 \leq k \leq n$, $\sum_{k=1}^{n} \omega_k^i = 1$, n, n, again being the number of decisions. In this case, the best decision is selected based on the class confidence indices rather than on the overall confidence indices.

Therefore, the best representative decision for a particular problem domain for a particular class can then be noted by finding the maximum weighting factor ω_m^i, so that $\omega_m^i = \max\omega_k^i$. The final decision is then expressed by $d_{Best} = d_m^i$.

2.6   Enhanced Majority Voting

Simple and weighted majority voting are very robust provided adequate number of classifiers are available to reach the correct consensus. There are various ways in which qualitative enhancement can be added to this framework. Rovatti et al.[23] have discussed a form of cooperation between the k-nearest neighbors (NN) approach to classification and their neural like property of adaptation. A tunable, high level k-nearest neighbor decision rule is defined that comprehends most previous generalizations of the common majority rule. ENCORE (Enhanced Consensus in Recognition) has been proposed by Fairhurst and Rahman[24]. This approach implements a decision consensus approach, but the quality of the consensus is evaluated in terms of the past track record of the consenting experts before it is accepted. The logical structure of this approach can be summarized as follows:

- Find the class $\omega(X)$ having the consensus support of the experts for any arbitrary pattern X.
- Find the corresponding sample confidence indices α_{ijk}, which denote the confidence of the ith expert in identifying the kth sample coming from the jth class.
- Apply the following rule:
  - The decision associated with the highest sample confidence value α is accepted as the final decision, provided the highest sample confidence value is not separated from the next highest confidence value assigned by a cooperating expert by an amount greater than (or equal to) a threshold, so that,

$$\alpha_{uwt} \sim \alpha_{vwt} \leq \acute{\psi}_c \qquad (4)$$

  where u and v are the top two cooperating experts, w is the class under consideration, t is the sample in question and $\acute{\psi}_c$ is the threshold.
  - In circumstances where the criteria of Eqn.(4) are not met, it is deemed that the top two cooperating experts show an unacceptable confidence gap and alternative solutions should be sought. In this case, the second group of consensus decisions are considered and the same process of applying Eqn.(4) to the corresponding sample confidence values is attempted. This process is repeated until all the consensus groups are exhausted.

  When this process has been exhausted, the consensus decision approach is abandoned and the decision combination approach changes. Now the top two decisions having the maximum sample confidence index are examined in terms of Eqn.(4). In circumstances where the criteria of Eqn.(4) are not met decision combination is attempted based on the criteria of Eqn.(5) so that,

$$\beta_{sw} \sim \beta_{tw} \leq \acute{\theta}_c \qquad (5)$$

where β is the class confidence index, s and t are the top two competing experts, w is the class under consideration by that particular expert and $\acute{\theta}_c$ is the threshold value. The motivation behind using this criterion is to give due preference to the strengths of particular experts in recognizing a particular class of patterns.

- In the event of a failure to reach a final decision at this stage, the criterion of Eqn.(6) can be applied.

$$\gamma_s \sim \gamma_w \leq \acute{\phi}_c \tag{6}$$

where γ is the overall confidence index, s and w are the top two competing experts and $\acute{\phi}_c$ is the corresponding threshold. If no decision can be arrived at even at this stage, either an arbitrary decision of accepting the decision of the first expert in the array is taken, or the pattern is rejected.

2.7   Ranked Majority Voting

It is entirely possible to include additional information derived from participating classifiers in reaching the final consensus. Instead of only using the final class labels to which a sample is estimated to belong, it is also possible to produce a ranked list of suggested decisions covering multiple classes. These ranked lists can then be manipulated to reach a final consensus. A very interesting approach to majority voting has been put forward by Ho et al.[1]. In this case, decisions by the classifiers have been represented as rankings of classes so that they are comparable across different types of classifiers and different instances of a problem. The rankings are combined by methods that either reduce or re-rank a given set of classes. An intersection method and a union method have been proposed for class set reduction. Three methods based on the highest rank, the Borda count, and logistic regression are proposed for class set re-ranking. Elsewhere, Ho et al.[25] emphasis the re-ranking of the ranked outputs delivered by the cooperating classifiers. In [26], Ho et al. described a concise and focused version of the ideas presented in [1], again emphasizing the substantial improvements achievable from these multiple expert systems. Duong[27] has discussed the problem of combination of forecasts employing a ranking and subset selection approach. The ranking and subset selection approach is suggested as a statistical procedure for ranking alternative forecasts. This simple method is shown to compare favorably with those based on other optimality criteria when applied to some real data.

2.8   Committee Methods

Mazurov et al.[28] have discussed theorems concerning the existence of p-commit-tee for an arbitrary finite system of sets and for the finite systems of half-spaces. The existence theorem for a discriminating committee consisting of affine functions which were used in the solution of the problem of pattern recognition has been presented in detail. Yu et al.[29] report a multiple expert decision combination method based on stacked generalization and committee methods. Kimura and Shridhar[30] have combined two algorithms for unconstrained handwritten numeral recognition. The first of their algorithms employs a modified quadratic discriminant function utilizing direction sensitive spatial features of the numeral image. The other algorithm utilisers features derived from the profile of the character in a structural configuration to recognized the numerals.

2.9   Regression

Ho et al.[31] described in detail the regression approach to the combination of decisions by multiple character recognition algorithms. Ho[32] reported an investigation on different strategies to coordinate and combine different alternative classifiers that can adapt to certain conditions in the input which concern both accuracy and speed. The design of such strategies is based on a detailed analysis of the classifiers' performances on test data using a parameterized defect model.

Table 1. Performance of the individual classifiers

Expert	Accepted	Recognized	Error	Rejected
FWS	97.35	78.76	18.59	2.65
MPC	97.62	85.78	11.84	2.38
BWS	95.50	72.31	23.19	4.50
MLP	95.13	82.31	12.82	4.87

Table 2. Performance of various majority voting systems

Combination Method	Accepted	Recognized	Error	Rejected
Simple Majority Voting	96.59	90.59	6.00	3.41
Weighted Majority Voting	96.85	90.64	6.21	3.15
Class-wise Weighted Majority Voting	96.86	90.70	6.16	3.14
Restricted Majority Voting (Top Choice)	95.68	88.97	6.71	4.32
Class-wise Best Decision Selection	96.76	89.64	6.79	3.24
Restricted Majority Voting (Generalized)	96.54	90.63	5.91	3.46
Enhanced Majority Voting (ENCORE)	97.14	90.91	6.23	2.86
Ranked Majority Voting (Borda Count)	96.99	90.77	6.22	3.01
Committee Methods	95.98	89.63	6.35	4.02
Regression Methods	97.68	90.85	6.83	2.32

3   A Sample Problem Domain

In order to compare some of these widely differing multiple classifier decision combination methods implementing forms of majority consensus, a sample problem domain of handwritten character recognition has been chosen. The source of the handwritten characters (numerals) was the database compiled by the

U.S. National Institute of Standards and Technology (NIST) [33], which contains samples of numerals 0 to 9. Four experts were chosen to be combined in the framework of the various chosen methods, which included a Binary Weighted Scheme (BWS), which employs a technique based on n-tuple sampling or memory network processing (Rahman and Fairhurst[34]), a Frequency Weighted Scheme (FWS), which calculates the relative frequencies of the sampled features indicating the probability distribution of the group of points or n-tuples (Rahman and Fairhurst[5]), a Multi-layer Perceptron Network (MLP), the familiar multilayer perceptron neural network structure, employing the standard error backpropagation algorithm (Rahman and Fairhurst[35]) and a Moment-based Pattern Classifiers (MPC), which is a maximum likelihood classifier, employing the nth order mathematical moments derived from the binarized patterns (Rahman and Fairhurst[36]).

4 Performance

Before reporting the performance of the proposed structure, it is important to assess the performance of the chosen experts individually on the selected problem. Table 1 presents the optimum performance achieved on the chosen database. Table 2 presents the results of decision combination using various decision combination schemes based on majority voting. It is clearly seen that some of these methods offer very high levels of top choice recognition (e.g. ENCORE, Regression Methods), and some offer very low levels of error rates (Restricted Majority Voting: Generalized Framework). Depending on what is required from the decision combination system, different methods can be selected in different problem domains.

From the short discussion presented so far, it is clear that the performances of these various approaches are directly related to their design emphasis. In some of these approaches, emphasis is given to assess how a consensus can be reached given the often conflicting opinions of these classifiers. Simple and Weighted Majority Methods are examples of this approach. On the other hand, other methods try to assess the 'appropriateness' or the 'suitability' of a classifier over other classifiers and favor its opinion over others. So it is seen that there are two ways of looking at this problem. One is to assume that the classifiers are cooperating with each other in reaching a final decision, the other is to assume that the classifiers are competing with each other to win an argument. Either of these approaches can be the 'most appropriate' solution to a particular problem, given that the best solution depends on the localized nature of the problem, and in this respect there is no global winner. However, a combination of these two approaches has been found to offer some advantages (ENCORE, for example, can be treated as a combination of Simple Majority and Restricted Majority techniques). Combination of decision combination methods is not a new concept (Paik et al.[37], Anzai et al.[38] etc.), but the use of this concept is relatively unexplored and preliminary results are very encouraging (Rahman and Fairhurst[24]).

A final note about the applicability of these majority voting techniques on document analysis applications. In addition to the obvious applications to character level recognition used an example in this paper, these techniques have been used in word level recognition, cursive recognition, signature recognition, PDA applications, automatic segmentation, automatic check processing, layout analysis, mail sorting, archiving, indexing and many more similar applications.

5   Conclusion

The main objective of the paper is to revisit the issue of Majority Voting in classifier design, to illustrate huge number of variations that are possible on the theme of majority voting, and to demonstrate their applicability in typical task domains. A discussion of the various multiple expert decision combination strategies implementing some form of majority voting in the context of character recognition has been presented. The review includes short descriptions of various methods and how they are related in terms of the underlying design philosophy. A comparative study of these methods on a typical handwritten character recognition problem is also included to show how, even with this apparently narrowly-defined framework, different strategic strands can be productively identified.

Acknowledgements. The authors gratefully acknowledge the support of the Advanced Technology Program (ATP) of National Institute of Standards and Technology (NIST, USA) and UK Engineering and Physical Sciences Research Council.

References

1. T. K. Ho, J. J. Hull, and S. N. Srihari. Decision combination in multiple classifier systems. *IEEE Trans. Pattern Analysis and Machine Intelligence*, 16(1):66–75, January 1994.
2. Y. S. Huang, K. Liu, and C. Y. Suen. The combination of multiple classifiers by a neural-network approach. *Int. Jour. of Pattern Recognition and Artificial Intelligence*, 9(3):579–597, 1995.
3. A. F. R. Rahman and M. C. Fairhurst. Serial combination of multiple experts: A unified evaluation. *Pattern Analysis and Applications*, 2:292–311, 1999.
4. A. F. R. Rahman and M. C. Fairhurst. Enhancing multiple expert decision combination strategies through exploitation of a priori information sources. *IEE Proc. on Vision, Image and Signal Processing*, 146(1):1–10, 1999.
5. A. F. R. Rahman and M. C. Fairhurst. Machine-printed character recognition revisited: Re-application of recent advances in handwritten character recognition research. *Special Issue on Document Image Processing and Multimedia Environments, Image & Vision Computing*, 16(12-13):819–842, 1998.
6. L. Lam, Y. S. Huang, and C. Y. Suen. *Combination of multiple classifier decisions for optical character recognition in Handbook of Character Recognition and Document Image Analysis*, pages 79–101. World Scientific Publishing Company, 1997. H. Bunke and P. S. P. Wang(Eds.).

7. J. Kittler, M. Hatef, R.P.W. Duin, and J. Matas. On combining classifiers. *IEEE Transactions on Pattern Analysis and Machine Intelligence*, 20(3):226–239, 1998.
8. L. Lam and C. Y. Suen. Application of majority voting to pattern recognition: An analysis of its behavior and performance. *IEEE Trans. Pattern Analysis and Machine Intelligence*, 27(5):553–568, 1997.
9. L. Lam and C. Y. Suen. A theoretical-analysis of the application of majority voting to pattern-recognition. In *Proc. 12th IAPR Int. Conf. on Pattern Recognition, Conf. B: Pattern Recognition and Neural Networks*, volume 2, pages 418–420, Jerusalem, Israel, 1994.
10. I. Todhunter. *A History of the Mathematical Theory of Probability from the Time of Pascal to that of Laplace.* Macmillan, Cambridge, UK, 1865.
11. N. C. de Condorcet. *Essai sur l'Application de l'Analyze à la Probabilité des Décisions Rendues à la Pluralité des Voix.* Imprimérie Royale, Paris, France, 1785.
12. C. Y. Suen, C. Nadal, T. A. Mai, R. Legault, and L. Lam. Recognition of totally unconstrained handwritten numerals based on the concept of multiple experts. In *Proc. IWFHR*, pages 131–143, Montréal, Canada, 1990.
13. G. S. Ng and H. Singh. Democracy in pattern classifications: Combinations of votes from various pattern classifiers. *Artificial Intelligence in Engineering*, 12(3):189–204, 1998.
14. A. Stajniak, J. Szostakowski, and S. Skoneczny. Mixed neural-traditional classifier for character recognition. In *Proc. Int. Conf. on Imaging Sciences and Display Technologies: International Society for Optical Engineering (SPIE)*, volume 2949, pages 102–110, Berlin, Germany, 1997.
15. A. Belaid and J. C. Anigbogu. Use of many classifiers for multifont text recognition. *Traitement du Signal*, 11(1):57–75, 1994.
16. J. R. Parker. Voting methods for multiple autonomous agents. In *Proc. 3rd Australian and New Zealand Conf. on Intelligent Information Systems*, pages 128–133, Perth, WA, Australia, 1995.
17. C. Ji and S. Ma. Combination of weak classfiers. *IEEE Trans. on Neural Networks*, 8(1):32–42, 1997.
18. E. Alpaydin. Improved classification accuracy by training multiple models and taking a vote. In *Sixth Italian Workshop. Neural Nets Wirn Vietri-93*, pages 180–185, 1994.
19. J. Kittler, A. Hojjatoleslami, and T. Windeatt. Weighting factors in multiple expert fusion. In *Proc. British Machine Vision Conference*, pages 41–50, 1997.
20. S. R. Gang, T. K. Woo, and I. C. Sung. Recognition of printed and handwritten numerals using multiple features and modularized neural networks. *Journal of the Korean Institute of Telematics*, 32B(10):101–1111, 1995.
21. A. F. R. Rahman and M. C. Fairhurst. Exploiting second order information to design a novel multiple expert decision combination platform for pattern classification. *Electronics Letters*, 33(6):476–477, 1997.
22. A. F. R. Rahman and M. C. Fairhurst. A New Multiple Expert Framework for Decision Fusion. In *Proc. 9th Int. Graphonomics Society Conference (IGS'99)*, pages 161–166, Singapore, 1999.
23. R. Rovatti, R. Ragazzoni, Z. M. Kovacs, and R. Guerrieri. Voting rules for k-nearest neighbors classifiers. *Neural Computation*, 7(3):594–605, 1995.
24. M. C. Fairhurst and A. F. R. Rahman. Enhancing Consensus in Multiple Expert Decision Fusion. *IEE Proc. on Vision, Image and Signal Processing*, 147(1):39–46, 2000.

25. T. K. Ho, J. J. Hull, and S. N. Srihari. *Combination of Decisions by Multiple Classifiers in Structured Document Image Analysis*, pages 188–202. S-V, 1992. H. S. Baird, H. Bunke and K. Yamamoto(Eds.).

26. T. K. Ho, J. J. Hull, and S. N. Srihari. On multiple classifier systems for pattern recognition. In *Proc. 11th ICPR*, pages 84–87, The Hague, Netherlands, 1992.

27. Q. P. Duong. The combination of forecasts: A ranking and subset selection approach. *Mathematical and Computer Modelling*, 12(9):1131–1143, 1989.

28. V. D. Mazurov, A. I. Krivonogov, and V. L. Kazantsev. Solving of optimisation and identification problems by the committee methods. *Pattern Recognition*, 20(4):371–378, 1987.

29. Y. H. Hu, J. M. Park, and T. Knoblock. Committee pattern classifiers. In *Proc. IEEE Int. Conf. on Acoustics, Speech, and Signal Processing*, pages 3389–3392, Munich, Germany, 1997.

30. F. Kimura and M. Shridhar. Handwritten numeral recognition based on multiple algorithms. *Pattern Recognition*, 24(10):969–983, 1991.

31. T. K. Ho, J. J. Hull, and S. N. Srihari. A regression approach to combination of decisions by multiple character recognition algorithms. In *Machine Vision Applications in Character Recognition and Industrial Inspection, Proc. SPIE 1661*, pages 137–145, 1992.

32. T. K. Ho. Adaptive coordination of multiple classifiers. In *Proc. of Int. Workshop on Document Analysis Systems*, pages 338–351, Malvern, Pennsylvalia, USA, 1996.

33. NIST Special Databases 1-3, 6-8, 19, 20, National Institute of Standards and Technology, Gaithersburg, MD 20899, USA.

34. A. F. R. Rahman and M. C. Fairhurst. An evaluation of multi-expert configurations for recognition of handwritten numerals. *Pattern Recognition*, 31(9):1255–1273, 1998.

35. A. F. R. Rahman and M. C. Fairhurst. Towards the design of a generic multiple expert image classification system capable of automatic self-configuration. In *Proc. Int. Conf. on Quality Control by Artificial Vision (QCAV'99)*, pages 259–264, Québec, Canada, 1999.

36. M. C. Fairhurst and A. F. R. Rahman. A generalised approach to the recognition of structurally similar handwritten characters. *IEE Proc. on Vision, Image and Signal Processing*, 144(1):15–22, 1997.

37. J. Paik, S. Jung, and Y. Lee. Multiple combined recognition system for automatic processing of credit card slip applications. In *Proceedings of the Second International Conference on Document Analysis and Recognition (Cat. No.93TH0578-5)*, pages 520–523, 1993.

38. Y. Anzai, H. Mori, M. Ito, and Y. Hayashi. A serial-parallel integrated information-processing model for complex human problem solving. In *Cognitive Engineering in the Design of Human-Computer Interaction and Expert Systems. Proceedings of the Second International Conference on Human-Computer Interaction. Vol.II*, pages 175–182, 1987.

Correcting for Variable Skew

A. Lawrence Spitz

Document Recognition Technologies, Inc.
616 Ramona Street, Suite 20
Palo Alto, California 94301, USA
`spitz@docrec.com`

Abstract. The proliferation of inexpensive sheet-feed scanners, particularly in fax machines, has led to a need to correct for the uneven paper feed rates during digitization if the images produced by these scanners are to be further analyzed. We develop a technique for detecting and compensating for this type of image distortion.

1 Introduction

Many techniques have been developed for detecting the dominant skew angle of printed documents [2]. However sometimes more than one skew angle is represented in the document image. Baird [3] points out that the paste-up of text columns may result in slightly (but significantly) different skew angles and notes the importance of segmenting the columns first in order that individual skew corrections can be applied to the individual columns. Spitz [6] and Antonacopoulos [1] have described techniques for detecting the presence of multiple discrete skew angles in a single document image. Spitz showed the angular distribution of the "power" (as defined by Baird) for both instances of multiple discrete skews. This is reproduced in Fig. 1.

This paper presents a solution to a different problem, that of documents which contain a continuously variable skew as a function of vertical distance along the page.

In Section 2, we describe the type and range of skew angle variability seen. Section 3 describes the segmentation of the image and determination of the dominant skew angle for the individual segments. Section 4 describes the correction of the skew for each of these segments. We discuss the re-assembly of the image in Section 5.

Throughout Sections 2 though 5 we will describe the algorithms using a much simplified page image specifically synthesized for this study because doing so makes the processes much easier to understand. In Section 6 we will provide a real-world example.

2 Image Characteristics

Inexpensive sheet-feed scanners often feed paper unevenly, that is as the page passes the CCD array from top to bottom, the left and right edges do not move at exactly the same rates. The effect of this is to produce a distorted image with continuously variable skew from top to bottom.

In order to simplify development and illustration of the techniques described here, we synthesized an number of images demonstrating variable skew, one of which is shown in Fig. 2 This image has been printed and scanned to introduce noise to the basic structure. Note that though this simulation is useful for didactic purposes it is an insufficiently accurate representation of "real-world" distortion because continuous variation of skew angle is not apparent due to the small number of nominally horizon-

D. Lopresti, J. Hu, and R. Kashi (Eds.): DAS 2002, LNCS 2423, pp. 179–187, 2002.

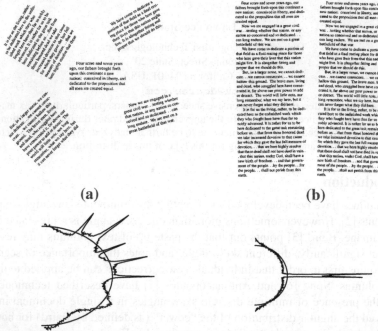

Fig. 1. Two document images and their respective angular power distribution. (a) shows five text blocks and five distinct peaks in the distribution. (b) illustrates the ability to detect small differences in skew. Note the double peak in the power distribution.

tal lines. Note that the lines to be made horizontal are dashed in order to simulate individual characters in the way that they generate pass codes and that the "diagonal" line will be able to demonstrate, by its continuity or lack of continuity, the degree to which distortion of the input image (in the digital domain) introduces artifacts.

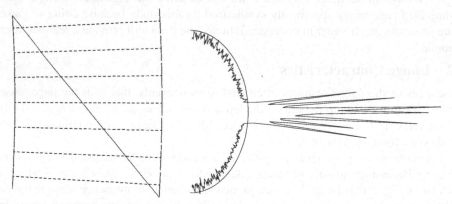

Fig. 2. Synthesized image with continuously variable

Note that most images that demonstrate variable skew do not exhibit the monotonic, and nearly linear, skew variation shown in Fig. 4 for the test image.

3   Skew Detection

Skew angle detection is fundamentally a two stage process. In the first stage one determines the locations of the features on which alignment quality will be assessed. In the second, various tests are applied to determine if a proposed alignment is a good one relative to a prior sample alignment or other standard. Depending on the choice of alignment features, the computational expense of calculating tentative alignments may be variously divided between the calculation of the alignment measure itself or in the testing of the quality of the particular alignment.

We adopt the method of testing rotational alignment developed and described by Baird [3], but we use a different set of fiducial points.

3.1   Fiducial Points

As we have described in earlier papers, we detect skew on the basis of the positions of white CCITT pass codes [6][7]. Pass codes are described by Hunter and Robinson [4] and are a part of the Group IV facsimile coding scheme. CCITT pass codes themselves do not carry color information; however it is easy to add. If the process of decompression is adding white pixels at the time a pass code is encountered in the compressed data stream, that pass code is labeled white. Hence the presence of a white pass code indicates the presence of the bottom of a black structure.

Text documents contain images of characters. Each character has at least one bottom point. A, H, K, M, N, Q, W, X, h, k, m, n and w have more than one bottom point. The bottom of most characters (except g, j, p, q, y) lie on a baseline. Thus character bottoms are a reasonable structure on which to determine an alignment.

Of course facsimile images can contain graphical elements other than character images such as rulings and logotypes. These structures too generate pass codes.

The white pass positions for the test document shown in Fig. 1 are shown in Fig. 3.

The calculation of alignment is made efficient by processing this relatively small number of fiducial points as representative of the entire image.

3.2   Alignment

Alignment of fiducial points is determined by overlaying the spatial distribution of fiducial points with parallel bins. This system of bins is rotated through the desired range of angles and the populations of each of the bins is calculated at each angle. For each angle the "power" of the alignment is calculated by computing the sum of squares of the bin populations. This power measurement is therefor maximized when the variance of the bin population is greatest since the total number of fiducial points is constant. The power is greatest when the largest proportion of fiducial points falls within the smallest number of bins.

3.3   Multiple Skew Angles

We have now detected the dominant skew angle, that is the angle at which a particular bin has the maximum population of passes. We then iteratively remove the passes

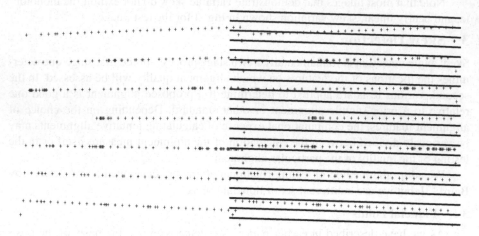

Fig. 3. White pass positions in the test documents and a set of rotationally aligned bins overlaying the fiducial points. Note that the actual bins would be much small than those.

found in that bin, leaving behind passes aligned at the same angle but at different positions on the page, and re-compute the dominant skew angle.

In the example shown in Fig. 2, we find seven dominant skew angles, one for each nominally horizontal line. Along with the skew angle we calculate the vertical position along the vertical centerline of the page at which this skew angle exists. If there is significant skew angle difference between adjacent points on the vertical centerline we interpolate to reduce this angular distance between samples. Currently we re-sample to reduce the inter-sample skew angle difference to less than 0.5 degrees.

We can demonstrate the distribution of skew with a plot of skew angle vs. vertical distance down the page measured on the vertical centerline. Such a plot is shown in Fig. 4. Note the filled squares denoting the original 7 detected skew angles, the skew profile, shown by the solid line, determined by fitting a curve to the detected skew angles. This skew profile is subsequently sampled at regular intervals in order to provide the basis for rotating, slicing and re-assembling the image.

For each skew angle thus determined we rotate the source image by the appropriate angle to correct for the skew. For the test image the original 7 skew angles are increased to 18. Ten of these 18 are shown in Fig. 5

Rotation is accomplished using the three-shear method due to Paeth [5]. Each shear is implemented by looping over the source pixels and distributing fractions to each of the destination pixels. This has an "anti-aliasing" effect.

4   Slicing the Image

For reasons of efficiency we wish to process the image in as few slices as possible consistent with maintaining image quality sufficient for further recognition processes such as OCR.

To this end we determine the minimum number of slices of constant height necessary to ensure that the maximum difference of skew angle from slice center to slice

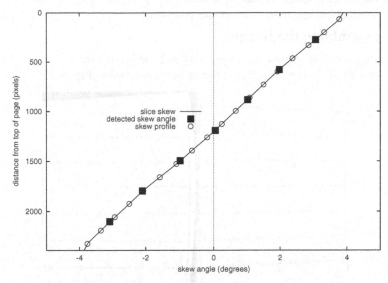

Fig. 4. Plot of detected skew angles, the skew profile that they define and the samples along the profile used for rotating the slices of the image.

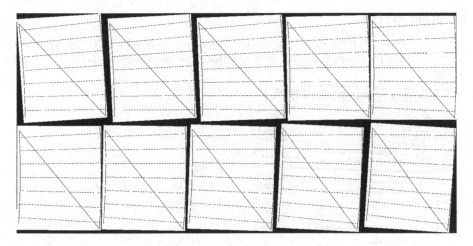

Fig. 5. Ten of the 18 rotated images resulting from finding the dominant skew angle in a test

center is less that a pre-determined threshold, in this instance 0.5 degrees. We constrain this number to never be less than the number of discrete skew angles detected earlier or greater than 100. Therefore at the maximum number of slices, necessary for the most severely warped images, a 200 spi facsimile of a letter or A4 page would result in slices that are approximately 22 pixels in height.

Once the number of horizontal slices is determined, the skew profile is sampled at equal intervals of vertical distance. Each sampling point is then associated with a vertical position and an angular rotation. For each such point the appropriately rotated image is cropped according to the slice center position.

5   Re-assembling the Image

The resulting set of images slices is then stacked from top to bottom.

The results of slicing and splicing the image are shown in Fig. 6.

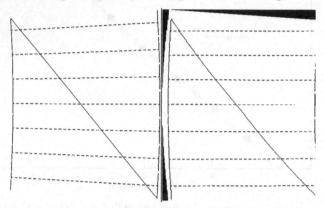

Fig. 6. Distorted and corrected test image.

6   Real World

Fig. 7 shows an example of a "real world" facsimile image which demonstrates variable skew. The pass code positions on which that skew determination is based is shown in Fig. 8.

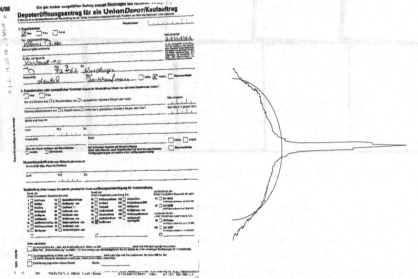

Fig. 7. An actual facsimile image demonstrating variable skew and the plot of the angular distribution of "power". Note the broad peak relative to those shown in Fig. 1.

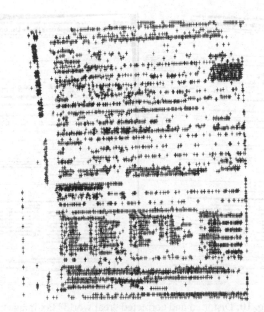

Fig. 8. White pass positions in the "real world" documents

The skew angles detected in the document as a function of vertical position on the page, the skew profile and the selected sampling points are shown in Fig. 9.

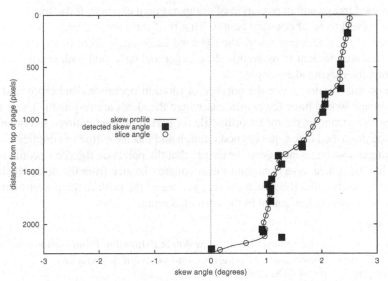

Fig. 9. Plot of detected skew angles, the skew profile that they define and the samples along the profile used for rotating the slices of the image.

Fig. 10 shows the facsimile document both before and after variable skew detection and correction.

Fig. 10. Distorted and corrected "real world" fax images.

7   Conclusions

It might be possible to achieve somewhat better results both in terms of the quality of the corrected image and in reduction of computational expense, if the slices taken were not constrained to be of constant height. That is, if there were a large range of the vertical span of the document where the detected skew angle were relatively constant it would be more efficient to make this slice larger and only deal with small slices in areas of rapidly varying skew angle.

To do this would reduce the number of rotation operations and crops and the resultant image would have fewer artifacts where the slices are re-joined. These may be very positive attributes deemed worthwhile for particular applications, but in our experience the described technique is good enough and has the virtue of simplicity.

It might also be advantageous to ensure that the points on the skew profile selected for slicing the image have minimum mean-square distance from the detected skew angles, thus ensuring that the structures that generated the peak in the power distribution become more nearly horizontal in the corrected image

References

1. Apostolos Antonacopoulos, "Local Skew Angle Estimation From Background Space in Text Regions", *International Conference on Document Analysis and Recognition*, pp 684-688. 1997.
2. Andrew D. Bagdanov, Junichi Kanai, "Evaluation of Document Image Skew Estimation Techniques", *SPIE*, pp 343-353, 1996.
3. Henry S. Baird, "The Skew Angle of Printed Documents", *SPSE Symposium on Hybrid Imaging Systems*, pp 21-24, 1987.

4. Roy Hunter & A. Harry Robinson, "International Digital Facsimile Coding Standards". *Proceedings of the IEEE*, Vol. 68, No. 7, pp 854-867, July 1980.
5. Alan W. Paeth, "A Fast Algorithm for General Raster Rotation", *Graphics Interface '86*, pp 77-81, 1986.
6. A. Lawrence Spitz, "Analysis of Compressed Document Images for Dominant Skew, Multiple Skew and Logotype Detection", *Computer Vision and Image Understanding,* 70, 3, pp 321-334, 1998.
7. A. Lawrence Spitz." Skew Determination in CCITT Group 4 Compressed Images", *Symposium on Document Analysis and Information Retrieval*, Las Vegas, Nevada, 1992.

Two Geometric Algorithms for Layout Analysis

Thomas M. Breuel

Xerox Palo Alto Research Center
3333 Coyote Hill Road
Palo Alto, CA 94304
tbreuel@parc.xerox.com

Abstract. This paper presents geometric algorithms for solving two key problems in layout analysis: finding a cover of the background whitespace of a document in terms of maximal empty rectangles, and finding constrained maximum likelihood matches of geometric text line models in the presence of geometric obstacles. The algorithms are considerably easier to implement than prior methods, they return globally optimal solutions, and they require no heuristics. The paper also introduces an evaluation function that reliably identifies maximal empty rectangles corresponding to column boundaries. Combining this evaluation function with the two geometric algorithms results in an easy-to-implement layout analysis system. Reliability of the system is demonstrated on documents from the UW3 database.

1 Introduction

A wide variety of algorithms for geometric layout analysis of document images have been proposed. Among them are morphology or "smearin g" based approaches, projection profiles (recursive X-Y cuts), texture-based analysis, analysis of the background structure, and others (for a review and references, see [6]). While layout analysis is a simpler problem than general image segmentation, it still raises challenging issues in geometric algorithms and image statistics.

This paper presents algorithms for addressing two key problems in geometric layout analysis. The first is an efficient and easy to implement algorithm for analyzing the whitespace or background structure of documents in terms of rectangular covers. Background structure analysis as an approach to document layout analysis has been described by a number of authors [13, 2, 12, 8, 1, 9]. The work by Baird *et al.* [2] analyzes background structure in terms of rectangular covers, a computationally convenient and compact representation of the background. However, past algorithms for computing such rectangular covers have been fairly difficult to implement, requiring a number of geometric data structures and dealing with special cases that arise during the sweep (Baird, personal communication). This has probably limited the widespread adoption of such methods despite the attractive properties that rectangular covers possess. The algorithm presented in this paper requires no geometric data structures to be implemented and no special cases to be considered; it can be expressed in less than 100 lines of Java code. In contrast to previous methods, it also returns solutions in order of decreasing quality.

D. Lopresti, J. Hu, and R. Kashi (Eds.): DAS 2002, LNCS 2423, pp. 188–199, 2002.
© Springer-Verlag Berlin Heidelberg 2002

The second algorithm presented here is a text line finding algorithm that works in the presence of "obstacles". That is, given a set of regions on the page that are known to be free of text lines (e.g., column separators) and a collection of character bounding boxes, the algorithm will find globally optimal maximum likelihood matches to text lines under a Gaussian error model, subject to the constraint that no text line crosses an obstacle. In contrast, many previous message to line finding (e.g., projection methods, Hough transform methods, etc.) either do not work reliably for multi-column documents or multiple text orientations on the same page, or they require a complete physical layout segmentation into disjoint text regions with uniform text line orientations prior to their application.

Each of the algorithms presented in this paper has useful applications in existing layout analysis systems. Taken together, these two algorithms permit us to take a new approach to document layout segmentation.

Traditional document layout analysis methods will generally first attempt to perform a complete global segmentation of the document into distinct geometric regions corresponding to entities like columns, headings, and paragraphs using features like proximity, texture, or whitespace. Each individual region is then considered separately for tasks like text line finding and OCR. The problem with this approach lies in the fact that obtaining a complete and reliable segmentation of a document into separate regions is quite difficult to achieve in general. Some decisions about which regions to combine may well involve semantic constraints on the output of an OCR system. However, in order to be able to pass the document to the OCR system in the first place, we must already have identified text lines, leading to circular dependencies among the processing steps.

In contrast, if we can perform text line finding in the presence of obstacles, it is not necessary to perform a complete segmentation of the document in order to perform OCR. Rather, all that is needed is the identification of vertical spaces or lines separating text in different columns. That problem turns out to be considerably simpler. It can be accomplished quite reliably using the whitespace analysis algorithm described in this paper using a novel evaluation function.

2   Whitespace Cover

2.1   Problem Definition

We define the maximal white rectangle problem as follows. Assume that we are given a collection of rectangles $C = \{r_0, \ldots, r_n\}$ in the plane, all contained within some given bounding rectangle r_b. In layout analysis, the r_i will usually correspond to the bounding boxes of connected components on the page, and the overall bounding rectangle r_b will represent the whole page. Also, assume that we are given an evaluation function for rectangles $Q : \mathbb{R}^4 \to \mathbb{R}$ satisfying, for any two rectangles r and r' that

$$r \subseteq r' \Rightarrow Q(r) \leq Q(r') \tag{1}$$

In the case described in [8], the Q function is simply the area of the rectangle, which is easily seen to satisfy the condition expressed in Equation 1. The maximal white

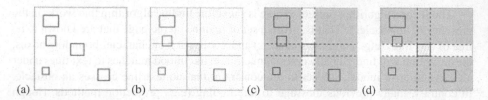

Fig. 1. Figure illustrating the recursion step of the branch-and-bound whitespace cover algorithm. See the text for an explanation.

rectangle problem is to find a rectangle $\hat{r} \subseteq r_b$ that maximizes $Q(T)$ among all the possible rectangles $r \subseteq r_b$, where r overlaps none of the rectangles in C. Or, expressed using mathematical notation:

$$\hat{r} = \hat{r}(C, r_b, Q) = \arg\max_{r \in U} Q(r) \quad \text{where} \quad U = \{r \subseteq r_b | \forall c \in C : r \cap c = \emptyset\} \quad (2)$$

2.2   Algorithm

As noted above, there are several algorithms for maximal empty rectangle problems, including those from computational geometry (e.g., [11]) and document analysis (e.g., [2]). Unfortunately, such algorithms tend to be fairly complex to implement and have not found widespread use.

The algorithm presented in this paper for the maximum empty rectangle problem can be used with obstacles that are points or rectangles. The key idea is analogous to quicksort or branch-and-bound methods. It is illustrated in Figure 1. Figure 1(a) shows the start of the algorithm: we are given an outer `bound` and a collection of rectangles (`obstacles`). If none of the obstacles are contained within `bound`, then we are done: the `bound` is itself the maximal rectangle given the obstacles. If one or more obstacles are contained within `bound`, we pick one of those rectangles as a "pivot" (Figure 1(b)). A good choice is a rectangle that is centrally located within the `bound`. Given that we know that the maximal rectangle cannot contain any of the `obstacles`, in particular, it cannot contain the pivot. Therefore, there are four possibilities for the solution to the maximal white rectangle problem: to the left and right of the pivot (Figure 1(c)) or above and below the pivot (Figure 1(d)). We compute the obstacles overlapping each of these four subrectangles and evaluate an upper bound on the quality of the maximal empty rectangles that is possible within each subrectangle; because of the monotonicity property (Equation 1), the quality function Q applied to the bounds of the subrectangles itself serves as an upper bound. The subrectangles and their associated obstacles and qualities are inserted into a priority queue and the above steps are repeated until the first obstacle-free rectangle appears at the top of the priority queue; this rectangle is the globally optimal solution to the maximal empty rectangle problem under the quality function Q. This algorithm is given in pseudo-code in Figure 2.

To obtain the n-best solutions, we can keep expanding nodes from the priority queue until we obtain n solutions in order of decreasing quality. However, many of those solutions will overlap substantially. The following greedy variant of the algorithm for

```
def find_whitespace(bound,rectangles):
    queue.enqueue(quality(bound),bound,rectangles)
    while not queue.is_empty():
        (q,r,obstacles) = queue.dequeue_max()
        if obstacles==[]:
            return r
        pivot = pick(obstacles)
        r0 = (pivot.x1,r.y0,r.x1,r.y1)
        r1 = (r.x0,r.y0,pivot.x0,r.y1)
        r2 = (r.x0,pivot.y1,r.x1,r.y1)
        r3 = (r.x0,r.y0,r.x1,pivot.y0)
        subrectangles = [r0,r1,r2,r3]
        for sub_r in subrectangles:
            sub_q = quality(sub_r)
            sub_obstacles =
                [list of u in obstacles if not overlaps(u,sub_r)]
            queue.enqueue(sub_q,sub_r,sub_obstacles)
```

Fig. 2. Pseudo-code for finding the globally optimal whitespace rectangle. A complete Java implementation is about 200 lines of code (statements).

finding the n best solutions addresses this. After we have found the maximal empty rectangle $\hat{r}$, we can add it to the list of obstacles and keep expanding. When we dequeue a search state, we check whether the list of obstacles has changed and, if so, recompute the quality of the node and re-enqueue it. This will result in a greedy cover of the whitespace with maximal rectangles and is considerably faster than restarting the algorithm.

Furthermore, rather than insisting on a cover of completely disjoint rectangles, we can allow for some fractional or absolute overlap among them. A careful implementation of finding such partially overlapping maximal empty rectangles might incorporate the overlap constraint into the computation of the upper bound during the partitioning process. However, the algorithm runs fast enough on real-world problems, and the number of solutions we desire is usually small enough, that it is sufficient merely to generate maximal empty rectangles in order of decreasing quality using the unmodified algorithm, test for overlap of any new solution with all the previously identified ones, and reject any new solution that overlaps too much with a previously found solution.

An application of this algorithm for finding a greedy covering of a document from the UW3 database with maximal empty rectangles is shown in Figure 7. Computation times for commonly occurring parameter settings using a C++ implementation of the algorithm on a 400MHz laptop are under a second. As it is, this algorithm could be used as a drop-in replacement for the whitespace cover algorithm used by [8], and it should be useful to anyone interested in implementing that kind of page segmentation system. However, below, this paper describes an alternative use of the algorithm that uses different evaluation criteria.

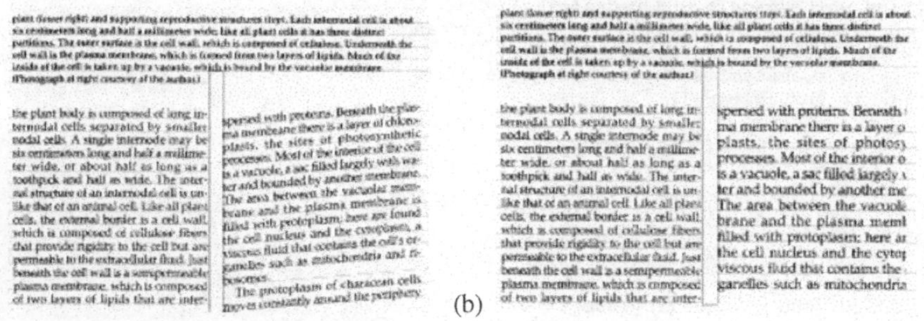

(a)   (b)

Fig. 3. Application of the constrained line finding algorithm to simulated variants of a page. Gutters (obstacles) were found automatically using the algorithm described in the paper and are shown in green. Text lines were found using the constrained line finder and are shown in faint red. (a) Two neighboring columns have different orientations (this often occurs on the two sides of a spine of a scanned book). (b) Two neighboring columns have different font sizes and, as a result, the baselines do not line up.

3   Constrained Line Finding

3.1   Problem Definition

We will now turn to a second geometric algorithm, one for finding text lines in the presence of obstacles. The "obstacles" will turn out to be the rectangles comprising the whitespace cover found by the algorithm described in the previous section and the evaluation criteria described in the next section. The constrained line finding algorithm is also linked with the algorithm described in the previous section by taking a similar algorithmic approach: branch-and-bound.

The problem that constrained line finding addresses in document analysis is the following. Many documents contain text in multiple columns. Some documents or document images may even contain text at multiple orientations, either because of complex document layouts, or (more commonly) because the two facing pages of a book were scanned at slightly different rotations within the same image. Text lines that are close to each other may therefore still have different line parameters. Some cases are illustrated in Figure 3.

Traditional approaches attempt to cope with such cases by first finding a complete and correct page segmentation and then performing line finding within each text block; that is, they take a hierarchical top-down approach. Unfortunately, finding a complete and correct page segmentation without knowledge of the line structure is difficult. Globally integrated solutions to page layout analysis, like those proposed by Liang et al. [10] avoid this issue, but appear to be complex to implement and so far have not found wide application.

Constrained line finding provides a simpler alternative. A constrained line finder only needs a list of obstacles that lines of text do not cross. These obstacles are generally gutters, and a few graphical elements such as figures or thin vertical lines. Based on the results presented below, finding gutters appears to be a much simpler problem than a complete (even if provisional) layout analysis, and even complex layouts tend

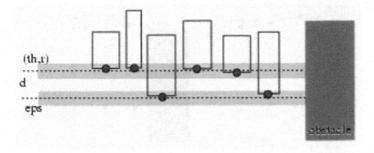

Fig. 4. The text line model used for constrained line finding.

to have a simple gutter structure (see the examples in Figure 7). Those gutters can be identified easily using the whitespace cover method described in the previous section. Furthermore, the constrained line finding method described in this paper can also be used together with orientation independent layout analysis techniques, allowing us to find text lines at arbitrary orientations even in incompletely segmented text.

The approach to constrained text line finding underlying the algorithm in this paper has previously been described for geometric object recognition [3], and applied to text line finding [5]. Let us represent each character on the page by the point at the bottom and center of its bounding box (the alignment point). In the absence of error, for most Roman fonts, each such point rests either on the baseline or on another line parallel to the baseline, the line of descenders. This is illustrated in Figure 4.

For finding "optimal" matches of text line models against the bounding boxes of a page, we use a robust least square model. That is, the contribution of each character to the overall match score of a text line is penalized by the square of the distance of the alignment point from the base line or line of descenders, up to a threshold. This match score corresponds to a maximum likelihood match in the presence of Gaussian error on location and in the presence of a uniform background of noise features, as shown in the literature [7].

Let us assume that lines are parameterized by their distance r from the origin and the orientation θ of their normal. An additional parameter, d, gives the distance of the line of descenders from the baseline. These three parameters (r, θ, d) then determine a text line model. If the alignment points of all connected components on the page are given by $\{p_1, \ldots, p_n\} \subseteq \mathbb{R}^2$, we can express the quality of match (monotonically related to the log likelihood) function as:

$$Q(r, \theta, d) = \sum_i \phi_\epsilon(\text{dist}(l_{r,\theta,d}, p_i)) \tag{3}$$

Here, $\text{dist}(\cdot, \cdot)$ is the Euclidean distance and ϕ is a threshold function

$$\phi_\epsilon(x) = \max(0, 1 - \frac{x^2}{\epsilon^2}) \tag{4}$$

Maximizing $Q(r, \theta, d)$ over all parameters gives us the globally optimal solution to the unconstrained line finding problem. For the constrained line finding problem, we

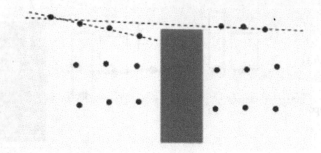

Fig. 5. Illustration of the constrained line finding problem with obstacles. The rectangle is the obstacle and the dots represent points to be matched by a line. Two candidates lines are shown: one dashed line matches four points but is stopped by the obstacle, another dashed line matches five points and narrowly avoids the obstacle.

consider line segments instead of lines and require finding a maximal line segment that does not intersect any of the given obstacles.

3.2 Algorithm

An algorithm for finding globally optimal solutions to the unconstrained text line finding problem has been presented in [5], based on previous work on branch-and-bound methods for geometric matching [4]. We will briefly review the unconstrained method here. The basic idea is to consider rectangular subsets (boxes; cartesian products of line parameter intervals) of the three-dimensional space of text line parameters and compute upper bounds on the value of the quality function achievable over those subsets. Subsets with large upper bounds are subdivided into smaller subsets and reevaluated. Eventually, the rectangular subsets arrived at in this process are small enough to bound the optimal solution to the optimization problem with any desired numerical accuracy. This is an instance of a branch and bound algorithm.

In order to be practical for geometric optimization problems, two difficulties need to be overcome: first, we need to be able to find an upper bound $\hat{Q}$ to the quality function Q over some region, and second, we need to be able to compute that upper bound efficiently. [4] describes the computation of the upper bound $\hat{Q}$ function for a box of line parameters $[\underline{r}, \overline{r}] \times [\underline{\theta}, \overline{\theta}]$. Let us review this approach briefly here. For the moment, to simplify the discussion, consider only the baseline, not the line of descenders. Consider the region L_B swept out by lines with parameters contained in the box of parameters $B = [\underline{r}, \overline{r}] \times [\underline{\theta}, \overline{\theta}]$. We use as our upper bound $\hat{Q}(L_B) = \max_{(r,\theta) \in B} Q(r, \theta)$. Taking advantage of the monotonicity of $\phi_\epsilon(x)$, this bound is easily seen to be

$$\hat{Q}(B) = \sum_i \min_{(r,\theta) \in B} \phi_\epsilon(\text{dist}(l_{r,\theta}, p_i)) \tag{5}$$

$$= \sum_i \phi_\epsilon(\text{dist}(L_B, p_i)) \tag{6}$$

```
def find_constrained_lines(linebox,points,obstacles):
    queue.enqueue(quality(linebox,points),linebox,points,obstacles)
    while not queue.is_empty():
        (q,linebox,points,obstacles) = queue.dequeue_max()
        if accurate_enough(linebox):
            return linebox
        excluded_obstacles =
            [list of obstacle in obstacles
                if linebox.can_not_intersect(obstacle)]
        if excluded_obstacles!=[]:
            ...split linebox at excluded obstacles and enqueue...
        sublineboxes = split(linebox)
        for sub_linebox in sublineboxes:
            sub_points =
                [list of point in points
                    if point.may_match(line)]
            sub_q = quality(sub_linebox,sub_points)
            queue.enqueue(sub_q,sub_linebox,sub_points,obstacles)
```

Fig. 6. Pseudo-code for finding the globally optimal constrained match of a line model against a set of points.

The region L_B is a bow-tie shaped region. It is bounded on four sides by lines given by the extreme values of the line parameter box. The fifth side is bounded by a small circular arc. For the computation of the upper bound $\hat{Q}(B)$, we therefore need to compute the distance of a point p from this region, or at least a lower bound. This computation can be simplified by bounding the circular arc using a fifth line. A lower bound on the distance $\text{dist}(L_B, p_i)$ can then be computed using five dot products and a combination of min and max operations, as described in more detail in [4]. For the computation of descender lines, we replace $\text{dist}(L_B, p)$ by $\min(\text{dist}(L_B, p), \text{dist}(L'_B, p))$, where L'_B is the bow-tie shaped region swept out by the line of descenders in parallel with the baseline (see [5] for more detail).

The second technique that makes implementing geometric matching problems using branch and bound methods simple and efficient is the use of matchlists. That is, for each box B of line parameters, we maintain a list of all and only the alignment points that make non-zero contributions to the quality function Q. We call this list the "matchlist". When the box B gets subdivided, only alignment points on the matchlist need to be considered.

Up to this point, this section has been a review of prior work on globally optimal line finding. Let us now turn to the question of how we introduce geometric obstacles into this framework to text line finding. When finding text lines with obstacles, we do not allow matches in which a text line model $l_{r,\theta,d}$ intersects an obstacle. This is illustrated in Figure 5. The figure shows two candidate lines (dashed). One line avoids the obstacle and matches points from both sides. Another line matches points on one side of the obstacle better, but cannot "pick up" alignment points on the other side of the obstacle. In fact, in the constrained textline finding problem, solutions are textline segments, not infinite lines.

Perhaps surprisingly, incorporating obstacles into the branch-and-bound textline finding algorithm is simple and does not noticeably increase the complexity of the algorithm on problems usually encountered in practice. The approach is as follows. During

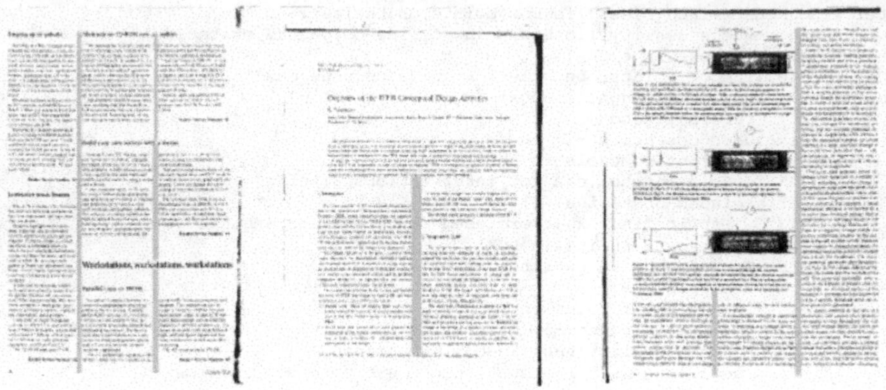

Fig. 7. Examples of the result of whitespace evaluation for the detection of column boundaries in documents with complex layouts (documents A00C, D050, and E002 from the UW3 database). Note that even complex layouts are described by a small collection of column separators.

the branch-and-bound evaluation, we consider successively smaller boxes of line parameters B. When these boxes are large, some of the lines implied by their parameters may intersect an obstacle and some may not. However, as the boxes of parameters get smaller and smaller, at some point, the lines corresponding to these parameter values will either all intersect an obstacle or will all fail to intersect an obstacle. In the case that all lines fail to intersect an obstacle, we simply remove the obstacle from further considerations in subsequent subdivisions of that box of parameters. In the case where all lines intersect an obstacle, we split the set of potentially matching alignment points into two subsets, those to the left of the obstacle and those to the right of the obstacle. We then continue the search with the same box B of line parameters and two separate matchlists, the matchlist for the alignment points to the left of the obstacle, and the matchlist for the alignment points to the right of the obstacle. The algorithm is given in pseudo-code in Figure 6.

This approach to line matching with obstacles uses the matchlists not just as an optimization, but also to structure the search and remove points from further consideration. The line segments that the algorithm finds are implicitly defined by the set of alignment points on a matchlist, the obstacles, and the line. This is a considerably more efficient approach than if we had attempted a search in the space of line segments directly. For finding obstacle-free line segments with baselines, this would have been a search over a five-dimensional parameter space, while the approach based on restricting matchlists requires only a search in the original three-dimensional space of parameters. As a result, using this approach, text line finding with obstacles runs in approximately the same amount of time as text line finding without obstacles.

4 Layout Analysis

So far, this paper has presented two geometric algorithms potentially useful in the implementation of document image analysis systems. The algorithm for the computation of whitespace covers can be used as an easy-to-implement drop-in replacement for the method used in [8]. In that work, rectangles with certain aspect ratios are preferred, and, overall, larger whitespace rectangles are preferred to smaller ones. Their evaluation function is based on statistical measurements on the distribution of whitespace rectangles in real documents, and it is intended to favor those rectangles that are meaningful horizontal or vertical separators.

To test the performance of evaluation functions based on area, aspect ratio, and position on the page, the whitespace coverage algorithm described above was applied to character bounding boxes obtained from document images in the UW3 database. For each document image, a collection of the 200 largest whitespace rectangles with pairwise overlap of less than 80% were extracted. This resulted, as expected, in a collection of whitespace rectangles that almost always completely covered the background, plus additional whitespace rectangles that intruded into text paragraphs. To arrive at a layout analysis, an evaluation function is needed that permits us to select only the rectangles whose union makes up the whitespace that isolates the components of the document layout.

To obtain such an evaluation function, a decision tree was trained to estimate the probability that a given whitespace rectangle is part of the page background. No formal evaluation of the performance was attempted, but the visual inspection showed that a significant fraction of the documents in the UW3 database could not be segmented fully using this approach. As reported in [8], tall whitespace rectangles were usually classified correctly, but for wide whitespace rectangles (those separating paragraphs or sections from one another), a significant number of positive and negative errors occurred. Ittner and Baird's system copes with these issues by computing the wide whitespace rectangles but ignoring spurious wide rectangles until later processing stages (they are not counted as incorrect in the evaluation of their method). Furthermore, visual inspection suggested that there were no rules or evaluation functions based just on the shape of the whitespace rectangles alone that would work reliably in all cases–the UW3 database contained such a diversity of documents that there were inherent ambiguities.

This means that, while evaluation functions based on the shape of whitespace rectangles alone may be useful and reliable for somewhat document collections, for very heterogeneous collections, we probably need another approach. Taken together, these results suggested taking an approach that classifies tall whitespace separately and that takes into account features other than just the shape and position of the whitespace rectangle in its evaluation. Furthermore, several observations suggest that wide whitespace, while sometimes visually salient, is neither necessary nor sufficient for the layout analysis of a document along the vertical axis. For example, paragraph breaks are indicated in many US-style documents by indentation, not additional whitespace, transitions from document headers to body text are most reliably indicated by changes in alignment (centering, left justification, right justification), and some section headings are indicated not by extra spacing but by changes in font size and style.

This then leads to the following four-step process for document layout analysis:

1. Find tall whitespace rectangles and evaluate them as candidates for gutters, column separators, etc.
2. Find text lines that respect the columnar structure of the document.
3. Identify vertical layout structure (titles, headings, paragraphs) based on the relationship (indentation, size, spacing, etc.) and content (font size and style etc.) of adjacent text lines
4. Determine reading order using both geometric and linguistic information.

The key idea for identifying gutters, which we take to mean here tall whitespace rectangles that are a meaningful part of a layout analysis, is to take into account, in addition to the shape and position of the rectangles, their proximity to neighboring text. This constraint is suggested both by document structure, as well as the observation that in a simple maximal white rectangle algorithm, many of the rectangles identified will be bordered only by a few textual components near their corners. Based on considerations of document layouts and readability, we can tentatively derive some rules that we would expect to apply to gutters (in future systems, we intend to base these constraints on statistical properties of pre-segmented document databases):

– gutters must have an aspect ratio of at least 1:3
– gutters must have a width of at least 1.5 times of the mode of the distribution of widths of inter-word spaces
– additionally, we may include prior knowledge on minimum text column widths defined by gutters
– gutters must be adjacent to at least four character-sized connected components on their left or their right side (gutters must separate something, otherwise we are not interested in them)

To test the feasibility of the approach, these rules were encoded into a whitespace evaluation function and the whitespace cover algorithm was applied to finding gutters on pages. To evaluate the performance, the method was applied to the 221 document pages in the "A" and "C" classes of the UW3 database. Among these are 73 pages with multiple columns. The input to the method consisted of word bounding boxes corresponding to the document images. After detection of whitespace rectangles representing the gutters, lines were extracted using the constrained line finding algorithm. The results were then displayed, overlaid with the ground truth, and visually inspected. Inspection showed no segmentation errors on the dataset. That is, no whitespace rectangle returned by the method split any line belonging to the same zone (a line was considered "split" if the whitespace rectangle intersected the baseline of the line), and all lines that were part of separate zones were separated by some whitespace rectangle. Sample segmentations achieved with this method are shown in Figure 7.

5   Discussion and Conclusions

This paper has presented two geometric algorithms. The first algorithm finds globally optimal solutions to the n-maximum empty rectangle problem in the presence of rectangular obstacles, under a wide class of quality functions (including area). The second algorithm finds globally optimal maximum likelihood solutions to the textline finding problem in the presence of obstacles. Both algorithms are easy to implement and practical and have uses in a variety of document analysis problems, as well as other areas of computational geometry.

These algorithms form the basis for an approach to document layout analysis that concentrates on the two arguably most salient and important aspects of layout: gutters (whitespace separating columns of text) and maximal segments of text lines that do not cross gutters. Paragraphs and other layout structure along the vertical dimension can then be found in a subsequent step. Applying this method to the UW3 database suggests very low segmentation error rates (no errors on a 223 page sample). The results also suggest that a description of pages in terms of column separators, text lines, and reading order, is a very compact and stable representation of the physical layout of a page and may be a better goal for the initial stages of layout analysis than traditional hierarchical representations.

References

1. H. S. Baird. Background structure in document images. In *H. Bunke, P. S. P. Wang, & H. S. Baird (Eds.), Document Image Analysis, World Scientific, Singapore*, pages 17–34, 1994.
2. H. S. Baird, S. E. Jones, and S. J. Fortune. Image segmentation by shape-directed covers. In *Proceedings of the Tenth International Conference on Pattern Recognition, Atlantic City, New Jersey*, pages 820–825, 1990.
3. Thomas M. Breuel. Fast Recognition using Adaptive Subdivisions of Transformation Space. In *Proceedings IEEE Conf. on Computer Vision and Pattern Recognition*, pages 445–451, 1992.
4. Thomas M. Breuel. Finding Lines under Bounded Error. *Pattern Recognition*, 29(1):167–178, 1996.
5. T.M. Breuel. Robust least square baseline finding using a branch and bound algorithm. In *Proceedings of the SPIE - The International Society for Optical Engineering*, page (in press), 2002.
6. R. Cattoni, T. Coianiz, S. Messelodi, and C. M. Modena. Geometric layout analysis techniques for document image understanding: a review. Technical report, IRST, Trento, Italy, 1998.
7. William Wells III. Statistical approaches to feature-based object recognition. *International Journal of Computer Vision*, 21(1/2):63–98, 1997.
8. D. Ittner and H. Baird. Language-free layout analysis, 1993.
9. K. Kise, A. Sato, and M. Iwata. Segmentation of page images using the area voronoi diagram. *Computer Vision and Image Understanding*, 70(3):370–82, June 1998.
10. J. Liang, I. T. Philips, and R. M. Haralick. An optimization methodology for document structure extraction on latin character documents. *Pattern Analysis and Machine Intelligence*, pages 719–734, 2001.
11. M. Orlowski. A new algorithm for the largest empty rectangle problem. *Algorithmica*, 5(1), 1990.
12. T. Pavlidis and J. Zhou. Page segementation by white streams. In *1st ICDAR, Saint-Malo*, pages 945–953, 1991.
13. J. P. Trincklin. *Conception d'un systéme d'analyse de documents*. PhD thesis, Thêse de doctorat, Université de Franche-Compté, 1984.

Text/Graphics Separation Revisited

Karl Tombre, Salvatore Tabbone, Loïc Pélissier, Bart Lamiroy, and
Philippe Dosch

LORIA, B.P. 239, 54506 Vandœuvre-lès-Nancy, France

Abstract. Text/graphics separation aims at segmenting the document
into two layers: a layer assumed to contain text and a layer containing
graphical objects. In this paper, we present a consolidation of a method
proposed by Fletcher and Kasturi, with a number of improvements to
make it more suitable for graphics-rich documents. We discuss the right
choice of thresholds for this method, and their stability. We also propose a post-processing step for retrieving text components touching the
graphics, through local segmentation of the distance skeleton.

1   Introduction

In document image analysis, the text/graphics separation process aims at segmenting the document into two layers: a layer assumed to contain text—
characters and annotations—and a layer containing graphical objects. As the
recognition tasks to be performed are quite different between these two layers,
most authors perform this separation very early in the document analysis chain,
which means that it is usually performed through image processing tools, with
limited knowledge about the presence of higher-level objects.

Many methods have been proposed for extracting text from cluttered background and segmenting the document image. One of the best known method is
that of Wong, Casey and Wahl [20], with its many adaptations and improvements [12]. However, whereas RLSA filtering has proved its efficiency in segmenting textual documents, its use in graphics-rich documents is less frequent;
one of the few methods we are aware of is that of Lu [13]. Other methods used for
text-rich documents include those based on white streams [18] and the top-down
methods using some kind of X–Y decomposition of the document [1,16].

In the special case of forms, text often touches the graphics, but the latter
are mainly horizontal and vertical lines, which gives the possibility to explicitly
look for these kinds of lines, with techniques such as the Hough transform, for
instance [10].

But in the general case of graphical documents, lines are more complex and
all these approaches are not very efficient. In this case, we are aware of three
basic families of methods for separating text and graphics:

– Some authors perform directional morphological filtering to locate all linear
  shapes and thus separate them from the other shapes, which are considered
  to be text. This works especially well for simple maps [14,15], although it

D. Lopresti, J. Hu, and R. Kashi (Eds.): DAS 2002, LNCS 2423, pp. 200–211, 2002.

remains to be seen how scalable the approach is when the complexity of the drawing grows.

- Similarly, other authors look for the lines, either on the distance transform [11], or on a vectorization of the document image [7].
- A third approach, used by many people, is based on the analysis of the connected components, which are filtered through a set of rules for determining to which layer they belong. One of the best known algorithms for performing this was proposed by Fletcher and Kasturi [9]. This method has proved to scale remarkably well with increasingly complex documents, although it is of course not able to directly separate text which is touching the graphics.

In this paper, we present a consolidation of the method proposed by Fletcher and Kasturi, with a number of improvements to make it more suitable for graphics-rich documents, with discussion about the choice of thresholds, and we propose a post-processing step for retrieving text components touching the graphics.

2   Separation through Analysis of Connected Components

Because of the scalability of the Fletcher & Kasturi method, we have chosen to base our own text/graphics separation on it, as we work with many kinds of complex graphics documents [8]. As Fletcher and Kasturi designed their method for mixed text–graphics documents, whereas we work with engineering drawings, maps, etc. we felt the need for adding an absolute constraint on the length and width of a text component; however, this does not add a new parameter to the method, as this constraint is set to $\sqrt{T_1}$ (see below).

The method yields good results, but there is still a problem with dashes and other elongated shapes. It is impossible to clearly discriminate, only on image features, a ¡¡ I ¿¿ or ¡¡ l ¿¿ character from a dash, for instance. We therefore propose to separate size filtering from shape filtering. As a consequence, we now have *three layers* at the end of the process, instead of two: small components, assumed to be text, large components, assumed to be graphics, and *small elongated components*, which are added to a specific layer and used at later stages both by dashed lines detection and by character string extraction.

Of course, another problem remains, that of text touching the graphics; we will come back to this in sections 3 and 4. The modified algorithm is the following—changes to the original Fletcher and Kasturi method are *emphasized*:

- compute connected components of the image, and the histogram of the sizes of the bounding boxes for all black components;
- find most populated area in this histogram, A_{mp} being the number of components in this area;
- compute average of histogram and let A_{avg} be the number of components having this average size;
- set a size threshold for bounding boxes, $T_1 = n \times \max(A_{mp}, A_{avg})$, and a maximum elongation threshold for the bounding boxes, T_2;

– filter the black connected components, adding to the text layer all those having an area lower than T_1, a $\frac{height}{width}$ ratio in the range $[\frac{1}{T_2}, T_2]$, *and both height and width lower than* $\sqrt{T_1}$, the other components being added to the graphics layer;

– *compute* **best enclosing rectangle**[1] *of each component labeled as text by previous step*;

– set a density threshold T_3 and an elongation threshold T_4;

– *Compute density of each "text" component with respect to its best enclosing rectangle and the elongation ratio of this rectangle—if the density is greater than T_3 and the elongation is greater than T_4, reclassify the component as "small elongated component", i.e. add it to the third layer.*

Figure 1 illustrates the results of the method on a drawing, with $T_1 = 1.5 \times \max(A_{mp}, A_{avg})$, $T_2 = 20$, $T_3 = 0.5$ and $T_4 = 2$. The small noise components are pruned by a simple pre-processing step.

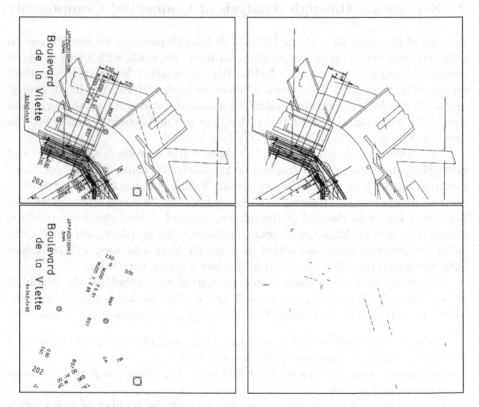

Fig. 1. A drawing and the three layers obtained by the method.

---

[1] And not bounding box!

In such a method, the stability of the thresholds is an important criterion for the robustness of the algorithm. In this case, T_1 is defined proportionnally to $\max(A_{mp}, A_{avg})$, the n factor being stable provided that there is only one character size. If the character size is very homogeneous, n can be set to 3, but for irregular sizes a lower value may be necessary for satisfying results. The T_2 set at 20 yields good results for all the documents we have worked on. The minimum density threshold T_3 must be set around 0.5 when the character contours are noisy. The minimal elongation factor T_4 is dependent of the kinds of dashes present in the drawing; in our case a value of 2 has proved to be satisfactory.

3   Extracting the Character Strings

Fletcher and Kasturi's method includes a method for grouping the characters into strings. This classically uses the Hough Transform (HT), working on the center of the bounding boxes of all components classified as text. The main steps are the following:

- compute average height H_{avg} of bounding boxes in the text layer, and set sampling step of the HT to $chdr \times H_{avg}$, where $chdr$ is a given parameter;
- look for all horizontal, vertical and diagonal alignments by voting in the (ρ, θ) space;
- segment each alignment into words:
  - compute mean height $\bar{h}$ of words in the alignment,
  - sort characters along main direction,
  - group into a word all successive characters separated by less than $\mu \times \bar{h}$, where μ is a given factor.
  We tested two options:
  1. process first the highest votes of the HT, and do not consider characters already grouped in a first alignment when processing lower votes;
  2. give the possibility to each character to be present in more than one word hypothesis, and wait until all votes are processed before eliminating multiple occurrences, by keeping the longest words.

Surprisingly, as illustrated by Fig. 2, it is difficult to choose a "best" option looking at our experimental results, whereas we expected the second option to be better than the first!

The two parameters of the method are $chdr$ and μ. $chdr$ adjusts the sampling step of the HT. It is difficult to find a stable value for it. When it is too low, the vote space is split into too many meshes, which may over-segment the strings. On the other hand, when the value gets too high, some separate strings may end up being merged.

μ adjusts the maximum distance allowed between characters in the same string. Of course, this may also over-segment or under-segment the strings. Our default value is 2.5, and this seems to be much more stable than $chdr$. Figure 3 illustrates the result with $\mu = 2.5$ and $chdr = 0.4$.

The method has still a number of limitations:

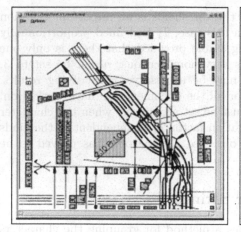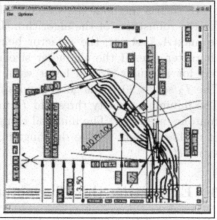

Fig. 2. String extraction — options 1 and 2.

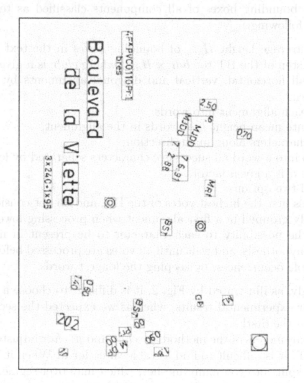

Fig. 3. String extraction.

- Short strings are not reliably detected, as there are not enough "votes" to discriminate them efficiently from artefacts.
- When there are several parallel strings, the method may find artificial diagonal alignments—however, this can be dealt with using heuristics on the privileged directions in the drawing.

- Punctuation signs, points on "i" characters and other accents, are not really aligned with the other characters in the string. To include them in the strings, we have to relax the parameters, thus opening up for wrong segmentations at other places.

However, despite these limitations, the results are sufficiently reliable to be usable as a basis for further processing, and for interactive edition if necessary.

4   Finding Characters Connected to the Graphics

One of the main drawbacks of methods based on connected components analysis is that they are unable to extract the characters wich touch the graphics, as they belong to the same connected component. By introducing some extra a priori knowledge, it is possible to actually perform this separation:

- If the shape of the lines is known a priori, which is the case in forms or tables, for instance, a specific line finder can extract the lines separating the areas in the table or the form; see for instance a vectorizer such as FAST [4].
- If the width of some of the strokes is known–typically, the width of writing on noisy backgrounds, or the width of the graphical lines in the drawing, it is possible to introduce some stroke modeling to retrieve one layer of strokes having a well-known width, thus separating it from other lines and strokes.

In this work, we propose a more general approach, where there is no need for this kind of a priori knowledge. Still, we use some assumptions:

- we assume that text is mostly present as strings, and not as isolated characters;
- we also assume that the complete strings are not touching the graphics, but that at least some of the characters have been found by the previous segmentation step.

4.1   Extension of the Strings

Our proposition is to start with the strings found by the previous step, and to extend them, looking for additional characters in specific search areas. Of course, as noted, we are aware of the fact that this strategy will not retrieve strings where all the characters are connected with the graphics, as there would be no "seed string" from which we could define a search area. Still, the presence of a single character connected to graphics occurs often enough for our strategy to increase significantly the performances of the segmentation, as we will see.

The HT gave a first idea about the direction of each string; however, as it "votes" for cells, this is not precise enough, and the first step is to determine more precisely the orientation of each string found, by computing the equation of the best line passing through all the characters. If the string has more than 4 points, this can be done through robust regression (median regression); for shorter strings we use linear regression, although we know that this is very sensitive to outliers.

Once the direction is found, we compute the enclosing rectangle of the string, along this direction; this gives us a much better representation of the string's location than the starting bounding box. From this rectangle, we compute search areas, taking into account the mean width of the characters and the mean spacing between characters in the string. Figure 4 illustrates the search areas defined in this way. When the string has only one character, the search area is a circle, as we have no specific direction for the string.

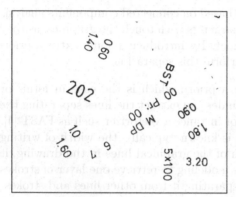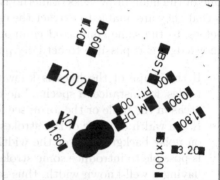

Fig. 4. Starting text layer and search areas for extending the strings.

4.2 Segmentation of the Skeleton

We first look in the third layer, that of small elongated shapes. If some of these shapes are included in a search area, they are added to the string.

We then look for possible characters connected to graphics in these search areas. This is done by computing the 3–4 distance skeleton in each search area, using Sanitti di Baja's algorithm [6]. The basic idea is then to segment the skeleton, reconstruct each part of the skeleton independently, and retrieve those part which are candidates to be characters to be added to the string. This is very similar to the idea proposed by Cao and Tan [2,3]; another possible approach is to use Voronoi tesselations [19].

For segmenting the skeleton, we based ourselves on a method proposed by Den Hartog [5], which identifies the points of the skeleton having multiple connectivity. However, in our case, this would over-segment the skeleton; therefore, we only segment the skeleton into subsets which are connected to the parts of the skeleton outside the search area by *one and only one multiple point*[2]. The

---

[2] This is a heuristic choice, which is based on the assumption that the character is only connected to the graphics at one location.

multiple points found in this way are the segmentation points of the skeleton. We do not take into account those parts of the skeleton which intersect the border of the search area.

Each part extracted by this segmentation is reconstructed using the inverse distance transform. Figure 5 illustrates the results of the method.

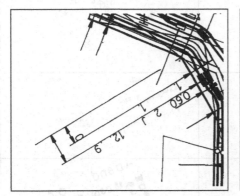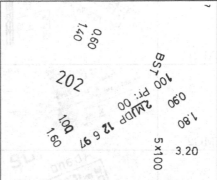

Fig. 5. Graphics layer where we segment the skeleton in the search areas defined in figure 4, and result of the string extraction.

Of course, the method has some limitations:

- as previously said, the method does not retrieve a string completely connected to the graphics, such as the 0.60 string, as there is no seed string;
- when the computed string orientation is not correct (which may happen for short strings, especially, as the regression is not robust in this case), we may miss some characters—in the figure, we fortunately retrieved the second 0 of the 1.00 string, but it might easily have been missed, as the orientation computed for the string is not correct (see Fig. 4), so that the search area is also wrong;
- whereas characters such as J in the string 2MJDP are retrieved inside the seed string M DP, it is not the case for the 1 character of string Pr:100, which intersects the search area both at the top and at the bottom.

Image	Nb. ch.	T/G	Retr.	Total	Errors
IMG1	63	50 (79%)	8/13	58 (92%)	7
IMG2	92	66 (72%)	5/16	71 (77%)	24
IMG3	93	78 (84%)	3/15	81 (87%)	5
IMG4	121	95 (78%)	9/26	104 (86%)	71
IMG5	31	7 (22%)	0/0	7 (22%)	1

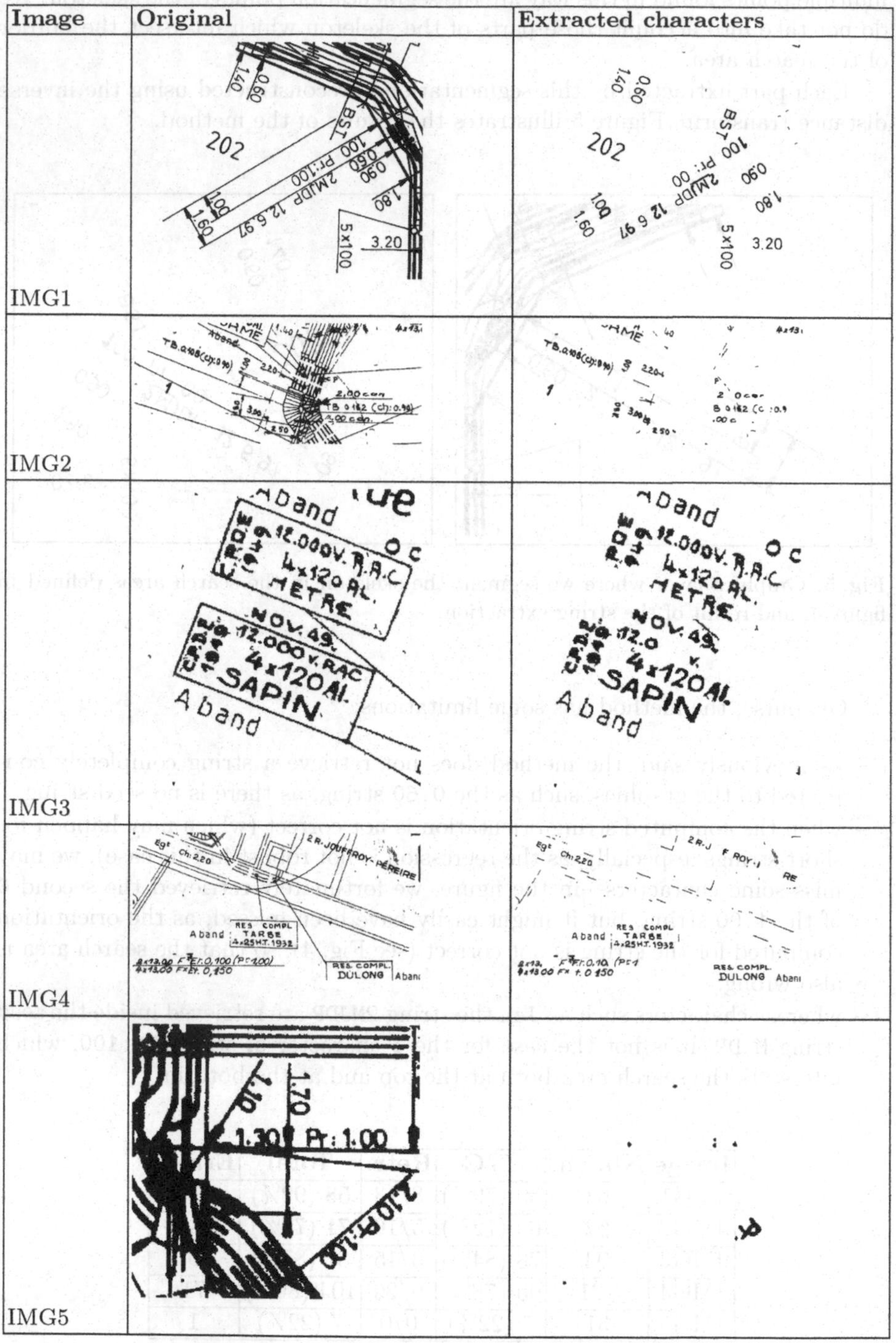

Image	Original	Extracted characters
IMG1		
IMG2		
IMG3		
IMG4		
IMG5		

Fig. 6. Some images and result of the segmentation.

5   Evaluation and Conclusion

We give here some quantitative measures on extracts from several drawings (Fig. 6). The **Nb. ch.** column indicates the number of characters counted by an operator, in each image. The **T/G** column shows the number of characters found by the text/graphics separation method described in Sect. 2, and the percentage of real characters thus found. The **Retr.** shows the number of characters retrieved by the method described in Sect. 4, out of the total number of connected characters. The **Total** column shows the total number of characters found after the retrieval step, and the corresponding percentage. The **Errors** column shows the number of components errouneously labeled as being text at the end of the whole process. It must be noted that most of these errors stem from the initial segmentation, not from the retrieval step.

We see that the string extension process improves the final segmentation by 5 to 10%, in general. The number of false detections in IMG2 and IMG4 stem from the dashed lines. We also included IMG5 to illustrate an extreme case: as previously said, when the whole strings are connected to the graphics, there are no seeds and no gains from the method ...

We still see room for a number of improvements:

- The statistics used in the Fletcher and Kasturi method to analyze the distributions of size and elongation are quite simple, even more or less empirical. This is especially true for threshold T_1. It might be interesting to proceed with a finer statistical analysis of the histograms.
- The elongation criterion we use (thresholds T_3 and T_4) works on the best enclosing rectangle. Although this is better than using the bounding box of the connected component, it is still a simple rectangle ... For shapes such as "l" or "t", or when the boundary of the shape is noisy, the best enclosing rectangle remains a rough feature, so that the elongation criterion is not very efficient. By allowing more computation time at this stage, we may go for better elongation descriptors, such as higher order moments.
- An interesting alternative to the Hough transform for extracting the character strings (Sect. 3) could be to use the algorithm based on a 3D neighborhood graph of all text components, proposed by Park et al. [17].

Acknowledgments. This work was supported by a research contract with EDF R&D. We are especially thankful to Raphaël Marc for support and fruitful discussions throughout the work on this contract.

References

[1] E. Appiani, F. Cesarini, A. M. Colla, M. Diligenti, M. Gori, S. Marinai, and G. Soda. Automatic document classification and indexing in high-volume applications. *International Journal on Document Analysis and Recognition*, 4(2):69–83, December 2001.

K. Tombre et al.

[2] R. Cao and C. L. Tan. Separation of Overlapping Text from Graphics. In *Proceedings of 6th International Conference on Document Analysis and Recognition, Seattle (USA)*, pages 44–48, September 2001.

[3] R. Cao and C. L. Tan. Text/Graphics Separation in Maps. In *Proceedings of 4th IAPR International Workshop on Graphics Recognition, Kingston, Ontario (Canada)*, pages 245–254, September 2001.

[4] A. K. Chhabra, V. Misra, and J. Arias. Detection of Horizontal Lines in Noisy Run Length Encoded Images: The FAST Method. In R. Kasturi and K. Tombre, editors, *Graphics Recognition—Methods and Applications*, volume 1072 of *Lecture Notes in Computer Science*, pages 35–48. Springer-Verlag, May 1996.

[5] J. E. den Hartog, T. K. ten Kate, and J. J. Gerbrands. An Alternative to Vectorization: Decomposition of Graphics into Primitives. In *Proceedings of Third Symposium on Document Analysis and Information Retrieval, Las Vegas*, April 1994.

[6] G. Sanniti di Baja. Well-Shaped, Stable, and Reversible Skeletons from the (3,4)-Distance Transform. *Journal of Visual Communication and Image Representation*, 5(1):107–115, 1994.

[7] D. Dori and L. Wenyin. Vector-Based Segmentation of Text Connected to Graphics in Engineering Drawings. In P. Perner, P. Wang, and A. Rosenfeld, editors, *Advances in Structural and Syntactial Pattern Recognition (Proceedings of 6th International SSPR Workshop, Leipzig, Germany)*, volume 1121 of *Lecture Notes in Computer Science*, pages 322–331. Springer-Verlag, August 1996.

[8] Ph. Dosch, K. Tombre, C. Ah-Soon, and G. Masini. A complete system for analysis of architectural drawings. *International Journal on Document Analysis and Recognition*, 3(2):102–116, December 2000.

[9] L. A. Fletcher and R. Kasturi. A Robust Algorithm for Text String Separation from Mixed Text/Graphics Images. *IEEE Transactions on PAMI*, 10(6):910–918, 1988.

[10] J. M. Gloger. Use of Hough Transform to Separate Merged Text/Graphics in Forms. In *Proceedings of 11th International Conference on Pattern Recognition, Den Haag (The Netherlands)*, volume 2, pages 268–271, 1992.

[11] T. Kaneko. Line Structure Extraction from Line-Drawing Images. *Pattern Recognition*, 25(9):963–973, 1992.

[12] D. X. Le, G. R. Thoma, and H. Wechsler. Classification of binary document images into textual or nontextual data blocks using neural network models. *Machine Vision and Applications*, 8:289–304, 1995.

[13] Z. Lu. Detection of Text Regions From Digital Engineering Drawings. *IEEE Transactions on PAMI*, 20(4):431–439, April 1998.

[14] H. Luo and I. Dinstein. Using Directional Mathematical Morphology for Separation of Character Strings from Text/Graphics Image. In *Shape, Structure and Pattern Recognition (Post-proceedings of IAPR Workshop on Syntactic and Structural Pattern Recognition, Nahariya, Israel)*, pages 372–381. World Scientific, 1994.

[15] Huizhu Luo and Rangachar Kasturi. Improved Directional Morphological Operations for Separation of Characters from Maps/Graphics. In K. Tombre and A. K. Chhabra, editors, *Graphics Recognition—Algorithms and Systems*, volume 1389 of *Lecture Notes in Computer Science*, pages 35–47. Springer-Verlag, April 1998.

[16] G. Nagy and S. Seth. Hierarchical Representation of Optically Scanned Documents. In *Proceedings of 7th International Conference on Pattern Recognition, Montréal (Canada)*, pages 347–349, 1984.

[17] H.-C. Park, S.-Y. Ok, Y.-J. Yu, and H.-G. Cho. A word extraction algorithm for machine-printed documents using a 3D neighborhood graph model. *International Journal on Document Analysis and Recognition*, 4(2):115–130, December 2001.

[18] T. Pavlidis and J. Zhou. Page Segmentation and Classification. *CVGIP: Graphical Models and Image Processing*, 54(6):484–496, November 1992.

[19] Y. Wang, I. T. Phillips, and R. Haralick. Using Area Voronoi Tessellation to Segment Characters Connected to Graphics. In *Proceedings of 4th IAPR International Workshop on Graphics Recognition, Kingston, Ontario (Canada)*, pages 147–153, September 2001.

[20] K. Y. Wong, R. G. Casey, and F. M. Wahl. Document Analysis System. *IBM Journal of Research and Development*, 26(6):647–656, 1982.

A Study on the Document Zone Content Classification Problem

Yalin Wang[1], Ihsin T. Phillips[2], and Robert M. Haralick[3]

[1] Dept. of Elect. Eng. Univ. of Washington
Seattle, WA 98195, US
ylwang@u.washington.edu

[2] Dept. of Comp. Science, Queens College, City Univ. of New York
Flushing, NY 11367, US
yun@image.cs.qc.edu

[3] The Graduate School, City Univ. Of New York
New York, NY 10016, US
haralick@gc.cuny.edu

Abstract. A document can be divided into zones on the basis of its content. For example, a zone can be either text or non-text. Given the segmented document zones, correctly determining the zone content type is very important for the subsequent processes within any document image understanding system. This paper describes an algorithm for the determination of zone type of a given zone within an input document image. In our zone classification algorithm, zones are represented as feature vectors. Each feature vector consists of a set of 25 measurements of pre-defined properties. A probabilistic model, decision tree, is used to classify each zone on the basis of its feature vector. Two methods are used to optimize the decision tree classifier to eliminate the data over-fitting problem. To enrich our probabilistic model, we incorporate context constraints for certain zones within their neighboring zones. We also model zone class context constraints as a Hidden Markov Model and used Viterbi algorithm to obtain optimal classification results. The training, pruning and testing data set for the algorithm include $1,600$ images drawn from the UWCDROM-III document image database. With a total of $24,177$ zones within the data set, the cross-validation method was used in the performance evaluation of the classifier. The classifier is able to classify each given scientific and technical document zone into one of the nine classes, 2 text classes (of font size $4 - 18$pt and font size $19 - 32$ pt), math, table, halftone, map/drawing, ruling, logo, and others. A zone content classification performance evaluation protocol is proposed. Using this protocol, our algorithm accuracy is 98.45% with a mean false alarm rate of 0.50%.

1 Introduction

A document is varied in content. It can contain numerous zones that may have text, math, figure zones, etc. Each of these zones has its own characteristic features. For example, a math zone may contain symbols like $=, +, \sum, \int, \cdots$, which a text zone may not contain. On the other hand, figure zones may not contain any symbols or text. Captions and pure text vary in font size and style. This paper describes an algorithm for the

D. Lopresti, J. Hu, and R. Kashi (Eds.): DAS 2002, LNCS 2423, pp. 212–223, 2002.
© Springer-Verlag Berlin Heidelberg 2002

determination of zone type of a given zone within a give document image. In the design of a zone classifier, a set of measurements of pre-defined properties of a given zone forms a feature vector. The features include mean of the run length mean and variance, spatial mean and variance, etc. A probabilistic model is used to classify each zone on the basis of its feature vector [1]. We employ a decision tree classifier in the classification process. Two methods are used to optimize the decision tree classifier to eliminate the data over-fitting problem. Furthermore, to enrich our probabilistic model, we incorporate context constraints within neighboring zones for some zones and we model zone class context constraints as a Hidden Markov Model and used Viterbi algorithm [2] to obtain optimal classification results.

Our earlier work, also using feature vectors, is described in Wang et. al [3] and Wang et. al [4]. There we used 69 features. Here we achieve better performance with 25 features. Liang et. al [5] developed a feature based zone classifier using only the knowledge of the widths and the heights of the connected components within a given zone. Chetverikov *et al.* [6] studied zone content classification using their general tool for texture analysis and document blocks are labeled as text or non-text using texture features derived from a feature based interaction map (FBIM). Le et. al [7] proposed an automated labeling of zones from scanned images with labels such as titles, authors, affiliations and abstracts. Their labeling is based on features calculated from optical character recognition (OCR) output, neural network models, machine learning methods, and a set of rules that is derived from an analysis of the page layout for each journal and from generic typesetting knowledge for English text.

We propose a set of performance evaluation criteria to evaluate the performance of our algorithm and a set of experiments were conducted. In the experiment, each zone is specified by a unique zone identification number, a rectangular box which encloses the zone and is represented by the coordinates of the leftmost-top and rightmost-bottom points, and the zone type. The zones are the zone ground-truth entities from UWCDROM-III document image database [8]. The database includes $1,600$ scientific and technical document images with a total of $24,177$ zones. The zone classes we consider are text with font size $\leq$ 18pt, text with font size $\geq$ 19pt, math, table, halftone, map/drawing, ruling, logo, and others. The examples of each class are shown in Figure1. Our algorithm accuracy rate is 98.45% and the mean false alarm rate is 0.50%.

The remaining of this paper is divided into 5 parts. In Section 2, we present the detail description of the feature vector used in the algorithm. In Section 3, we give a brief description of the classification procedure. The performance evaluation protocol and experimental results are reported in Section 4. The feature reduction analysis is presented in Section 5. Our conclusion and statement of future work are discussed in Section 6.

2   Features for Zone Content Classification

Every zone in the document is a rectangular area. Black pixels are assumed to be foreground and the white pixels are background. For each zone, run length and spatial features are computed for each line along two different canonical directions: horizontal, diagonal. These two directions are shown in Figure 2. In the notations, we use subscript

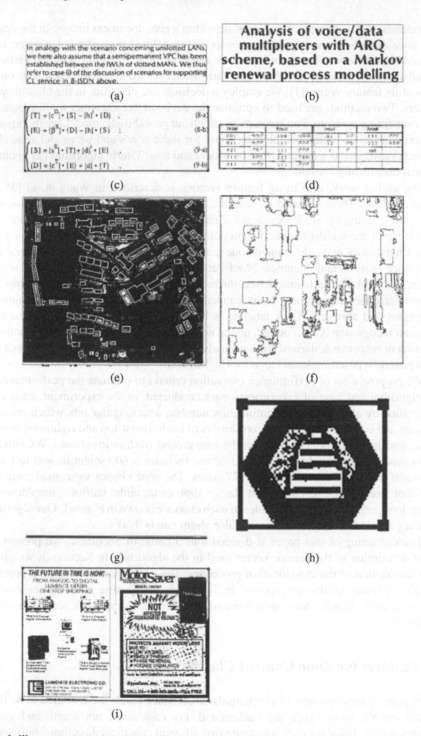

Fig. 1. Illustrates examples of nine zone content classes.(a) Text 1 class; (b)Text 2 class; (c) Math class; (d) Table class; (e) Halftone class; (f) Map/drawing class; (g) Ruling class; (h) Logo class; (i) Others class.

h and d to represent two directions. When to discriminate foreground and background features is necessary, we use superscript 0 and 1 to represent foreground and background features, respectively. For example, $rlmean_h^0$ represents background run length mean feature computed in horizontal direction. A total of 25 features are computed for each zone. In the following, we describe each feature in detail.

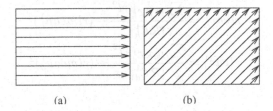

(a)   (b)

Fig. 2. Illustrates the two directions in which we compute run length and spatial features.(a) horizontal; (b) diagonal.

2.1   Run Length Features

A *run length* is a list of contiguous foreground or background pixels in a given direction. A total of 10 run length features are used, they include foreground/background run length mean and variance in each of the two directions.

Let $\mathcal{RL}_h^1$ and $\mathcal{RL}_d^1$ denote the foreground run length sets on the two directions. $|\mathcal{RL}_h^1|$, and $|\mathcal{RL}_d^1|$ constitute the first 2 features.

The next four features include foreground and background run length mean features on two directions in a given zone. Denote them as $rlmean_h^0$, $rlmean_d^0$, $rlmean_h^1$ and $rlmean_d^1$.

$$rlmean_h^0 = \frac{1}{|\mathcal{RL}_h^0|} \sum_{rl \in \mathcal{RL}_h^0} rl, rlmean_d^0 = \frac{1}{|\mathcal{RL}_d^0|} \sum_{rl \in \mathcal{RL}_d^0} rl$$

$$rlmean_h^1 = \frac{1}{|\mathcal{RL}_h^0|} \sum_{rl \in \mathcal{RL}_h^0} rl, rlmean_d^1 = \frac{1}{|\mathcal{RL}_d^0|} \sum_{rl \in \mathcal{RL}_d^0} rl$$

The next four features are foreground and background run length variance features on the two directions in a given zone. Denote them as $rlvar_h^0$, $rlvar_d^0$, $rlvar_h^1$ and $rlvar_d^1$. They can be obtained by calculating the mean of the squares of all the run lengths in the zone and subtracting them by the square of the run length mean. Specifically, they can be computed by the equations below.

$$rlvar_h^0 = \frac{\sum_{rl \in \mathcal{RL}_h^0} rl^2}{|\mathcal{RL}_h^0|} - (rlmean_h^0)^2$$

$$rlvar_d^0 = \frac{\sum_{rl \in \mathcal{RL}_d^0} rl^2}{|\mathcal{RL}_d^0|} - (rlmean_d^0)^2$$

$$rlvar_h^1 = \frac{\sum_{rl \in \mathcal{RL}_h^1} rl^2}{|\mathcal{RL}_h^1|} - (rlmean_h^1)^2$$

$$rlvar_d^1 = \frac{\sum_{rl \in \mathcal{RL}_d^1} rl^2}{|\mathcal{RL}_d^1|} - (rlmean_d^1)^2$$

2.2   Spatial Features

Four spatial features are designed to capture the foreground pixel distribution information. We denote the foreground pixel set in a given zone as $\mathcal{F}$. Spatial mean, μ, and spatial variance, δ, can be defined as

$$\mu = \frac{1}{|\mathcal{F}|} \sum_{p \in \mathcal{F}} w_p \qquad \delta = \frac{1}{|\mathcal{F}|} \sum_{p \in \mathcal{F}} (w_p - \mu)^2$$

where w_p is a weight assigned to each foreground pixel p. With two directions, we obtain four features.

As shown in Figure 2, we have two different directions to compute the run lengths. In each direction, we start computing from a point on a zone border and continue at a given direction until we hit another zone border again. We call such a computation route as a *run segment*. For every run segment the sum of foreground run lengths gives the *run segment projection*. Given a direction, each foreground pixel belongs and only belongs to one run segment. We associate each foreground pixel with a weight of run segment projection. We let the foreground pixels in the same run segment have the same weights so we have two different weight definitions according to each direction. We denote the starting and ending pixel coordinates of a horizontal run segment as $(x_{h,1}, y_{h,1})$, $(x_{h,2}, y_{h,2})$. We denote by $(x_{d,1}, y_{d,1})$, $(x_{d,1}, y_{d,1})$ the starting and ending pixel coordinates of a diagonal run segment.

The weights for horizontal and diagonal directions are denoted as w_h and w_d, $w_h = y_{h,1}$ and $w_d = y_{d,2} - x_{d,2}$.

Denote the set of run segments in two directions as $\mathcal{L}_h$ and $\mathcal{L}_d$. For a run segment, say, l_h, we denote its horizontal run segment projection on it as $proj_{h,l}$. In our algorithm, we compute spatial means and spatial variances as follows.

$$spmean_h = \frac{1}{|\mathcal{F}|} \sum_{l \in \mathcal{L}_h} w_h \times proj_{h,l}$$

$$spmean_d = \frac{1}{|\mathcal{F}|} \sum_{l \in \mathcal{L}_d} w_d \times proj_{d,l}$$

$$spvar_h = \frac{1}{|\mathcal{F}|} \sum_{l \in \mathcal{L}_h} [proj_{h,l} \times (w_l - spmean_h)^2]$$

$$spvar_d = \frac{1}{|\mathcal{F}|} \sum_{l \in \mathcal{L}_d} [proj_{d,l} \times (w_d - spmean_d)^2]$$

2.3 Autocorrelation Features

For each run segment, we define four functions: run segment projection, number of foreground run lengths, run length mean and spatial mean. We get 8 features by computing their autocorrelation functions using Fourier transform.

Denote the set of run length in a horizontal and a diagonal run segment as $\mathcal{RL}_{h,l}$ and $\mathcal{RL}_{d,l}$. Run segment projection function has been defined earlier, which are $proj_{h,l}$ and $proj_{d,l}$. The function of the number of foreground runs on each run segment are straightforward. The function of run length mean on each run segment can be defined as follows.

$$rlmean_{h,l} = \frac{proj_{h,l}}{|\mathcal{RL}_{h,l}|}, \qquad rlmean_{d,l} = \frac{proj_{d,l}}{|\mathcal{RL}_{d,l}|}.$$

Let $(x_{h,s}, y_{h,s})$, $(x_{h,e}, y_{h,e})$ be the two end points of a horizontal run length, and $(x_{d,s}, y_{d,s})$, $(x_{d,e}, y_{d,e})$ be the two end points of the diagonal run length. The definition of pos and $leng$ functions are given as

$$\begin{aligned} pos_{h,rl} &= x_{h,s}, & leng_{h,rl} &= x_{h,e} - x_{h,s} \\ pos_{d,rl} &= x_{d,s}, & leng_{d,rl} &= x_{d,e} - x_{d,s} \end{aligned} \tag{1}$$

The spatial mean function for each line can be defined as follows.

$$spmean_{h,l} = \frac{1}{proj_{h,rl}} \Big(\sum_{rl \in \mathcal{RL}_{h,l}} pos_{h,rl} \times leng_{h,rl} +$$

$$\frac{1}{2} \Big(\sum_{rl \in \mathcal{RL}_{h,l}} (leng_{h,rl})^2 - proj_{h,rl} \Big) \Big)$$

$$spmean_{r,l} = \frac{1}{proj_{d,rl}} \Big(\sum_{rl \in \mathcal{RL}_{d,l}} pos_{d,rl} \times leng_{d,rl} +$$

$$\frac{1}{2} \Big(\sum_{rl \in \mathcal{RL}_{d,l}} (leng_{d,rl})^2 - proj_{d,rl} \Big) \Big)$$

After we compute one function on each run segment, we can get a sequence of values, indexed by the run segment number. Using the Fast Fourier Transform [9], we can get the autocorrelation functions value for every function. Each feature is the slope of the tangent to the autocorrelation function values whose indexes are close to 0. We used general linear least squares method [9] to compute the slope of the points near 0.

2.4 Background Features

Although some background analysis techniques can be found in the literature([10],[11]), none of them, to our knowledge, has extensively studied the statistical characteristics of their background structure. Our signature-like background features are designed to give us more information on the distributions of the big foreground chunks in a given zone. We define a *large horizontal blank block* and a *large vertical blank block* as in [4]. The background feature is the total area of large horizontal and large vertical blank blocks, A.

2.5 Text Glyph Feature

A glyph is a connected component in a given zone. A text glyph is a character candidate glyph. Most of zones have some text glyphs. The information of how many text glyphs a given zone has is also an useful feature. The number of text glyphs in this zone, W, normalized by the zone area is the text glyph feature.

The so-called text glyphs are not from any OCR output. They are outputs of a statistical glyph filter. The inputs of this filter are the glyphs after finding connected component operation. The statistical glyph filter classifies each connected component into one of two classes: text glyph and non-text glyph. The filter uses a statistical method to classify glyphs and was extensively trained on UWCDROM-III document image database.

2.6 Column Width Ratio Feature

It is a common observation that math zones and figure zones have a smaller width compared to text zones. For any zone, the quotient of the zone width to the width of its column is calculated as $\frac{C}{Width_{column}}$, where C is the zone width and $Width_{column}$ is the width of the text column in which the zone is.

3 Classification Process

A decision tree classifier makes the assignment through a hierarchical, tree-like decision procedure. For the construction of a decision tree [1], we need a training set of feature vectors with true class labels. At each node, the discriminant function splits the training subset into two subsets and generates child nodes. A discriminant threshold is chosen at each node such that it minimizes an impurity value of the distribution mode at that node. The process is repeated at each newly generated child node until a stopping condition is satisfied and the node is declared as a leaf node on a majority vote.

In building a decision tree classifier, there is a risk of memorizing the training data, in the sense that nodes near the bottom of the tree represent the noise in the sample, As mentioned in [12], some methods were employed to make better classification. We used two methods [4] to eliminate data over-fitting in decision tree classifier.

To further improve the zone classification result, we want to make use of context constraint in some zone set. We model context constraint as a Markov Chain and use the Viterbi algorithm([2]) to find the most likely state sequence. To apply the Viterbi algorithm([2]), we have to know the probability that each zone belongs to each class. This probability is readily estimated from the training data set by decision tree structure. The details can be found in [4].

4 Experiments and Results

A hold-out method is used for the error estimation in our experiment. We divided the data set into 9 parts. We trained the decision tree on the first 4 parts, pruned the tree using another 4 parts, and then tested on the last 1 part. To train the Markov model, we trained on the first 8 parts and tested it on the last 1 part. Continue this procedure, each time omitting one part from the training data and then testing on the omitted one part from the training data and testing on the omitted part. Then the combined 9 part results are put together to estimate the total error rate [1].

Table 1. Possible true- and detected-state combination for two classes

True Class	Assigned Class	
	a	b
a	P_{aa}	P_{ab}
b	P_{ba}	P_{bb}

The output of the decision tree is compared with the zone labels from the ground truth in order to evaluate the performance of the algorithm. A contingency table is computed to indicate the number of zones of a particular class label that are identified as members of one of the nine classes. The rows of the contingency table represent the true classes and the columns represent the assigned classes. We compute four rates here: *Correct Recognition Rate (CR), Mis-recognition Rate (MR), False Alarm Rate (FR), Accuracy Rate (AR)*. Suppose we only have two classes: a and b. The possible true- and detected-state combination is shown in Table 1. We compute the four rates for class a as follows:

$$CR = \frac{P_{aa}}{P_{aa} + P_{ab}}, MR = \frac{P_{ab}}{P_{aa} + P_{ab}}$$
$$FR = \frac{P_{ba}}{P_{ba} + P_{bb}}, AR = \frac{P_{aa} + P_{bb}}{P_{aa} + P_{ab} + P_{bb} + P_{ba}}$$

In our experiment, the training and testing data set was drawn from the scientific document pages in the University of Washington document image database III [8]. It has $1,600$ scientific and technical document pages with a total of $24,177$ zones. The class labels for each of the zones are obtained from the database. These zones belonged to nine different classes. For a total of $24,177$ zones, the accuracy rate was 98.43% and mean false alarm rate was 0.50%, as shown in Table 2.

In Figure 3, we show some failed cases of our experiment. Figure 3(a) is a Table zone misclassified as Math zone due to the presence of many numerals and operators.

Table 2. Contingency table showing the number of zones of a particular class that are assigned as members of each possible zone class in UWCDROM-III. In the table, $T_1, T_2, M, T, H, MD,$ R, L, O represent text with font size $\leq$ 18pt., text with font size $\geq$ 19pt., math, table, halftone, map/drawing zone, ruling, logo, others, respectively. The rows represent the ground truth numbers while the columns represent the detection numbers.

	T1	T2	M	T	H	M/D	R	L	O	CR	MR
T1	21426	23	40	7	1	7	1	3	3	99.60%	0.40%
T2	19	104	1	0	1	2	0	0	1	81.25%	18.75%
M	47	1	686	2	0	18	1	1	2	90.50%	9.50%
T	6	0	4	162	0	35	0	1	2	77.14%	22.86%
H	1	0	1	1	345	27	0	0	0	92.00%	8.00%
M/D	2	3	20	20	28	648	1	1	5	89.01%	10.99%
R	3	0	2	0	0	2	424	0	1	98.15%	1.85%
L	7	3	1	0	0	0	0	2	0	15.38%	84.62%
O	4	0	2	0	2	7	1	0	6	27.27%	72.73%
FR	3.34%	0.12%	0.30%	0.13%	0.13%	0.42%	0.02%	0.02%	0.06%		

Figure 3(b) is a Map/Drawing zone misclassified as Table zone in that the content of the figure is just a table. Figure 3(c) shows a most frequent error of our current system. Our system classified a Math zone into Text 1 zone class. Sometimes our system still lacks a good ability to detect such a single line math equation zone which, even worse sometimes, includes some description words. Figure 3(d) shows an error example in which a Math zone was misclassified as a table zone because of its sparse nature.

5   Feature Reduction Analysis

In our early work [3] [4], we used a feature vector consisting of 69 features and got very good results. In our recent work, we tried to reduce the unnecessary features from the feature vector while keeping a good performance. By analysis and experiments, a total of 44 features were eliminated.

As shown in Figure 4, there were four feature computation directions. Since the images in UWCDROM-III are all de-skewed already, there do not exist strong variations in different directions. We changed the four directions to the current two directions 2. It directly removed 32 features from the feature vector.

Some features are redundant. For example, there were four background features, background run length number in the two given directions, a fraction of black pixels to the total number of pixels and total area of large horizontal and large vertical blank blocks. Since the feature, total area of large horizontal and large vertical blank blocks, is computed using the other three feature information, we eliminated the other three features. There were two zone area related features, zone bounding box area and a fraction of the number of text glyphs to the zone bounding box area. There are dependent features so we eliminated the first of them.

There were 16 features computed by autocorrelation function. We defined four functions which are computed in two different directions. The features are the slope of the

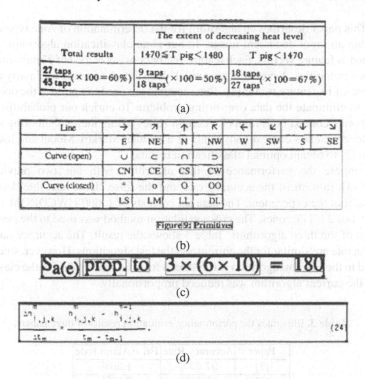

(a)

(b)

Figure 9: Primitives

(c)

(d)

Fig. 3. Illustrates some failed examples. (a). Table zone misclassified as Math zone; (b). Map/drawing zone misclassified as Table zone; (c). Math zone misclassified as Text 1 zone; (d). Math zone misclassified as Table zone.

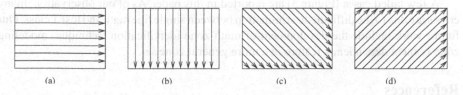

(a)   (b)   (c)   (d)

Fig. 4. Illustrates the four directions in which we computed run length and spatial features in our earlier work [3][4]. (a) horizontal; (b) vertical; (c) left-diagonal; (d) right-diagonal.

tangent to the autocorrelation function values whose indexes are close 0 and, the index for which the autocorrelation function goes to 10% of its maximum value. By experimenting, we eliminated 8 of them. From the experimental results, we believe our feature reduction was successful.

6   Conclusion

Given the segmented document zones, correctly determining the zone content type is very important for the subsequent processes within any document image understanding system. This paper describes an algorithm for the determination of zone type of a given zone within an input document image. In our zone classification algorithm, zones are represented as feature vectors. Each feature vector consists of a set of 25 measurements of pre-defined properties. A probabilistic model, decision tree, is used to classify each zone on the basis of its feature vector [1]. Two methods are used to optimize the decision tree classifier to eliminate the data over-fitting problem. To enrich our probabilistic model, we incorporate context constraints for certain zones within their neighboring zones. We also model zone class context constraints as a Hidden Markov Model and used Viterbi algorithm [2] to obtain optimal classification results.

To compare the performance of this algorithm with our two previous algorithms [3][4], in term of the accuracy rate and the false alarm rate, the identical data set was used in the experiment. The data set consists of $1,600$ UWCDROM-III images with a total of $24,177$ zones. The cross-validation method was used in the performance evaluation of the three algorithms. Table 3 shows the result. The accuracy rate and the false alarm rate are similar for the current and the last algorithms. However, since the features used in the current algorithm was reduced from 69 features to 25, the classification speed of the current algorithm was reduced proportionally.

Table 3. Illustrates the performance evaluation results of three papers.

Paper	Accuracy Rate	False Alarm Rate
[3]	97.53%	1.26%
[4]	98.52%	0.53%
This Paper	98.53%	0.50%

A few failed cases (Figure 3) are reported in this paper. As of our observation, many errors are due to the difficult discrimination between single line math and text 1 class. Our future work include the development of math zone identification technique, modeling zone content dependency feature in a more general zone set.

References

1. R. Haralick and L. Shapiro. *Computer and Robot Vision*, volume 1. Addison Wesley, 1997.
2. L. R. Rabiner. A tutorial on hidden markov models and selected applications in speech recognition. *Proceedings of the IEEE*, 77:257–285, February 1989.
3. Y. Wang, R. Haralick, and I. T. Phillips. Improvement of zone content classification by using background analysis. In *Fourth IAPR International Workshop on Document Analysis Systems. (DAS2000)*, Rio de Janeiro, Brazil, December 2000.
4. Y. Wang, R. Haralick, and I. T. Phillips. Zone content classification and its performance evaluation. In *Sixth International Conference on Document Analysis and Recognition(ICDAR01)*, pages 540–544, Seattle, WA, September 2001.
5. J. Liang, R. Haralick, and I. T. Phillips. Document zone classification using sizes of connected components. *Document Recognition III, SPIE'96*, pages 150–157, 1996.
6. D. Chetverikov, J. Liang, J. Komuves, and R. Haralick. Zone classification using texture features. In *Proc. International Conference on Pattern Recognition*, pages 676–680, Vienna, 1996.

7. D. X. Le, J. Kim, G. Pearson, and G. R. Thom. Automated labeling of zones from scanned documents. *Proceedings SDIUT99*, pages 219–226, 1999.
8. I. Phillips. Users' reference manual. *CD-ROM, UW-III Document Image Database-III*, 1995.
9. W. Press, B. Flannery, S. Teukolsky, and W. Vetterling. *Numerical Recipes in C*. Cambridge University Press, 1988.
10. A. Antonacopoulos. Page segmentation using the description of the background. *Computer Vision and Image Understanding*, pages 350–369, June 1998.
11. H. S. Baird. Background structure in document images. *Document Image Analysis*, pages 17–34, 1994.
12. W. Buntine. Learning classification trees. *Statistics and Computing journal*, pages 63–76, 1992.

Logical Labeling of Document Images Using Layout Graph Matching with Adaptive Learning

Jian Liang and David Doermann

Institute for Advanced Computer Studies
University of Maryland at College Park
{lj, doermann}@cfar.umd.edu

Abstract. Logical structure analysis of document images is an important problem in document image understanding. In this paper, we propose a graph matching approach to label logical components on a document page. Our system is able to learn a model for a document class, use this model to label document images through graph matching, and adaptively improve the model with error feed back. We tested our method on journal/proceeding article title pages. The experimental results show promising accuracy, and confirm the ability of adaptive learning.

1 Introduction

A typical document analysis system consists of page segmentation, optical character recognition (OCR), and logical structure understanding. The interest in the logical structure has been inspired by the emergence and popularity of common representation standards such as XML. With such standards, it is possible to encode complicated structural information together with content. The logical structure extracted from existing documents and expressed in XML format will greatly enhance the way the content can be used. In addition to traditional full text search, structured search and browsing, routing, database input, data mining, and document reformatting will be possible. Most current document analysis systems, however, cannot achieve this goal. Their output is typically no more than an unstructured text stream, although some systems try to make the output document layout similar to the original page by controlling font sizes, font styles, and text block positions. We need new tools to understand the logical structure of document images.

The task of logical labeling is to label segmented blocks on a document image as title, author, header, text column, etc. The set of labels will depend on document classes and/or applications. Logical labeling techniques can be roughly characterized as either zone-based or structure-based. Zone-based techniques [1][8] classify zones individually based on features of each zone. Structure-based techniques incorporate global constraints such as position. These techniques can further be classified as either top-down decision based [3][7], or bottom-up inference-based techniques [2][5]. Global optimization techniques [6][9] are often hybrids of the first two.

Based on our observation that page layouts tend to be consistent within a document class, we create a layout graph model for each visually distinct document class. Logical labeling is accomplished through a matching from a candidate page to a model.

D. Lopresti, J. Hu, and R. Kashi (Eds.): DAS 2002, LNCS 2423, pp. 224–235, 2002.

2 System Overview

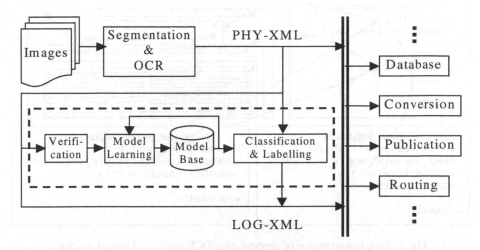

Fig. 1. System overview

Fig. 1 shows an overview of our document analysis system. First, document images are processed by a segmentation-and-OCR engine. We assume that the results are reasonably good. In particular, mild over-segmentation is acceptable, while under-segmentation which crosses logical content is not welcome. The outcome XML file (PHY-XML in the figure) contains information about the physical layout and text content of the original document page. The LOG-XML in the figure stands for logical structure XML file, which contains information about document class and logical labels corresponding to the PHY-XML file.

Our focus is on the logical labeling modules inside the dashed line frame. There are three working processes:

1. *Model Initialization*: At the beginning, there is no model in the model base. The user needs to provide ground truth LOG-XML files corresponding to the PHY-XML files, which are taken by the model learning module to learn an initial document model. Document models are represented by layout graphs (see section 3).

2. *Logical Labeling and Adaptive Model Learning*: Once there is a model in the model base, a new document image (represented by a PHY-XML file after segmentation and OCR) can be first converted into a candidate layout graph, then matched to the model in order to assign logical labels to each block, resulting in a LOG-XML file. The PHY-XML and LOG-XML files can be used by downstream applications. If there is any error, the user verifies the PHY-XML and LOG-XML files. The verification results, along with the model, are handed over to the model learning module to improve the model.

3. *Classification and Labeling*: More than one document model is stored in model base, each representing a document class. An incoming document (represented by a PHY-XML file after segmentation and OCR) is converted to a candidate layout graph and matched to all models. The best match gives both the labeling and the classification result. The verification and adaptive model learning remain the same.

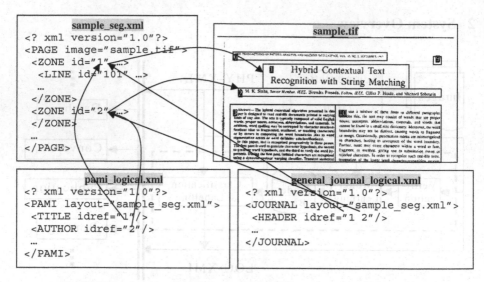

Fig. 2. XML representation of segmentation-OCR results and logical structure

Fig. 2 shows fragments of an example document page (*sample.tif*), the corresponding PHY-XML file (*sample_seg.xml*), and two LOG-XML files (*pami_logical.xml* and *general_journal_logical.xml*).

The PHY-XML file has a hierarchical structure, starting with a PAGE, down to ZONEs, LINEs, WORDs, and ending at CHARs. Each element has attributes describing its bounding box and average font size. The CHAR element has a character code attribute.

Each PHY-XML file can have more than one logical view. In *pami_logical.xml*, the TITLE and the AUTHOR are distinguished; but in *general_journal_logical.xml*, it is enough to identify the HEADER. Multiple logical views could be obtained through simple conversion: the combining of TITLE and AUTHOR into HEADER; or using multiple models: a PAMI model, and a GENERAL_JOURNAL model. Since the PAMI model has to achieve a finer resolution than the general one, it is more likely to produce errors. Therefore, if a general logical structure is the final goal, it would be better to use a general model.

As a simple sample application, we use XML stylesheets to translate the PHY-XML and LOG-XML files into other formats, such as HTML. Different tags can be assigned for text with different logical labels such that they are displayed with different font size/style and alignment. Depending on the application, different stylesheets can be designed. As an example, Fig. 3 shows one original document page and the converted HTML result.

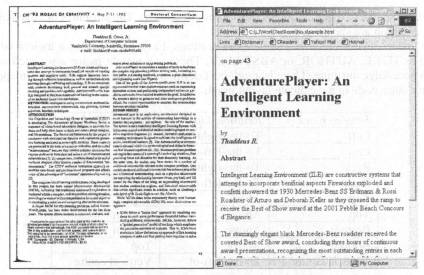

Fig. 3. Original document page and converted HTML result

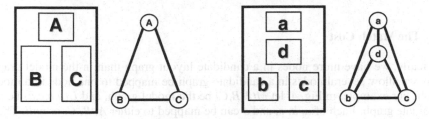

Fig. 4. Example layout and layout graphs

3 Layout Graph Matching

3.1 Layout Graph

A layout graph is a fully connected attributed relational graph. Each *node* corresponds to a segmented block on a page. The attributes of a node are the position and size of the bounding box, and the normalized font size (*small*, *middle*, or *large* as compared to the average font size over the whole page). An *edge* between a pair of nodes reflects the spatial relationship between two corresponding blocks in the image. We decompose this spatial relation into relations between block edges. For example, the relation between two vertical edges is normalized as *left-of*, *aligned*, or *right-of*. Similarly, the relation between two horizontal edges is *above*, *aligned*, or *below*. With 9 normalized edge relations (4 for left/right edges, 4 for top/bottom edges, and 1 for vertical central lines) we can describe the spatial relation between two blocks. If the distance between two block edges is within a threshold (we used 20 pixels for 300DPI images), they are regarded as *aligned*. The threshold depends on the skew of the image, and the document class.

Fig. 4 shows two layout graphs (attributes not shown). The attributes of edge AB in the left graph are shown in Fig. 5.

A model layout graph has some extra features. Each node carries a logical label, such as TITLE, AUTHOR, or ABSTRACT. There is a weight factor associated with each node/edge attribute. There is a *null*-cost defined for each node if it is not mapped to any other node in a candidate layout graph in a match.

Edge of block A	Relationship	Edge of block B
Left	To-the-right-of	Left
Left	To-the-left-of	Right
Right	To-the-right-of	Right
Right	To-the-left-of	Left
Top	Above	Top
Top	Above	Bottom
Bottom	Above	Bottom
Bottom	Above	Top
Vertical centre	To-the-left-of	Vertical centre

Fig. 5. Example edge attributes

3.2 The Match Cost

Typically, we have more nodes in a candidate layout graph than in the model graph. Thus we allow several nodes in a candidate graph be mapped to one node in a model graph. For example, in Fig. 4, let $M(A,B,C)$ be the model graph, and $U(a,b,c,d)$ be the candidate graph. Each of a, b, c, and d can be mapped to either A, B, C, or *null*. There are $4^4=256$ possible mappings. Here are two examples:

$$(A\text{-}a, B\text{-}b, C\text{-}c, A\text{-}d), (A\text{-}\Phi, B\text{-}d, C\text{-}a, \Phi\text{-}b, \Phi\text{-}c)$$

We need a metric to measure which mapping is the best. For a given mapping, an intermediate layout graph, T, is first constructed based on U such that the mapping between T and M is 1-1. Then a cost is computed for the 1-1 mapping and defined as the quality measurement of the mapping between U and M. The best match is the one with minimal cost.

Let $U = \{u_i\}_{i=1}^{K}$ be the candidate layout graph, $M = \{m_i\}_{i=1}^{L}$ be the model layout graph. The N-1 mapping from U to M is $f:U \to M$. The inverse mapping is defined as $f^{-1}(m) = \{u \mid u \in U, f(u) = m\}$. For a given subset of layout graph nodes, S, define a grouping operation g such that $g(S)$ represents a grouped node. In particular, the bounding box of $g(S)$ is the union of bounding boxes of nodes in S, and the font size of $g(S)$ is the average of font sizes of nodes in S weighed by character numbers of each node. If S is a null set, $g(S)$ is simply null, too. Then, the intermediate layout graph, T, is defined as $T = \bigcup_{m \in M} g(f^{-1}(m))$, where $g(f^{-1}(m))$ is the grouped node corresponding to m. Once nodes of T are determined, the edge attributes (i.e., spatial relationship between nodes in T) are computed. After that, T is fully determined.

Now the mapping from T to M is a 1-1 mapping, $h:T \to M$, deduced from $f:U \to M$. The match cost is defined as follows:

For a pair of mapped nodes, the cost is defined as the sum of differences between corresponding attributes, weighted by the weight factors in model node. If a model node is mapped to Φ, then a *null-cost* is incurred.

A cost is similarly defined for a pair of edges. A zero cost is defined if an edge is mapped to Φ.

The graph match cost is the sum of all node pair costs and edge pair costs. That is

$$C(T,M,h) = \sum_{t \in T} C_{t,h(t)} + \sum_{t \in T} \sum_{s \in T} C_{ts,h(t)h(s)} , \tag{1}$$

where $C_{t,h(t)}$ is the node pair cost,, and $C_{ts,h(t)h(s)}$ is the edge pair cost.

Once the best match is found, the logical label associated with each node m in the model is assigned to every node of $g(f^{-1}(m))$ in the candidate layout graph. If we have more than one model, each will give its best match and cost for a given U.

Given one model and one candidate, logical labeling is simply the search for the best match. Given multiple models, page classification is equivalent to the selection of the model with lowest match cost. The key is to find proper attributes and weights.

4   Finding the Match

Graph matching in general is NP-hard, and is itself an interesting problem. Practical solutions either employ branch and bound search with the help of heuristics, or non-linear optimization techniques [4]. It is even more difficult to do N-1 matching as required in our approach.

Our approach is a two-step approximate solution that aims at sub-optimal N-1 match. First, we search for the best 1-1 match from U to M, where U is the candidate graph, and M is the model graph. There are usually some unmatched nodes left in the candidate graph. In the second step, they are grouped to the matched nodes to form the intermediate graph, T. The match between T and M is a 1-1 mapping, determined by the best 1-1 mapping from U to M. Different grouping schemes result in different T. We search for the scheme that results in the best 1-1 match from T to M. From this grouping we can go back to get the sub-optimal N-1 match from U to M. Although in general it is sub-optimal, in our experiments it is usually satisfactory.

To address the computational expense involved in the first step, we took advantage of the fact that 1-1 match cost can be computed in an incremental way, and designed an efficient branch-and-bound search strategy. In experiments, the search took usually less than one second.

In the second step, we dramatically decreased the number of possible grouping schemes using the constraint that nodes in T should not overlap. The search in second step usually takes tens of milliseconds. Our assumption is that different logical parts on a page do not overlap, which is satisfied in most Manhattan style publications such as journals, proceedings, and business documents. Since this constraint is associated with each edge in the model graph, it is possible to relax it for some edges while keeping it for the rest. In our experiments, however, we imposed the non-overlapping constraint universally.

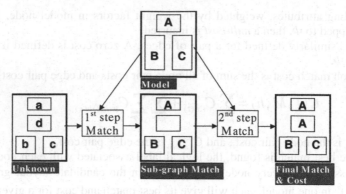

Fig. 6. Two-step N-1 graph matching procedure

5 Adaptive Model Learning

The model layout graph plays a key role in our matching procedure. If a model is ill defined, not only the result will be bad, but also the search for the best match may take a long time. It is important to find the appropriate features and weight factors. In our design, it is not too hard to write and/or adjust a model completely manually. However it is more time/cost efficient if accomplished automatically. In our previous work [10] we focused on the initialization of a model from a set of ground truth samples. Recently we continued to study adaptive model learning. For example, if the mistakenly labeled "author" is above "title", we could increase the weight associated with their vertical spatial relationship to force "author" be placed below "title". Inspired by the error back propagation learning methods in training neural networks, we designed an adaptive learning algorithm for improving models.

Given a model, a sample segmentation, and the ground truth mapping between them, we start out finding the N-1 match between the segmentation and the model using the methods we presented in the section above. We then compare the result with the ground truth. If they are different, it means the false match somehow has a lower cost than the true match. Then we need to modify the model. The step size of the modification is small to avoid abrupt jumps.

To summarize, our model updating policy is the following (see Fig. 7):

Let G be the feature in ground truth, R be the feature in match result, M be the feature in model, and W be the weight factor.

If $G=R$, leave M and W intact.

Else, bias M towards G by a small preset step.

And if $|M-G| < |M-R|$, increase W by a small preset amount.

Or, i.e., $|M-G| > |M-R|$, decrease W by a small preset amount.

With the adaptive learning ability, it is possible to initialize a model with only one sample image, then to improve the model as new samples come in one at a time. If any errors occur, there could be different strategy as to how much training should be done. The sample could be used only once to improve the model, it could be trained upon until no error (unnecessarily the first error) occurs, or it could be trained upon for a certain times. Alternatively a number of the most recent seen samples are all passed into the training procedure to avoid over fitting to the new sample.

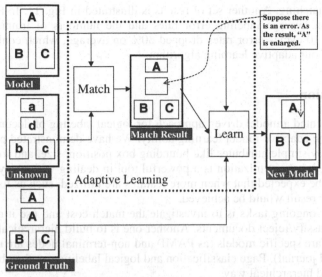

Fig. 7. Adaptive model learning procedure

6   Experiments

Our data set in this experiment consists of 80 title pages from 4 journal/conference proceedings, 20 pages from each. All of them are black-and-white images scanned at 300 DPI. In Fig. 8 four representative pages are shown. They share a common layout of general two-column journal title pages, yet slight differences exist in running headers, footers, page numbers, etc. Segmentation is done by off the shelf commercial OCR product from ScanSoft. We only used the position of segmented blocks, not OCR result or font information.

We adopted the leave-one-out strategy to achieve near real life testing environment. That is, for each one of the 20 pages, we pick it out as testing sample for once and use the other 19 as training samples. In this way we can get 20 testing results and then average them out. More precisely, suppose

1. $S = \{P_j; j=1,\ldots,\|S\|\}$ is the set of all sample pages, where P_j is the jth page plus ground truth labels.
2. For each $s=1,\ldots,\|S\|$, S is divided into two subsets: $TE_s = \{P_s\}$, and $TR_s = S - TE_s$.
3. The ith generation model for testing sample Ps is learned as
   if i=1 $m_s^{(i)} = $ Initialize(TR_s),
   otherwise $m_s^{(i)} = $ Improve$(TR_s, m_s^{(i-1)})$
4. The ith generation testing result for sample P_s is $R_s^{(i)} = $ Match $(P_s, m_s^{(i)})$.
5. The ith generation error count is $e_s^{(i)} = $ Compare$(R_s^{(i)}, P_s)$.
6. The number of blocks in P_s is b_s.
7. The ith generation average error rate is defined as $E_s^{(i)} = \sum_{s=1}^{\|S\|} e_s^{(i)} \Big/ \sum_{s=1}^{\|S\|} b_s$.

Fig. 10 (a) shows one sample page; (b) shows a visualization of the model; (c) is the labeling result after first step sub-graph matching; and (d) is the final result after second step matching. Another set of results is illustrated in Fig. 11. In Fig. 9 the relation between average labeling error rates and the numbers of training cycles is shown. After 10 cycles error rates dropped 30% on average, which confirms the effectiveness of our adaptive learning algorithm.

7 Conclusion

We have presented a model driven approach for logical labeling of document images, focusing on the adaptive model learning ability. We have demonstrated promising results using only simple attributes like bounding box position, size, and font size. This suggests that global optimization is a powerful tool in dealing with noisy and variant data. It could be expected that when more features are utilized, such as font style, text content, better result would be achieved.

One of our ongoing tasks is to investigate the match cost and use it as a distance measure to classify/reject documents. Another one is to build hierarchical model base whose leaves are specific models (as PAMI) and non-terminal nodes are unified models (as general journal). Page classification and logical labeling can then be done in an integrated, and hierarchical way.

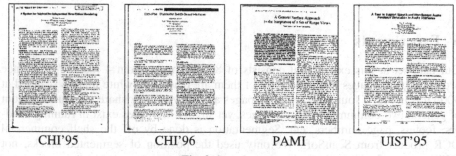

CHI'95   CHI'96   PAMI   UIST'95

Fig. 8. Sample pages

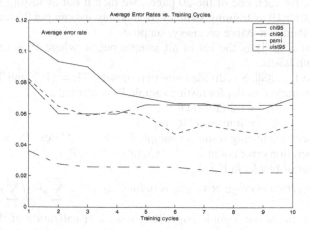

Fig. 9. Average error rates vs. training cycles

(a) Original image with
segmentation box overlaid

(b) Visualization of model

(c) Result of sub-graph matching

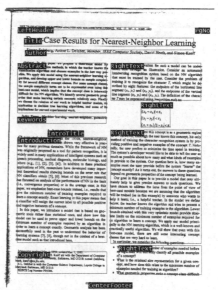

(d) Final result of N-1 graph matching

Fig. 10. Example image, model, and labeling result (I)

234   J. Liang and D. Doermann

(a) Original image with segmentation box overlaid

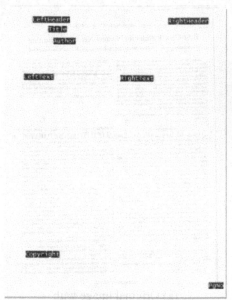

(b) Visualization of model

(c) Result of sub-graph matching

(d) Final result of N-1 graph matching

Fig. 11. Example image, model, and labeling result (II)

References

1. O. Altamura, F. Esposito, and D. Malerba. "Transforming paper documents into xml format with WISDOM++". Journal of Document Analysis and Recognition, 2000, 3(2):175–198.
2. T. A. Bayer and H. Walischewski. "Experiments on extracting structural information from paper documents using syntactic pattern analysis". In Proceedings of The Third International Conference on Document Analysis And Recognition, 1995, pp. 476–479.
3. A. Dengel, R. Bleisinger, F. Fein, R. Hoch, F. Hones, and M. Malburg. "OfficeMAID – a system for office mail analysis, interpretation and delivery". In International Workshop on Document Analysis Systems, 1994, pp. 253–276.
4. S. Gold and A. Rangarajan. "A graduated assignment algorithm for graph matching". IEEE Trans. Pattern Anal. Machine Intell., 1996, 18(4):377–388.
5. T. Hu and R. Ingold. "A mixed approach toward an efficient logical structure recognition from document images". Electronic Publishing, 1993, 6(4):457–468.
6. Y. Ishitani. "Model-based information extraction method tolerant of OCR errors for document images". In Proceedings of The Sixth International Conference on Document Analysis And Recognition, 2001, pp. 908–915.
7. M. Krishnamoorthy, G. Nagy, S. Seth, and M. Viswananthan. "Syntactic segmentation and labeling of digitized pp. from technical journals". IEEE Transactions On Pattern Analysis And Machine Intelligence, 1993, 15(7):737–747.
8. G. I. Palermo and Y. A. Dimitriadis. "Structured document labeling and rule extraction using a new recurrent fuzzy-neural system". In Proceedings of The Fifth International Conference on Document Analysis And Recognition, 1999, pp. 181–184.
9. H. Walischewske. "Learning regions of interest in postal automation". In Proceedings of The Fifth International Conference on Document Analysis And Recognition, 1999, pp. 317–340.
10. J. Liang and D. Doermann. "Page classification through logical labeling". (To be published) In Proceedings of The International Conference of Pattern Recognition, 2002.

A Ground-Truthing Tool for Layout Analysis Performance Evaluation

A. Antonacopoulos and H. Meng

PRImA Group, Department of Computer Science, University of Liverpool
Peach Street, Liverpool, L69 7ZF, United Kingdom
http://www.csc.liv.ac.uk/~prima

Abstract. There is a significant need for performance evaluation of Layout Analysis methods. The greatest stumbling block is the lack of sufficient ground truth. In particular, there is currently no ground-truth for the evaluation of the performance of page segmentation methods dealing with complex-shaped regions and documents with non-uniformly oriented regions.

This paper describes a new, flexible, ground-truthing tool. It is fast and easy to use as it performs page segmentation to obtain a first description of regions. The ground-truthing system allows for the editing (merging, splitting and shape alteration) of each of the region outlines obtained from page segmentation. The resulting ground-truth regions are described in terms of isothetic polygons to ensure flexibility and wide applicability. The system also provides for the labelling of each of the ground truth regions according to the type of their content and their logical function. The former can be used to evaluate page classification, while the latter can be used in assessing logical layout structure extraction.

1 Introduction

Layout Analysis is a key phase in any document image analysis and recognition system. Layout Analysis comprises three main stages: *page segmentation*, *page classification* and *layout structure extraction*. Page segmentation identifies the regions of interest in the document image, typically coherent printed regions such as text paragraphs or columns, graphics, images, and line art. Page classification determines the type of the content of the identified regions of interest. The goal of the third stage is to describe the structure of the layout in terms of geometric and topological properties of regions (physical layout structure) and, possibly, also in terms of the function of each region (logical layout structure). The latter may be deduced from the physical layout structure but more often than not it requires additional information about the fonts used and the recognised content of each region.

Over the last two decades, a plethora of layout analysis—page segmentation in particular—methods have been reported in the literature. It can be argued that the field is now beginning to mature and yet new methods are being proposed claiming to outperform existing ones. Frequently, each algorithm is devised with a specific application in mind and is fine-tuned to the test image data set used by its authors,

D. Lopresti, J. Hu, and R. Kashi (Eds.): DAS 2002, LNCS 2423, pp. 236–244, 2002.
© Springer-Verlag Berlin Heidelberg 2002

thus making a direct comparison with other algorithms difficult. The need for objective performance evaluation of Layout Analysis algorithms is evident.

In the wider field of Document Image Analysis, significant activity has concentrated on evaluating OCR results [1][2]. In the case of OCR the comparison of experimental results with ground truth is straightforward (ASCII characters) and lends itself to more elaborate analysis using string-matching theory to calculate errors and associated costs. Consequently, it is possible to automate OCR evaluation using large-scale test-databases [3].

A page segmentation evaluation system based on OCR results was proposed as a result of extensive experience in OCR evaluation at UNLV [4]. Although the OCR-based approach has the benefit of allowing for black box testing of complete (OCR-oriented) systems, it does not provide enough detailed information for researchers in Layout Analysis. In addition, there is not always a direct correspondence between segmentation performance and errors in the OCR result. Finally, this method ignores the non-textual entities on the page.

The other category of page segmentation performance evaluation approaches comprises methods that compare *regions* (segmentation result and ground-truth). There are two kinds of region-based approaches: *pixel-based* and *geometric description-based*. A flexible approach that deals with non-rectangular regions has been developed at Xerox [5]. This approach circumvents the problem of comparing regions when different geometric representation schemes are used, by performing a pixel-level comparison of regions (result and ground truth). The pixel-based comparison, however, is considerably slower than if a description-based comparison were to be used. Furthermore, although halftones are taken into account there is no provision for other non-textual components on a page.

A new layout analysis performance evaluation framework based on *geometric* comparison of regions is being developed at the University of Liverpool [6]. The regions are represented by their contours (as isothetic polygons), enabling fast and efficient comparison of segmentation results with ground truth (there is no need for image accesses). The main benefit of that system is that it can describe complex layouts and compare them (using an interval-based description [8]) with efficiency very close to that of comparing rectangles.

For any performance evaluation approach, the Achilles' heel is the availability of ground truth. As ground-truthing cannot (by definition) be fully automated, it remains a laborious and, therefore, expensive process. One approach is to use synthetic data [3]. It is the authors' opinion, however, that for the realistic evaluation of layout analysis methods, 'real' scanned documents give a better insight. Furthermore, it should be noted that there is currently no ground truth available for the evaluation of methods analysing complex layouts having non-rectangular regions.

For OCR evaluation, definitive ground truth can be relatively easily generated by typing (albeit still time-consuming). In the case of region-based evaluation approaches, however, ground-truthing is not as straightforward. In the pixel-based approach, every pixel of each region has to be correctly labelled, a potentially difficult and very laborious task in the case of complex layouts. In the geometric comparison approach, a flexible and accurate description of regions is essential.

This paper presents a tool that generates ground truth using a flexible page segmentation approach [7] as a first step. This tool facilitates the editing (correction) of region contours (isothetic polygons) and also enables the specification of the type and function of each region (to evaluate page classification and logical labelling).

A brief description of the new performance evaluation framework and the description of regions is given in the next section, The required ground truth is specified in Section 3. Each of the aspects of the ground-truthing system is described in Section 4 and its subsections. The paper concludes with a discussion in Section 5.

2   Performance Evaluation Framework

The motivation for the new performance evaluation framework is to provide *detailed information for developers* on both the local (page) and the global (whole data set) levels. This in contrast to benchmarking where one is only interested in comparative analysis where a final performance figure suffices. The new framework enables the evaluation of algorithms under an increased number of significant conditions that were not possible under past approaches. Such conditions include complex layouts with non-rectangular regions and regions with non-uniform orientations. The description of each region (and of the page as a whole) is based on interval structures [6] readily obtained from isothetic polygon contours. In this description, the area of a region is represented by a number of rectangular horizontal intervals whose height is determined by the corners of the contour polygon [8]. This (interval structure) representation of regions is very accurate and flexible since each region can have any size, shape and orientation without affecting the analysis method. Furthermore, the interval structure makes checking for inclusion and overlaps, and calculation of area, possible with very few operations.

3   Ground Truth

Region representation is of fundamental importance in any performance evaluation system. A region is defined here to be the smallest logical entity on the page. For Layout Analysis performance evaluation, a region is a paragraph in terms of text (body text, header, footnote, page number, caption etc.), or a graphic region (halftone, line-art, images, horizontal/vertical ruling etc.). Composite elements of a document, such as tables or figures with embedded text, are considered each as a single (composite) region.

The choice of a region representation scheme is crucial for efficiency and accuracy. While rectangles (bounding boxes) enable the simplest region comparisons, they are not suitable for complex-shaped regions. In the performance evaluation framework mentioned above, any region can be represented by an interval structure derived from an isothetic polygon. Isothetic polygons describe regions flexibly and they can be easily used in the context of other performance evaluation applications [9] as well as in the system mentioned above. Simplicity is also retained as for rectangular regions the isothetic polygon would be in essence a bounding box.

To ensure simplicity and wide applicability as outlined above, the chosen ground truth representation of a region is an isothetic polygon.

The ground truth generated by the tool described in this paper includes the following for each region: its description in terms of an isothetic polygon (a list of vertices in anti-clockwise sequence), the type of its contents, and its functional (logical) label.

4   The System

The input to the system is a page image. At the moment, only binary images are supported. Regions of interest are identified using a page segmentation method. The objective is to identify regions in the image as close as possible to the target regions. Naturally, no page segmentation method would produce perfect results. Therefore, it is desirable that the inevitable errors are as straightforward as possible.

The page segmentation method used here is the white tiles method [7]. Apart from its ability to identify and describe complex-shaped regions in different orientations, it is also fast and produces isothetic polygons. If required, another page segmentation method can be used, either in addition or as a replacement.

Having an initial description of the regions, the user has the option to edit individual polygons, merge polygons that should be part of the same region, and split polygons that should represent different regions.

When the user is satisfied with the representation of the regions, further information (type of region contents and functional label) can be specified for each of the polygons in the description of the page.

The following sections describe these processes in more detail.

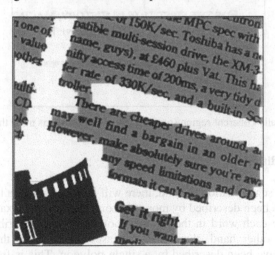

Fig. 1. An example of region description after page segmentation.

4.1   Page Segmentation

The white tiles page segmentation method [7] is part of the white tile approach that also performs page classification [8] and region orientation estimation [10], using the description of the background space. It is equally applicable to the segmentation of images of document pages having both traditional and complex layouts. The underlining idea is to efficiently produce a flexible description (by means of tiles) of the background space that surrounds the printed regions in the page image under conditions such as the presence of non-rectangular regions and regions with different orientations. Using this description of space, the contours of printed regions are identified with significant accuracy. The white tiles approach is fast as there is no need for skew detection and correction, and only few simple operations are performed on the description of the background (not on the pixel-based data).

In the ground-truthing system, the white tiles page segmentation method is set to slightly over-segment regions. This ensures that the number of inadvertent mergings of regions of different types is kept to a minimum.

At the end of the page segmentation process, all printed regions on the page image are represented by isothetic polygons. An example of the description of part of a page can be seen in Figure 1.

Fig. 2. A logically coherent region (running footer) described as more than one region.

4.2   Region Editing

As with any page segmentation method, there will be cases where a logically coherent printed region has been described by more than one polygon. An example can be seen in Figure 2 where each word in the running footer has been described by a separate polygon. On the other hand, there may be cases where more than one logically distinct regions have been described by a single polygon. This is frequently the case with paragraphs in a single column when there is no extra spacing between the paragraphs (see Figure 1).

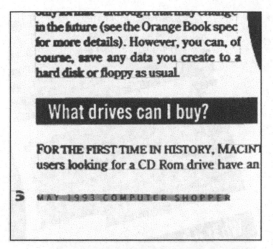

Fig. 3. The resulting single region after merging.

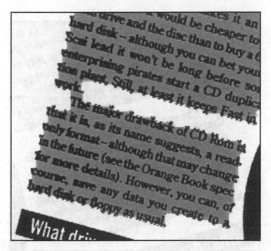

Fig. 4. More than one paragraph in a column described as one region.

The system provides editing facilities for merging and splitting polygonal regions. In addition, the position of each vertex of a polygon can be adjusted (by clicking and dragging) to ensure the regions are accurately described to the user's satisfaction. It is important to mention here that the system makes no assumptions about the orientation of the regions and about their shape. The system can be used to ground-truth skewed images as well.

Merging regions
When two or more regions resulting from page segmentation must be merged, the user selects the corresponding polygons and clicks on the 'merge' button. The merging process sorts all selected polygons according to their position and starts

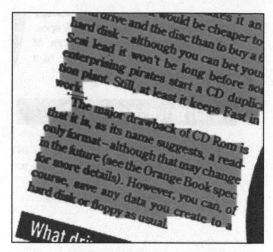

Fig. 5. Placement of a line indicating the direction and position of splitting.

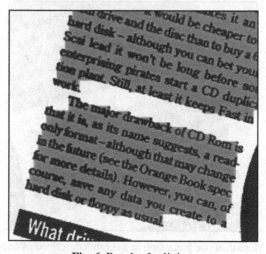

Fig. 6. Result of splitting.

merging them into an aggregate polygon, one at a time, starting from the top-left-most one. The resulting polygon has the same structure (list of vertices ordered anti-clockwise) as the polygons resulting from page segmentation.

The aggregate polygon resulting from merging the words in the running footer of Figure 2 can be seen in Figure 3.

Splitting Regions
The division (splitting) of an identified region into two separate regions is slightly more complicated than the merging operation described above. The operation involves the examination of the background space along the split direction so that each of the resulting regions does not contain excess space.

First, the user selects the polygon corresponding to the region to be split. For instance, one may wish to split the column in Figure 4 into separate paragraphs. Then they place a line indicating the direction of the split (see Figure 5) and click the 'split' button.

The system first calculates the intersection of the splitting line with the selected polygon. Within the polygon boundary either side of the split line, black pixels are counted along the direction of the split line (there should be no black pixels along the split line itself. As soon as the first black pixels are encountered along parallel lines on either side of the split line, the boundaries of the new polygons (where the split will occur) are fixed to these lines. New vertices are inserted in the original polygon at its intersections with the lines denoting the split positions. To ensure conformity with other polygons, the vertices are ordered so that the resulting two polygons will have their vertices ordered anti-clockwise. The result from the splitting of the region in Figure 4 can be seen in Figure 6.

Region Labelling
Once the regions are correctly described by the polygons (after editing), the user can enter further information about the regions. By right-clicking in a region they can select the option to associate a region with its content type and logical label. A dialog box appears that is filled in with the necessary information and optional comments. For ease of use, regions that have been indicated by the user as completely edited and specified are drawn in a different colour.

5   Concluding Remarks

A ground-truthing system for layout Analysis performance evaluation has been described in its context (the system is currently in the last stages of development and it is anticipated that it will be ready for demonstration at DAS'02). The system addresses a significant need to produce ground truth, especially for complex layouts (where no ground truth exists at the moment).

Flexibility is one of the main advantages of this system. The choice of region representation (isothetic polygons) enables accurate description and the resulting ground truth is not only applicable to the performance evaluation framework described here. Furthermore, the page segmentation method can be changed or enhanced, or even use the results of alternative methods, each better tuned perhaps to different types of documents.

The system is implemented in Visual C++ and works on PCs. This choice was made in order to ensure wide compatibility and enhanced performance. The system will be made available to the document analysis community.

References

[1]   G. Nagy, "Document Image Analysis: Automated Performance Evaluation", Document Image Analysis Systems, A.L. Spitz and A. Dengel (eds.), World Scientific, 1995.

[2]   C.H. Lee and T. Kanungo, "The architecture of TRUEVIZ: A groundTRUth / metadata Editing and VisualiZing toolkit", *Symposium on Document Image Understanding Technology*, April 23 –25, 2001, Columbia, Maryland,

[3]   I.T. Philips, S. Chen and R.M. Haralick, "CD-ROM Document Database Standard", Proceedings of 2nd International Conference on Document Analysis and Recognition (ICDAR'93), Tsukuba, Japan, 1993, pp. 478–483.

[4]   J. Kanai, S.V. Rice, T.A. Nartker and G. Nagy, "Automated Evaluation of OCR Zoning", IEEE Transactions on Pattern Recognition and Machine Intelligence, Vol. 17, No. 1, January, 1995, pp. 86–90.

[5]   B.A. Yanikoglu and L. Vincent, "Pink Panther: A Complete Environment for Ground-Truthing and Benchmarking Document Page Segmentation", Pattern Recognition, Vol. 31, No. 9, 1998, pp. 1191–1204.

[6]   A. Antonacopoulos and A Brough, "Methodology for Flexible and Efficient Analysis of the Performance of Page Segmentation Algorithms", Proceedings of 5th International Conference on Document Analysis and Recognition (ICDAR'99), Bangalore, India, 1999, IEEE-CS Press, pp. 451–454.

[7]   A. Antonacopoulos, "Page Segmentation Using the Description of the Background", Computer Vision and Image Understanding, Special issue on Document Analysis and Retrieval, Vol. 70, No. 3, June 1998, pp. 350–369.

[8]   A. Antonacopoulos and R.T. Ritchings, "Representation and Classification of Complex-Shaped Printed Regions Using White Tiles", Proceedings of 3rd International Conference on Document Analysis and Recognition (ICDAR'95), Montreal, Canada, 1995, Vol. 2, pp. 1132–1135.

[9]   B. Gatos, S.L. Mantzaris and A. Antonacopoulos, "First International Newspaper Contest", Proceedings of the 6th International Conference on Document Analysis and Recognition (ICDAR2001), Seattle, USA, September 2001, pp. 1190–1194.

[10] A. Antonacopoulos, "Local Skew Angle Estimation from Background Space in Text Regions", Proceedings of the 4th International Conference on Document Analysis and Recognition (ICDAR'97), Ulm, Germany, August 18–20, 1997, IEEE-CS Press, pp. 684–688.

Simple Layout Segmentation of Gray-Scale Document Images

A. Suvichakorn, S. Watcharabusaracum, and W. Sinthupinyo

National Electronics and Computer Technology Center,
112 Phahol Yothin Road, Klong Luang, Pathumthani 12120, Thailand

Abstract. A simple yet effective layout segmentation of document images is proposed in this paper. First, $n \times n$ blocks are roughly labeled as background, line, text, images, graphics or mixed class. For blocks in mixed class, they are split into 4 sub-blocks and the process repeats until no mixed class is found. By exploiting Savitzky-Golay derivative filter in the classification, the computation of features is kept to the minimum. Next, the boundaries of each object are refined. The experimental results yields a satisfactory results as a pre-process prior to OCR.

1 Introduction: Problems Stated

Like most Optical Character Recognition(OCR) systems, Thai OCR is suffered from compound documents, particularly in magazines or newspapers. For example, by doing connected component analysis for recognition, big objects such as images will cause memory run-out. In addition, lines or parts of graphic result in dropping of recognition accuracy. Thus, an effective layout segmentation is required as a pre-process to the OCR. The segmentation is also expected to duplicate the original document's layout to electronic form. On the other hand, the algorithm should not affect much in computation time of the system.

Therefore, a simple yet effective layout segmentation is proposed. The algorithm exploits texture-based multiscale segmentation and a set of post-processing rules to refine object boundaries. The computation is at a low level, by deriving classification's features from Savitzky-Golay filter[1], but the accuracy rate is *comparable* to those using DCT or wavelet decomposition[2] in recent techniques.

This paper is organized as follows. In section 2, the algorithm is described. Next, the experimental results and the conclusion of this study will be presented in sections 3 and 4 respectively.

2 Algorithm

The Classifier consists of two parts: *block classification* and *boundary refinement*. In block classification, each block is labled as background, line, text, images or graphics. Then, boundary refinement is applied to obtain accurate boundaries of each object. In this part, tables are also extracted from graphic objects using a set of rules.

D. Lopresti, J. Hu, and R. Kashi (Eds.): DAS 2002, LNCS 2423, pp. 245–248, 2002.

2.1   Block Classification

We starts the block classification with an initial block size of 64×64 pixels. In each block, 5 features are calculated to catagorize the block as background, text, lines, graphics or images. Blocks, which contains many objects and do not fall in any stated classes are assigned to an intermediate class. Such cases will be analyzed by splitting the block into 4 sub-blocks. The process continues until no intermediate class is found or the block size is 16×16 pixels. The smaller block size than this provides not enough information for classifying and may confuse the classifier what it actually contains.

Classification's Features. Since one requirement of the segmentation is minimum computation, the features we selected here are easy to compute but have high performance in classification. First, mean(μ) and standard deviation(σ) of intensity(I) are used to separate background and images from text and graphics.

Note here that text in non-white background may have μ and σ close to those of images. Moreover, such text could not be recognized correctly without binarization. To solve the problem, we calculate active pixels(α), using the method of adaptive thresholding in binarization, to find amounts of pixels that should be active or black when the binarization is applied.

$$\alpha = \sum_{blocksize} (I < \mu - k \cdot \sigma), \tag{1}$$

where k is a weighting factor. This is the easiest way to compute thresholds. The faster and more effective can be found in the most recent research [3].

Next, we will find more features to classify text and graphics. These two classes have similar global characteristics in sense of μ and σ. However, we can use *uniqueness* of character's pattern to separate them. Thus, we introduce two features derived from 1-D Savitzky-Golay filter, which is well-known for its low computation time. Here, we use the filter to find the second derivatives of average intensity, calculated in X ($I_{av,x}$) and Y ($I_{av,y}$) direction. This is different from typical derivative filter, such as the Sobel filter, because the Savitzky-Golay filter also performs noise filtering while it finds the derivatives. Therefore, we can adjust the parameters of the filter, e.g. degree and window's width(M), to gain the suitable *texture* characteristics like edges or frequency response of the image blocks.

The equation of the two parameters, namely D_x and D_y are described briefly below.

$$D_x = \sum_{blockwidth} a_2; \tag{2}$$

$$D_y = \sum_{blockheight} a_2; \tag{3}$$

where a_2 is the second coefficient of the Savitzky-Golay filter, which equals to its second derivative. Let f denote input vector ($f_{i-M}, \ldots, f_{i+M}$) at the position i in the I_{av} stream. Then, a_2 can be expressed symbollicaly as

$$a_2 = \{(\mathbf{A}^T\mathbf{A})^{-1}(\mathbf{A}^T\boldsymbol{f})\}_3 \qquad (4)$$

The notation $\{\}_3$ denotes the third element of vector $\boldsymbol{a}$ and $\boldsymbol{f}$ is $(I_{av,x})$ and $(I_{av,y})$ in equations 2 and 3, respectively. $\mathbf{A}$ is a design matrix, which is known *a priori*. Hence, we can compute the coefficients $(\mathbf{A}^T\mathbf{A})^{-1}\mathbf{A}^T$ prior to the filtering operation. The computation of $\mathbf{A}$ and its relation to the filter's degree and width are described in [1].

Classifier's Performance. In the learning process, we supervised the system with the training sets that are manually labeled. The output of the process is a decision tree, which minimizes misclassification error of the labeled data set by the Baysian approach. The trees are designed especially for each block size.

Let K be the number of classes. The misclassification error is defined as:

$$Error = \sum_i^K \sum_j^K P(\text{assigned class} = i \text{ and true class} = j) \qquad (5)$$

3   Boundary Refinement

Block information does not identify large objects such as headings or big pictures, etc. As a result, an image block containing parts of such objects will be classified incorrectly. Also, some times only parts of text occurs in a block and is labeled as graphics. Moreover, it is necessary to identify the image's or the textual column's coordinates to the OCR system. Consequently, the boundary refinement is applied to find the whole objects' boundaries.

- **The First Stride**: Region growing is applied to the label map in order to group blocks with same labels and change maybe-mislabeled blocks. For example, if a text block is enclosed by graphics, it is likely to be graphics. Besides, the graphic blocks close to images are possible to be edges or parts of images.
- **Textual Column Separation**: We calculate the best path that has minimum $\sum_{column} D_x$ less than a pre-defined threshold at 64×64 pixels block size. Next, we calculate the sum of the block's intensity in the path. The column is split at the highest (white) intensity column.
- **Closed Table Extraction**: Here, groups of vertical(high D_x, low D_y) and horizontal (high D_y, low D_x) lines with text within areconsidered. The lines are tracked to find inclided angles of the tables and rotate the region. We judge whether it is a table by significant peaks of intensity sum in X and Y direction. The table structure can be recognized by the algorithm in [4].

4   Experimental Results

20 Scanned images of pages from magazines, text books and newspapers were used as training images and another 20 images were used as test images. The

images were 8-bit gray scale, 200 dpi and had size of 1500 × 2000 pixels for newspapers and 2200 × 1600 pixels for others. The algorithm was written in Borland Builder C++ 5.0 and run on PentiumII - 500 MHz. The computation time was approximately 2 seconds. The Savitzky-Golay filter has the second degree and 11 pixels width. The approches we compare with are described in [2].

Table 1. Comparision of average misclassification errors in percent

Part I Only	Part I& Part II	Sobel Filter	DCT Bit rate	Wavelet (Haar)
10.40	9.59	13.10	10.15	18.50

We propose the algorithm as a choice instead of those hard-computing approaches. The results shown are comparable with the recent techniques and are a reliable guidance to identify the positions of objects. When apply to Thai OCR, the memory runout is clearly solved. Moreover, the algorithm increases a few recognition rate, because it disposes those parts of graphic that disturb the recognition system. The coordinates of the object, using corner positions of blocks, can provide information to duplicate the document's layout. However, due to limitation in block separation, if text is close to other objects less than 16 pixels, some characters will be lost. Though the result is satisfactory for OCR, the research recently continues on appropriate utilizing the filter's parameters at different degrees or window width. Faster and more effective region refinement is also helpful.

5   Conclusion

A new choice for document segmentation has been proposed in this paper. The algorithm is simple yet effective as a pre-processing of OCR.

References

1. A. Savitzky and M.J.E. Golay, Smoothing and differentiation of data by simplified least squares procedure. Analytical Chemistry **36** (1964) 1627–1639
2. I. Keslassy, M. Kalman, D. Wang, and B. Girod, Classification of Compound Images Based on Transform Coefficient Likelihood. Proc. ICIP 2001 (2001)
3. In-Kwon Kim, Dong-Wook Jung and Rae-Hong Park Document image binarization based on topographic analysis using a water flow model. Pattern Recognition, **35** (1) (2002) 265–277
4. Sarin Watcharabusaracum and Wasin Sinthupinyo Unknown Table Image Recognition. Proc. SNLP - Orietal COCOSDA 2002 (2002) 201–204

Detecting Tables in HTML Documents

Yalin Wang[1] and Jianying Hu[2]

[1] Dept. of Electrical Engineering, Univ. of Washington,
Seattle, WA 98195, US
ylwang@u.washington.edu
[2] Avaya Labs Research, 233 Mount Airy road,
Basking Ridge, NJ 07920, US
jianhu@avaya.com

Abstract. Table is a commonly used presentation scheme for describing relational information. Table understanding on the web has many potential applications including web mining, knowledge management, and web content summarization and delivery to narrow-bandwidth devices. Although in HTML documents tables are generally marked as `<table>` elements, a `<table>` element does not necessarily indicate the presence of a *genuine* relational table. Thus the important first step in table understanding in the web domain is the detection of the genuine tables. In our earlier work we designed a basic rule-based algorithm to detect genuine tables in major news and corporate home pages as part of a web content filtering system. In this paper we investigate a machine learning based approach that is trainable and thus can be automatically generalized to including any domain. Various features reflecting the layout as well as content characteristics of tables are explored. The system is tested on a large database which consists of 1,393 HTML files collected from hundreds of different web sites from various domains and contains over 10,000 leaf `<table>` elements. Experiments were conducted using the cross validation method. The machine learning based approach outperformed the rule-based system and achieved an F-measure of 95.88%.

1 Introduction

The increasing ubiquity of the Internet has brought about a constantly increasing amount of online publications. As a compact and efficient way to present relational information, tables are used frequently in web documents. Since tables are inherently concise as well as information rich, the automatic understanding of tables has many applications including knowledge management, information retrieval, web mining, summarization, and content delivery to mobile devices. The processes of table understanding in web documents include table detection, functional and structural analysis and finally table interpretation [3].

In this paper, we concentrate on the problem of table detection. The web provides users with great possibilities to use their own style of communication and expressions. In particular, people use the `<table>` tag not only for relational information display but also to create any type of multiple-column layout to

D. Lopresti, J. Hu, and R. Kashi (Eds.): DAS 2002, LNCS 2423, pp. 249–260, 2002.

facilitate easy viewing, thus the presence of the <table> tag does not necessarily indicate the presence of a true relational table. In this paper, we define *genuine* tables to be document entities where a two dimensional grid is semantically significant in conveying the logical relations among the cells [2]. Conversely, *Non-genuine* tables are document entities where <table> tags are used as a mechanism for grouping contents into clusters for easy viewing only. Examples of a genuine table and a non-genuine table can be found in Figure 1. While genuine tables in web documents could also be created without the use of <table> tags at all, we do not consider such cases in this article as they seem very rare from our experience. Thus, in this study, *Table detection* refers to the technique which classifies a document entity enclosed by the <table></table> tags as a genuine or non-genuine table.

Several researchers have reported their work on web table detection . Chen *et al.* used heuristic rules and cell similarities to identify tables and tested their algorithm on 918 tables form airline information web pages [1]. Yoshida *et al.* proposed a method to integrate WWW tables according to the category of objects presented in each table [4]. Their algorithm was evaluated on 175 tables.

In our earlier work, we proposed a rule-based algorithm for identifying genuinely tabular information as part of a web content filtering system for content delivery to mobile devices [2]. The algorithm was designed for major news and corporate web site home pages. It was tested on 75 web site front-pages and achieved an F-measure of 88.05%. While it worked reasonably well for the system it was designed for, it has the disadvantage that it is domain dependent and difficult to extend because of its reliance on hand-crafted rules.

To summarize, previous methods for web table detection all relied on heuristic rules and were only tested on a database that is either very small [2,4], or highly domain specific [1].

In this paper, we propose a new machine learning based approach for table detection from generic web documents. While many learning algorithms have been developed and tested for document analysis and information retrieval applications, there seems to be strong indication that good document representation including feature selection is more important than choosing a particular learning algorithm [12]. Thus in this work our emphasis is on identifying features that best capture the characteristics of a genuine table compared to a non-genuine one. In particular, we introduce a set of novel features which reflect the layout as well as content characteristics of tables. These features are then used in a tree classifier trained on thousands of examples. To facilitate the training and evaluation of the table classifier, we constructed a large web table ground truth database consisting of $1,393$ HTML files containing $11,477$ leaf <table> elements. Experiments on this database using the cross validation method demonstrate a significant performance improvement over the previously developed rule-based system.

The rest of the paper is organized as follows. We describe our feature set in Section 2, followed by a brief description of the decision tree classifier in Section 3. Section 4 explains the data collection process. Experimental results are then reported in Section 5 and we conclude with future directions in Section 6.

2   Features for Web Table Detection

Past research has clearly indicated that layout and content are two important aspects in table understanding [3]. Our features were designed to capture both of these aspects. In particular, we developed 16 features which can be categorized into three groups: seven layout features, eight content type features and one word group feature. In the first two groups, we attempt to capture the global composition of tables as well as the consistency within the whole table and across rows and columns. With the last feature, we investigate the discriminative power of words enclosed in tables using well developed text categorization techniques.

Before feature extraction, each HTML document is first parsed into a document hierarchy tree using Java Swing XML parser with W3C HTML 3.2 DTD [2]. A <table> node is said to be a *leaf table* if and only if there are no <table> nodes among its children [2]. Our experience indicates that almost all genuine tables are leaf tables. Thus in this study only leaf tables are considered candidates for genuine tables and are passed on to the feature extraction stage. In the following we describe each feature in detail.

2.1   Layout Features

In HTML documents, although tags like <TR> and <TD> (or <TH>) may be assumed to delimit table rows and table cells, they are not always reliable indicators of the number of rows and columns in a table. Variations can be caused by spanning cells created using <ROWSPAN> and <COLSPAN> tags. Other tags such as <BR> could be used to move content into the next row. To extract layout features reliably, we maintain a matrix to record all the cell spanning information and serve as a pseudo rendering of the table. Layout features based on row or column numbers are then computed from this matrix.

Given a table T, we compute the following four layout features:

- (1) and (2): Average number of columns, computed as the average number of cells per row, and the standard deviation.
- (3) and (4): Average number of rows, computed as the average number of cells per column, and the standard deviation.

Since the majority of tables in web documents contain characters, we compute three more layout features based on cell length in terms of number of characters:

- (5) and (6): Average overall cell length and the standard deviation.
- (7): Average *Cumulative length consistency, CLC*.

The last feature is designed to measure the cell length consistency along either row or column directions. It is inspired by the fact that most genuine tables demonstrate certain consistency either along the row or the column direction, but usually not both, while non-genuine tables often show no consistency in either direction. First, the average cumulative within-row length consistency,

CLC_r, is computed as follows. Let the set of cell lengths of the cells from row i be $\mathcal{R}_i$, $i = 1, \ldots, r$ (considering only non-spanning cells), and the the mean cell length for row $\mathcal{R}_i$ be m_i:

1. Compute cumulative length consistency within each $\mathcal{R}_i$: $CLC_i = \sum_{cl \in \mathcal{R}_i} LC_{cl}$. Here LC_{cl} is defined as: $LC_{cl} = 0.5 - D$, where $D = min\{\frac{|cl - m_i|}{m_i}, 1.0\}$. Intuitively, LC_{cl} measures the degree of consistency between cl and the mean cell length, with -0.5 indicating extreme inconsistency and 0.5 indicating extreme consistency. When most cells within $\mathcal{R}_i$ are consistent, the cumulative measure CLC_i is positive, indicating a more or less consistent row.
2. Take the average across all rows: $CLC_r = \frac{1}{r} \sum_{i=1}^{r} CLC_i$.

After the within-row length consistency CLC_r is computed, the within-column length consistency CLC_c is computed in a similar manner. Finally, the overall cumulative length consistency is computed as $CLC = max(CLC_r, CLC_c)$.

2.2   Content Type Features

Web documents are inherently multi-media and have more types of content than any traditional document. For example, the content within a `<table>` element could include hyperlinks, images, forms, alphabetical or numerical strings, etc. Because of the relational information it needs to convey, a genuine table is more likely to contain alpha or numerical strings than, say, images. The content type feature was designed to reflect such characteristics.

We define the set of content types $\mathcal{T} =$ {Image, Form, Hyperlink, Alphabetical, Digit, Empty, Others}. Our content type features include:

 - (1) - (7): The histogram of content type for a given table. This contributes 7 features to the feature set;
 - (8): Average *content type consistency*, CTC.

The last feature is similar to the cell length consistency feature. First, within-row content type consistency CTC_r is computed as follows. Let the set of cell type of the cells from row i as $\mathcal{T}_i$, $i = 1, \ldots, r$ (again, considering only non-spanning cells), and the dominant type for $\mathcal{T}_i$ be DT_i:

1. Compute the cumulative type consistency with each row $\mathcal{R}_i$, $i = 1, \ldots, r$: $CTC_i = \sum_{ct \in \mathcal{R}_i} D$, where $D = 1$ if ct is equal to DT_i and $D = -1$, otherwise.
2. Take the average across all rows: $CTC_r = \frac{1}{r} \sum_{i=1}^{r} CTC_i$.

The within-column type consistency is then computed in a similar manner. Finally, the overall cumulative type consistency is computed as: $CTC = max(CTC_r, CTC_c)$.

2.3   Word Group Feature

If we look at the enclosed text in a table and treat it as a "mini-document", table classification could be viewed as a text categorization problem with two broad categories: genuine tables and non-genuine tables. In order to explore the the potential discriminative power of table text at the word level, we experimented with several text categorization techniques.

Text categorization is a well studied problem in the IR community and many algorithms have been developed over the years (e.g., [6,7]). For our application, we are particularly interested in algorithms with the following characteristics. First, it has to be able to handle documents with dramatically differing lengths (some tables are very short while others can be more than a page long). Second, it has to work well on collections with a very skewed distribution (there are many more non-genuine tables than genuine ones). Finally, since we are looking for a feature that can be incorporated along with other features, it should ideally produce a continuous confidence score rather than a binary decision. In particular, we experimented with three different approaches: vector space, naive Bayes and weighted kNN. The details regarding each approach are given below.

Vector Space Approach. After morphing [9] and removing the infrequent words, we obtain the set of words found in the training data, $\mathcal{W}$. We then construct weight vectors representing genuine and non-genuine tables and compare that against the frequency vector from each new incoming table.

Let $\mathcal{Z}$ represent the non-negative integer set. The following functions are defined on set $\mathcal{W}$.

- $df^G : \mathcal{W} \rightarrow \mathcal{Z}$, where $df^G(w_i)$ is the number of genuine tables which include word w_i, $i = 1, ..., |\mathcal{W}|$;
- $tf^G : \mathcal{W} \rightarrow \mathcal{Z}$, where $tf^G(w_i)$ is the number of times word w_i, $i = 1, ..., |\mathcal{W}|$, appears in genuine tables;
- $df^N : \mathcal{W} \rightarrow \mathcal{Z}$, where $df^N(w_i)$ is the number of non-genuine tables which include word w_i, $i = 1, ..., |\mathcal{W}|$;
- $tf^N : \mathcal{W} \rightarrow \mathcal{Z}$, where $tf^N(w_i)$ is the number of times word w_i, $i = 1, ..., |\mathcal{W}|$, appears in non-genuine tables.
- $tf^T : \mathcal{W} \rightarrow \mathcal{Z}$, where $tf^T(w_i)$ is the number of times word w_i, $w_i \in \mathcal{W}$ appears in a new test table.

To simplify the notations, in the following discussion, we will use df_i^G, tf_i^G, df_i^N and tf_i^N to represent $df^G(w_i)$, $tf^G(w_i)$, $df^N(w_i)$ and $tf^N(w_i)$, respectively.

Let N^G, N^N be the number of genuine tables and non-genuine tables in the training collection, respectively and let $C = \max(N^G, N^N)$. Without loss of generality, we assume $N^G \neq 0$ and $N^N \neq 0$. For each word w_i in $\mathcal{W}$, $i = 1, ..., |\mathcal{W}|$, two weights, p_i^G and p_i^N are computed:

$$p_i^G = \begin{cases} tf_i^G log(\frac{df_i^G}{N^G} \frac{N^N}{df_i^N} + 1), & \text{when } df_i^N \neq 0 \\ tf_i^G log(\frac{df_i^G}{N^G} C + 1), & \text{when } df_i^N = 0 \end{cases} \tag{1}$$

$$p_i^N = \begin{cases} tf_i^N log(\frac{df_i^N}{N^N} \frac{N^G}{df_i^G} + 1), & \text{when } df_i^G \neq 0 \\ tf_i^N log(\frac{df_i^N}{N^N} C + 1), & \text{when } df_i^G = 0 \end{cases} \qquad (2)$$

As can be seen from the formulas, the definitions of these weights were derived from the traditional $tf * idf$ measures used in informational retrieval [6], with some adjustments made for the particular problem at hand.

Given a new incoming table, let us denote the set including all the words in it as $\mathcal{W}_n$. Since we only need to consider the words that are present in both $\mathcal{W}$ and $\mathcal{W}_n$, we first compute the *effective word set*: $\mathcal{W}_e = \mathcal{W} \cap \mathcal{W}_n$. Let the words in $\mathcal{W}_e$ be represented as w_{m_k}, where $m_k, k = 1, ..., |\mathcal{W}_e|$, are indexes to the words from set $\mathcal{W} = \{w_1, w_2, ..., w_{|\mathcal{W}|}\}$. we define the following weight vectors:

- Vector representing the genuine table class: $\vec{G_S} = \left(\frac{p_{m_1}^G}{U}, \frac{p_{m_2}^G}{U}, \cdots, \frac{p_{m_{|\mathcal{W}_e|}}^G}{U} \right)$,

  where U is the cosine normalization term: $U = \sqrt{\sum_{k=1}^{|\mathcal{W}_e|} p_{m_k}^G \times p_{m_k}^G}$.

- Vector representing the non-genuine table class: $\vec{N_S} = \left(\frac{p_{m_1}^N}{V}, \frac{p_{m_2}^N}{V}, \cdots, \frac{p_{m_{|\mathcal{W}_e|}}^N}{V} \right)$, where V is the cosine normalization term: $V = \sqrt{\sum_{k=1}^{|\mathcal{W}_e|} p_{m_k}^N \times p_{m_k}^N}$.

- Vector representing the new incoming table: $\vec{I_T} = \left(tf_{m_1}^T, tf_{m_2}^T, \cdots, tf_{m_{|\mathcal{W}_e|}}^T \right)$.

Finally, the word group feature is defined as the ratio of the two dot products:

$$W_{vs} = \begin{cases} \frac{\vec{I_T} \cdot \vec{G_S}}{\vec{I_T} \cdot \vec{N_S}}, & \text{when } \vec{I_T} \cdot \vec{N_S} \neq 0 \\ 1, & \text{when } \vec{I_T} \cdot \vec{G_S} = 0 \text{ and } \vec{I_T} \cdot \vec{N_S} = 0 \\ 10, & \text{when } \vec{I_T} \cdot \vec{G_S} \neq 0 \text{ and } \vec{I_T} \cdot \vec{N_S} = 0 \end{cases} \qquad (3)$$

Naive Bayes Approach. In the Bayesian learning framework, it is assumed that text data has been generated by a parametric model, and a set of training data is used to calculate Bayes optimal estimates of the model parameters. Then, using these estimates, Bayes rule is used to turn the generative model around and compute the probability of each class given an input document.

Word clustering is commonly used in a Bayes approach to achieve more reliable parameter estimation. For this purpose we implemented the distributional clustering method introduced by Baker and McCallum [8]. First stop words and words that only occur in less than 0.1% of the documents are removed. The resulting vocabulary has roughly 8000 words. Then distribution clustering is applied to group similar words together. Here the similarity between two words w_t and w_s is measured as the similarity between the class variable distributions they induce: $P(C|w_t)$ and $P(C|w_s)$, and computed as the average KL divergence between the two distributions. (see [8] for more details).

Assume the whole vocabulary has been clustered into M clusters. Let w_s represent a word cluster, and $C = \{g, n\}$ represent the set of class labels (g

for for genuine, n for non-genuine), the class conditional probabilities are (using Laplacian prior for smoothing):

$$P(w_s|C = g) = \frac{tf^G(w_s) + 1}{M + \sum_{i=1}^{M} tf^G(w_i)}; \quad (4)$$

$$P(w_s|C = n) = \frac{tf^N(w_s) + 1}{M + \sum_{i=1}^{M} tf^N(w_i)}. \quad (5)$$

The prior probabilities for the two classes are: $P(C = g) = \frac{N^G}{N^G + N^N}$ and $P(C = n) = \frac{N^N}{N^G + N^N}$.

Given a new table d_i, let $d_{i,k}$ represent the kth word cluster. Based on the Bayes assumption, the posterior probabilities are computed as:

$$P(C = g|d_i) = \frac{P(C = g)P(d_i|C = g)}{P(d_i)} \quad (6)$$

$$\sim \frac{P(C = g) \prod_{k=1}^{|d_i|} P(w_{i,k}|C = g)}{P(d_i)}; \quad (7)$$

$$P(C = n|d_i) = \frac{P(C = n)P(d_i|C = n)}{P(d_i)} \quad (8)$$

$$\sim \frac{P(C = n) \prod_{k=1}^{|d_i|} P(w_{i,k}|C = n)}{P(d_i)}. \quad (9)$$

Finally, the word group feature is defined as the ratio between the two:

$$W_{nb} = \frac{P(C = g) \prod_{k=1}^{|d_i|} P(w_{i,k}|C = g)}{P(C = n) \prod_{k=1}^{|d_i|} P(w_{i,k}|C = n)} = \frac{N^G}{N^N} \prod_{k=1}^{|d_i|} \frac{P(w_{i,k}|C = g)}{P(w_{i,k}|C = n)}. \quad (10)$$

Weighted kNN Approach. kNN stands for k-nearest neighbor classification, a well known statistical approach. It has been applied extensively to text categorization and is one of the top-performing methods [7]. Its principle is quite simple: given a test document, the system finds the k nearest neighbors among the training documents, and uses the category labels of these neighbors to compute the likelihood score of each candidate category. The similarity score of each neighbor document to the test documents is used as the weight for the category it belongs to. The category receiving the highest score is then assigned to the test document.

In our application the above procedure is modified slightly to generate the word group feature. First, for efficiency purpose, the same preprocessing and word clustering operations as described in the previous section is applied, which results in M word clusters. Then each table is represented by an M dimensional vector composed of the term frequencies of the M word clusters. The similarity score between two tables is defined to be the cosine value ($[0, 1]$) between the two corresponding vectors. For a new incoming table d_i, let the k training tables that are most similar to d_i be represented by $d_{i,j}, j = 1, ..., k$. Furthermore, let $sim(d_i, d_{i,j})$ represent the similarity score between d_i and $d_{i,j}$, and $C(d_{i,j})$ equals 1.0 if $d_{i,j}$ is genuine and -1.0 otherwise, the word group feature is defined as:

$$W_{knn} = \frac{\sum_{j=1}^{k} C(d_{i,j}) sim(d_i, d_{i,j})}{\sum_{j=1}^{k} sim(d_i, d_{i,j})}. \tag{11}$$

3   Classification Scheme

Various classification schemes have been widely used in web document processing and proved to be promising for web information retrieval [11]. For the table detection task, we decided to use a decision tree classifier because of the highly non-homogeneous nature of our features. Another advantage of using a tree classifier is that no assumptions of feature independence are required.

An implementation of the decision tree allowing continuous feature values described by Haralick and Shapiro [5] was used for our experiments. The decision tree is constructed using a training set of feature vectors with true class labels. At each node, a discriminant threshold is chosen such that it minimizes an impurity value. The learned discriminant function splits the training subset into two subsets and generates two child nodes. The process is repeated at each newly generated child node until a stopping condition is satisfied, and the node is declared as a terminal node based on a majority vote. The maximum impurity reduction, the maximum depth of the tree, and minimum number of samples are used as stopping conditions.

4   Data Collection and Ground Truthing

Instead of working within a specific domain, our goal of data collection was to get tables of as many different varieties as possible from the web. At the same time, we also needed to insure that enough samples of genuine tables were collected for training purpose. Because of the latter practical constraint we biased the data collection process somewhat towards web pages that are more likely to contain genuine tables. A set of key words often associated with tables were composed and used to retrieve and download web pages using the Google search engine. Three directories on Google were searched: the business directory and news directory using key words: {`table`, `stock`, `bonds`, `figure`, `schedule`, `weather`, `score`, `service`, `results`, `value`}, and the science directory using key words {`table`, `results`, `value`}. A total of 2,851 web pages were downloaded in this manner and we ground truthed 1,393 HTML pages out of these (chosen randomly among all the HTML pages). The resulting database contains 14,609 `<table>` elements, out of which 11,477 are leaf `<table>` elements. Among the leaf `<table>` elements, 1,740 (15%) are genuine tables and the remaining 9,737 are non-genuine tables.

5   Experiments

A hold-out method is used to evaluate our table classifier. We randomly divided
the data set into nine parts. The decision tree was trained on eight parts and
then tested on the remaining one part. This procedure was repeated nine times,
each time with a different choice for the test part. Then the combined nine part
results are averaged to arrive at the overall performance measures [5].

The output of the classifier is compared with the ground truth and the standard performance measures precision (P), recall (R) and F-measure (F) are computed. Let N_{gg}, N_{gn}, N_{ng} represent the number of samples in the categories "genuine classified as genuine", "genuine classified as non-genuine", and "non-genuine
classified as genuine", respectively, the performance measures are defined as:

$$R = \frac{N_{gg}}{N_{gg} + N_{gn}} \qquad P = \frac{N_{gg}}{N_{gg} + N_{ng}} \qquad F = \frac{R + P}{2}.$$

For comparison among different features we report the performance measures
when the best F-measure is achieved. The results of the table detection algorithm
using various features and feature combinations are given in Table 1. For both
the naive Bayes based and the kNN based word group features, 120 word clusters
were used ($M = 120$).

Table 1. Experimental results using various feature groups

	L	T	LT	LTW-VS	LTW-NB	LTW-KNN
R (%)	87.24	90.80	94.20	94.25	95.46	89.60
P (%)	88.15	95.70	97.27	97.50	94.64	95.94
F (%)	87.70	93.25	95.73	95.88	95.05	92.77

L: Layout features only.
T: Content type features only.
LT: Layout and content type features.
LTW-VS: Layout, content type and vector space based word group features.
LTW-NB: Layout, content type and naive Bayes based word group features.
LTW-KNN: Layout, content type and kNN based word group features.

As seen from the table, content type features performed better than layout
features as a single group, achieving an F-measure of 93.25%. However, when the
two groups were combined the F-measure was improved substantially to 95.73%,
reconfirming the importance of combining layout and content features in table
detection.

Among the different approaches for the word group feature, the vector space
based approach gave the best performance when combined with layout and content features. However even in this case the addition of the word group feature
brought about only a very small improvement. This indicates that the text enclosed in tables is not very discriminative, at least not at the word level. One
possible reason is that the categories "genuine" and "non-genuine" are too broad
for traditional text categorization techniques to be highly effective.

Overall, the best results were produced with the combination of layout, content type and vector space based word group features, achieving an F-measure of 95.88%. Figure 1 shows two examples of correctly classified tables, where Figure 1(a) is a genuine table and Figure 1(b) is a non-genuine table.

1961 (4-9-1)			
Date	Opponent	W/L	Score
Sept. 17	PITTSBURGH	W	27-24
Sept. 24	MINNESOTA	W	21-7
Oct. 1	Cleveland	L	25-7
Oct. 8	Minnesota	W	28-0
Oct. 15	N Y GIANTS	L	31-10
Oct. 22	PHILADELPHIA	L	43-7
Oct. 29	N Y. Giants	W	17-16
Nov. 5	ST LOUIS	L	31-17
Nov. 12	Pittsburgh	L	37-7
Nov. 19	WASHINGTON	T	28-28
Nov. 26	Philadelphia	L	35-13
Dec. 3	CLEVELAND	L	38-17
Dec. 10	St Louis	L	31-13
Dec. 17	Washington	L	34-24

Worldwide Sugar Sites

Links by Country	Prices, Reports & Subscriptions
Links to worldwide sugar industry sites	Sugar Prices, Physical, News
Agriculture	**Equipment & Machinery**
Fertilizers, Seeds, Agri Inputs	Sugar Manufacturing, Processing
Processing & Refining	**Financial Services**
Sugar Cane Millers, Sugar Beet Processors	Sugar Export/Import, Finance, Insurance
Traders & Brokers	**Associations & Organisations**
Physical, International, Futures	Consumers, Trade Bodies, Producers
Logistics & Packing	**Industrial Sugar Users**
Supervision, Bags, Shipping	Confectionery, Beverages
Government & Policy	**Research & Technical**
Environment, Tariffs, Health, Trade	Trade, Field, History, Factory

(a)   (b)

Fig. 1. Examples of correctly classified tables: (a) a genuine table; (b) a non-genuine table

Figure 2 shows a few examples where our algorithm failed. Figure 2(a) was misclassified as a non-genuine table, likely because its cell lengths are highly inconsistent and it has many hyperlinks which is unusual for genuine tables. Figure 2(b) was misclassified as non-genuine because its HTML source code contains only two <tr> tags. Instead of the <tr> tag, the author used <p> tags to place the multiple table rows in separate lines. This points to the need for a more carefully designed pseudo-rendering process.

Figure 2(c) shows a non-genuine table misclassified as genuine. A close examination reveals that it indeed has good consistency along the row direction. In fact, one could even argue that this is indeed a genuine table, with implicit row headers of *Title, Name, Company Affiliation* and *Phone Number*. This example demonstrates one of the most difficult challenges in table understanding, namely the ambiguous nature of many table instances (see [10] for a more detailed analysis on that).

Figure 2(d) was also misclassified as a genuine table. This is a case where layout features and the kind of shallow content features we used are not enough – deeper semantic analysis would be needed in order to identify the lack of logical coherence which makes it a non-genuine table.

For comparison, we tested the previously developed rule-based system [2] on the same database. The initial results (shown in Table 2 under "Original Rule Based") were very poor. After carefully studying the results from the initial experiment we realized that most of the errors were caused by a rule imposing a hard limit on cell lengths in genuine tables. After deleting that rule the rule-based

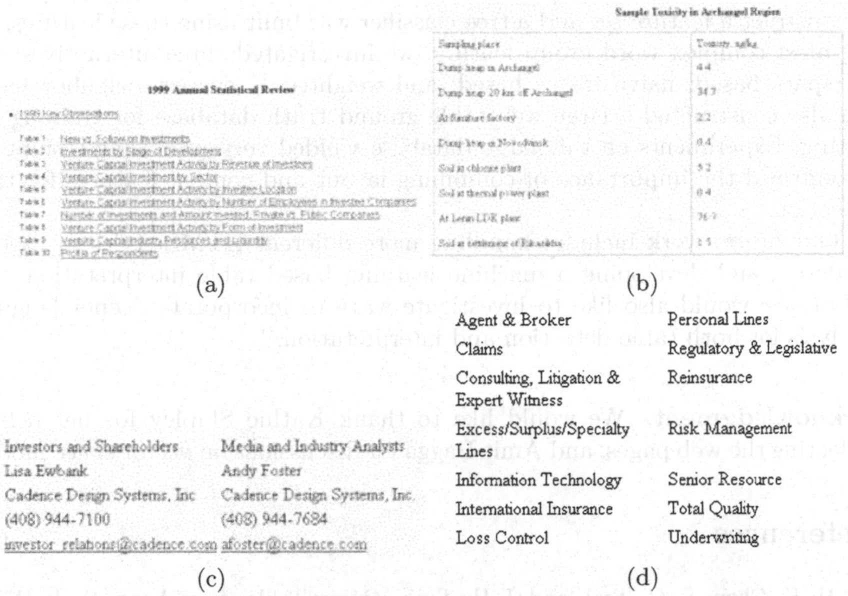

Sample Toxicity in Archangel Region

Sampling place	Toxicity, mg/kg
Dump heap in Archangel	4.4
Dump heap 20 km of Archangel	34.7
At furniture factory	2.2
Dump heap in Novodvinsk	0.4
Soil at chlorine plant	5.2
Soil at thermal power plant	0.4
At Lenin LDK plant	76.7
Soil in settlement of Eskariabis	2.5

1999 Annual Statistical Review

- 1999 New Observations

Table 1   New vc Follow-on Investments
Table 2   Investments by Stage of Development
Table 3   Venture Capital Investment Activity by Revenue of Investees
Table 4   Venture Capital Investment by Sector
Table 5   Venture Capital Investment Activity by Investee Location
Table 6   Venture Capital Investment Activity by Number of Employees in Investee Companies
Table 7   Number of Investments and Amount Invested, Private vs. Public Companies
Table 8   Venture Capital Investment Activity by Form of Investment
Table 9   Venture Capital Industry Resources and Liquidity
Table 10 Profile of Respondents

(a)

(b)

Investors and Shareholders	Media and Industry Analysts
Lisa Ewbank	Andy Foster
Cadence Design Systems, Inc	Cadence Design Systems, Inc.
(408) 944-7100	(408) 944-7684
investor_relations@cadence.com	afoster@cadence.com

(c)

Agent & Broker	Personal Lines
Claims	Regulatory & Legislative
Consulting, Litigation & Expert Witness	Reinsurance
Excess/Surplus/Specialty Lines	Risk Management
Information Technology	Senior Resource
International Insurance	Total Quality
Loss Control	Underwriting

(d)

Fig. 2. Examples of misclassified tables: (a), (b) genuine tables misclassified as non-genuine; (c), (d) non-genuine tables misclassified as genuine

system achieved much improved results (shown in Table 2 under "Modified Rule Based"). However, the proposed machine learning based method still performs considerably better in comparison. This demonstrates that systems based on hand-crafted rules tend to be brittle and do not generalize well. In this case, even after careful manual adjustment in a new database, it still does not work as well as an automatically trained classifier.

Table 2. Experimental results of the rule based system

	Original Rule Based	Modified Rule Based
R (%)	48.16	95.80
P (%)	75.70	79.46
F (%)	61.93	87.63

A direct comparison to other previous results [1,4] is not possible currently because of the lack of access to their system. However, our test database is clearly more general and far larger than the ones used in [1] and [4], while our precision and recall rates are both higher.

6   Conclusion and Future Work

We present a machine learning based table detection algorithm for HTML documents. Layout features, content type features and word group features were used to construct a feature set and a tree classifier was built using these features. For the most complex word group feature, we investigated three alternatives: vector space based, naive Bayes based, and weighted K nearest neighbor based. We also constructed a large web table ground truth database for training and testing. Experiments on this large database yielded very promising results and reconfirmed the importance of combining layout and content features for table detection.

Our future work includes handling more different HTML styles in pseudo-rendering and developing a machine learning based table interpretation algorithm. We would also like to investigate ways to incorporate deeper language analysis for both table detection and interpretation.

Acknowledgment. We would like to thank Kathie Shipley for her help in collecting the web pages, and Amit Bagga for discussions on vector space models.

References

1. H.-H. Chen, S.-C. Tsai, and J.-H. Tsai: Mining Tables from Large Scale HTML Texts. In: The 18th Int. Conference on Computational Linguistics, Saarbrücken, Germany, July 2000.
2. G. Penn, J. Hu, H. Luo, and R. McDonald: Flexible Web Document Analysis for Delivery to Narrow-Bandwidth Devices. In: ICDAR2001, Seattle, WA, USA, September 2001.
3. M. Hurst: Layout and Language: Challenges for Table Understanding on the Web. In: First International Workshop on Web Document Analysis, Seattle, WA, USA, September 2001, http://www.csc.liv.ac.uk/ wda2001.
4. M. Yoshida, K. Torisawa, and J. Tsujii: A Method to Integrate Tables of the World Wide Web. In: First International Workshop on Web Document Analysis, Seattle, WA, USA, September 2001, http://www.csc.liv.ac.uk/ wda2001/.
5. R. Haralick and L. Shapiro: Computer and Robot Vision. Addison Wesley, 1992.
6. T. Joachims: A Probabilistic Analysis of the Rocchio Algorithm with TFIDF for Text Categorization. In: The 14th International Conference on Machine Learning, Nashville, Tennessee, 1997.
7. Y. Yang and X. Liu: A Re-Examination of Text Categorization Methods, In: SIGIR'99, Berkeley, California, 1999.
8. D. Baker and A.K. McCallum: Distributional Clustering of Words for Text Classification, In: SIGIR'98, Melbourne, Australia, 1998.
9. M. F. Porter: An Algorithm for Suffix Stripping. In: Program, Vol. 14, no.3, 1980.
10. J. Hu, R. Kashi, D. Lopresti, G. Nagy, and G. Wilfong: Why Table Ground-Truthing is Hard. In: ICDAR2001, Seattle, WA, September 2001.
11. A. McCallum, K. Nigam, J. Rennie, and K. Seymore: Automating the Construction of Internet Portals with Machine Learning. In: Information Retrieval Journal, vol. 3, 2000.
12. D. Mladenic: Text-learning and related intelligent agents. In: IEEE Expert, July-August 1999.

Document-Form Identification Using Constellation Matching of Keywords Abstracted by Character Recognition

Hiroshi Sako[1], Naohiro Furukawa[1], Masakazu Fujio[1], and Shigeru Watanabe[2]

[1] Central Research Laboratory, Hitachi, Ltd.
1-280 Higashi-Koigakubo, Kokubunji, Tokyo 185-8601, JAPAN
[2] Mechatronics Systems Division, Hitachi, Ltd.
1 Ikegami, Haruoka, Owariasahi, Aichi 488-8501, JAPAN
sakou@crl.hitachi.co.jp

Abstract. A document-form identification method based on constellation matching of targets is proposed. Mathematical analysis shows that the method achieves a high identification rate by preparing plural targets. The method consists of two parts: (i) extraction of targets such as important keywords in a document by template matching between recogised characters and word strings in a keyword dictionary, and (ii) analysis of the positional or semantic relationship between the targets by point-pattern matching between these targets and word location information in the keyword dictionary. All characters in the document are recognised by means of a conventional character-recognition method. An automatic keyword-determination method, which is necessary for making a keyword dictionary beforehand, is also proposed. This method selects the most suitable keywords from a general word dictionary by measuring the uniqueness of keywords and the stability of their recognition. Experiments using 671 sample documents with 107 different forms in total confirmed that (i) the keyword-determination method can determine sets of keywords automatically in 92.5% of 107 different forms and (ii) that the form-identification method can correctly identify 97.1% of 671 document samples at a rejection rate 2.9%.

1 Introduction

Though e-X [X: banking, cash, commerce, etc.] is very popular now, people are still using paper application forms and banknotes at windows or counters of banks, city halls, etc. This is because direct manipulation of such forms is very easy for most people. Senior people, especially, who are not familiar with personal computers, are not easy beneficiaries of e-X. Therefore, a hybrid system that can accept both electronic applications and paper applications would be most convenient. Such a system would apply document analysis technology to interpret the content information described by characters on a paper application into codes. The codes are then stored together with corresponding information from the electronic application.

This study focuses mainly on technology for document identification. For example, such technology could be applied for discriminating the kind of application

D. Lopresti, J. Hu, and R. Kashi (Eds.): DAS 2002, LNCS 2423, pp. 261–271, 2002.
© Springer-Verlag Berlin Heidelberg 2002

slip handled at a counter at a bank, and it could work on a system composed of a scanner and a personal computer. Moreover, in Japan, some automated teller machines (ATMs) need a function for remitting money (e.g. to pay the public utility charges) as well as a withdrawal function. These machines must recognise the kind of remittance form submitted. By identifying the form and using the knowledge of its frame structure, the machines can read the information, such as the amount of money to be sent, the time of payment, the remitter and the remittee, which is written at specific places of the form.

Conventional methods for identifying an application form are mainly based on the dimensions of the form and the characteristics of the frame structure. The characteristics [1]-[4] include the number of frame strokes and the relative positional or absolute spatial relationship of the frames. The relationship is sometimes expressed as a tree [2]. One of the advantages of these methods is that the processing speed is very fast because the image processing (such as matching with dictionary frame templates) is very simple. However, these methods might not be applicable to forms with a similar frame structure because their essential principle is based on the structure difference. Other related studies include layout analysis methods [5][6] based on the location of fields and logos. The relationship between fields is sometimes expressed as graphs [5]. While these studies are mainly concerned with layout analysis for reading items in known forms, this paper focuses on the identification of the unknown forms.

To discriminate similar forms, a method based on constellation matching of keywords is proposed. The keywords are abstracted by character recognition and template (character string) matching. One of the advantages of this method is that the system interprets all character images into their category codes, which can be used not only for string matching to extract the keywords but also for initial reading of the written items at the same time. The items include the amount of money and the time of payment on the remittance sheet, for example. In this paper, firstly, the concept of constellation matching is explained. Secondly, a form identification method based on constellation matching of keywords and a method for selecting unique and valuable keywords to recognise each form are explained in Chapter 3. Finally, experimental results on 671 real document-forms are given in Chapter 4.

2   Constellation Matching

2.1   Structure

Template pattern matching and point pattern matching are simple but very useful techniques for identifying an input object. The techniques have therefore been implemented into real-time image-processing system in industrial and OCR products in the form of hardware in the 70's and software in the 90's. Generally speaking, the combination of these techniques can achieve good performance with high recognition rate and low error rate, because the template pattern matching can check the existence of characteristic patterns in the image or essential words (keywords) in the document, and the point pattern matching can analyse the geometrical relationship between these patterns or the semantic relationship between these words. In other words, the combination makes it possible to recognise an input image or a document by abstracting essential patterns or important words. This combined method [7] is referred as constellation matching hereafter because targets such as characteristic patterns or essential words are like fixed stars in a constellation.

Constellation matching is composed of two parts as shown in Fig. 1. (1) Template pattern matching (character string matching) extracts important targets such as keywords of the document. (2) Point pattern matching analyses positional or semantic relationship between the targets.

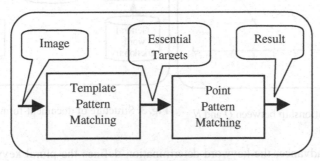

Fig. 1. Constellation matching

2.2 Mathematical Analysis

Generally speaking, constellation matching can statistically achieve good performance with high recognition rate and low error rate, because the number of targets is usually plural and it is possible to make a decision by detected targets even if some of targets are lost. To estimate recognition rate approximately, it is assumed that detection rate q of an individual target is identical for all targets in the object. Thus, the final recognition rate Q is represented as the probability of detecting more than a threshold number of detected targets M out of a number of the expected targets N. Therefore, by using the probability function of a binomial distribution, probability Q is expressed as

$$Q = \Sigma_{i=M,N}\, {}_N C_i * q^i * (1.0 - q)^{N-i}. \tag{1}$$

Fig. 2 shows the relationship between Q and N when $M = N/2$. It can be seen that Q is larger than individual detection rate q since probability Q is the summation of the probabilities for every combination of detected CPs (Characteristic Patterns, i.e., targets or keywords) whose number exceeds M. Thus, constellation matching has the advantage that it has higher recognition rate than conventional methods using a single target.

3 Document-Form Identification

3.1 Structure

As shown in Fig. 3, the document-form identification system is composed of three main parts: keyword determination, keyword dictionary and document-form identi-

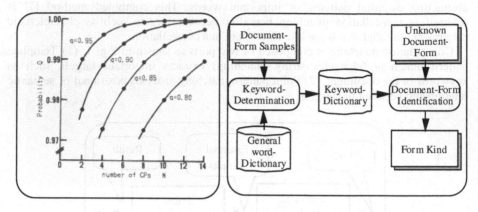

Fig. 2. Relationship between Q and N **Fig. 3.** Structure of document-form identification

fication. In advance, the keyword determination defines the plural keywords in each individual document-form and stores them in the keyword dictionary. For each document-form, the set of keywords must be unique because the difference between sets of keywords is essential for discriminating the form.

A binary image of the form to be identified is put into the form identification part and the form structure is analysed. Then, the binary connected components are detected as character candidates, and they are put into a character classifier. The detected character category codes are matched with all sets of keywords in the keyword dictionary, and the kind of the document-form with the biggest number of matched keywords is regarded as the kind of the input form.

3.2 Form Identification

The identification of the document-form is one of the new applications of constellation matching [9]. As mentioned before, this task is very important in document-reading systems to realise automation equipments such as special ATMs, because the items to be read might depend on the kind of document. Therefore, to complete the document-reading, the identification of a document-form is indispensable. The developed document identification system is composed of two steps as shown in Fig. 4. (i) Character recognition and string matching to detect keywords (i.e., template pattern matching). (ii) Analysis of locational relationship between the keywords to identify the document-form (i.e., point pattern matching).

In the step (i), the input document image is analysed and decomposed [10][11] into several character-line images surrounded by line frames as shown in Fig. 5. The character-line image in each field is separated into connected components as character candidates, which are all examined by a character classifier and are transformed into the corresponding character category codes. However, in the separation process, it is very difficult to separate the character-line image into characters one by one correctly because the components of a Japanese Kanji character are usually Kanji characters

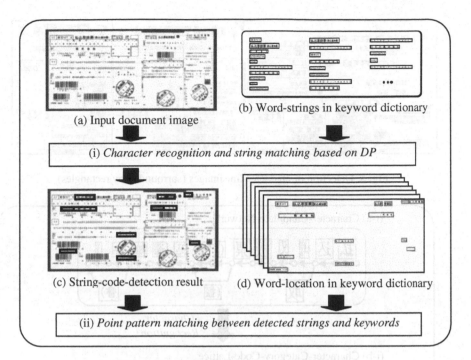

(a) Input document image

(b) Word-strings in keyword dictionary

(i) *Character recognition and string matching based on DP*

(c) String-code-detection result

(d) Word-location in keyword dictionary

(ii) *Point pattern matching between detected strings and keywords*

Fig. 4. Document-form identification

themselves. To cope with this difficulty, many ways of separation are executed so as to be one correct separation within them (so-called "over-segmentation" [8]). As shown in Fig. 6(i-a), one way of separation is expressed by one path of the network. In the process, joined characters, if any, are also separated by the rule-based method [12] using shape analysis of the joined parts of the strokes. Each character-string image in the document-form is mapped onto the network. In the character-recognition process, all connected components in the network are classified into character category codes. The classification is executed under the assumption that the category of an examined character should exist within categories of characters that express dictionary keywords. This assumption can effectively reduce both processing time and the number of misclassified cases. Since the first candidate from the classifier might not be correct, plural candidates are kept in a table (Fig. 6(i-b)). This table is made for every path expressed in the network.

To detect keywords, the detected character category codes (detected strings) are matched with each keyword string in a keyword dictionary prepared as *a priori* knowledge. The keyword-dictionary in Fig. 4(b) is made of popular pre-printed words and proper nouns, which are automatically determined and gathered from sample document-forms in advance. The string matching method is based on a special type of DP (Dynamic Programming) [9], [13]-[15], which allows fluctuations

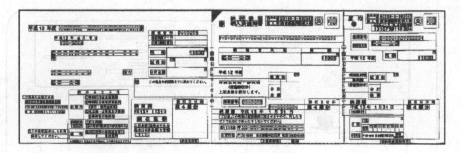

Fig. 5. Detection of character-line images (surrounded by rectangles)

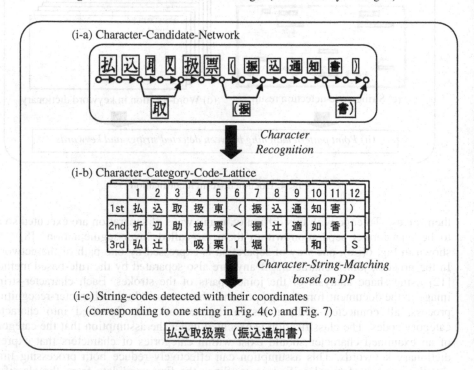

Fig. 6. Character recognition and string matching based on DP

such as insertion, deletion and substitution of one character, because the character segmentation and recognition are not always perfect. Penalty P of the detected keyword is defined by taking account of both the degree of fluctuations and the rank of candidates of the character recognition. The matching score of keyword S_{kw} is calculated using penalty P as follows:

$$S_{kw} = 1 - (P / L) ,\qquad (2)$$

where L is the number of characters of the corresponding dictionary keyword in one kind of form. Fig. 7 shows a magnified image including detected strings, and the image is a part of the detection result in Fig. 4(c).

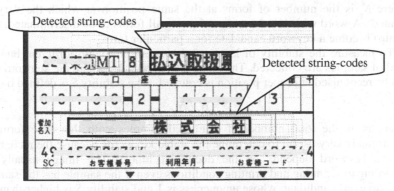

Fig. 7. Result of string code detection

In the step (ii), the detected strings in Fig. 4(c) are estimated by referring to each set of keywords and their locational information as shown in the keyword-dictionary (d). The estimation is based on the average matching scores of the keywords that are detected just at the same positions of the dictionary keywords. The average matching score S^j_c in the dictionary form j is calculated by

$$S^j_c = (1 / D_j) \sum_{i=1, Dj} S^{ij}_{kw}, \qquad (3)$$

where D_j is the total number of detected keywords located correctly on the keyword-dictionary of the form j, and S^{ij}_{kw} indicates the matching score of the ith keyword in the keyword-dictionary of the form j. Finally, the kind of the dictionary form having the maximum S^j_c determines the kind of form.

3.3 Keyword Determination

A keyword dictionary, which must be prepared in advance, is a kind of abstract of content such as pre-printed titles of fields and pre-printed words in notes and instructions on each kind of document. Each abstract is expressed by a combination of such unique keywords or popular words that have a unique positional relationship. In this section, the method for determining these keywords is explained.

The requirement is that the method must determine the keywords: (1) which can identify each document-form and (2) which can be easily recognised by the character classifier when the form identification is being executed. The approach [16] to satisfy requirements (1) and (2) is to measure the degree of uniqueness of each keyword and to measure the degree of recognition stability of the keyword.

In the measurement of the uniqueness, a similar procedure of the form identification (Section 3.2), which is composed of the form structure analysis and the recognition of the character string in each field, is executed. The difference is that this measurement uses a general word dictionary, which stores several thousand general words, in order to detect a unique set of keywords for each document-form. Samples with different format are collected at first. The degree of uniqueness U of a word is then defined by

$$U = 1 / N_u, \qquad (4)$$

where N_u is the number of forms at the same position at which the very word is located. A word with $U = 1$ is very unique to all forms to be discriminated; therefore, it must become a keyword candidate for a particular form.

To measure the stability of keyword detection, physically different but the same kind of samples are collected. The number of forms, N_s, where the keyword candidate can be recognised at proper position is counted. The stability S is defined by

$$S = N_s / N_t,$$ (5)

where N_t is the total number of examined samples with the same format. This definition is very useful to determine the stable keywords because the recognition rate of the keyword depends on the document image. The image usually changes according to scanning and printing conditions even if the sample has the same format. The keyword candidate, whose uniqueness is 1 and stability S is higher than a certain value, is selected as one of keywords of the form, and they are stored to the keyword-dictionary in advance. Note that each document-form can have plural keywords in the dictionary. The desirable number of keywords is estimated from the final recognition rate Q formulated in Equ. 1.

A serious problem encountered in the real world is that requirements (1) and (2) must also be satisfied under the circumstance that we cannot collect many samples but only single sample of a document-form because hundreds of new document-forms are produced in public and private organisations every year, and it's impossible to ask them to collect many samples in every different kind of form. To solve this problem, the perturbation method is used to increase the number of samples virtually. The perturbation can be realised by binarising the grey image of the document-form at several levels around an optimum threshold level and by slightly shifting and skewing the image of the form intentionally. These kinds of images of the form are added and used in the keyword determination.

4 Experiments Using Real Document Samples

To evaluate the effectiveness of the perturbation method and to measure the correct identification rate, 671 document samples were prepared in total and they include 107 kinds of document-forms. Also, about 4500 words were prepared in the general word dictionary to evaluate the accuracy of keyword determination.

4.1 Evaluation of Keyword Determination

To measure the effectiveness of the perturbation method, the following four data subsets were prepared from original samples. Each dataset includes 16 kinds of forms. The datasets are listed below:

DS0: one sample for each kind of form (1x16 samples in total),
DS1: nine randomly selected samples for each kind of form (9x16 samples),
DS2: nine samples generated by perturbing the sample for each kind of form in dataset DS0 (9x16 samples),
DS3: another one randomly selected sample for each kind of form (1x16 samples).

Figs 8(a), (b) and (c) show the results of the document-form identification for the samples in DS3 by using sets of the keywords that are determined from datasets DS0, DS1 and DS2, respectively. The figures show the number of forms that can be identified correctly as well as the number of rejected forms. They are plotted when the threshold value for the average score S^j_c changes from 0.1 to 0.9. Though the number of samples is small, it is possible to conclude the followings.

(1) Increasing the number of samples for each kind of form increases the identification rate and decreases the rejection rate and error rate even when the threshold for the average score S^j_c is high [Figs. 8(b) vs. 8(a)].
(2) The comparison of the identification rate using the keywords determined by DS2 with that by DS0 [Figs. 8(c) vs. 8(a)] shows that the perturbation method improves the identification rate and its stability significantly, and the identification rate using the keywords determined by DS2 is comparable with that by DS1 [Figs. 8(c) vs. 8(b)].

The keyword determination rate is 92.5%, which means that the sets of keywords can be determined in 99 kinds out of 107 kinds of document-forms. The determination failure is mainly caused by the failure to detect the character string images by the structure analysis. The keywords in these failure forms are prepared manually to complete the evaluation of the document-form identification in the next section.

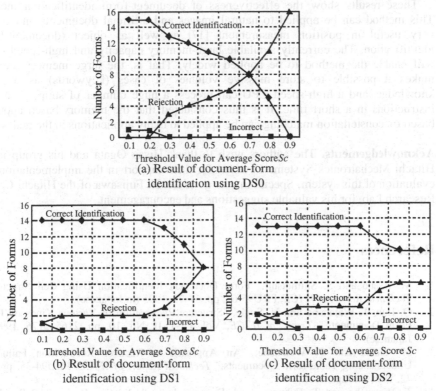

(a) Result of document-form
identification using DS0

(b) Result of document-form
identification using DS1

(c) Result of document-form
identification using DS2

Fig. 8. Effect of perturbation method

4.2 Evaluation of Document-Form Identification

An evaluation of document-form identification based on 671 document samples showed 97.1% correct identification with 2.9% rejection and 0% error rates. The main reason for the rejection is the detection failure of line frames, which makes it difficult to detect the character-line images correctly. Apart from this rejection, the method can realise reliable document identification without any errors in this sample size.

5 Concluding Remarks

A document-form identification method (based on the constellation matching of keywords) and a method for determining the keywords (based on the uniqueness of keywords and the stability to their recognition) are proposed.   To increase the identification rate in the case that plural samples for each document-form cannot be collected, a perturbation method is also proposed. Experiments using 671 sample documents with 107 different forms in total confirmed that (i) the keyword-determination method can determine sets of keywords in 92.5% of 107 different forms and (ii) the form-identification method can correctly identify 97.1% of 671 document samples with the rejection rate 2.9%.

These results show the effectiveness of document-form identification method. This method can be applied to natural images and artificial documents and can be very useful in position measurement [17] as well as object (document-form) identification. The currently available large-memory capacity and high-speed CPUs will enable the method to be applied widely. That is, the large memory capacity makes it possible to store massive volumes of cases (keywords) as *a priori* knowledge, and a high-speed CPU can process a huge number of simple matching instructions in a short time. It is thus considered that the memory-based approach based on constellation matching can be applied to many applications in the real world.

Acknowledgements. The authors wish to thank Hisao Ogata and his group in the Hitachi Mechatronics Systems Division for their support in the implementation and evaluation of this system. Special thanks go to Dr. H. Fujisawa of the Hitachi Central Research Lab. for his valuable suggestions and encouragement.

References

1.   M. Asano and S. Shimotsuji, "Form Document Identification Using Cell Structures," *Technical Report of IEICE*, PRU95-61, pp. 67–72, 1995 (in Japanese).
2.   Q. Luo, T. Watanabe and N. Sugie, "Structure Recognition of Various Kinds of Table-Form Documents," *Trans. of IEICE*, Vol, J76-D-II, No. 10, pp. 2165–2176, 1993 (in Japanese).
3.   M. Ishida and T. Watanabe, "An Approach to Recover Recognition Failure in Understanding Table-form Documents," *Technical Report of IEICE*, PRU94-35, pp. 65–72, 1994 (in Japanese).
4.   T. Watanabe and T. Fukumura, "A Framework for Validating Recognized Results In Understanding Table-form Document Images," *Proc. of ICDAR '95*, pp. 536–539, 1995.

5. F. Cesarini, M. Gori, S. Marinai and G. Soda, "INFORMys: A Flexible Invoice-Like Form-Reader System," *IEEE Trans. on PAMI*, Vol.20, No. 7, pp. 730–745, 1998.
6. S.L. Lam and S. N. Srihari, "Multi-Domain Document Layout Understanding," *Proc. of ICDAR '93*, pp. 497–501, 1993.
7. H. Sako, M. Fujio and N. Furukawa, "The Constellation Matching and Its Application," *Proc. of ICIP 2001*, pp. 790–793, 2001.
8. H. Fujisawa, Y. Nakano and K. Kurino, "Segmentation Methods for Character Recognition: From Segmentation to Document Structure Analysis," *Proc. of the IEEE*, Vol. 80, No. 7, pp. 1079–1092, 1992.
9. N. Furukawa, A, Imaizumi, M. Fujio and H. Sako, "Document Form Identification Using Constellation Matching," *Technical Report of IEICE*, PRMU2001-125, pp. 85–92, 2001. (in Japanese)
10. H. Shinjo, K. Nakashima, M. Koga, K. Marukawa, Y. Shima and E. Hadano, "A Method for Connecting Disappeared Junction Patterns on Frame Lines in Form Documents," *Proc. of ICDAR '97*, pp. 667–670, 1997.
11. H. Shinjo, E. Hadano, K. Marukawa, Y. Shima and H. Sako, "A Recursive Analysis for Form Cell Recognition," *Proc. of ICDAR 2001*, pp. 694–698, 2001.
12. H. Ikeda, Y. Ogawa, M. Koga, H. Nishimura, H. Sako and H. Fujisawa, "A Recognition Method for Touching Japanese Handwritten Characters," *Proc. of ICDAR '99*, pp. 641–644, 1999.
13. F. Kimura, M. Shridhar and Z. Chen, "Improvements of a lexicon directed algorithm for recognition of unconstrained handwritten words," *Proc. of ICDAR '93*, pp. 18-22, 1993.
14. F. Kimura, S. Tsuruoka, Y. Miyake and M. Shridhar, "A lexicon directed algorithm for recognition of unconstrained handwritten words," *IEICE Trans. Info. & Syst.*, Vol. E77-D, No. 7, pp. 785–793, 1994. (in Japanese)
15. H. Bunke, "A fast algorithm for finding the nearest neighbor of a word in a dictionary," *Report of Institut fur Informatik und Angewandte Mathematik, Universitat Bern*, 1993.
16. M. Fujio, N. Furukawa, S. Watanabe and H. Sako, "Automatic Generation of Keyword Dictionary for Efficient Document Form Identification," *Technical Report of IEICE*, PRMU2001-126, pp. 93–98, 2001 (in Japanese).
17. H. Sakou, T. Miyatake, S. Kashioka and M. Ejiri, "A Position Recognition Algorithm for Semiconductor Alignment Based on Structural Pattern Matching," *IEEE Trans. Acoustic, Speech, Signal Processing*, ASSP-37, pp. 2148–2157, Dec. 1989.

Table Detection via Probability Optimization

Yalin Wang[1], Ihsin T. Phillips[2], and Robert M. Haralick[3]

[1] Dept. of Elect. Eng. Univ. of Washington
Seattle, WA 98195, US
ylwang@u.washington.edu

[2] Dept. of Comp. Science, Queens College, City Univ. of New York
Flushing, NY 11367, US
yun@image.cs.qc.edu

[3] The Graduate School, City Univ. Of New York
New York, NY 10016, US
haralick@gc.cuny.edu

Abstract. In this paper, we define the table detection problem as a probability optimization problem. We begin, as we do in our previous algorithm, finding and validating each detected table candidates. We proceed to compute a set of probability measurements for each of the table entities. The computation of the probability measurements takes into consideration tables, table text separators and table neighboring text blocks. Then, an iterative updating method is used to optimize the page segmentation probability to obtain the final result. This new algorithm shows a great improvement over our previous algorithm. The training and testing data set for the algorithm include $1,125$ document pages having 518 table entities and a total of $10,934$ cell entities. Compared with our previous work, it raised the accuracy rate to 95.67% from 90.32% and to 97.05% from 92.04%.

1 Introduction

With the large number of existing documents and the increasing speed in the production of multitude new documents, finding efficient methods to process these documents for their content retrieval and storage becomes critical. For the last three decades, the document image analysis researchers have successfully developed many outstanding methods for character recognition, page segmentation and understand of text-based documents. Most of these methods were not designed to handle documents containing complex objects, such as tables. Tables are compact and efficient for presenting relational information and most of the documents produced today contain various types of tables. Thus, table structure extraction is an important problem in the document layout analysis field. A few table detection algorithms have been published in the recent literature ([1]–[2]). However, the performance of these reported algorithms are not yet good enough for commercial usage.

Among the recently published table detection algorithms, some of them are either using a predefined table layout structures [3][4], or relying on complex heuristics for detecting tables ([5], [6], [7]). Klein et. al. [7] use a signal model to detect tables. Hu et. al. [2] describe an algorithm which detects tables based on computing an optimal partitioning of an input document into some number of tables. They use a dynamic

D. Lopresti, J. Hu, and R. Kashi (Eds.): DAS 2002, LNCS 2423, pp. 272–282, 2002.
© Springer-Verlag Berlin Heidelberg 2002

programming technique to solve the optimization problem. Their algorithm works for both ASCII and image documents, and according to their global evaluation protocol, the algorithm yields a recall rate of 83% for 25 ASCII documents and 81% for 25 scanned images, and a precision rate of 91% and at 93%, respectively.

Our early table detection work [1] is based on a background analysis, has a coarse to fine hierarchy structure and is a probability based algorithm. It determines the table candidates by finding the large horizontal blank blocks [8] within the document and then statistically validates if the candidates are table entities. Due to the non-iterative nature of this algorithm, its accuracy was not high enough. Figure 1 shows two of failed examples of the earlier algorithm. Figure 1(a) is a false alarm example (b) is a misdetection example.

In this paper, we define the table detection problem as a probability optimization problem. We begin, as we did in our previous algorithm, finding and validating each detected table candidates. We proceed to compute a set of probability measurements for each of the table entities. The computation of the probability measurements takes into consideration tables, table text separators and table neighboring text blocks. Then, an iterative updating method is used to optimize the page segmentation probability to obtain the final result. This new algorithm shows a great improvement over our previous algorithm.

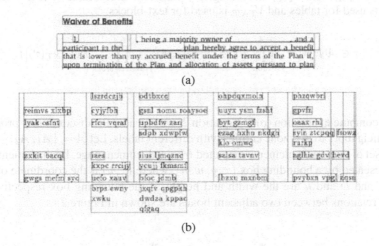

Fig. 1. Examples of table detection research of our early research; (a) a false alarm example; (b) a misdetection example.

The remainder of the paper is organized as follows. We give the problem statement in Section 2. The probability estimation details are described in Section 3. We present our algorithm details in Section 4. The experimental results are reported in Section 5 and we conclude with our future directions in Section 6.

2 Table Detection Problem

Let $\mathcal{A}$ be a set of zone entities. Let $\mathcal{L}$ be a set of content labels, {table, text-block}. Function $f : \mathcal{A} \to \mathcal{L}$ assigns each element of $\mathcal{A}$ with a label. Function $V : \wp(\mathcal{A}) \to \Lambda$ computes measurements made on subset of $\mathcal{A}$, where Λ is the measurement space.

We define a probability of labeling and measurement function as

$$P(V(\tau) : \tau \in \mathcal{A}, f | \mathcal{A}) = P(V(\tau) : \tau \in \mathcal{A}, | f, \mathcal{A}) P(f | \mathcal{A}) \tag{1}$$

By making the assumption of conditional independence that when the label $f_\tau, \tau \in \mathcal{A}$ is known, no knowledge of other labels will alter the probability of $V(\tau)$, we can decompose the probability in Equation 1 into

$$P(V(\tau) : \tau \in \mathcal{A} | f, \mathcal{A}) = \underbrace{\prod_{\tau \in \mathcal{A}} P(V(\tau) | f, \mathcal{A}}_{(a)} \underbrace{P(f | \mathcal{A})}_{(b)} \tag{2}$$

Expression (a) in Equation 2 can be computed by applying different measurement functions V_{TAB} and V_{TXT} according to f function values, table or text-block, where V_{TAB} is used for tables and V_{TXT} is used for text-blocks.

$$P(V(\tau) : \tau \in \mathcal{A} | f, \mathcal{A}) = \prod_{\substack{\tau \in \mathcal{A} \\ f_\tau = table}} P(V_{TAB}(\tau) | f, \mathcal{A}) \prod_{\substack{\tau \in \mathcal{A} \\ f_\tau = text-block}} P(V_{TXT}(\tau) | f, \mathcal{A}) P(f | \mathcal{A}) \tag{3}$$

To compute expression (b) in Equation 2, we consider the discontinuity property between neighbors to two zone entities with different labels. Let $\mathcal{A} = \{A_1, A_2, \cdots, A_M\}$ be the set of document elements extracted from a document page. Each element $A_i \in \mathcal{A}$ is represented by a bounding box (x, y, w, h), where (x, y) is the coordinate of top-left corner, and w and h are the width and height of the bounding box respectively. The spatial relations between two adjacent boxes are shown in Figure 2.

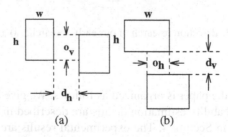

(a)   (b)

Fig. 2. Illustrates the spatial relations between two bounding boxes that are (a) horizontally adjacent (b) vertically adjacent.

For a pair of bounding boxes $a(x_a, y_a, w_a, h_a)$ and $b(x_b, y_b, w_b, h_b)$, the horizontal distance $d_h(a, b)$ and vertical distance $d_v(a, b)$ between them are defined as

$$d_h(a, b) = \begin{cases} x_b - x_a - w_a & \text{if } x_b > x_a + w_a \\ x_a - x_b - w_b & \text{if } x_a > x_b + w_b \\ 0 & \text{otherwise} \end{cases} \tag{4}$$

$$d_v(a, b) = \begin{cases} y_b - y_a - h_a & \text{if } y_b > y_a + h_a \\ y_a - y_b - h_b & \text{if } y_a > y_b + h_b \\ 0 & \text{otherwise} \end{cases} \tag{5}$$

The horizontal overlap $o_h(a, b)$ and vertical overlap $o_v(a, b)$ between a and b are defined as

$$o_h(a, b) = \begin{cases} x_a + w_a - x_b & \text{if } x_b > x_a, x_b < x_a + w_a \\ x_b + w_b - x_a & \text{if } x_a > x_b, x_a < x_b + w_b \\ 0 & \text{otherwise} \end{cases} \tag{6}$$

$$o_v(a, b) = \begin{cases} y_a + h_a - y_b & \text{if } y_b > y_a, y_b < y_a + h_a \\ y_b + h_b - y_a & \text{if } y_a > y_b, y_a < y_b + h_b \\ 0 & \text{otherwise} \end{cases} \tag{7}$$

Let $A_a = (x_a, y_a, w_a, h_a)$ and $A_b = (x_b, y_b, w_b, h_b)$ be two zone entities.

- We define A_b as a *right neighbor* of A_a if $A_b \neq A_a, x_b > x_a$, and $o_v(a, b) > 0$. Let B_a be the set of right neighbors of A_a. Zone entities A_a and A_b are called *horizontally adjacent* if

$$A_b = \arg \min_{A_i \in B_a} (d_h(a, i) | x_i > x_a, o_v(a, i) > 0). \tag{8}$$

- We define A_b as a *lower neighbor* of A_a if $A_b \neq A_a, y_b > y_a$, and $o_h(a, b) > 0$. Let B_a be the set of right neighbors of A_a. Zone entities A_a and A_b are called *vertically adjacent* if

$$A_b = \arg \min_{A_i \in B_a} (d_v(a, i) | y_i > y_a, o_h(a, i) > 0). \tag{9}$$

The neighbor set is defined as

$$\mathcal{N} = \{(v_a, v_b) | v_a \text{ and } v_b \text{ horizontally or vertically adjacent}, v_a \in \mathcal{V}, v_b \in \mathcal{V}\}$$

Assuming the conditional independence between each neighborhood relationship, expression (b) in Equation 2 can be computed as

$$P(f | \mathcal{A}) = \prod_{\{p, q\} \in \mathcal{N}} P_{\{p, q\}}(f_p, f_q | p, q) \tag{10}$$

where $P_{\{p, q\}}(f_p, f_q | p, q)$ has the property

$$P_{\{p, q\}}(f_p, f_q | p, q) = \begin{cases} P_{\{p, q\}}(f_p, f_q | p, q) & f_p \neq f_q \\ 0 & f_p = f_q \end{cases} \tag{11}$$

Equation 3 can be written as

$$P(V(\tau) : \tau \in \mathcal{A}|f, \mathcal{A}) =$$

$$\prod_{\substack{\tau \in \mathcal{A} \\ f_\tau = table}} P(V_{TAB}(\tau)|f, \mathcal{A}) \prod_{\substack{\tau \in \mathcal{A} \\ f_\tau = text-block}} P(V_{TXT}(\tau)|f, \mathcal{A}) \prod_{\{p,q\} \in \mathcal{N}} P(f_p, f_q|p, q)$$

(12)

The table detection problem can be formulated as follows: *Given initial set $\mathcal{A}^0$, find a new set $\mathcal{A}^s$ and a labeling function $f^s : A^s \to L$, that maximizes the probability:*

$$P(V(\tau) : \tau \in \mathcal{A}^I|f^s, \mathcal{A}^s) =$$

$$\prod_{\substack{\tau \in \mathcal{A}^s \\ f^s_\tau = table}} P(V_{TAB}(\tau)|f^s, \mathcal{A}^s) \prod_{\substack{\tau \in \mathcal{A}^s \\ f^s_\tau = text-block}} P(V_{TXT}(\tau)|f^s, \mathcal{A}^s) \prod_{\{p,q\} \in \mathcal{N}} P(f^s_p, f^s_q|p, q)$$

(13)

Our goal is to maximize the probability in Equation 12 by iteratively updating $\mathcal{A}^k$ and f^k. Our table detection system works as follows: we used our early research [1] to get preliminary table detection results. Then we systematically adjust the labeling to maximize the probability until no further improvement can be made.

3   Probability Estimation

3.1   Table and Text Separator Probability

Given a table, t and its vertically adjacent neighboring text block B, we compute the probability of the separator between them being a table and text separator as

$$P(f_t, f_B|t, B) = P(TableTextSeparator|o_h(t, B), d_v(t, B))$$

where the definitions of $d_v(t, B)$ and $o_h(t, B)$ can be found at Equation 5 and Equation 6.

3.2   Table Measurement Probability

To facilitate table detection, we applied our table decomposition algorithm [1] on each detected table. Based on the table decomposition results, three features are computed. These features are given below.

- Ratio of total large vertical blank block [8] and large horizontal blank block [8] areas over identified table area. Let t be an identified table and $\mathcal{B}$ be the set of large horizontal and vertical blank blocks and in it, $ra = \frac{\sum_{\beta \in \mathcal{B}} Area(\beta)}{Area(t)}$;
- Maximum difference of the cell baselines in a row. Denote the set of the cells in a row i as $\mathcal{RC}_i$, $\mathcal{RC}_i = \{c_{i,1}, c_{i,2}, ..., c_{i,i_m}\}$. Denote the set of $\mathcal{RC}_i$ as $\mathcal{RC}$, $\mathcal{RC} = \{\mathcal{RC}_i, i = 1, ..., m\}$, where m is the row number in the table. Let $baseline(c)$ be the y coordinate of the cell entity bottom line, $mc = \max_{\mathcal{RC}_i \in \mathcal{RC}} (\max_{c_{i,j} \in \mathcal{RC}_i} (baseline(c_{i,j})) - \min_{c_{i,j} \in \mathcal{RC}_i} (baseline(c_{i,j})))$;

– Accumulated difference of the justification in all columns. Denote the set of cells in a column, i, in the table $CC_i = \{c_{i,1}, c_{i,2}, ..., c_{i,i_n}\}$. Denote the set of CC_i as CC, $CC = \{CC_i, i = 1, ..., n\}$, where n is the column number in the table. Let $x_{i,j}, y_{i,j}, w_{i,j}, h_{i,j}$ represent the bounding box of the cell $c_{i,j} \in CC_i$. We estimate the justification of a column, $i, i = 1, ..., n$, by computing the vertical projection of the left, center, and right edge of $c_{i,j}, j = 1, ..., i_n$,

$$C_{left}[i] = max_{c_{i,j} \in CC_i}(x_{i,j}) - min_{c_{i,j} \in CC_i}(x_{i,j})$$
$$C_{center}[i] = max_{c_{i,j} \in CC_i}(x_{i,j} + w_{i,j}/2) - min_{c_{i,j} \in CC_i}(x_{i,j} + w_{i,j}/2)$$
$$C_{right}[i] = max_{c_{i,j} \in CC_i}(x_{i,j} + w_{i,j}) - min_{c_{i,j} \in CC_i}(x_{i,j} + w_{i,j})$$
$$J_i = min\{C_{left}[i], C_{center}[i], C_{right}[i]\}$$

The accumulated difference of the justification in all columns, mj, is computed as: $mj = \sum_{i=1}^{n} J_i$.

Finally, we can compute the table consistent probability for table t as

$$P(V_{TAB}(t)) = P(consistency(t)|ra(t), mc(t), mj(t))$$

3.3 Text Block Measurement Probability

A text block, in general, has a homogeneous inter-line spacing and an alignment type (such as left-justified, etc.) Given a detected text block B, we compute the probability that B has homogeneous inter-line spacing, and a text alignment type. We define leading as inter-line spacing. As in Liang et. al.' [9], we compute text block measurement probability as

$$P(V_{TXT}(B)) = P(V_{TXT}(B)|Leading(B), Alignment(B))$$

By making the assumption of conditional independence, we can rewrite the above equation as

$$P(V_{TXT}(B)) = P(V_{TXT}(B)|Leading(B))P(V_{TXT}(B)|Alignment(B))$$

Let $B = (l_1, ..., l_n)$ be an extracted block. $D_B = (d(1), d(2), ..., d(n-1))$ is a sequence of inter-line space distances, where $d(j)$ is the space distance between l_j and l_{j+1}. We compute the median and the maximum value of the elements of D_B. The probability is

$$P(V_{TXT}(B)|Leading(B)) = P(median(D_B), max(D_B)|Leading(B)).$$

Given a text block B that consists of a group of text lines $B = (l_1, l_2, \cdots, l_n)$, we determine the text alignment of B by observing the alignment of the text line edges. Let e_{li} be the left edge of the text line l_i and let e_{ci} and e_{ri} be the center and right edges of the line box respectively. Let E_l be the left edges of text line 2 to n, such that $E_l = \{e_{li}|2 \le i \le n\}$. E_c is the center edges of text line 2 to $n-1$, and E_r is the right edges of text line 1 to $n-1$. We first estimate the median of E_l, then compute the absolute deviation D_l of the elements of E_l from its median,

$$D_l = \{d_i | d_i = |e_{li} - \text{median}(E_l)|, 2 \leq i \leq n\}.$$

Similarly, we estimate the absolute deviation of the center edges and right edges: D_c and D_r. Then, we compute the probability of B being left, center, right, or both justified by observing the mean absolute deviation of the left, center and right edges,

$$P(V_{TXT}(B)|Alignment(B)) = P(\text{mean}(D_l), \text{mean}(D_c), \text{mean}(D_r)|Alignment(B)). \tag{14}$$

4   Table Detection Algorithm

Figure 3 shows our algorithm diagram. Given a labeled page, first we estimate its segmentation probability. For each table, we consider several adjustments, which are to keep it as a table, to grow the table to include its upper and lower neighbors, to merge the table with its upper and lower neighbors and label it as text block. For each adjustment, we compute the new probability. We select the adjustment which produces the biggest improvement upon the initial page segmentation probability. This process is repeated until no improvement can be made. The details of the algorithm are described below.

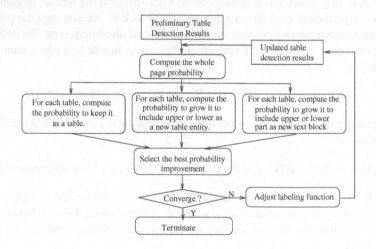

Fig. 3. Overview of the table detection algorithm

Algorithm 41 *Table Optimization*

1. The input data to the algorithm are our previous table detection [1] and text block segmentation results. They are a set of block entities, $\mathcal{A}^0$ and function $f^0 : \mathcal{A}^0 \rightarrow \mathcal{L}$;

2. Set $k = 0$;
3. For each hypothesized table, $i, i = 1, ..., N$, where N is the number of tables in $\mathcal{A}^k$. Compute the different probabilities under different adjustments.
   - Keep the table. Compute the probability $P_{(i,1)}$ following Equation 12;
   - Merge table i with its upper text neighbor and label it as a new table. Compute the new probability $P_{(i,2)}$ following Equation 12;
   - Merge table i with its upper text neighbor and label it as a new text block. Compute the new probability $P_{(i,3)}$ following Equation 12;
   - Merge table i with its lower text neighbor and label it as a new table. Compute the new probability $P_{(i,4)}$ following Equation 12;
   - Merge table i with its lower text neighbor and label it as a new text block. Compute the new probability $P_{(i,5)}$ following Equation 12.
4. Compute $P_{max} = max(P_{(i,j)}), i = 1, ..., N, j = 1, ..., 5$ and get its appropriate adjustment *action*.
5. If the *action* is to keep the table, then, return the labeling result $\mathcal{A}^k$ as $\mathcal{A}^s$ and stop the algorithm.
6. If the *action* is not to keep the table, then take the adjustment *action* and we get $\mathcal{A}^{k+1}$ and $f^{k+1} : \mathcal{A}^{k+1} \rightarrow \mathcal{L}$.
7. Set $k = k + 1$ and go back to 3.

5   Experimental Results

Our test data set has $1,125$ document pages [1]. All of them are machine printed, noise free data. Among them, 565 pages are real data from different business and law books. Another 560 pages are synthetic data generated using the method described in [1]. A hold-out cross validation experiment [10] was conducted on all the data with $N = 9$. Discrete lookup tables were used to represent the estimated joint and conditional probabilities used at each of the algorithm decision steps.

Suppose we are given two sets $\mathcal{G} = \{G_1, G_2, ..., G_M\}$ for ground-truthed foreground table related entities, e.g. cell entities, and $\mathcal{D} = \{D_1, D_2, ..., D_N\}$ for detected table related entities. The algorithm performance evaluation can be done by solving the correspondence problem between the two sets. Performance metrics developed in [11] can be directly computed in each rectangular layout structure set. The performance evaluation was done on the cell level. The numbers and percentages of miss, false, correct, splitting, merging and spurious detections on real data set and on the whole data set are shown in Table 1 and Table 2, respectively. Compared with our early work [1], we improved the detection result rates from 90.32% to 95.67% and from 92.04% to 97.05% in the whole data set. For the real data set, we improved the detection result rates from 89.69% to 96.76% and from 93.12% to 93.86%.

Figure 4 shows a few table detection examples. Figure 4(a), (b) are the correct detection results of Figure 1(a), (b), respectively. In Figure 4(a), our algorithm grows the original table and include its lower neighbor and construct a new table entity. In Figure 4(b), our algorithm eliminates the originally detected table and merge it with its lower neighbor and construct a new text block entity. Figure 4(c), (d) illustrate some failed

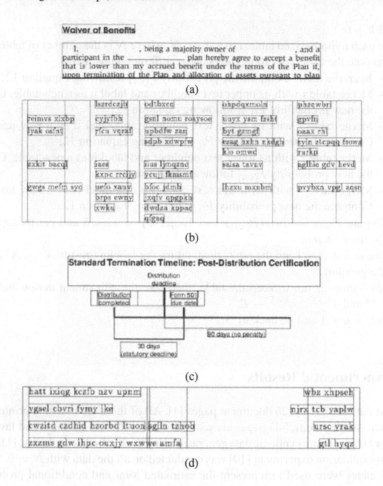

Fig. 4. Illustrates the table detection results; (a), (b) Correct table detection results; (c), (d) failed table detection results.

examples. Figure 4(c) shows a false alarm example. Some texts in a figure are detected as a table entity. Figure 4(d) shows an error example where our table decomposition algorithm failed.

6 Conclusion and Future Work

In this paper, we formulated table detection problem in the whole page segmentation framework. We tried to improve table detection result by optimizing the whole page segmentation probability, including table entities, text block entities and the separators between them. We used iterative updating method to improve the probability. We implemented our algorithm and tested on a data set which includes $1,125$ document pages with $10,934$ table cell entities. Among them, 565 pages are real data from differ-

Table 1. Cell level performance of the table detection algorithm on real data set.

	Total	Correct	Splitting	Merging	Mis-False	Spurious
Ground Truth	679	657	3	15	4	0
		(96.76%)	(0.44%)	(2.21%)	(0.59%)	(0.00%)
Detected	700	657	6	7	30	0
		(93.86%)	(0.86%)	(1.00%)	(4.29%)	(0.00%)

Table 2. Cell level performance of the table detection algorithm on the whole data set.

	Total	Correct	Splitting	Merging	Mis-False	Spurious
Ground Truth	10934	10461	132	45	296	0
		(95.67%)	(1.21%)	(0.41%)	(2.71%)	(0.00%)
Detected	10779	10461	264	18	36	0
		(97.05%)	(2.45%)	(0.17%)	(0.33%)	(0.00%)

ent business and law books. Another 560 pages are synthetic data generated using the method described in [1]. The experimental results demonstrated the improvement of our algorithm.

As shown in Figure 4(d), our current table decomposition algorithm needs further refined, incorporating some additional information carrying features. Our formulation has the potential to be useful to other more general page segmentation problems, for example, to segment text, figure and images, etc. We will study this in the future.

References

1. Y. Wang, I. T. Phillips, and R. Haralick. Automatic table ground truth generation and a background-analysis-based table structure extraction method. In *Sixth International Conference on Document Analysis and Recognition(ICDAR01)*, pages 528–532, Seattle, WA, September 2001.
2. J. Hu, R. Kashi, D. Lopresti, and G. Wilfong. Medium-independent table detection. In *SPIE Document Recognition and Retrieval VII*, pages 291–302, San Jose, California, January 2000.
3. E. Green and M. Krishnamoorthy. Model-based analysis of printed tables. In *Proceedings of the 3rd ICDAR*, pages 214–217, Canada, August 1995.
4. J. H. Shamilian, H. S. Baird, and T. L. Wood. A retargetable table reader. In *Proceedings of the 4th ICDAR*, pages 158–163, Germany, August 1997.
5. T. G. Kieninger. Table structure recognition based on robust block segmentation. *Document Recognition V.*, pages 22–32, January 1998.
6. T. Kieninger and A. Dengel. Applying the t-rec table recognition system to the business letter domain. In *Sixth International Conference on Document Analysis and Recognition(ICDAR01)*, pages 518–522, Seattle, WA, September 2001.
7. B. Klein, S. Gokkus, T. Kieninger, and A. Dengel. Three approaches to "industrial" table spotting. In *Sixth International Conference on Document Analysis and Recognition(ICDAR01)*, pages 513–517, Seattle, WA, September 2001.

8. Y. Wang, R. Haralick, and I. T. Phillips. Improvement of zone content classification by using background analysis. In *Fourth IAPR International Workshop on Document Analysis Systems. (DAS2000)*, Rio de Janeiro, Brazil, December 2000.

9. J. Liang, I. T. Phillips, and R. M. Haralick. Consistent partition and labeling of text blocks. *Journal of Pattern Analysis and Applications*, 3:196–208, 2000.

10. R. Haralick and L. Shapiro. *Computer and Robot Vision*, volume 1. Addison Wesley, 1997.

11. J. Liang. *Document Structure Analysis and Performance Evaluation*. Ph.D thesis, Univ. of Washington, Seattle, WA, 1999.

Complex Table Form Analysis Using Graph Grammar

Akira Amano[1] and Naoki Asada[2]

[1] Kyoto University, Kyoto 606-8501, Japan,
amano@i.kyoto-u.ac.jp
[2] Hiroshima City University, Hiroshima 731-3194, Japan,
asada@its.hiroshima-cu.ac.jp

Abstract. Various kinds of complex table forms are used for many purposes, e.g. application forms. This paper presents a graph grammar based approach to the complex table form structure analysis. In our study, field types are classified into four, i.e. blank, insertion, indication, explanation, and four kinds of indication patterns are defined between indication and blank or insertion. Then, two dimensional relations between horizontally and vertically adjacent fields are described by graph representation and those reduction procedures are defined as production rules. We have designed 56 meta rules from which 6745 rules are generated for a complex table form analysis. Experimental results have shown that 31 kinds of different table forms are successfully analyzed using two types of meta grammar.

1 Introduction

Various kinds of form documents are in circulation around us such as research grant application sheets to which we need to fill in appropriate data to send some information to others.

One popular type of form document is table form document which are widely used in Japanese public documents. Although many researches have been done for automated table processing[1], there are few researches which extracts semantic (structural) information. Among them, production system based systems[2][3][4] have been proposed, yet, they have drawback that modification of structural knowledge is annoying. Practically, it is very important to adapt structural knowledge to each document type, as there exist large variety of table form documents.

For this problem, system using grammatical representation for the structural knowledge have been proposed. In the system proposed by Rahgozar et. al.[5], graph grammar is used for the representation of the knowledge. However, document structure considered in this system is quite simple compared to prior ones such as [2].

We have proposed table form structure analysis system using ordinary one dimensional grammar[6]. In this system, simple grammar is used for the analysis of complex document structure. As the grammar is very simple, it is easy to

D. Lopresti, J. Hu, and R. Kashi (Eds.): DAS 2002, LNCS 2423, pp. 283–286, 2002.
© Springer-Verlag Berlin Heidelberg 2002

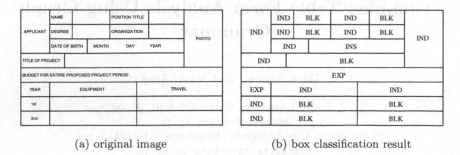

(a) original image   (b) box classification result

Fig. 1. An example of table form document.

modify and maintain consistency of them. However, as the table form documents have two dimensional structure, the structure analysis part of the system handles two dimensional information which are not described in the grammar. Thus, some part of the structural knowledge were embedded in the analysis part of the system, that leads to difficulty in modifying structural knowledge in some case.

In this paper, we propose table form structure analysis system based on graph grammar which can handle complex table structure. As the structural knowledge is fully expressed in the grammar, we can easily modify it to suit various kinds of documents.

2   Document Structure

The system deals with documents that consist of rectangular fields formed by horizontal and vertical rules as shown in Fig.1(a). In this paper, each field is called *box* which is considered as a primitive element of document structure. Boxes are classified into four types, BLK(blank box to be filled-in), INS(insertion box to be inserted or pasted between preprinted letters), IND(indication box that indicates other boxes) and EXP(general explanation box) according to the database. Figure 1(b) shows the box types of Fig.1(a).

Box indication patterns considered in our system is same as those in [2]. The indication box plays an important role in the document structure analysis; that is, the function of the blank and insertion boxes are determined by the left or upper adjacent indication box, and such a horizontal or vertical relation is always established when both boxes have the same height or width, respectively. This means that the unification of an indication box and its associated blank or insertion one forms a rectangular block like a box, so we call it a *compound box*. This unification also takes place in the situation that a compound box is associated with adjacent indication box. Note that, there are two types of unification; one is one dimensional unification in which one indication box and one associated box is unified, and the other is two dimensional unification in which two indication boxes placed above and left of their associated box are unified.

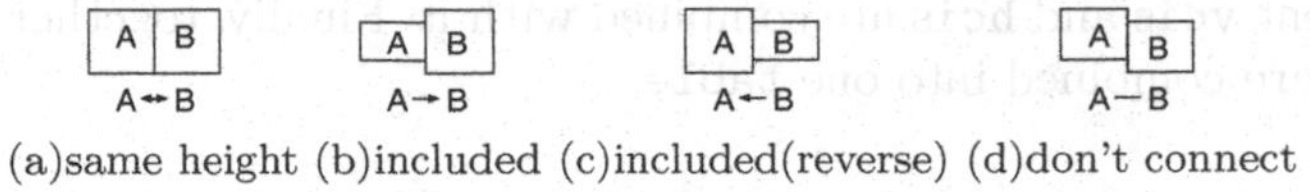

A B
A↔B
A B
A→B
A B
A←B
A B
A—B
(a)same height (b)included (c)included(reverse) (d)don't connect

Fig. 2. Symbols for adjacent box connectivity. (edge going to the right only)

3 Document Structure Grammar

Two dimensional document structure can naturally be denoted by graph grammar. Graph grammar is a four-tuple $\{\Sigma, \Delta, \mathrm{S}, \mathrm{P}\}$ where Σ is node labels of 4 box types and 9 compound box types, and Δ is edge labels shown in Fig.2. Note that each edge has direction attribute, therefore, edge label becomes combination of four edge types(a,b,c,d) and four edge directions(l,r,u,d). S is starting symbol `document` which represents whole document. P denotes a set of productions that are of the form $p = (L, R, E)$ where L and R are lhs and rhs graphs of the production rule p respectively, and E is a set of embedding rules. Embedding rules are of the form $\{v_1, e_1, n_1, v_2, e_2\}$ where edge labeled e_1 from node v_1 to node of the label n_1 in rhs is replaced with the edge label e_2 from node v_2.

For example, adjacent `IND` and `BLK` boxes in upper left part of Fig.1 becomes `hicb` (horizontal indication compound box) as shown in upper part of Fig.3 and corresponding production rule is shown in lower part of the figure. Note that, a set of production rules for producing `hicb` from `IND` and `BLK` are used according to the variety of combination of edge label. Afterwards, `Hicbs` are converted to `gcbs` (general compound boxes) by another set of rules, and they are combined to one `gcb`. Finally, leftmost `IND` and adjacent `gcb` become `hicb` and it is converted into a `gcb`.

For the two dimensional part, first, two `IND` and one `BLK` boxes in left top corner are converted into `vci` (vertical cell indication), `hci` (horizontal cell indication) and `cel` (cell box) as shown in upper part of Fig.4 and corresponding production rule is shown in lower part of the figure. Similary, `IND` boxes are converted into `vci` and `hci` boxes, and `BLK` or `INS` boxes are converted into `cel` boxes by another set of rules. Afterwards, every `cels` are combined into one `cel`,

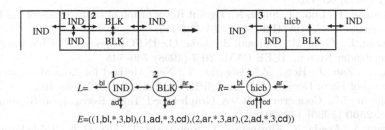

1
IND
2
BLK
IND
IND
IND
BLK
3
hicb
IND
IND
IND
BLK
L=
bl
IND
BLK
ar
ad
ad
R=
bl
hicb
ar
cd
cd
E=((1,bl,*,3,bl),(1,ad,*,3,cd),(2,ar,*,3,ar),(2,ad,*,3,cd))

Fig. 3. A production rule for compound box.

and adjacent vcis and hcis are combined with it. Finally, together with left top EXP, they are combined into one table.

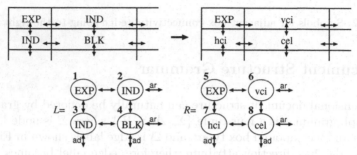

$E=((2,ar,*,6,ar),(3,ad,*,7,ad),(4,ar,*,8,ar),(4,ad,*,8,ad))$

Fig. 4. A production rule for table.

Finally, we used 6745 rules to analyze Fig.1. Note that they are generated from 56 meta rules as they are combinations of geometrical and logical box relations. Experimentally, 31 table form documents were successfully analyzed with two types of meta grammar.

4   Conclusion

In this paper, we revealed that the graph grammar can be a powerful tool for structure analysis system of complex table form documents. We have shown that the system can deal with complex table forms considered in prior systems. Owing to its ability of expressing 2 dimensional relations, the grammar can easily be extended to deal with various complex table forms.

References

1. Lopresti, D., Nagy, G.: A Tabular Survey of Automated Table Processing. LNCS **1941** (2000) 93–120.
2. Watanabe, T., Luo, Q., Sugie, N.: Layout Recognition of Multi-Kinds of Table-Form Documents. IEEE PAMI **17** 4 (1995) 432–445.
3. Cesarini, F., Gori, M., Marinai, S., Soda, G.: INFORMys: A Flexible Invoice-Like Form-Reader System. IEEE PAMI **20** 7 (1998) 730–745.
4. Bing, L., Zao, J., Hong, Z., Ostgathe, T.: New Method for Logical Structure Extraction of Form Document Image. SPIE Proc. **3651** (1999) 183–193.
5. Rahgozar, M., Cooperman, R.: A Graph-based Table Recognition System. SPIE Proc. **2660** (1996) 192–203.
6. Amano, A., Asada, N., Motoyama, T., Sumiyoshi, T., Suzuki, K.: Table Form Document Synthesis by Grammar-Based Structure Analysis. 6th ICDAR (2001) 533–537.

Detection Approaches for Table Semantics in Text

Saleh Alrashed and W.A. Gray

Department of Computer Science, Cardiff University,
Cardiff, Wales, UK.
{scmsa1,wag}@cs.cf.ac.uk

Abstract. When linking information presented in documents as tables with data held in databases, it is important to determine as much information about the table and its content. Such an integrated use of Web-based data requires information about its organization and meaning i.e. the semantics of the table. This paper describes approaches that can be used to detect and extract the semantics for a table held in the text. Our objective is to detect and extract table semantics that are buried in the text. For this goal to be achieved, a domain ontology that covers the semantics of the term used in this table must be available to the information system. The overall aim is to link this tabular information in an interoperable environment containing database and other structures information. ...

1 Introduction

The amount of online structured, semi-structured and unstructured data is growing rapidly. The reasons for this are the growth of e-commerce, e-services, e-government and e-library, areas which publish a very large amount of data on the internet in tabular form. Web pages can be designed as static html pages or as dynamic web page. A dynamic web page gives its user the ability to query an associated database, with the result being represented as either an html table or an XML document. Joining these tables from different sources will leads to semantic conflicts. The information needed to detect semantic conflicts when combining tables is often buried deep within the text of the documents associated with the table or in the web site itself . In order to resolve problems caused by semantic conflict, an information system must be able to ensure semantic interoperability by discovering and utilizing this contextual information. The goal of this research is to enable the discovery and effective use of context information. The context of a piece of data in a table is the metadata relating to its meaning.

D. Lopresti, J. Hu, and R. Kashi (Eds.): DAS 2002, LNCS 2423, pp. 287–290, 2002.
© Springer-Verlag Berlin Heidelberg 2002

2   Semantics and Representational Conflicts

When trying to integrate data from different sources drawn from the same domain, semantic conflicts and representational conflicts can occur. Semantic conflicts are related to differences in the metadata of the table (attributes, names etc). Such a conflict occurs when different data names represent the same data (synonyms), the same name represents a different data domain (homonyms), or a hidden semantic relationship exists between two or more terminologies. For example the relationship between cost and price or between profit and net-profit, and the similarity between car, vehicle and truck cannot be understood unless we use a domain knowledge base to relate these terms. To overcome conflicts we use semantic metadata, which provides information about the meaning of the available data and any semantic relationships . The sources of semantic information can include ontologies.

Representational conflicts occur due to the way data is represented and in particular the measurement unit being used. These conflicts are concerned with the values of an attribute. If we have two attributes, which are semantically the same, they are not in conflict when their values are represented in the same way, i.e. in the same units. This is important, if we are bringing attributes together. Thus representational metadata provides information about the meaning of the values of an attribute, its representational relationships and units of representation.

3   Semantic and Representation Detection Framework

SRD (Semantic and Representation Detection framework) is a proposed system for discovering and interpreting the context information about tables present in a document containing tabular data. (Fig. 1) shows the proposed system architecture of the SRD system, which will extract and structure the context data about a table held within a textual document.

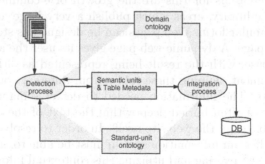

Fig. 1. Semantic and representation detection framework

It consist of five units; namely: detection process – analyses the content of the document and detects the beneficial context information about tables present in a document containing tabular data; domain ontology - provides information about the representation and description of the data on the basis of the model and details about how to convert between different representations; standard-unit ontology – used in discovering some of the value representations in the text; semantic units and table metadata – represent extracted semantics and representation information which is stored for further processing; integration unit – integrates semantic units and table metadata with the corresponding data from a database. In this paper we concentrate on the detection process subunit.

3.1   Detection Process

This process analyses the content of a document and detects the useful context information about tables present in a document containing tabular data. We divide this process into three parts; context detection, context extraction, and context representation.

Context detection. There are a number of approaches that can be used to analyze a document which contains tabular data to detect contextual information about the table.

A. Text searching:Use the table headings as keywords to search for related semantics in the adjacent paragraphs to the table. We know that the table header or table metadata indicates the main concepts that the table represents, therefore concentrating on the table metadata insures the correctness and accuracy of the detected contexts.

   B. Augmenting header using an ontology: In many situations the table header alone is not enough to describe the semantics of that table. Another approach is then used, namely: the table header is used to extract the corresponding concept from the domain ontology and search for that concept and all related synonyms in the text.

C. Table data: In some cases, the author explains some of the table data immediately after or before the table itself. Therefore searching the surrounding paragraphs might lead us to some of the table semantics.

D. Table title: Another approach is to take the table title and search for the phrase "figure x" in the text. We can also use the table title which informs that this table is about car prices which leads us to an understanding that the field name "value" is equivalent to "price". We can then search for both value and price in the adjacent document context.

Context extraction. After detecting the corresponding context in a document, these contexts will be extracted and kept for farther processing.These contexts will have no meaning until they have been mapped to a corresponding concepts in the domain ontology.

Extraction algorithm. After selecting the approach to take, the first thing is to decide which part of the document to search. Logically the author is going to describe the table either before or after. We can also search for the table figure number in other paragraphs. After identifying the section to be searched in detail, a search will start looking for the column headers and their synonyms until it finds matching words followed by a mathematical operator $(+, *, = \ldots)$ or (is, are ...). If no mathematical operators found than this sentence will be stored for further assessment by the user.

Representing the extracted contexts. After detecting and extracting the corresponding contexts, our internal model represents them in two ways; as semantic units or as table metadata. This can then be used to link corresponding information in different tables together.

3.2   Semantic Units

A semantic unit represents a data item together with its underlying semantic context. This consists of a flexible set of meta-attributes that describe the meaning of the data item. However, because we cannot describe all modeling assumptions the semantic context always has to be recognized as being a partial representation. In addition, each semantic unit has a concept label associated with it that specifies the relationship between the unit and the real world aspects it describes. These labels have to be taken from the ontology. Our Semantic Unit represents a value v as: "(C , V , ST)" where C represents the knowledge concept derived from the domain ontology which represents the corresponding value, V represents the value, and ST represents the semantic contexts that have been discovered in the text.

3.3   Table Metadata

The table metadata describes the full table with its corresponding contexts. This metadata is enhanced with any semantic context found in the text.

4   Related Work

Christof Bornhovd proposed a representation model for explicit description of implicitly described semi-structured data, and used this model for the integration of heterogeneous data sources from the web. In this model they don't distinguish between semantic and representational contexts and don't support the conversion of data between different contexts. Thus our proposal extends their work by supporting the conversion between different representational values.

5   Conclusion

In this paper we have described the architecture of a system for the discovery and resolution of semantic and representational conflicts and have shown the differences between them and when these occur. Also we have described the different approaches that can be used to detect the table semantics by using the domain ontology. After detection and extraction of the corresponding contexts, our internal model represents them in two ways; as semantic units or as table metadata. This can then be used to link corresponding information in different tables together.

A Theoretical Foundation and a Method for Document Table Structure Extraction and Decompositon

Howard Wasserman, Keitaro Yukawa, Bon Sy, Kui-Lam Kwok, and
Ihsin Tsaiyun Phillips

Department of Computer Science
Queens College, the City University of New York
65-30 Kissena Boulevard
Flushing, New York 11367-1597
howard@umedia.cs.qc.edu, yukawa@picasso.cs.qc.edu, bon@bunny.cs.qc.edu,
kwok@ir.cs.qc.edu, ihsin_phillips@qc.edu

1 Introduction

The algorithm described in this paper is designed to detect potential table regions in the document, to decide whether a potential table region is, in fact, a table, and, when it is, to analyze the table structure. The decision and analysis phases of the algorithm and the resulting system are based primarily on a precise definition of table, and it is such a definition that is discussed in this paper. An adequate definition need not be complete in the sense of encompassing all possible structures that might be deemed to be tables, but it should encompass most such structures, it should include essential features of tables, and it should exclude features never or very rarely possessed by tables.

The remainder of the paper is organized as follows. The table definition is omitted due to the page limitation. Please contact the author for detail. We describe the propose table region detection algorithm in details Section 2, and we conclude with our future directions in Section 3.

2 The Proposed Table Region Detection Algorithm

Typical document image analysis and recognition systems consist of the following main modules—scanning/digitization, page physical layout analysis, page logical layout analysis, and the output formatting modules. Within the page layout analysis module are typically included sub-modules that extract text-words, text-lines, text-paragraphs, text-columns, as well as sub-modules for non-text region extraction and labeling. In this section we outline our proposed algorithm for table region detection which will become a component of an overall document table-understanding system within any OCR system. Our algorithm takes as input a set of word boxes, the result of the word segmentation technique in [11], produces from this set an initial set of "black boxes" which is subsequently

D. Lopresti, J. Hu, and R. Kashi (Eds.): DAS 2002, LNCS 2423, pp. 291–294, 2002.
© Springer-Verlag Berlin Heidelberg 2002

processed by the following modules discussed in this section: word-box consolidation and text-line elimination module, vertical-range module, horizontal-range module, and table-region extraction module, yielding a final set of potential table-region bounding boxes which constitutes suitable input for a table decomposition algorithm.

2.1   Problem Statement

Given is a set of word boxes $\mathbf{W} = \{b_i : b_i = (x_i, y_i, w_i, h_i)\}$ where (x_i, y_i) is the coordinates of the upper-left corner of the word box b_i, w_i is the width of b_i, and h_i is the height of b_i, with the requirement that $0 \leq x_i, w_i \leq$ width of a given document page P and $0 \leq y_i, h_i \leq$ height of the given document page P. The problem is to *compute* the collection of potential table regions on the given document page: $\mathbf{T} = \{T_i : T_i \subseteq \mathbf{W}, T_i$ a potential table region $\}$ such that for each pair i, j with $i \neq j, T_i \cap T_j = \emptyset$.

2.2   Test Data

The initial test data set for the algorithm will be taken from recent proceedings of scientific conferences that are available to the public in PDF file format. These PDF files will be converted into TIFF image format. We intend to collect at least 100 instances of such test data, some of which will include tables, and some not, to insure objective testing.

2.3   Overall Description

The input to the algorithm is a set $\mathbf{W}$ of word boxes. The output of the algorithm is the set of potential table regions. The algorithm consists of the following modules in the stated order: a *word-box consolidation and text-line elimination module*, a *vertical-range module*, a *horizontal-range module*, and a *table-region extraction module*.

The set, $\mathbf{W}$, of word boxes is passed as input to a word-box consolidation and text-line elimination module, producing a reduced set of (combined) word boxes called "black boxes". This set of black boxes is then passed to a vertical-range module which, using horizontal projection profiles, produces vertical ranges of potential table regions. For each vertical range produced, the set of black boxes in it is passed to a horizontal-range module which, using vertical projection profiles, produces horizontal ranges of potential table regions. The computed vertical and horizontal ranges are passed to a table-region extraction module, which produces the final set of potential table-region bounding boxes.

2.4   Word-Box Consolidation and Text-Line Elimination

Let $\mathbf{W}$ be the input set of word boxes. For each $b_i \in \mathbf{W}$ that has a right neighbor, compute its right gap box g_i. Let $\mathbf{RG} = \{g_i\}$ be the set of all right gap boxes.

Small, inter-word gap boxes are then eliminated as follows. Compute the gap-width histogram to determine a threshold value ρ for inter-word gap widths. Consider each word box to be an initial "black box". Then, iteratively, delete each $g_i \in \mathbf{RG}$ whose width is less than the threshold ρ, and for each deleted gap box g_i, horizontally merge the two adjacent black boxes together with the gap box g_i into a longer black box. Let the resulting set of black boxes be $\mathbf{B}$.

Black boxes for regular text lines are subsequently eliminated as follows. Compute a histogram of the widths of black boxes in $\mathbf{B}$. Then determine a threshold from the histogram to eliminate black boxes for regular text lines—in so doing, the following observation may be used: table entries are normally less than half the average width of text lines. Then eliminate the black boxes in $\mathbf{B}$ whose width is greater than the threshold. (Remark: If a black box has a width not greater than the threshold but follows a run of one or more text-line black boxes, it is normally not a table entry.)

2.5   Computation of Vertical and Horizontal Ranges of Potential Table Regions

The fundamental idea behind the following two modules is to compute vertical and horizontal projection profiles of the black boxes, and then detect patterns of profiles suggesting potential table regions (PTRs) using finite automata.

Vertical Range Modules. Compute a horizontal projection profile, HP, of the black boxes in $\mathbf{B}$.

Then do the following preprocessing to clean up the horizontal profile by eliminating short, noisy black boxes: Compute a histogram of lengths of runs of 1's (here and subsequently "1" symbolically denotes any positive number). Compute a threshold, ρ, such that those runs of 1's of length less than ρ should be eliminated. Eliminate those short runs of 1's by turning the 1's to 0's. Let the resulting, cleaned up, horizontal profile be P'.

In the next step, parameters for a finite automaton to detect vertical ranges of potential table regions (PTRs) are computed: Compute a histogram of runs of 1's from P', and determine the parameter values pertaining to heights of black boxes, to be used in the finite automaton to detect PTRs. Compute a histogram of runs of 0's from P', and determine the parameter values pertaining to heights of inter-line, inter-row, and inter-table white gaps, to be used in the finite automaton to detect PTRs.

Construct the finite automaton using the computed parameters, and then apply the finite automaton to detect the vertical ranges of PTRs.

Horizontal Range Modules. For each vertical range of a PTR detected, do the following:

Compute a vertical projection profile, VP, for the black boxes in $\mathbf{B}$. Do a clean-up processing on VP similar to that done in the vertical-range detection module. Compute histograms of lengths of runs of 0's and 1's, and obtain thresholds. Apply a "non-maximum suppression" technique using the thresholds to obtain an accentuated vertical profile. Apply a finite automaton technique to detect columns and column boundaries of the PTR.

2.6 Table Region Extraction

Using the vertical and horizontal PTR ranges computed, return the set of word boxes falling within the intersection of the two ranges.

References

1. Y. Wang, I. T. Phillips, and R. Haralick. Automatic table ground truth generation and a background-analysis-based table structure extraction method. *Sixth International Conference on Document Analysis and Recognition(ICDAR01)*, pages 528–532, September 2001.
2. E. Green and M. Krishnamoorthy. Model-based analysis of printed tables. *Proceedings of the 3rd ICDAR*, pages 214–217, August 1995.
3. J. H. Shamilian, H. S. Baird, and T. L. Wood. A retargetable table reader. *Proceedings of the 4th ICDAR*, pages 158–163, August 1997.
4. T. G. Kieninger. Table structure recognition based on robust block segmentation. *Document Recognition V.*, pages 22–32, January 1998.
5. T. Kieninger and A. Dengel. Applying the t-rec table recognition system to the business letter domain. *Sixth International Conference on Document Analysis and Recognition(ICDAR01)*, pages 518–522, September 2001.
6. B. Klein, S. Gokkus, T. Kieninger, and A. Dengel. Three approaches to "industrial" table spotting. *Sixth International Conference on Document Analysis and Recognition(ICDAR01)*, pages 513–517, September 2001.
7. K. Zuyev. "Table image segmentation". Proceedings of ICDAR, Germany, 1997. pp.705–708, 1997.
8. J. Hu, R. Kashi, D. Lopresti and G. Wilfong. A system for understanding and reformulating tables. *Proc. 4th IAPR Intl. Workshop on Document Analysis Systems - DAS'2000.* pp.361–372, 2000.
9. J. Hu, R. Kashi, D. Lopresti, and G. Wilfong. Medium-independent table detection. *SPIE Document Recognition and Retrieval VII*, pages 291–302, January 2000.
10. J. Liang, I. T. Phillips, and R. M. Haralick. Consistent partition and labeling of text blocks. *Journal of Pattern Analysis and Applications*, 3:196–208, 2000.
11. Yalin Wang, Ihsin. T. Phillips, Robert M. Haralick, Statistical-based Approach to Word Segmentation. *Proceedings of the 15th International Conference on Pattern Recognition(ICPR2000)*, Barcelona, Span, September 3–7, 2000, p.555–558.
12. Jisheng Liang, Ihsin. T. Phillips, and Robert M. Haralick, "An Optimization Methodology for Document Structure Extraction on Latin Character Documents", the Journal of IEEE Transactions for Pattern Analysis and Machine Intelligence, 2000.
13. Jisheng Liang, Ihsin. T. Phillips, and Robert M. Haralick, "Performance Evaluation of Document Structure Extraction Algorithms", the Journal of computer Vision and Image Understanding, 2000.

Fuzzy Segmentation of Characters in Web Images Based on Human Colour Perception

A. Antonacopoulos and D. Karatzas

PRImA Group, Department of Computer Science, University of Liverpool
Peach Street, Liverpool, L69 7ZF, United Kingdom
http://www.csc.liv.ac.uk/~prima

Abstract. This paper describes a new approach for the segmentation of characters in images on Web pages. In common with the authors' previous work in this subject, this approach attempts to emulate the ability of humans to differentiate between colours. In this case, pixels of similar colour are first grouped using a colour distance defined in a perceptually uniform colour space (as opposed to the commonly used RGB). The resulting colour connected components are then grouped to form larger (character-like) regions with the aid of a fuzzy propinquity measure. This measure expresses the likelihood for merging two components based on two features. The first feature is the colour distance in the $L^*a^*b^*$ colour space. The second feature expresses the topological relationship of two components. The results of the method indicate a better performance than the previous method devised by the authors and comparable (possibly better) performance to other existing methods.

1 Introduction

Text is routinely created in image form (headers, banners etc.) on Web pages, as an attempt to overcome the stylistic limitations of HTML. This text, however, has a potentially high semantic value in terms of indexing and searching for the corresponding Web pages. As current search engine technology does not allow for text extraction and recognition in images (see [1] for a list of indexing and ranking criteria for different search engines), the text in image form is ignored. Moreover, it is desirable to obtain a uniform representation (e.g. UNICODE) of all *visible* text on a Web page. This uniform representation can be used by a number of applications such as voice browsing [2] and automated content analysis [3] for viewing on small screen devices such as PDAs.

There has been a provision for specifying the text included in images, in the form of ALT tags in HTML. However, a study conducted by the authors [4], assessing the impact and consequences of text contained in images indicates that the ALT tag strategy is not effective. It was found that the textual description (ALT tags) of 56% of images on Web pages was incomplete, wrong or did not exist at all. This can be a serious matter since, of the total number of words visible on a Web page, 17% are in image form (most often semantically important text). Worse still, 76% of these words in image form do not appear elsewhere in the encoded text. These results agree with earlier findings [5] and clearly indicate an alarming trend.

D. Lopresti, J. Hu, and R. Kashi (Eds.): DAS 2002, LNCS 2423, pp. 295–306, 2002.
© Springer-Verlag Berlin Heidelberg 2002

It can be seen from the above that there is a significant need for methods to extract and recognise the text in images on Web pages. However, this is a challenging problem for the following reasons. First, these (sometimes complex) colour images tend to be of low resolution (usually just 72 dpi) and the font-size used for text is very small (about 5pt–7pt). Such conditions clearly pose a challenge to traditional OCR, which works with 300dpi images (mostly bilevel) and character sizes of usually 10pt or larger. Moreover, images on Web pages tend to have various artefacts due to colour quantization and lossy compression [6].

It should be mentioned that text in Web images is of quite different nature than text in video, for instance. In principle, although methods attempting to extract text from video (e.g., [7]) could be applied to a subset of Web images, they make restricting assumptions about the nature of embedded text (e.g., colour uniformity). As such assumptions are, more often than not, invalid for text in Web images, such methods are not directly discussed here.

Previous attempts to extract text from Web images mainly assume that the characters are of uniform (or almost uniform) colour, work with a relatively small number of colours (reducing the original colours if necessary) and restrict all their operations in the *RGB* colour space [8][9][10]. A novel method that is based on information on the way humans perceive colour differences has been proposed by the authors [11]. That method works on full colour images and uses different colour spaces in order to approximate the way humans perceive colour. It comprises the splitting of the image into layers of similar colour by means of histogram analysis and the merging of the resulting components using criteria drawn from human colour discrimination observations.

This paper describes a new method for segmenting character regions in Web images. In contrast to the authors' previous method [11], it is a bottom-up approach. This is an alternative method devised in an attempt to emulate even closer the way humans differentiate between text and background regions. Information on the ability of humans to discriminate between colours is used throughout the process. Pixels of similar colour (as humans see it) are merged into components and a fuzzy inference mechanism that uses a 'propinquity' measure is devised to group components into larger character-like regions.

The colour segmentation method and each of its constituent operations are examined in the next section and its subsections. Experimental results are presented and discussed, concluding the paper.

2 Colour Segmentation Method

The basic assumption of this paper is that, in contrast to other objects in general scenes, text in image form can always be easily separated (visually) from the background. It can be argued that this assumption holds true for all text, even more so for text intended to make an impact on the reader. The colour of the text in Web images and its visual separation from the background are chosen by the designer (consciously or subconsciously) according to how humans perceive it to 'stand out'.

To emulate human colour differentiation, a colour distance measure is defined in an alternative colour space. This distance measure is used first to identify colour connected components and then, combined with a new topological feature (using a fuzzy inference system), it is used to aggregate components into larger entities (characters).

Each of the processes of the system is described in a separate subsection below. First, the colour measure is described in the context of colour spaces and human colour perception. The connected components labelling process using this colour distance is described next. The two features (colour distance and a measure of spatial proximity) from which the new 'propinquity' measure is derived are presented in Section 2.3. Finally, the fuzzy inference system that computes the propinquity measure is the subject of Section 2.4 before the description of the last stage of colour connected component aggregation (Section 2.5).

2.1 Colour Distance

To model human colour perception in the form of a colour distance measure, requires an examination of the different colour spaces in terms of their perceptual uniformity. The *RGB* colour system, which is by far the most frequently used system in image analysis applications, lacks a straightforward measurement method for *perceived* colour difference. This is due to the fact that colours having equal distances in the *RGB* colour space may not necessarily be perceived by humans as having equal distances.[1] A more suitable colour system would be one that exhibits perceptual uniformity. The CIE (Commission Internationale de l'Eclairage) has standardised two colour systems ($L^*a^*b^*$ and $L^*u^*v^*$) based upon the CIE *XYZ* colour system [12][13]. These colour systems offer a significant improvement over the perceptual non-uniformity of *XYZ* [14] and are a more appropriate choice to use in that aspect than *RGB* (which is also perceptually non-uniform, as mentioned before).

The measure used to express the perceived colour distance in the current implementation of this method is the Euclidean distance in the $L^*a^*b^*$ colour space ($L^*u^*v^*$ has also been tried, and gives similar results). In order to convert from the *RGB* to the $L^*a^*b^*$ colour space, an intermediate conversion to *XYZ* is necessary. This is not a straightforward task, since the *RGB* colour system is by definition hardware-dependent, resulting in the same *RGB*-coded colour being reproduced on each system slightly differently (based on the specific hardware parameters). On the other hand, the *XYZ* colour system is based directly on characteristics of human vision (the spectral composition of the *XYZ* components corresponds to the colour matching characteristics of human vision) and therefore designed to be totally hardware-independent. In reality, the vast majority of monitors conform to certain specifications, set out by the standard *ITU-R recommendation BT.709* [15], so the conversion suggested by *Rec.709* can be safely used and is the one used for this method. The conversion from *XYZ* to $L^*a^*b^*$ is straightforward and well documented.

---

[1] For example, assume that two colours have RGB (Euclidean) distance δ. Humans find it more difficult to differentiate between the two colours if they both lie in the green band than if the two colours lie in the red-orange band (with the distance remaining δ in both cases). This is because humans are more sensitive to the red-orange wavelengths than they are to the green ones.

2.2 Colour Connected Component Identification

Colour connected component labelling is performed in order to identify components of similar colour. These components will form the basis for the subsequent aggregation process (see Section 2.5). It should be noted that although the aggregation process that follows would still work with pixels rather than connected components as input, using connected components significantly reduces the number of mergers and subsequently the computational load of the whole process.

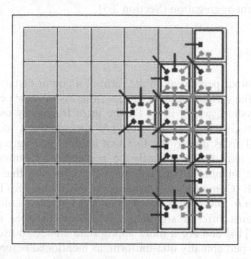

Fig. 1. A connected component (white) and its external and internal connections to its neighbouring components (shown in dark and light grey). Black lines indicate the external connections (to pixels belonging to different components) and light grey lines the internal connections (to pixels of the same component)

The idea behind this pre-processing step is to group pixels into components, if and only if a human being cannot discriminate between their colours. The rationale at this stage is to avoid wrong groupings of pixels as – this is true for all bottom-up techniques – early errors have potentially significant impact on the final results.

The identification of colour connected components is performed using a one-pass segmentation algorithm adapted from a previously proposed algorithm used for binary images [16]. For each pixel, the colour distance to its adjoining (if any) connected components is computed and the pixel is assigned to the component with which the colour distance has the smallest value. If the pixel in question has a distance greater than a threshold to all its neighbouring connected components, a new component is created from that pixel.

The threshold below which two colours are considered similar was experimentally determined and set to *20* in the current implementation. In fact, it was determined as the maximum threshold for which no character was merged with any part of the background. It should be noted, since the images in the training data set include cases containing text very similar to the surrounding background in terms of hue, luminance or saturation, this threshold is believed to be appropriate for the vast majority of text in Web images. Finally, the chosen threshold is small enough to conform to the opening statement that only colours that cannot be differentiated by humans should be grouped together.

2.3 Propinquity Features

The subsequent aggregation of the connected components produced by the initial labelling process into larger components is based on a fuzzy inference system (see next section) that outputs a *propinquity* measure. This measure expresses how close two components are in terms of colour and topology.

The propinquity measure defined here is based on two features: a colour similarity measure and a measure expressing the degree of 'connectivity' between two components. The colour distance measure described above (Section 2.1) is used to assess whether two components have perceptually different colours or not.

The degree of connectivity between two components is expressed by the *connections ratio* feature. A *connection* is defined here as a link between a pixel and any one of its 8-neighbours, each pixel thus having 8 connections. A connection can be either internal (i.e., both the pixel in question and the neighbour belong to the same component) or external (i.e. the neighbour is a pixel of another component). Figure 1 illustrates the external and internal connections of a given component to its neighbouring components.

Given any two components a and b, the connections ratio, denoted as $CR_{a,b}$, is defined as

$$CR_{a,b} = \frac{C_{a,b}}{\min(Ce_a, Ce_b)} \tag{1}$$

where $C_{a,b}$ is the number of (external) connections of component a to pixels of component b, and Ce_a and Ce_b refer to the total number of external connections (to all neighbouring components) of components a and b, respectively. The connections ratio is therefore the number of connections between the two components, divided by the total number of external connections of the component with the smaller boundary. The connections ratio ranges from $0 - 1$.

In terms of practical significance, the connections ratio is far more descriptive of the topological relationship between two components than other spatial distance measures (e.g., the Euclidean distance between their centroids). A small connections ratio indicates loosely linked components, a medium value indicates components connected only at one side, and a large connections ratio indicates that one component is almost included in the other. Moreover, the connections ratio provides a direct indication of whether two components are neighbouring or not in the first place, since it will equal zero if the components are disjoint.

2.4 Fuzzy Inference

A fuzzy inference system has been designed to combine the two features described above into a single value indicating the degree to which two components can be merged to form a larger one. The $L^*a^*b^*$ colour distance and the connections ratio described in the previous sections form the input to the fuzzy inference system. The output, called the *propinquity* between the two participating components, is a value ranging between zero and one, representing how close the two components are in terms of their colour and topology in the image. Each of the inputs and the output are coded in a number of membership functions described below, and the relationship between them is defined with a set of rules.

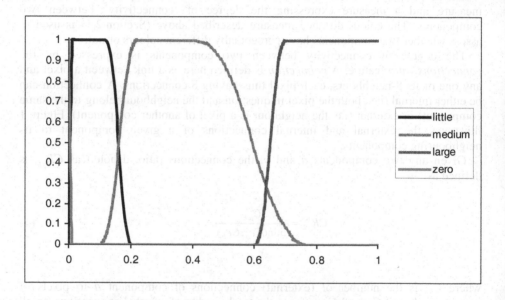

Fig. 2. Membership functions for connections ratio input

The membership functions defined for the connections ratio input can be seen in Figure 2. The components that should be combined are those that correspond to parts of characters. Due to the fact that characters consist of continuous strokes, the components in question should only partially touch each other. For this reason, a *medium* membership function is defined between *0.1* and *0.75*. It is considered advantageous for two components to have a connections ratio that falls in that range in order to combine them. This fact is reflected in the rules comprising the fuzzy inference system, which favour a connectivity ratio in the *medium* region, rather than one in the *small* or *large* regions. Furthermore, a membership function called *zero* is defined, in order to facilitate the different handling of components that do not touch at all, and should not be considered for merging.

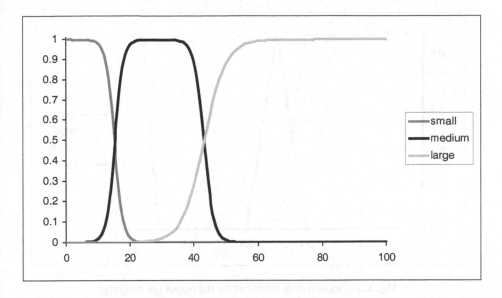

Fig. 3. The membership functions for the colour distance input

There are three membership functions defined for the $L^*a^*b^*$ colour distance input, namely *small*, *medium* and *large* (see Figure 3). The *small* membership function is defined between *0* and *15*. Colours having an $L^*a^*b^*$ distance less than *15* cannot be discriminated by a human being, therefore a colour distance falling in the small range is being favoured by the rules of the fuzzy inference system. In contrast, a large membership function has been defined for colour distances above *43*. Components having a colour distance in that range are considered as the most inappropriate candidates to be merged. The middle range, described by the medium membership function, is where there is no high confidence about whether two components should be merged or not. In that case, the rules of the system give more credence to the connections ratio feature. The thresholds of *15* and *43* were experimentally determined, as the ones that minimise the number of wrong mergers.

The single output of the fuzzy inference system, the propinquity, is defined with the help of five membership functions (see Figure 4). There are two membership functions at the edges of the possible output values range, namely *zero* and *definite*, and three middle range membership functions: *small*, *medium* and *large*. This set of membership functions allows for a high degree of flexibility in defining the rules of the system, while it encapsulates all the possible output cases.

The fuzzy inference surface, picturing the relationship defined by the rules of the system between the two inputs and the propinquity output can be seen in Figure 5. The fuzzy inference system is designed in such a way, that a propinquity of *0.5* can be used as a threshold in deciding whether two components should be considered for merging or not.

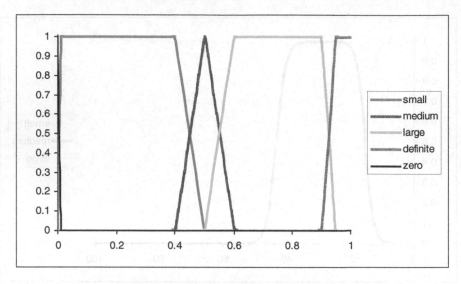

Fig. 4. The membership functions for the output (propinquity)

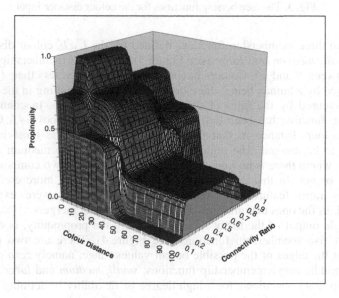

Fig. 5. The fuzzy inference system surface

2.5 Colour Component Aggregation

The merging algorithm considers pairs of connected components, and based on the propinquity output of the fuzzy inference system, combines them or not. All components produced by the initial colour connected components identification process are considered.

For each connected component, the propinquity to each of the neighbouring components is computed, and if it is greater than a set threshold, a possible merger is identified. A sorted list of all possible mergers is maintained, based on the computed propinquity value. The algorithm proceeds to merge the components with the largest propinquity value, and updates the list after each merger, including possible mergers between the newly created component and its neighbours. Only the necessary propinquity values are recalculated after each merger, keeping the number of computations to a minimum. The process continues in an iterative manner, as long as there are merger candidates in the sorted list having propinquity greater that the threshold. The threshold for propinquity is set (as a direct result of the design of the membership functions) to be 0.5.

3 Results and Discussion

The colour segmentation method was evaluated using a variety of images collected from different Websites. The test set comprises 124 images, which are divided into four categories: (a) Multicoloured text over multicoloured background (24 images), (b) Multicoloured text over single-coloured background (15 images), (c) Single-coloured text over multicoloured background (30 images) and (d) Single-coloured text over single-coloured background (55 images). This distribution reflects the occurrence of images on Web documents. The number of colours in the images ranges from two to several thousand and the bits per pixel are in the range from 8 to 24. A width of four pixels was defined as the minimum for any character to be considered readable.

The evaluation of the segmentation method was performed by visual inspection. This assessment can be subjective for the following reasons. First, the borders of the characters are not precisely defined in most of the cases (due to anti-aliasing or other artefacts e.g. artefacts caused by compression). Second, no other information is available about which pixel belongs to a character and which to the background (no ground truth information is available for Web images). For this reason, in cases where it is not clear whether a character-like component contains any pixel of the background or not, the evaluator decides on the outcome based on whether by seeing the component on its own he/she can understand the character or not. The foundation for this is that even if a few pixels have been misclassified, as long as the overall shape can still be recognised, the character would be identifiable by OCR software.

The following rules apply regarding the characterisation of the results. Each character contained in the image is characterised as identified, partially identified or missed. Identified characters are those that are described by a single component. Partially identified ones are the characters described by more than one component, as long as each of those components contain only pixels of the character in question (not any background pixels). If two or more characters are described by only one component (thus merged together), yet no part of the background is merged in the same component, then they are also characterised as partially identified. Finally, missed are the characters for which no component or combination of components exists that describes them completely without containing pixels of the background as well.

The algorithm was tested with images of each of the four categories. In category (a) 223 out of 420 readable characters (53.10%) were correctly identified, 79 characters (18.57%) were partially identified and 119 characters (28.33%) were missed. In addition, out of the 487 non-readable characters of this category, the method was able to identify 245 and partially identify 129. In category (b) the method correctly identified 284 out of 419 characters (67.78%) while 88 (21.00%) were partially identified and 47 (11.22%) missed. There were no non-readable characters in this category. In category (c) 443 (72.74%) out of 609 readable characters were identified, 115 (18.88%) partially identified and 51 (8.37%) missed. In this category, the method was also able to identify 130 and partially identify 186 out of 388 non-readable characters. Finally, in category (d) 572 (73.71%) out of 776 readable characters were identified, 197 (25.39%) partially identified and 7 (0.9%) missed. In addition, 127 out of 227 non-readable characters were identified and 53 partially identified.

Fig. 6. An image containing gradient text blended with the background and the corresponding results

Fig. 7. An image containing multi-coloured characters over multi-coloured background and the corresponding results

The results mentioned above reflect the increasing difficulty in categories where the text and/or the background are multi-coloured. In figures 6 to 9, a number of images of the test set can be seen, along with the corresponding results. The black characters denote correctly identified ones, whereas the grey ones (red in the original) partially identified ones.

In conclusion, a new approach for the segmentation of characters in images on Web pages is described. The method is an attempt to emulate the ability of humans to differentiate between colours. A fuzzy propinquity measure is used to express the likelihood for merging two components, based on topological and colour similarity

Fig. 8. An image containing shadowed and outlined characters and the corresponding results

Fig. 9. An image containing single-colour characters over multi-coloured background and the corresponding results

features. The results of the method indicate a better performance than the previous method devised by the authors and comparable performance to other existing methods. Continuous work is concentrating on the possibilities to enhance the propinquity measure by adding more features and in the further optimisation of the fuzzy inference system. Results over a large test set indicate potential for better performance.

Acknowledgement. The authors would like to express their gratitude to Hewlett-Packard for their substantial equipment donation in support of this project.

References

1. Search Engine Watch, http://www.searchenginewatch.com
2. M.K. Brown, "Web Page Analysis for Voice Browsing", *Proceedings of the 1st International Workshop on Web Document Analysis (WDA'2001)*, Seattle, USA, September 2001, pp. 59-61.
3. G. Penn, J. Hu, H. Luo and R. McDonald, "Flexible Web Document Analysis for Delivery to Narrow-Bandwidth Devices", *Proceedings of the 6th International Conference on Document Analysis and Recognition (ICDAR'01)*, Seattle, USA, September 2001, pp. 1074–1078.
4. A. Antonacopoulos, D. Karatzas and J. Ortiz Lopez, "Accessing Textual Information Embedded in Internet Images", *Proceedings of SPIE Internet Imaging II*, San Jose, USA, January 24-26, 2001, pp.198-205.

5. J. Zhou and D. Lopresti, "Extracting Text from WWW Images", *Proceedings of the 4th International Conference on Document Analysis and Recognition (ICDAR'97)*, Ulm, Germany, August, 1997

6. D. Lopresti and J. Zhou, "Document Analysis and the World Wide Web", *Proceedings of the 2nd IAPR Workshop on Document Analysis Systems (DAS'96)*, Marven, Pennsylvania, October 1996, pp. 417–424.

7. H. Li; D. Doermann and O. Kia, "Automatic text detection and tracking in digital video", *IEEE Transactions on Image Processing*, vol. 9, issue 1, Jan. 2000, pp. 147-156.

8. D. Lopresti and J. Zhou, "Locating and Recognizing Text in WWW Images", *Information Retrieval*, **2** (2/3), May 2000, pp. 177–206.

9. A.K. Jain and B. Yu, "Automatic Text Location in Images and Video Frames", *Pattern Recognition*, vol 31, no. 12, 1998, pp.2055-2076.

10. A. Antonacopoulos and F. Delporte, "Automated Interpretation of Visual Representations: Extracting textual Information from WWW Images", *Visual Representations and Interpretations*, R. Paton and I Neilson (eds.), Springer, London, 1999.

11. A. Antonacopoulos and D. Karatzas "An Anthropocentric Approach to Text Extraction from WWW Images", *Proceedings of the 4th IAPR Workshop on Document Analysis Systems (DAS'2000)*, Rio de Janeiro, Brazil, December 2000, pp. 515–526.

12. R. C. Carter and E. C. Carter, "CIE L*u*v* Color-Difference Equations for Self-Luminous Displays," *Color Research and Applications*, vol. 8, 1983, pp. 252-253.

13. K. McLaren, "The development of CIE 1976 (L*a*b*) Uniform Colour Space and Colour-diference Formlua," *Journal of the Society of Dyers and Colourists*, vol. 92, 1976, pp. 338-341.

14. G. Wyszecki and W. S. Stiles, *Color Science - Concepts and Methods, Quantitative Data Formulas*. John Wiley, New York, 1967.

15. *Basic Parameter Values for the HDTV Standard for the Studio and for International Programme Exchange*, ITU-R Recommendation BT.709 [formely CCIR Rec.709] Geneva, Switzerland: ITU 1990.

16. A. Antonacopoulos, "Page Segmentation Using the Description of the Background", *Computer Vision and Image Understanding*, vol. 70, 1998, pp. 350-369.

Word and Sentence Extraction Using Irregular Pyramid

Poh Kok Loo[1] and Chew Lim Tan[2]

[1]School of the Built Environment & Design, Singapore Polytechnic,
Singapore 139651
[2]School of Computing, National University of Singapore,
Singapore 117543

Abstract. This paper presents the result of our continued work on a further enhancement to our previous proposed algorithm. Moving beyond the extraction of word groups and based on the same irregular pyramid structure the new proposed algorithm groups the extracted words into sentences. The uniqueness of the algorithm is in its ability to process text of a wide variation in terms of size, font, orientation and layout on the same document image. No assumption is made on any specified document type. The algorithm is based on the irregular pyramid structure with the application of four fundamental concepts. The first is the inclusion of background information. The second is the concept of closeness where text information within a group is close to each other, in terms of spatial distance, as compared to other text areas. The third is the "majority win" strategy that is more suitable under the greatly varying environment than a constant threshold value. The final concept is the uniformity and continuity among words belonging to the same sentence.

1 Introduction

In today's environment, document that one has to read and process is growing at an exponential rate. The requirement to be able to extract and summarise text information on a document with speed and accuracy is increasingly important. Although most of the information has already been digitized, the transformation of the imaged document's text content into a symbolic form for reuse still remains as a very active research area [1]. Before the text content can be recognized by an OCR system and converted into a symbolic form, it must be extracted from the imaged document. There have been many studies about text extraction. Some focuses on the extraction of characters [2], a few works directly on the word level [3], [4] and others direct their attention to layout analysis [5]. Our algorithm will perform the extraction task starting from the word level and progress into the layout analysis to extract sentences. Some techniques make use of a model to guide the extraction where the specific type of document under process is known in advance. Others will base on just the raw input data, which is what our algorithm will do. Due to the complexity of the problem and the vast variety of methods, it is not easy to categorize all methods. Nevertheless, in our context we will categorize them into non-pyramid and pyramid techniques. The majority of the proposed methods fall under the non-pyramid techniques.

D. Lopresti, J. Hu, and R. Kashi (Eds.): DAS 2002, LNCS 2423, pp. 307–318, 2002.

Most non-pyramid techniques perform detailed spatial analysis of the text area. Assumption about the physical spatial property of the image is required. In most cases, text images must be aligned or grouped in a homogeneous direction (i.e. horizontally or vertically). Most of them require the application of further skew correction technique [3], [5] before the content can be extracted properly. The statistically based approach proposed by Wang, Phillips and Haralick [4] require the inter-glyph and inter-word distances in its probability computation that are horizontally aligned. The splitting and merging technique as proposed by Wong, Casy and Wahl [6] requires text information to be separable in the horizontal or vertical direction. Others rely on the detailed analysis of the inter-component spacing. The labelling algorithm [7] also requires the alteration in the image horizontal scale to facilitate the extraction.

In the pyramid category, the majority of the proposed methods make use of the regular pyramid structure. Most of these studies require connected component analysis. A strong assumption of disjoint components is needed to ensure correct extraction of text images [8]. In our algorithm, no connected component analysis is required. The aggregation of pixels into characters and character into words is done through the natural grouping of pixels and regions. This proposed algorithm has no assumption in terms of the size, font, orientation and layout of text images. Although the regular pyramid shares the same benefit as in irregular pyramid with the ability to carry out image abstraction in achieving reduced computation cost and permitting local analysis of image features, it suffers from its rigid contraction scheme and there exists the shift dependent problem [9]. Due to the effect of the fixed decimation function (eg. summation of 4 pixels into 1) in a regular pyramid the coarse representation of the image will be distorted if the original image is shifted. For irregular pyramids, in particular, the stochastic pyramid as proposed by Kropatsch [10], only local information is required in its decimation. Large decimation ratio is obtained and thus results in a faster pyramid construction time. The shift dependence problem no longer exists, since its structure is flexible enough to match with the input content. The content of the image will control the aggregation process. To date there are only a handful of studies on irregular pyramids. Some address the issues of increasing the efficiency in building the pyramid through the reduction of pyramid levels [11]. Others use the pyramid structure to perform region segmentation [12], [13], edge detection [11], or connected component analysis [7]. No direct attempt is made to use the irregular pyramid to extract logical text group from a text image in existing works. This paper will propose an algorithm based on the irregular pyramid to perform text extraction. This is the result of our continued work on a further enhancement to our previous proposed algorithm [14].

2 Fundamental Concepts

There are a few basic concepts that our algorithm relies on. They are the inclusion of background information, concept of "closeness", density of a word region, majority "win" strategy and the directional uniformity and continuity among words in a sentence. The following subsections describe these concepts in detail.

2.1 Inclusion of Background Information

This is one of the unique features of our algorithm. Unlike most of the proposed methods, we include the background information in the processing. Background information are those white areas (ie. for a binary image) surrounding the actual black foreground where the actual text images are. Most researchers focus their attention only on the actual text image and discard the background information. In our algorithm, the main focus is still the foreground data, but the background information is also processed with a lower priority. Unlike the other methods where the strong assumption of horizontal alignment allows strict geometric analysis among text region, it is too complex or even not possible for our algorithm to base on this analysis to achieve our objective. In order to process text images of any size and orientation, we need the background region to guide the algorithm to perform the extraction. Clues about how various fragments of the text image are held together are in the background area.

2.2 Concept of 'Closeness''

We have discussed how English texts are formed and arranged in terms of the proximity among the characters and words but exactly what kind of distance is considered "close". If we are processing text with a common font, size and orientation, then perhaps it is possible to find a value in defining "closeness". Some papers [12], [15] have explored the possibility to compute such a value for their extraction activity with certain degree of success. Nevertheless, the method is quite restrictive in terms of the kind of document it can process. Once there is a considerable mixture of fonts or sizes and the orientation gets very irregular, than the likelihood of getting such a value become impossible. In our algorithm, instead of attempting to compute this value, we define a general concept of "closeness".

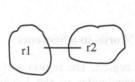

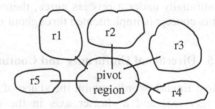

Fig. 1. 'Closeness'' between two regions   **Fig. 2.** "Closeness" among multiple regions

Two regions are considered "close" if they are next to each other. Multiple regions are considered "close" if they are "close" to a common pivot region. The pivot region is like a pulling force to attract all neighboring regions together. There is no computation of any distance. Figures 1 and 2 are the diagrams showing these two cases. No attempt is made to define what is "close" beyond the immediate surrounding. Regions just need to be present in the neighborhood to be "close".

2.3 Density of a Word Region

In our algorithm, a word region is defined as a collection of pixel points. It includes both foreground and background pixels. It is a regional area enclosing a complete word comprising of multiple characters. The mass of the region is defined as the total number of black pixels. The area of the region is defined as the total number of pixel points including both black and white pixels. The density of this region is computed as the mass over the total area of the region. This value indirectly reflects how much background information is used to enclose a complete word. A larger density value shows that the characters in the word are placed closer together. In contrast a smaller density indicates a loosely positioned character within the word. This density value is independent of the size, font and orientation of the text. To capitalize on this property, our algorithm has made use of the density value in two different ways. The first is used as a value to determine whether a word region has been formed or it is still a region holding word fragment. A complete word region is formed by many smaller regions. Each smaller region will hold different fragments of the word. As compared to a complete word region, the density of a region containing word fragments varies greatly among its neighboring regions. Such variation in density becomes a suitable condition to determine word formation. The second is used as a criterion to determine a correct word formation among a group of neighboring words. This leads us to our next concept.

2.4 Majority "Win" Strategy

Since our algorithm has no restriction to the kind of document it can process, the variation over the text image feature will vary greatly. The possibility to make global decision by using some constant factor becomes very low. There is simply no way to enforce a common condition that all can follow. Under such a scenario, the next best strategy is to get the majority agreement. If the majority of the members among the community under a process agree, then the members in question should agree also. This concept is implemented throughout our algorithm.

2.5 Directional Uniformity and Continuity among Words in a Sentence

Most English words exhibit the shape of an elongated region. The region will have a longer axis and a shorter axis in the direction perpendicular to the longer axis. Directional path of a word region is defined as the path along the longer axis. As we examine such a directional path of all words in a sentence, usually we can find uniformity in terms of the direction. All words in a sentence will follow the same direction. This is a common scenario observed in most text documents.

But there can be situations where there is no directional uniformity among words within a sentence. This frequently occurs in advertisements or posters where words are aligned in different orientations to have the artistic effect. Words in the same sentence can be positioned in different directions. Although uniformity has lost in this instance, there is still some form of continuity among the words belonging to the same sentence. Regardless of how artistic is the words' arrangement, continuity among words will still exist to allow human reader to relate such group of words. Figure 3 shows two examples. In our algorithm, two words are considered continuous if the projections of their directional paths intersect. Regardless of where the intersection points are, as long as they lie within the image boundary they are considered valid. By basing on the property of uniformity and continuity, words can be grouped to form sentence.

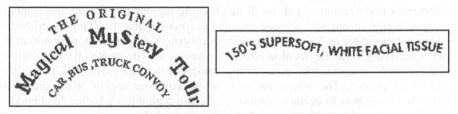

Fig. 3. Words uniformity and continuity in a sentence

3 Irregular Pyramid Structure

One key feature in our algorithm is the use of an irregular pyramid structure to represent the image content. In addition to just image representation, the algorithm uses this structure for its entire extraction process. Without the pyramid structure, some of our concepts cannot be realized. The present research makes use of an irregular variant, which is adapted from Kropatsch's irregular pyramid [11], [16].

The main use of a pyramid structure is to hold an image content. The structure is formed by a set of resolution levels. Starting from the base where the original image resides, each successively higher pyramid level will hold a transformed image content of a lower resolution. The image content of the lower pyramid level is condensed and represented by a smaller set of data point at the higher pyramid level. The resulting pyramid will be a structure holding successively coarser version of the image from the lower pyramid level till the pyramid apex. The construction of any pyramid structure involves three main components. They are the input image, a transformation function and an output image. An input image from a lower pyramid level is fed into a transformation function where the resulting output image is produced and placed on a higher pyramid level. The objective of the transformation function is to analyze and summarize the content of the input image and produce a smaller and yet representative set of image data point to form the output image. Unlike regular pyramid, the transformation function for an irregular pyramid structure is more complex. Instead of predetermining the number of data points to be transformed onto the next level, a decimation process is used to decimate un-qualified data points. Only data points that satisfy the criteria are promoted to the next level. Besides the decimation process, irregular pyramid also has two other processes that are not required in a regular pyramid construction. These are the explicit selection of children and neighbors. Due to the constancy nature in a regular pyramid transformation process that is known in advance, the children and neighbor can easily be determined. In an irregular pyramid, this must be maintained explicitly with the survivor. The number of children and neighbors that a survivor must maintain will vary.

In our algorithm, the objective is to extract a word group of any size, font or orientation. A region that encloses such a word group can be of any irregular size and shape. Our strategy is first to identify the potential center of a word group (ie. local maximal among the neighboring regions). With this central region as the survivor we assign the neighboring non-surviving regions (ie. fragments of the word group) to become its children. Another way to view this is to allow the center of the word group to become a pivot region to pull in all neighboring regions that are the fragments of the word group. In order to achieve this, the decimation and the claiming criteria in our algorithm are set as follows. The decimation criterion is to allow region with the largest surviving value (ie. local maximal) to survive and decimate all other regions. Each region is assigned with a surviving value equal to its own mass plus all its neighboring masses. The motivation is to allow a heavier region or a region with many mass neighbors to become a survivor. Such a region has a higher likelihood of being the center of a word group and thus become a better pivot region. As for the claiming rule, the criterion is to permit a region that has an unstable density with respect to its neighboring region to claim more children than a stable region.

4 The Algorithm

Our proposed algorithm is divided into two main sections. The first is for the extraction of word groups. The other is the concatenation of words into a sentence. Both processes are based on the same pyramid structure. In the algorithm, each data point on a pyramid level represents a region. Each individual region will maintain a list of attributes. The attributes are the area of the region, mass of the region, the children list, the neighbor list, a surviving value and the growing directional value. Figure 4 contains the pusedo code of the main algorithm for word extraction. As compared to our previous proposed method in [14], we have made revision to some of the old procedures and added a few new procedures. Below will only highlight the details of the revision and addition.

4.1 The Revision and Addition in the Word Extraction Process

In our previous algorithm there are two main stages in the child selection process. On pyramid level 0 and 1, a survivor will claim all neighboring non-survivors (ie. mass or non-mass region) if there is no other survivor claiming for the same non-survivor. If conflict arises, preference is given to the survivor with a larger surviving value. We call this 'general' claiming of neighboring regions. Starting from level 2 and onwards, a more elaborate child selection process is used and we call this the 'special' claiming. A survivor will first claim all neighboring regions with mass. A non-mass region will only be considered if it helps in the stability of the region's density. The assumption is that on level 0 and 1 there is less possibility to locate a complete word group and thus should encourage more growing. The growing process will slow down from level 2 and onwards as the likelihood to locate a word group is higher.

After we have experimented with more test images we discover that this leads to the problem of "over growing" and "under growing" of the word region. "Over growing"

```
 1:  Create pyramid base level with (original image)
 2:  Pick survivors
 3:  Select children for each survivor
 4:  For (each pyramid level where
         -    the total number of pixel > 1 AND
         -    more word groups continue to form in the last pyramid level)
 5:     { Create pyramid higher level with (previously formed level)
 6:        Update the survivor neighborhood list
 7:        Assign pulling status (ie. general/special) to each region
 8:        Adjust the pulling status (ie. "smoothing")
 9:        Assign surviving value to each region
10:        Pick survivors for the next higher pyramid level
11:        Select children for each survivor  }
```

Fig. 4. The word extraction algorithm

occurs when more than one correct word groups are merged. The region has over grown to include more than one word. This will usually happen when the word size is too small. On the other hand when the word size is too big, it will result in "under growing". A region is "under grown" if it fails to enclose the entire word group. Fragments of the word are extracted as isolated regions. The key reason to the above problems is the timing in switching from "general" to "special" claiming. The purpose for "general" claiming is to bridge the spacing gap in between characters. As a survivor claims or pulls in non-mass blank region, it is using the blank region to grow outwards to bring more word's fragment into the neighborhood. As a result when the size of the word is small, word region may have already been formed at a very early stage of the pyramid level. If we continue to allow "general" claiming, then the word region will continue to grow outwards and chances of growing into other word group will occur. This is the result of "over growing". The scenario of "under growing" is the exact opposite. If the switch from "general" to "special" claiming or pulling is done too early (ie. before the word's fragments are in the neighborhood), then fragments that belong to the same word may remain as an isolated region. Figure 5 shows an overgrown word group where all individual words are erroneously grouped together as one "word". Figure 5 also shows an under grown word where part of the letter "i" and the letter "B" are detached from the word groups.

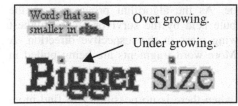

Fig. 5. Problem with over/under growing   **Fig. 6.** Result with the amended algorithm

In order to solve this problem, the algorithm is amended to include a "pulling" status flag for each region. The flag will indicate whether a survivor should use "general" or "special" pulling (ie. pulling of neighboring mass or non-mass non-survivors) to claim its neighboring children. This will allow individual survivors to grow independently from each other depending on their own local situation. Instead of every one following a rigid global decision, the survivors will make their own local decision. In order to make the decision, the survivor will analyze its immediate neighbors. Density is again used as the factor for the decision. If the density of the region formed by merging the survivors and all its surrounding neighbors stay within an acceptable range of the average density of all its neighboring regions, then the region is considered stable and no further growing is required. In contrast, the survivor will continue to grow until the density reaches a stable level. This is achieved in the newly added function on line 7 of figure 4. Although with the above setting we have solved the "over/under growing" problem, a side effect occurs. As the algorithm allows individual survivors to grow at their own rate, the locality of growing becomes random. In order to ensure local growing consistency among neighboring regions, the algorithm is modified to include another processing step (ie. line 8). The purpose is to perform some "smoothing" over the pulling status of the neighboring survivors. A region will maintain its original pulling status if the majority of its neighboring regions also have the same pulling status. This will enforce nearby regions, usually belonging to the same word group, to have the same pulling status. Figure 6 is the result of the new algorithm.

4.2 Sentence Extraction Process

In order to assist the extraction of sentences, an additional attribute called the growing directional weight is added. This attribute is used to retain and reflect the growing path of a word region. It is an array of 8 entries containing the total mass in a specified growing direction. The growing direction is categorized into 8 segments. Just like the 8-connectivity direction, it comprises of top, top-right, right, bottom-right, bottom, bottom-left, left and top-left.

As a survivor is promoted to a higher pyramid level, it retains its original directional weight from the lower level. Using this set of weight as the base, it analyzes all the child regions. By taking the center of mass of the overall region (ie. all regions covered by the survivor) as the pivot point, the direction of where the child is located is computed. Each child is grouped under one of the directions mentioned above. The algorithm will now compare the directional mass inherited from the lower level by the survivor in a specified direction with the total mass of all children in that direction. It will retain the maximal value. As the algorithm progresses up the pyramid level, the directional weight attribute held by the survivor on the highest pyramid level will reflect the largest growing mass in the respective direction. A higher mass value reflects more growing. More word fragments are being pulled in from that direction.

Once the word extraction process stops when there is no possibility to find more word groups (ie. the same number of word groups on two consecutive levels), the extraction of sentence will begin. Figure 7 shows the main algorithm for the extraction of sentences. The new objective is to continue to grow the word region in order for words that belongs to the same sentence to merge as one bigger region. In another words the algorithm must allow words to grow into the correct neighboring regions for words belonging to the same sentence to merge. The algorithm will continue to grow a word region (ie. pull in more blank region), but only in 2 directions. They are the directions with the highest mass value in the directional weight attribute. It reflects that the formed word group is oriented along the 2 directions. There exist cases where no clear directional path can be found. This usually occurs in words that are very short in length (eg. in, of, is, etc). In this situation, the algorithm will examine the surrounding of such a word. The growing direction of the word is determined by the growing direction of the set of closest neighboring word region. The majority win concept is used. The word is assigned with the most frequently occurring growing direction among its neighboring word regions. If no maximum mode exists, the growing direction of the closest word region is used. Unlike word extraction where the closeness among regions is the immediate neighborhood (ie. two regions are next to each other), in sentence extraction all word regions are isolated with a distance apart. As a result the "closeness" definition is redefined as the shortest Euclidean distance between the boundaries of two regions.

```
1:   For (each pyramid level where
  -      the total number of pixel > 1 AND
  -      (the first merging of word group has not occurred OR
  -      more word groups continue to form in the last pyramid level))
2:   {  Create pyramid higher level with (previously formed level)
3:       Update the survivor neighborhood list
4:       Assign pulling status (sentence) to each region
5:       Assign surviving value to each region
6:       Pick survivors for the next higher pyramid level
7:       Select children (sentence) for each survivor  }
```

Fig. 7. The sentence extraction algorithm

The task of growing a word region is to pull in more blank regions along the detected directions. Although the original 8 directional segments are used, further refinement is required. Problem will occur if we have the long word group as shown in figure 8. If the growing direction for the word group is on the left and right, by following the original directional segment all blank regions that are located in A and B will grow together. This is not desirable. Chances for this word group to grow into the wrong region (ie. up and down) are high. As a result, refinement is made in the algorithm to allow a more pointed and targeted growing direction. This will permit the growing of region B only.

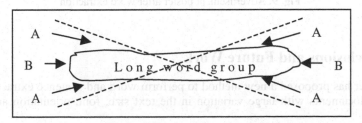

Fig. 8. Targeted growing direction

As we can see in the sentence extraction main algorithm in figure 7, it is almost the same as the word extraction process. The only changes are in the assignment of pulling status, selection of child and the stopping criteria for the entire process. The basic operations are the same as in word extraction, but the attribute in focus and the criteria used are different. Instead of using regional density, the algorithm will make use of the directional weight in its analysis. The criterion used to select children is amended to select only children in the growing directional path. This criterion also allows the growing to be more targeted and pointed towards the growing direction. For the stopping criteria, it is a 2-stage process. In the first stage the growing will begin and continue until it encounters the first merging of words. In the second stage, the growing will proceed until it has detected no further merging of word regions in two consecutive levels.

5   Experimental Results

We now report some of our test cases. In order for our system to focus only on text extraction, large graphically objects are removed through a pre-processing stage [8]. All images are converted to binary images by a thresholding algorithm. The first test case is an advertisement poster with text of varying sizes in the same sentence and aligned in a non-traditional orientation (ie. non-horizontal). This has demonstrated the capability of the algorithm to extract word of different sizes on the same document and even with varying orientation. Figure 9 shows the result of the word extraction. Figure 10 illustrates the merging of words to form their respective sentences. All word groups are correctly merged to the correct sentence. The second test case is a newspaper advertisement for toys. Figures 11 show the output results. All sentences are correctly identified including the three sloping texts, represented by a bounding box for each sentence.

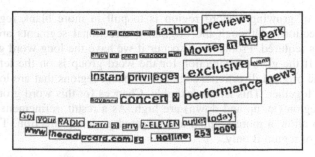

Fig. 9. Advertisement poster after word extraction

6   Conclusions and Future Work

This paper has proposed a new method to perform word and sentence extraction from imaged documents with large variation in the text size, font, orientation and layout

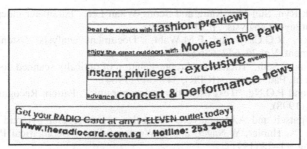

Fig. 10. Advertisement poster after sentence extraction

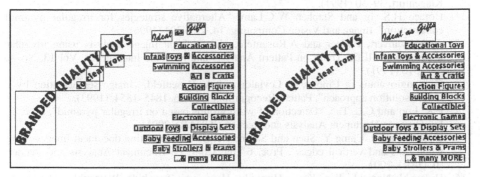

Fig. 11. Toys advertisement after word (ie, left) and sentence (ie. right) extraction

within the same document. The entire algorithm is based on the irregular pyramid structure with the application of four fundamental concepts. Through the process of building the irregular pyramid structure, the algorithm achieves the task of merging characters into words, and words into sentences. It also illustrates the ability to process words of varying orientations and layout where many existing techniques have avoided. Our next task of research is to build a complete system. Starting from the pre-processing to binarize the input image and the elimination of large graphical objects, to the extraction of words and sentences, and finally the correction of text alignment in a form that is acceptable by an OCR system.

References

1. G. Nagy, "Twenty years of document image analysis in PAMI", IEEE Trans. PAMI, Vol. 22, No. 1, 38–62, (Jan 2000).
2. Richard G. Casey and Eric Lecolinet, "A survey of methods and strategies in character segmentation", IEEE Trans. PAMI, Vol. 18, No. 7, (July 1996).
3. U. Pal and B.B. Chaudhuri, "Automatic separation of words in multi-lingual muti-script Indian documents", In Proc. 4th Int. Conf. On Document Analysis and Recogn. (ICDAR '97).
4. Yalin Wang, Ihsin T. Phillips and Robert Haralick, "Statistical-based approach to word segmentation", Proceedings of the ICPR 2000.

5. Dae-Seok Ryu, Sun-Mee Kang and Seong-Whan Lee, "Parameter-independent geometric document layout analysis", IEEE, (2000).
6. K.Y.Wong, R.G.Casy and F.M.Wahl, "Document analysis system", IBM J. Res. Development, Vol 26, 642–656 (1982).
7. G.Nagy and S.Seth, "Hierarchical representation of optically scanned documents", In Proc. 7th Int. Conf. Patt. Recogn. (ICPR), 347–349 (1984).
8. C.L.Tan and P.O.Ng, "Text extraction using pyramid", Pattern Recognition, Vol. 31, No. 1, 63–72 (1998).
9. W.G.Kropatsch and A.Montanvert, "Irregular versus regular pyramid structures", In U. Eckhardt, A. Hubler, W.Nagel, and G.Werner, editors, Geometrical Problems of Image Processing, 11–22 (1991).
10. W.G.Kropatsch, "Irregular pyramids", Proceedings of the 15th OAGM meeting in Klagenfurt, 39–50 (1991).
11. Horace H.S. Ip and Stephen W.C.Lam, "Alternative strategies for irregular pyramid construction", Image and Vision Computing, 14, 297–304 (1996).
12. A. Montanvert, P.Meer and A.Rosenfeld, "Hierarchical image analysis using irregular tessellations", IEEE Trans. on Pattern Analysis and Machine Intelligence, Vol 13, No. 4, 307–316 (1991).
13. G. Bongiovanni, L. Cinque, S. Levialdi and A. Rosenfeld, "Image segmentation by a multiresolution approach", Pattern Recognition, Vol. 26, 1845–1854, (1993).
14. P.K. Loo and C.L. Tan, "Detection of word groups based on irregular pyramid", Proc. 6th Int. Conf. on Document Analysis and Recogn (ICDAR), 2001.
15. Boulos Waked, Ching Y. Suen and Sabine Bergler, "Segmenting document images using white runs and vertical edges", Proc. 6th Int. Conf. on Document Analysis and Recogn (ICDAR), 2001.
16. Hideyuki Negishi, Jien Kato, Hiroyuki Hase and Toyohide Watanable, "Character Extraction from Noisy Background for an Automatic Reference System", In Proc. 5th Int. Conf. On Document Analysis and Recogn. (ICDAR), 143–146 (1999).

Word Searching in Document Images Using Word Portion Matching

Yue Lu and Chew Lim Tan

Department of Computer Science, School of Computing
National University of Singapore, Kent Ridge, Singapore 117543
{luy,tancl}@comp.nus.edu.sg

Abstract. An approach with the capability of searching a word portion in document images is proposed in this paper, to facilitate the detection and location of the user-specified query words. A feature string is synthesized according to the character sequence in the user-specified word, and each word image extracted from documents are represented by a feature string. Then, an inexact string matching technology is utilized to measure the similarity between the two feature strings, based on which we can estimate how the document word image is relevant to the user-specified word and decide whether its portion is the same as the user-specified word. Experimental results on real document images show that it is a promising approach, which is capable of detecting and locating the document words that entirely match or partially match with the user-specified word.

1 Introduction

With the rapid development of computer technology, digital documents have become popular for storage and transmission, instead of the traditional paper documents. The most widespread format for these digital documents is the text in which the characters of the documents are represented by the machine-readable codes(e.g. ASCII codes). The majority of the newly generated documents are in the text format. On the other hand, to make billions of volumes of traditional paper documents available and accessible in the format of digital domain, they are scanned and converted to digital images by the digitization equipment.

Although the technology of Optical Character Recognition(OCR) may be utilized to automatically transfer the digital images of these documents to their machine-readable text format, the OCR has still its inherent weaknesses in the recognition ability, especially for the poor quality document images. Generally speaking, manual correction/proofing of the OCR results is usually unavoidable, which is typically not cost effective for transferring a huge amount of paper documents to their text format. Moreover, the technology of layout analysis is still immature for the documents with complicated layouts. As a result, storing these documents in the image format has become an alternative way in many cases. Nowadays, many digital documents are in the image format. It is therefore

D. Lopresti, J. Hu, and R. Kashi (Eds.): DAS 2002, LNCS 2423, pp. 319–328, 2002.
© Springer-Verlag Berlin Heidelberg 2002

of significant meaning to study the strategies of retrieving information from these document images.

Motivated by the fact that the OCR accuracy requirements for information retrieval are considerably lower than for many document processing applications, the methods with the ability of tolerating recognition errors of OCR have been researched[1,2]. However, the layout analysis and character segmentation are unavoidable in these OCR-based methods. In recent years, a number of attempts have been made to avoid the use of OCR for retrieving information from document images[3,4].

Searching and locating a user specified keyword in the image format documents has its practical value for document information retrieval. For example, by using this technique the user can locate a specified word in the document images without the requirement of OCRing the entire document.

In the case where there are a large number of image documents in the Internet, the user has to download each one to see its contents before knowing whether the document is relevant to his interest. The image based keyword searching technology is capable of notifying the user whether a document image contains words of interest to him, and indicating which documents are worth downloading, prior to transmitting the document images through the Internet.

Some image-based approaches to searching keyword in handwritten[5,6] and printed[7,8,9,10,11] documents have been reported in the past years. To avoid the difficulties of segmenting connected characters in a word image, segmentation-free methods were applied in these approaches. For example, the hidden Markov model and Viterbi dynamic programming algorithm are widely used to recognize keywords. However, these approaches have their disadvantages. Although DeCurtins' approach[7] and Chen's approach[9,10] are capable of searching a word portion, it can only process the predefined keywords, and the pre-training procedure is unavoidable. In our previous word searching system[11], a weighted Hausdorff distance is used to measure the dissimilarity between word images. Although it can cope with any words the user specified, it cannot deal with the problem of portion matching. As a result, the approach is not able to search the word "images" while the user keys in a word "image", because they are considered as different words from the image standpoint.

In this paper, we propose an approach based on partial word image matching, which has the ability of searching the words in the document images if their portions match the user-specified words. For example, it can detect the words such as "knows" and "unknown" while the user keys in the query word "know". A feature string is synthesized according to the the character sequence in the user-specified word, and each word image extracted from documents are represented by a feature string. Then, an inexact string matching technology is utilized to measure the similarity between the two feature strings. Based on the similarity measurement we can estimate how the document word image is relevant to the user specified word. Experiments have been conducted to detect and locate the user-specified words in real document images. The results show that it is a promising approach with the capability of word portion searching.

2   Feature String

To search a user-specified word in a document image, the feature string of the user-specified word is first generated by synthesizing the feature of each character in the word. Then it is matched with the feature string of each word image bounded in the document. According to the matching scoring the corresponding word image is decided whether its portion is the same as the user-specified word.

To extract the feature string of a word image, we scan the word image column by column, and give each column a code. Different code represents different feature as indicated below:

&: there is no image pixel in the column. It corresponds to the blank space between characters generally.

1: upper long vertical strokes. There is only one vertical stroke in the column. Its length is greater than the x-height of the word image, and it is located above the base line.

2: lower long vertical strokes. There is only one vertical stroke in the column. Its length is greater than the x-height of the word image, and it is located below the mean line.

3: vertical strokes. There is only one vertical stroke in the column, and its length is shorter than the x-height of the word image but longer than half of the x-height of the word image.

4: short vertical strokes at the upper-side of the mid-zone. There is in the column only one vertical stroke whose length is shorter than half of the x-height of the word image, and it is located at the upper-side of the mid-zone.

5: short vertical strokes at the lower-side of the mid-zone. There is in the column only one vertical stroke whose length is shorter than half of the x-height of the word image, and it is located at the lower-side of the mid-zone.

6: there are two strokes in the scanned column.

7: there are three or more strokes in the scanned column.

Then, the adjacent neighboring features with the same codes are merged to one code. Figure 1 shows an example of extracting the feature codes from the word image "able".

To achieve the ability of dealing with different fonts, the features used to represent a character should be independent of typefaces. It is a basic necessity to avoid the effect of serif in a printed character. Our observation found that a feature code produced by serif can be eliminated by analyzing its preceding and succeeding features. Fox example, a feature '5' in a feature subsequence '35&' is normally generated by a right-side serif of characters such as 'a', 'd', 'h', 'm', 'n', 'u', etc. Therefore, we can remove straightforward the feature '5' from a feature subsequence '35&', as shown in Figure 1.

Based on the feature extraction described above, we can give each character a feature sequence. For example, the feature sequence of character 'b' is '163', and that of character 'p' is '263'. The feature string of a user specified word can be generated by synthesizing the feature sequence of each characters in the word and inserting a special feature '&' among them to identify a spacing gap.

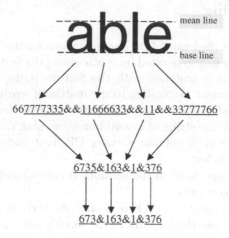

Fig. 1. Feature string

3   Inexact Feature Matching

Based on the above processing, each word image is described by a feature string. The procedure of searching word image has become measuring the similarity between the string $S=[S_1, S_2, \ldots, S_n]$ representing the features of the user-specified word and the string $T=[T_1, T_2, \ldots, T_m]$ representing the features of the word image extracted from the document. Matching word portion becomes evaluating the similarity between the feature string S with the sub-sequence of the feature string T.

In a word image, it is common that two or more adjacent characters are connected with each other, which is possibly caused by low scanning resolution or poor printing quality. This will result in the deletion of the feature '&' in the corresponding feature string, compared to its standard feature string. Moreover, noise effect will undoubtedly produce the substitution or insertion of features in the feature string of the word image. The deletion, insertion and substitution are very similar to the course of evolutionary mutations of DNA sequences in molecular biology.

Drawing inspiration from the alignment problem of two DNA sequences, we apply the technology of inexact string matching to evaluate the similarity between the feature string of the user-specified word and that of the word image extracted from document. From the standpoint of string alignment[12], two opposing features that mismatch correspond to a substitution; a space contained in the first string corresponds to an insertion of the opposing feature into the first string; and a space in the second string corresponds to a deletion of the opposing features from the first string. The insertion and deletion are the reverse of each other. A dash("-") is therefore used to represent a space feature inserted into the corresponding positions in the strings for the situation of deletion. Notice that we use 'spacing' to represent the gap in the word image, whereas we use 'space' to represent the inserted feature in the feature string. Their concepts are completely different.

Definition 1 For a string S of length n and a string T of length m, $V(i,j)$ is defined to be the similarity value of the prefixes $[S_1, S_2, \ldots, S_i]$ and $[T_1, T_2, \ldots, T_j]$. The similarity of S and T is precisely the value $V(n,m)$.

Definition 2 Let $\Sigma=\{\&,1,2,3,4,5,6,7\}$ be the feature set of the strings S and T, and let Σ' be Σ with the added feature "-" denoting a space. Then, for any two features x, y in Σ', $\sigma(x,y)$ denotes the score obtained by aligning the feature x against the feature y.

The similarity of two strings S and T can be computed by dynamic programming with recurrences. The base conditions are :

$\forall i,j$:

$$\begin{cases} V(i,0) = 0 \\ V(0,j) = 0 \end{cases} \tag{1}$$

The general recurrence relation is:

for $1 \leq i \leq n, 1 \leq j \leq m$:

$$V(i,j) = max \begin{cases} 0 \\ V(i-1,j-1) + \sigma(S_i, T_j) \\ V(i-1,j) + \sigma(S_i, -) \\ V(i,j-1) + \sigma(-, T_j) \end{cases} \tag{2}$$

The zero in the above recurrence implements the operation of 'restarting' the recurrence, which can make sure that the unmatched prefixes are discarded from the computation.

We choose the matching scoring between any two features x and y in Σ' as:

$$\sigma(x,y) \begin{cases} \geq 0 & \text{if } x \text{ is same as/similar to } y \\ \leq 0 & \text{else} \end{cases} \tag{3}$$

In the experiments, the scoring of matching any feature in Σ with the space '-' is defined as:

$$\sigma(S_k, -) = \sigma(-, T_k) = -2 \quad for \ S_k, T_k \in \Sigma \tag{4}$$

while the scoring between any feature in Σ is defined in Table 1.

The problem can be evaluated systematically using a tabular computation. In this approach, a bottom-up approach is used to compute $V(i,j)$. We first compute $V(i,j)$ for the smallest possible values for i and j, and then compute the value of $V(i,j)$ for increasing values of i and j. This computation is organized with a dynamic program table of size $(n+1) \times (m+1)$. The table holds the values of $V(i,j)$ for the choices of i and j(see Table 2). Note that the string S corresponds to the horizontal axis of the table, while the string T corresponds to the vertical axis. The values in row zero and column zero are filled in directly from the base conditions for $V(i,j)$. After that, the remaining $n \times m$ sub-table

Table 1. Scoring between features

*	1	2	3	4	5	6	7
*	30	0	0	0	0	0	0	0
1		3	-3	1	-2	-2	-3	-3
2			3	1	-2	-2	-3	-3
3				3	-1	-1	-3	-3
4					3	-2	-3	-3
5						3	-3	-3
6							3	-3
7								3

is filled in one row at a time, in the order of increasing i. Within each row, the cells are filled in the order of increasing j.

The following pseudo code describes the algorithm:

for $i = 1$ to n do
begin
    for $j = 1$ to m do
    begin
        calculate $V(i, j)$ using $V(i - 1, j - 1)$,
            $V(i, j - 1)$, and $V(i - 1, j)$
    end
end

The entire dynamic programming table for computing the similarity between a string of length n and a string of length m, can be obtained in $O(nm)$ time, since only three comparisons and arithmetic operations are needed per cell.

Table 2 illustrates the scoring table computing from the feature strings of the word image "enabled" and the user specified word "able". It can be seen that the maximum scoring achieved in the table corresponds to the matching of character sequence "able" in the word "enabled".

Then, the maximum scoring is normalized as:

$$score = \max_{\forall i,j} V(i, j)/V_s^*(n, n) \tag{5}$$

where $V_s^*(n, n)$ is the matching score between the string S and itself.

If the score is greater than a predefined threshold δ, then we recognize that a portion of the word image matches the user-specified word.

4 Experiments

To verify the validity of the proposed approach of word portion matching, we use it to detect and locate the user-specified words in the real document images. The document images are selected from the scanned books and students' theses that are provided by the Central Library of the National University of Singapore.

Table 2. Scoring table for computing $V(i,j)$

		-	a				b				l		e		
			6	7	3	&	1	6	3	&	1	&	3	7	6
	-	0	0	0	0	0	0	0	0	0	0	0	0	0	0
	3	0	0	0	3	1	1	0	3	1	1	0	3	1	0
e	7	0	0	3	1	3	1	0	1	3	1	1	1	6	4
	6	0	3	1	0	1	0	4	2	1	0	1	0	4	9
	&	0	1	3	1	3	1	2	4	5	3	3	1	2	7
	3	0	0	1	6	4	4	2	5	4	6	4	6	4	5
n	4	0	0	0	4	6	4	2	3	5	4	6	4	3	3
	5	0	0	0	3	4	7	5	5	3	6	4	9	7	5
	&	0	0	0	1	6	5	7	5	8	6	9	7	9	7
	6	0	3	1	0	4	3	8	6	6	5	7	6	7	12
a	7	0	1	6	4	2	1	6	5	6	4	5	4	9	10
	3	0	0	4	9	7	5	4	9	7	7	5	8	7	8
	&	0	0	2	7	12	10	8	7	12	10	10	8	8	7
	1	0	0	0	5	10	15	13	11	10	15	13	11	9	7
b	6	0	3	1	3	8	13	18	16	14	13	15	13	11	12
	3	0	1	0	4	6	11	16	21	19	17	15	18	16	14
	&	0	0	1	2	7	9	14	19	24	22	20	18	18	16
l	1	0	0	0	2	5	10	12	17	22	7	25	23	2	19
	&	0	0	0	0	5	8	10	15	20	25	30	28	26	24
	3	0	0	0	3	3	6	8	13	18	23	28	33	3	29
e	7	0	0	3	1	3	4	6	11	16	21	26	31	36	34
	6	0	3	1	0	1	2	7	9	14	19	24	29	34	39
	&	0	1	3	1	3	1	5	7	12	17	22	27	32	37
	3	0	0	1	6	4	4	3	8	10	15	20	25	30	35
d	6	0	3	1	4	6	4	7	6	8	13	18	23	28	33
	1	0	1	0	2	4	9	7	8	6	11	16	21	26	21

maximum scoring (value 39 circled)

A connected component detecting algorithm is applied to identify all of the connected components in the document image first. The positional relations among the connected components are then utilized to bound the word images. The feature string of each word image is extracted for matching with the feature string of the user-specified word.

When a user keys in a specified word, the system generates its corresponding feature string according to the character sequence. The feature string is matched with each feature string of document words to measure the similarity between them. Figure 2 demonstrates one example, in which the words "processing" and "processed" are detected and located successfully in the document image within the bounding rectangles while the user keys in the word "process" for searching. Another example is given in Figure 3, in which the words "enabled" and "unable" are detected and located in the document image while the user inputs the word "able" for searching.

To evaluate the performance of the system, 25 images of scanned books and 324 images of scanned students' theses are included in the test. 100 words are selected to search their corresponding words and variations from the document images. The system achieves an average precision ranging from 91.57% to 99.21% and an average recall ranging from 87.38% to 97.12% depending on different threshold δ, as shown in Table 3.

A lower δ results in higher recall but at the expense of lower precision. The reverse is true for a higher δ. Thus, if the goal is to retrieve as many relevant

Table 3. Performance vs. Threshold δ

Threshold δ	0.75	0.8	0.85	0.9	0.95
Recall	97.12%	95.23%	91.52%	89.26%	87.38%
Precision	91.57%	92.29%	94.60%	98.73%	99.21%

words as possible, then a lower δ should be set. On the other hand, for low tolerance to precision, then δ should be raised.

Experiments found that the present approach is able to deal with most commonly used fonts, but it cannot handle italic fonts. This is caused by the shortcoming of the features used to represent the word image, in which the features are obtained by vertically scanning the image column by column.

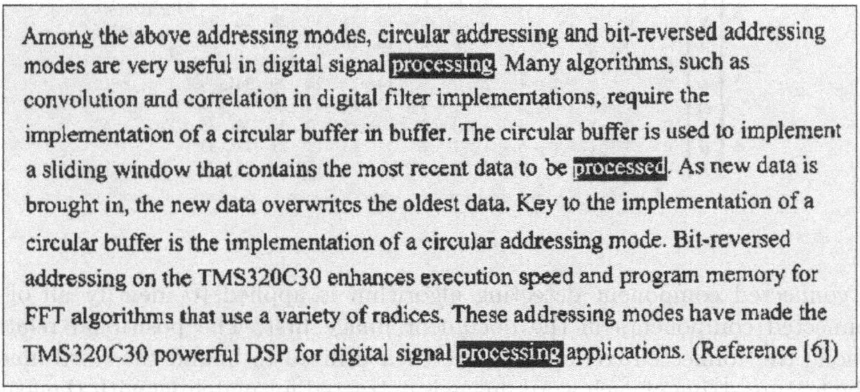

Among the above addressing modes, circular addressing and bit-reversed addressing modes are very useful in digital signal processing. Many algorithms, such as convolution and correlation in digital filter implementations, require the implementation of a circular buffer in buffer. The circular buffer is used to implement a sliding window that contains the most recent data to be processed. As new data is brought in, the new data overwrites the oldest data. Key to the implementation of a circular buffer is the implementation of a circular addressing mode. Bit-reversed addressing on the TMS320C30 enhances execution speed and program memory for FFT algorithms that use a variety of radices. These addressing modes have made the TMS320C30 powerful DSP for digital signal processing applications. (Reference [6])

Fig. 2. Result of searching word "process"

5   Conclusions

We proposed in this paper an approach for word portion searching based on the technique of inexact matching. The user specified word and the word image extracted from documents are represented by two feature strings first. Then, an inexact string matching technique is utilized to measure the similarity between the two feature strings. The present approach has the ability to search words in document images, whose portions match with the user-specified words. The experimental results show that it is a promising approach for word image searching.

However, the present approach cannot handle the italic word image due to the inherent shortcoming of the feature string used to represent the word image. Further work is to overcome the limitation by using a new feature string which is applicable to all typefaces.

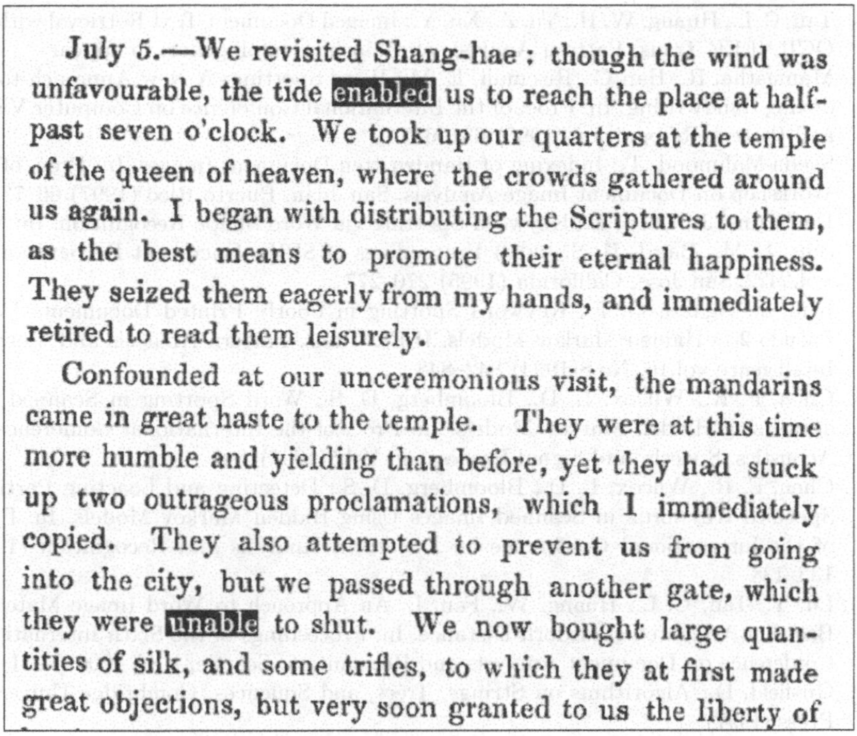

July 5.—We revisited Shang-hae : though the wind was unfavourable, the tide `enabled` us to reach the place at half-past seven o'clock. We took up our quarters at the temple of the queen of heaven, where the crowds gathered around us again. I began with distributing the Scriptures to them, as the best means to promote their eternal happiness. They seized them eagerly from my hands, and immediately retired to read them leisurely.

Confounded at our unceremonious visit, the mandarins came in great haste to the temple. They were at this time more humble and yielding than before, yet they had stuck up two outrageous proclamations, which I immediately copied. They also attempted to prevent us from going into the city, but we passed through another gate, which they were `unable` to shut. We now bought large quantities of silk, and some trifles, to which they at first made great objections, but very soon granted to us the liberty of

Fig. 3. Result of searching word "able"

In addition, from the analysis of recall, it has been found that most of the missing words are caused by the incorrect word bounding(fragmentation mostly). It is therefore necessary to improve the word bounding performance of the system.

Acknowledgements. This project is supported by the Agency for Science, Technology and Research, and Ministry of Education of Singapore under research grant R255-000-071-112/303.

References

1. Ishitani, Y.: Model-based Information Extraction Method Tolerant of OCR Errors for Document Images. In: Proc. of the Sixth International Conference on Document Analysis and Recognition, Seattle, USA (2001) 908–915
2. Ohtam, M., Takasu, A., Adachi, J.: Retrieval Methods for English Text with Mis-recognized OCR Characters. In: Proc. of the Fourth International Conference on Document Analysis and Recognition, Ulm, Germany (1997) 950–956
3. Doermann, D.: The Indexing and Retrieval od Document Images: A Survey. Computer Vision and Image Understanding, Vol.70, No.3 (1998) 287–298

4. Tan, C. L., Huang, W. H., Yu, Z., Xu, Y.: Imaged Document Text Retrieval without OCR. IEEE Trans. Pattern Analysis and Machine Intelligence, to appear
5. Manmatha, R., Han C., Riseman, E. M.: Word Spotting: A New Approach to Indexing Handwriting. In: Proc. of the International Conference on Computer Vision and Pattern Recognition (1996) 631–637
6. Syeda-Mahmood, T.: Indexing of Handwritten Document Images. In: Proc. of the Workshop on Document Image Analysis. San Juan, Puerto Rico (1997) 66–73
7. DeCurtins, J., Chen, E.: Keyword Spotting via Word Shape Recognition. In: Vincent, L. M., Baird, H. S. (eds.) Proceedings of SPIE, Document Recognition II, Vol.2422, San Jose, California (1995) 270–277
8. Kuo, S., Agazzi, O. F.: Keyword Spotting in Poorly Printed Documents Using Pseudo 2-D Hidden Markov Models. IEEE Trans. Pattern Analysis and Machine Intelligence vol.16, No.8(1994) 842–848
9. Chen, F. R., Wilcox, L. D., Bloomberg, D. S.: Word Spotting in Scanned Images Using Hidden Markov Models. In: Proc. of the International Conference on Acoustics, Speech, and Signal Processing, Vol.5(1993) 1–4
10. Chen, F. R., Wilcox, L. D., Bloomberg, D. S.: Detecting and Loacting Partially Specified Keywords in Scanned Images Using Hidden Markov Models. In: Proc. of the International Conference on Document Analysis and Recognition (1993) 133–138
11. Lu, Y., Tan, C. L., Huang, W., Fan, L: An Approach to Word Image Matching Based on Weighted Hausdorff Distance. In: Proceedings of the Sixth International Conference on Document Analysis and Recognition, Seattle, USA (2001) 921–925
12. Gusfield, D.: Algorithms on Strings, Trees, and Squences. Combridge University Press (1997)

Scene Text Extraction in Complex Images

Hye-Ran Byun[1], Myung-Cheol Roh[2], Kil-Cheon Kim[1], Yeong-Woo Choi[3] and
Seong-Whan Lee[2]

[1]Dept. of Computer Science, Yonsei University, Seoul, Korea
{hrbyun, kimkch}@cs.yonsei.ac.kr
[2]Dept. of Computer Science and Engineering, Korea University, Seoul, Korea
{mcroh, swlee}@image.korea.ac.kr
[3]Dept. of Computer Science, Sookmyung Woman's University, Seoul, Korea
ywchoi@sookmyung.ac.kr

Abstract. Text extraction and recognition from still and moving images have many important applications. But, when a source image is an ordinary natural scene, text extraction becomes very complicated and difficult. In this paper, we suggest text extraction methods based on color and gray information. The method using the color image is processed by color reduction, color clustering, and text region extraction and verifications. The method using the gray-level image is processed by edge detection, long line removal, repetitive run-length smearing (RLS), and text region extraction and verifications. Combining two approaches improves the extraction accuracies both in simple and in complex images. Also, estimating skew and perspective of the extracted text regions are considered.

1 Introduction

Texts in natural scene images often contain the important summarized information about the scene. If we could find these items accurately in real time, we can design the vision systems for assisting navigation of the moving robots or the blinds. Much of the previous research has focused on the text extraction with the gray-level images. Zhong *et al.* [1] used a spatial variance by assuming that it is lower in the background regions than in the text regions. But, the ascending and descending characters are not well detected on their test images. Ohya *et al.* [2] presented a method with several restrictions on the texts such as they should be upright without slant or skew, distinctive to the background regions, and uniform in their gray values. After a local thresholding, a relaxation algorithm is used for the component merging. Several kinds of the natural images were tested, and the extraction results are dependent on the text slant or tilt. Lienhart *et al.* [3] extracted the text regions using block matching after splitting and merging the connected components. Their method also has restrictions on size, gray values, and directions of the texts, and it also has difficulties in finding texts with skewed or with several colors on the same texts.

D. Lopresti, J. Hu, and R. Kashi (Eds.): DAS 2002, LNCS 2423, pp. 329–340, 2002.
© Springer-Verlag Berlin Heidelberg 2002

In recent years there have been several approaches for extracting the text regions on color images. Haralick *et al.* [4] proposed a method using a differential top-hats morphological operator. The method shows robustness to the light changes. H. K. Kim [5] presented a method based on color segmentation and color clustering with video frames, and the characters are assumed to lying horizontally with similar colors and size. But, the method used too many ad-hoc thresholds. Jain *et al.* [6] presented two different methods and combined the results with complex color images. The first method used color quantization and connected components analysis on each quantized color plane. The second method used a spatial variance on the converted gray-level image. P. K. Kim [7] presented a method for complex color images. By using local quantization of the colors, text regions mixed with the backgrounds are removed. This method improved the extraction accuracy, but it requires plenty of computation time.

In this paper we extract text regions of natural scene images with two different methods, one in color image and the other in gray-level image. Then, we combine the two methods. Compared to the previous approaches to solve the same or similar problems, our approach has the following distinctive features: 1) To improve the color clustering results a new method is used in RGB color space; 2) To emphasize only the text regions accurately, line components surrounding text regions are removed and repetitive RLS is applied on the gray-level image; and 3) Estimating skew and perspective of the extracted text region is proposed.

2   Text Extractions in Color Images

The extraction method in color images consists of three steps: preprocessing, color clustering, and text region extraction and verification. We assume the colors of the characters in the same text regions are similar in this paper.

2.1   Preprocessing

The preprocessing consists of geometrical clustering, color reduction, and noise reduction. The input image size is 320x240, and the depth of each pixel is 24 bits. To reduce computation time the color reduction is needed and performed by dropping several lower bits of each pixel. During this process, the similar colors that we want to be clustered into the same color are often clustered into different colors. Thus, we first use a geometrical clustering. The geometrical clustering fills the pixels horizontally between the vertical edges with the same color. The vertical edges are found using equations (1) to (3) with a 3x3 mask as shown in figure 1. Equation (1) defines the strength of the vertical edge based on the Euclidean distance, D, defined by (2). The $v_0, ..., v_8$ represents the pixels, and v_R, v_G, v_B are the color components of each pixel. Figure 2 compares the results without and with the geometrical clustering. The edges produced by the proposed method are more accurate and clear. To save the computation, only the filling between the vertical edges is used.

$$E(v_0) = D(v_1, v_3) + 2 * D(v_4, v_5) + D(v_6, v_8) \tag{1}$$

$$D(v_1, v_2) = \sqrt{(v_{1_R} - v_{2_R})^2 + (v_{1_G} - v_{2_G})^2 + (v_{1_B} - v_{2_B})^2} \tag{2}$$

$$v = (v_R, v_G, v_B) \tag{3}$$

v_1	v_2	v_3
v_4	v_0	v_5
v_6	v_7	v_8

Fig. 1. Edge detection mask for the geometrical clustering

Fig. 2. Edge detection results: a given image (left), edge detection without (middle), and with (right) the geometrical clustering

The color reduction is realized by dropping the lower six bits of each RGB component. Thus, the reduced color image can represent up to 64 colors. During this process, a connected component like a stroke in the characters frequently gets disconnected due to noise. A 3x3 mask is used to eliminate the noise and to improve the connectivity of the strokes. The center pixel of the mask is compared with the neighboring pixels. If the number of pixels that have the same color with the center pixel is less than a given threshold, the center pixel is considered as a noise, and is substituted by the majority color in the mask.

2.2 Color Clustering

Since the image contents are sensitive to shading and surface reflections, the pixels in the same text components can be clustered into different colors during the color reduction. Also, since using all the color planes resulting from the color reduction requires a heavy computational cost, the color clustering is performed to reduce the number of color planes.

For 6-bit color clustering, a color histogram is first calculated. Then, the first color for the clustering is selected from the colors that are located at the corner points in the RGB color space with a largest color histogram. If there is no color at the corner points, then the colors located at the nearest to the corner points are the candidates. The nearest color to this beginning color is found by measuring the Euclidean distance between the two colors. If the distance is 1, the two colors are merged into the color with a larger histogram. The next color for clustering is selected by finding the longest distance from the previous merged color. This process is continued until the number of remaining colors is less than a given value, 3 in this paper, or until no more colors are merged. In this way, two complementary or near complementary colors that are usually texts and backgrounds in the natural scene images are rarely merged. Figure 3 shows a result of the color clustering: 30 colors remain after the color reduction, but only 6 colors remain by applying the proposed clustering method. Figure 4 shows the image of the color clustering. Thus, the image can be separated into 6 color planes. For each color plane, a morphological closing with 3x3 structuring element is applied to improve the connectivity of the strokes in the characters.

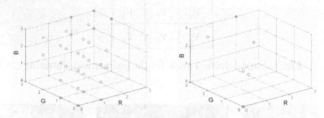

Fig. 3. Results of color reduction (left) and color clustering (right) in RGB color space

Fig. 4. Original image (left) and its clustering result (right)

2.3 Extracting Text Candidates

For each color plane we determine connected components and its size, bounding box of each component and its size, location and aspect ratio. Figure 5 shows the connected components and their bounding boxes. We only show four planes out of six color planes in the above clustering results.

Fig. 5. Bounding boxes of the connected components for each color plane

Then, the connected component is removed when its size is too big or its width or height of the bounding box is too large or too small. The bounding boxes with its height smaller than 7 or larger than 90 pixels are removed. Figure 6 shows the results for each color plane and we can see many of the non-text components are removed.

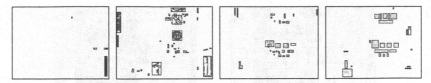

Fig. 6. Removal of non-text components by considering component size, width or height

Next, the remaining boxes are merged to make characters or text lines. Closeness and overlapping ratios between the bounding boxes are examined for merging, and its results are shown in figure 7.

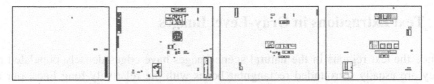

Fig. 7. Merging bounding boxes to make characters or text regions

We again remove some of the bounding boxes by considering the pixel density of the bounding box. The pixel density of the candidate text region is usually larger than that of the non-text bounding box. Figure 8 shows the results.

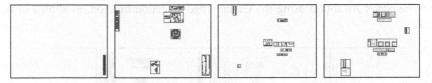

Fig. 8. Removal of the merged boxes as non-texts

Since the text regions usually contain densely packed edges compared to other regions, some of the bounding boxes are further removed by considering the edge distribution. As an example, a region on a wall painted with the same color due to noise or light influence can be easily removed. Figure 9 shows the result. Only three planes maintain the bounding boxes of the candidate text regions with this removal.

Fig. 9. After verifying each box with edge distribution

Finally, considering the overlapping ratio of the bounding boxes combines the results from each color plane. Figure 10 shows the combined result, before and after.

Fig. 10. Bounding boxes obtained in each color plane (left) and their combined results (right)

3   Text Extractions in Gray-Level Images

Since the text regions in the natural scene images have edges densely populated and they are usually surrounded rectangular boxes with the relatively long lines, our approach finds the text regions based on the edge density, and removes the long line elements that can border the text regions during the region emphasis. Also, the long line elements around the text regions are used for the skew and perspective estimations. There are four steps in this approach: preprocessing, text region extraction, verification, and skew/perspective estimations.

A median filter is applied to the 320x240 gray-level image for the preprocessing, then the edges are found using the Canny edge detection method, as shown in figure 11(a).

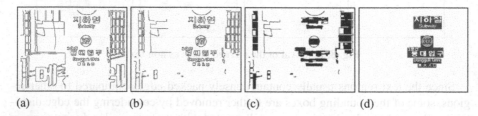

(a)   (b)   (c)   (d)

Fig. 11. Images of (a) edges, (b) long lines removed, (c) RLS applied, (d) extraction results

3.1   Extracting Text Regions

The long line components are first found and removed in the edge image. The long line components include horizontal or vertical lines, quadrilaterals with long lines, and broken lines with long horizontal or vertical components. The 8-directional edge following is performed and the histograms of each direction are obtained. Horizontal or vertical longs lines have the dominant histograms only in one direction. Quadrilaterals have dominant histograms usually in two directions. And, the broken lines also have the dominant histograms in two or three directions. Since the 8-directional histogram bins can be different according to the starting point of the edge following, we also consider 4-directional bins by adding the opposite direction bins together. Then the long line elements will become the connected components with the dominant values of the histograms in either one or two directions both in 8 and 4-directional bins. Figure 11(b) shows the result with the long lines removed.

Then, repetitive RLS is applied to emphasize the text regions, since the edge density of the text regions is usually high. The RLS is applied iteratively since there are various distances between text edges due to size variations in fonts and various interdistances between character strokes. By increasing the run length from small to large horizontally and vertically the text regions are emphasized more accurately. The results are shown in figure 11(c).

3.2 Verifying Candidate Regions

After applying repetitive RLS, we remove the connected components by analyzing the components and their bounding boxes. First, component with a large number of pixels is removed. Those components, for example, can be leaves on a tree or tiles on a wall with dense edges. Also, component with a small number of pixels is removed, since even though the regions are texts they can be hardly recognized due to their small size. Then, we further removed the components when its size is too small comparing to the size of its bounding box. Also, if there are components that have a large aspect ratio or whose widths or heights are less than 5 pixels, they are removed. The results are shown in figure 11(d).

3.3 Skew and Perspective Estimations

After the text regions are extracted, the skew and perspective of the regions are estimated. The long lines surrounding or around the text regions are used to estimate the skew angle. By using a least mean square method to each line component, slope, location, and mean square errors are found.

For the skew estimation, we first apply a simple smoothing to the line elements to remove small bumps, holes, and disconnections. Since we are currently focusing on extracting the horizontal text lines, only the lines with small slopes are smoothed. For each smoothed line element 10 points are sampled for the slope and location estimations. The sample points are obtained by dividing the line components by 10 equal distances. When there exists a line that is almost straight but with small abrupt branches as shown in line 3 of figure 12(a), the slope of this line can be found by sampling 10 points only from the component region that has the maximum histogram in the 4-directional bins. The 10 sampling coordinates are applied to the least mean square method. During this process a component with either a curve or with many branches can be discarded by removing a line with a large mean square error. The line 4 in figure 12(b) is removed due to its high error value.

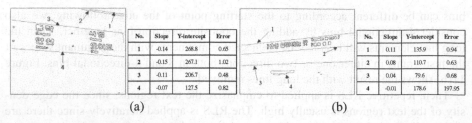

No.	Slope	Y-intercept	Error
1	-0.14	268.8	0.65
2	-0.15	267.1	1.02
3	-0.11	206.7	0.48
4	-0.07	127.5	0.82

No.	Slope	Y-intercept	Error
1	0.11	135.9	0.94
2	0.08	110.7	0.63
3	0.04	79.6	0.68
4	-0.01	178.6	197.95

(a)   (b)

Fig. 12. Examples of finding slopes, locations, and mean square errors

For an accurate estimation of the skew angle the lines are merged when they are located in the vicinity of the same text region. For the lines with small mean square errors we consider both slope and location (Y-intercept) for merging. First, the slopes of the two lines are compared, and when they are very similar, two lines are candidates for merging. Then, the locations are compared, and when they are in close proximity, they are merged. The merged line has slope and location though averaging the two candidate lines. In figure 12(a), lines 1 and 2 are merged, but lines 3 and 4 are not.

When there are two lines surrounding a center of the text box, the skew angle and perspective can be measured. If the slopes of the two lines are very similar, we regard the text region has only skew and the skew angle is used for the correction. But, when the slopes are not similar, there is a perspective. The perspective can be measured by finding four intersection points with two vertical end lines of the image and by subtracting the two vertical distances. When there is only one line located near a text box, only the skew angle can be estimated. The skew and perspective of the text regions are estimated from the lines 1 and 2 of figure 13. The line 3 is not used. The skewed images are corrected by applying shearing transformations as shown in figure 14.

No.	①	②	③
Skew	6.65	6.65	4.74
Perspective	9.57	9.57	9.57

Fig. 13. Examples of skew and perspective estimations

Fig. 14. Skew image (left) and its corrected result (right)

4 Combining Two Approaches

The color-based method is sensitive to the lighting conditions, and the gray-based method is sensitive to the complexity of the background. The former is rather robust to the background complexity, and the latter robust to the lighting conditions. Thus, combining two methods can complement the shortcomings of each method. When the extracted text regions in each method have similar locations and sizes, we conclude the regions as the correct ones and the verification by the other method is skipped. But, when a region is detected as the text region only in one method, this region is verified by the other method. Verifying this local region only can reduce the effect of surrounding edges/objects in the gray-based method, and can expect the improvement of the color clustering in the color-based method. Combining the two methods is shown in figure 15.

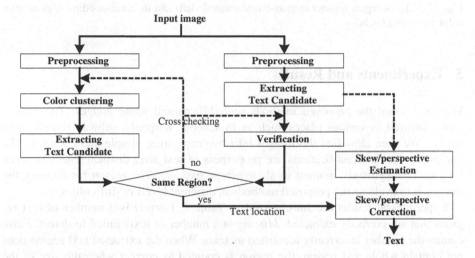

Fig. 15. Combining two methods

When a candidate text region is only detected in the color-based method, that local region is verified. Figure 16(a) shows the regions that are extracted on the color-based method and figure 16(b) shows the corresponding regions with the repetitive RLS is applied on the gray-based method. Since the density of the connected component and the ratio of the bounding boxes in figure 16(b) are not similar to those of the text, these regions are rejected.

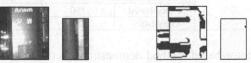

Fig. 16. False accepted regions with color-based method (left) and its corresponding regions after repetitive RLS applied (right)

When a text region is detected only in the gray-based method, the verification is also applied to that local region. Figure 17(a) shows the candidate text regions found in the gray-based method, and figure 17(b) shows their color clustering results in the color-based method. The color clustering results of these local regions are better than the result obtained by color clustering on the whole image. This is because the number of colors remaining after the color clustering is restricted to only two or three. But, for the whole image, the number of colors remained after the clustering can be larger than two or three. Thus, the regions in figure 17 are verified as non-texts by color-based verification.

Fig. 17. False accepted regions in gray-based method (left) and its corresponding regions after color clustering (right)

5 Experiments and Results

We have tested the proposed methods with 120 natural scene images. The images were captured in various places such as in schools, hospitals, subway stations, and streets. We then classified the images into two categories, simple and complex. The guidelines for the classifications are properness of text size, distinctiveness between texts and backgrounds, amount of skew/perspective, *etc*. The reason for dividing the images is to evaluate the proposed methods in different levels of difficulties.

Experimental results are summarized in Table 1. *Correct* is a number of text regions that are correctly extracted. *Missing* is a number of texts failed to detect. *False* counts the number incorrectly identified as texts. When the extracted text region does not contain whole text region, the region is counted as *correct* when the size of the extracted text region is more than two-third of the correct regions. Otherwise, it is counted as *false*.

Table 1. Extraction results with simple and complex test images

	Total number	Method	*Correct*	*False*	*Missing*
Simple images	255	Combining	202	124	53
		Color-based	194	156	61
		Gray-based	210	151	45
Complex images	235	Combining	177	207	58
		Color-based	190	282	45
		Gray-based	165	201	70

From Table 1, color-based method demonstrates better results than the gray-based method for complex images, but it has more false detections. The gray-based method has better performance for simple images. The color-based method gives steady performance on both simple and complex images. Also, the results of the combining method are better than that of each method. The number of false detected regions is significantly reduced, and the number of missing is also reduced.

Figure 18 shows the extraction results. The results show that the color-based method continues to make errors where surface reflection is strong, while the gray-based method fails when the background is complex. In the bottom images of figure 18, the first image is a combined result that does not require cross verifications. The second underwent the cross verifications since some of the bounding-boxes do not coincide in the two results. We can see the usefulness of the cross validations at the bottom images in figure 18.

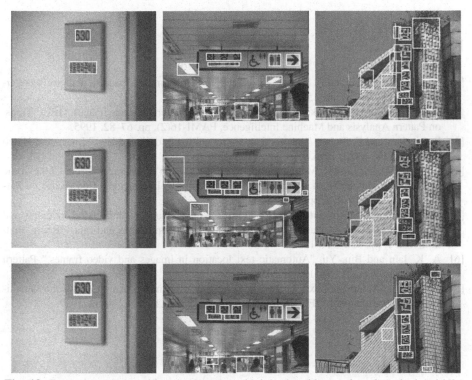

Fig. 18. Extraction results with color-based method (top), with gray-based method (middle), and combined results (bottom)

6   Conclusions

We attempted to extract texts from natural scene images with only a few restrictions. We suggested two different methods for the text extraction, and a method for estimating skew and perspective of the candidate text regions was proposed. Our approach has the following distinctive features: 1) To improve the color clustering results a new method is used in RGB color space; 2) To emphasize only the text regions accurately, line components surrounding text regions are removed and repetitive RLS is applied on the gray-level image; and 3) Estimating skew and perspective of the extracted text region is proposed. With these features our approach shows the improved extraction accuracies both in simple and in complex images in the experiments.

Acknowledgements. This research was supported as a Brain Neuroinformatics Research Program sponsored by Korean Ministry of Science and Technology (M1-0107-00-0009).

References

[1] Y. Zhong, K. Karu and A. K. Jain, "Locating Text in Complex Images," Pattern Recognition, Vol. 28, No. 10, pp. 1523–1535, 1995.

[2] J. Ohya, A. Shio and S. Akamatsu, "Recognizing characters in scene images," IEEE Trans. on Pattern Analysis and Machine Intelligence, PAMI-16(2), pp. 67–82, 1995.

[3] R. Lienhart and F. Stuber, "Automatic text recognition in digital videos," Image and Video Processing IV, SPIE, 1996.

[4] L. Gu, N. Tanaka and R. M. Haralick, "Robust Extraction of Characters from Color Scene Image using Mathematical Morphology," Proceedings of International Conference on Pattern Recognition, Vol. 2, pp. 1002–1004, 1998.

[5] H. K. Kim, "Efficient automatic text location method and content-based indexing and structuring of video database," Journal of Visual Communications and Image Representation, Vol. 7, pp. 336–344, 1996.

[6] A. K. Jain and Bin. Yu, "Automatic text location in images and video frames," Pattern Recognition, Vol. 31, No. 12, pp. 2055–2076, 1998.

[7] P. K. Kim, "Automatic Text Location in Complex Color Images using Local Color Quantization," Proceedings of IEEE Region 10 Conference, Vol. 1, pp. 629–632, 1999.

Text Extraction in Digital News Video Using Morphology

Hyeran Byun[1], Inyoung Jang[1], and Yeongwoo Choi[2]

[1]Visual Information Processing Lab., Dept. of Computer Science, Yonsei University,
134, Shinchon-Dong, Seodaemun-Gu, Seoul, Korea, 120-749
{hrbyun, stefano}@cs.yonsei.ac.kr
[2]Image Processing Lab., Dept. of Computer Science, Sookmyung Women's University,
Chungpa-Dong 2, Yongsan-Gu, Seoul, Korea, 140-742
ywchoi@sookmyung.ac.kr

Abstract. In this paper, a new method is presented to extract both superimposed and embedded scene texts in digital news videos. The algorithm is summarized in the following three steps : preprocessing, extracting candidate regions, and filtering candidate regions. For the first preprocessing step, a color image is converted into a gray-level image and a modified local adaptive thresholding is applied to the contrast-stretched image. In the second step, various morphological operations and Geo-correction method are applied to remove non-text components while retaining the text components. In the third filtering step, non-text components are removed based on the characteristics of each candidate component such as the number of pixels and the bounding box of each connected component Acceptable results have been obtained using the proposed method on 300 domestic news images with a recognition rate of 93.6%. Also, the proposed method gives good performance on the various kinds of images such as foreign news and film videos.

1 Introduction

In recent years the amount of digital video used has risen dramatically to keep pace with the increasing use of the internet and consequently an automated method is needed for indexing digital video databases. Up to now most of digital video indexing is done by human operators. This is an inefficient process due to the need of time and manpower for dealing with massive digital videos. Also, there is a room for making errors on account of the subjective decisions of the human operator. To avoid these inefficiencies and errors, automatic shot segmentation and text extraction have been studied [7,11,12,14]. However, since the automatic methods of shot segmentation alone have limitations for the complete digital video indexing, the research on the text extraction is also needed. Textual information, both superimposed and embedded scene texts, appearing in a digital video can be a crucial clue for helping the video indexing [1–5]. Also, there have been various approaches [1–5,7,11,12,15] for the correct extraction of textual information. In general, typical obstacles are variations in

D. Lopresti, J. Hu, and R. Kashi (Eds.): DAS 2002, LNCS 2423, pp. 341–352, 2002.

size and font, the orientation and positioning of the characters, different textures, un-constrained illumination, and irregular background and color gradients on the character stroke [5,6]. To overcome some of these difficulties, this paper proposes morphological operations and Geo-correction method to extract text regions.

2   Related Works

There are various approaches for extracting and recognizing texts on the image. If the text is in binary images, such as book pages, it can be segmented by identifying the foreground pixels in each horizontal line [8]. But, to extract text regions in complex video frames or scene images we need more advanced approaches. Various advanced methods have been proposed to extract texts from the complex images.

Zhong et al. [9] presented two methods for extracting texts from the complex color images, and combined the methods together. The first method used color image with color quantization and the connected components analysis on each quantized color plane. Heuristic filters for removing non-text components are developed and used. The second method used spatial variance on a gray-level image by assuming that the spatial variance in the background region is lower than that in the text regions. In their approach, the ascending and descending characters are not well detected.

Ohya et al. [10] presented a method to extract text in scene images. In their approach, several assumptions on the characters are used: they should be upright without slant or skew, distinctive between texts and background regions, and uniform in their gray values. Their method first segments image using a local thresholding method for detecting patterns of candidate characters. Then, the differences in the gray values between text and background regions are evaluated. Finally, the similarity to a set of character categories is measured, and component merging is performed by using a relational operation. They tested several kinds of images such as road signs, automobile license plates, and signboards of shops with various sizes, and gray-level under unconstrained illumination conditions. This method is not independent on text slant or tilt.

H. K. Kim [11] presented automatic text detection and location method for color video frames. In his paper, characters are assumed to lying on a horizontal way with uniform color and size. The algorithm first performs color segmentation by quantizing the image using the color histogram. The most dominant color is segmented by clustering colors. In color clustering, selecting color space and distance metrics are critical factors for the results. Then, heuristic filtering is applied to the candidate text regions. This method used too many ad-hoc thresholds.

M. A. Smith [12] proposed a method for extracting textual information from consecutive video frames. In this approach, the characters are assumed to lying on a horizontal line. The algorithm first extracts the high contrast regions using thresholding and vertical edge detection. Then, the non-text regions are removed and the broken regions are merged using a smoothing filter, and the candidate text regions are detected. Finally, the filtering is performed by considering the following criteria: the pixel density of the candidate text region, the ratio of the minor to the major axis of the bounding box, the local intensity histogram. In this approach, texts with different contrast are not well extracted.

P. K. Kim [14] presented a text location method in complex color images. A local color quantization is applied for each color separately. The algorithm consists of four phases: converting the input color image into a 256 color image, contour following using a local color quantization, extracting a connected component, and filtering. An intermingled text regions with backgrounds, which may happen in the global color quantization, is excluded by using local color quantization. This method improved the detection rate of texts, but it requires plenty of processing time.

3   The Proposed Method

The proposed method is composed of three steps as shown in Fig 1: preprocessing (step 1), extracting candidate text regions (step 2), and filtering candidate text regions (step 3). In the preprocessing step, a color image is converted into a gray-level image and applies histogram stretching method to enhance the contrast of the image. Then, a modified local adaptive thresholding is applied to the contrast enhanced image. In the text extraction step, various image processing methods based on morphological operations are applied to remove non-text components while retaining the text components. In the final filtering step, the characteristics of each connected component are used.

In this paper, morphology operation is applied to the modified local adaptive thresholded image to emphasize the false positive component, which can be easily decided as a text while not a text region. Then, morphology operation and Geo-correction filtering which is proposed in this paper are applied to the modified local adaptive thresholded image to emphasize both text and text-like component. Text components, which we want to extract, are mainly remained and false positive components are mostly removed by means of obtaining difference image. Opening with 3x3 structuring element and (OpenClose + CloseOpen)/2 are used for extracting the false positive component, and (OpenClose + CloseOpen)/2 and Geo-correction are used for extracting both text and text-like components. In this paper, text region is assumed as comprising at least three consecutive characters and lies on a horizontal direction.

3.1   Characteristics of Text Appearing in News Video

Text may appear as a superimposed text or a scene text in digital video. The superimposed text is added to a video after finishing the video shooting in a post processing stage by artificially, while the scene text is recorded with the scene without

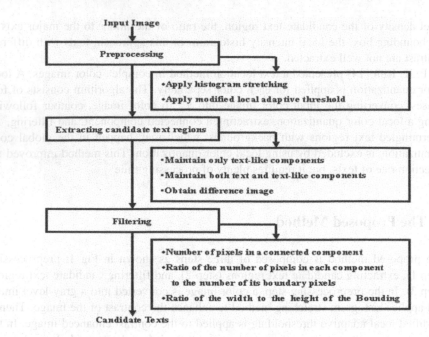

Fig. 1. Steps of the proposed method

any intention. Superimposed text extraction is more important than scene text extraction. The reason is that the superimposed text in video implies a mostly condensed and important content, whereas scene text usually appears without any intend. Thus, superimposed text is more appropriate for indexing and retrieval than scene text. However, text extraction in scenery image, needless to say scene text is the most important and very difficult to extract as much owing to infinite diversity of its appearance in direction, slant, occlusion and unconstrained illumination. Though appearance of superimposed text also has as much of the same difficulty as scene text, extraction of the superimposed text is less complicated than scene text since, the superimposed text has made for the purpose of reading and catching a viewer's eye easily. In this paper, extraction of the superimposed text has been focused and its features are described as follows [15]:

- Contrast between text as foreground and non-text as background is high because the superimposed text has made with intend for easy reading.
- Text is upright and monochrome in most cases.
- Each character piles up into a text line at a uniform interval with a horizontal direction.
- Text has the following restrictions in size: smaller than entire image size and bigger than a certain size as it can be seen.

3.2 Preprocessing

In text extraction, input images for preprocessing are color [10,12,13,15] or gray level images [11,14]. Zhong et al. [9] employed both the color and the gray-level images for their hybrid approach. The shortcoming on using the color image is that text regions and background can be merged [14]. Therefore, the proposed method uses the gray-level image for text extraction and will use the contrast between text and background and the shape of text. The RGB components of the input color image are converted into gray-level image.

A histogram stretching method is applied to the gray-level image to enhance the contrast of the input image. This is done to emphasize the brightness difference in the text region between text strokes and their background. A modified local adaptive thresholding is applied to the contrast enhanced image. The block size used is (Width/30)*(Height/30). The local threshold, T, is computed by considering mean, m, and standard deviation, σ, of the pixel values in each block as given in (1). User input variable, k, can be controlled by the types of video sources such as news, sports, cinemas, commercials, etc. The modification of our method to the original local adaptive thresholding is in setting the thresholded values: when the pixel value is less than T, it is set to zero, but when the value is greater than or equal to T, the gray value of the pixel is remained.

$$T = m + \sigma * k \qquad (1)$$

3.3 Extracting Candidate Text Regions

3.3.1 Maintaining Only Text-Like Components

In this paper, text components are exactly the text, which is appearing on an image, and text-like components are something, which can be easily presumed as a text even not a text. In this subsection, morphological opening and (OpenClose + CloseOpen)/2 operations are consecutively applied to the semi-thresholded image. First, the semi-thresholded image is binarized by converting non-zero values to 255 to apply binary morphological operations. 3x3 structuring element is used for opening. This 3x3 structuring element is selected based on analyzing the character width on a video image. In the opening process, the erosion is applied to remove noises and text-like components, and then the dilation is performed to recover the remaining objects that can be damaged during the erosion operation, as shown in Fig 4 (c) and (d). Then the gray value of semi-thresholded image is copied into the pixels with the gray value of 255 in binary image which is the result of the opening operation. (OpenClose + CloseOpen)/2 operation is applied to the above result using 1x5 structuring element as shown in Fig 2. (OpenClose + CloseOpen)/2 operation is a gray level morphology operation. Opening and closing operations are consecutively applied to the input image and closing and opening operations are consecutively applied to the input image apart from the former, after that an average is calculated between these two images.

Fig. 2. Structuring element for OpenClose or CloseOpen

Erosion and dilation used in (OpenClose + CloseOpen)/2 operation to the gray level image in this paper are shown in Fig 3. In the erosion, subtract pixel values in structuring element from pixel values in input image. After substraction, pixel values smaller than the central pixel value are remained as it is and bigger than the central pixel value are substituted as the central pixel value as shown in Fig 3-(a).

In the dilation, the pixel value bigger than the central pixel value are remained as it is and smaller than the central pixel value are substituted as the central pixel value as shown in Fig 3-(b) after the summation of pixel values in input image and pixel values in structuring element. Therefore,the image will be more brightened after applying dilation and more darkened after applying erosion in the gray level image.

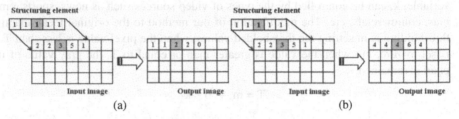

(a)   (b)

Fig. 3. Gray level morphology operation used in this paper, (a) Erosion in gray-level morphology, (b) Dilation in gray-level morphology

The (OpenClose + CloseOpen)/2 operation based on the above morphological operations will reduce the noise in the background by OpenClose and fill out the holes in the remaining objects by CloseOpen operation [13]. This operation is performed only in a horizontal direction using the 1x5 structuring element to detect the horizontal text lines. The results of each morphological operations are shown in Fig 4.

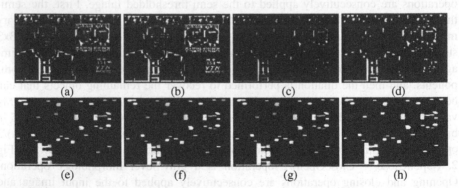

(a)   (b)   (c)   (d)

(e)   (f)   (g)   (h)

Fig. 4. Results for each morphological operation, (a) Semi-thresholded image, (b) Binarized image, (c) Erosion applied, (d) Dilation applied (e) OpenClose applied, (f) CloseOpen applied, (g) (OpenClose+CloseOpen)/2, (h) Binarization of (g)

3.3.2 Maintaining Both Text and Text-Like Components

In this step, (OpenClose + CloseOpen)/2 and Geo-correction method are applied. First, (OpenClose + CloseOpen)/2 operations are applied to remove noise in the background and to fill out the holes in the object. Then, the result image is binarized by setting a non-zero gray value to 255 and then the Geo-correction filtering is performed (refer to Fig 6-(e)). The Geo-correction shown in Fig 5 is needed for further recovering the text candidate components by connecting the separated components that can be resulted by the erosion operation in the previous morphological operations. It is performed along the horizontal and vertical directions. In the proposed method, the threshold for the vertical direction is set smaller than the threshold for the horizontal direction, since most of texts are lying on horizontal direction in news image. The threshold value 20 for the horizontal and the value 5 for the vertical direction chosen by experiments are used.

The Geo-correction filtering fills and connects the intermediate pixels by 255 as follows. Each pixel is scanned from left to right and top to bottom. If the pixel value is 255, begin scanning the consecutive pixels continuously until zero appears, and then count the number of zeros until reaching out pixel value of the next 255. If the number of pixel values having zero is below the given threshold, these pixels are converted into 255 in order to connect two lines. And if the number is above the threshold, maintain the pixel value as it is.

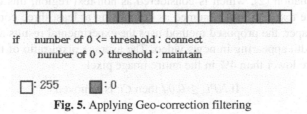

if   number of 0 <= threshold : connect
      number of 0 > threshold : maintain

☐ : 255   ■ : 0

Fig. 5. Applying Geo-correction filtering

3.3.3 Obtaining Difference Image

The binary image obtained by extracting false positive text components using morphology has mostly non-text components, and the binary image obtained by maintaining both text and text-like components using morphology has both the text candidates and the non-text components. Text components are mainly remained and false positive components are mostly removed as shown in Fig 6-(f) by means of obtaining difference between these two images. We set negative pixel values to 0.

3.4 Filtering Text Candidates

The non-text or the noise components are needed to be removed. A connected component labeling is performed first, and then the filtering is applied. Three features are used for filtering and the proper threshold values in each filtering are selected by the experiment. Since these values are measured as ratios, they are not affected by the

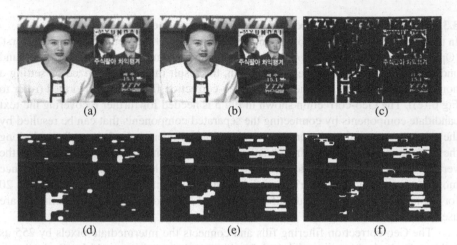

Fig. 6. Snapshots of the preprocessing and text region extractions, (a) Input image, (b) Contrast stretched result, (c) Semi-thresholded image, (d) Sub step 1, (e) Sub step 2, (f) Subtracting (d) from (e)

entire image size. First, the number of pixels(*NPi*) in each connected component(*Ci*) is considered. When the number of pixels in each connected component is too small as shown in equation (2), which is considered as non-text region, this component is removed. Since text region is assumed as comprising at least three consecutive characters in this paper, the proposed method uses the experimental results about the average character width appearing in news video. The average pixel ratio of three consecutive characters are lower than 4% in the entire image pixel.

$$\text{If } NPi \leq 0.04 \text{ then } Ci \text{ is removed} \tag{2}$$

$$\text{else } Ci \text{ is retained}$$

Second, the ratio between the number of pixels in each component and the number of its boundary pixels(*NBi*) is used. This is based on the experimental result that the ratio between the number of pixels in each component and the number of its boundary pixels below some ration is assumed as text component. The ratio 0.23 is obtained by the experiment and the component with the ratio less than 0.23 is removed.

$$\text{If } NBi \leq 0.23 \text{ then } Ci \text{ is removed} \tag{3}$$

$$\text{else } Ci \text{ is retained}$$

Third, the ratio between the width and the height of the bounding box of each component is used. If this ratio is less then the given threshold, the component will be removed. This is based on the assumption that the text line is assumed as comprising at least three consecutive characters and most of characters appearing in news video lies on a horizontal direction. Thus, the ratio 0.66 is obtained after the experiment about width and height of character appearing in news video.

if *Height/Width* ≤ *0.66* then *Ci* is removed   (4)

else *Ci* is retained

4   Experimental Results

The proposed algorithm has been implemented using Microsoft Visual C++ 6.0 on PC with 866MHz Pentium processor. The proposed algorithm is evaluated using 300 color images of Korean news clips (MBC, SBS, KBS, YTN) and 100 color images of English news clips (CNN, BBC, Bloomberg). Also, 100 film video clips, which include subtitles, and 50 commercial TV clips are evaluated to make a comparison among the different kinds of video. The image size is 320*210. Each image data is randomly captured on the consecutive frames. Three performance criteria are used to evaluate the results: correct extraction rate, practical extraction rate, and error rate. The practical extraction rate is a rate of finding text regions within a permitted tolerance of region judged by human. The error rate is defined as a rate of finding non-text components as texts and missing texts together. The extracted text line is counted as one text. These three criteria are stated as follows.

Correct extraction rate = Nct / Tn (5)

Practical extraction rate = $(Nct + Npt) / Tnt$

Error rate = $(Nnr + Nmt) / Tnt$

Where,   *Tnt*: the total number of texts in test images

Nct: the number of texts correctly extracted

Npt: the number of texts extracted in a permitted tolerance

Nnr: the number of extracted non-text regions

Nmt: the number of missing texts

| (a) | (b) | (c) | (d) |

Fig. 7. Examples of three performance criteria, (a) Correct extraction, (b) Practical extraction, (c) Finding non-texts as text, (d) Missing texts

Fig 7-(a) shows the example of correct extraction, which is the case of finding all text line appearing in an image. Fig 7-(b) shows the example of practical extraction, which is the case of finding text line and keyword for video indexing even though there are some partial errors. The partial errors are due to not recovering sufficiently while applying morphology operations. Figure 7-(c) shows the example of finding non-text component as text. This error is caused by high contrast between foreground and background, and these high contrast components have not removed during the modified local adaptive threshold phase. Figure 7-(d) shows the example of missing texts. This error is caused by low contrast between foreground and background, and these low contrast components have removed during the modified local adaptive threshold phase. In the proposed method, the main reasons of the error are due to the tiny text in the image, the low contrast between the text and the background, and also due to the large horizontal distance between the same text components.

Table 1. Recognition rate of test data

	Nct		Npt		Nnr + Nmt	
	Number	%	Number	%	Number	%
Korean news	533	77.5%	533+110	93.6%	46+42	12.8%
English news	291	76.5%	291+43	88.1%	6+45	13.4%
Film video	132	73.7%	132+43	97.7%	2+4	3.3%
Commercial video	66	49.3%	66+29	70.9%	8+39	35.1%

The reason why the proposed method classifies the test data as Korean and English news in the evaluation phase is that the height of each character in English news video can be different while the height in Korean news video is almost the same. This characteristic may cause the error during the modified local adaptive threshold and also has a close relation with the extraction rate. As we can see the above test result, the extraction rate of the Korean news was a little bit higher than the English news. In the film video images, the practical extraction rate was higher and the correct extraction rate was lower than the news video images. This is because of the complicated backgrounds in the film video images even though those images have a regular character size than the news video images. In the commercial video images, the extraction rate was not better than the news video images, since the commercial video images easily contain the texts with variations in size and font, skewed, different textures, unconstrained illumination, *etc.* The commercial video images contain many of the scene texts and thus the modified local adaptive threshold has not segmented the image well. Consequently, the proposed method gives higher extraction rate on the superimposed texts in the news videos, but it has limitations on finding the scene texts with complex backgrounds.

Fig. 8. Text extraction results

5   Conclusions

A new method has proposed for extracting text specially well for the superimposed texts from digital video news images. In the proposed method, several morphological operations are used: eliminating text-like components by applying erosion, dilation, and (OpenClose + CloseOpen)/2 operations, maintaining text components using (OpenClose + CloseOpen)/2 and Geo-correction operations, and subtracting two result images. The OpenClose, CloseOpen and their combined operations can reduce noises and remove holes in each connected component. The proposed Geo-correction method is also efficient for conserving and compensating the candidate text components that can be damaged by the morphological operations. The experimental results show that the proposed method shows good performance in extracting texts in news video with the correct extraction rate of 77.5%, the practical extraction rate of 93.6% and the error rate of 12.8%. The proposed method also has tested with movies and commercial videos by adjusting the structuring elements of the morphological operations to the width of the character, and the initial results are very promising. We need to develop this research to modify and refine for the extraction of the scene texts with various kinds of images and video frames.

Acknowlegdements. This research was supported as a Brain Neuroinformatics Research Program sponsored by Korean Ministry of Science and Technology (M1-0107-00-0009).

References

1. Jae-Chang Shim, Chitra Dorai, and Ruud Bolle, Automatic Text Extraction from Video for Content-Based Annotation and Retrieval, *Proceedings of Fourteenth International Conference on Pattern Recognition*, Vol. 1, pp. 618–620 , 1998.
2. Anil K. Jain and Bin Yu, Automatic text location in images and video frames, *Pattern Recognition,* Vol. 31, No. 12, pp. 2055–2076, 1998.
3. H.Kuwano, Y.Taniguchi, H.Arai, M.Mori, S.Kuraka-ke, and H.Kojima, Telop-on-demand: video structuring and retrieval based on text recognition, *IEEE International Conference on Multimedia and Expo*, Vol. 2, pp. 759-762, 2000.
4. U. Gargi, S. Antani, and R. Kasturi, Indexing text events in digital video databases, *Proceedings of Fourteenth International Conference on Pattern Recognition*, Vol. 1, pp. 916–918, 1998.
5. Sameer Antani, Ullas Gargi, David Crandall, Tarak Gandhi, and Rangachar Kasturi, Extraction of Text in Video, *Dept. of Computer. Science and Eng., Pennsylvania State Univ., Technical Report*, CSE-99-016, 1999.
6. S. Messelodi and C.M. Modena, Automatic identification and skew estimation of text lines in real scene images, *Pattern Recognition*, Vol. 32, pp. 791–810, 1999.
7. S. Antani, D. Crandall, and R. Kasturi , Robust extraction of text in video, *Proceedings of 15th International Conference on Pattern Recognition*, Vol. 1, pp. 831–834, 2000.
8. Y. Lu, Machine printed character segmentation-An overview, *Pattern Recognition*, Vol. 28, pp. 67–80, 1995.
9. Y. Zhong, K. Karu, and A. K. Jain, Locating text in complex color images, *Pattern Recognition*, Vol. 28, pp. 1523–1535, 1995.
10. J. Ohya, A. Shio, and S. Akamatsu, Recognizing characters in scene images, *IEEE Trans on Pattern Analysis and Machine Intelligence*. PAMI-16, pp.214–220, 1994.
11. H. K. Kim, Efficient automatic text location method and content-based indexing and structuring of video database, *J. Visual Commun. Image Representation*, Vol. 7, pp. 336–344, 1996.
12. M. A. Smith and T. Kanade, Video skimming for quick browsing base on audio and image characterization, *Technical Report CMU-CS-95-186, Carnegie Mellon University*, July 1995.
13. J. Serra, Image Analysis and Mathematical Morphology. New York: Academic, 1982.
14. Pyeoung-Kee Kim, Automatic Text Location in Complex Color Images using Local Color Quantization, *TENCON 99. Proceedings of the IEEE Region 10 Conference*, Vol. 1, pp. 629–632, 1999.
15. R. Lienhart and F. Stuber, Automatic text recognition in digital videos, *SPIE Image and Video Processing IV*, pp 2666–2669, 1996

Retrieval by Layout Similarity of Documents Represented with MXY Trees

Francesca Cesarini, Simone Marinai, and Giovanni Soda

Dipartimento di Sistemi e Informatica – Università di Firenze
Via S.Marta, 3 – 50139 Firenze – Italy
{cesarini,simone,giovanni}@dsi.unifi.it

Abstract. Document image retrieval can be carried out either processing the converted text (obtained with OCR) or by measuring the layout
similarity of images. We describe a system for document image retrieval
based on layout similarity. The layout is described by means of a tree-
based representation: the Modified X-Y tree. Each page in the database
is represented by a feature vector containing both global features of the
page and a vectorial representation of its layout that is derived from the
corresponding MXY tree. Occurrences of tree patterns are handled similarly to index terms in Information Retrieval in order to compute the
similarity. When retrieving relevant documents, the images in the collection are sorted on the basis of a measure that is the combination of two
values describing the similarity of global features and of the occurrences
of tree patterns. The system is applied to the retrieval of documents belonging to digital libraries. Tests of the system are made on a data-set of
more than 600 pages belonging to a journal of the 19th Century, and to
a collection of monographs printed in the same Century and containing
more than 600 pages.

1 Introduction

The document image database described in this paper is used to store books
and journals in digital libraries. In the last few years the largest public libraries
in the world have digitized and stored in electronic format collections of books
and journals. These documents can be browsed and retrieved on the basis of
meta-data describing their content. Most of this information (e.g. title, authors,
publishing date) is manually selected from catalog cards. Sometimes the pages
are processed with OCRs in order to allow the user to retrieve documents on
the basis of their textual content. In this case the retrieval by (imprecise) text
content is possible with techniques derived from Information Retrieval (IR). Few
systems allow the user to retrieve pages by layout similarity, with approaches
somehow similar to those applied in Content Based Image Retrieval (CBIR).
Document image retrieval is a research field that lies at the borderline between
classic IR [1] and CBIR [2]. Two recent papers [3,4] investigated past research
and future trends in document image retrieval. Most work in document image
retrieval has been based on the processing of converted text with IR-based techniques [3]. Fewer methods approached the retrieval by layout similarity, and

D. Lopresti, J. Hu, and R. Kashi (Eds.): DAS 2002, LNCS 2423, pp. 353–364, 2002.

related approaches have been considered for document page classification. The retrieval by layout similarity is useful for locating some meaningful pages in unlabeled collections of scanned pages. For instance, if a query page corresponds to the beginning of a chapter, then the retrieved pages are likely to provide information on the chapters in a book or collection of books. Illustrations in a book can be retrieved by using a page with an image as a query page.

A general framework for document image retrieval has been proposed in [5]. The system allows users to retrieve documents on the basis of both global features of the page and features based on blocks extracted by layout analysis packages. Global features include texture orientation, gray level difference histogram, and color features. The block-based features use a weighted area overlap measure between segmented regions. More recently, the combination of global (page-level) and local features has been furtherly investigated for computing visual similarity between document images for page classification [6]. In the latter approach a fixed-size feature vector is obtained by extracting some specific features in the regions defined by a grid overlapped to the page. Similarly, the method discussed in [7] takes into account a fixed grid partitioning of the page and uses features computed from the textual zones. A grid-based approach to construct a feature vector computed from the density of connected components was considered also in [8]. In order to overcome some problems related to the choice of an optimal grid size, a page classification method based on an MXY tree decomposition of the page has been recently proposed in [9]. This method relies on a MXY tree [10] built from a segmented image where the blocks are obtained with a commercial OCR. The MXY tree is afterwards encoded into a fixed size vector that is used as input to an MLP-based classifier.

In the document image retrieval system described in this paper we use an MXY tree based document representation with an approach tightly related with the page classification proposed in [9]. The pages are first segmented with a layout analysis tool provided with an OCR package[1]. Blocks extracted by this tool are afterwards arranged in an MXY tree describing the page layout. A DBMS is used in order to store relevant information of digitized books and also for maintaining the MXY tree of the page. At the end of a session of database population, appropriate feature vectors describing both the global features of the page and the MXY tree structure are stored in the database. During retrieval, a query by example approach is considered. To this purpose the user first selects one sample page by browsing the collection; afterwards a comparison of the query feature vector with vectors in the database is performed with an appropriate similarity measure, and retrieved documents are shown to the user.

The paper is organized as follows: in the next section we describe the method for document image retrieval that has been implemented in the system described in Section 3. Experimental results on a first data set containing more than 1200 pages are reported in Section 4, while concluding remarks are in Section 5.

---

[1] The OCR used is FineReader Engine 4.0.

Fig. 1. User interface showing the result of the retrieval based on a query page shown on the left. The nine pages reported on the right are those with an higher similarity measure (reported over each image).

2   Document Image Retrieval

Document images are retrieved in our system by using a "query by example" approach: given a sample page the system computes the layout similarity of the page with all the pages in the database. Pages in the database are afterwards ranked on the basis of this similarity and shown to the user as system's answer (Fig. 1). The page similarity is computed considering the distance between feature vectors describing the layout. Each feature vector contains two main groups of features. The first group contains global features describing the position and size of the printed part of the page with respect to the other pages belonging to the same book. The second group of features describes the layout of the page and is obtained from its MXY tree [10]. The page similarity is computed with an appropriate combination of two measures that operate independently for each group of features. In this section we describe the two parts of the feature vector and the similarity measure that we introduced in order to deal with this representation.

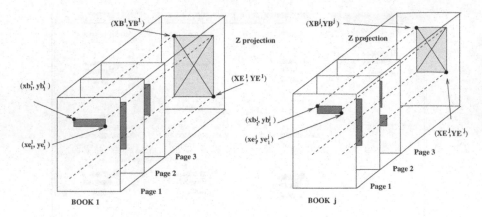

Fig. 2. Computation of the "book bounding box" by taking into account a Z-projection.

2.1   Global Features

The pages inserted in the database are first processed with layout analysis tools in order to extract homogeneous blocks. The layout is afterwards described by means of an MXY tree. This description has been demonstrated to be adequate for the classification of journal pages, where page layouts are quite complex and MXY trees are usually composed by several nodes [9]. When considering digitized books, there are some pages whose layout is made by an unique block. Typical examples are *regular pages*, corresponding to pages containing continuous text (the narrative part of the book). Other pages composed by a single text block contain for instance short dedications. These layouts can be recognized with some features describing the position and size of the printed part of the page (represented in the MXY tree root) with respect to the document image. Heterogeneous collections contain different books with variable size. However, users are usually interested in pages with a given layout independently from the book size. In order to use features invariant with respect to the book size, the root position and the size of each page are normalized with respect to the bounding box of all the book pages. The computation of such a "book bounding box" is equivalent to the extraction of the bounding box of the image that is obtained by projecting all the book pages in a Z-direction (see Fig. 2). In so doing we are able to obtain features that are invariant with respect to different book sizes and different book locations in the scanner.

The features can be computed in the following way. Let (xb_i^j, yb_i^j) and (xe_i^j, ye_i^j) be the top-left and bottom-right points of the bounding box of page P_i in book B_j. The "book bounding box" can be simply computed by Eq. 1:

$$
\begin{aligned}
XB^j &= \min_{P_i \in B_j} \left(xb_i^j\right) & YB^j &= \min_{P_i \in B_j} \left(yb_i^j\right) \\
XE^j &= \max_{P_i \in B_j} \left(xe_i^j\right) & YE^j &= \max_{P_i \in B_j} \left(ye_i^j\right)
\end{aligned}
\tag{1}
$$

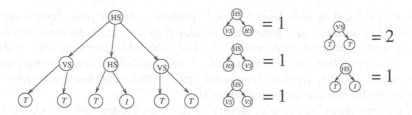

Fig. 3. A simple MXY tree; in the right part of the figure we show the balanced tree patterns in the tree, with the corresponding occurrences.

The page location can be described by computing the normalized position of the page center ($\overline{x}_i^j = \frac{xb_i^j + xe_i^j}{2}$, $\overline{y}_i^j = \frac{yb_i^j + ye_i^j}{2}$) with respect to the "Book Bounding Box" (Eq. 2):

$$x_i^j = \frac{\overline{x}_i^j - XB^j}{XE^j - XB^j} \qquad y_i^j = \frac{\overline{y}_i^j - YB^j}{YE^j - YB^j} \qquad (2)$$

The normalized width (w_i^j) and height (h_i^j) of page P_i in book B_j can be computed in the same fashion (Eq. 3):

$$w_i^j = \frac{xe_i^j - xb_i^j}{XE^j - XB^j} \qquad h_i^j = \frac{ye_i^j - yb_i^j}{YE^j - YB^j} \qquad (3)$$

2.2 MXY Tree Similarity

The layout similarity is computed on the basis of the similarity between MXY trees corresponding to the query and to the pages in the database. Although some limits of the XY decomposition have been pointed out in the literature, this representation is very appropriate when dealing with documents with a *Manhattan* layout and when the pages are not subjected to large skews. Digitized pages of both books and journals are examples of documents where these hypotheses are verified, and the XY tree representation is a good choice. In particular, MXY trees (that decompose the document image also along horizontal and vertical lines) have been demonstrated to be effective when dealing with documents containing ruling lines [9,10]. The MXY trees have been encoded into a fixed-size feature vector for page classification by taking into account occurrences of *tree-patterns* made by three nodes [9]. This approach is motivated by the observation that similar layouts frequently contain common sub-trees in the corresponding MXY tree. Trees composed by three nodes can have two basic structures: the first pattern has root and two children, whereas the second pattern (denoted as *balanced tree-pattern*, Fig. 3) is made by a root, a child, and a child of the second node.

MXY tree nodes contain symbolic attributes describing the purpose of the node. Basically, internal nodes represent the cut strategy considered (we can have horizontal/vertical cuts along either spaces or lines), whereas leaves correspond to homogeneous blocks in the page (text, image, horizontal/vertical line). Since node labels are in a fixed number, the number of possible *tree-patterns* (denoted with TP) is fixed as well. Under these hypotheses, similar pages have some *tree-patterns* in common, and sometimes similar pages contain the same number of occurrences of a given *tree-pattern* (for instance table pages usually contain a large number of *tree-patterns* with lines). Unfortunately, there are some patterns that appear roughly in every document, and in this case these patterns are not very useful for measuring page similarities.

These peculiarities are very similar to the use of index terms in classic Information Retrieval. We extended the vector model approach, used in IR for dealing with textual documents, to our representation based on *tree-patterns*. The vector model of IR (see [1], Chapter 2) is based on a vectorial description of the document textual contents. The vector items are related to the occurrences of index terms, that usually correspond to words in the text of the document. Vector values are weighted in order to provide more importance to most discriminant terms. One common approach relies on the well known *tf-idf* weighting scheme. Basically, index terms that are present in many documents of the collection have a lower weight since their presence is not discriminant. In our approach, the vector model is used in order to describe the page layout. To this purpose, the page is described by means of the MXY tree representation, and occurrences of *tree-patterns* are used instead of word-based index terms. The extension of *tf-idf* weighting to this case is straightforward: the weight assigned to the k-th *tree-pattern* in the tree T_j corresponding to page P_i is computed by Eq. 4.

$$w_{i,k} = f_{i,k} \cdot log\left(\frac{N}{n_k}\right) \tag{4}$$

where $f_{i,k}$ is the frequency of the k-th *tree-pattern* in T_j normalized with respect to the maximum *tree-pattern* frequency in T_j, N is the total number of pages, and n_k is the number of trees containing the k-th *tree-pattern*.

2.3 Similarity Computation

The similarity between two pages is computed by taking into account the corresponding feature vectors that are made by two parts. The feature vector describing page P_i in book B_j can be represented as follows:

$$\boxed{T\,|\,L\,|\,I\,|\,x_i^j\,|\,y_i^j\,|\,w_i^j\,|\,h_i^j\,\|\,w_{i,1}\,|\,\ldots\,|\,w_{i,k}\,|\,\ldots\,|\,w_{i,TP}}$$

The first seven values correspond to global features (Section 2.1). (T,L,I) are binary values describing the tree root. $(x_i^j, y_i^j, w_i^j, h_i^j)$ describe the position and size of the tree root (Eqs. 2 and 3). In a page containing a unique block the corresponding MXY tree is made by a unique node that can be a text block, a line, or an image block. These three cases are described with a mutual exclusion in T,L,I values (e.g. $T = 1, L = 0, I = 0$ corresponds to a text block). When the page contains more blocks, then the root does not correspond to a single block, and in this case the three values are all set to zero.

The rest of the vector contains an encoding of the MXY tree associated to the page (Section 2.2): $w_{i,k}$ $k = 1,\ldots,TP$ are the weights associated to the occurrences of *tree-patterns* (Eq. 4).

The similarity between a query page q and a generic page p in the database is computed by combining two similarity measures for the two components of the feature vector. Let $\mathcal{F}$ be the feature vector space, and $V \in \mathcal{F}$ be a generic vector in $\mathcal{F}$. We indicate with V_{GL} and V_{XY} the two sub-vectors contained in V. Let $Q \in \mathcal{F}$ and $P \in \mathcal{F}$ be the feature vectors corresponding to the query page q and to the page p, respectively. The similarity between q and p can be computed by Eq. 5

$$Sim(P, Q) = \alpha \cdot SimEuc(P_{GL}, Q_{GL}) + \beta \cdot SimCos(P_{XY}, Q_{XY}) \qquad (5)$$

The similarity between P_{GL} and Q_{GL} is computed by using the Euclidean distance between the two sub-vectors (Eq. 6). The distance is divided by the maximum value that can reached ($\sqrt{6}$). $SimEuc$ has higher values (close to 1) when the pages are similar and the two sub-vectors are the same.

$$SimEuc(P_{GL}, Q_{GL}) = 1 - \frac{\sqrt{\sum_{i=1}^{7}(P_{GL}[i] - Q_{GL}[i])^2}}{\sqrt{6}} \qquad (6)$$

The similarity between P_{XY} and Q_{XY} is computed by taking into account the *cosine of the angle* between the two vectors (Eq. 7)

$$SimCos(P_{XY}, Q_{XY}) = \frac{P_{XY} \times Q_{XY}}{|P_{XY}| \cdot |Q_{XY}|} = \frac{\sum_{i=1}^{TP}(P_{XY}[i] \cdot Q_{XY}[i])}{\sqrt{\sum_{i=1}^{TP} P_{XY}[i]^2} \cdot \sqrt{\sum_{i=1}^{TP} Q_{XY}[i]^2}} \qquad (7)$$

The two parameters α and β are used in order to weight the contribution of the two parts to the overall similarity measure. Several tests have been made by varying the values of α and β as it will discussed in Section 4.

3 System Architecture

When designing a retrieval system that can easily scale up to large document collections, the use of a robust and reliable data-base management system (DBMS) is essential. The use of a standard DBMS is in contrast with approaches where all the information is kept in the file system. When dealing with large image collections one critical issue is related to image storage. One approach relies on the use of appropriate DBMSs that are able to store images. One intermediate strategy is based on the use of a DBMS for storing information about images, and to use customized approaches for image storage. In Digital Libraries, the image repositories are already defined and are usually based on complex organizations (based on standard file systems), where most difficulties are related to the use of appropriate hardware equipments (like juke-boxes for keeping large collections of CD-ROMS) [11].

To facilitate the integration with existing solutions we designed a system for computing the layout similarity, whereas document images are stored in the file system (this is clearly one of the main limits of the current implementation). We used the Java language for the user interface and the retrieval algorithms. The

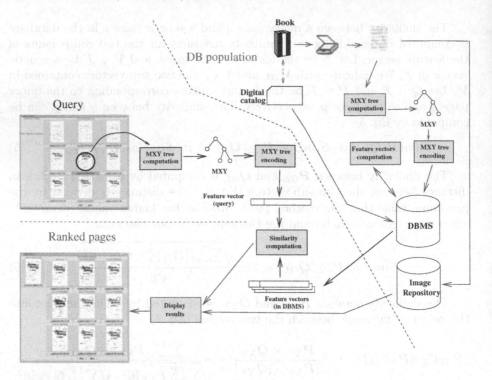

Fig. 4. System architecture.

DBMS currently used is IBM's DB2 [12], and the interface with the retrieval system is made through standard JDBC methods. The use of a DBMS for the storage of layout information allows us to obtain a dynamic system to which data (scanned books) can be easily added and removed. This is in contrast with static systems where the addition of new documents is a complex task. To support the dynamic updating of database contents, the MXY tree of each page is stored in the DBMS as well. The MXY trees are used at the end of an update session ("DB population" in Figure 4) in order to compute feature vectors on the basis of Eq. 4. When the user makes a query, the system computes the MXY tree of the sample page, and obtains the corresponding feature vector. According to Eq. 5 the pages are ranked by comparing the corresponding feature vectors with the vector computed for the sample page. Lastly, images of most relevant pages are retrieved from the image repository. The DBMS contains four tables: *Book*, *Page*, *XYNode*, and *Vector*. The *Book* table contains all the information useful for book identification. The main purpose of the table *Page* is to link together each page of a given book with the corresponding image file. The table *XYNode* is the largest table in the DBMS as it contains all the nodes of all the MXY trees in the database. Lastly, the *Vector* table contains the feature vectors corresponding to each document image.

4   Experimental Results

In this section we discuss the system evaluation that has been carried out using two sets of document images. The first set of images contains several issues of a journal, the second set contains a collection of books.

The evaluation of image retrieval systems is difficult for the peculiarities of the tasks required by users as well as for semantic ambiguities in defining image similarity [2]. In Information Retrieval, *Precision* and *Recall* are traditionally used for performance evaluation, and can be defined as follows (e.g. [1], page 75): $Precision = \frac{N_{RetRel}}{N_{Ret}}$, $Recall = \frac{N_{RetRel}}{N_{Rel}}$, where N_{Ret} is the number of retrieved documents, N_{Rel} is the number of relevant documents, and N_{RetRel} is the number of relevant documents in the set of retrieved documents.

There are two main limitations to the use of Precision and Recall in the field of image retrieval [2]. First, the selection of a relevant set in an image database is much more problematic than in a text database Second, image databases usually do not return an undifferentiated set of "relevant" results, but a ranked list of all the documents in the collection sorted on the basis of their similarity with respect to the query. In document image retrieval the first problem is less critical than in more general CBIR systems, since frequently the relevance of a document with respect to a given query can be defined unambiguously. This assumption is true for the experiments reported in this paper, since all the pages in the collection belong to some user-defined classes, and consequently one page is clearly deemed to be relevant when its class corresponds to the query page class. However, the difficulty in computing Precision and Recall on the basis of a sorting of the complete collection of pages is an issue in our experiments as well. To provide an evaluation of the retrieval effectiveness, we introduce a measure (*accuracy*) that is appropriate in the problem at hand. Let N_{Ans} be the number of pages in the answer set. We can define the accuracy as follows:

$$Acc = \frac{N_{RetRel}}{min(N_{Ans}, N_{Rel})} \tag{8}$$

This approach is appropriate when dealing with systems (like the one proposed in this paper) that provide to the user a ranked list of the N_{Ans} most relevant retrieved documents.

Table 1. Average accuracy on all the experiments when taking into account different values for α and β.

α	0	0.3	0.5	0.7	1
β	1	0.7	0.5	0.3	0
Acc	0.390	0.862	0.854	0.866	0.822

The aim of the tests described in this section is the evaluation of the system accuracy when different values of α and β are considered in Eq. 5. As illustrated in the following, the choice of these parameters is not too critical, provided that a contribution of both parts of the similarity measure are considered. The experiments have been made on two data sets that are representative of the material stored in digital libraries. The first experiments have been made inserting in the system a collection of documents containing several issues of the journal "The American Missionary" belonging to the on-line digital library *Making of America*[2]. In the second group of experiments we inserted in the database four scanned books of the 19th Century, containing 621 pages. These books have been downloaded from the on-line digital library hosted by the "*Bibliotèque Nationale de France*" (BNF)[3]. Examples of pages corresponding to each class are shown in Tables 2,3. For each test we used each page in the database as a query page, and we evaluated the accuracy on the basis of the classes of retrieved pages. Table 1 contains the average accuracy obtained for the whole set of documents when taking into account some values of α and β, and fixing $N_{Ans} = 10$ (similar results have been achieved with $N_{Ans} = 50$). More detailed results are shown in tables 2,3 whose numerical values correspond to the average accuracy computed for all the documents in a given class. Global accuracy values reported in table 1 give us two main messages. First, the best results are achieved when taking into account both similarity measures ($\alpha \neq 0$ and $\beta \neq 0$). In contrast, when considering only the MXY-tree based similarity ($\alpha = 0$) or the similarity relying on global features only ($\beta = 0$) lower values of *Acc* are reached. Second, the choice of appropriate values for α and β is not critical, since in a wide interval $[(\alpha = 0.3, \beta = 0.7), (\alpha = 0.7, \beta = 0.3)]$ the global accuracy is very similar.

Table 2. Average accuracy for pages in classes that are recognized better with the MXY tree based similarity.

Class (Book/Journal)	Advert (J)	Issue (B)	Sect0 (B)	Receipts (J)	Text2 (B)
$\alpha = 0, \beta = 1$	0.880	0.245	0.667	0.852	0.832
$\alpha = 1, \beta = 0$	0.700	0.204	0.667	0.604	0.768
$\alpha = 0.5, \beta = 0.5$	0.847	0.245	0.555	0.863	0.839
# pages	104	7	3	118	31
Class description	Two columns with pictures (advertisement)	Two columns with a centered title	Small text block	List of items on two columns	Two columns

A detailed analysis of results obtained for each class is reported in Tables 2 and 3. In particular, Table 2 contains classes with a complex layout, and in this case it is quite natural that the results obtained considering only the MXY tree encoding are better than those obtained when considering global features only.

---

[2] Document images can be downloaded from the web site of the collection: *http://cdl.library.cornell.edu/moa/*

[3] The web site of the collection is: *http://gallica.bnf.fr/*

One exception is class *Sect0* that presents a simple layout but is recognized with the same accuracy by both methods. Global features (Table 3) are appropriate when dealing with pages whose tree is made by a unique node (e.g. classes *Regular* and *Text1*). In this case the Accuracy is very low in columns where $\alpha = 0$, whereas higher values are obtained by setting $\alpha = 1$ and $\beta = 0$.

Table 3. Average accuracy for pages in classes that are recognized better with global features.

Class (Book/Journal)	Index (J)	Regular (J)	Text1 (B)	SecM1 (B)	First (J)
$\alpha = 0, \beta = 1$	0.895	0.081	0.064	0.015	0.876
$\alpha = 1, \beta = 0$	0.953	0.800	0.927	0.854	0.938
$\alpha = 0.5, \beta = 0.5$	0.907	0.791	0.925	0.407	0.942
# pages	107	172	478	26	107
Class description	Index with a large picture on top	Simple text on a single column	Simple text on a single column	Subsection title	First page of a chapter (one column)
Class (Book/Journal)	SecS1 (B)	Image (B)	ITLPa (B)	SecE1 (B)	Title (B)
$\alpha = 0, \beta = 1$	0.530	0.500	0.125	0.247	0.125
$\alpha = 1, \beta = 0$	0.770	0.750	0.313	0.296	0.312
$\alpha = 0.5, \beta = 0.5$	0.726	0.500	0.250	0.796	0.312
# pages	27	4	7	26	4
Class description	First page of a section	One large image	Table of contents	Last page of a section	Book title

5 Conclusions

We described a system for document image retrieval on the basis of layout similarity. Pages are represented with both global features and features related to the MXY tree layout representation. The similarity is computed by combining the similarity measures that are defined for both types of features. In the case of global features we take into account a similarity that is based on the Euclidean distance between feature vectors. When dealing with MXY trees, the occurrences of some predefined *tree-patterns* are first counted in each tree. Afterwards, these occurrences are stored in a feature vector obtained with the *tf-idf* weighting scheme, and the similarity is evaluated by computing the *cosine of the angle* between the two vectors.

Future work concerns the implementation of a "query by sketch" approach, where the user can easily perform a query by drawing an ideal page sample. Moreover, we plan to add further retrieval strategies to this general framework by taking into account also information that can be extracted from the textual content of the page.

Acknowledgments. We would like to thank M. Ardinghi and S. Matucci for their work in the implementation of various parts of the system.

References

1. R. Baeza-Yates and B. Ribeiro-Neto, *Modern Information Retrieval*. Addison Wesley, 1999.
2. A. Smeulders, M. Worring, S. Santini, A. Gupta, and R. Jain, "Content-based image retrieval at the end of the early years," in *IEEE Trans. PAMI*, vol. 22, pp. 1349–1380, December 2000.
3. D. Doermann, "The indexing and retrieval of document images: A survey," *Computer Vision and Image Understanding*, vol. 70, pp. 287–298, June 1998.
4. M. Mitra and B. B. Chaudhuri, "Information retireval from documents: a survey," *Information Retrieval*, vol. 2, pp. 141–163, 2000.
5. D. Doermann, J. Sauvola, H. Kauniskangas, C. Shin, M. Pietikainen, and A. Rosenfeld, "The development of a general framework for intelligent document image retrieval," in *Document Analysis Systems*, pp. 605–632, 1996.
6. C. Shin and D. Doermann, "Classification of document page images based on visual similarity of layout structures," in *SPIE 2000*, pp. 182–190, 2000.
7. J.Hu, R.Kashi, and G.Wilfong, "Comparision and classification of documents based on layout similarity," *Information Retrieval*, vol. 2, pp. 227–243, May 2000.
8. J. F. Cullen, J. J. Hull, and P. E. Hart, "Document image database retrieval and browsing using texture analysis," in *Proceedings of the 4th International Conference on Document Analysis and Recognition*, pp. 718–721, 1997.
9. F. Cesarini, M. Lastri, S. Marinai, and G. Soda, "Encoding of modified X-Y trees for document classification," in *Proceedings of the Sixth International Conference on Document Analysis and Recognition*, pp. 1131–1136, 2001.
10. F. Cesarini, M. Gori, S. Marinai, and G. Soda, "Structured document segmentation and representation by the modified X-Y tree," in *Proc. of ICDAR '99*, pp. 563–566, 1999.
11. W. Y. Arms, *Digital Libraries*. MIT Press, 2000.
12. G. Baklarz and B. Wong, *DB2 Universal Database V7.1*. Prentice Hall, 2000.

Automatic Indexing of Newspaper Microfilm Images

Qing Hong Liu and Chew Lim Tan

School of Computing
National University of Singapore
Kent Ridge Singapore 117543

Abstract. This paper describes a proposed document analysis system that aims at automatic indexing of digitized images of old newspaper microfilms. This is done by extracting news headlines from microfilm images. The headlines are then converted to machine readable text by OCR to serve as indices to the respective news articles. A major challenge to us is the poor image quality of the microfilm as most images are usually inadequately illuminated and considerably dirty. To overcome the problem we propose a new effective method for separating characters from noisy background since conventional threshold selection techniques are inadequate to deal with these kinds of images. A Run Length Smearing Algorithm (RLSA) is then applied to the headline extraction. Experimental results confirm the validity of the approach.

1 Motivation

Many libraries archive old issues of newspapers in microfilm format. Locating a news article among a huge collection of microfilms proves to be too laborious and sometimes impossible if there is no clue to the date or period of the publication of the news article in question. Today many digital libraries digitize microfilm images to facilitate access. However, the contents of the digitized images are not indexed and thus searching a news article in the large document image database will still be a daunting task. A project was thus proposed in conjunction with our Singapore National Library to do an automatic indexing of the news articles by extracting headlines from digitized microfilm images to serve as news indices. This task can be divided into two main parts: image analysis and pattern recognition. The first part is to extract headline areas from the microfilm images and the second part is to apply Optical Character Recognition (OCR) on the extracted headline areas and turn them into the corresponding texts for indexing. This paper focuses on the first part. Headline extraction is done through a layout analysis of the microfilm images. Most research on layout analysis has largely assumed relatively clean images. Old newspapers' microfilm images, however present a challenge. Many of the microfilm images archived in Singapore National Library are dated as old as over a hundred years ago. Figure 1 shows one of the microfilm images. Adequate pre-processing of the images is thus necessary before headline extraction can be carried out. To extract the headline of the newspaper microfilm images, a Run Length Smearing Algorithm (RLSA) is applied.

D. Lopresti, J. Hu, and R. Kashi (Eds.): DAS 2002, LNCS 2423, pp. 365–375, 2002.
© Springer-Verlag Berlin Heidelberg 2002

The remainder of the paper is organized as follows: Section 2 will describe the pre-processing for image binarization and noise removal. Section 3 will discuss our method for headline extraction. Section 4 will present our experimental results. Finally we outline some observations and conclude the paper.

2   Precrocessing

Various preprocessing methods to deal with noisy document images have been reported in the literature. Hybrid methods as proposed by Hideyyuki et al [1] and James L. Fisher [2] require adequate capturing of images. O'Gorman [3] uses connectivity-preserving method to binarize the document images. These methods were tried but found inadequate for our microfilm images because of their poor quality with low illumination and excessive noise. Separating text and graphics from their background is usually done by thresholding. If the text sections have enough contrast with the background, they can be thresholded directly using methods proposed so far [2][4]. However in view of the considerable overlaps of gray level ranges between the text, graphics and the background, in our image data, poor segmentation results after trying theses methods. Thus, we experimented three stages of preprocessing, namely, histogram transformation, adaptive binarization and noise filtration. Histogram transformation is used to improve the contrast ratio of the microfilm images without changing the histogram distribution of the images for the later preprocessing. An adaptive binarization method is then applied for converting the original image to binary image with reasonable noise removal. The last step in the preprocessing is applying a kFill filter [5] to remove the pepper and salt noise to get considerably noise-free images.

2.1   Histogram Transformation

Because of the narrow range of the gray scale values of the microfilm image content, a linear transformation is adopted to increase the visual contrast. This entails the stretching of the nonzero input intensity range, $x \in [x_{min}, x_{max}]$ to an output intensity range $y \in [0, y_{max}]$ by a linear function to take advantage of the full dynamic range.

As a result, the interval is stretched to cover the full range of the gray level and the transformation is applied without altering the image appearance. Figure 2 shows the result of thresholding without histogram transfer. In contrast, figures 3 and 4 show the significant improvements with histogram transformation.

2.2   Adaptive Binarization

While the idea of binarization is simple, poor image quality can make binarization difficult. Because of the low contrast of microfilm images, it is difficult to resolve foreground from the background. Furthermore, spatial non-uniformity is even worse in the background intensity in that the images appears light at some areas while dark at some other areas in one single image.

A local adaptive binarization technique is thus applied to counter the effects of non-uniform background intensity values. Here we divide the original image into subimages. Depending on the degree of the non-uniformity of the original image, the image size of $N \times M$ is divided into $N / n \times M / m$ subimages of size $n \times m$. In each sub-image, we do a discriminant analysis [6] to determine the optimal threshold within each sub-image. Sub-images with small measures of class separation are said to contain only one class; no threshold is calculated for these sub-images and the threshold is taken as the average of thresholds in the neighboring sub-images. Finally the sub-image thresholds are interpolated among sub-images for all pixels and each pixel value is binarized with the respect to the threshold at pixel.

Let $P(i)$ be the histogram probabilities of the observed gray values i, where i ranges from 1 to I:

$$P(i) = \frac{\#\{(r,c) \mid Gray-value(r,c)=i\}}{\#R \times C}. \tag{1}$$

where $R \times C$ is the spatial domain of the image. Let σ_W^2 be the weighted sum of group variances, that is, the within-group variance. Let $\sigma_1^2(t)$ be the variance of the group with values less than or equal to t and $\sigma_2^2(t)$ be the variance of the group with values greater than t. Let $q_1(t)$ be the probability for the group with values less than or equal to t and $q_2(t)$ be the probability for the group with values greater than t. Let $\mu_1(t)$ be the mean for the first group and $\mu_2(t)$ be the mean for the second group. Then the within-group variance σ_W^2 is defined by

$$\sigma_w^2(t) = q_1(t)\sigma_1^2(t) + q_2(t)\sigma_2^2(t). \tag{2}$$

where

$$q_1(t) = \sum_{i=1}^{t} P(i). \tag{3}$$

$$q_2(t) = \sum_{i=t+1}^{I} P(i). \tag{4}$$

$$\mu_1(t) = \sum_{i=1}^{t} iP(i)/q_1(t). \tag{5}$$

$$\sigma_1^2(t) = \sum_{i=1}^{t} [i - \mu_1(t)]^2 P(i)/q_1(t). \tag{6}$$

$$\mu_2(t) = \sum_{i=t+1}^{I} iP(i)/q_2(t) \cdot \tag{7}$$

$$\sigma_2^2(t) = \sum_{i=t+1}^{I} [i - \mu_1(t)]^2 P(i)/q_2(t) \cdot \tag{8}$$

The best threshold t can be determined by a sequential search through all possible values of t to locate the threshold t that minimizes $\sigma_w^2(t)$.Compared with several other local adaptive threshold methods [7] this method is parameter independent and also computationally inexpensive.

2.3 Noise Reduction

Binarized images often contain a large amount of salt and pepper noise and James L. Fisher's [2] study shows that noise adversely affects image compression efficiency and degrades OCR performance. A more general filter, called kFill [5] is designed to reduce the isolated noise and noise on contours up to a selected limit in size. The filter is implemented as follows:

In a window of size $k \times k$, the filling operations are applied in the raster-scan order. The interior window, the core, consists of $(k-2) \times (k-2)$ pixels and $4(k-1)$ pixels on the boundary that is referred to as the neighborhood. The filling operation sets all values of the core to ON or OFF, depending on the pixel values in the neighborhood. The criteria to fill with ON (OFF) requires that all core pixels to be OFF (ON) and is dependent on three variables m, g and c of the neighborhood. For a fill value equal to ON (OFF), m equals to the number of ON (OFF) pixels in the neighborhood, g denotes the number of connected groups of ON pixels in the neighborhood, c represents the number of corner pixels that are ON (OFF). The window size k determines the values of m and c.

The noise reduction is performed iteratively. Each iteration consists of two sub-iterations, one performing ON fills and the other OFF fills. When no filling occurs in the consecutive sub-iterations, the process stops automatically.

Filling occurs when the following conditions are satisfied:

$$(g = 1) \text{ AND} [(m > 3k - 4) \text{ OR} \{(m = 3k - 4) \text{ AND} (c = 2)\}] \tag{9}$$

where $(m > 3k\text{-}4)$ controls the degree of smoothing: A reduction of the threshold for m leads to enhanced smoothing; $\{(m = 3k\text{-}4) \text{ AND} (c = 2)\}$is to ensure that the corners less than $90°$ are not rounded. If this condition is left out, greater noise can be reduced but corners may be rounded. $(g = 1)$ ensures that filling does not change connectivity. If this condition is absent, a greater smoothing will occur but the number of distinct regions will not remain constant. The filter is designed specifically for binary text to remove noise while retaining text integrity, especially to maintain corners of characters.

3 Headline Extraction

Headline extraction requires proper block segmentation and classification. Looking for possible existing methods for our current application, we found the work by Wahl *et al* [8] who placed the graphics as the same category with pictures. On the other hand, Fisher *et al* [2] made use of computation of statistical properties of connected components. In yet another approach, Fletcher and Kasturi [4] applied a Hough transform to link connected components into a logical character string in order to discriminate them from graphics, which is relatively independent of changes in font, size and the string orientation of text. Because of the huge amount of large images in the image store, the above methods prove to be too computationally expensive for our microfilm images.

At an early stage in the document understanding process, it is essential to identify text, image and graphics regions, as a physical segmentation of the page, so that each region can be processed appropriately. Most of these techniques for page segmentation rely on prior knowledge or assumptions about the generic document layout structure and textual and graphical attributes, e.g. rectangularity of major blocks, regularity of horizontal and vertical spaces, and text line orientation, etc. While utilizing knowledge of the layout and structure of document results in a simple, elegant and efficient page decomposition system, such knowledge is not readily available in our present project. This is because the entire microfilm collection at the National library spans over 100 years of newspapers where layouts have changed over all these years. There are thus a great variety of different layouts and structures in the image database. To address the above problems, we try to do away with the costly layout analysis. To do so, we adopt a rule-based approach to identify headlines automatically. The following approach is proposed that is not dependent on any particular layout.

3.1 Run Length Smearing

Run length smoothing algorithm (RLSA) [9] is used here to segment the document into regions. It entails the following steps: a horizontal smoothing (smear), a vertical smoothing, a logical AND operation, and an additional horizontal smoothing. In the first horizontal smoothing operation, if the distance between two adjacent black pixels (on the same horizontal scan line) is less than a threshold H, then the two pixels are joined by changing all the intervening white pixels to black ones, and the resulting image is stored. The same original image is then smoothed in the vertical direction, joining together vertically adjacent black pixels whose distance is less than a threshold V. This vertically smoothed image is then logically ANDed with the horizontally smoothed image, and the resulting image is smoothed horizontally one more time, again using the threshold H, to produce the RLSA image.

Different RLSA images are obtained with different values of H and V. A very small H value simply smoothes individual characters. Increasing the value of H can put individual characters together to form a word (word level) and further increase of H can smear a sentence (processing in a sentence level). An even larger value of H can merge the sentence together. Similar comments hold for the magnitude of V. Appropriate choice of the values of the thresholding parameters H and V is thus important. They are found empirically through experimentation.

3.2 Labeling

Using a row and run tracking method [4], the following algorithm detects connected components in the RLSA image:

Scan through the image pixel by pixel across each row in order:

- If the pixel has no connected neighbors with the same value that have already been labeled, create a new unique label and assign it to that pixel.
- If the pixel has exactly one label among its connected neighbors with the same value that has already been labeled, give it that label.
- If the pixel has two or more connected neighbors with the same value but different labels, choose one of the labels and remember that these labels are equivalent.

Resolve the equivalence by making another pass through the image and labeling each pixel with a unique label for its equivalence class. Based on the RLSA image, we can then establish boundaries around and calculate statistics of the regions using connected components. A rule based block classification is used for classifying each block into one of these types, namely, text, horizontal /vertical lines, graphics and picture.

Let the upper-left corner of an image block be the origin of coordinates. The following measures are applied on each block

- Minimum and maximum x and y coordinates of a block $(x_{min}, y_{min}, x_{max}, y_{max})$;
- Number of white pixels corresponding to the block of the RLSA image (N)

The following features are adopted for block classification:

- Height of each block, $H = y_{max} - y_{min}$;
- Width of each block, $W = x_{max} - x_{min}$;
- Density of white pixels in a block, $D = N/(H \times W)$;

Newspaper headlines often contain characters of a certain font and a larger size, which are different from the text. Let H_m and W_m denote the height and width of the most likely height of connected components, which can be determined by thresholding. Let D_a represent the minimum density of the connected components, and $d_1, d_2, d_3, d_4, e_1, e_2, e_3$, and e_4 be appropriate tolerance coefficients.

- Rule1: if, the block $H > e_1 H_m$ then it belongs to text paragraph or graphics.

- Rule2: if $e_1 H_m < H < e_2 H_m$ and $e_3 W_m < W < e_4 W_m$ then it belongs to the title or text block.
- Rule3: under rule2: if $d_1 D_a < D < d_2 D_a$ then it belongs to the title
- Rule4: under rule2: if $d_3 D_a < D < d_4 D_a$ then it belongs to the text block.

Rule1 aims to distinguish the graphics and connected text block from the image while Rule2 is used to remove horizontal and vertical lines. Rule3 and rule4 are to differentiate the headline from the text block.

4 Experimental Result

40 images of old newspaper microfilms with the width ranging from 1800 to 2400 pixels and the height ranging from 2500 to 3500 pixels were tested in our experiments. We used three different approaches to pre-process the images before applying the headline extraction discussed in section 3. The three approaches are (1) Conventional binarization based on the normal threshold [10]; (2) Histogram transformation discussed in section 2.1 above followed by Otsu method [11](Various adaptive binarization methods including Niblack method [12] were also attempted and our final choice is Otsu Method.); and (3) The three-stage image preprocessing method described in section 3. Table 1 shows the experimental results in terms of precision and recall rates defined below:

$$\text{Precision} = \frac{\text{No. of headline characters correctly extracted by the system}}{\text{No. of characters (headline or non - headline) extracted by the system}} \quad (10)$$

$$\text{Recall} = \frac{\text{No. of headline characters correctly extracted by the system}}{\text{Actual no. of headline characters in the document page}}. \quad (11)$$

Table 1. Experiment results of three methods

Image No.	Recall Rate			Precision Rate		
	Conv	Otsu	Our	Conv	Otsu	Our
1	98.2	100	100	95.2	100	100
2	50.2	70.5	80.8	96.5	100	100
3	78.2	80.3	90.5	93.1	95.3	97.1
4	80.2	84.4	86.1	89.7	90.8	91.2
5	75.3	80.2	87.5	90.1	92.5	94.6
6	60.5	79.7	89.1	92.1	93.1	95.2
7	53.3	60.9	79.8	78.2	80.1	80.5
8	73.4	78.5	81.9	82.5	83.7	85.2
9	80.7	83.4	91.2	87.4	89.6	93.4

10	56.5	62.6	70.5	76.6	79.8	82.3
11	72.4	77.1	84.5	80.4	84.2	88.6
12	79.6	80.4	92.4	81.8	89.9	95.8
13	51.2	70.5	77.6	67.7	72.4	86.9
14	60.3	70.9	78.5	70.1	80.3	85.4
15	78.2	80.0	85.1	85.9	86.6	89.7
16	69.5	74.3	82.3	77.1	85.4	89.8
17	58.4	68.9	73.2	64.3	77.8	80.5
18	74.7	80.6	83.5	80.3	83.7	87.9
19	81.6	84.7	90.2	90.4	90.4	95.4
20	75.1	80.5	84.8	83.5	88.1	90.1
21	68.9	73.3	80	75.6	79.1	88.2
22	60.8	65.4	75.6	79.2	80.3	89.3
23	76	81.2	86.3	81.8	84.9	92.7
24	78.5	86.4	90.1	87.4	90.5	92.8
25	62.3	70.6	79.3	71.7	80.3	84.5
26	55.8	62.7	71.9	71.2	79.2	82.3
27	72.4	80.7	89.5	83.3	89.9	92.6
28	69.4	78.6	87.3	74.5	85.6	89.5
29	66.1	76.4	88.5	70.4	80.8	88.9
30	53.2	69.7	79.7	61.6	79.5	85.8
31	66.7	77.9	80.4	71.9	80.7	90.3
32	70.3	78.1	90.2	81.5	89.6	92.1
33	62.4	79	85.6	77.2	80.0	86.2
34	70.2	83.5	89.9	77.1	87.3	93.7
35	58.3	61.2	77.9	64.8	72.7	80.3
36	67.8	72.3	85.2	73.2	78.4	89.6
37	78.3	84.5	87.0	83.4	87.8	92.4
38	72.6	78.9	84.8	84.1	85.4	91.3
39	60.4	73.5	85.2	73.5	84.9	87.3
40	78.2	84.1	88.4	86.4	89.6	94.3
Ave.	68.5	76.5	84.4	79	84.9	89.7

5 Conclusion and Discussion

We propose a document analysis system that extracts news headlines from microfilm images to do automatic indexing of news articles. The poor image quality of the old newspapers presented us several challenges. First, there is a need to properly binarize the image and to remove the excessive noise present. Second, a fast and effective way of identifying and extracting headlines is required without the costly layout analysis in view of the huge collection of images to be processed.

From the experiments that we have conducted, we have the following observations.

- The method of histogram transformation has significantly improved the final output despite the extremely poor and non-uniform illumination of the microfilm images and present good results.

- Adaptive binarization approach is effective for extracting text area from noisy background, even though the histogram of the image is unimodal and the gray levels of the text parts overlap with the background.

- Our headline extraction method works well even with skewed images of up to 5°. Fig 6 and 7 show the examples.

- The pre-processing step has achieved a significant improvement in headline extraction. The average recall and precision rates are 84.4% and 89.7% as compared to those of 76.5% and 84.9% for Otsu method and 68.5% and 79% for conventional approach.

- The recall rate of the headline is not always 100% in the result shown in table 1. Because some of the headlines are too close to the vertical or horizontal line and were thus regarded as the graphical or text block.

Acknowledgements. This project is supported in part by the Agency for Science, Technology and Research (A*STAR) and Ministry of Education, Singapore under grant R-252-000-071-112/303. We thank National Library Board, Singapore, for permission to use their microfilm images.

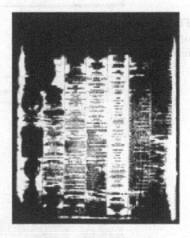

Fig. 1. One image of microfilm (T=115)

Fig. 2. Result of thresholding image of Fig. 1

Fig. 3. Result of thresholding image of Fig 1 using Otsu method after

Fig. 4. Result of thresholding image of Fig 1 using Niblack method after histogram transformation

Fig. 5. Result of thresholding image of Fig 1 using our method after histogram   transformation

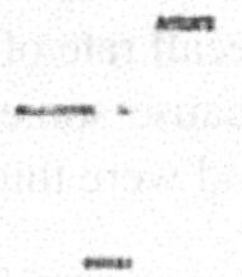

Fig. 6. Extracted headline of the microfilm

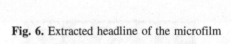

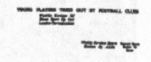

Fig. 7. Skewed newspaper microfilm image image

Fig. 8. Detected headline of skewed image Fig. 7

References

1. Hideyuki Negishi etc. "Character Extraction from Noisy Background for an automatic Reference System" ICDAR pp. 143–146, 1999
2. James L.Fisher, Stuart C.Hinds .etc "A Rule-Based System for Document Image Segmentation" IEEE Trans. Pattern Matching, 567–572,1990
3. L.O'Gorman "Binarization and multithresholding of Document images using Connectivity" CVGIP: Graphical Model and Image Processing Vol.56, No. 6 November, pp. 494–506, 1994
4. L.A. Flecher and R.Kasturi," A robust algorithm for text string separation from mixed text/graphics images" IEEE Trans. Pattern Anal. Machine Intel. Vol. 10 no. 6, pp. 910–918, Nov 1988
5. L.O'Gorman "Image and document processing techniques for the Right Pages Electronic library system" in Pro.11th Int. Conf. Pattern Recognition(ICPR) Aug 1992, pp. 260–263.
6. Y. Liu, R. Fenrich, S.N. Srihari, An object attribute thresholding algorithm for document image binarization, International Conference on Document Analysis and Recognition, ICDAR '93, Japan, 1993, pp. 278–281.
7. M.A. Forrester, etc "Evaluation of potential approach to improve digitized image quality at the patent and trademark office" MITRE Corp., McLean, VA, Working Paper WP-87W00277, July 1987.
8. F.M. Wahl, K.Y. Wong, and R.G.Casey "Block segmentation and text extraction in mixed text / image documents", Computer vision, Graphics, Image Processing, vol 20, pp. 375–390, 1982.
9. K.Y.Wong, R.G.Casey, and F.M.Wahl, "Document analysis system", IBM J.Res.Develop, vol.26, no. 6, pp. 647–656, Nov.1983.
10. T. Pavlidis: Algorithms for graphics and image processing, Computer Science Press, 1982.
11. Otsu, N., "A threshold selection Method from Gray-Level Histogram" IEEE Trans. System, Man and Cybernetics, Vol. SMC-9, No. 1, pp. 62–66, Jan 1979
12. W.Niblack,"An Introduction to Image Processing", Prentice-Hall, Englewood Cliff, NJ, pp. 115–116,1986.

Improving Document Retrieval
by Automatic Query Expansion
Using Collaborative Learning of Term-Based Concepts

Stefan Klink, Armin Hust, Markus Junker, and Andreas Dengel

German Research Center for Artificial Intelligence (DFKI, GmbH)
P.O. Box 2080, 67608 Kaiserslautern, Germany
{Stefan.Klink, Armin.Hust, Markus.Junker,
Andreas.Dengel}@dfki.de
http://www.dfki.de/~klink

Abstract. Query expansion methods have been studied for a long time – with debatable success in many instances. In this paper, a new approach is presented based on using term concepts learned by other queries. Two important issues with query expansion are addressed: the selection and the weighing of additional search terms. In contrast to other methods, the regarded query is expanded by adding those terms which are most similar to the *concept* of individual query terms, rather than selecting terms that are similar to the complete query or that are directly similar to the query terms. Experiments have shown that this kind of query expansion results in notable improvements of the retrieval effectiveness if measured the recall/precision in comparison to the standard vector space model and to the pseudo relevance feedback. This approach can be used to improve the retrieval of documents in Digital Libraries, in Document Management Systems, in the WWW etc.

1 Introduction

As the Internet and Digital Libraries become more and more popular, the growing number of documents has raised the problem called information overload. Typical search engines index billions of pages across a variety of categories, and return results ranked by expected topical relevance. But only a small percentage of these pages may be of a specific interest.

In Information Retrieval (IR) the number of retrieved documents is related to the number of appropriate search terms. Retrieval with short queries is typical in Web search [13], but it is much harder as compared to retrieval with long queries. This is because shorter queries often provide less information for retrieval. Modern IR systems therefore integrate thesaurus browsers to find additional search terms [24].

However, the aim of the retrieval activity is not to retrieve a large number of documents. Rather, users are interested in a high usefulness of the retrieved documents.

Another problem which is typical for the Web and for Digital Libraries is that the terminology used in defining queries is often different to the terminology used in the

D. Lopresti, J. Hu, and R. Kashi (Eds.): DAS 2002, LNCS 2423, pp. 376–387, 2002.

representing documents. Even if some users have the same information need they rarely use the same terminology in their queries. Many intelligent retrieval approaches [5, 18, 23] have tried to bridge this terminological gap.

Research on automatic query expansion (or modification) was already under way before the 60's when initial requests were enlarged in the grounds of statistical evidence [30]. The idea was to obtain additional relevant documents through expanded queries based on the co-occurrence of the terms. However, this kind of automatic query expansion has not been very successful. The retrieval effectiveness of the expanded queries was often not greater than, or even less than the effectiveness of the original queries [21, 22, 31].

One idea involves the use of a relevance feedback environment where the system retrieves documents that may be relevant to a user's query. The user judges the relevance of one or more of the retrieved documents and these judgments are fed back to the system to improve the initial search result. This cycle of relevance feedback can be iterated until the user is satisfied with the retrieved documents. In this case, we can say that the more feedback is given to the system the better is the search effectiveness of the system. This behavior is verified by [4]. He has shown that the recall/precision effectiveness is proportional to the log of the number of relevant feedback documents.

But in a traditional relevance feedback environment the user voted documents are appropriate to the complete query. That means that the complete query is adapted to the users needs. If another user has the same intention but uses a different terminology or just one word more or less in his query then the traditional feedback environment doesn't recognize any similarities in these situations.

Another idea to solve the terminology problem is to use query concepts. The system called 'Rule Based Information Retrieval by Computer' (RUBIC) [1, 5, 18] uses production rules to capture user query concepts. In RUBIC, a set of related production rules is represented as an AND/OR tree, called a rule base tree. RUBIC allows the definition of detailed queries starting at a conceptual level. The retrieval output is determined by fuzzy evaluation of the AND/OR tree. To find proper weight values, Kim and Raghavan developed a neural network (NN) model in which the weights for the rules can be adjusted by users' relevance feedback. Their approach is different from the previous NN approaches for IR in two aspects [12, 14]. First, they handle relations between concepts and Boolean expressions in which weighted terms are involved. Second, they do not use their own network model but an already proven model in terms of its performance.

But the crucial problem of a rule-based system still exists: the automatic production of proper rules and the learning of appropriate structures of rules, not just the weights.

2   Query Expansion

The crucial point in query expansion is the question: Which terms (or phrases) should be included in the query formulation? If the query formulation is to be expanded by additional terms there are two problems that are to be solved, namely how are these terms selected and how are the parameters estimated for these terms.

Many terms used in human communication are ambiguous or have several meanings [20]. But in most cases these ambiguities are resolved automatically without noticing the ambiguity. The way this is done by humans is still an open problem of psychological research, but it is almost certain, that the context in which a term occurs plays a central role.

Most attempts at automatically expanding queries failed to improve the retrieval effectiveness and it was often concluded that automatic query expansion based on statistical data was unable to improve the retrieval effectiveness substantial [22].

But this could have several reasons. Term-based query expansion approaches are mostly using hand-made thesauri or just plain co-occurrence data. They often do not use learning technologies for the query terms. On the other hand, those who use learning technologies (Neural Networks, Support Vector Machines, etc.) are query-based. That means these systems learn concepts (or additional terms) for the complete query.

In contrast to learning complete queries, the vital advantage of using term-based concepts is that other users can profit from learned concepts even if the same query is never used before. A statistical evaluation of log files has shown that the probability that a searcher uses exactly the same query than a previous searcher is much lower then the probability that parts of the query (phrases or terms) occurs in previous queries. So, even if a searcher never used the given search term, the probability that other searchers had used it is very high and then he can profit from the learned concept.

3   Traditional Document Retrieval

The task of traditional document retrieval is to retrieve documents which are relevant to a given query from a fixed set of documents, i.e. a document database. In a common way to deal with documents as well as queries, they are represented using a set of index terms (simply called terms) by ignoring their positions in documents and queries. Terms are determined based on words of documents in the database, usually during pre-processing phases where some normalization procedures are incorporated (e.g. stemming and stop-word elimination).

In the following, t_i ($1 \leq i \leq M$) and d_j ($1 \leq j \leq N$) represent a term and a document in the database, respectively, where M is the number of terms and N is the number of documents.

3.1   Vector Space Model

The most popular and the simplest retrieval model is the vector space model (VSM) [5]. In the VSM, a document d_j is represented as a M dimensional vector

$$d_j = (w_{1j}, \dots, w_{Mj})^T \tag{1}$$

where T indicates the transpose, w_{ij} is a weight of a term t_i in a document d_j. A query is likewise represented as

$$q_k = (w_{1k}, ..., w_{ik}, ..., w_{Mk})^T, \quad 1 \leq k \leq L \tag{2}$$

where w_{ik} is a weight of a term t_i in a query q_k.

These weights are computed by the standard normalized tf · idf weighting scheme [27] as follows:

$$w_{ij} = tf_{ij} * idf_i \tag{3}$$

where tf_{ij} is the weight calculated using the term frequency f_{ij} and idf_i is the weight calculated using the inverse of the document frequency.

The result of the retrieval is represented as a list of documents ranked according to their similarity to the query. The similarity $sim(d_j, q_k)$ between a document d_j and a query q_k is measured by the standard cosine of the angle between d_j and q_k:

$$sim(d_j, q_k) = \frac{d_j^T q_k}{\|d_j\| \|q_k\|} \tag{4}$$

where $\|\cdot\|$ is the Euclidean norm of a vector.

3.2 Pseudo Relevance Feedback

A well-known method to obtain the terms for a query expansion is the pseudo relevance feedback [18]. Here, in a first step, documents are ranked with an original query, like in the VSM. Then, the highly ranked documents are assumed to be relevant and their terms are incorporated into original query. In the second step, the documents are ranked again by using the new expanded query.

In this paper, we employ (like in Kise et al. [15]) a simple variant of the pseudo relevance feedback:

Let $\mathbb{E}$ be a set of document vectors for expansion given by

$$\mathbb{E} = \left\{ d_j^+ \mid \frac{sim(d_j^+, q)}{\max_i sim(d_i, q)} \geq \theta \right\} \tag{5}$$

where q is an original query vector and τ is a threshold of the similarity. The sum d_s of the document vectors in

$$d_s = \sum_{d_j^+ \in \mathbb{E}} d_j^+ \tag{6}$$

can be considered as enriched information about the original query. Then, the expanded query vector q' is obtained by

$$q' = \frac{q}{\|q\|} + \alpha \frac{d_s}{\|d_s\|} \tag{7}$$

where α is a parameter for controlling the weight of the newly incorporated component. Finally, the documents are ranked again according to the similarity $sim(d_j, q')$ to the expanded query.

4 Learning Term-Based Concepts

A problem of the standard VSM is that a query is often too short to rank documents appropriately. To cope with this problem, our approach is to enrich the original query by expanding it with terms occurring in the documents of the collection. But in contrast to traditional pseudo relevance feedback methods, where the top i ranked documents are assumed to be relevant and then all their terms are incorporated into the expanded query, a different technique is used to compute the relevant documents as follows:

Let $q = t_1 \dots t_n$ be the user query containing the terms $t_1 \dots t_n$
and $q = (w_1, \dots, w_i, \dots, w_M)^T$ be the vector representation of this query.
Let $Q = \{q_1, \dots, q_m\}$ be the set of all previous queries $q_1, \dots, q_m$
and D_k^+ be the set of relevant documents of the query q_k.

The goal is now to learn for each term t_i a concept c_i ($1 \leq i \leq n$) with the help of previous queries and their appropriate relevant documents. For this, the term t_i is searched in all previous queries and if it is found, the relevant documents of these queries are used to learn the concept.

Due to the VSM, a concept is also a weighted vector of terms and calculated with:

$$c_i = \tau_i (0,\dots,w_i,\dots,0)^T + \delta_i \sum_{t_i \in q_k} D_k^+ \qquad (8)$$

where $0 \leq \tau_i, \delta_i \leq 1$ are weights for the original term and the additional terms, respectively.

The expanded query vector is obtained by the sum of all term-based concepts:

$$q' = \sum_{i=1}^{n} c_i \qquad (9)$$

Before applying the expanded query, it is normalized by

$$q'' = \frac{q'}{\|q'\|} \qquad (10)$$

For this approach, the complete documents (e.g. all term weights of the document vector) are summed up and added to the query. Although, in some papers it is reported that using just the top ranked terms is sufficient or sometimes better, experiments with this approach on our collections have shown that the more words are used to learn the concepts the better are the results. So, the decision was made to use always all terms of the documents and not only some (top ranked) terms.

If no ground truth of relevant documents is available, relevance feedback techniques can be used to get the ground truth. Then, concepts are learned by adding terms from retrieved relevant documents.

5 Experiments and Results

Section 5.1 describes the test collections, section 5.2 describes our evaluation methods, and section 5.3 presents the results

5.1 Test Collections

For our comparison we used four standard test collections: CACM (collection of titles and abstracts from the journal 'Communications of the ACM'), CR (congressional report), FR (federal register) and NPL (also known as the VASWANI). These collections are contained in the TREC disks [9]. All collections are provided with queries and their ground truth (a list of documents relevant to each query). For these collections, terms used for document representation were obtained by stemming and eliminating stop words.

Table 1 lists statistics about the collections after stemming and eliminated stop words. In addition to the number of documents, a difference among the collections is the document length: CACM and NPL consists of abstracts, while CR and FR contain much longer documents.

Queries in the TREC collections are mostly provided in a structured format with several fields. In this paper, the "title" (the shortest representation) is used for the CR and NPL collection whereas the "desc" (description; medium length) is used for the CACM and FR collection.

Table 1. Statistics about collections used for experiments

	CACM	CR	FR	NPL
# documents	3204	27922	19789	11429
# queries	52	34	112	93
# different terms	3029	45717	50866	4415
avg doc length [terms]	25.8	672.8	863.7	21.8
avg query length [terms]	10.9	3.1	9.8	6.6

5.2 Evaluation

The following paragraphs describe some basic evaluation methods used in this paper. For further information and a more detailed description see Kise et al [15].

5.2.1 Average Precision
A common way to evaluate the performance of retrieval methods is to compute the (interpolated) precision at some recall levels. This results in a number of recall/precision points which are displayed in recall/precision graphs [5]. However, it is sometimes convenient for us to have a single value that summarizes the performance. The average precision (non-interpolated) over all relevant documents [5, 7] is a measure resulting in a single value. The definition is as follows:

As described in section 3, the result of retrieval is represented as the ranked list of documents. Let $r(i)$ be the rank of the i-th relevant document counted from the top of the list. The precision for this document is calculated by $i/r(i)$. The precision values for all documents relevant to a query are averaged to obtain a single value for the query. The average precision over all relevant documents is then obtained by averaging the respective values over all queries.

5.2.2 Statistical Test

The next step for the evaluation is to compare the values of the average precision obtained by different methods [15]. An important question here is whether the difference in the average precision is really meaningful or just by chance. In order to make such a distinction, it is necessary to apply a statistical test.

Several statistical tests have been applied to the task of information retrieval [11,33]. In this paper, we utilize the test called "macro t-test" [33] (called paired t-test in [11]). The following is a summary of the test described in [15]:

Let a_i and b_i be the scores (e.g., the average precision) of retrieval methods A and B for a query i and define $d_i = a_i - b_i$. The test can be applied under the assumptions that the model is additive, i.e., $d_i = \mu + \varepsilon_i$ where μ is the population mean and ε_i is an error, and that the errors are normally distributed. The null hypothesis here is $\mu = 0$ (A performs equivalently to B in terms of the average precision), and the alternative hypothesis is $\mu > 0$ (A performs better than B).
It is known that the Student's t-statistic

$$t = \frac{\bar{d}}{\sqrt{s^2/n}} \tag{11}$$

follows the t-distribution with the degree of freedom of $n - 1$, where n is the number of samples (queries), $\bar{d}$ and s^2 are the sample mean and the variance:

$$\bar{d} = \frac{1}{n} \sum_{i=1}^{n} d_i, \qquad s^2 = \frac{1}{n-1} \sum_{i=1}^{n} (d_i - \bar{d})^2 \tag{12}$$

By looking up the value of t in the t-distribution, we can obtain the P-value, i.e., the probability of observing the sample results d_i ($1 \le i \le N$) under the assumption that the null hypothesis is true. The P-value is compared to a predetermined significance level σ in order to decide whether the null hypothesis should be rejected or not. As significance levels, we utilize 0.05 and 0.01.

5.3 Results and Comparison to the Standard

In this section the results of the experiments are presented. Results were evaluated using the average precision over all queries. Recall/precision graphs were generated and then significance tests were applied to the results.

5.3.1 Recall and Precision

As described above, term weights in both documents and queries are determined according to the normalized tf·idf weighting scheme and the similarity is calculated by the VSM cosine measure, see also formula (3).

The results of the pseudo relevance feedback are depending on the two parameters β (weight) and θ (similarity threshold). To get the best results, we were varying β from 0 to 5.0 with step 0.1 and θ from 0.0 to 1.0 with step 0.05. For each collection, best individual β and θ are calculated such that their average precision is highest:

Table 2. Best values for pseudo relevance feedback parameters

	CACM	CR	FR	NPL
β (weight)	1.70	1.50	0.30	2.00
θ (sim. threshold)	0.35	0.75	0.00	0.45

The results for the concept-based queries are calculated as follows: For each individual query, all concepts of the terms within this query are learned by using all other queries with the help of their relevant documents (leave-one-out test) and the expanded query is used to calculate the new recall/precision result. Of course, the relevant documents of the current query are not used to learn the concepts.

The results of our concept-based expansion are also depending on weights. For the experiments described in this paper we just used the default value: $\tau_i = \delta_i = 1$.

Figure 1 shows the recall/precision results of the original query with the standard vector space model (red line, VSM), the pseudo relevance feedback (blue line, PRF) and the expanded query using learned concepts (green line, concepts).

The recall/precision graphs in figure 1 indicate that the automatic query expansion method based on learned concepts yields a considerable improvement in the retrieval effectiveness in 3 collections over all recall points compared to the standard vector space model and to the pseudo relevance feedback method (except with the NPL collection). There is no indication that the improvement is depending on the size of the collection, the number of documents nor on the number or size of the queries. The method performs good on CACM but only somewhat better than the VSM on the NPL. On FR it performs better than on the CR collection. Looking at the figures the impression could arise that our method performs better with longer queries. But experiments with the CR collection have shown that 'title' queries result a better precision than 'description' or 'narrative' queries. This behavior is in contrast to the first impression of the figures.

Additionally, as described above, the more words and the more documents are used to learn the concept the better are the results. Experiments have shown that the precision continues to increase as more documents are used.

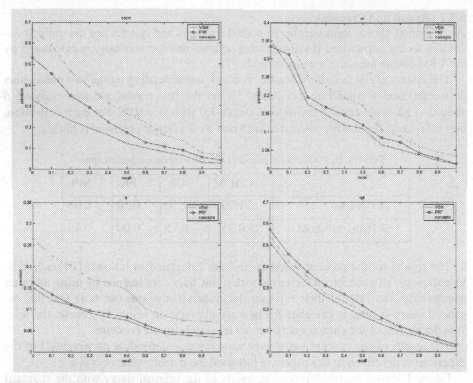

Fig. 1. recall / precision of CACM, CR, FR, and NPL

5.3.2 Statistical tests

The results above are very exciting. But in order to be sure that these results are really meaningful and not just by chance, it is necessary to apply a statistical test. As described above, we used the "macro t-test". The results of the macro t-test for all pairs of methods are shown in table 3. The meaning of the symbols such as "", ">" and "~" is summarized at the bottom of the table. For example, the symbol "<" was obtained in the case of the concept method compared to the VSM for the NPL collection. This indicates that, at the significance level $\sigma = 0.05$, the null hypothesis "concept method performs equivalently to the VSM" is rejected and the alternative hypothesis "concept method performs better than the VSM" is accepted. (At $\sigma = 0.01$, however, the null hypothesis cannot be rejected.)

Roughly speaking, "A $\gg$ ($\ll$) B", "A > (<) B" and "A~B" indicate that "A is almost guaranteed to be better (worse) than B", "A is likely to be better (worse) than B" and "A is equivalent to B", respectively.

The macro t-tests confirm our results. Our new method for expanding queries which is based on term-based concepts outperforms the standard VSM and the pseudo-relevance feedback (except on the NPL collection).

Due to the low P-values in the '$\gg$' cases it is proved that the results are not obtained by chance and that the improvements are significant.

Table 3. Results of the macro t-test.

methods (A vs. B)	CACM	CR	FR	NPL
PRF vs. VSM	≫	~	~	≫
concepts vs. PRF	≫	>	≫	<
concepts vs. VSM	≫	≫	≫	>

$$\gg, \ll \; : \qquad \text{P-value} \le 0.01$$
$$>, < \; : \quad 0.01 \le \quad \text{P-value} \le 0.05$$
$$\sim \; : \quad 0.05 \le \quad \text{P-value}$$

6 Conclusions and Future Work

We have described an approach for bridging the terminology gap between user queries and potential answer documents using term-based concepts. In this approach for all query terms concepts are learned from previous queries and relevant answer documents. A new query is transformed by replacing the original query terms by the learned concepts. This is in contrast to traditional query expansion methods which do not take into account previous queries but mostly rely on term statistics of the underlying document collection or hand-made thesauri.

Our experiments made on four standard test collections with different sizes and different document types have shown considerable improvements vs. the original queries in the standard vector space model and vs. the pseudo relevance feedback (here, except on the NPL collection). This is true even through the parameters for pseudo relevance feedback were optimized, while for our approach we did not touch the parameters. The improvements seem not to depend on the type nor on the size of the collection and they are not obtained by chance.

The vital advantage of the approach is that in a multi-user scenario users can benefit from concepts learned by other users. The approach is expected to perform better as more users and queries are involved. It can be used to improve the retrieval of documents in Digital Libraries, Document Management Systems, WWW etc.

In the near future it is planned to make some experiments on the influence of the weights τ_i and δ_i (cmp. equation (8)), and to develop functions for calculating these parameters for each individual concept. Further experiments are planned using user-voted relevance feedback instead of collection-given ground-truth to test the performance on 'real-life' data. For this we are currently collecting queries and click data from a search engine [10].

The approach on passage-based retrieval by Kise [15] has shown good improvements vs. LSI and Density Distribution. Instead of using the complete relevant documents for expanding the query or using the n top ranked terms, an interesting idea for the future is to use just terms of relevant passages within the documents. This should increase the quality of the expanded queries.

7 Acknowledgements

This work was supported by the German Ministry for Education and Research, bmb+f (Grant: 01 IN 902 B8).

References

1. Aalbersberg I.J.: Incremental relevance feedback. In *Proceedings of the Annual Int. ACM SIGIR Conference on Research and Development in Information Retrieval*, pp. 11 - 22, 1992
2. Allan J.: Incremental relevance feedback for information filtering. In *Proceedings of the 19th Annual Int. ACM SIGIR Conference on Research and Development in Information Retrieval*, pp. 270 - 278, 1996
3. Alsaffar A.H., Deogun J.S., Raghavan V.V., Sever H: Concept-based retrieval with minimal term sets. In Z.W. Ras and A. Skowon, editors, *Foundation of Intelligent Systems: 11th Int. Symposium*, ISMIS'99, pp. 114-122, Springer, Warsaw, Poland, June 1999
4. Buckley C., Salton G., Allen J.: The effect of adding relevance information in a relevance feedback environment. In *Proceedings of the 17th Annual Int. ACM SIGIR Conference on Research and Development in Information Retrieval*, pp. 292 - 300, 1994
5. Baeza-Yates R., Ribeiro-Neto B.: *Modern Information Retrieval*. Addison-Wesley Pub. Co., 1999. ISBN 020139829X
6. Croft W.B.: Approaches to intelligent information retrieval. *Information Processing and Management*, 1987, Vol.23, No.4, pp. 249-254
7. ftp://ftp.cs.cornell.edu/pub/smart/
8. Harman D.: Towards Interactive Query Expansion. In: Chiaramella Y. (editor): *11th International Conference on Research and Development in Information Retrieval*, pp. 321 – 331, Grenoble, France, 1988
9. http://trec.nist.gov/
10. http://phibot.org/
11. Hull D.: Using Statistical Testing in the Evaluation of Retrieval Experiments. In *Proceedings of the 16th Annual Int. ACM SIGIR Conference on Research and Development in Information Retrieval*, pp. 329 - 338, 1993
12. Iwayama M.: Relevance Feedback with a Small Number of Relevance Judgments: Incremental Relevance Feedback vs. Document Clustering. In *Proceedings of the 23rd Annual Int. ACM SIGIR Conference on Research and Development in Information Retrieval*, pp. 10 - 16, Athens, Greece, July 2000
13. Jansen B.J., Spink A., Bateman J. and Saracevic T.: Real Life Information Retrieval: A Study of User Queries on the Web, In *SIGIR Forum*, Vol. 31, pp. 5-17, 1988
14. Kim M., Raghavan V.: Adaptive concept-based Retrieval Using a Neural Network, In *Proceedings of ACM SIGIR Workshop on Mathematical/Formal Methods in Information Retrieval*, Athens, Greece, July 2000
15. Kise K., Junker M., Dengel A., Matsumoto K.: Passage-Based Document Retrieval as a Tool for Text Mining with User's Information Needs, In *Proceedings of the 4th International Conference of Discovery Science*, pp. 155-169, Washington, DC, USA, November 2001

16. Kwok K.: Query Modification and Expansion in a Network with Adaptive Architecture. In *Proceedings of the 14th Annual Int. ACM SIGIR Conference on Research and Development in Information Retrieval*, pp. 192 - 201, 1991

17. Lu F., Johnsten Th., Raghavan V.V., Traylor D.: Enhancing Internet Search Engines to Achieve Concept-based Retrieval, In *Proceedings of Inforum'99*, Oakridge, USA

18. Manning C.D. and Schütze H.: *Foundations of Statistical Natural Language Processing*, MIT Press, 1999

19. Maglano V., Beaulieu M., Robertson S., : Evaluation of interfaces for IRS: modeling end-user search behaviour. *20th Colloquium on Information Retrieval*, Grenoble, 1988

20. McCune B.P., Tong R.M., Dean J.S., Shapiro D.G.: RUBRIC: A System for Rule-Based Information Retrieval, In *IEEE Transaction on Software Engineering*, Vol. SE-11, No.9, September 1985

21. Minker J., Wilson, G.A. Zimmerman, B.H.: An evaluation of query expansion by the addition of clustered terms for a document retrieval system, *Information Storage and Retrieval*, vol. 8(6), pp. 329-348, 1972

22. Peat H.J., Willet, P.: The limitations of term co-occurrence data for query expansion in document retrieval systems, *Journal of the ASIS*, vol. 42(5), pp. 378-383, 1991

23. Pirkola A.: Studies on Linguistic Problems and Methods in Text Retrieval: The Effects of Anaphor and Ellipsis Resolution in Proximity Searching, and Translation and query Structuring Methods in Cross-Language Retrieval, *PhD dissertation*, Department of Information Studies, University of Tampere. Acta Universitatis Tamperensis 672. ISBN 951-44-4582-1; ISSN 1455-1616. June 1999

24. Qiu Y.: ISIR: an integrated system for information retrieval, In *Proceedings of 14th IR Colloqium*, British Computer Society, Lancaster, 1992

25. van Rijsbergen C.J., Harper D.H., etal.: The Selection of Good Search Terms. *Information Processing and Management* 17, pp. 77-91, 1981

26. Resnik P.: Using information content to evaluate semantic similarity in a taxonomy. In *Proceedings of the 14th Int. Joint Conference on Artificial Intelligence*, pp. 448-453, 1995

27. Salton G., Buckley C.: Term weighting approaches in automatic text retrieval. Information *Processing & Management* 24(5), pp. 513 - 523, 1988

28. Salton G., Buckley C.: Improving Retrieval Performance by Relevance Feedback. *Journal of the American Society for Information Science* 41(4), pp. 288 – 297, 1990

29. Sanderson M., Croft B.: Deriving concept hierarchies from text. In *Proceedings of the 22nd Annual Int. ACM SIGIR Conference on Research and Development in Information Retrieval*, pp. 206 - 213, Berkeley, CA, August 1999

30. Sparck-Jones K.: Notes and references on early classification work. In *SIGIR Forum*, vol. 25(1), pp. 10-17, 1991

31. Smeaton A.F., van Rijsbergen C.J.: The retrieval effects of query expansion on a feedback document retrieval system. *The Computer Journal*, vol. 26(3), pp. 239 – 246, 1983

32. Stucky D.,: Unterstützung der Anfrageformulierung bei Internet-Suchmaschinen durch User Relevance Feedback, *diploma thesis*, German Research Center of Artificial Intelligence (DFKI), Kaiserslautern, November 2000

33. Yang Y. and Liu X.: A Re-Examination of Text Categorization Methods. In *Proceedings of the 22nd Annual Int. ACM SIGIR Conference on Research and Development in Information Retrieval*, pp. 42 - 49, Berkeley, CA, August 1999

Spotting Where to Read on Pages – Retrieval of Relevant Parts from Page Images

Koichi Kise, Masaaki Tsujino, and Keinosuke Matsumoto

Department of Computer and Systems Sciences,
Graduate School of Engineering, Osaka Prefecture University
1-1 Gakuencho, Sakai, Osaka 599-8531 Japan
kise@cs.osakafu-u.ac.jp

Abstract. This paper presents a new method of document image retrieval that is capable of spotting parts of page images relevant to a user's query. This enables us to improve the usability of retrieval, since a user can find where to read on retrieved pages. The effectiveness of retrieval can also be improved because the method is little influenced by irrelevant parts on pages. The method is based on the assumption that parts of page images which densely contain keywords in a query are relevant to it. The characteristics of the proposed method are as follows: (1) Two-dimensional density distributions of keywords are calculated for ranking parts of page images, (2) The method relies only on the distribution of characters so as not to be affected by the errors of layout analysis. Based on the experimental results of retrieving Japanese newspaper articles, we have shown that the proposed method is superior to a method without the function of dealing with parts, and sometimes equivalent to a method of electronic document retrieval that works on error-free text.

1 Introduction

Document image retrieval is a task to retrieve document images relevant to user's information needs. This technology allows us to replace a huge amount of paper documents with document images, and thus enables us to solve the problem of space occupied by paper documents.

Although a number of researches have been made on document image retrieval [1], there is still room for improvement. We focus here on the problems of *indexing*, *retrieval* and *presentation*.

Indexing. Users' information needs are typically represented as keywords, while the database stores document images. This gap between symbols (character codes) and signals (pixels) poses the problem of indexing. Since manual indexing is prohibitive, automatic indexing should be employed. Researchers have proposed a number of methods ranging from the indexing based on text produced by OCR [2] to the indexing based on the image features [3,4,5]. The problem here is how to obtain the robustness against low-quality images. For instance, in case that the indexing based on OCR results is employed,

D. Lopresti, J. Hu, and R. Kashi (Eds.): DAS 2002, LNCS 2423, pp. 388–399, 2002.
© Springer-Verlag Berlin Heidelberg 2002

it is necessary to cope with OCR errors. The OCR errors are not limited to the misrecognition of individual characters, but include the errors in layout analysis and identification of reading order.

Retrieval. The effectiveness of document (or page) ranking is an important problem of retrieval, though most of the existing methods deal mainly with keyword spotting on page images. In order to obtain the ranking, we should define and utilize a measure of similarity between a user's query (a set of keywords) and a page image, according to the spotted keywords.

Presentation. It seems that the problem of presentation is often overlooked. This problem is caused by the disparity between the size of page images and the size of images that can be displayed. For example, newspaper pages scanned with the resolution of, say, 200 dpi, are too large for ordinary displays. Images of A4 pages could cause the same problem if we use PDA's. Thus it is important to locate where to read on pages in addition to select pages which contain information relevant to a query.

In the field of electronic document retrieval, researchers have faced the similar problems of document ranking and presentation, and proposed the scheme called "passage retrieval" [6,7] to solve the problems. The task of passage retrieval is to retrieve not whole documents but their parts, or *passages* relevant to a query. This enables us to solve the problem of presentation in a natural way. It has also been shown that, as compared to the similarity based on whole documents, the similarity based on passages improves the quality of document ranking [9]. This suggests that the problems of document image retrieval could also be solved by applying passage retrieval.

In this paper, we experimentally validate the above suggestion. We propose a method of passage retrieval for document images by extending our method [8,9] for electronic documents. In the context of document image retrieval, passages correspond to parts of page images. The characteristic features of the proposed method are as follows:

- For indexing, we do not employ the results of neither layout analysis nor identification of reading order so as to obtain the robustness against errors. Document images are indexed based only on character positions and codes obtained by segmentation and recognition of characters.
- We assume that parts of page images are relevant to a query if these parts *densely* contain keywords in a query. Two-dimensional distributions called "density distributions of keywords" are calculated for finding such parts.

The organization of this paper is as follows. In Sect. 2, we give an overview of the related work in the fields of both electronic documents and document images. Section 3 describes the proposed method of retrieving parts of document images. In Sect. 4, we experimentally evaluate the proposed method in comparison with a standard method of electronic document retrieval.

2   Related Work

2.1   Retrieval of Electronic Documents

Since the mid 90's, researchers in the field of information retrieval have proposed a retrieval scheme called "passage retrieval" [6,7]. Passage retrieval is advantageous to conventional document retrieval in the following points:

1. It provides us the direct access to passages, which relieves us from the burden of finding relevant parts in the retrieved documents.
2. It improves the ranking of documents as follows. In general, long documents contain multiple topics. Even if a topic in such documents is relevant to a query, the rest may be irrelevant. This results in disturbing document ranking by conventional document retrieval, since there is no way to distinguish relevant topics from irrelevant topics. On the other hand, passage retrieval enables us to avoid the influence of irrelevant topics in documents.

The authors have also proposed a method of passage retrieval called "density distribution". The density distribution was first introduced to locate the explanation of a word in long documents [10] and applied to passage retrieval by the authors [8,9]. In this paper, we extend this method to be applicable to the retrieval of page images.

2.2   Retrieval of Document Images

In the field of document image retrieval, a central issue has been how to locate words on page images. This would be because, after locating words, the task of document image retrieval is considered to be equivalent to that of electronic document retrieval. For the retrieval of page images written in ideograms such as Kanji characters, we can also consider the possibility of locating characters. Words and characters can be located in several ways including the application of OCR [4], utilization of a special set of symbols such as "character shape coding" [3], and the matching with real-valued feature vectors [4,5].

However, if we build systems of document image retrieval by replacing the function of locating words in electronic document retrieval, we will suffer the similar difficulties about the selection of relevant parts as well as the influence of irrelevant parts.

We consider that the layout of pages provides us fruitful hints for solving these problems in the document image domain. This is because words and characters in the same topic are laid out closer with one another on a page. The method proposed in this paper embodies this idea without suffering from the errors of layout analysis.

3   Retrieval of Image Parts

3.1   Overview

The proposed method employs three types of processing: indexing, retrieval and presentation. The process of indexing is applied to document images in advance

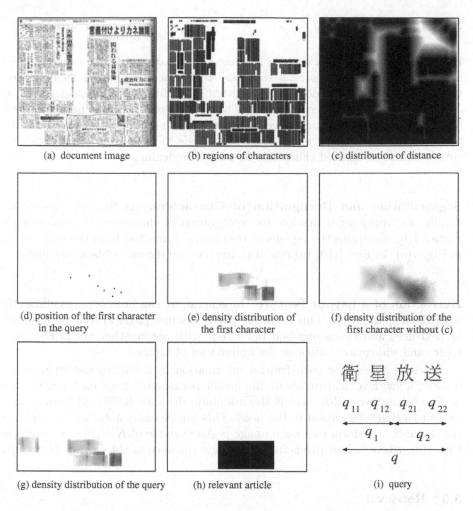

(a) document image   (b) regions of characters   (c) distribution of distance

(d) position of the first character in the query   (e) density distribution of the first character   (f) density distribution of the first character without (c)

(g) density distribution of the query   (h) relevant article   (i) query

Fig. 1. Examples of processing results

of receiving a query. Every time a query is received, the process of retrieval starts to find relevant parts of images, which are then displayed by the process of presentation. The current implementation is just for Japanese printed documents, though we consider that central ideas of the method are independent of the type of languages.

In what follows, each step of processing is explained using examples shown in Fig. 1. In Fig. 1(a), a page of a newspaper that contains an article about "satellite broadcasting" is shown. Figure 1(i) illustrates four Kanji characters (q_{11}, q_{12}, q_{21}, q_{22}) which mean "satellite broadcasting". Taken as input the query in Fig. 1(i), the method produces the density distribution of the query as shown in Fig. 1(g) based on the intermediate results of Figs. 1 (b),(c),(d) and (e). Figure 1(h) illustrates the correct region of the article about "satellite broadcasting"; the output (Fig. 1(g)) agrees well with the correct region.

3.2   Indexing

For documents written in western languages, it is natural to take words as units of indexing, because it is relatively easy to extract them from page images. On the other hand, for documents written in agglutinative languages such as Japanese, it is difficult to extract words because there is no space between them. Morphological analysis is required to identify words from a sequence of characters. Instead of applying morphological analysis to recognized characters[1], we simply utilize recognized characters as units of indexing.

Segmentation and Recognition of Characters. As the first step of indexing, we apply segmentation and recognition of characters to page images. Figure 1(b) illustrates the regions of characters segmented from the page image in Fig. 1(a). In Fig. 1(b), regions of characters are shown as black rectangles.

Extraction of a Layout Feature. In general, we can browse pages efficiently with the help of layout. This would be partly because physical components such as text-lines and characters laid out closer with one another are of the same topic, and wide space indicates the boundaries of topics.

In order to employ such fruitful information in a way robust to noise on images, a low level feature about the layout is extracted from each page image p. The feature we utilize here is the minimum distance $K^{(p)}(x,y)$ from a pixel (x,y) to a character closest to the pixel. This can be easily obtained by applying the distance transform to a page image p. An example of $K^{(p)}(x,y)$ is shown in Fig. 1(c), where lighter pixels indicate longer distance to the closest characters.

3.3   Retrieval

Query Processing. The first step of retrieval is the processing of a query. Since a user may represent a query as sentences or phrases, we first apply morphological analysis to extract as keywords nouns from a query. Then each keyword is further decomposed into characters.

For example, a query q (*satellite broadcasting*) shown in Fig. 1(i) is decomposed into two keywords q_1 (*satellite*) and q_2 (*broadcasting*). The first keyword q_1 consists of two characters q_{11} and q_{12} in Fig. 1(i), and the second keyword q_2 includes two characters q_{21} and q_{22}.

In the following, keywords extracted from a query q are represented as $\{q_1, ..., q_n\}$, and characters contained in a keyword q_i are represented as $\{q_{i1}, ..., q_{im}\}$.

---

[1] This is not a trivial task because morphological analyzers are not designed to deal with errors of character recognition.

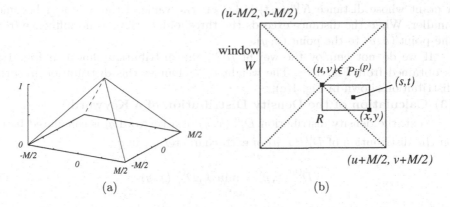

Fig. 2. Window function and points (u, v), (x, y) and (s, t)

Calculation of Density Distributions. The role of this step is to calculate the density distribution of a query for each page in order to obtain information for spotting relevant parts. The processing consists of the following four steps.

(1) Locating Characters on Pages

As shown in Fig. 1(b), character regions are represented as rectangles. We indicate positions of characters using the centers of rectangles. In this step, we first find all positions of each character q_{ij} on pages. An example is shown in Fig. 1(d). In the following, the positions of a character q_{ij} in a page image p are represented by a set of points $P_{ij}^{(p)} = \{(u, v)\}$ where (u, v) indicates the center of a rectangle.

(2) Calculation of the Density Distribution of a Character

The density distribution $D_{ij}^{(p)}(x, y)$ of a character q_{ij} is obtained by smoothing the distribution of points $P_{ij}^{(p)}$ with the distance $K^{(p)}(x, y)$. Figure 1(e) illustrates the density distribution obtained from Fig. 1(d) with Fig. 1(c). In Fig. 1(e), darker regions contain the character more densely. The distribution is given by

$$D_{ij}^{(p)}(x, y) = \sum_{(u,v) \in P_{ij}^{(p)}} W(x - u, y - v)\alpha^{(p)}(x, y, u, v) \ , \qquad (1)$$

where W is a window function for smoothing, and $\alpha^{(p)}$ is a weight obtained from $K^{(p)}(x, y)$. As a window function, we utilize a square pyramid shown in Fig. 2(a) where M is the window width.

The weight $\alpha^{(p)}$ is to control the influence of a point (u, v) on the distribution using the distance $K^{(p)}(s, t)$:

$$\alpha^{(p)}(x, y, u, v) = \begin{cases} T - \max_{(s,t) \in R} K^{(p)}(s, t) & \text{if } \max_{(s,t) \in R} K^{(p)}(s, t) < T \ , \\ 0 & \text{otherwise} \ , \end{cases} \qquad (2)$$

where T is a threshold and (s, t) is the point within the rectangle R defined by two points (u, v) and (x, y) as shown in Fig. 2(b). If the rectangle R includes a point whose distance $K^{(p)}(s,t)$ is larger, the value of the weight α becomes smaller. When the distance exceeds the threshold T, there is no influence from the point (u,v) to the point (x,y).

If we do not employ the weight $\alpha^{(p)}$, the distribution shown in Fig. 1(f) is obtained from Fig. 1(d). The weight $\alpha^{(p)}$ changes this distribution into the distribution shown in Fig. 1(e).

(3) Calculation of the Density Distribution of a Keyword

Next, the density distribution $D_i^{(p)}(x,y)$ of a keyword q_i is calculated based on the distribution of $D_{ij}^{(p)}(x,y)$ of each character q_{ij} in q_i:

$$D_i^{(p)}(x,y) = \min_j \beta_{ij} D_{ij}^{(p)}(x,y) \; . \tag{3}$$

The operation "min" is applied to the distributions of characters, because we are interested in the *co-occurrence* of characters to identify a keyword.

In (3), β_{ij} indicates the weight of $D_{ij}^{(p)}$ which represents the importance of a character q_{ij} for the identification of a keyword q_i. If a character q_{ij} is ubiquitous on pages, its distribution conveys little information for the identification, and thus a small weight is used[2]. The above notion can be expressed as:

$$\beta_{ij} = \sum_{p,x,y} (\max_{p,x,y} D_{ij}^{(p)}(x,y) - D_{ij}^{(p)}(x,y)) \; . \tag{4}$$

(4) Calculation of the Density Distribution of a Query

As the last step, the density distribution of a whole query q is calculated based on the distributions of keywords q_i as follows:

$$D^{(p)}(x,y) = \max_i D_i^{(p)}(x,y) \; . \tag{5}$$

This time, the operation "max" is applied since the parts which contain one of the keywords would be relevant to a query.

3.4   Presentation

Each page image p is now associated with its density distribution $D^{(p)}(x,y)$ of a query. In our method, the maximum of the density distribution in a page image:

$$\max_{x,y} D^{(p)}(x,y) \tag{6}$$

is employed as a score of a page image. Page images in the database are ranked according to their score (in descending order of the score). Then the top-ranked page image is presented to a user by displaying its part whose density is the maximum.

---

[2] The aim of the weight β_{ij} is similar to the *inverse document frequency (IDF)* that is often employed for term weighting in IR systems.

Table 1. Queries used in the experiments

query id	keywords(translation)	no. of relevant articles
1	任天堂 (Nintendo), セガ (Sega)	4
2	農薬 (agricultural chemical)	3
3	液晶 (liquid crystal)	3
4	減税 (tax reduction)	4
5	衛星 (satellite), 放送 (broadcasting)	3
6	賃貸 (rent), 住宅 (house)	4
7	核兵器 (nuclear weapon)	4

Table 2. Statistics on page images and queries for experiments

no. of pages	25
no. of articles	249
size of page images	$8,000 \times 6,000$ pixels
scanning resolution	800 dpi
size of characters in body text regions	50×50 pixels
no. of queries	7
ave. no. of relevant articles for a query	3.57 articles
ave. no. of keywords in a query	1.48 keywords
ave. no. of characters in a keyword	2.2 characters

4 Experimental Results

4.1 Data for Experiments

We prepared the data of page images and queries based on a test collection available for evaluation of Japanese information retrieval (IR) systems. The collection we utilized is called BMIR-J2 [12], which consists of 50 queries for 5,080 articles of Mainichi Shinbun newspaper issued in 1994 and the groundtruth (relevance judgements) for the queries.

Based on BMIR-J2, we prepared the document image database with the groundtruth. The queries in BMIR-J2 are classified into several types. We utilized the queries which belong to the basic type as listed in Table 1. Next, we randomly selected, for each query, three to four articles whose subjects are relevant to it. Then, pages that contain those articles were obtained from the microcopy of the newspaper. In the scanned pages, the parts which do not correspond to 5,080 articles of BMIR-J2 were manually erased. The statistics on page images and queries are shown in Table 2.

The results of character segmentation and recognition were obtained using a commercial OCR. The recognition rate for the characters in the queries was 74.1% and the false alarm rate was 2.3%. We consider that such a low recognition rate was due to the quality of the images which were obtained not from the original pages but from the microcopy pages.

In the processing of queries, we applied a Japanese morphological analyzer JUMAN [13] to obtain keywords.

4.2   Methods for Comparison

Since the electronic version of articles are also available, we can apply a standard IR method for the same set of queries and articles. In the experiments, we employed as a method of comparison the vector space model(VSM) with the tf–idf term weighting [11]. The VSM is applied to the recognized text as well as to the clean (error-free) text. In the following, the VSM applied to the clean text is referred to as "VSM" and the VSM to the recognized text is referred to as "VSM (OCR)".

In addition to them, we employed a modified version of the proposed method in order to evaluate the effectiveness of taking image parts into account. The modification is to exclude the function for dealing with image parts as follows. For each character q_{ij} in a keyword q_i, the weight tf_{ij}, which corresponds to D_{ij} in (1), is computed as

$$\text{tf}_{ij} = (\text{the number of occurrence of } q_{ij} \text{ in a page}) \ . \tag{7}$$

The weight w_i for a keyword q_i is then given by

$$w_i = \min_j (\text{idf}_{ij} \cdot \text{tf}_{ij}) \ , \tag{8}$$

which corresponds to (3). In (8), idf_{ij} is the inverse document frequency given by

$$\text{idf}_{ij} = \log \frac{N}{N_{ij}} \ , \tag{9}$$

where N and N_{ij} represent the number of all pages in the database and the number of pages that contain the character q_{ij}, respectively. Finally, the score of a page is obtained by

$$\max_i w_i \ , \tag{10}$$

which corresponds to (5). In the following, this method is called "MOD".

4.3   Criteria for Evaluation

A common way to evaluate the performance of retrieval methods is to compute recall and precision [11]. Let X, Y be a set of retrieved documents and a set of relevant documents, respectively. The recall R and the precision P is defined as $R = |X \cap Y|/|Y|$, $P = |X \cap Y|/|X|$. When we have multiple queries for evaluation, the precision for each query is calculated at some fixed points of recall (recall levels) with the help of interpolation, and then averaged over all queries at each recall level. Since this produces some points of recall and precision for each method, they are typically shown in recall-precision graphs.

In addition to the recall-precision graphs, it is sometimes convenient to have a single value that summarizes the performance. For this purpose, we utilized *the average precision (non-interpolated) over all relevant documents* [11].

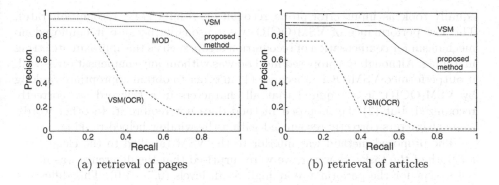

(a) retrieval of pages   (b) retrieval of articles

Fig. 3. Experimental results

4.4 Tasks

In this paper, we have two retrieval tasks, i.e., retrieval of pages and that of articles. For the task of retrieval of pages, methods were required to rank *pages* for evaluation. In the proposed method, for example, the ranking was obtained according to the score defined by (6). For the task of retrieval of articles, on the other hand, *articles* were ranked according to the score. Although there is no obstacle to compute the score of articles by the VSM, it is not possible for the proposed method, because there is no way to obtain the exact regions of articles by itself. In order to compute as well the score of articles for the proposed method, the regions of articles were prepared beforehand and the score of each article was determined as the maximum of the density distribution $D^{(p)}(x, y)$ within its region.

4.5 Values of Parameters

The proposed method employs two parameters: the window width M in Fig. 2 and the threshold T in (2). The values of these parameters were experimentally determined as follows. Since the number of queries was small, we applied leave-one-out, which means that values of the parameters for i-th query were determined using the data for all queries except for the i-th query. We examined all the combination of the values for $M = 100 \sim 3,000$ with the step of 50 and $T = 10 \sim 100$ with the step of 10 to obtain the best values in terms of the average precision for retrieval of pages.

4.6 Results and Discussion

The results of experiments are shown in Fig. 3. Because MOD is only for page ranking, its result is shown only for the task of "retrieval of pages".

As shown in Fig. 3, the proposed method was superior to VSM(OCR) for both of the tasks (retrieval of pages and articles), though these two methods equally took as input error-prone recognition results (74% recognition rate). The low performance of VSM(OCR) was reasonable because it employed no mechanism for compensation of recognition errors such as the approximate string matching. Although the proposed method was without any compensation as well, it outperformed VSM(OCR), because (1) in order to obtain appropriate ranking by VSM(OCR), it is required that all characters in a keyword are correctly recognized, but (2) the proposed method does not require it. In other words, some characters correctly recognized within the window helped ranking.

The proposed method was inferior to the VSM (applied to the clean text) for both of the tasks. However, we were surprised that the difference was not so big except for the performance at high recall levels (0.7 – 1.0). This difference at high recall levels was caused mainly by the errors of character recognition. Some relevant documents contain only a few characters of a keyword, so that the performance was influenced by the errors. Thus in order to improve the performance at high recall levels, it is required to employ a method to cope with recognition errors.

Finally, let us compare the proposed method with MOD on the task of page retrieval. The graph in Fig. 3(a) shows a small but clear difference at all recall levels. This indicates that the the proposed method which takes into account the locality of occurrence of characters and keywords enables us to improve precision of retrieval.

5   Conclusion

We have presented a method of document image retrieval which enables us to spot where to read on pages. The characteristics of the proposed method are as follows:

1. The method realizes the notion that relevance of parts of images can be measured by the density distributions of keywords,
2. The method relies only on the distribution of characters so as to obtain the robustness against errors of layout analysis.

From the experiments on the retrieval of both pages and articles, it has been shown that the proposed method outperforms the methods (VSM and MOD) that also work on recognized characters. It has also been shown that at low and middle recall levels the proposed method is almost equivalent to the VSM that works on error-free text.

Due to the difficulty of preparing the groundtruth for the articles on pages, the number of pages and articles were too small to draw a definite conclusion. In addition, the documents employed in the experiments were limited only to those written in Japanese, though we consider that the fundamental notions of the method are independent of languages. Thus the future work is to scale up the experiments as well as to apply the method to documents written in other languages.

Acknowledgment. This research was supported in part by Grant-in-Aid for Scientific Research (C) and (B) from Japan Society for the Promotion of Science (No.14580453, No.14380182). We used BMIR-J2 based on the Mainichi Shinbun CD-ROM'94 data collection, as well as a Japanese morphological analyzer JUMAN. We are grateful to those who permitted us to use their materials and programs.

References

1. Doermann, D.: The Indexing and Retrieval of Document Images: A Survey, *Computer Vision and Image Processing*, Vol. 70, No. 3, pp.287–298, 1998.
2. Ohta, M., Takasu, A., Adachi, J.: Retrieval Methods for English-Text with Missrecognized OCR Characters, *Proc. of the 4th ICDAR*, pp.957–961, 1997.
3. Smeaton, A. F., Spitz, A. L.: Using Character Shape Coding for Information Retrieval, *Proc. of 4th ICDAR*, pp.974–978, 1997.
4. Ohta, Y., Mori, R., Sakai, T.: Retrieval of Chinese Character Sequence Using Pictorial Features — The Case of Names on Visiting Cards —, *Trans. IECE, Japan*, Vol. J64-D, No. 11, pp.997–1004, 1981 (in Japanese).
5. Nakanishi, T, Omachi, S., Aso, H.: High Precision Keyword Search System Adapted to Low Quality Document Images, *Tech. Report of IEICE*, PRMU98-232, 1999 (in Japanese).
6. Salton, G., Singhal, A., Mitra, M.: Automatic Text Decomposition Using Text Segments and Text Themes, in *Proc. Hypertext '96*, pp.53-65, 1996.
7. Callan, J. P.: Passage-Level Evidence in Document Retrieval, in *Proc. SIGIR '94*, pp.302-310,1994.
8. Kise, K., Mizuno, H., Yamaguchi, M., Matsumoto, K.: On the Use of Density Distribution of Keywords for Automated Generation of Hypertext Links from Arbitrary Parts of Documents, in *Proc. of the 5th ICDAR*, pp.301–304, 1999.
9. Kise, K., Junker, M., Dengel, A., Matsumoto, K.: Experimental Evaluation of Passage-Based Document Retrieval, in *Proc. of the 6th ICDAR*, pp.592–596, 2001.
10. Kurohashi, S., Shiraki, N., Nagao, M.: A Method for Detecting Important Descriptions of a Word Based on Its Density Distribution in Text, *Trans. Information Processing Society of Japan*, Vol.38, No.4, pp.845–853, 1997 (In Japanese).
11. Baeza-Yates, R., Ribeiro-Neto, B.: *Modern Information Retrieval*, Addison-Wesley Pub. Co., 1999.
12. Sakai, T., et al.: BMIR-J2: A Test Collection for Evaluation of Japanese Information Retrieval Systems, *SIGIR Forum*, Vol.33, No.1, pp.13–17, 1999.
13. ⟨ URL:http://www-nagao.kuee.kyoto-u.ac.jp/nl-resource/juman-e.html ⟩.

Mining Documents for Complex Semantic Relations by the Use of Context Classification

Andreas Schmidt and Markus Junker

German Research Center for Artificial Intelligence (DFKI)
P.O. Box 2080, 67608 Kaiserslautern / Germany
{schmidt,junker}@dfki.uni-kl.de

Abstract. Causal relations symbolize one of the most important document organization and knowledge representation principles. Consequently, the identification of cause-effect chains for later evaluation represents a valuable document analysis task. This work introduces a prototype implementation of a causal relation management and evaluation system which functions as a framework for mining documents for causal relations. The central part describes a new approach of classifying passages of documents as relevant considering the causal relations under inspection. The "Context Classification by Distance-Weighted Relevance Feedback" method combines passage retrieval and relevance feedback techniques and extends both of them with regard to the local contextual nature of causal relations. A wide range of parameter settings is evaluated in various experiments and the results are discussed on the basis of recall-precision figures. It is shown that the trained context classifier represents a good means for identifying relevant passages not only for already seen causal relations but also for new ones.

1 Introduction

Mining documents for causal relations [1] represents a worthwile document analysis task and can be regarded as a predecessor step towards "knowledge-based document analysis and understanding" [2] and semantic net constructions for a better understanding and superior view of the context of document collections.

Figure 1 shows a semantic net which reflects cause-effect chains that are typical for applications in the economic science domain, i.e. the so-called "Scenario-Management" [3]. The goal of this paper is to automatically identify passages that contain attributes such as "domestic demand" and "interest rate" as causes and / or effects of a specific causal relation, i.e. "influence: interest rate influences domestic demand" and to incrementally learn a classifier by relevance feedback. The application of this algorithm helps to mine new relations from text collections and makes it possible to build up a causal semantic net.

The subsequent work consists of four sections. First of all, the "System Design of the Causal Relation Management and Evaluation System" (CRMES) section describes the main steps of the causal relation mining process and the respective CRMES application. Then, the "Context Classification by Distance-Weighted Relevance Feedback" chapter details the theoretic background of the new developed algorithm.

D. Lopresti, J. Hu, and R. Kashi (Eds.): DAS 2002, LNCS 2423, pp. 400–411, 2002.
© Springer-Verlag Berlin Heidelberg 2002

The forth chapter describes the experimental design followed by a discussion of the experimental results. The last chapter concludes the paper with a summary of the results and an outlook for future research.

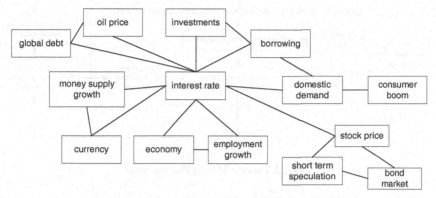

Fig. 1. Causal Relations visualized as a Semantic Net

2   System Design of the Causal-Relation-Management and Evaluation System

This chapter describes the overall process and application scenario for the "Causal-Relation Management and Evaluation System" (CRMES)[1]. Figure 2 gives an overview of the passage mining process steps. Figure 3 depicts a screenshot of the CRMES. Input to the CRMES is a base text collection. Several retrieval models - here a boolean retrieval model and a passage vector-space model with and without relevance feedback, and a parameter base for full parametrization control the system behavior. Furthermore a set of distance-weighted context relevance feedback classifiers and a set of causal relation attributes consisting of cause- and effect-terms influence the specific contextual causal relation setting.

Given one is interested in a causal relation with the cause being "interest rate" and the effect not further defined (A) q_{CE}:[CAUSE="interest rate" $\Rightarrow$ EFFECT=""]. With respect to the retrieval model (B), the parameter base (C) and the current distance-weighted relevance feedback context classifier (D), CRMES returns a ranked list of passages that may contain relevant causal relations. Passage by passage (E) can be browsed through (F) and may be manually judged relevant or irrelevant by the user (G). The resulting relevant or irrelevant terms of the passage are listed under "Rel. Passage" or "Irrel. Passage" respectively. These judgements are input to the modification of the context relevance feedback classifier as described below.

---

[1] CRMES is part of ongoing research in the "Adaptive READ" project of the German Research Center for Artificial Intelligence (DFKI): http://www.adaptive-read.de

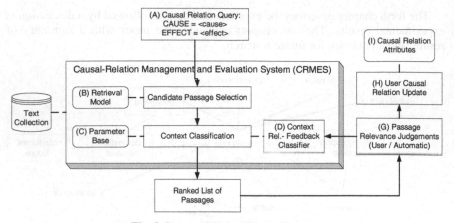

Fig. 2. Passage Mining Process Steps

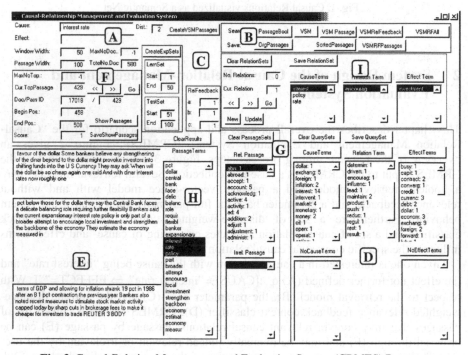

Fig. 3. Causal-Relation Management and Evaluation System (CRMES) Prototype

Furthermore the user can manually update the causal relation attribute set by highlighting relevant passage terms (H) and store them for future reference (I). This way, CRMES not only learns to fine-tune its relevance feedback context classifier with each new relevance judgement, but also extends its knowledge about new relations. The system can also be run in batch mode by using predetermined relevant and irrelevant passages and specific experimental parameter settings. The batch mode was actually used for the following experiments.

3   Context Classification by Distance-Weighted Relevance Feedback

The new developed "Context Classification by Distance Weighted Relevance Feedback" combines Rocchio relevance feedback methods (see [4], pp. 118) with passage retrieval approaches [5]. First of all the conventional "Document Vector Space Model" [6] as a representation of texts is applied on passage level resulting in a new derivate "Passage Vector Space Model". Second the new Rocchio relevance feedback method incorporates the "distance-weighted" idea in such a way that terms occurring close to query terms are weighted more and as such are more important candidates for query term expansion than those that stand further apart.

Additional relevance feedback and query expansion techniques that base on probabilistic text models can be found in [7]. Other applications of term selection for automatic query expansion are described in [8]. While the term expansion technique in this paper base on learning a classifier, [9] shows interesting approaches in the fields of reinforcement learning. Last but not least, [10] gives a detailed survey of a complete different view how to extract information from texts.

3.1   Passage Vector Space Model

A passage vector space model PVSM consists of a triple

$$PVSM=(P, Q, R(p_j, q_l))   \qquad (1)$$

where $P = \{p_1, ..., p_M\}$ is a set of M passages – representing the text-collection, $Q = \{q_1, ..., q_k\}$ is a set of k queries and R is a ranking function which defines an ordering among passages with regard to queries. Let $T = \{t_1, ..., t_N\}$ be the set of all index terms that occur in P where P may be preprocessed to eliminate stopwords (such as "the", "a", etc.).

On the basis of term-occurrence counts, a passage-term frequency matrix PTF: (T x P) is constructed where $PTF(t_i, p_j)$ is the raw frequency of term t_i within passage p_j. The passage-term frequency matrix PTF may be dampened by a dampening function f to reflect the fact that more occurrences of a term indicate higher importance but not as much as the raw frequency might suggest. Typical dampening functions are square root: dPTF=f(PTF) = sqrt(PTF) or log: dPTF=f(PTF)=1+log(PTF). The second frequency count captures the importance of terms across the whole collection. The inverse passage term frequency is defined as

$$iptf_i = \log \frac{M}{pf_i}   \qquad (2)$$

where $M = |P|$ number of passages in the collection and pf_i is the number of passages that term t_i occurs in. IPTF gives full weight for terms that occur in ONE passage and zero weight for those that occur in ALL passages.

The definition of weights w=w(t$_i$, p$_j$) which are associated to the index terms t$_i$ and passages p$_j$ combine various combinations of the term-occurrence and passage frequency counts into several PTF.IPTF weighting schemes (similar to the ones based on documents in [4] and [6]). This work uses the subsequent weighting scheme

$$w_{i,k} = dptf_{i,k} \times iptf_i \times \frac{1}{|\vec{w}_k|} . \tag{3}$$

Now each passage p$_j$ and query q$_l$ can be represented by a passage-weight vector.

$$\vec{p}_j = (w_{1,j}, ..., w_{n,j}) \text{ and } \vec{q}_l = (w_{1,l}, ..., w_{n,l}) \tag{4}$$

Finally, a ranking function R needs to be defined which expresses the similarity sim(p$_j$, q$_l$) between passages and queries. We have chosen the normalized COSINE-similarity[2]

$$R : sim(\vec{p}_j, \vec{q}_l) = \frac{\vec{p}_j \bullet \vec{q}_l}{|\vec{p}_j| \times |\vec{q}_l|} = \frac{\sum_{i=1}^{n} w_{i,j} \times w_{i,l}}{\sqrt{\sum_{i=1}^{n} w_{i,j}^2} \times \sqrt{\sum_{i=1}^{n} w_{i,l}^2}} . \tag{5}$$

3.2   Rocchio-Relevance Feedback as a Distance-Weighted Context Classification Method

The conventional Rocchio-Relevance Feedback utilizes all terms of manual or automatic judged relevant / irrelevant passages P$_{Train,rel}$ / P$_{Train,irrel}$ to expand an original query q$_0$ into an extended query q$_{RF}$

$$\vec{q}_{RF} = \alpha\vec{q}_0 + \frac{\beta}{|P_{Train,rel}|} \sum_{p_j \in P_{Train,rel}} \vec{p}_{dist,j} - \frac{\gamma}{|P_{Train,irrel}|} \sum_{p_j \in P_{Train,irrel}} \vec{p}_{dist,j} \tag{6}$$

where $\vec{p}_{dist,j}$ equals the original non-distance-weighted passage vector $\vec{p}_j$ and the Rocchio multipliers α, β, γ parametrize the feedback strategy with the following special cases:

- no feedback: α>0   β=0   γ=0
- pure positive feedback: α=0   β>0   γ=0
- pure negative feedback: α=0   β=0   γ>0

The new distance-weighted relevance feedback computation is based on the assumption that terms t$_i$ which are closer to cause-effect terms q$_0$ characterize the causal relation in a better way than terms that are further apart.

Figure 4 depicts a symbolic causal relation context where the x-axis represent the position of terms and the y-axis assigns a distance-weighted weight to each term t$_i$ according to a given window-weight function win_fun ∈ {"rectangular", "triangular", "hanning"} and relative to a queried causal relation q$_0$ = (q$_{0,1}$, q$_{0,2}$, ...). The window functions are placed at each position of all q$_{0,j}$ with their normalized maximum amounting to one so that the resulting distance-weighted passage vector amounts to

---

[2] For other similarity measures like DICE coefficient etc. see [4]

$$\vec{P}_{dist} = \left(w_{1,p}, w_{2,p}, ..., w_{n,p} \right) \tag{7}$$

$$w_{i,p} = \sum_{q_{0,j} \in \bar{q}_0} wf(q_{0,j}, t_i); \qquad wf(q,t) = win\_fun(dist(q,t)) \tag{8}$$

with dist(q,t) being the distance between q and t in number of terms.

The three window types allow for different explanations of the impact of terms t_i with respect to the distance they have to q_0. By using the rectangular window it is assumed that all terms within the window width have the same impact on the classification of the causal relation. The triangular window reflects a linear correlation between impact and distance while the hanning window allows closer terms to be of relative more importance than terms that are further apart. The baseline parametrization consists of the rectangular window function with a window-width equal to the passage length.

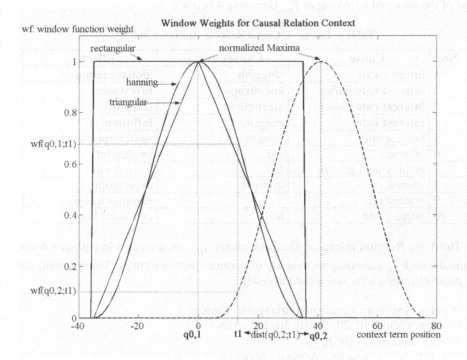

Fig. 4. Distance-Weighted Relevance Feedback Computation

4   Experimental Design

The experimental design is based on running the CRMES system in batch mode where the base text-collection – the REUTERS21578 corpus [11] – consists of 21578 news stories from REUTERS. This collection was transfered into document vector-space representation.

In a first step, all passages that fulfilled a specific causal relation attribute, here: CAUSE = "interest rate" were retrieved and transferred into a passage vector-space model. This procedure translates into posing an initial query q_0 and receiving a ground-truth passageset P_{GT} where each passage is manually judged relevant or irrelevant.

The second step involved the selection of the training- and test-set, P_{Train} and P_{Test}, that were taken aside from P_{GT} for training and testing the distance-weighted context classifier. Altogether four sets were created represented by $P_{Train} = P_{Train,rel} \cup P_{Train,irrel}$ and $P_{Test} = P_{Test,rel} \cup P_{Test,irrel}$ with $P_{Test} \cap P_{Train} = \emptyset$. Table 1 shows an extract of ten causal relation attributes that were part of P_{Train}. Bold rows indicate attributes that also were part of the retrieved testpassages P_{Test} (see table 4 below).

Table 1. Extract of Causal Relation Attributes in P_{Train}

No.	Cause$_{Train}$	Connective$_{Train}$	Effect$_{Train}$
1	**interest rate**	**sluggish**	**global economy**
2	**interest rate policy**	**encourage**	**investment**
3	**interest rate policy**	**strengthen**	**economy**
4	**interest rate**	**reignite**	**inflation**
5	interest rate	curtails	short term speculation
6	oil price	led	interest rate
7	employment growth	led	interest rate
8	interest rate	improve	expectation
9	interest rate		earnings margin
10	interest rate	lead	consumer boom

Third, the Rocchio relevance feedback vector $\vec{q}_{RF}$ as described in equation 6 was trained with P_{Train} according to a variety of parametrization settings. Three dimensions of parametrization were researched in detail:

1. Window functions: rectangular, triangular, hanning
2. Window widths: 10, 20, 30, 40, 50, 100 terms
3. Rocchio multipliers $[\alpha, \beta, \gamma]$:
    [1, 0, 0]:   baseline, original query only
    [0, 1, 0]:   only relevant passages are considered
    [0, 1, 1]:   relevant and irrelevant passages are considered equal; original query is not considered
    [0, 1, 0.5]:   irrelevant passages are considered less important than relevant passages; the original query is neglected
    [1, 1, 1]:   all equal

To reflect an untrained system, the baseline settings consisted of the parametrization set window-function = rectangular (distance between q_0 and respective terms is not taken into consideration) , window-width=100 terms (equals passage width) and Rocchio multiplier = [1, 0, 0] (unexpanded query only). The combination of all parameter settings (three window-functions, six window-widths, five Rocchio sets) led to the sum of 90 different Rocchio relevance feedback vectors.

Finally during the test-phase, the similarity between each relevance feedback vector q_{RF} and each passage $p_{Test,i} \in P_{Test}$ were calculated and ranked using the ranking function R: $sim(p_{Test,j}, q_{RF})$ resulting in a ranked passage list $RP=(rp_1, rp_2, ...)$ where rp_i =p_j with p_j being i-th ranked. The ranked passage list consisted of passages $rp_{i,rel}$ that were relevant, $RP_{rel}=(rp_{1,rel}, ..., rp_{n,rel})$, and passages $rp_{j,irrel}$ that were irrelevant, $P_{irrel} = (rp_{1,irrel}, ..., rp_{m,irrel})$, so that $RP=RP_{rel} \cup RP_{irrel}$.
In order to compare the results, three scenarios were calculated as follows:
1. Modification of the Window Functions:
   fixed window widths and Rocchio-sets; variable window functions
2. Modification of the Window Width:
   fixed window functions and Rocchio-sets; variable window widths
3. Modification of the Rocchio-Set:
   fixed window functions and window widths; variable Rocchio-sets

5   Experimental Results

The results are visualized by precision-recall graphs with precisions being interpolated at 11 standard recall levels. The n-th level $recall_n$ consists of the share of top n ranked relevant passages $|RP_{n,rel}|$ with regard to all relevant testpassages $|P_{Test,rel}|$. The n-th level $precision_n$ is the fraction of $|RP_{n,rel}|$ considering both relevant and irrelevant top n ranked passages $|RP_n|$. Average precision AveP functions as an aggregated measure for comparing the results of the overall classification / retrieval algorithm.

$$recall_n = \frac{|RP_{n,rel}|}{|P_{Test,rel}|} \; ; \; precision_n = \frac{|RP_{n,rel}|}{|RP_n|} \tag{9}$$

$$AveP = \frac{1}{n}\sum_{i=1}^{n} precision_n \tag{10}$$

Figure 5 shows the precision-recall graphs that correspond to the best two and the worst two average precision results - including the baseline as a representative for the untrained classifier. The corresponding parameter settings can be found in tables 2 and 3. Let the experiment consist of 50 testpassages, $|P_{Test}| = 50$, where 26 of them are judged relevant, $|P_{Test,rel}| = 26$. As an example for interpreting the precision-recall graphs, let the goal be to retrieve 50% of all relevant passages which translates into a recall of 50% or a $|RP_n| = recall_n / |P_{Test,rel}| = 50\% \times 26 = 13$ relevant passages. The untrained classifier reflected by the baseline precision-recall graph reaches a precision of 48% at 50% recall. The total number of ranked passages which needs to be seen amounts to $|RP| = |RP_n| / precision_n = 13 / 48\% = 27$ passages. The best trained classifier reflected by the Top 1 precision-recall graph reaches a precision of 86% at a recall level of 50% so that the necessary total number of ranked passages amount to |RP| = 13 / 86% = 15 passages only. Compared to the baseline, the best trained classifier allows for a cut of almost half the size in ranked passages to be seen.

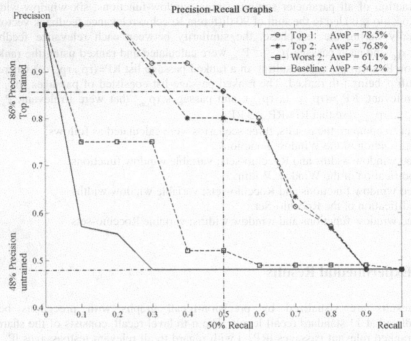

Fig. 5. Best / Worst Precision-Recall Graphs

The parameter settings leading to the best five and the worst five average precisions out of the total 90 parameter settings are listed in tables 2 and 3. The optimization trend seems to be to use a small window-width together with the relevant terms feeded back only (Rocchio-Parameterset = [0, 1, 0]), while the choice of the window function does not seem to have such a big impact.

Table 2. Top five parameter settings

No.	AveP	Window-Type	Window-Width	Rocchio-Parameterset		
				α	β	γ
1	0,785	rectangular	10	0	1	0
2	0,768	hanning	20	0	1	0
3	0,767	triangular	20	0	1	0
4	0,763	rectangular	20	0	1	0
5	0,762	triangular	30	0	1	0

Table 3. Worst five parameter settings

No.	AveP	Window-Type	Window-Width	Rocchio-Parameterset		
				α	β	γ
1	0,542	rectangular	100	1	0	0
2	0,611	rectangular	30	0	1	1
3	0,611	rectangular	30	1	1	1
4	0,623	rectangular	40	0	1	1
5	0,623	rectangular	40	1	1	1

Figure 6 breaks the results of the preceding chapter down on cause-effect level. The "Training Phase" figure section shows the direct cause-effect relations that were part of the passages used to construct the distance-weighted context classifier by considering all fifty training passages. The five bold causal attributes reflect the situation where only ten passages were considered for training (baseline setting).

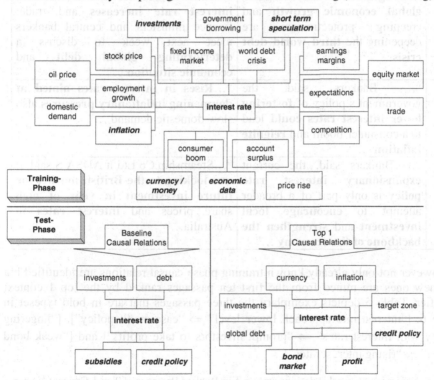

Fig. 6. Comparison of Causal Relations Context Classifier Parametrizations

The "Test Phase" lower part of the figure depicts the cause-effect relations when taking the top ten ranked passages of the baseline context classifier ("No. 1" parameter settings in table 3) and the top 1 context classifier ("No. 1" parameter settings in table 2). Figure 6 confirms the results of the preceding chapter. The optimized parametrization of the top 1 context classifier contains eight cause-effect relations while the baseline classifier returns only four among the first ten ranked passages.

Table 4 juxtaposes three sample relations that were part of both training and test passages. Passage set one depicts a typical "same-direction" relation with Train: ["**High** interest rate" ⟹ "**sluggish** global economic growth"] and Test: ["interest rate **increases**" ⟹ "**deteriorating** global debt and economic situation"]. Passage set two shows a counter-direction with Train: ["**lower** interest rates" ⟹ "**reignite** inflation"] and Test: ["**rise** in interest rates" ⟹ "**dampening** inflationary pressure"]. Passage set three exemplifies a similarity-based relation where "interest rate policy" in the training passage is set similar to "interest rate" in the test passage.

Table 4. Causal Relations in both Training and Test Passages

	Training Passage	Test Passage
1	"... **High interest rates sluggish global economic growth** and creeping protectionism are deepening the **third world debt crisis** ..."	"...Amid **new concerns about** inflation, **interest rate increases** and trade, finance ministers and central bankers meet next week to discuss a **deteriorating global debt** and economic situation..."
2	"... Bankers said, the government s policy of **fostering lower interest rates could** lead to a consumer boom and **reignite inflation** ..."	"...**Rises in interest rates aimed at dampening inflationary pressures** also slow domestic demand ..."
3	"... Bankers said, the current **expansionary interest rate policy** is only part of a broader attempt to **encourage local investment** and **strengthen the backbone of the economy** ..."	"...Steamship Co Ltd lt ADSA S said, it was **looking to the British market for future investment in view of** high share prices and **interest rates** in Australia..."

However not only already known training phase causal relations are identified but also new ones are mined from the first ten passages ranked by the top 1 context classifier. Table 5 depicts exemplary the three passages that are in bold typeset in figure 6: ["interest rate approach lower level" ⟹ "ease credit policy"], ["lingering anxiety with interest rates" ⟹ "prompt investors to take profits"] and ["weak bond market" ⟹ "rising interest rates"].

Table 5. New mined Causal Relations among Top-Ranked Passages of Top 1 Concept Vector

	Test Passage
1	"... there is little room left for the central bank to further **ease its credit policy as interest rate** levels are now **approaching their lower limit** ..."
2	"... Wall Street s **lingering anxiety with interest rates** and inflation **prompting investors to take profits** ..."
3	"... A **weak bond market ignited concern about rising interest rates** and inflation ..."

6 Conclusion and Outlook

This work presented the "Causal Relation Management and Evaluation System" as a prototype implementation for identifying and managing causal relations in text collections. The new developed method of "Context Classification by Distance-Weighted Relevance Feedback" demonstrated good performance for classifying passages as containing not only already seen relevant causal relations but also unseen examples of causal relations. Consequently, this new approach may be regarded as a worthwile contribution for developing a new kind of knowledge-centered document analysis systems.

Future research may deal with the transitivity of known relations, i.e. "[a⟹b ∧ b⟹c] : ⟹ [a⟹c]", and the vector-space similarity of terms, i.e. "[a⟹b ∧ sim(a,c) ∧ sim(b,d)] :⟹ [c⟹d]" to capture a wider spectrum of document understanding and knowledge representation. Another fruitful undertaking may be the application of the new developed context classifier in other research areas that base on the contextual nature of relational elements, such as word-sense disambiguation.

References

1. P.G. Meyer. The relevance of causality. in: *E. Couper-Kuhlen. Cause – Condition-Concession – Contrast: Cognitive and Discourse Perspective.* Mouton de Gruyter, Berlin, New-York, 2000, pp. 9–34
2. C. Wenzel, H. Maus. An Approach to Context-driven Document Analysis and Understanding. in: *4th IAPR International Workshop On Document Analysis Systems – DAS'2000*, Rio de Janeiro, Brazil, Dec. 2000, pp. 121–133
3. J. Gausemeier, A. Fink, O. Schlake. Szenario-Management: Planen und Führen mit Szenarien, 2. Edition, Hanser Verlag München, 1996
4. R. Baeze-Yates, B. Ribeiro-Neto. Modern Information Retrieval. Addison-Wesley, 1999
5. K. Kise et al. Passage-Based Document Retrieval as a Tool for Text Mining with User's Information Needs. in: *K. P. Jantke, A. Shinohara (eds.) Discovery Science, 4th International Conference, DS 2001,* Washington. Lecture Notes in Computer Science, Springer-Verlag, 2001, pp. 155–169
6. C. D. Manning, H. Schütze. Foundations of Statistical Natural Language Processing. The MIT Press, Cambridge, 2000
7. Y. Ogawa et al. Structuring and Expanding Queries in the Probabilistic Model. in: *Proceedings of the 9th Text Retrieval Conference (TREC-9).* NIST Special Publication, 2001
8. M. Adriani, C.J. van Rijsbergen. Informative term selection for automatic query expansion. in: *S. Abiteboul, A.-M. Vercoustre (eds.). ECDL 1999,* Springer-Verlag, Berlin-Heidelberg, pp. 311–322
9. L. Kaelbling, M. Littman. Reinforcement Learning: A Survey. in: *Journal of Artificial Intelligence Research 4 (1996),* pp. 237–285, Morgan Kaufmann Publishers
10. I. Muslea. Extraction Patterns for Information Extraction Tasks: A Survey. in: *American Association for Artificial Intelligence, 1999*
11. REUTERS Corpus: http://about.reuters.com/researchandstandards/corpus/

Hairetes: A Search Engine for OCR Documents

Kazem Taghva and Jeffrey Coombs

Information Science Research Institute
University of Nevada, Las Vegas
taghva@isri.unlv.edu

Abstract. In this paper, we report on the architecture and preliminary implementation of our search engine, Hairetes. This engine is based on an extended concept of *Retrieval by General Logical Imaging* (RbGLI). In this extension, word similarity measures are computed by EMIM and Bayes' theorem.

1 Introduction

During the 1990's the Information Science Research Institute (ISRI) at the University of Nevada, Las Vegas conducted a series of large scale OCR tests to better understand OCR accuracy with respect to retrieval effectiveness [13,14,15,16]. These tests generally imply that average precision and recall are not affected by OCR errors. They also imply that certain ranking algorithms can produce marked variability in document ranking. These ranking problems are essentially due to normalization factors such as document length which one can overcome by using length normalization as defined by Singhal [12].

One of the more interesting experiments we conducted was the role of OCR errors with respect to feedback [14]. This experiment showed that in the manually corrected collection, average precision keeps improving as more terms are added to queries. But in the OCR collection, precision values level off after a certain number of term expansions. Further analysis showed that this complication was a result of a few "difficult to retrieve" documents within the OCR collection. Consequently, one can assume for documents with low OCR accuracy (such as handwritten texts, faxes, or nth-generation photocopies) that the retrieval may require more effort.

Putting OCR issues aside for a moment and concentrating on retrieval concepts based on statistical models, one observes that *term mismatch* has played an important role in hindering the user from finding relevant documents [2]. Typically, a document is not retrieved unless the query and document have some terms in common. Many approaches such as *latent semantic indexing*, use of thesauri, and query expansions were developed to address the term mismatch problem [1,5,6]. One of the more recent and promising approaches is *Retrieval by General Logical Imaging* (RbGLI) proposed by Crestani and Van Rijsbergen [3, 4,11]. This technique is heavily dependent on the assumption that a measure of similarity on the term space can be evaluated. Hairetes is an implementation of this idea extended by OCR word similarities adopted from OCRSpell [18]. We

D. Lopresti, J. Hu, and R. Kashi (Eds.): DAS 2002, LNCS 2423, pp. 412–422, 2002.

believe by augmenting RbGLI with similarities based on OCR errors, we can provide an environment to study retrieval effectiveness from poorly recognized document collections.

This paper is organized into six sections. Section one is this Introduction. Section two covers some basic material on index construction. Section three shows how word similarity calculations are performed. Sections four and five are short discussions on query processing and compression. Finally, section six is the conclusion and a prospectus of future work.

2   Document Information

In building a search engine for OCR, one needs to take into consideration the type of problems that OCR errors cause and an alternative way of displaying information. In this section, we will give a modified version of a typical construction following [19].

The information associated with the collection is kept in three structures. The first structure keeps the document information. Each record in this structure looks like:

doc no.	doc weight	summary	doc-type	words	image bit	image	categories

Summary is a pointer to the document summary. Doc-type can be ASCII, OCR-ASCII, OCR with word bounding boxes, or some other possibility. words are pointers to the words in the document. The fields image and categories contain pointers to images and categories.

The doc weight in search engines represents the length of the document. This length is typically the number of distinct terms in a document or the frequency of the term with the highest occurrence [8,9]. It is shown in [13,14] that these sorts of length estimation cause problems when the collection is predominantly OCR text. Singhal [12] defined the length of the document as byte size and showed that this notion of length works well with OCR collections. In our engine, we use this length measure.

The second structure is the lexicon with records of the form:

word t	word no.	f_t	max sim	similar	max OCR-related	OCR-related	Excp

f_t is the number of documents in which word t occurs. Max sim is the number of non-empty pointers to similar terms. Similar contains pointers to similar words. Max OCR-related is the number of non-empty pointers to OCR related terms. OCR-related contains pointers to OCR related terms. Excp is an exception bit indicating that the term is an acronym, proper noun, garbage string, etc.

The third structure contains the posting for each word. These postings contain document word occurrence plus other useful information such as word position in the document and bounding box coordinates.

2.1   Creating an Inverted File

The inverted file is built following [19].

1. /*initialization*/
   a) create an empty lexicon S.
   b) create an empty temporary file.
2. /* process text and write temporary file */
   For each document D_d in the collection $1 \leq d \leq N$
   a) Read D_d, parsing it into index terms.
   b) for each index term $t \in D_d$
      i. let $f_{d,t}$ be the frequency in D_d of term t.
      ii. search S for t.
      iii. if t is not in S, insert it.
      iv. write a record $(t,d,f_{d,t})$ to the temporary file, where t is represented by the word number.
      v. call acronym(t).
         call graphic-text-recognizer(t) if t is OCR text.
         call proper-noun(t).
         If any return "yes", set Excp, the exception-bit, to 1 in the lexicon entry for t.
   c) /* Populate Document-info record */
      i. enter doc-num and doc-type.
      ii. enter document weight as $bytesize^{0.375}$ [12].
      iii. generate summary.
      iv. compress and store this document posting and make the pointers to the word in the document point to this location in the document posting file.
3. /* Internal sorting to make runs */
   Let k be the number of records that can be held in memory.
   a) Read k records from the temporary file.
   b) sort into nondecreasing t order, and for equal values of t, nondecreasing d order.
   c) write the sorted run back to the temporary file.
   d) repeat until there are no more runs to be sorted.
4. /* Merging */
   Pairwise search runs in the temporary file until it is one sorted run.

3   Word Similarity Calculation

Word similarity has been studied in the field of information retrieval for a long time. Thesauri construction is an example of word similarity efforts. Most of the automatic word similarity procedures depend on word frequency and co-occurrence. In the case of OCR errors, word similarity represents the closeness of a misrecognized word to other correctly recognized words in the collection. We typically need to divide the indexed terms into two groups of correctly recognized and incorrectly recognized words. This can be done with the help of a dictionary or, as we recently discovered, with dimensionality reduction techniques [17].

3.1 Apply a Dimensionality Reduction

Hence we will define a constant `Doc-Dim-Reduction` which can be changed and experimented with. For example, if `Doc-Dim-Reduction` = 3, then we will only look at the words occurring in 3 or more of the documents. We can then divide the lexicon into 2 sets of words: The set `Correct` will contain words with $f_t \geq 3$ or `Excp` = 1, and the set `Suspect` will be the complement of `Correct`.

3.2 Apply EMIM

We will then apply EMIM (*Expected Mutual Information Measure*) on the `Correct` list to generate `similar`, the similar-words' field in the lexicon:

word t	word no.	f_t	max sim	similar	max OCR-related	OCR-related	Excp
t_1				$x_1 \ldots x_n$			
t_2				$y_1 \ldots y_m$			
$\ldots$				$\ldots$			

where x_1 is the most similar to term t_1 and x_n is least similar, and y_1 is most similar to t_2 while y_m is the least similar to t_2.

EMIM is defined as:

$$EMIM(t_1, t_2) = \sum_{i=0}^{1} \sum_{j=0}^{1} r(t_1^* = i, t_2^* = j) \log_2 \left(\frac{r(t_1^* = i, t_2^* = j)}{p(t_1^* = i)p(t_2^* = j)} \right).$$

Here the expressions t_1^* and t_2^* represent functions from terms t_1 and t_2 to the set $\{0,1\}$ where 0 indicates the absence and 1 the presence of a term in a document. Thus $p(t_1^* = i)$ is the probability that t_1^* returns the value i, and $r(t_1^* = i, t_2^* = j)$ is the probability that t_1^* and t_2^* return the values i and j respectively. If i and j take the value 1, then $r(t_1^* = 1, t_2^* = 1)$ is the probability that t_1 and t_2 will co-occur in a given document.

Van Rijsbergen in [10] shows that EMIM can be estimated in the following way. First define the contingency table:

	$t_l \in doc_k$	$t_l \notin doc_k$	
$t_m \in doc_k$	n_{11}	n_{01}	$n_{.1} = tf_m$
$t_m \notin doc_k$	n_{10}	n_{00}	$n_{.0}$
	$n_{1.} = tf_l$	$n_{0.}$	N

The value n_{11} is the number of documents in which both terms t_l and t_m occur (that is, $t_l^* = 1$ and $t_m^* = 1$), n_{01} the number of documents in which t_m occurs but t_l does not, n_{10} the number of documents containing t_l but not t_m, and n_{00} is the number of documents in which neither term occurs. The value $n_{1.}$ is the total number of documents in which t_l appears, that is, $n_{1.}$ is the *term frequency* tf_l of t_l. The expression $n_{0.}$ stands for the number of documents in which t_l does *not* occur, which is the same as $N - tf_l$ where N is the total number of documents in the collection.

Any item in the contingency table can be calculated *given* that n_{11} and the values of tf_m, tf_l, and N are known. The marginal values are easy to calculate since tf_m and tf_l are the term frequencies of t_m and t_l, which are available from the inverted file, and N is the total number of documents in the collection. Getting n_{11}, however, may prove to be computationally expensive and may require sophisticated estimation techniques to calculate effeciently.

Van Rijsbergen uses the contingency table definitions to state an estimate for EMIM which is strictly monotone to that measure:

$$\widehat{EMIM} = n_{11} \log_2 \frac{n_{11}}{tf_l tf_m} + n_{10} \log_2 \frac{n_{10}}{tf_l n_{.0}} + n_{01} \log_2 \frac{n_{01}}{n_{0.} tf_m} + n_{00} \log_2 \frac{n_{00}}{n_{0.} n_{.0}}.$$

According to Van Rijsbergen, the first term indicates the similarity of the two terms, the second and third measure dissimilarity, and the last term is likely to be constant in large samples. Also, we must define $0 \, log \, 0 = 0$.

Consider as an example the following document collection from [19]:

1. Pease porridge hot. Pease porridge cold.
2. Pease porridge in the pot.
3. Nine days old.
4. Some like it hot. Some like it cold.
5. Some like it in the pot.
6. Nine days old.

The contingency table for term 1 (*pease*) and term 2 (*porridge*) is:

$$
\begin{array}{r|c|c|c}
 & \multicolumn{2}{c}{pease} & \\
\hline
porridge & 2 & 0 & 2 \\
\hline
 & 0 & 4 & 4 \\
\hline
 & 2 & 4 & 6
\end{array}
$$

and the $\widehat{EMIM}$ values for other terms with respect to *pease* are:

	$\widehat{EMIM}$		$\widehat{EMIM}$
pease,porridge	-10.00	pease,nine	-10.00
pease,hot	-14.32	pease,days	-10.00
pease,cold	-14.32	pease,old	-10.00
pease,in	-14.32	pease,some	-10.00
pease,the	-14.32	pease,like	-10.00
pease,pot	-14.32	pease,it	-10.00

where, for example, $\widehat{EMIM}$ for *pease* and *porridge* is calculated as

$$\widehat{EMIM}(pease, porridge) = 2\log\frac{2}{4} + 0\log\frac{0}{8} + 0\log\frac{0}{8} + 4\log\frac{4}{16} = -10$$

So, the "closest" terms to *pease* are *porridge, nine, days, old, some, like,* and *it*.

3.3 OCR Similarity

Our next goal is to create the OCR-related terms entries for the lexicon, such that:

		OCR-related words:	
C_j	...	$S_1 \ldots S_m$	...

where each S_i is a **Suspect** term and C_j is a **Correct** term in the lexicon.

To construct these entries, a spelling correction system developed by ISRI especially for OCR text errors called *OCRSpell* can be used. OCRSpell is similar to a spell-checking program such as ISpell [7] but with the ability to help correct errors typically generated by OCR software.

In particular OCRSpell attempts to identify and suggest corrections for segmentation and classification errors resulting from the OCR process. Segmentation errors encompass such errors as recognizing single letters as multiple characters, for example, reading 'rn' for 'm', reading multiple characters as single letters, e.g., 'ci' for 'd', and incorrect concatenation and division of terms, such as recognizing 'c at' for 'cat'. Classification errors are errors such as replacing 'o' with '9' in 'J9hn'.

OCRSpell uses a specially designed parser, domain specific dictionaries, and a statistical device mapping word generator to create a list of word candidates as replacements for incorrect terms. Also provided with each replacement candidate is a probability that the corrected term is in fact the correction for that particular incorrect term. For example, if OCRSpell is given an expression such as "iiien", it produces the output:

```
@(#) Ispell Output Emulator Version 1.0.00 08/17/95
iiien
  original word: iiien
***********************************
amen      0.000359
man       0.000530
mien      0.000190
men       0.012714
iii-en    0.002057
***********************************
```

This output indicates that OCRSpell believes that there is a probability of 0.000359 that "amen" is the correct replacement for "iiien", a 0.000530 probability that "man" is the correct replacement, and so on. Further details of the OCRSpell system are available in [18].

To use OCRSpell to generate the OCR-related entries, however, we must note that the output of OCRSpell gives us $P(C_j|S_i)$, the conditional probability that C_j is the **Correct** term given we started with the **Suspect** term S_i. For the OCR-related terms, however, we want a measure like $P(S_i|C_j)$, the conditional probability S_i is the term we want given we have C_j.

We can use Bayes' Theorem to get this from the OCRSpell results:

$$P(S_i|C_j) = \frac{P(S_i) \cdot P(C_j|S_i)}{P(S_1) \cdot P(C_j|S_1) + \cdots + P(S_k) \cdot P(C_j|S_k)}$$

but the difficulty here is getting all the information needed to make the calculation. There are two problems here: (1) how to get $P(C_j|S_k)$ for all k, and (2) how to get all the $P(S_k)$'s.

With regard to the first problem, consider the output from OCRSpell for the Suspect term *iiien* listed earlier. What this output gives us is:

$$P(C_1 = amen|S = iiien) = 0.000359$$
$$P(C_2 = man|S = iiien) = 0.000530$$
$$P(C_3 = mien|S = iiien) = 0.000190$$
$$P(C_4 = men|S = iiien) = 0.012714$$
$$P(C_5 = iii - en|S = iiien) = 0.002057$$

However, what we really need in order to use Bayes' rule is a list for all k of the probabilities $P(C_j|S_k)$ for a specific C_j. For example, we want to know for all k $P(C_i = men|S_k)$, that is, the probability that *men* is Correct for each given Suspect term that OCRSpell claims is similar to *men* in the document collection.

One way to get this information is to maintain a Term Probability B^+-tree (or some other appropriate data structure) during the lexicon building phase. When the first occurrence of a Suspect term is discovered, OCRSpell should be run on the term, and for each Correct term having non-zero probability, that term should be added/updated to the B^+-tree with an entry consisting of the Suspect word and associated probability. Hence the entry for *men* in the Term Probability B^+-Tree would look like:

$$\boxed{\text{men} \parallel \text{iiien } 0.012714 \mid \text{mqn } 0.007673 \mid \ldots}$$

This entry is updated when *iiien* is first discovered in the document collection and again when *mqn* and subsequent Suspect terms are found.

In general, the procedure is as follows: Suppose the lexicon L of Correct terms exists, and there exists a list of Suspect terms SW. Create a useful data structure, like a B^+-tree, called B. Add items from SW to B in this way:

> for each term s in SW
>> for each Correct term c returned by OCRSpell(s)
>>> if c is in L
>>>> add c to B if not there
>>>> add s and its probability to c's entry in B

For the second problem of defining $P(S_k)$, we may use the *inverse document frequency (idf)*

$$P(S_k) = idf(S_k) = -\log \frac{f_{S_k}}{N}$$

since the lexicon entry of Suspect words will contain the frequency they occur in the collection. Now, to calculate the probabilities of the OCR-related terms, let c be a Correct term in B (our Term Probability B^+-Tree) and s_i one of c's Suspect terms and p_i its probability. That is, going back to the previous example:

c	s_1	p_1	s_2	p_2	
men	iiien	0.012714	mqn	0.007673	...

Let E be the number of OCR-related words entered in c's lexicon so far. A procedure (not necessarily the most efficient) to select the OCR-related word entries for the lexicon would be:

for each Correct term c in B
$E = 0$
    for each Suspect term entry s_i in c's entry in B
        calculate $P(s_i|c) := \dfrac{idf(s_i)\cdot p_i}{\sum_{k=0} idf(s_k)\cdot p_k}$
        if $E < m$,
           add a pointer to s_i and
           add $P(s_i|c)$ to c's entry in the lexicon.
           $E = E + 1$
        else if $P(s_i|c) > min(P(s_k|c))$
        (where the $P(s_k|c)$'s are values already entered under c),
           replace the minimal s_k and $P(s_k|c)$ with s_i and $P(s_i|c)$

4   Query Processing

We plan orginally to construct Hairetes using *Retrieval by General Logical Imaging (RbGLI)*. Later we will implement a *vector space* version. For more about RbGLI see [2,3,4].

4.1   Opinionated Function

First, we define the *opinionated-function* as follows:

opinionated-function $(f_t, total\_no, POS)$
    return $((-\log \frac{f_t}{N}) \cdot (2^{total\_no - POS}))$

where f_t is the number of documents containing the term t, *total_no* is the total number of terms similar to t listed in t's lexicon entry, and *POS* is the position of a term t'_i in t's lexicon entry:

term		no.	similar words:		
t	...	N	$t'_1 \ldots t'_m$		...

where t'_1 through t'_m are pointers to terms similar to t. N is a binary number indicating the number of non-empty pointers. For example 1111000000 means there are four such pointers.

4.2 Query Process

We want to retrieve r documents in response to a query. We will keep an array called the *accumulator (A)* to keep track of the similarity between the documents and the query. So, if this array is indexed with the document number, it is more likely that most of the similarities will be zero. Among the non-zero similarities we want to select the top r documents following the model of a *heap*.

Let's assume we have query Q:

1. Set $A \leftarrow \phi$, where A is the accumulator array.
2. For each query term $t \in Q$,
   a) search the lexicon
   b) record f_t and the address I_t, the inverted file entry for t.
   c) set $P(t) = -\log \frac{f_t}{N}$
   d) read the inverted file entry I_t.
      i. For each pair $(d, f_{d,t})$ in I_t
         If $A_d \notin A$ then
            set $A_d \leftarrow 0$
            set $A \leftarrow A + A_d$
         set $A_d \leftarrow A_d + P(t)$
      ii. look at the list of terms similar to t, call them $t_1, \ldots, t_k$
         A. sort this list on word no.
         B. look at the list of the words in d and identify among $t_1, \ldots, t_k$ those terms which are *not* in d and call these $t'_1, \ldots, t'_l$.
         C. for each t'_i look in the lexicon for the word t in the t'_i list of words.
         D. if found, set
            opinionated-value $\leftarrow$ *opinionated-function*$(f_{t'_i}, TOT, POS)$
            where TOT is the total number of words in the similar-word list for t'_i and POS is the position of t in the similar-word list for t'_i.
         E. set $A_d \leftarrow A_d + $ opinionated-value
      iii. Assume $t'_1, \ldots, t'_l$ are the list of OCR-related terms of term t with probabilities $p_1, \ldots, p_l$. For each t_i in this list
         A. read I_t, the inverted file entry. For each $(d, f_{d,t})$ in this list
            if $A_d \notin A$ then
               set $A_d \leftarrow 0$
               set $A \leftarrow A + A_d$
            set $A_d \leftarrow A_d + \left(-\log \frac{f_{t_i}}{N} \times p_i \right)$
3. For each $A_d \in A$, set $A_d \leftarrow \frac{A_d}{weight-of-d}$ from the document info file
4. select the r documents with the highest A_d value.

5 Compression of Files

As it was pointed out in Section 2, OCR collections require certain considerations to compensate for errors. Index size and image display are two prominent factors. The compression of the postings and bounding boxes has to be taken into consideration for a manageable and efficient system. We mainly rely on unary and γ-code [19] to compress these entries. For the sake of completeness, we define these two codes here.

Example: The unary code for a number x is defined as $(x - 1)$ 1-bits followed by a 0-bit. So if x is 9, the unary code is 111111110. The γ-code for x is defined as follows for $x = 9$:

1. Take $\lfloor \log x \rfloor$.
   $\lfloor \log 9 \rfloor = 3$.
2. represent $1 + \lfloor \log x \rfloor$ as a unary code.
   $1 + \lfloor \log x \rfloor = 1 + 3 = 4$ has code 1110.
3. calculate $x - 2^{\lfloor \log x \rfloor}$.
   $9 - 2^3 = 9 - 8 = 1$.
4. Now represent $x - 2^{\lfloor \log x \rfloor}$ as $\lfloor \log x \rfloor$ binary code.
   In our example, $9 - 2^3 = 1$ is represented as 001.
5. So the code for 9 is 1110 001.

To decode example 1110 001, extract the unary code, in this case 1110, which is 4. Treat the next 3 $(4 - 1 = 3)$ bits as a binary code, in this case 001, which is the binary code for 1. The original number is $2^{4-1} + 1 = 8 + 1 = 9$.

We can use γ-code to compress the posting and bounding boxes for each term. As an example, suppose document number 10 has 5 words as shown below:

doc.	no. words	word no.	occurrences of word 50 in doc	x_1	y_1	x_2	y_2	x_3	y_3
10	5	50	3	10	15	302	47	614	312
		75	2	12	18	300	320		
		...	...						

We compress the information for these 5 words as follows:

(γ-code 5)(γ-code 50)(γ-code 3)(unary x_1)(unary y_1)(unary x_2)(unary y_2)
(unary x_3)(unary y_3)(γ-code 75)(γ-code 2)(unary x_1)(unary y_1)...

6   Conclusion and Future Work

Statistically-based information retrieval engines are robust enough to deal with typical OCR errors in text. If the collection is poor in quality, then certain documents may be hard to locate and retrieve. Hairetes is designed to address this problem and avoid the extreme variability in the the ranked result set.

Hairetes is currently being implemented and we hope to report on its performance in the near future.

References

[1] Jean Aitchison, Alan Gilchrist, and David Bawden. *Thesaurus Construction and Use : A Practical Manual*. Fitzroy Dearborn, 4th edition, 2000.

[2] Fabio Crestani. Exploiting the similarity of non-matching terms at retrieval time. *Journal of Information Retrieval*, pages 25–45, 2000.

[3] Fabio Crestani and C.J. Van Rijsbergen. A study of kinematics in information retrieval. *ACM Transactions on Information Systems*, 16:225–255, 1998.

[4] Fabio Crestani, Ian Ruthven, M. Sanderson, and C.J. van Rijsbergen. The troubles with using a logical model of ir on a large collection of documents. experimenting retrieval by logical imaging on trec. In *Proceedings of the Fourth Text Retrieval Conference (TREC-4)*, 1995.

[5] Scott C. Deerwester, Susan T. Dumais, Thomas K. Landauer, George W. Furnas, and Richard A. Harshman. Indexing by latent semantic analysis. *Journal of the American Society of Information Science*, 41(6):391–407, 1990.

[6] William B. Frakes. Stemming algorithms. In William B. Frakes and Ricardo Baeza-Yates, editors, *Information Retrieval: Data Structures and Algorithms*, pages 131–160. Prentice Hall, 1992.

[7] R. E. Gorin, Pace Willisson, Walt Buehring, Geoff Kuenning, et al. Ispell, a free software package for spell checking files. The UNIX community, 1971. version 2.0.02.

[8] Donna K. Harman. Ranking algorithms. In William B. Frakes and Ricardo Baeza-Yates, editors, *Information Retrieval: Data Structures and Algorithms*, pages 363–392. Prentice Hall, 1992.

[9] Donna K. Harman. Relevance feedback and other query modification techniques. In William B. Frakes and Ricardo Baeza-Yates, editors, *Information Retrieval: Data Structures and Algorithms*, pages 241–263. Prentice Hall, 1992.

[10] C. J. Van Rijsbergen. A theoretical basis for the use of co-occurrence data in information retrieval. *Journal of Documentation*, 33(2):106–109, June 1977.

[11] C. J. Van Rijsbergen. A non-classical logic for information retrieval. *The Computer Journal*, 29:481–485, 1986.

[12] Amit Singhal, Gerard Salton, and Chris Buckley. Length normalization in degraded text collections. In *Proc. of SDAIR-96 5th Annual Symposium on Document Analysis and Information Retrieval*, pages 149–162, Las Vegas, NV, 1996.

[13] Kazem Taghva, Julie Borsack, and Allen Condit. Results of applying probabilistic IR to OCR text. In *Proc. 17th Intl. ACM/SIGIR Conf. on Research and Development in Information Retrieval*, pages 202–211, Dublin, Ireland, July 1994.

[14] Kazem Taghva, Julie Borsack, and Allen Condit. Effects of OCR errors on ranking and feedback using the vector space model. *Inf. Proc. and Management*, 32(3):317–327, 1996.

[15] Kazem Taghva, Julie Borsack, and Allen Condit. Evaluation of model-based retrieval effectiveness with OCR text. *ACM Transactions on Information Systems*, 14(1):64–93, January 1996.

[16] Kazem Taghva, Julie Borsack, Allen Condit, and Srinivas Erva. The effects of noisy data on text retrieval. *J. American Soc. for Inf. Sci.*, 45(1):50–58, January 1994.

[17] Kazem Taghva, Thomas A. Nartker, and Julie Borsack. Recognize, categorize, and retrieve. In *Proc. of the Symposium on Document Image Understanding Technology*, pages 227–232, Columbia, MD, April 2001. Laboratory for Language and Media Processing, University of Maryland.

[18] Kazem Taghva and Eric Stofsky. Ocrspell: An interactive spelling correction system for OCR errors in text. *Intl. Journal on Document Analysis and Recognition*, 3(3):125–137, March 2001.

[19] I. Witten, A. Moffat, and T. Bell. *Managing Gigabytes: Compressing and indexing documents and images*. Morgan Kaufmann, 2nd edition, 1999.

Text Verification in an Automated System for the Extraction of Bibliographic Data

George R. Thoma, Glenn Ford, Daniel Le, and Zhirong Li

National Library of Medicine
Bethesda, Maryland

Abstract. An essential stage in any text extraction system is the manual verification of the printed material converted by OCR. This proves to be the most labor-intensive step in the process. In a system built and deployed at the National Library of Medicine to automatically extract bibliographic data from scanned biomedical journals, alternative means were considered to validate the text. This paper describes two approaches and gives preliminary performance data.

1 Introduction

The manual verification of the text produced by any OCR system, or one that is a sequence of document image analysis and understanding (DIAU) processes, is an essential stage to ensure the accuracy of the extracted text. At the R&D center of the National Library of Medicine, we have developed a DIAU-based system[1] that automatically extracts significant bibliographic data from scanned biomedical journals to populate MEDLINE®, the library's flagship database used worldwide by biomedical scientists and clinicians. The final step prior to accepting the bibliographic record thus created is a manual check for accuracy by human operators. Following a brief description of the overall data extraction system in Section 2, we discuss alternative approaches for the design of the workstation used by the text verification operators.

2 Overall System: Brief Description

The DIAU-based system, code-named MARS for *Medical Article Records System*, consists of both automated and operator-controlled subsystems as shown in Figure 1. The schematic shows automated processes as boxes with thin boundaries, and manual workstations with thick boundaries. The workflow is initiated at the CheckIn stage where a supervisor scans the barcode on a journal issue arriving at the production facility. This barcode number, called the "MRI", is routinely affixed to every journal issue by NLM staff. It therefore serves as a unique key to identify the issue, all the pages scanned in that issue, and indeed the outputs of all processes performed on

D. Lopresti, J. Hu, and R. Kashi (Eds.): DAS 2002, LNCS 2423, pp. 423–432, 2002.

those page images. The scanning operator captures the first page of every article in the issue, since this page contains the fields we seek to extract automatically. The resulting TIFF images go into a file server and associated data into the MARS database for which the underlying DBMS is Microsoft's SQL Server. The OCR system accesses the TIFF images and produces the corresponding text as well as other data descriptive of the text characters such as bounding boxes, attributes (bold, italic, underlined), confidence level, font style and size, and others. The automatic zoning[2] (Autozone) module then blocks out the contiguous text using features derived from the OCR output data, followed by the automated labeling[3] (Autolabel) module that identifies the zones as the fields of interest (article title, author names, affiliations, abstract). The Autoreformat[4] module then reorganizes the syntax of the zone contents to adhere to MEDLINE conventions (e.g., author name *John A. Smith* becomes *Smith JA* for pre-2002 journal issues, and *Smith John A* for 2002 and later).

At this point, two lexicon-enabled modules operate on the data to reduce the burden on the operator performing the final checking and verification of the data: ConfidenceEdit that modifies the incorrect confidence levels assigned to the characters by the OCR system, and PatternMatch[5,6] that corrects institutional affiliations whose text, usually italicized and in small font size, is frequently recognized incorrectly by the OCR system. PatternMatch relies on a combination of two matching techniques: whole word matching (which compares the entire OCR output word with each word in a lexicon of words found in the affiliation fields from 230,000 journal articles) and 'probability matching' (that scores matched words according to a calculated confidence value and frequency of occurrence.).

Some data essential to a complete bibliographic record in MEDLINE cannot be automatically extracted, such as NIH Grant Numbers and Databank Accession Numbers. The major reason is that they appear in pages other than the scanned first page of the article. Such data is manually entered by a pair of "Edit" operators, a double-key process that ensures a high degree of accuracy. An EditDiff module then correlates these different entries and notes differences.

The output of the automated processes and the EditDiff module are then presented to the "Reconcile" operator who verifies the text and corrects errors. Following this text verification stage, the data is transmitted by the Upload module to the NLM's DCMS (Data Creation Maintenance System) which is later accessed by NLM indexers to add medical subject headings (MeSH terms) and keywords, thereby completing the bibliographic record for the MEDLINE database. The Admin workstation shown is used by the production supervisor to send a journal issue back to an earlier processing stage in case of errors.

The focus of this paper is the design of the Reconcile workstation.

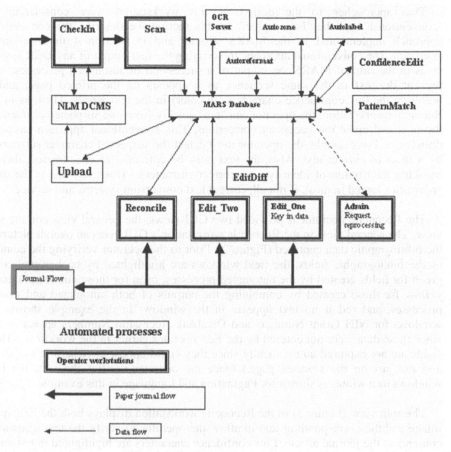

Fig. 1. MARS general schematic.

3 Reconcile Workstation

The purpose of the text verification or Reconcile workstation is to enable an operator to check the accuracy of the bibliographic data extracted by the automated processes, as well as that entered manually by the Edit operator. Any errors are corrected at this stage before the citation is uploaded to the DCMS database. Desirable features of a text verification workstation include: (a) all text must be presented for verification, whether automatically or manually generated in upstream processes; (b) the original bitmapped document image must be displayed for reference; (c) characters detected with low confidence by the OCR must be highlighted so the operator may focus on them; (d) navigation between fields and from one character to another must be rapid; (e) optionally, aids such as lexicon-based pattern matching systems may be provided to correct errors.

Two approaches to the design of this workstation were considered: the 'conventional' and the 'Isomorphic.' In this section we describe the conventional approach implemented in the MARS system, and in Section 4 the Isomorphic approach. The conventional approach to verifying the text output of any OCR system, or as in the case of MARS the output of a succession of automated processes, is to present the text in the same sequence as it appears on the printed page, and to highlight the low confidence characters (in color) in the text words. Then, as in our Reconcile workstation, the operator can "tab" quickly from one suspected character to the next and make the necessary corrections. This conventional approach has some drawbacks. For example, the operator must detect the suspected character surrounded by a mass of correct text. Also, the text must be corrected as encountered, thereby breaking the rhythm of identifying incorrect characters. However, this is the usual approach adopted in most, if not all, current text conversion systems and services.

The Reconcile operator is provided two GUI views: the general view and the split view. The general view in the Reconcile workstation's GUI gives an overall picture of the bibliographic data captured (Figure 2). Prior to the operator verifying the contents of the bibliographic fields, the field windows are highlighted by background color: green for fields created by the automated processes, cyan for those entered manually, yellow for those created by combining the outputs of both automated and manual processes, and red if no text appears in the window. In the example shown, the windows for NIH Grant Numbers and Databank Accession Numbers appear in red, since these data were not entered by the Edit operator earlier in the workflow. (These fields are not captured automatically since they could appear anywhere in the article and not just on the scanned page.) Once the operator verifies the text, the field windows turn white, as shown for Pagination and Language in this example.

The split view (Figure 3) in the Reconcile workstation displays both the bitmapped image and the corresponding text to allow the operator to verify the text against the contents of the journal article. Low confidence characters are highlighted in red on the text to attract the operator's attention.

The Reconcile workstation provides the operator several additional functions: the operator may rename a field labeled incorrectly; activate a standalone OCR system to extract the field contents through the image or, alternatively, type in the text; if a page image is missing or duplicated, the operator may insert the missing page, or delete a duplicate; and if there are 'invalid' characters, the Reconcile software will convert them to the form required in MEDLINE.

Many of the functions in the Reconcile workstation are provided by a program called Character Verification[7], a module that allows the Reconcile operator to view the bitmapped document images and to verify the text in all the fields, both entered by the Edit operator, and that from the automated processes. It is based on two ActiveX controls, the Eastman Kodak Image ActiveX Control and Microsoft's Rich Text Editor ActiveX control, both embedded in the Reconcile software.

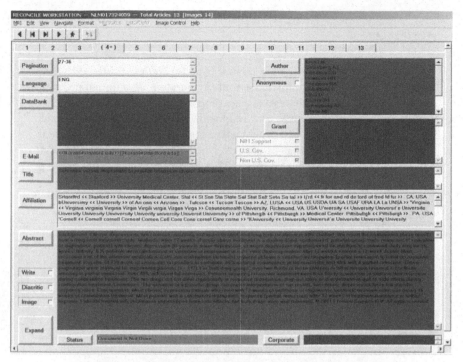

Fig. 2. General view for all bibliographic fields in an article.

The Eastman Kodak Image control provides the functionality for the operator to view the image and perform manipulations such as rotation, and zooming in or out. It also provides a bounding box showing the area on the image that corresponds to the text that the operator is focusing on.

Character Verification also allows the operator to edit the field contents. The design of this editor is based on the Microsoft Rich Text Editor, and is derived from its heavily used functions such as copy, cut, paste, search and replace. The software can also relate the position of the text characters to the corresponding ones in the image, provide confidence levels, and allow the operator to enter diacritical marks, Greek letters, mathematical signs, change the first character of a selected word to upper case while leaving the rest in lower case, convert case, and complete words in the affiliation field from a partial output.

Character Verification and Reconcile's main program communicate via methods and events. Reconcile sets or gets the methods to instruct Character Verification. In turn, Character Verification fires events back to Reconcile to provide the information. It retrieves the OCR output for every article (bibliographic) field, including text contents (character codes), confidence levels and character coordinates, from the MARS database, and the images from a file server.

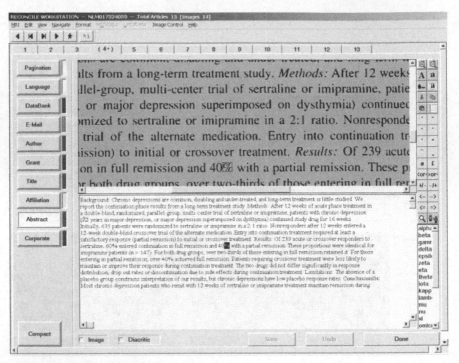

Fig. 3. Split view shows both the bitmapped image and corresponding text. Low confidence characters are highlighted in the text window.

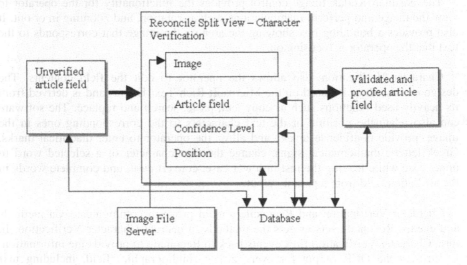

Fig. 4. Character Verification displays label text, confidence and character position.

Character Verification also provides the results of the PatternMatch[5,6] program to the operator in a word list to choose from. An example is given in Figure 5 showing optional words in a dropdown box for the operator to select in an affiliation field.

4   Isomorphic Method for Text Verification

To overcome the drawbacks in the conventional approach to text verification (noted in Section 3), we investigated an alternate method involving the simultaneous display of like characters. The hypothesis is that an operator would pick the odd one out quicker than reading through large numbers of words on the screen, would be required to do fewer keystrokes, and would experience lower eyestrain. These factors, we believe, would help achieve higher productivity. Proprietary systems, either commercial or research products, with similar functionality have been reported[8-10], but did not appear to allow for easy integration into our production system.

Our Isomorphic ("having the same form or appearance") method involves grouping like characters (drawn from a number of pages or journal issues at the same time) and displaying them in groups in a single window, as shown in Figure 6. Each character appears in its "edit box." Only low confidence **A - Z** and **0 – 9** characters, of the same type, would be displayed in groups. The example shows a set of characters in the edit boxes, mostly **e**'s, some of them a misreading of an **s** or an **E** as shown in the corresponding bitmapped images right above the edit boxes. Since context is important to detect poorly captured character shapes, the system must provide the display of the image fragment (a word or phrase) that provides the context in which the (presumably) incorrect character appears. Such context will particularly help distinguish letters or numbers that appear similar, e.g., 1, I or 0,O.

Our Isomorphic system is designed with the following functions:

An Automatic Context display of the TIFF image is available when any of the edit boxes is focused on.

By clicking on an edit box, or using the F1 thru F9 keys, the operator can correct the character. In Figure 6, the bitmap of each low confidence character appears above the edit text boxes. In case of ambiguity, the operator may type in a '?' that invokes the image fragment to provide the necessary context.

To continue, the operator can select **Next>>** and load the next batch of 9 characters, or select **<<Previous** for a second look at the previous 9. By selecting Next>>, all characters are set to high confidence.

All characters are displayed at low confidence, in case of an accidental clicking of the Next>> button.

Clicking OK will stop processing.

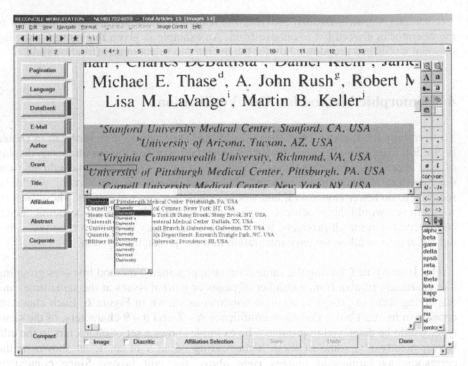

Fig. 5. Operator can select alternative words in an affiliation field.

The Isomorphic system is implemented using Visual C++ with the Eastman Kodak Image libraries. Following the software development, we conducted a performance study using this system for reconciling, and measured the residual error rate and the time taken for correcting and verifying all the characters from a complete journal issue at a time. Should further tests conclusively prove that the accuracy and time saved are an improvement over the current verification method, this module will be incorporated in the Reconcile workstation software.

5 Test Results

Tests were conducted to determine the speed advantages of using the Isomorphic system over the conventional method. The Title and Abstract fields from 122 articles were selected for the tests. These fields were picked for the following reasons.

- These two fields account for nearly 99% of the OCR output data.
- The text in these fields is not reformatted.
- These fields have relatively good OCR data, unlike, say, the affiliation field that shows a high error rate on account of a preponderance of characters that are in italics and small sized fonts.

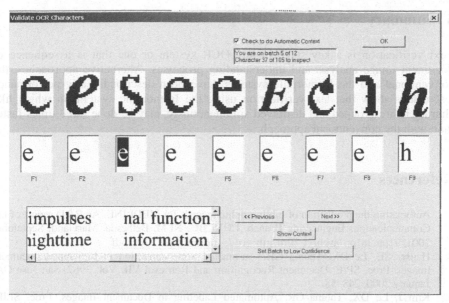

Fig. 6. GUI for Isomorphic method.

Two operators conducted the tests independently. The results presented in Figure 7 show that the Isomorphic approach is approximately three times as fast as the conventional method. For a normal daily work output of 600 bibliographic records, this corresponds to a saving of about 7 labor hours per day for the correction/verification of the Title and Abstract fields.

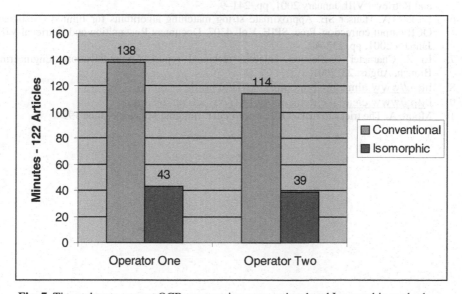

Fig. 7. Time taken to correct OCR errors using conventional and Isomorphic methods.

6 Summary

Text verification is a key stage in any OCR system or one that is a sequence of document image analysis and understanding processes. Alternative approaches, the conventional and the Isomorphic systems, have been described. Early performance test results show that text verification using the Isomorphic system, in which like characters are grouped and displayed simultaneously, may be done three times faster than with the conventional approach.

References

1. Automating the production of bibliographic records for MEDLINE. An R&D report of the Communications Engineering Branch, LHNCBC, NLM. Bethesda, Maryland. September 2001, 91pp. http://archive.nlm.nih.gov/~thoma/mars2001.pdf
2. Hauser SE, Le DX, Thoma GR. Automated zone correction in bitmapped document images. Proc. SPIE: Document Recognition and Retrieval VII, Vol. 3967, San Jose CA, January 2000, 248–58.
3. Kim J, Le DX, Thoma GR. Automated Labeling in Document Images. Proc. SPIE: Document Recognition and Retrieval VIII, Vol. 4307, San Jose CA, January 2001, 111–22.
4. Ford GM, Hauser SE, Thoma GR. Automatic reformatting of OCR text from biomedical journal articles. Proc.1999 Symposium on Document Image Understanding Technology, College Park, MD: University of Maryland Institute for Advances in Computer Studies; 321–25.
5. Ford G, Hauser SE, Le DX, Thoma GR. Pattern matching techniques for correcting low confidence OCR words in a known context. Proc. SPIE, Vol. 4307, Document Recognition and Retrieval VIII, January 2001, pp. 241–9.
6. Lasko TA, Hauser SE. Approximate string matching algorithms for limited-vocabulary OCR output correction. Proc. SPIE, Vol. 4307, Document Recognition and Retrieval VIII, January 2001, pp. 232–40.
7. Li Z. Character verification. Internal technical report, Communications Engineering Branch, August 23, 2001.
8. http://www.almaden.ibm.com/DARE/ui.html
9. http://www.clearlake.ibm.com/gov/ifp/sk_advantage.html
10. Moore A. The tricks to make OCR work better. Imaging Magazine. June 1994.

smartFIX: A Requirements-Driven System for Document Analysis and Understanding

Andreas R. Dengel and Bertin Klein

German Research Center for Artificial Intelligence (DFKI)
P.O.Box 2080
D-67608 Kaiserslautern, Germany
{dengel,klein}@dfki.de

Abstract. Although the internet offers a wide-spread platform for information interchange, day-to-day work in large companies still means the processing of tens of thousands of printed documents every day. This paper presents the system *smartFIX* which is a document analysis and understanding system developed by the DFKI spin-off INSIDERS. It permits the processing of documents ranging from fixed format forms to unstructured letters of any format. Apart from the architecture, the main components and system characteristics, we also show some results when applying *smartFIX* to medical bills and prescriptions.

1 Introduction

About 1.2 million printed medical bills arrive at the 35 German private health insurance companies every day. Those bills amount to 10% of the German health insurance market and they are actually maintained by printed paper bills. Figure 1 shows examples of such printed bills. Until recently the processing of these bills was done almost completely manually. In addition to the tedious task of initiating every single payment by transcribing a number of data fields from varying locations on the paper documents into a computer, this had the serious disadvantage that only a small number of inconsistent and overpriced bills were discovered. Conservative estimates predict savings in the range of several hundred million Euros each year if this process could be automated reliably.

About two years ago, a consortium of German private health insurance companies ran a public benchmark test of systems for Document Analysis and Understanding (DAU) for the respective private insurance sector. The benchmark was clearly won by *smartFIX* (smart For Information eXtraction). *smartFIX* was developed by a spin-off company of the DAU group at DFKI, INSIDERS (www.insiders-ag.de • founded in 1999 by the first author), thinking that the available DAU technology after a decade of focused research was ready to construct a versatile and adaptive DAU system [1, 2, 3]. After the premise of the identification of a viable type of application scenarios, the well-directed research on a feasible combination of available methods and completion with new methods could be successfully accomplished. This background probably explains the clear suitability of *smartFIX* for the project, which INSIDERS and four insurance companies started after the benchmark: the development of a standard product for the analysis of printed medical bills: *smartFIX healthcare*. *smartFIX* was

D. Lopresti, J. Hu, and R. Kashi (Eds.): DAS 2002, LNCS 2423, pp. 433–444, 2002.

the result of several man-years investment. The brainpower in *smartFIX healthcare* can be estimated in a larger dimension.

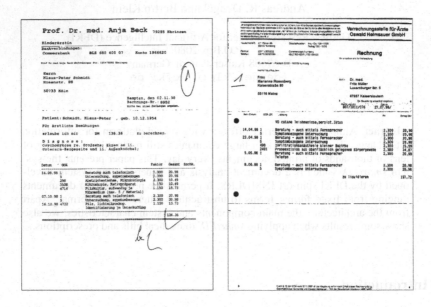

Fig. 1. Examples of medical bills common in Germany

The first two important facts about the health insurance domain are:

1. Bills are more complex than forms.
2. Every single bill is inspected by a human operator.

Therefore, the DAU task for bills requires more than the more simple methods that suffice for forms - a challenge for the DAU technology developers in the project. But at the same time, the insurance auditors can be assured, that the economic success does not only start after a distant breakthrough, but every little successfully implemented DAU step reduces the human operators workload right away. Every correctly recognized data item saves typing and can be logically and numerically checked. Diagnoses can be automatically coded into ICD 10 (the international standard code for diagnoses). Actually, even with no recognition results, the efficient user interface of the result viewer facilitates the processing of scanned bills.

Nowadays, at least since the CommonKADS projects series [4], it is known how indispensable the analysis of the intended application is for successful knowledge-intensive software projects. Facing the needs of a group of companies, this requirements-centered approach is even more important and challenging, e.g. the number of example documents, which the companies' representatives thought to convey their needs, rapidly grew to much more than 10000. So, the original ideas underlying

smartFIX were refined with the needs of the insurance companies. Actually, many of the requirements only became clearer to us whilst the project progressed.
The insurance companies required from *smartFIX healthcare*:

1. Verified economic advantages (qualitative, quantitative)
2. Economic reliability (error recovery, error rate, error statistics)
3. Scalability
4. Adaptability to their workflow (people, tasks, databases, archives)

The advantages remained to be verified. Scalability had already been targeted and was almost available: *smartFIX* is a distributed system, CORBA on networked PCs, which can easily spread its single-analysis processes over many CPUs and still be controlled from one desktop. One aspect of reliability is achieved with a central transaction memory database. Thus, the only remaining tasks were to extend and adapt *smartFIX* to the insurers workflow requirements and to learn about reliability in terms of stable error-rates.

For the design of a DAU system we came to the following guiding principles. But still the most basic finding is that the design should not be technology-driven, but explicitly requirements-driven, and thus finally user-driven [4]:

1. Compositionality: A versatile system has to have a significant spectrum of different basic DAU components, one paradigm alone will almost surely fail to solve a real problem. – Complex methods, which at first glance are very hard to conceive, are obtained from deliberate, small combinations of simple methods. [3]
2. Practice principle: There is no way to get around errors. Thus it is important to help users to discover, judge, and either tolerate, or to correct errors. This is especially critical as the user in every day practice is left alone with the control of the system and the responsibility for its results. – The real DAU technology must be powerfully accompanied by technology for logging, tracing, visualizing, interactive testing, statistics.
3. Epistemological adequacy: The basic DAU components must be bundled to greater analysis scripts which are made available to the user. The user has to perceive document characteristics and map those to the scripts. Thus the scripts must be meaningful to the user, easy to memorize and use. Good script metaphors also guide the perception of the document characteristics. Later these scripts might report success or error messages. – This long standing AI principle implies that so-called "syntactic sugar" can actually make a difference.
4. Constructivism: The philosophic principle of constructivism says that every knowledgeable agent, human or machine, has a different account of reality and there is no objective truth at all. For a DAU system it means: (a) That every scenario will always require at least one aspect, which is outside of the capabilities of the system at hand. Thus it is important to allow users access to manipulate intermediate results. (b) That two persons at a time (and even often one person at two times) disagree on facts significantly often (cf. TREC human evaluators cross comparison [5]). Thus it is important that the DAU system gives feedback and continuously makes transparent, which information it receives from a user and how this information is used.

In general, *smartFIX* is not limited to the domain of medical bills but rather can be applied to other forms and unstructured documents as well. In the following, we will describe the major characteristics of the system including architecture, main components as well as some technical aspects. At the end of the paper, we will show runtime results of *smartFIX* PKV applied to medical bills based on an recent evaluation of a large private health insurance company processing several tens of thousands of bills and prescriptions every day.

2 System Architecture

The capabilities of *smartFIX* PKV are diverse, and so is its architecture. The architecture, i.e. the main components, are shown in Figure 2. This section's overview is succeeded in the following sections by a sketch of the *DocumentManager* through which the system is instructed and after that an explanation of the most central DAU component, the *analyzer*.

To apply *smartFIX* PKV to a new DAU problem, it is necessary to pin down the specific document types and the "what and how" of information extraction. The resulting "document information" –one synonym is "processing knowledge"– is configured with the *DocumentManager*.

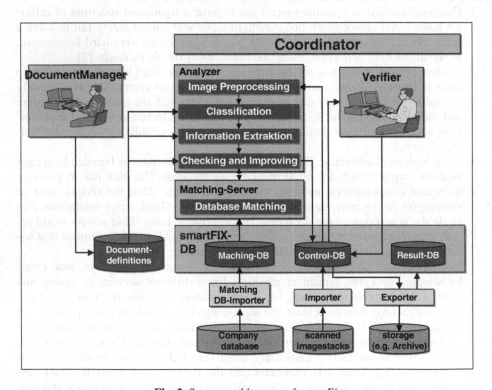

Fig. 2. System architecture of *smartFix*

Then the system can be started with the *coordinator*. This program provides a control panel, from which DAU-processes, i.e. *analyzers*, can be started on a freely-configurable network of PCs; one *analyzer* per CPU as a rule of thumb. The *coordinator* also starts some other processes, first now, two database processes used by the analyzers: the *Matching-Server* provides very fast retrieval ("matching") on company knowledge from the *matching data base*. The *matching data base*, mostly contractual data, is a working copy, which can be updated with a handy tool, the *matching data base importer*, from company databases. The *control data base* is the central working memory of *smartFIX*. It could be called the blackboard of the whole architecture.

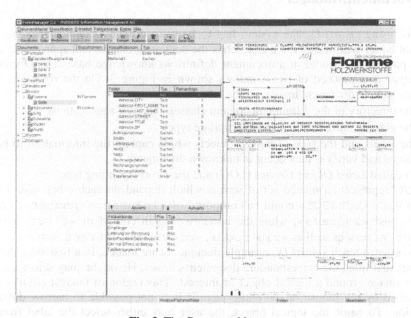

Fig. 3. The *DocumentManager*

The *coordinator* controls an *importer* process, which transfers document images from a predefined source into the *control data base*, together with possibly known information. Any idling *analyzer* will check out, process and check in again documents in the *control data base*. Successful information extraction provided, human agents who are logged on with a *verifier* process, are prompted the DAU results. With the database it is assured, that not a single bit is lost, even in the event of a power cut. Finished documents are transferred out of the system by an *exporter,* typically into archive systems.

This is the main architecture of *smartFIX*. There are some more components, many of which implement much of the user-driven principle, but space prohibits really elaborating on them. The complicated information for spotting and extracting tables is handled by a *TableTool* which follows the approach we proposed in [10] to keep the *DocumentManager* simpler. *Verifiers* can have different priorities and rights assigned and can log the user-actions. They provide online access to the fast databases, aiding the manual completion of missing data. Amongst other things, the freely configurable workflow logic allows intermediate processing results to be externalized with a *user exit* process. The format is configurable, mostly XML. The intermediate results can thus be checked and changed with external software and then be reintegrated into regular processing. The workflow also allows for tricky DAU processes, where, for example, documents are analyzed to a first level and in a second run from the first level to a second level. Online and offline, a number of tools enable the overview and tracing the status, progress and statistics of the involved processes.

3 DocumentManager

Before using *smartFIX,* the system has to be trained. The *DocumentManager* is a special editor with which the user teaches the document classes and appropriate reference patterns are stored in a document definitions knowledge base. The *Document-Manager* is composed of five windows shown in Figure 3. On the right is a user-chosen sample document image, on the left:

- The directory of the different document classes and their aggregations
- The classification features and appropriate types
- The labels and the type of logical objects which capture the information to be extracted and verify if they occur in unknown documents
- So-called *Label Object Groups* (*LOG*) and their corresponding type

A *LOG* represents a named set of scripts which depend on each other, e.g. a LOG <SERVICE SUBJECT> could be composed of <insurance number>, <person>, and <address>, while the latter two again consist of <first name>, <last name> as well as <zip code>, <city>, and <street name>.

In order to teach *smartFIX,* example documents are loaded. In a first step, the user defines and links the corresponding document classes. He or she may select a region in the image around a logical object of interest. This region of interest (ROI) can be described by the mouse or the entire page if it is not possible to narrow down the position. To name the logical object, the user may either select the label from the existing list in the window or could add a new label. In addition, the user has to define the corresponding type which addresses the analysis agent to be applied for extracting the contained information. For that purpose, *smartFIX* offers various agents. The most significant are:

- ADDRESS describes an appropriate grammar of how German addresses typically look like.
- CHECK BOX
- BAR CODE
- SEARCH PATTERN addresses a *key string* (including synonyms and acronyms from an associated thesaurus) to which a corresponding *value string* has to be found. For example (see Fig. 4), the value of the logical object <bill no.> (in German <rechnungs-nr.>) is a numerical expression located within a certain word distance in the image.
- ASSOCIATION relates to information which might not be in a document but rather stored in a data base.
- TABLE allows the description of the logical structure of tables including optional columns.

- TEXT addresses logical objects which can be defined as regular expressions and are captured within free text, e.g. "my insurance number is BG/1495-H".

All logical objects which are defined are related to ranges of values, e.g. lexical knowledge, regular expressions, or numerical constraints, depending on their type. For example, each column of a table is linked to the corresponding set of values, i.e. the logical object <product> which represents a table column name is linked with all valid product names in a data base.

Another issue which holds for all names of logical objects is the fact that they are all only representatives, i.e. variables with possible instantiations. Instantiations may be synonyms and acronyms stored in an attached thesaurus, e.g.,

```
<total amount>=
{"amount","sum", ..}:= NUM{1-5}I.I NUM{2}I{"DM","€"}
<product> =
{"artefact","item", ..}:= ref [product data base/names]
```

After defining all logical objects and the corresponding ROIs, it is possible to support the analysis further by defining LOGs. Consequently, the reference pattern is stored in a knowledge base for later analysis.

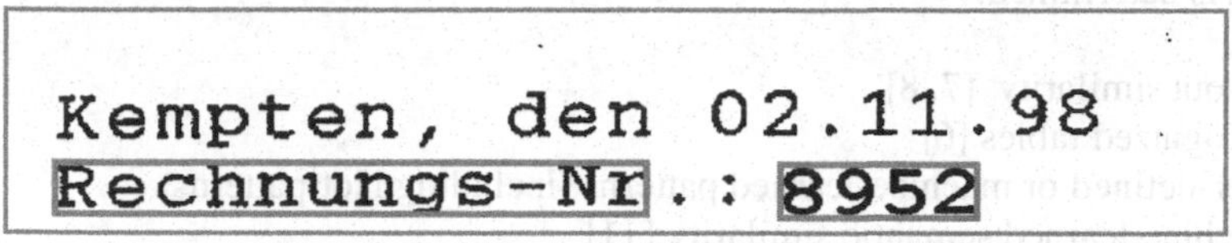

```
Kempten, den 02.11.98
Rechnungs-Nr.: 8952
```

Fig. 4. Typical constellation of numerical data close to a meaningful keyword.

4 Analyzer

The *analyzer* processes do the real DAU processing. Every running *analyzer* pulls the *control data base* for documents to process. After finishing with a document it is labeled and put back into the *control data base* (the label is like the address of the next necessary processing stage, e.g. *verifier*, and the labels flexibly implement the internal workflow).

For one page the analysis progresses in roughly four stages:

1. Image pre-processing,
2. Classification,
3. Information extraction,
4. Improvement.

OCR is called lazily, i.e. it is called for segments only when their character content is needed. As a matter of fact, the four phases are not always clearly distinguished. E.g. after the classification it is possible to have found that the image must be scaled.

4.1 Image Pre-processing

Image pre-processing consists of five optional steps. Each step can be individually switched on and off and tuned with parameters:

1. Removal of graphical lines (vertical and horizontal)
2. Optimization of matrix printed characters
3. Despeckle
4. Deskew (±10° landscape and portrait)
5. Correction of upside-down

The pre-processed images are stored for the later visualization of the extraction results (with *verifiers*).

4.2 Classification

The classification runs in predefined phases and searches the following features until a class is determined:

1. Layout similarity [7, 8]
2. Recognized tables [6]
3. User-defined or machine-learned patterns (including Not-patterns)
4. Machine-learned semantic similarity [11]
5. Document size

The known classes and their features are configured using the *DocumentManager*. The classes can be set up so that non-classified documents are sent to a *verifier* for manual classification, or run through a default information extraction first.

The classification also has to deal with the collation of pages to documents. The most reliable method, interspersing different documents with easy-to-recognize dividing pages at scanning, is sometimes not possible. Therefore *smartFIX healthcare* provides a collation-machinery, which is not really sophisticated but confusing to explain without using many examples.

4.3 Information Extraction

Information extraction is performed according to the "scripts" selected and configured for the respective document class with the *DocumentManager*. Scripts have a type and a name. According to their type scripts perform a specific action referring to the page at hand, after which they provide a value under their name. Where this is important, scripts can be assigned priorities to constrain the sequence in which they are run. Simple extraction scripts search the image of the page. The complex extraction scripts use complicated user-provided and built-in knowledge. The data scripts are simply providing access to logical page data. These three categories of script types are explained in the following.

Simple extraction scripts types.
1. "Text" and "Combination": extract characters in a specified area. The combination script sends the extracted characters later to have it split into components with the support of database lookups. It is possible to have the area initially cleared from form preprints.
2. "Checkbox": two different algorithms can be chosen, to determine whether a checkbox area is ticked.
3. "Pattern search": either on the whole page or in an area, a regular expression is either searched directly, or searched in the configurable surroundings (direction and distance) of a prior regular expression match or thesaurus synonyms match.
4. "Address": a specific script for the extraction of German addresses, split into standard pieces. A regular expression may be used to exclude strings from the search space.
5. "Anchor": does a pattern search and after matching it triggers other linked scripts, which then run in an area relative to the position of the match.
6. "Format": currently simply measures and evaluates to A4, A5, or A6.

Value script types. With the choice of one of the following scripts it is possible to access page information: "Document class": Evaluates to the result of the classification. "Document ID": evaluates to the unique identifier of the document (which often allows access to further related external archive data). "Task ID": evaluates to the task which the document belongs to.
A "free value script" does nothing, but can be set later with a value from a database lookup. This might be helpful as a variable for further database lookups, for automatic checks, or as an additional information for human verifiers.

Complex extraction script types. "Association": skims for occurrences of patterns from a possibly huge database. Several fields of the database can be mixed. Prior successful scripts can be used to restrict the search space of database field combinations. This is a powerful tool e.g. to find exceptionally formatted senders' addresses, if they are only known in a customer database.
"Fixed table": extracts a table according to user-defined layout rules.
"Free table": is a comprehensive analyzer in its own right. According to a complex knowledge configuration with the *TableTool*, this script extracts tables of different layouts, even spanning more than one page, rather intelligently. Extracts also table-related data like sum total. [6]

4.4   Improving

The improving module, newly based on a constraint solver [9], checks consistencies, searches optima, and fills in deducible information. It exploits the user defined *Labeled Object Groups* (LOG), user provided auxiliary conditions and finishes the "Association" scripts. The main idea is that the results of all the single scripts, which are fuzzy and unsafe, can be constrained step by step to more specific and reliable results, with local auxiliary conditions and interdependency conditions. The improving module heavily uses the *matching server* process.

With the local auxiliary conditions the system estimates a level of reliability for every single piece of extracted information, which is used in the *verifier* as colored backgrounds green, light blue, blue, to gain human attention.

LOGs relate different scripts (i.e. their values) together, by a reference to databases. The results of two scripts for a name and a contract number are rather unsafe after simple extraction. But their combination most often allows the determination of the one right name and contract number. Also the "Combination" scripts, introduced before, are processed in this module. In their case, the difference is only, that name and number and perhaps more data are concatenated in one string, possibly permutated.

The "Association" scripts are not much different. Mainly for their calculation it is possible and sometimes necessary to consider their position on the page.

Auxiliary conditions need not only be local, but can also relate two or more script values analytically, in which case they work like LOGs. E.g. all the fields in a summation column sum up to the sum total below the column. Available predicates and functions address arithmetic, dates, checkboxes, strings. Some of the auxiliary conditions can generate correction hypotheses or fill empty fields (e.g. a wrong or empty OCR result in a summation column) others only work as a filter. Via CORBA or COM users can also call user-implemented condition functions (returning a string).

Note: this intelligence is also automatically available in the *verifier*, so that after the typing of missing information, deducible information is provided by the system.

This should be enough explanation on the improving module. There are some more details, like e.g. the role and configuration of thresholds.

5   Results

smartFIX was successfully installed at the insurances' sites and connected to their workflow. It was configured to distinguish about 50 different types of mostly unstructured documents, like hospital bills, dentist bills, medicament bills etc. All bills and prescriptions capture valuable information for establishing a patient history, for guiding internal processes, or for generating statistics. Information items that *smartFIX* was configured for comprise: (a) insurance number, (b) name of patient, (c) date, (d) service period, (e) diagnosis, (f) medical services table, (g) duration of treatment, (h) name and address of doctor, altogether a number of 107, out of which about 20 are to be found on average depending on the respective document type.

For an evaluation, we considered a representative stack of 525 documents as they arrived at one of the largest health insurance companies in Germany. The test comprised of classification into classes reimbursement form (RF), prescription (P), dentists bills (D), hospital bills (H), bills from medical doctors (M), and others (O) while the latter ones had to be sub-classified into another 20 classes. The following Table 1 shows the classification results:

Table 1. Classification results of *smartFIX healthcare*.

RF	95%	D	100%	M	92%
P	96%	H	94%	O	73%

The classification rate over all classes was 92%. Note that rejects are no problem because they are treated by the user at the verifier. The error rate was less than 0.1%.

In addition, the various ROIs were searched and the captured information extracted. For the evaluation, two aspects were of importance: The extraction rates as well as savings in time. The extraction for all fields (a) to (h) was 81 % and saved an average of 64% of time compared to manual input.

In addition to the results of information extraction, the special modules included in *smartFIX healthcare* verify the correctness of the service information shown on the bill. This means, to do a numerical cross check of single service fees, the so called factors as well as the various amounts shown on the bill. And finally, *smartFIX healthcare* checks whether the service positions shown on each bill fit into the German scale of charges and fees, the so-called GOÄ which is law.

This result is just one example presented to the reader. *smartFIX* runs at more than a dozen of customers sites, with very different configurations. A huge number of very different documents were classified and their information extracted to date. Note for example, that at one company the classification rate went down to 30 % last year. They were happy. Without changing the system configuration, they strained the system with a variety of new and complicated input documents, which could of course not be classified; and which should not be classified. And this is what *smartFIX* did not do, correctly. Statistics are not important, the customers satisfaction is.

6 Summary and Future Work

We have given an overview of a commercial document analysis system, *smartFIX*, which is the result of the exploitation of research results from the DFKI, their non-trivial combination and additional research by the start-up company INSIDERS. The system is able to process stacks of mixed-format documents including forms, invoices, letters, all of which may contain machine-written or hand-printed information. The system is installed at about two dozens of customers analyzing several hundred thousands of document pages every day. The purpose of *smartFIX* is in the distribution (classification) of scanned incoming mail and the extraction of information relevant for the user or customer. *smartFIX* has some special features. It processes unsorted incoming mail of any format and independent of the degree of structure or preprints. Furthermore it is not limited to a small number of sorted and separated document types. *smartFIX* classifies all documents and therefore is independent of pre-sorting. Images are combined automatically into single- or multi-page documents.

Recently, we have been working on some improvements and additional features of *smartFIX*. The first addresses the restructuring of the system into smaller modules which then allow for more flexible mixing, which in turn allows to serve new and more complex application scenarios.

The second addresses a new paradigm for the *DocumentManager* with full access to all *analyzer* features, so that the effect of every single configuration-information can be immediately tried out interactively. This will look and feel like a software engineering environment with full debugging support.

A third important improvement is dedicated to what we call "adaptivity". "Adaptivity" aims to reduce the human effort to maintain applications and to configure the system for new applications. We work on learning tools and domain assessment tools.

Learning tools aid, because it is simpler to just provide examples, than determine the right features and explicate them to the system. Domain assessment tools aid determination of relevant features, by allowing the evaluation of e.g. the average distance between two consecutive words on 1000 sample documents.

References

1. A. Dengel, R. Bleisinger, R. Hoch, F. Hönes, M. Malburg and F. Fein, OfficeMAID — A System for Automatic Mail Analysis, Interpretation and Delivery, Proceedings DAS94, Int'l Association for Pattern Recognition Workshop on Document Analysis Systems, Kaiserslautern (Oct. 1994), pp. 253–276.
2. S. Baumann, M. Ben Hadj Ali, A. Dengel, T. Jäger, M. Malburg, A. Weigel, C. Wenzel, Message Extraction from Printed Documents A Complete Solution. In: Proc. of the 4.th International Conference on Document Analysis and Recognition (ICDAR), Ulm, Germany, 1997.
3. A. Dengel and K. Hinkelmann, The Specialist Board – a technology workbench for document analysis and understanding. In M. M. Tanik, F.B. Bastani, D. Gibson, and P.J. Fielding, editors, Integrated Design and Process Technology – IDPT96, Proc. of the 2nd World Conference, Austin, TX, USA, 1996.
4. G. Schreiber, H. Akkermans, A. Anjewierden, R. de Hoog, N. Shadbolt, W. Van de Velde, and B. Wielinga. Knowledge Engineering and Management – The CommonKADS Methodology. The MIT Press, Cambridge, Massachusetts, London, England, 1999.
5. http://trec.nist.gov/
6. B. Klein, S. Gökkus, T. Kieninger, A. Dengel, Three Approaches to "Industrial" Table Spotting. In: Proc. of the 6.th International Conference on Document Analysis and Recognition (ICDAR), Seattle, USA, 2001.
7. A. Dengel and F. Dubiel, Computer Understanding of Document Structure, International Journal of Imaging Systems & Technology (IJIST), Special Issue on Document Analysis & Recognition, Vol. 7, No. 4, 1996, pp. 271–278.
8. F. Dubiel and A. Dengel, FormClas — OCR-Free Classification of Forms, in: J.J. Hull, S. Liebowitz (eds.) Document Analysis Systems II, World Scientific Publishing Co. Inc., Singapore, 1998, pp. 189–208.
9. A. Fordan, Constraint Solving over OCR Graphs. In: Proc. Of the 14th International Conference on Applications of Prolog (INAP), Tokyo, Japan, 2001.
10. T. Kieninger and A. Dengel, A Paper-to-HTML Table Converting System, Proceedings DAS98, Int'l Association for Pattern Recognition Workshop on Document Analysis Systems, Nagano, Japan, Nov. 1998, pp. 356–365.
11. M. Junker and A. Dengel, Preventing overfitting in learning text patterns for document categorization, ICAPR2001, 2nd Intern'l Conference on Advances in Pattern Recognition, Rio de Janeiro, Brazil, March 2001.

Multi-scale Document Description Using Rectangular Granulometries

Andrew D. Bagdanov and Marcel Worring

Intelligent Sensory Information Systems
University of Amsterdam, Kruislaan 403, 1098 SJ Amsterdam
The Netherlands
{andrew, worring}@science.uva.nl

Abstract. When comparing documents images based on visual similarity it is difficult to determine the correct scale and features for document representation. We report on new form of multivariate granulometries based on rectangles of varying size and aspect ratio. These rectangular granulometries are used to probe the layout structure of document images, and the rectangular size distributions derived from them are used as descriptors for document images. Feature selection is used to reduce the dimensionality and redundancy of the size distributions, while preserving the essence of the visual appearance of a document. Experimental results indicate that rectangular size distributions are an effective way to characterize visual similarity of document images and provide insightful interpretation of classification and retrieval results in the original image space rather than the abstract feature space.

1 Introduction

There are many applications in document image understanding where it is necessary to compare documents according to visual appearance before attempting high–level understanding of document content. Example applications include document genre classification, duplicate document detection, and document image retrieval.

Genre classification is useful for grouping documents for routing through office workflows, as well as identifying the type of document before applying class–specific strategies for document understanding [1]. Document image retrieval systems are of particular interest in some application areas [2]. Given an example image as a query, a document image retrieval system should return a ranked list of visually similar documents from an indexed collection. In document collections automatic conversion of documents is often expensive or impossible. In such cases image retrieval may be the only feasible means of providing access to a document database.

Whether document images are to be classified into a number of known document genres, or ranked by similarity to documents in a document database, it is necessary to establish meaningful measures of visual similarity between documents. To that end we must first define an appropriate document representation.

D. Lopresti, J. Hu, and R. Kashi (Eds.): DAS 2002, LNCS 2423, pp. 445–456, 2002.

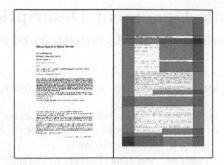

Fig. 1. Characterizing document images as a union of rectangles.

Consider the document shown in figure 1. The visual appearance of a document is determined by the foreground and background pixels in the document image. Document segmentation techniques using structural decompositions of the *background* are common in the literature on document understanding [3]. The background of a document image can be represented by rectangular regions of various sizes. Analysis of the structure of such rectangular decompositions can be used to derive useful descriptors of the appearance of document images. While most of the visual content of a document image can be described by analyzing the background in this way, for some documents it is necessary to perform the same type of decompositional analysis on the foreground. The most obvious example of this are documents containing reverse "video" regions.

The proper scale to use for document representation depends on the application, and hence a generic representation of visual content must be multi–scale. Some researchers, in fact, advocate exploration of an entire scale–space of potential document segmentations before committing to a single one [4]. Most techniques based on a single layout segmentation fail to take the multi–scale nature of visual perception into account. For documents this multi–scale nature is implicit in the scales distinguishing characters, words, textlines, paragraphs, columns, etc.

Our approach for representing visual content is based on morphological granulometric analysis of document images. A granulometry can be thought of as a morphological sieve, where objects not conforming to a particular size and shape are removed at each level of the sieving process. They were first introduced by Matheron for characterizing the probabilistic nature of random sets [5]. Granulometries, and the corresponding measurements taken on them, have been applied to problems of texture classification [6], image segmentation [7], and filtering [8]. Recent work by Vincent has shown how granulometries can be effectively and efficiently applied, particularly in the binary image domain [9].

The rest of this paper is organized as follows. We give in the next section a brief introduction to granulometries and the multivariate extensions used in our approach. Next, a description of our representation of document images derived from measurements on these granulometric filters is described. We also show how these measurements may be used to interpret the important features distinguishing between visually distinct document classes. To illustrate the effectiveness of our representation, we have applied our technique to the problems of document genre classification and document image retrieval. The results of these experiments are given in section 4.

2   Rectangular Granulometries

In this section we describe the properties of granulometries. Formally, a *granulometry* on $\mathcal{P}(R \times R)$, where $\mathcal{P}(X)$ is the power set of X, is a family of operators:

$$\Psi_t : \mathcal{P}(R \times R) \longrightarrow \mathcal{P}(R \times R)$$

satisfying for any $S \in \mathcal{P}(R \times R)$

A1: $\Psi_t(S) \subset S$ for all $t > 0$ (Ψ_t is anti–extensive)
A2: For $S \subset S'$, $\Psi_t(S) \subset \Psi_t(S')$ (Ψ_t is increasing).
A3: $\Psi_t \circ \Psi_{t'} = \Psi_{t'} \circ \Psi_t = \Psi_{\max(t,t')}$ for all $t, t' > 0$.

Of particular interest are granulometries generated by openings by scaled versions of a single convex structuring element B, i.e.

$$\Psi_t(S) = S \circ tB .$$

To capture the vertically and horizontally aligned regions of varying aspect ratios we use multivariate, rectangular granulometries to characterize document images. Let H and V be horizontal and vertical line segments of unit length centered at the origin. We define each opening in the rectangular granulometry as:

$$\Psi_{x,y}(S) = S \circ (yV \oplus xH).$$

The above definition makes use of the fact that any rectangle may be written as a dilation of its orthogonal horizontal and vertical components. Note that any increasing function $f(x)$ induces a univariate granulometry $\{\Psi_{x,f(x)}\}$ satisfying A1–A3. The extension to rectangular openings allows us to capture the information from all rectangular granulometries in a single parameterized family of operators. Figure 2 gives some example openings of this type for a document image.

3   Document Representation

In this section we describe our method for representing document images using measurements taken on rectangular granulometries. Note that it is not the openings constituting the rectangular granulometries described above, nor the filtered versions of the image S that are of most interest in describing the visual appearance of document images, but rather the *measurements* taken on the filtered images $\Psi_{x,y}(S)$.

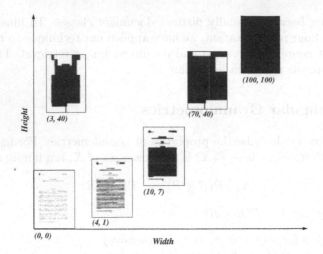

Fig. 2. Some examples of $\Psi_{x,y}(S)$ for a document S for various values of x and y. The multi–scale nature of documents is evident in the different structural relationships emerging at different levels in the granulometry: characters are merged into words, words into lines, and lines into textblocks. Eventually the margins are breached and the entire document is opened.

3.1   Rectangular Size Distributions

Maragos [6] has described two useful measurements for granulometries, the size distribution and pattern spectrum, which have subsequently been extended to multivariate granulometries [10]. We define the rectangular size distribution induced by the granulometry $G = \{\Psi_{x,y}\}$ on image S as:

$$\Phi_G(x, y, S) = \frac{A(S) - A(\Psi_{x,y}(S)))}{A(S)},$$

$A(X)$ denoting the area of set X. $\Phi_G(x, y, S)$ is a cumulative probability distribution, i.e. $\Phi_G(x, y, S)$ is the probability that an arbitrary pixel in S is opened by a rectangle of size $x \times y$ or smaller.

As mentioned in the introduction, documents with regions containing reverse video text, i.e. white text against a black background, are not thoroughly captured by the openings $\Psi_{x,y}$. To account for this, we extend the rectangular size distributions downward to include openings of the foreground. The definition becomes:

$$\Phi_G(x, y, S) = \begin{cases} \frac{A(S) - A(\Psi_{x,y}(S)))}{A(S)} & \text{if } x, y \geq 0 \\ \frac{A(S^c) - A(\Psi_{x,y}(S^c)))}{A(S^c)} & \text{if } x, y < 0 \end{cases}$$

The pattern spectrum is defined as the derivative of $\Phi_G(x, y, S)$, for which we have two choices in the case of rectangular granulometries. For document images there is no *a priori* evidence for preferring either horizontal or vertical

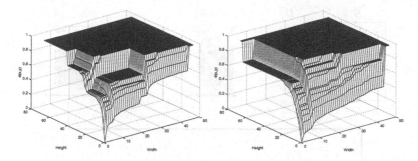

Fig. 3. Example rectangular size distributions for two documents from different genres in our test database. Note the prominent flat plateau regions indicating regions of stability in the granulometry. These most likely correspond to typographical parameters such as margin width, inter–line distance, etc. The size distribution on the left is constructed from the document shown in figure 1, and the one on the right from the document used to construct the example openings in figure 2.

directional derivatives, e.g. preferring emphasis on inter–column gap over inter–line spacing, and for now we concentrate on using the size distribution as our document representation.

Figure 3 gives two example size distributions. In these examples, we only plot the size distribution in the first quadrant, i.e. for $x, y > 0$. We see that the rectangular size distribution captures much information about the document image. Of specific interest are the plateau regions in the size distribution, which indicate islands of stability most likely corresponding to specific typographical features such as inter–line spacing, paragraph spacing, and inter–column gap.

3.2 Efficiency

It is not feasible to exhaust the entire parameter space for rectangular size distributions in a naïve way. This is especially true for document images, which tend to be large. We can take advantage of several properties of rectangular granulometries and size distributions in order to make their computation more tractable.

First, each rectangular opening may be decomposed into linear erosions and dilations as follows:

$$\begin{aligned}
\Psi_{x,y}(S) &= S \circ (yV \oplus xH) \\
&= (S \ominus (yV \oplus xH)) \oplus (yV \oplus xH) \\
&= (((S \ominus yV) \ominus xH) \oplus yV) \oplus xH.
\end{aligned} \tag{1}$$

This eliminates the need to directly open a document image by rectangles of all sizes. Instead, the opening is incrementally constructed by the orthogonal components of each rectangle, which are increasing linearly in size rather than quadratically.

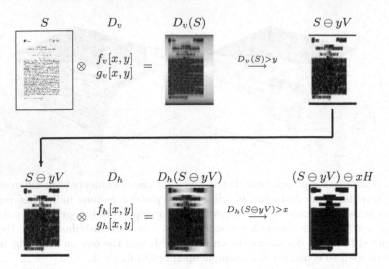

Fig. 4. Efficient computation of an arbitrary rectangular opening. Distance transforms are used to effectively encode all possible vertical and horizontal erosions. By thresholding these distance images we can obtain each desired erosion. The $\otimes$ operator is used above to indicate the application of the recursive filters described in equations 2 and 3. The first part of the opening, $(S \ominus yV) \ominus xH$, is illustrated above. The opening is completed by performing the same steps on $((S \ominus yV) \ominus xH)^c$.

Next, we can eliminate the need to erode and dilate the image by structuring elements increasing linearly in size. Using linear distance transforms for vertical and horizontal directions we can generate all needed erosions and dilations for each rectangular opening. The horizontal distance transform of an image S is defined as:

$$D_h(S, x, y) = \min\{\Delta x \mid (x \pm \Delta x, y) \in S\},$$

and the vertical distance transform as:

$$D_v(S, x, y) = \min\{\Delta y \mid (x, y \pm \Delta y) \in S\}.$$

These transforms can be efficiently performed using the following recursive forward/backward filter pairs defined on image S:

$$D_h \begin{cases} f_h[x, y] = \min\{f[x - 1, y] + 1, \ S(x, y)\} \\ g_h[x, y] = \min\{f[x, y], \ g[x + 1, y] + 1\} \end{cases} \tag{2}$$

$$D_v \begin{cases} f_v[x, y] = \min\{f[x, y - 1] + 1, \ S(x, y)\} \\ g_v[x, y] = \min\{f[x, y], \ g[x, y + 1] + 1\} \end{cases} \tag{3}$$

The use of these distance transforms to generate erosions of the original image represents a significant savings in computation time. To generate a vertical or horizontal erosion of arbitrary size we only have to apply two fixed–size recursive neighborhood operations, rather than eroding by structuring elements increasing in size. In this way each opening can be incrementally constructed as illustrated in figure 4.

Lastly, since rectangular size distributions are monotonically increasing in both parameters, i.e. if $x' \geq x$ and $y' \geq y$ then $\Phi_G(x', y', S) \geq \Phi_G(x, y, S)$, we can recursively search the parameter space, eliminating the need to explore large, flat regions.

3.3 Feature Space Reduction and Interpretation

The multi–scale representation developed in the previous two subsections captures much structural information about document images, but does little toward reducing the overall complexity of the problem. To that end we describe in this subsection our approach to dimensionality reduction, which also leads to interesting qualitative interpretations in the original document image space.

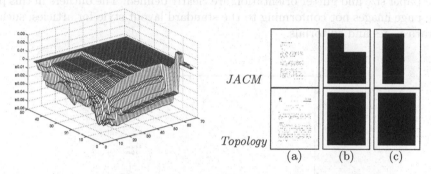

Fig. 5. Interpreting the PCA results. On the left are shown the coefficients in the principle eigenvector mapped back into the original feature space of the size distribution (i.e. the same feature space as shown in the examples given in figure 3). On the right, individual openings are interpreted: (a) shows the original images, (b) an opening emphasizing the presence of the *Topology* logotype, and (c) an opening emphasizing the differences in margins.

The dimensionality of the entire size distribution is too large to be applied effectively in a statistical pattern recognition setting. Some feature selection or reduction strategy must be applied. Principle Component Analysis (PCA) is a well–known approach to feature reduction, and can be applied to rectangular size distributions to reduce the dimensionality of our document representation, while preserving the maximum amount of variance in a document collection. The principle component mapping defines a rotation of the original feature space using the eigenvectors of the covariance matrix of the dataset. Since each eigenvector is of the same dimensionality as the original feature space, we can visualize them individually in the same way as size distributions. Figure 5 shows the coefficients of the first principle component computed for a two–class subset of our four document genres.

From inspection of the plot on the left in figure 5 it is evident that it is not necessary to sample much of the parameter space in order to account for most of the variance in the entire sample. In particular, most of the large openings do not contribute at all to the variance in the first principle component mapping. By selecting a coefficient of high magnitude in the first principle component, we can compute the corresponding opening $\Psi_{x,y}(S)$ on document images from our test sample. This allows us to interpret features important for distinguishing between documents in the original image space. The opening shown in figure 5b emphasizes the presence of the logotype appearing in the upper right corner of *Topology* articles, while in figure 5c the differences in margins are emphasized.

The principle component mapping is also useful for visualizing an entire genre of document images. Figure 6 shows a sample class of document images (from the *Journal of the ACM*) after mapping to the first two principle components. The clusters in the low–dimensional space represent the gross typographical differences between document images from this class. In this case, clusters indicating the paper size and gutter orientation are clearly defined. The outliers in this plot are page images not conforming to the standard layout style for articles, such as errata pages and editorials.

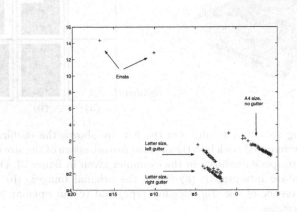

Fig. 6. The first two principle components for two document classes.

4   Experimental Results

To illustrate the effectiveness of rectangular granulometries, we have applied the technique to the problems of document genre classification and document image retrieval. A total of 537 PDF documents were collected from several digital libraries. The sample contains documents from four different journals, which determine the genres in our classification problem, and relevance for document retrieval. Note that these genres are not necessarily determined by visual similarity. Since we are using an inherently *logical* definition of document genre, i.e. coming from the same publication, there may be significantly different visual sub–genres within each genre (see figure 6). However, this does give us a non–subjective division of our document collection.

We consider only the first page of each document, as it contains most of the visually significant features for discriminating between document genres. The first page of each PDF document was converted to an image and subsampled to 1/4 of its original size. The rectangular size distribution described in section 2 was then computed for each image. Each quadrant of the size distribution is then sampled to form a rectangular size distribution of size 41×61. The resulting dimensionality of our feature space is 5002.

4.1 Genre Classification

Table 1 gives the estimated classification accuracy for a training sample of 30 documents selected randomly from each document genre, with the remaining documents used as an independent test set. Estimated classification accuracy is shown for 5, 7, and 10 principle components computed from the training sample, and for a 1-nearest neighbor, quadratic discriminant, and linear discriminant classifier. These results indicate that, even with relatively few principle components, rectangular granulometries are capable of capturing the relevant differences between document genres.

Table 1. Genre classification results for 30 training samples per class and various numbers of principle components. Classification accuracy is estimated by averaging over 50 experimental trials. The PCA is performed independently for each trial.

Classifier	# PCs		
	5	7	10
1-Nearest Neighbor	94%	95%	98%
Quadratic Discriminant	93%	94%	98%
Linear Discriminant	76%	80%	93%

4.2 Document Image Retrieval

For the document image retrieval experiments, a single document image is given as a query, and a ranked list of relevant documents is returned. We use the rectangular size distributions described above as the representation for each document. Document ranking is computed using the Euclidean distance from the size distribution of the query document. For evaluation, a document is considered relevant if it belongs to the same genre as the query document (i.e. it is from the same publication).

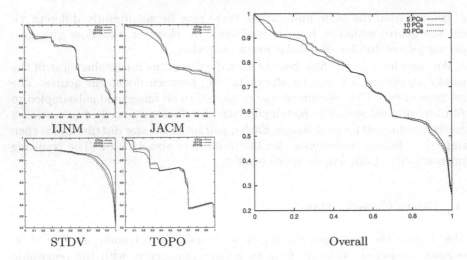

Fig. 7. Average precision and recall plots for each genre in the test database. Results on the entire feature space and with 5, 10, and 20 principle components are shown. The graphs on the left show the precision and recall for each individual class, while the plot on the right gives the overall average precision and recall.

Precision and recall statistics can be used to measure the performance of retrieval systems. They are defined as:

$$\text{Precision} = \frac{\text{\# relevant documents retrieved}}{\text{\# documents retrieved}}$$

$$\text{Recall} = \frac{\text{\# relevant documents retrieved}}{\text{\# relevant documents}}$$

Rather than computing the overall precision, it is more useful to sample the precision and recall at several cutoff points. For a given recall rate, we can determine what the resulting precision is. That is, how many non–relevant documents must we inspect before finding that fraction of relevant documents.

Figure 7 gives the average precision/recall graphs for each document genre in our database. The graphs were constructed by using each document in a genre as a query, ranking all documents in the database against it, and computing the precision at each recall level. These individual precision/recall statistics are then averaged to form the final graph.

The graphs in figure 7 give a good indication of how well each individual genre is characterized by the rectangular size distribution representation, and also indicates the overall precision and recall for the entire dataset. The overall precision/recall graph is constructed by averaging the precision and recall rates over all classes. This graph indicates that, on average, 50% of all relevant documents can be retrieved with a precision of about 80%.

All of the precision/recall graphs have a characteristic plunging tail, indicating that there are some queries where relevant documents appear near the end of the ranked list. It is illustrative to examine some specific examples of this phenomenon. Figure 8 gives some example query images along with the highest ranked relevant document returned, excluding the query document itself, and the lowest ranked relevant document returned. In most cases these low ranking relevant documents represent pathologically different visual sub–classes of the document genre.

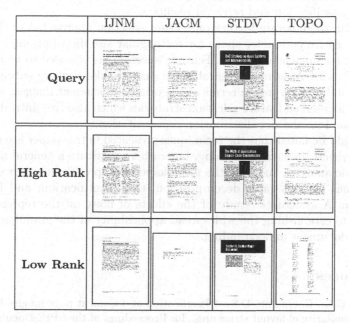

Fig. 8. Some illustrative query examples. A sample query image for each genre is shown, along with the highest and lowest ranked relevant images from the relevant genre. In most cases the least relevant document is pathologically different the query.

5   Conclusions

We have reported on an extension to multivariate granulometries that uses rectangles of varying scale and aspect ratio to characterize the visual content of document images. Rectangular size distributions are an effective way to describe the visual structure of document images, and by employing morphological decomposition techniques they can be efficiently computed. Experiments have shown that size distributions can be used to discriminate between specific document genres. Principle component analysis can be used to reduce the dimensionality of multivariate size distributions, while preserving their discriminating power. One of the attractive aspects of rectangular size distributions is the ability, even under dimensionality reduction, to interpret significant features back in the original image space.

Document retrieval experiments also indicate the effectiveness of rectangular size distributions for capturing visual similarity of documents. For our document database 50% of relevant documents can be retrieved with a precision of approximately 80%.

Principle component analysis has proved useful for accentuating the important features in size distributions. A non–linear PCA approach which maximizes inter–class variance while minimizing intra–class variance will certainly improve both the classification and retrieval results.

We plan to elaborate further on feature selection approaches in the near future. The entire parameter space for rectangular size distributions is expensive to sample for document images. Feature selection, as opposed to feature reduction such as PCA, is more desirable because of this. Feature subsets are also more natural to interpret in terms of the original document images. Research in currently focused on feature selection strategies which also (re–)introduce spatial information into the size distribution representation.

It should be noted that the techniques presented in this paper are not limited solely to visual similarity matching, but rather constitute a general approach to multi–scale analysis. As such, the granulometric approach may prove useful for applications such as table decomposition, text identification, and layout segmentation. A systematic study of the effects of noise on the representation is essential to establishing the widespread applicability of the granulometric technique to document understanding.

References

1. Shin, C.K., Doermann, D.S.: Classification of document page images based on visual similarity of layout structures. In: Proceedings of the SPIE Document Recognition and Retrieval VII. (2000)
2. Doermann, D.S.: The indexing and retrieval of document images: A survey. Computer Vision and Image Understanding **70** (1998)
3. Antonacopoulos, A.: Page segmentation using the description of the background. Computer Vision and Image Understanding **70** (1998) 350–369
4. Breuel, T.: Thomas m. breuel. layout analysis by exploring the space of segmentation parameters. In: Proceedings of the Fourth International Workshop on Document Analysis Systems (DAS'2000). (2000)
5. Matheron, G.: Random Sets and Integral Geometry. John Wiley & Sons, New York (1975)
6. Maragos, P.: Pattern spectrum and multiscale shape representation. IEEE Transactions on Pattern Analysis and Machine Intelligence **11** (1989) 701–716
7. Dougherty, E.R., Pelz, J., Sand, F., Lent, A.: Morphological image segmentation by local granulometric size distributions. J. Electronic Imaging **1** (1992)
8. Haralick, R.M., Katz, P.L., Dougherty, E.R.: Model-based morphology: the opening spectrum. Graphical Models and Image Processing **57** (1995) 1–12
9. Vincent, L.: Granulometries and opening trees. Fundamenta Informatica **41** (2000) 57–90
10. Batman, S., Dougherty, E.R., Sand, F.: Heterogeneous morphological granulometries. Pattern Recognition **33** (2000) 1047–1057

Machine Learning of Generalized Document Templates
for Data Extraction

Janusz Wnek

Science Applications International Corporation
1953 Gallows Road, Vienna, VA 22182, U.S.A.
Janusz.Wnek@saic.com

Abstract. The purpose of this research is to reverse engineer the process of encoding data in structured documents and subsequently automate the process of extracting it. We assume a broad category of structured documents for processing that goes beyond form processing. In fact, the documents may have flexible layouts and consist of multiple and varying numbers of pages. The data extraction method (DataX) employs general templates generated by the Inductive Template Generator (InTeGen). The InTeGen method utilizes inductive learning from examples of documents with identified data elements. Both methods achieve high automation with minimal user's input.

1 Introduction

Understanding documents is a relatively easy task for an intelligent human reader most of the time. This is due to the fact that the documents are prepared using some common assumptions about structuring them, and authors' intend to convey information in ways allowing readers accurate and efficient interpretation. The problem is, to what degree is it possible to reverse engineer the process of encoding data in documents and subsequently automate the process of extracting the data.

The main objective for creating most documents is to communicate visual information. Characters, combined in words, sentences, and paragraphs, have been intentionally placed on documents. We have found that a fundamental utility for reverse engineering of the process of encoding data in documents is provided by optical character recognition (OCR). Specifically, OCR-based features, i.e. characters, make ultimate sense in recognizing textual constructs, as opposed to other features, such as bounding boxes resulting from connected component analysis, frequency/distribution profiles, texture analysis, and other image processing artifacts.

Based on recognized character contents and its layout one can build even more meaningful constructs, such as words and phrases, and relate them with each other. We understand that this process is a subsequent, important element in reverse engineering the document encoding process. Words and phrases become elementary symbols in machine document processing. Understanding their relative usage enriches document representation. Now, given the set of symbolic elements related to each other via a set of defined relations, an intelligent system can learn patterns in their

D. Lopresti, J. Hu, and R. Kashi (Eds.): DAS 2002, LNCS 2423, pp. 457–468, 2002.
© Springer-Verlag Berlin Heidelberg 2002

arrangement. Generalized pattern descriptions can be induced from exemplary definitions of data elements on some instance documents.

Generalization is a powerful knowledge transformation that allows learning of general descriptions that govern data element arrangement. The descriptions of symbol arrangements become the underlying representation for document structures. They disclose intentions of document authors with regard to data composition.

Fig. 1 illustrates the process of reverse engineering a document design as specified in the InTeGen method. It is assumed that each document file consists of ordered images of single pages, assembled in a prior process. One at a time, a template is "learned" for each document type. In the first two steps, the document image is extended with a symbolic description of its contents; i.e., with document text and relations between identified visual/textual constructs. Given the document image and OCR'd text, a user defines data elements on the image. This procedure involves drawing boundaries around the character strings constituting the data elements.

Data element (DE) definitions communicate *user's goals* for processing a particular document type at the moment. Refining goals can be realized by adding or removing definitions at a later time. Next, the symbolic representations of the document and data element definitions are input to a learning module. Given the first instance of a document, the symbolic information is simply stored in a document template. Processing the following instances involves assimilation into the template. More specifically, common textual patterns are found in both the new document and the current template, and the general patterns are stored as a new template description.

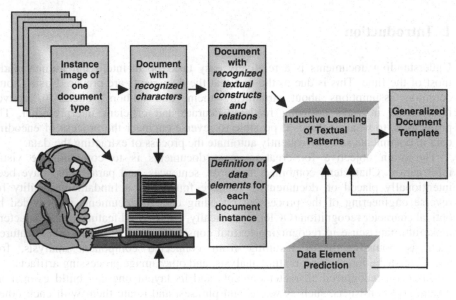

Fig. 1. Reverse engineering the document design process: Inductive Template Generator – InTeGen

After each incremental template refinement, the InTeGen process is bootstrapped with the newly refined template. The template is utilized in predicting data elements of unprocessed training documents. First, the predicted data elements serve in assisting the user when defining data elements on new documents of the same type. Second, the predicted data elements are utilized in evaluating capabilities of the current template, before the decision about assimilating new documents into the template is made.

The Generalized Document Template represents the original design of one document type with regard to the guidelines provided by the user in the form of data element definitions. Accurate formulation of the hypothesis depends on consistency in specification of data elements across the document type and the user definitions of data element boundaries.

In summary, the goal of the combined InTeGen-DataX system is to automatically "learn" complex document structures, store them in general templates, and utilize them in a data extraction process. Reverse engineering of a document design is realized by a combination of optical character recognition, reconstruction and understanding of document components, and relating them to original intend by utilizing user's input.

2 Inductive Template Generator: Document and Data Structures

Historically, document conversion systems have focused on two major types of applications: full-text databases and forms processing. Examples of full-text applications include correspondence tracking and litigation support. Major forms processing applications (domains) include health care forms, tax forms, and the U.S. Census. There is a large class of applications that lies between these two major types. These applications involve processing flexible forms. Examples include bills of lading, invoices, insurance notifications and mortgage documentation. Such applications typically are characterized by a large number of document variants. Today, most forms processing applications are designed to recognize and capture data from a small number of form types. Even the most versatile operations typically process at most a few dozen forms. The flexible form applications, in contrast, typically involve hundreds to thousands of document variants.

In order to facilitate processing of flexible form documents, a *generalized document template* is introduced to represent a generalized document model. The generalized document template captures characteristics of the complete document as opposed to page (or form) templates that generalize single pages only. A generalized document template contains generalized descriptions of data elements. A data element is a logical unit that defines an object for extraction. We assume that data elements contain one or more lines of textual information and can be enclosed in a rectangular bounding box. The bounding box provides necessary grouping of all words relevant to the data element. In the remainder of the paper we refer to the generalized document template simply as the *template*.

Defining a data element is a very simple operation which involves drawing a bounding box around the data element and selecting a predefined name for that data element (Fig. 2). The data element description and a necessary context are both acquired from the document and maintained automatically. Keywords, key phrases, or the layout of a data element on a page can provide the context.

Data extraction from new documents, i.e. documents not used for training is based on the application of the template. The context enables finding the data element on the document and helps in determining the scope of the data element.

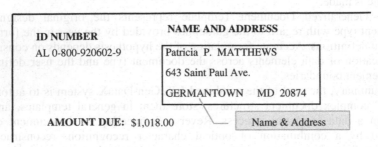

Fig. 2. A document fragment with a user-defined data element.

In the template generation process, a document is described at several levels of abstraction: page, line, word, and character levels. *Page level* consists of descriptions of all pages included in the document. These are simply page dimensions and margin offsets. *Line level* consists of the total number of document lines; vertical offsets to line bases from the beginning of the document, and numbers of words in each line. An OCR engine predetermines division of a document into lines. *Word level* consists of the total number of document words, horizontal offsets to words' start and end measuring from the line beginning, and number of characters in each word. *Character level* consists of the total number of document characters, horizontal offsets to characters, their widths and heights, as well as the complete document text.

A template represents a generalized document description. In the template, each data element is represented by a list of alternative descriptions. Alternative descriptions represent various patterns in DE contexts that are significantly different. For example, if documents from the same class use different captions to tag the same data element then the system may use two or more alternative descriptions to represent the changing captions.

A single description contains four attribute types: physical, lexical, contextual, and control type.

Physical attributes include ranges of vertical and horizontal positions in the document, width range, height range, maximal width and height including white space available. Positions, widths, and heights are measured in pixels. Other physical attributes include number of lines, word position in the line from both left and right, number of words in the line, and number of characters in the first word.

Lexical attributes correspond to document description at the three levels: line level, word level and character level. *Line level* consists of the total number of DE lines; vertical offsets to line bases from the beginning of each DE, and numbers of words in each DE line. *Word level* consists of the total number of DE words, horizontal offsets to words' start and end from DE line beginning, and number of characters in each word. *Character level* consists of the total number of DE characters, horizontal offsets to characters, their widths and heights, as well as the complete DE text. The text consists of words separated by single spaces. Lexical description provides an example of data element contents. It does not contain any generalized information.

Contextual attributes include number of words in the context, and actual words with distance and utility measurements. The words are naturally ordered in a sequence according to the line order produced by an OCR and read from left to right. The distances are grouped into two categories: pixel and word distances. *Pixel distance* describes span (in pixels) between the context word and the DE origin, i.e. the beginning of the first DE word. Two ranges in vertical (x) and horizontal (y) dimensions represent the pixel distance. Word distances are stated using the number of words between the context word and the first DE word. Two word distances are used: sequential and vertical. *Sequential word distance* counts words as they were read line by line, from left to right. *Vertical word distance* counts the number of lines containing words intersecting the column delineated by the width of the context word. For each vertical distance, the number of occurrences (frequency) in various documents is collected.

The distances are whole numbers. Positive numbers indicate that the context word is after the first DE word. Negative number indicates that the context word is before the first DE word. The order depends on the type of distance. For pixel distances, "before" means that the context word is above in vertical dimension and to the left in horizontal dimension. For sequential word distance, "before" means that the context word is closer to the beginning of the document than the DE word. For vertical word distance, "before" means that the context word is above DE.

The utility of a context word indicates the usefulness of the word for searching purposes. Four values are being assigned: best, good, fair, and poor. Best utility is assigned to words that precisely identify a DE by themselves and are unique. Good utility is assigned to words that precisely identify a DE (in terms of the search method, e.g. starting from the top of the document) but are not unique. Fair utility is assigned to unique words that occasionally may fail the search. Poor utility is assigned to words that should not be used in searches.

Table 1. Context word utility with regard to potential search precision and uniqueness within the document.

Utility	Search Precision	Uniqueness
Best	+	+
Good	+	−
Fair	−	+
Poor	−	−

Control attributes include word types for selected DE words (e.g. first words in each DE line), indices of the first DE line, word, and character; generalization counter, and DE identifier in the domain. Word types categorize words into several classes, such as: numeric with various combinations of related characters (e.g., +, −, #, %, etc.), alphabetic (ALL CAPS, all lower case, mixed, etc.), alphanumeric, dates, etc. Generalized word types may have one or more values.

3 Inductive Template Generator: The Method

A template for a given document class is built in an incremental way from examples of documents (training documents) and data element definitions. The documents are first assembled from scanned and OCR'd pages, and stored in the document description data structure. For each document, a user defines a set of data elements by drawing bounding boxes on the document image. At the minimum, DE definitions consist of five numbers only: vertical and horizontal position of the bounding box origin, width, height, and data element identifier.

3.1 Induction

The procedure for generalizing templates iterates through the list of data element definitions and generalizes each data element description. Generalization of DE descriptions is performed independently of each other.

Given the *first training* document and a set of data element definitions, InTeGen initializes the template by copying the document description to the template description, and by constructing and attaching initial data element descriptors to the template for each data element. Each DE descriptor is constructed based on its definition and document contents: filling out the descriptor involves extraction of relevant lexical descriptors from the document description, determining values of physical and control attributes, and constructing contextual attributes. Initially, contextual attributes comprise all document words. For each attribute, all types of distance measurements are taken, i.e. pixel distance, sequential and vertical word distances. Copying the document description to the template is simple because both document and template descriptions share the same data structures.

Given the *next training* document and the set of DE definitions, generalization with the template occurs unconditionally. The following training documents may or may not be generalized with the template depending on template generality, or in other words, the template's capability of correctly predicting the place and scope of its data elements. Template generalization equates to generalization of any of the DE descriptions. In order to determine if a template covers DE descriptions from the training document, a prediction test is conducted for each DE. The template's DE description is generalized only if it is not capable of correctly predicting the given DE on the training document.

DE description generalization involves generalization of particular attributes. For physical and control attributes expanding the range of measured values is sufficient. The selection of this type of generalization was dictated by the nature of document attributes, values of which are continuous rather than discrete. For example, assuming that DE sequential word distances for the first two documents were 5 and 8, the generalized distance results in a range between 5 and 8. This means that if the third document distance value is 7 then the third document is covered by that condition.

Generalization of context attributes involves intersecting two sequences of words and then, for the common words, generalizing their values. For example, given the two sequences of words, T_CAi, D_CAi, below, describing contextual attribute (CA) of data element (i) on template (T) and document (D), their generalization results in T_CAi. Spacing between words was added to highlight the method of aligning words.

Table 2. Generalization of two sequences.

T_CAi:	w1		w2	$w3$	w4	w5	w6		w7	w̲8̲
D_CAi:	w1	w̲8̲	w2		w4		w6	$w3$	w7	w8
T_CAi:	**w1**		**w2**		**w4**		**w6**		**w7**	**w8**

The method for aligning words incorporates three general preference criteria for selecting words for alignment. Additional criteria may be added based on document characteristics in a particular document domain. The general preference criteria include:

1. Words in the template are more significant then those in the document (unless the template was not generalized yet).

2. Alignment should maximize the number of common words.

3. Alignment should take into consideration keywords or key phrases delimiting identifiable sections of a document.

After DE generalization, the DE description is evaluated with regard to its utility. There are two criteria for testing DE description utility. The first is based on description evaluation, and the second is based on performance evaluation. If both tests are passed then the DE description replaces the previous one in the generalized template. If any of the tests fails, then a new alternative description is created.

Description evaluation involves determining the amount of change in context close to DE. The change is determined by comparing sequence word distances in the last two generalizations. If the distance to the word immediately proceeding DE or the distance to the word immediately following DE increased by more than predefined thresholds, then a new alternative rule is added. The threshold values are determined empirically for the given document-processing domain.

Performance evaluation involves testing prediction capability using the recently generalized DE description. The document that was recently used for generalization serves as a testing material. This procedure allows for producing consistent and complete descriptions with regard to the training set of documents.

In some cases a data element may show a high degree of variability in addition to not having precisely defined boundaries. For example, a data element may consist of a varied number of lines with some other data immediately following it. The attached data may easily be construed as an integral part of the DE especially when it takes place optionally. In order to detect ambiguous boundaries, InTeGen learns the structure of the edit phrases that delimit a data element.

The procedure for generalizing templates takes advantage of failing some prediction tests to learn the edit phrases. Edit phrases consist of the difference between the predicted text and the defined text. The phrases are generalized, stored and utilized when predicting data elements. The edit phrase data structure consists of a location attribute, a generalized text of the phrase, and a generalization counter. The generalized text of the edit phrase stores actual words if they reappear, or word types for varied phrase words.

3.2 Prediction

Prediction plays an important role in building a generalized template (InTeGen) and actual data extraction from new documents (DataX). Given the fact that during template generation data element definitions are available from a user as an integral part of the training set, DE definitions may also serve as a basis for comparison with predicted values. Feedback produced that way is invaluable for an automated system. It provides a means for detecting the need for performing generalization, and once generalization is done, the verification of a template's utility. As a result of such verification, it may lead to follow-up actions such as building alternative descriptions.

Given data element id, the data element prediction procedure selects the DE description from the template. DE description is by itself disjunctive. It consists of alternative descriptions covering variations in the DE context observed on different training documents. The procedure has to decide which alternative description is best for making prediction on the given document. In order to do this, it performs partial prediction based on all of the alternative descriptions and then selects one to complete the prediction process. In the case where no alternative description can be successfully applied, the procedure reports failure.

The prediction process breaks down into two stages: finding the origin of the data element on the current document and determining its size. Finding the DE origin is simplified to finding the first word of the data element, which is facilitated by the DE description constructed in the learning phase. This task involves selecting the proper search phrase to address the first word, applying one of the distances to find candidate words, and determining the best candidate based on testing the first word properties. Once the first word is known, the origin of the DE bounding box is also known. Determining DE size is based again on measurements and characteristics gathered during the learning phase and stored in DE description.

Finding the DE origin consists of searches for the DE using context phrases located before or after the data element. Regularly, one of the searches succeeds in finding a reliable phrase that is located in consistent proximity from the data element that yields anticipated DE origin. If the two searches do not yield an anticipated DE origin, a range of words for examination is constructed, and the DE origin is decided based on sequential location in the target document and data type of the DE first word. If there is no valid context phrase before or after the DE, or it is not possible to predict using the sequence distance, context phrases above and under are examined, and the vertical distance may be applied to predict the DE origin.

In the process of finding DE origin, a procedure is employed to search for context phrases. Based on the template description, it constructs a multi-word context phrase that precisely addresses DE. The phrase has to be close to the DE to assure the most precise reconstruction of DE location. In order to assure that the context phrase is not mismatched within the currently processed document, a unique landmark in close proximity to the phrase is being used. The unique landmark is a word that was assigned the best search utility during template learning. The procedure returns the address of the word nearest to the DE origin.

4 Evaluation

The InTeGen-DataX method has been implemented in the ML-FromForms system. The system is capable of processing variety of flexible form documents. The system integrates various image processing and document understanding components including, inductive document classifier for recognizing document types (Wnek, 1999). Fig. 3 presents a sample of documents that can be processed by ML-FromForms (only first pages of multiple-page documents are shown). For some applications, templates for several hundred of document types have been created and data successfully extracted.

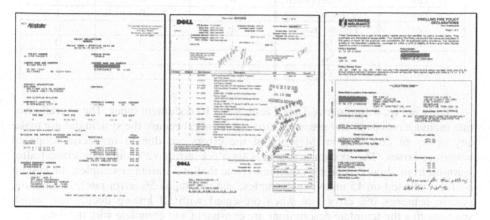

Fig. 3. Examples of insurance and invoice documents used for template training and data extraction. ML-FromForms is capable of extracting any machine-printed, data element identifiable on such pages.

The main objective for the testing was to establish prediction accuracy of the DataX method, i.e. accuracy of finding and extracting data elements from documents similar to those presented in Fig. 3. OCR accuracy was not of our concern, hence ground truth data was easy to create and consisted only of bounding boxes and identifiers of defined data elements. Another two objectives for testing was to establish approximate number of training examples required to achieve a desired prediction accuracy, and to confirm system's stability on known (training) data.

There may be many other factors that influence prediction accuracy in general. First of all, not all documents or their parts may qualify as having flexible layouts. Therefore, not all data elements may be extracted from them. Second, document image quality and OCR accuracy may influence both quality of data element prediction accuracy, as well as data element contents.

Our testing involved 10 selected document types for which ground truth data was created. For each document type up to 11 data elements were defined, totaling 103 data elements in all document types. Ground truth data was created for 20 documents in each type. In all, 2,060 data elements were defined. In each train-test session, the system was trained using from 1 to 20 training examples and evaluated using all 20 documents.

Three error types were measured: omission error, commission error, and precision error. Table 3 defines the error types for various occurrences of defined and predicted pairs of data elements (DE). Precision errors capture imprecision in extracting data element, i.e. too small or too large bounding box. This error type is usually of lesser concern to users than the errors of commission or omission because it may be corrected by post processing.

Table 3. Error types used in determining data element prediction accuracy.

DE defined	DE predicted	Omission Error	Commission Error	Precision Error
Yes	Yes, exact match	0	0	0
Yes	Yes, partial match	0	0	1
Yes	Yes, no match	1	1	0
Yes	No	1	0	0
No	No	0	0	0
No	Yes	0	1	0

Charts in Fig. 4 summarize DataX testing for 10 document types. The overall error rate includes omission and precision error rates only, because the system did not make any errors of commission. Majority of the errors are due to imprecise scope of bounding boxes. The system makes less than 5% errors (2% omission errors) after learning from about 5 training examples. (Note that at 5 training examples, the system is still evaluated on 15 unknown examples, and maintains 5% error rate). In addition, system achieves 0% error rate when presented with all known documents, which suggests that the template descriptions are consistent and complete with the data.

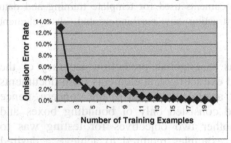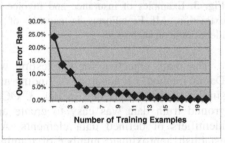

Fig. 4. Data element prediction accuracy.

5 Related Research

The document reverse engineering process may take many different forms and extent of automation. Some systems may have such knowledge preprogrammed, others, more flexible, may use some declarative representation for modeling document domains. Document models may be acquired in a variety of ways too. Some systems may require explicit rule coding for finding data elements. Others, through a graphical user interface, may support template design. Still, all data descriptions have to be detected and input by a user. Overall, application of form processing methods to complex documents may require manual or semi-manual preparation of complicated models, which makes them prohibitively expensive due to labor costs.

For example, Koppen et al. (1998) describe a system for an automated evaluation of invoices. The purpose of the system is to detect and recognize price entries of item tables in invoices. The system is not model-driven but it makes many assumptions about the structure of the invoices and data elements constituting a table. It does not attempt to extract other, non-table like date elements. Consequently, the system seems to be restricted to a very specific category of documents.

Bayer and Mogg-Schneider (1997) describe a more flexible system for processing invoices. The system consists of two components, OCR tool and data extraction component that contains declarative knowledge about the domain. The system uses special language for describing objects in structured documents. The drawback of the method is that document models have to be carefully crafted and described by a document engineer. In a selected domain of insurance invoices, the system achieved 50% automation rate with an error rate below 1% on selected data elements. Even though the system has a potential for processing diverse documents, the document definition process seems to be complex.

In contrast to those systems, the InTeGen method completely automates the process of document definition through machine learning. The method is applicable to a variety of flexible form documents, and provides easy and fast document definition. The only drawback of the method, the necessity of defining models for each document type, is offset by the simple and expeditious document definition process.

In a broader sense, the InTeGen method is related to the automated discovery of logical structure in text documents (Esposito et al., 1994; Cesarini et al, 1999). The aim of automated discovery of logical structure is to create a hierarchy of logical components of a document from given physical instances of the document. Most of the methods target specific types of documents, such as technical papers or office documents. Each approach assumes some degree of prior knowledge of the style of a document.

Another fundamental distinction in various approaches stems from the relative roles of content and layout in the definition of a logical structure. A logical structure is more content-oriented if its definition relies more heavily on internal meaning. A layout-oriented structure relies more heavily on visual presentation. Therefore, in content-oriented methods, OCR data is analyzed and utilized; whereas, in layout-oriented methods, image-processing methods, such as segmentation, projection profiles, texture analysis, play the major role (Dengel, 1992, Summers, 1995).

6 Conclusions

Data extraction from context-form type documents is a difficult problem because of the indefinite structure of such documents. Data fields do not have fixed locations and characteristics on a page, and may flow between pages of documents. These documents are frequently beyond the capability of the currently commercially available forms processing systems, which require significant user involvement in the process of defining fields for extraction. The process requires competence and is time consuming. The user has to: (1) learn how to operate a new system, (2) discover patterns in data format, and (3) learn ways of transferring this knowledge to the document processing system. The third requirement may be extremely time consuming and often frustrating given the system constraints. Moreover, the user's input, calculations and estimations may often be imprecise and lead to system errors.

The InTeGen-DataX method offers several advantages over the earlier methods. The most important feature manifests itself in the minimal user's involvement in the process of defining fields for extraction. The user is only required to identify what the location of the object of extraction is. The user is not required to provide any additional characterization of the object. All necessary information needed to characterize the object and its context is acquired automatically. It minimizes human effort and chances for introducing errors. Additionally, the system supports data element definition process by predicting DEs based on currently defined templates. This feature greatly speeds up template development, and assures template quality.

The next advantage results from robust generalization of training examples. The example documents are real documents as opposed to synthetic document models. This way the system encounters not only variability in data arrangement but also possible noise. By processing and filtering out noisy descriptions, the system becomes immune to noise when processing subsequent documents. In addition, machine learning makes it feasible to include the template generation module in a real-time system, and acquire knowledge about new document cases during production. The input can be directed from key-from-image processing of failed documents. This creates opportunity for the document processing system to become instantly responsive to incoming variations in document designs.

Finally, the symbolic descriptive patterns are language independent. The method could be integrated with versatile OCR devices that process documents in different languages, e.g. Latin, Cyrillic, Greek, Arabic, Japanese, or Chinese.

References

Bayer, T., Mogg-Schneider, H., "A Generic System for Processing Invoices," *Proc. Int. Conf. on Doc. Analysis and Recognition*, pp.740–744, IEEE Computer Society Press, 1997.

Cesarini, F., Francesconi, E., Gori, M., and Soda, G., "A Two Level Knowledge Approach for Understanding Documents of a Multi-Class Domain," *Proc. Int. Conf. on Doc. Analysis and Recognition*, pp.135–138, IEEE Computer Society Press, 1999.

Dengel, A., "ANASTASIL: A System for Low-Level and High-Level Geometric Analysis of Printed Documents" in *Structured Document Image Analysis*, Springer-Verlag, Berlin, 1992.

Esposito, F., Malerba, D., and Semeraro, G., "Multistrategy Learning for Document Recognition," *Applied Artificial Intelligence*, Vol. 8, pp.33–94, 1994.

Koppen, M., Waldostl, D., and Nickolay, B., "A System for the Evaluation of Invoices," in *Document Analysis Systems II*, pp. 223–241, World Scientific, 1998.

Summers, K., "Near-Wordless Document Structure Classification," *Proc. Int. Conf. On Document Analysis and Recognition*, IEEE Computer Society Press, 1995.

Wnek, J., "Learning to Identify Hundreds of Flex-form Documents," *Proc. of SPIE, Document Recognition and Retrieval VI*, D. Lopresti and J. Zhou (Eds.), Vol. 3651, pp. 173–182, 1999.

Configuration REcognition Model for Complex Reverse Engineering Methods: *2(CREM)*

Karim Hadjar, Oliver Hitz, Lyse Robadey, and Rolf Ingold

DIUF, University of Fribourg,
Chemin du Musée 3, 1700 Fribourg, Switzerland,
{firstname.lastname}@unifr.ch

Abstract. This paper describes *2(CREM)*, a recognition method to be applied on documents with complex structures allowing incremental learning in an interactive environment. The classification is driven by a model, which contains a static as well as a dynamic part and evolves by use. The first prototype of *2(CREM)* has been tested on four different phases of newspaper image analysis: line segment recognition, frame recognition, line merging into blocks, and logical labeling. Some promising experimental results are reported.

1 Introduction

In the field of document recognition many improvements have been made during the last decade. However, there is still a lack especially in recognizing complex structured documents, such as newspapers or magazines.

The first layout analysis methods were focused on simple document structures [1]. Some recent works show a great interest in complex layout analysis [2, 3,4], and introduce the concept of learning-based algorithms [5].

Currently known approaches rely on document models, which are either set up by hand or generated automatically in a previous learning step that needs a lot of ground-truthed data [6]. The drawback is that such models do not accommodate easily to new situations, a condition that is very important when dealing with complex document structures.

Human beings are able to cope with new situations using their knowledge. They learn from experiences and improve their knowledge incrementally. Given the variety of different types of documents, the same strategy should be applied to document recognition by computers.

We believe that *interactive incremental learning* is an important issue for document recognition. It is one of the main goals of the CIDRE[1] project, which aims at building a semi automatic document recognition system that constructs its knowledge incrementally through the interaction with the user. Our previous work was devoted to software architecture issues [7,8] as well as logical structure and font recognition algorithms [9,10].

---

[1] CIDRE stands for Cooperative and Interactive Document Reverse Engineering and is supported by the Swiss National Fund for Scientific Research, code 2000-059356.99-1.

D. Lopresti, J. Hu, and R. Kashi (Eds.): DAS 2002, LNCS 2423, pp. 469–479, 2002.
© Springer-Verlag Berlin Heidelberg 2002

In this paper we introduce *2(CREM)*, which stands for Configuration REcogntion Model for Complex Reverse Engineering Methods. It is an interactive recognition method for complex structured documents based on incremental learning.

This paper is organized as follows: in section 2 we introduce the principles of *2(CREM)*. Section 3 is devoted to the experimental part and the results obtained. Finally in section 4 we conclude our work and give some perspectives for future work.

2   *2(CREM)* Principles

The goal of *2(CREM)* is to classify document primitives named "objects". Depending on the application, these objects can be line segments, frames, text lines, etc.

An object is associated with different attributes such as position and size, font definition, neighborhood relation etc. Not all attributes are necessary to classify an object. Some classification tasks use a subset of the available attributes. In *2(CREM)*, such attributes are called "relevant attributes". They are defined in the static part of a *2(CREM)* model, as illustrated in figure 1. The static part therefore defines all possible features that can be used for classification.

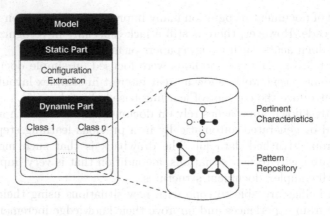

Fig. 1. The model of *2(CREM)*.

The set of features is called "configurations". In the dynamic part of a model, reference configurations are stored for every class. These configurations represent the knowledge of the model and are called "patterns".

A configuration consists of different kinds of characteristics associated to the object to be classified or to other objects referred to by neighborhood relations. The dynamic part contains a set of relevant attributes per class.

The classification procedure of the *2(CREM)* is illustrated on figure 2. For every object to classify, we extract a configuration according to the static part

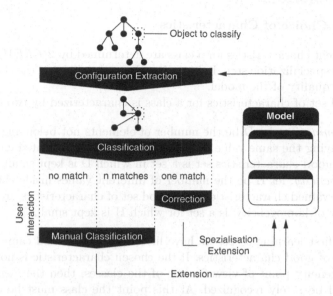

Fig. 2. Architecture of *2(CREM)*.

of the model. This configuration is then compared to the patterns of each class, by taking into account the pertinent characteristics.

This comparison produces three possible alternatives:

- The configuration matches exactly one class: this is the ideal case. The system classified the object. User interaction is possible to correct erroneous classifications.
- The configuration matches multiple classes: there is no discriminating characteristic among the classes. User interaction is required to resolve this ambiguity.
- The configuration does not match any class: the object is classified as "unknown". User interaction is required to classify the object.

The system displays the results by highlighting objects that do not belong to a unique class. The user can then label the object manually; by doing so, he does not only solve the problem of this object, but he also modifies the model, allowing thus other objects to be reclassified according to this incremental learning.

User interactions modify the model in a threefold manner:

- Extension: when a previously unknown configuration is classified by the user, it becomes a pattern. The model is therefore extended with new knowledge.
- Specialization: when a configuration is classified incorrectly or ambiguously by the system and the user solves the conflict, a characteristic is added to the set of pertinent characteristics. This results in a more specialized model.
- Generalization: unknown configurations are also the result of a model which is too discriminating. In this case, characteristics can be removed from the set of pertinent characteristics to render the model more general.

For a more formal description of this method please refer to [11].

2.1 The Choice of Characteristics

The pertinent characteristics for a class are determined by *2(CREM)*, during the creation or specialization step. In both situations, the choice of the characteristics affects the quality of the model.

A good set of characteristics for a class is characterized by two criteria:

– *Discrimination*: let D be the number of elements not belonging to the class and having the same value as class pattern for the evaluated characteristics set. A good characteristics set is a set in which D is kept small.
– *Homogeneity*: let H be the number of different values inside class members for the valued characteristic set. A good set of characteristics, from the point of view of homogeneity, is a set for which H is kept small.

In the first learning steps, we have little information and cannot guarantee the choice of good characteristics. If the chosen characteristic is not good from the homogeneity point of view for one of the classes, then the members of the classes will be rarely recognized. At this point the class must be extended by adding new patterns.

One solution would be to try all the combinations of the characteristics and to choose those minimizing the number of patterns but this leads to exponential growth. Therefore a greedy algorithm is used to determine a set of characteristics for each class according to its patterns, its members and the characteristics not belonging to it.

2.2 Example

We will illustrate *2(CREM)* on a simplified document classification example shown figure 3.

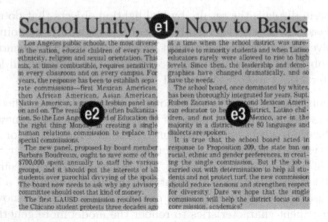

Fig. 3. Document example with three objects.

The static part of the chosen model is defined by two attributes that are the type and the font of the objects. Every object is represented by a list of "attribute-value" pairs that correspond to its configuration:

- $e_1 = \{(\text{Type} : \text{textblock}), (\text{Font} : \text{big})\}$
- $e_2 = \{(\text{Type} : \text{textblock}), (\text{Font} : \text{small})\}$
- $e_3 = \{(\text{Type} : \text{textblock}), (\text{Font} : \text{small})\}$

As we can notice, both e_2 and e_3 configurations are equivalent. Now we simulate the interactive classification process.

Only the static part of our model contains data (staticpart = {Type, Font}). No information about any classes is available yet, since there are no discriminating attributes and patterns.

At the beginning the system finds no class for any object of the document.

Step 1

- The user classifies interactively object e_1 as "title".
- The system updates the dynamic part of its model :
  - class "title"
    * $\text{pattern}_1 = \{(\text{Type} : \text{textblock}), (\text{Font} : \text{big})\}$
    * discriminating attributes $= 0$
- The configuration of object e_1 has become $pattern_1$ of the "title" class.

As there is a discriminating attribute in the model for the class "title", the system classifies every object in the class "title".

Step 2

- The user classifies object e_2 in the class "paragraph".
- The system updates the model's dynamic part:
  - class "title"
    * $\text{pattern}_1 = \{(\text{Type} : \text{textblock}), (\text{Font} : \text{big})\}$
    * discriminating attributes $= \text{Font}$
  - class "paragraph"
    * $\text{pattern}_1 = \{(\text{Type} : \text{textblock}), (\text{Font} : \text{small})\}$
    * discriminatingattributes $= \{\text{Font}\}$
- The only potential discriminating attribute was "Font" and the configuration has become pattern_1 of the class "paragraph".

Object e_1 is classified "title" and objects e_2 and e_3 are classified "paragraph".

3   Tests & Results

The first prototype of *2(CREM)* has been tested on four different applications: thread recognition, frame recognition, text lines merging into blocks and logical labeling.

All the experiments described were conducted on a set of pages from the Los Angeles Times (LAT) newspaper (see figure 4) using the XMIllum environment [8]. All the information (of the document as well as of the model) is represented in XML. The tool allows the user to browse throw the recognition results, to correct them manually and thus to adapt the document model incrementally.

The formal description of the four applications is based on graphs; please refer to [11] for more details.

Fig. 4. Page sample of LAT.

3.1 2(CREM) Applied to Segmentation

Thread Recognition. Concerning thread recognition, we distinguish three types of threads: thread internal separator, thread external separator and thread underline. The first one is used inside articles (often for putting eye-catchers), the second one is used to delimitate articles, and the third one is used to indicate a title or a subject (figure 5).

least 2 square miles must be treated every year until the Great Basin air agency determines that federal **Please see WATER, A8**

ences are based more on personalities than policies—undercuts U.S. hopes for a quick start to peace **Please see KOSOVO, A4**

④

Asian Americans Finding Cracks in the Glass Ceiling

■ **Business:** But because of societal and cultural barriers, top management jobs are still elusive for many.

By DON LEE
TIMES STAFF WRITER

Robert Nakasone grew up as one of a handful of Asian Americans in the San Fernando Valley community of of Tujunga. That, he says, forced him to assimilate early and prepared him for the corporate world.

But as he moved up the ladder at Toys R Us, the third-generation Japanese American also kept a reminder of his family's history—a brown government blanket issued

officer at the $11-billion toy company based in New Jersey, becoming the sole Asian American CEO of a Fortune 500 company that he or she did not found.

"I just didn't feel myself as being

REACHING CRITICAL MASS
Asian Americans in California
■ Last in a series

a minority," said Nakasone, a graduate of Claremont Men's College and the University of Chicago

Fig. 5. Examples of thread types: (1), (2) and (3) are internal separators while (4) is an external separator.

The results of the thread recognition on 81 pages of the LAT are shown in table 1.

Table 1. Thread recognition results.

Thread	External Separator	Internal Separator	Underline
Recognized	90%	81%	90%
Misclassified	1%	1%	5%
Unknown	9%	18%	5%
Conflicts	0%	0%	0%

The "unknown" entry represents objects that have not been assigned to any class; the "conflicts" entry corresponds to objects assigned to more than one class. Finally, objects that were classified wrong are reported in the row "misclassified".

Frame Recognition. For the frames, we have identified two main classes which a frame may belong to:

- external separator frames separate articles from each other;
- internal separator frames are found inside articles.

The results of the frame recognition process applied on 114 pages of the LAT are shown in table 2.

Table 2. Frame recognition results.

Frames	External Separator	Internal Separator
Recognized	98%	83%
Misclassified	1%	15%
Unknown	0%	2%
Conflicts	2%	0%

Line Merging. For the line merging application, the objects to be classified are couples of neighboring text lines relatively to a vertical axis and the classes are "merging" or "not merging". Using incremental learning the system builds the whole set of possible configurations. *2(CREM)* outperforms the traditional line merging algorithms based on fixed rules.

On 29 pages of the LAT the following results have been obtained for line merging:

The presentation of the results is a little bit different, because instead of counting the number of couples of lines correctly classified, we counted the number of blocks correctly segmented. We reached 99.2% of success with only 6 incorrectly segmented blocks out of 752 blocks. These mistakes are configurations not faced during the training phase.

3.2   *2(CREM)* Applied to Logical Structure

2(CREM) has also been applied to the logical structure recognition problem and more precisely to logical labeling of text blocks. In complex documents, the diversity of labels is important. We have classified text blocks in 14 different classes: basic text, title, subtitle, author, author's function, summary, source, etc.

Table 3 shows the results for the logical structure recognition. Due to the number of classes, only the most relevant ones have been represented in our results: basic text, title, authors, summary, and source. The results of the other classes have been grouped under column "others".

Table 3. Logical structure recognition results.

Logical labeling	Basic text	Titles	Authors	Summary	Sources	Others
Recognized	90%	69%	96%	84%	94%	75%
Misclassified	0%	7%	3%	2%	3%	2%
Unknown	5%	18%	1%	0%	3%	15%
Conflicts	5%	6%	0%	14%	0%	8%

3.3 Convergence of the Model

At the beginning, no object is recognized and we would like the model to recognize almost all objects presented after the learning step. We can say that our method converges if for a finite set of objects and corrections it succeeds to build a model capable to classify correctly all set's objects. This is illustrated in figure 6.

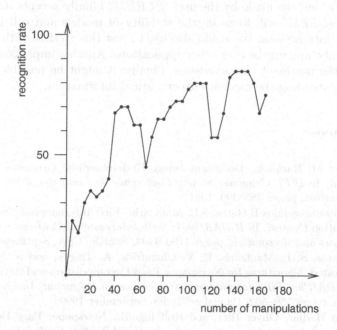

Fig. 6. Recognition rate vs. the number of manipulations.

From our observation, we believe that if the choice of the characteristics of the static part is pertinent, then the method converges; because if two objects do not belong to the same class, the system should find a characteristic which can be used to distinguish them.

In practice, the method does not converge if we can't find characteristics allowing to distinguish objects from different classes or if we cannot try all the subsets of characteristics for each class.

All the applications developed above have required only a few manipulations in order to reach an acceptable recognition rate.

4   Conclusion

In this paper we describe a classification method featuring interactive incremental learning named *2(CREM)*. Encouraging experimental results are reported concerning its application for recognition of complex structured documents.

Collecting ground-truthed documents has become a major concern of our research community. We believe that *2(CREM)* can be used successfully as a tool to build ground-truthed repositories: instead of manually labeling documents, users can, through some mouse clicks, easily produce ground-truthed data.

Several improvements are required to make *2(CREM)* more reliable and practicable. At the present stage, there is a total trust in the user actions, so that if there is a mistake made by the user *2(CREM)* blindly accepts it. Our future work on *2(CREM)* will focus on the stability of models and will handle erroneous user interactions. We would also like to test this method with other types of documents, and maybe even other applications. Another important issue is the choice of the pertinent characteristics. Finally, it might be possible to perform better by extending the models with statistical information.

References

[1] Robert M. Haralick. Document Image Understanding: Geometric and Logical Layout. In *IEEE Computer Society Conference on Computer Vision and Pattern Recognition*, pages 385–390, 1994.

[2] A. Antonacopoulos B.Gatos, S.L. Mantzaris. First International Newspaper Segmentation Contest. In *ICDAR'2001: Sixth International Conference on Document Analysis and Recognition*, pages 1190–1194, Seattle, USA, September 2001.

[3] B. Gatos, S. L. Mantzaris, K. V. Chandrios, A. Tsigris, and S. J. Perantonis. Integrated Algorithms for Newspaper Page Decomposition and Article Tracking. In *ICDAR'99: Fifth International Conference on Document Analysis and Recognition*, pages 559–562, Bangalore, India, September 1999.

[4] Karim Hadjar, Oliver Hitz, and Rolf Ingold. Newspaper Page Decomposition Using a Split and Merge Approach. In *ICDAR'2001: Sixth International Conference on Document Analysis and Recognition*, pages 1186–1189, Seattle, USA, September 2001.

[5] Pierre Heroux, Eric Trupin, and Yves Lecourtier. Modélisation et classification pour la rétroconversion des documents. In *CIFED'2000: Colloque International Francophone sur l'Ecrit et le Document*, pages 413–421, Lyon, France, jul 2000.

[6] J. Hu, R. Kashi, D. Lopresti, G. Nagy, and G. Wilfong. Why Table Ground Truthing is Hard. In *ICDAR'2001: Sixth International Conference on Document Analysis and Recognition*, pages 129–133, Seattle, USA, September 2001.

[7] Frédéric Bapst. *Reconnaissance de documents assisté: architecture logicielle et intégration de savoir-faire.* PhD thesis, University of Fribourg, 1998.

[8] Oliver Hitz, Lyse Robadey, and Rolf Ingold. An Architecture for Editing Document Recognition Results Using XML. In *DAS'2000: 4th International Workshop on Document Analysis Systems*, pages 385–396, Rio de Janeiro, Brazil, December 2000.

[9] Rolf Brugger, Abdelwahab Zramdini, and Rolf Ingold. Modeling Documents for Structure Recognition Using Generalized N-Grams. In *ICDAR'97: Fourth International Conference on Document Analysis and Recognition*, pages 56–61, Ulm, Germany, August 1997.

[10] Abdelwahab Zramdini. *Study of Optical Font Recognition Based on Global Typographical Features*. PhD thesis, University of Fribourg, 1995.

[11] Lyse Robadey. *Une méthode de reconnaissance structurelle de documents complexes basée sur des patterns bidimensionnels*. PhD thesis, University of Fribourg, 2001.

Electronic Document Publishing Using DjVu

Artem Mikheev[1], Luc Vincent[1], Mike Hawrylycz[1], and
Léon Bottou[2]

[1] Lizardtech Software, 1008 Western Avenue,
Seattle WA 98105, USA
lvincent@lizardtech.com
http://www.lizardtech.com
[2] NEC Research Institute, 4 Independence Way,
Princeton, NJ 08540–6634, USA
leon@bottou.org

Abstract. Online access to complex compound documents with client side search and browsing capability is one of the key requirements of effective content management. "DjVu" (Déjà Vu) is a highly efficient document image compression methodology, a file format, and a delivery platform that, when considered together, has shown to effectively address these issues [1]. Originally developed for scanned color documents, the DjVu technology was recently expanded to electronic documents. The small file sizes and very efficient document browsing make DjVu a compelling alternative to such document interchange formats as PostScript or PDF. In addition, DjVu offers a uniform viewing experience for electronic or scanned original documents, on any platform, over any connection speed, which is ideal for digital libraries and electronic publishing. This paper describes the basics of DjVu encoding, with emphasis on the particular challenges posed by electronic sources. The DjVu Virtual Printer Driver we implemented as "Universal DjVu Converter" is then introduced. Basic performance statistics are given, and enterprise workflow applications of this technology are highlighted.

1   Scanned Document Publishing and DjVu

Document image processing for the Internet, including storage, presentation, and transmission systems for complex compound documents is one of the fundamental challenges of current content management systems. Enterprise applications, including corporate Intranet usage and internal workflow management systems require rapid transmission and feature-rich viewing that enable users to quickly access and browse important documents. The advent of wireless communications only further stresses the technology required to address these problems as transmission costs remain significant and the processing capacity of portable client devices is limited.

In parallel, digital libraries are becoming a more accepted form of information archiving, search, retrieval, and taxonomy. However, online document libraries will succeed only to the extent that they prove adequate and effective

D. Lopresti, J. Hu, and R. Kashi (Eds.): DAS 2002, LNCS 2423, pp. 480–490, 2002.

for common and mass usage. A key to surmounting these technological hurdles is understanding the workflow of the document storage, transmission, and viewing and the adoption of standards and applications that perform naturally at each stage of the process.

The last several years have seen a growing demand for technology that could handle *color* documents, whether scanned or electronic, in an effective manner. Such applications as online digital libraries with ancient or historical documents, online catalogs for e-commerce sites, online publishing, forms processing, and scientific publication, are in need of an efficient compression technique for color documents. The availability of low-cost, high quality color scanners, the recent emergence of high-speed production color scanners, and the appearance of ultra high resolution digital cameras open the door to such applications.

Compression technology for bitonal (black and white) document images has a long history [2]. It is the basis of a large and fast growing industry with widely accepted standards (Group 3, MMR/Group 4), as well as still emerging standards (JBIG1, JBIG2). Standard color image compression algorithms are grossly inadequate for the type of applications mentioned earlier because associated file sizes are still excessively large if one wants to preserve the readability of the text: compressed with JPEG, a color image of a typical magazine page scanned at 100dpi (dots per inch) is around 100–200KB, and is barely readable. The same page at 300dpi is of acceptable quality, but occupies at least 500KB to 1 MB. These sizes are impractical for online document browsing, even with broadband connections.

A notable observation about document encoding is that preserving the readability of the text and the sharpness of line art requires high resolution (typically 300–600dpi) and the preservation of sharp edges. On the other hand, preserving the appearance of continuous-tone images and background paper textures does not require as high a resolution (typically, 100dpi is sufficient). An obvious way to take advantage of this is to *segment* these elements into separate layers. The foreground layer would contain the text and line drawings, while the background layer would contain continuous-tone pictures and background textures. This multi-layer raster representation is a key element in various emerging document interchange products and standards such as MRC, TIFF-FX, JPEG2000 (part 6), and of course DjVu! The separation method brings another considerable advantage to DjVu: since the text layer is separated, it can be stored in a chunk at the beginning of the image file and decoded by the viewer as soon as it arrives in the client machine. Along with the DjVu "Hidden Text Layer", this enables immediate access for text search and retrieval applications.

The general requirements for an acceptable user experience may be described as follows: The text and line diagrams should appear on the display after only a few seconds delay. This means that the text layer must fit within 20–40KB, under the assumption of a 56KB/sec modem connection. The pictures and other background items would subsequently appear, improving the image quality as more bits arrive. The overall size of the file should be in the order of 50–100KB to bound the overall transmission time and storage requirements.

Thanks to its outstanding compression capabilities, excellent image quality, simple and effective file format, and highly efficient viewing and browsing, DjVu has proven to provide a content delivery platform that can successfully meet all the challenges mentioned above [1,3,4,5,6]. With DjVu, pages scanned at 300dpi in full color can be compressed down to 30–80KB files from 25MB originals with excellent quality. This puts the size of high-quality scanned pages in the same order of magnitude as a typical HTML page. Like HTML pages, DjVu pages are displayed progressively within a web browser window, via a custom plugin. Panning, zooming, and navigation is highly efficient, even though pages are internally kept in a partially decoded representation, which requires only about 2MB of cache. In short, the DjVu technology has all the features required to provide an excellent end-user experience when browsing collections of complex color documents.

2   DjVu Encoding Basics

The basic idea behind DjVu is to separate the text from the background and pictures and to use different techniques to compress each of those components. Traditional methods are either designed to compress natural images with few edges (JPEG), or to compress black and white document images almost entirely composed of sharp edges (Group 3, MMR/Group 4, and JBIG1). The DjVu technique combines the best of both approaches. A foreground/background separation algorithm segments images into separately compressed layers:

- The **background layer** contains a low resolution (typically 100 dpi.) background image representing details that are best encoded using a continuous tone technique. This usually includes the document background and the pictures. For the background and foreground images, DjVu uses a progressive, wavelet-based compression algorithm called *IW44* or *DjVuPhoto*. IW44 offers many key advantages over existing continuous-tone image compression methods that are particularly useful for efficient panning and zooming of large images.
- The **foreground layer** contains a high resolution bitonal *mask image* (typically 300 to 600 dpi) that accurately defines the shape of details with sharp edges such as text and line-art. The optional color information is either encoded as a solid color per connected component in the mask, or as a very low resolution *foreground image* (typically 25 dpi) whose colors are applied using the mask as a stencil. The bitonal mask image is encoded with a new bi-level image compression algorithm dubbed *JB2* or *DjVuBitonal*. It is a variation on AT&T's proposal to the emerging JBIG2 standard. The basic idea of JB2 is to locate individual shapes on the page (such as characters), and to use a shape clustering algorithm to find similarities between shapes [7,8].

The DjVu encoder was designed to be as generic as possible. The only information it requires about the document is its scanning resolution. This puts an extraordinary constraint on the segmentation algorithms used to obtain the foreground/background separation. Most of the details are beyond the scope of this aritcle and the reader is referred to [9].

3   DjVu for Electronic Documents

Scanned documents and documents of electronic source origin present distinct challenges for encoding. While DjVu was initially designed for scanned documents, it soon became apparent that it could also significantly improve the compression rate and speed of rendering of electronic documents such as PostScript, PDF or MSWord. These document description languages are generally slow to render, may produce very large files and are often platform dependent (mostly because of the fonts and character sets they rely on).

Converting such documents into DjVu can be done by first rendering them into a high-resolution color raster image and then converting it to DjVu. However, relying on a purely pixel-based intermediate representation is less than ideal in that it disregards essential information about the document, such as what is text and what is not. This information could be used to significantly improve conversion quality, which, for electronic documents, is essential. In addition, intermediate pixel-based representations are expensive to compute and require large amounts of RAM. One would therefore like the conversion process to work directly on the existing *structured page information* [10], that is, high level objects such as text, fonts, colors, embedded images, etc., instead of pixels.

Structured page information for electronic documents is used in a large variety of file formats such as the MSWord .doc files, PDF files, or PostScript files. Printing such files converts the structured information into a list of drawing operations such as "fill a rectangle", "draw a line", "draw an image" or "draw a piece of text". This can be interpreted as an ordered list of predefined graphic objects, which can—and often do—overlap. The challenge is to efficiently turn this ordered list into only two layers, for subsequent DJVu compression.

A novel and general framework for unifying the concepts underlying scanned and electronic DjVu segmentation was recently presented in [9]. The authors show how a concept known as the Minimum Description Length (MDL) principle [11] can be used as a type of universal segmentation tool to determine which objects are defined in the foreground and background for both scanned and electronic documents. In essence the MDL principle works by minimizing the overall coding cost. This coding cost is the sum of the number of bits necessary to encode the image (*the encoding bit cost*) and the number of bits necessary to encode the discrepancy between the encoded image and the original image (*the discrepancy bit cost*). This general approach can be successfully used on raster data (scanned documents) as well as electronic documents, albeit using substantially different algorithms.

Though DjVu converted file sizes vary depending on the type of electronic document converted to DjVu, file sizes generally compare favorably. As a rule of thumb, one can expect a file size reduction of a factor 2 to 50. This is somewhat remarkable considering that the originals were electronic. The resulting DjVu files are a completely portable version of their original electronic counterparts: they do not depend on any system-specific objects such as fonts; like all DjVu files, they are very efficient to transmit, display, store, and they can be viewed on any platform. In addition, they contain a *hidden text layer* that is a faithful representation of the text in the original electronic document, and is key for search and retrieval. This makes DjVu an excellent document interchange format.

Our electronic to DjVu document conversion framework and algorithms are referred to as *DjVuDigital*. Current implementations include a Ghostscript driver [12], which enables the creation of DjVu from PostScript and PDF, and a Windows Virtual Printer Driver, which we now describe.

4   The DjVu Virtual Printer Driver

An important class of a file format conversion applications are called Virtual Printer Drivers (VPD). These are applications that configure as if they were standard system or network printers, but serve the role of file format interchange devices. There are many brands and variations of VPDs currently on the market that allow conversion between most of the commonly used graphic file formats. Adobe PDFWriter^{TM} is essentially a VPD converting Postscript or MSWord documents into PDF. Below we describe the steps and workflow of the Lizardtech Software DjVu VPD. The details are given with respect to an implementation on the Microsoft Windows architecture, but the principles are the same for most operating systems.

4.1   Representation of Printed Output in Metafile Form

Most popular Windows applications have printing functionality: the user is able to specify the specific printer device and output the document to that device. The first step in converting an electronic document to DjVu is the representation of the structured page information as an Enhanced Metafile. Enhanced Metafiles are used in the DjVu VPD to store a picture created by using the Win32 GDI functions.

The Windows Enhanced Metafile format (EMF) is used to represent both scalable vector and bitmap graphics under Windows. This format is widely used in Windows applications for clipboard, client-server data exchange and within the Windows spooler. An EMF file consists of the following elements: a header, a table of handles to GDI objects, a private palette, and an array of metafile records. EMF facilitates a device independence description of objects. It gives a uniform object representation whether it appears on a printer, a plotter, the desktop, or in the client area of any Win32-based application. In this respect, one can think of EMFs as the Windows equivalent of Adobe PostScript files. An example is shown in Fig. 1.

Although there are many ways for the application to perform printing to a document, the two main methods are:

1. Print by rasterizing consecutive vertical bands of the document. Then send the representation of those bands in the bitmap form to the printer.
2. Print by drawing separate drawing elements on the printer device context.

The second method leads to much faster printing in most cases and is used by most modern applications. One consequence of this method is that the corresponding generated EMF contains a sequence of overlapping drawing elements that need to be rendered. While, at first, this may seem like a drawback, it is quite advantageous to the algorithm used by the VPD.

The size of the metafile generated depends greatly on the content of the source electronic document. For example, let us consider printing the front page of the Web site CNN (http://www.cnn.com) using Internet Explorer 5.5. Depending on daily variations on the site, the typical Metafile it produces is 2.5MB in size, which is somewhat typical for letter-size documents printed at 300dpi. This metafile contains about 60,000 different records, however only 8,000 of them represent drawing elements. Rarely, documents can produce metafiles of extremely large size. In one instance, we came across a 1-page document which generated a metafile of close to 100MB! This particular metafile contained 5 Million records, about 450,000 of which corresponding to the actual drawing elements.

```
⊞  1: ENHMETAHEADER
   2: SelectObject(hDC, GetStockObject(BLACK_PEN));, 12 bytes
   3: SelectObject(hDC, GetStockObject(WHITE_BRUSH));, 12 byt
   4: SelectObject(hDC, GetStockObject(DEVICE_DEFAULT_FONT)
   5: MoveToEx(hDC, 0, 0, NULL);, 16 bytes
   6: SetBrushOrgEx(hDC, 0, 0, NULL);, 16 bytes
   7: SetICMMode(hDC, 1);, 12 bytes
   8: SetColorSpace(hDC, GetStockObject(0x14 /*Unknown*/));, 1
   9: // Unknown record [119], 20 bytes
  10: SetViewportOrgEx(hDC, 0, 0, NULL);, 16 bytes
  11: SaveDC(hDC);, 8 bytes
  12: SetViewportOrgEx(hDC, 0, 0, NULL);, 16 bytes
  13: DeleteObject(hRegion);, 64 bytes
  14: hObj[1]=CreateSolidBrush(0x2FFFFFF);, 24 bytes
  15: SelectObject(hDC, hObj[1]);, 12 bytes
  16: SelectObject(hDC, GetStockObject(NULL_PEN));, 12 bytes
  17: SetROP2(hDC, R2_COPYPEN);, 12 bytes
  18: SetBkMode(hDC, OPAQUE);, 12 bytes
  19: Polygon(hDC, Points_1, 4);, 44 bytes
  20: SetBkMode(hDC, OPAQUE);, 12 bytes
```

Fig. 1. Realization of an Enhanced Metafile (EMF) and representative EMF commands.

DjVu documents being raster-based, they contain a certain resolution value, which needs to be specified before conversion. Currently acceptable values are in the range 50 to 4,800 dpi, with 400 dpi being the default. After conversion, the DjVu document will have physical dimensions defined by the printing application. These dimensions are easily computed from the user-specified resolution and the dimensions stored in the metafile.

4.2   Parsing the Metafile and Record Classification

The enhanced metafile is a sequence of records representing drawing operations applied to a specific Windows Device Context. These records are accessed using standard Win32 API calls. Some EMF records correspond to mode setting operations: they do not modify actual graphic content, but are important in that they determine how subsequent record should be rendered. Records that actually modify pixels of the Metafile Device Context are parsed, rendered, and then a decision is made whether they belong to the foreground or background DjVu layer.

This is complicated by the fact that, in order for overlaps to be accurately processed, EMF records need to be considered in reverse drawing order, that is, starting from the EMF record corresponding to the *last* element that should be drawn (topmost drawing element). For more information on this process, see [10]. For each page, two segmented layers are produced, which can then be sent to the back-end DjVu compressor. This back-end is essentially identical as the one used for scanned documents. In particular, it should be noted that it takes advantage of redundancy across pages in the JB2 compression, and also avoids spending any bits on IW44 compressed background regions that will be covered by foreground pixels.

Text capture is performed concurrently, without the need for any OCR. Indeed, EMF files contain bounding box and text character information. This information is parsed as essentially another object of the structured page information, and enables the DjVu "hidden text layer" to be easily created.

4.3   Overview of Virtual Printer Driver Workflow

The DjVu Virtual Printer Driver we implemented seamlessly installs like any system printer. Once installed, the process of conversion to DjVu starts after the user has selected a "Print" command from the host application's print menu. When the visible local or network printers are displayed, the user selects "DjVu VPD" from the drop down list. This causes the Windows application to generate an EMF file and then brings up the interface shown in Fig. 2. This interface includes a preview pane, which makes it easy to correct any application-specific settings required for producing the desired output.

At this point, the user has to specify the main conversion parameters: resolution, whether or not to include the hidden text layer, and final orientation of the document. The "Advanced Parameters" dialog box, shown in Fig. 3, allows the user to fine tune conversion for the specific document variation. In particular, control is given for the quality of the background encoding, the relative weight of importance of foreground versus background, and the limitations on the color

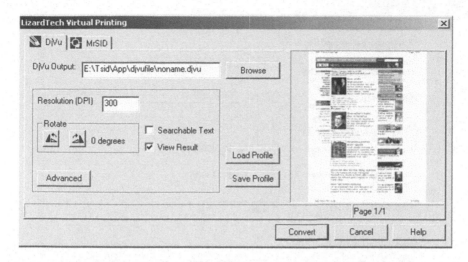

Fig. 2. Main Screen of DjVu Virtual Printer Driver

palate to be used. In 99% of cases, these advanced options do not need to be changed from their defaults.

5   Results and Conclusions

Extensive tests were conducted during the development of the VPD, analyzing both image quality upon conversion and printer performance. We found that the VPD performed well on a broad sample of document types, with specialized document types such as high resolution maps, or images with very large numbers of objects sometimes requiring tuning of the parameter settings for optimal results. The bulk of the tests were on desktop workstation running Pentium-4/1.4GHz with 256MB RAM. Documents of many several types were used for these tests, Fig. 4 showing some representative document types.

For each document class the original and converted sizes were recorded as well as the time to convert. The results shown in Table 1 were found to be typical expected performance.

Our results indicate that the DjVu VPD successfully converts almost all Windows type documents. Long PowerPoint documents including complex backgrounds sometimes take a long time to convert, owing to the inefficient way shaded backgrounds are represented in EMF records. This type of driver could have enormous benefit to the digital libraries and in enterprise applications where archival and business critical documents need to be published in a readily accessible manner.

The ability to capture searchable text is an extremely attractive feature in the above applications. As the text layer can be carried along with the encoded document, DjVu is easily integrated with document search and content management systems.

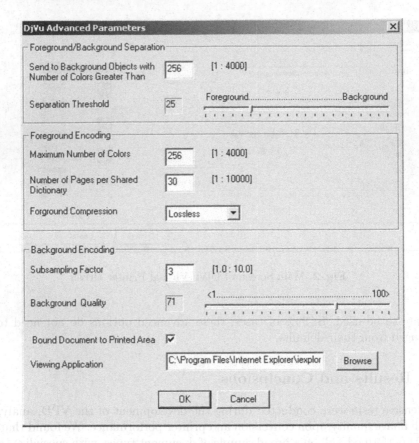

Fig. 3. Advanced Parameter Screen of Virtual Printer Driver

Table 1. Comparative size and conversion times using the VPD for several common document types, shown in Fig. 4. Performance data was obtained on a Pentium 4, 1.4GHz.

Document Name	Format	Number of Pages	Original Size	**DjVu** Size	Time to Convert
NY Times	PDF	92	25.9 MB	8.57 MB	12 m 32 s
HBS Review	PDF	132	8.75 MB	4.63 MB	11 m 5 s
Vector Map	PDF	1	1.67 MB	117 KB	19 s
Slides	PowerPoint	23	1.7 MB	1.05 MB	5 m 32 s
BBC Web page	HTML	3	174 KB	116 KB	14 s

A remarkable property of DjVu is the extreme file size reduction possible. This makes DjVu a natural choice in wireless and very constrained bandwidth situations. The DjVu VPD and its underlying technology could play an important role in the large scale preparation of documents for this use. With the recent

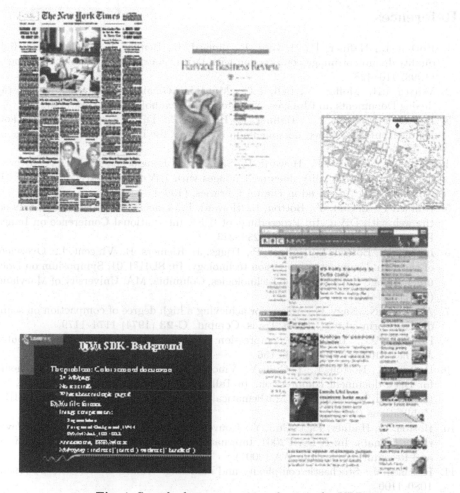

Fig. 4. Sample documents printed using the VPD

addition of electronic document conversion to its portfolio, DjVu becomes a serious, powerful document interchange format, able to address the needs of a wide range of users.

A full range of DjVu authoring products, from non-commercial software packages to full-feature, advanced packages designed for enterprise users, are available from Lizardtech Software, http://www.lizardtech.com. The technology is also partly available as open source at http://djvu.sourceforge.net. In addition, a growing number of third-party tools, from imaging packages such as *IrfanView* (http://www.irfanview.com)to searching and indexing engines such as the *Realview DjVu Index Filter* (http://www.realview.com.au),are supporting DjVu. The web site http://www.djvuzone.org is dedicated to the DjVu community, with news, documentations and many links to Digital libraries which use DjVu.

References

1. Bottou, L., Haffner, P., Howard, P., Simard, P., Bengio, Y., LeCun, Y.: High quality document image compression with DjVu. Journal of Electronic Imaging **7** (1998) 410–428
2. Witten, I.H., Moffat, A., Bell, T.C.: Managing Gigabytes: Compressing and Indexing Documents and Images. Van Nostrand Reinhold, New York (1994)
3. LeCun, Y., Bottou, L., , Haffner, P., Howard, P.: DjVu: a compression method for distributing scanned documents in color over the internet. In: Proceedings of Color 6, IST. (1998)
4. Bottou, L., Haffner, P., Howard, P., Simard, P., Bengio, Y., LeCun, Y.: Browsing through high quality document images with DjVu. In: Proceedings of IEEE Conference on Advanced in Digital Libraries. (1998)
5. Haffner, P., LeCun, Y., Bottou, L., Howard, P., Vincent, P.: Color documents on the web with DjVu. In: Proceedings of IEEE International Conference on Image Processing, Kobe, Japan (1999) 239–243
6. LeCun, Y., Bottou, L., Haffner, P., Triggs, J., Riemers, B., Vincent, L.: Overview of the djvu document compression technology. In: SDIUT'01, Symposium on Document Image Understanding Technologies, Columbia, MA, University of Maryland (2001) 119–122
7. Ascher, R.N., Nagy, G.: Means for achieving a high degree of compaction on scan-digitized printed text. IEEE Trans. Comput. **C-23** (1974) 1174–1179
8. Howard, P.G.: Text image compression using soft pattern matching. Computer Journal **40(2/3)** (1997) 146–156
9. Haffner, P., Bottou, L., LeCun, Y., Vincent, L.: A general segmentation scheme for DjVu document compression. In Talbot, H., Berman, M., eds.: ISMM'02, International Symposium on Mathematical Morphology, Sydney, Australia, CSIRO Publications (2002)
10. Bottou, L., Haffner, P., LeCun, Y.: Conversion of digital documents to multilayer raster formats. In: ICDAR'2001, International Conference on Document Analysis and Recognition, Seattle, WA (2001)
11. Rissanen, J.: Stochastic complexity and modeling. Annals of Statistics **14** (1986) 1080–1100
12. GhostScript: Home page at http://www.ghostscript.com (2002)

DAN: An Automatic Segmentation and Classification Engine for Paper Documents

L. Cinque, S. Levialdi, A. Malizia, and F. De Rosa

Dept. of Information Science,
Universita' "La Sapienza" di Roma Via Salaria 113, 00198 Roma, Italy
{cinque,levialdi,malizia,derosa}@dsi.uniroma1.it

Abstract. The paper documents recognition is fundamental for office automation becoming every day a more powerful tool in those fields where information is still on paper. Document recognition follows from data acquisition, from both journals, and entire books in order to transform them in digital objects. We present a new system DAN (Document Analysis on Network) for Document recognition that follows the Open Source methodologies, XML description for documents segmentation and classification, which turns to be beneficial in terms of classification precision, and general-purpose availability.

1 Introduction

The document analysis field is related to the semi-automatic management of paper documents. Such automation systems have been used in several fields: typically cataloguing and storing of documents, blueprints, faxing servers, character recognition software. Many different approaches have been used and standards are still lacking. Typical problems of document analysis systems are: layout segmentation, syntactic parsing, but also the selective extraction of information such as document types and semantic contents [1,2]. Most document processing packages are designed either for document recognition (i.e., indexing and archiving of document images) or for data acquisition (i.e., extracting data from filled forms). Document recognition is essentially the process of converting paper documents into digital images and indexing such data. Images are stored as data files (typically as TIFF files) and together with indexes are stored in a content management system. Most forms oriented products available on the market today instead require the user to redesign his forms in order to achieve acceptable recognition rates. In our case we can show that our model will work both with document images and forms. A central question is how to evaluate the effectiveness of such complex document analysis systems involving rather distinct components. In addition, we are interested in comparing different document categorization algorithms by their effectiveness [3,4,5]. A lot of different approaches have been proposed in the Document Analysis field. The existing works could be classified into three main classes: top-down systems, bottom-up systems, and mixed systems.

D. Lopresti, J. Hu, and R. Kashi (Eds.): DAS 2002, LNCS 2423, pp. 491–502, 2002.

Top-down methods start from the original image, and, using cut operations obtain regions, which have to be catalogued [6,7,8]. In order to be efficient, this method needs a priori information, which leads to a non-general approach. Bottom-up systems start from small parts of the document image, and then merge regions having similar characteristics [9,10]. Mixed systems instead optimize the use of both bottom-up and top-down methods in order to avoid their limititations [11,12]. Our approach, as shown in the following paragraphs, falls in the mixed systems class.

2   System Architecture Overview

Our system uses a split and merge technique similar to the approach that has been obtained by Nagy's X-Y cut algorithm [13], but instead of working top-down, we use the recognized horizontal and vertical lines to cut the image into small regions, merging with a quad-tree technique and image processing algorithms. We have built a system based onto these different phases, in order to perform the document classification in a modular and efficient way. The DAN (Document Analisys on Network) system is based onto the Segmentation and Classification engine, which takes a document as input, and performs an automatic classification, which is then presented to the end user with an interface called DANEditor. The DANEditor allows users to evaluate the automatic classification performed by the system and edit the textual annotation for indexing. The user can also edit the recognized regions by the classification engine and adjust their values and sizes. The output of these phase is an XML file which could be imported in a server with an xml DB for indexing and querying. The Figure (1) shows the DANEditor module, with it's tools for annotating and edit the automatic recognized region sizes and properties.

3   Segmentation and Classification Engine

The DAN system architecture includes four main components: the preprocessor (1), the split module (2), the merge module (3) and the classification module (4) as shown in Figure (2). The preprocessing algorithm (1) component is performed in order to enhance the quality of input data, removing portions of the image, which could be considered as noise. Moreover in this phase the original image of the document is loaded into main memory so obtain better computation performances. The Split module (2) takes input from the preprocessing phase and applies a particular quad-tree technique in order to split the document into small blocks. Then the Split module passes its result to the Merge module (3), which applies pre-classification criterion merging similar regions into big regions. We use local operators with variable thresholds in order to compute the pre-classification phase. Finally the engine of our system is in the Classification module (4) which executes the classification procedure according to the classification logic. In fact, the "brain" of our system is this classification engine, which

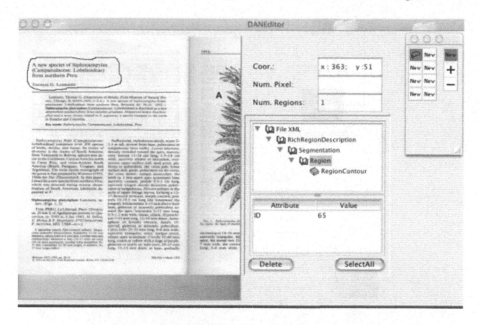

Fig. 1. Annotation and Editor tool diagram.

outputs segmented regions and their attributes, like type and size, in an XML file.

4   Split and Merge Phases

In this section we will explain, the details of the documents segmentation phases. We will show the techniques used for preprocessing, splitting and then merging the regions, with pre-classification information. It is important to understand that all of these phases are optimized for using them in a general environment without "a priori" knowledge of the documents format or size.

4.1   Preprocessing

In a production environment, the preprocessing stage of the recognition process may be very important in order to enhance the quality of the input data. The preprocessing phase performs two steps: loads the scanned image in main memory and computes the gray-level histogram extracting the three parameters discussed below. This approach is due to the fact that we want to reduce the amount of computations in the preprocessing phase obtaining a quick response method. Starting from a 256 gray levels document we compute the RI1 parameter, as the maximum value in the first half of the gray-level histogram. This value is not the absolute maximum of the histogram function, but considering intervals in a window of $\varepsilon = 5$ gray levels length. Then for the RI2 parameter we compute it in the same way but on the other half of the histogram, thus considering the

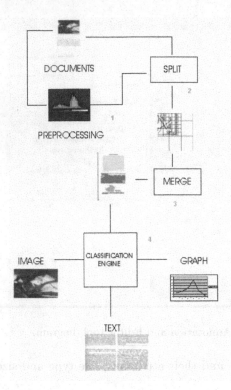

Fig. 2. Segmentation and Classification Engine architecture diagram.

whitening colors. Finally the last parameter RI3, which represents the point of separation between background and text, is the minimum between the RI1 and RI2 parameter. The use of these parameters will help in the split and merge phase in order to let our method adapt to different documents.

4.2   Split

The split procedure is based on two functions: the mean and the variance of scanned documents. Using the mean function we set a window (ranging along x and y coords) of pixels and compute the value:

$$f_m(i,j) = \left[\frac{\sum_i \sum_j f(i,j)}{(x_w - x_i + 1)(y_w - y_i + 1)} \right], \tag{1}$$

with $f(i,j)$ representing the gray-level values of the image pixels and (x_i, y_i), (x_w, y_w) the pixels between the chosen window in which we apply the mean operator.

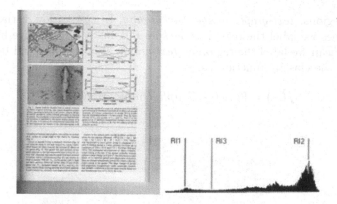

Fig. 3. Original document and its gray-levels histogram, we can see also the three parameters *RI*1, *RI*2, *RI*3.

Calling that mean value $f_m(i,j)$, we can compute the variance operator for every pixels of the document image, as described in the above function:

$$f_v(i,j) = \left[\sqrt{\frac{\sum_i \sum_j (f(i,j) - f_m(i,j))^2}{(x_w - x_i + 1)(y_w - y_i + 1)}} \right] \qquad (2)$$

During the split phase, the whole image of the document is split according to the extracted vertical and horizontal lines as well as the boundaries of recognized images. This results in many small zones (block sizes are within a range depending on the size of the image). We have decided to use an already known technique but modeling it with our specific parameters. This technique is known as *quad-tree*[14]. We use the quad-tree decomposition to perform spatial segmentation by assigning a condition by which nodes are split, according with the Ojala and Pietikainen idea [15]. We also added a post-processing routine for adjoining similar spatially adjacent nodes with different parents. A final block grouping stage can be added to merge all similar blocks to obtain arbitrarily shaped regions.

In order to choose if going on with splitting or stop the method we use the mean and variance operators. We simulate a split step in four regions, and using the mean and variance of the regions we find if these values are in a range; more deeply we have a variable threshold range (depending on the pre-processing phase) in order to distinguish low variance regions (thus with less information); moreover ranges are adaptive depending on the region area, in fact ranges are related to the inverse of region areas thus enhancing precision with wider regions. Finally we define the result of the split procedure so that:

$$\cup_i r_i = I \quad and \quad \cap_i r_i = \emptyset \qquad (3)$$

We apply labels to regions in order to pre-classify them. These pre-classification is useful to pass information to the merge phase. We define three class of regions: *text-graph*, *image*, *background*. In case of low variance and low mean values we label the region as *background*, instead if we have high variance and low mean we label the region as *text-graph*; else the label will be *image*. Let we define the classify function as:

$$f(r_i) = \{Text - Graph, Image, Background\}. \tag{4}$$

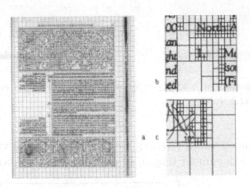

Fig. 4. Original document after the split phase (a), and two highlighted particulars (b) and (c)

4.3 Merge

The split operation results in a heavily over-segmented image. The goal of the merge operation is to join neighboring zones to form bigger rectangular zones. The first phase of merging consists of connecting neighbors regions with the same pre-classification value. Let's define the merge procedure above descript in terms of a boolean function regarding the r_i and r_j generic regions:

$$R = \{r_i | r_i \in I, \exists k \in P | \forall i, f(r_i) = k, \forall (i,j) C(i,j)\} \tag{5}$$

$$C(i,j) = \{(f(r_i) = f(r_j)) \wedge adjacent(i,j)\} \tag{6}$$

$$P = \{Text - Graph, Image, Background\} \tag{7}$$

Using only pre-classification we don't have all the information we need, but with this approach we follow one of the targets of our method, the computing performance efficiency. The second step of the merging phase is the Union phase. The Union procedure will be used to enhance the pre-classification results. First of all, the regions, which are in the external edges of the document, are removed, then all other regions will be consider for the further phase. Now let's introduce the Macro-Regions, as those regions with a spanned area greater than a threshold, which is related to the document region sizing. All the adjacent Macro-Regions with the same pre-classification values will be merged thus obtaining our segmentation.

Fig. 5. Original document after the first phase of the merge and its highlighted particular.

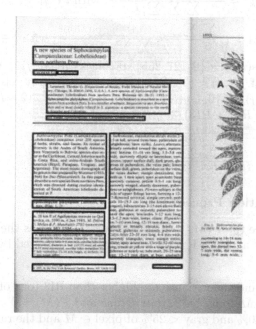

Fig. 6. Original document after the second phase of the Merge, the "Union" phase.

5   Region Classification

Now, regions of interest has been segmented, so we have to catalogue them . In order to catalogue regions we introduce global operators, which are universally used in Image Processing. These global operators will work on the entire segmented areas. In order to interpret in a precise manner all these regions, more operators than in the split and merge phase, are required.

5.1   Global Operators

The selected global operators are: the mean, which is applied to the region with the median, the threshold that computes the values of the darkness pixels in the region, the variance which is an average square difference, the gray-levels which consists of the grays, blacks and white pixels, edges that are related to color variations in the document and ratio which is the ratio between the region and the enclosing rectangle.

- $mean(M_k) = \frac{\sum_l \sum_i \sum_j f(i,j)}{\sum_l \sum_i \sum_j 1}$, with $l \in M_k$, with M_k is a Macro-Region
- $median(M_k) = min_m m | \sum_{k=0}^m f_k(R) \leq \sum_l \sum_i \sum_j \frac{1}{2} f_k(R) = \#\{(i,j)|f(i,j)=k\}$
- $threshold(M_k) = \frac{\sum_l \sum_i \sum_{j|f(i,j)>k} 255}{\sum_l \sum_i \sum_j 1}$, with $l \in R$
- $variance(M_k) = \sqrt{\frac{\sum_l \sum_i \sum_j (f(i,j)-mean(M_k))^2}{\sum_l \sum_i \sum_j 1}}$, with $l \in R$
- $gray - levels(i,j) = \{0, 127, 255\}$, 0 (black) if $f(i,j) < (2*RI1+RI3)/3$, 255 (white) if $f(i,j) < (2*RI2+RI3)/3$, 127 (gray) else
- edges $g(i,j) = \{0, 1, g(i,j-1)\}$, 0 if $f(i,j) < (2*R21+RI3)/3$, 1 if $f(i,j) < (2*RI1+RI3)/3$, $g(i,j-1)$ else
- $edge(M_k) = \frac{\#\{(i,j)|g(i,j)\neq g(i,j-1)\}*256}{\#\{(i,j)\}}$
- $ratio(M_k) = \frac{\sum_l \sum_i \sum_j 1}{(Rx_f-Rx_i+1)(Ry_f-Ry_i+1)}$, with $l \in R$

5.2   Classification Procedure

We will introduce the $F(M) = \{Text, Graph, Image\}$ as the classification function, where M is a Macro-Region, which will be valorized by the following procedure:

1. if the mean and the variance are higher than RI3 (one of the pre-processing parameters) M could be *Text* or *Graph* and $F(M) = \emptyset$
2. if (white > 40% and gray < 25% of pixel $\in M$ and the ratio is less than 60% of threshold(M)) then $F(M) = Text$
3. else if (gray > 25% or mean is higher then RI3) then $F(M) = Image$
4. else $F(M) = Graph$
5. if $F(M)$ is $\emptyset$ then M is removed (could be background or border).

The DAN system produces an XML (eXtensible Markup Language) description of the regions recognized with the above procedure, which is useful for creating a standard base query system. In fact the user can define a query module based on standard HTML+XML source code using the system output. Moreover users can build their own central repository and acquire different documents in different states or cities and then using Internet to upload the XML region descriptions to a central repository. The users can interact with an Internet Browser in order to produce queries onto the central repository, thus obtaining interesting documents. An example of the XML file produced and the DocRegionDescription DTD (Document Type Definition) used are shown in the following code examples.

Example of an XML file produced by DAN

```
<?xml version="1.0"?>
<!-- XML example -->
<!DOCTYPE DRD SYSTEM "DRD.dtd">
<DRD  FName="2.tif" W="640" H="480">
<Segmentation Type="Auto" Algo="Cinque-Levialdi-Malizia-DeRosa">
<Region ID="1" type="TEXT">
 <NumPixels Num="144"/>
 <Size x1="52" x2="75" y1="5" y2="8"/>
 <Barycenter x="463" y="17"/>
</Region>
</Segmentation>
</DRD>
```

Example of the DocRegionDescription DTD used by DAN

```
<?xml version="1.0" encoding="us-ascii"?>
<!-- DTD "DRD" version 0.93 -->
<!ELEMENT DRD (Segmentation+)>
<!ATTLIST DRD
        Version    CDATA    #IMPLIED
        FileName   CDATA    #REQUIRED
        Height     CDATA    #REQUIRED
        Width      CDATA    #REQUIRED>
<!ELEMENT Segmentation (Region+)>
<!ATTLIST Segmentation
        Type    (Auto | Manual)    #IMPLIED
        Param1    CDATA    #IMPLIED
        Param2    CDATA    #IMPLIED
        Param3    CDATA    #IMPLIED
        Algo    CDATA    #IMPLIED>
<!ELEMENT Region ((NumPixels | Barycenter | Size | Shape| Label)+)>
<!ATTLIST Region
        ID    CDATA    #REQUIRED
        Type    CDATA    #REQUIRED>
<!ELEMENT NumPixels EMPTY>
<!ATTLIST NumPixels
        Num    CDATA    #REQUIRED>
<!ELEMENT Barycenter EMPTY>
<!ATTLIST Barycenter
        x    CDATA    #REQUIRED
        y    CDATA    #REQUIRED>
<!ELEMENT Size EMPTY>
<!ATTLIST Size
        x1    CDATA    #REQUIRED
        y1    CDATA    #REQUIRED
        x2    CDATA    #REQUIRED
        y2    CDATA    #REQUIRED>
```

```
<!ELEMENT Shape EMPTY>
<!ATTLIST Shape
        Shape   CDATA   #REQUIRED>
<!ELEMENT Label EMPTY>
<!ATTLIST Label
        Label   CDATA   #REQUIRED>
```

5.3 Noise Reduction

We have also improved our system with noise reduction of original document caused by scanning, borders, extra pages and transparencies. Scanning is a very important issue, and we have considered images scanned at 200-400 dpi range. Using the RI_i (described in preprocessing phase) we avoid the problem of having scanned images darker or lighter than the original paper; in fact the problem of acquisition could affect splitting parameters causing errors. Borders are often obtained from photocopies or central part of two pages magazines or books. In order to avoid errors of this kind, like black borders, we use a post-process routine. This routine uses Macro-Regions which are a small number thus having good computation performances. The routine finds a central region and tries to enlarge that region joining it to Macro-Regions with at least one edge into the central region. Extra pages are caused acquiring not only the original page but also part of another page in a two pages book or magazine. Different techniques exist in order to correct this problem; we choose to eliminate all the regions that after the merge phase are adjacent to external borders. Transparencies are originated by thin paper or very old ink absorbed by the paper. We have avoided this problem, which can cause region detection errors, by the use of the RI_i parameters, in fact these parameters help our method to understand where information are in a manner which is independent from gray-levels absolute values thus avoiding errors from transparencies.

6   Experimental Results

We have tested our system over the UW-II database that is the second in series of document image databases produced by the Intelligent Systems Laboratory, at the University of Washington, Seattle, Washington, USA. UW-II is designed and constructed by a team of undergraduate and graduate students, led by Dr. Ihsin Phillips and Dr. Robert Haralick at the Intelligent Systems Laboratory. The database contains 624 English journal document pages (43 complete articles) and 63 MEMO pages. All pages are scanned pages.

Each document in the database has been taken from scientific journals and contains text, graphs and images. The average sizes of documents are 2500 x 3000 pixels and about 1 MB of storage required for each document. We can see in table 1, a sample of 8 documents taken from the database. The fields respectively indicate D (Document ID), R (Regions number), C R (Correctly Recognized), N C R (Not Correctly Recognized), T B D (To Be Defined, this are regions for which our system hasn't enough information to decide if they're text, graph or image). This sample even with this low number of documents is an important example of the results obtained over the entire database because of the different qualities of the selected documents.

Table 1. A sample of 8 eigth docs extracted from the database.

D	R	C R	N C R	T B D
1	14	14	0	0
2	8	8	0	0
3	10	9	1	0
4	11	8	3	0
5	5	5	0	0
6	10	8	2	0
7	9	7	2	0
8	8	6	1	1
TOTAL	75	65	9	1

We have tested our method over the entire database (600 images) obtaining an 84% of correctly recognized regions, 14% of not correctly recognized and 2% to be defined. The 84% of correctly recognized regions could be sub dived into a 59% of entirely recognized and 25% of partially recognized, which means a single text regions was interpreted as two text regions (this usually happens in titles where there are many spaces).

Table 2. Values over the entire database.

D	R	C R	N C R	T B D
600	5625	4725	788	112

7   Conclusion and Further Works

This paper presents our approach for segmenting and classifying documents. In this approach we have worked on the reduction of the split operations using a pre-processing routines. In future this work could be improved in sub-classification, such as the title and subtitle detection inside text block, table recognition, and the use of some OCR technique in the text regions. Moreover the system could be improved adapting parameters to specific fields of applications where documents are of a certain type, thus we could obtain a better percentage of correctly recognized regions. The goal is general document recognition system that assists the user in recognizing documents also using segmentation algorithm [16] for classifying image regions, and some shape algorithm [17] in order to model documents with convex regions, which are more precise representation than the rectangular ones. Finally, our DAN system may be consider as an automatic documents recognition system with region segmentation and classification, with the chance of semi-automatic or interactive action by the user; thus this system should be very suitable for automatic recognition of image database and batch acquisition of multiple documents types and formats.

References

1. F. Bapst, R. Brugger, and R. Ingold. Towards an Interactive Document Recognition System. *Internal working paper* 95– 09, IIUF-Université de Fribourg, March 1995.
2. B. Gatos, S. L. Mantzaris, K. V. Chandrios, A. Tsigris, and S. J. Perantonis. Integrated algorithms for newspaper page decomposition and article tracking. In *ICDAR'99: Fifth International Conference on Document Analysis and Recogntion*, pages 559–562, Bangalore, India, Sept. 1999.
3. D. Lewis. Representation and Learning in Information Retrieval. *PhD thesis*, Department of Computer Science, University of Massachusetts, 1992.
4. Y. Yang and J. Pedersen. A Comparative Study on Feature Selection in Text Categorization. *Machine Learning. Proceedings of the 14th International Conference (ICML 97)*, pages 412-420, Nashville, TE, USA, July 6–12 1997.
5. M. Junker and R. Hoch. An Experimental Evaluation of OCR Text Representations for Learning Document Classi- fiers.*International Journal on Document Analysis and Recognition*, 1(2):116–122, June 1998.
6. G. Nagy, S. Seth, S. Stoddard. Document analysis with an expert system.*Pattern Recognition*, Vol. 19 N.1, pp 149–159, 1986.
7. K. C. Fan, L. S. Wang, Y. K. Yang. Page segmentation and identification for intelligent signal processing. *Signal Processing*, Vol 45 N.2, pp 329–346, 1995.
8. T. Pavlidis, J. Zhou. Page segmentation and classification. Graphical Models and Image Processing. *CVGIP*, Vol 54, pp 484–496, November 1992.
9. L. Fletcher, R. Katsuri. A robust algorithm for text string separation from mixed text/graphics images. *IEEE Transaction on Pattern Analysis and Machine Intelligence*, Vol 10, pp 910–918, 1998.
10. J. Litcher, F. Hones. Layout extraction of mixed mode document. *IEEE Transaction on Machine Vision and Application*,Vol 6, pp 477–486, 1994.
11. L. O'Gorman, R. Katsuri. Document image analysis. *IEEE Computer Society*. Press Los Alamos, California, pp 161–181, 1995.
12. F. Esposito, D. Malerba, G. Semeraro, E. Annese, G. Scafuro. An experimental page layout recognition system for office document automatic classification: an integrated approach for inductive generalization. *Proceedings of 10th ICPR*, pp 557–562.
13. G. Nagy, S. Seth, and M. Viswanathan. A prototype document image analysis system for technical journals. *Computer*, 25(7):10–22, July 1992
14. M. Span, R. Wilson. A quad-tree approach to image segmentation which combines statistical and spatial information. *Pattern Recognition*, Vol.18:257–269,1985.
15. T. Ojala, M. Pietikainen. Unsupervised texture segmentation using feature distributions. *Pattern Recognition*, Vol.32:477–486,1999.
16. L. Cinque, F. Lecca, S. Levialdi, S. Tanimoto – "Retrieval of images using Rich Region Descriptions". *Proceeding of the International Conference of Pattern Recognition*, Brisbane, Australia, 1998, Volume I, pp. 899–109.
17. L. Cinque, S. Levialdi, A. Malizia, K.A. Olsen. "A Multidimensional Image Browser". *Journal of Visual Language and Computing*,Vol. 9, 1998.

Document Reverse Engineering: From Paper to XML

Kyong-Ho Lee[1], Yoon-Chul Choy[2], Sung-Bae Cho[2], Xiao Tang[1], and
Victor McCrary[1]

[1] National Institute of Standards and Technology, 100 Bureau Drive, Gaithersburg,
MD 20889, USA
{kyongho, xiao.tang, victor.mccrary@nist.gov
[2] Dept. Computer Science, Yonsei Univ., 134 Shinchon-dong, Seodaemun-ku, Seoul, 120-
749, Korea
{ycchoy, sbcho}@cs.yonsei.ac.kr

1 Introduction

Since XML has the advantage of embedding logical structure information into documents, it is widely used as the universal format for structured documents on the Web. This makes it attractive to convert paper-based documents with logical hierarchy into XML representations automatically. Document image analysis and understanding [1] consists of two phases: geometric and logical structure analysis. Because the two phases take different kinds of data as input, it may not be desirable to apply the same method to them. Targeting technical journal document with multiple pages, we present a hybridization of knowledge-based and syntactic methods for geometric and logical structure analysis of document images.

Sophisticated geometric structure analysis is a prerequisite for logical structure analysis that recognizes logical components and their hierarchy. The geometric properties of document images are different according to the type of the document. Even the documents of the same type can differ from each other. The formalism to reflect geometric characteristics that are publication-specific as well as class-specific is very important. For geometric structure analysis, we present a knowledge-based method that can handle more sophisticated problems than previous works.

Logical components such as headers or paragraphs are identified from document images based on their geometric characteristics of the corresponding text regions. The logical components that are directly identifiable from geometric characteristics of text regions are called primary structures and the ones such as *Section* that can be identified through grouping components together are called secondary structures [2]. For XML documents with logical hierarchy, secondary structures as well as primary structures should be extracted from multi-page documents. We present a syntactic method for logical structure analysis. Normally, a text region composing a document image functions as a header or a body, which corresponds to a title or a paragraph, respectively. Headers and bodies may be classified into various kinds according to the geometric characteristics of the corresponding text region. We define headers and bodies as functional components, and a tree with nodes of headers and bodies as a functional structure tree.

D. Lopresti, J. Hu, and R. Kashi (Eds.): DAS 2002, LNCS 2423, pp. 503–506, 2002.
© Springer-Verlag Berlin Heidelberg 2002

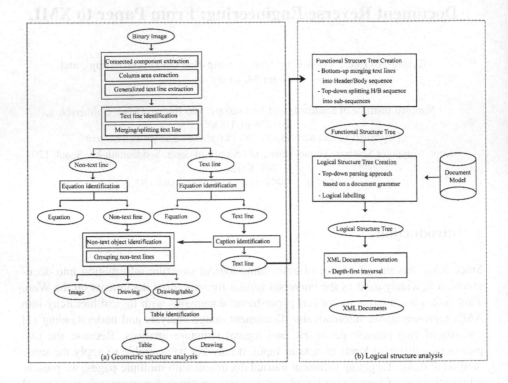

Fig. 1. A flow diagram for the proposed document analysis process

To improve in the processing speed of logical structure analysis, compared with previous related works of which the basic units are text lines, the proposed method takes a functional structure tree.

2 Document Structure Analysis

As shown in Fig. 1(a), the geometric structure method is composed of two stages: region segmentation and identification. The knowledge base has been constructed using the characteristics of a technical journal publication. First, it categorizes the types of document images into title and body pages, and examines the characteristics of each type. Regions of the document image are divided into complex layout objects such as text lines, equations, images, drawings, and tables. The knowledge base is expressed with 91 rules, based on a careful examination of geometric characteristics of layout objects. The result of segmentation process does not usually have a one-to-one matching with composite layout components. A figure object contains many small regions that correspond to image or drawing regions. Based on the hybrid of top-down and bottom-up techniques, the proposed method identifies non-text objects such as images, drawings and tables, as well as text objects such as text lines and equations by splitting and grouping segmented regions into composite components.

```
element_declaration ::= "<!ELEMENT", element_type (content_model | geometric_property), ">"
element_type ::= generic_identifier
content_model ::= model_group
model_group ::= "(", content_token (connector, content_token)*, ")", occurrence_indicator?
content_token ::= element_token | model_group
element_token ::= generic_identifier, occurrence_indicator?
generic_identifier ::= name
name ::= name_start_character, name_character*
name_character ::= name_start_character | digit
name_start_character ::= "A" | ... | "Z" | "a" | ... | "z"
digit ::= "0" | "1" | "2" | "3" | "4" | "5" | "6" | "7" | "8" | "9"
connector ::= "," | "|" | "&"
occurrence_indicator ::= "?" | "+" | "*"
geometric_property ::= "#", "(", functional_structure_type, column_type, line_height, line_number,
    space_before, space_after, black_pixel_density, justification, ")"
functional_structure_type ::= "FUNCTION_TYPE:", funtional_type_indicator
funtional_type_indicator ::= "HEADER" | "BODY"
column_type ::= "COLUMN_TYPE:", column_type_indicator
column_type_indicator ::= "SINGLE" | "DOUBLE"
line_height ::= min_line_height, max_line_height
min_line_height ::= "MIN_LINE_HEIGHT:", real
max_line_height ::= "MAX_LINE_HEIGHT:", real
line_number ::= min_line_number, max_line_number
min_line_number ::= "MIN_LINE_NUMBER:", integer
max_line_number ::= "MAX_LINE_NUMBER:", integer
space_before ::= min_space_before, max_space_before
min_space_before ::= "MIN_SPACE_BEFORE:", real
max_space_before ::= "MAX_SPACE_BEFORE:", real
space_after ::= min_space_after, max_space_after
min_space_after ::= "MIN_SPACE_AFTER:", real
max_space_after ::= "MAX_SPACE_AFTER:", real
black_pixel_density ::= min_black_pixel_density, max_black_pixel_density
min_black_pixel_density ::= "MIN_BLACK_PIXEL_DENSITY:", real
max_black_pixel_density ::= "MAX_BLACK_PIXEL_DENSITY:", real
justification ::= "JUSTIFY:", justification_indicator
justification_indicator ::= "LEFT" | "RIGHT" | "CENTER" | "INDENT"
integer ::= digit+
real ::= ".", digit+ | digit+, ".", digit*
```

1. Generate a header/body sequence.
   (a) Group together text lines into various kinds of header and body based on the principles of Gestalt psychology.
2. Split the header/body sequence into subsequences.
   (a) Find repetitive headers that form repetitive patterns, or the header which corresponds to a lower level header.
   (b) Split the sequence into subsequences at the next lower level: the sequence becomes the parent of subsequences.
3. Repeat step 2 until no changes are generated.

(a) Document model

(b) Algorithm for a functional structure tree

Fig. 2. The proposed document model and algorithm for creating a functional structure tree

The proposed method for logical structure analysis takes as input a set of text lines from geometric analysis of each multi-page document as shown in Fig 1 (b). A document model is proposed as shown in Fig. 2 (a). For secondary structures, the model expresses such information as their names and frequency, and ordering information among them in the form of regular expressions. The model defines the required and optional contents of secondary structures, specified by sub-element names. Additionally, it defines order among the contents and their occurrence. As geometric conditions that primary structures should satisfy, the model describes geometric characteristics such as column type, the number and height of text lines, the space before and after a text region, the density distribution of a black pixel, and alignment.

As shown in Fig. 1(b), the logical analysis method is composed of three phases. First is the creation step of a functional structure tree where text lines are merged into a sequence of headers and bodies, and by splitting the sequence repeatedly a hierarchical tree is created. A sequence of header and body is created by merging adjacent text lines that have similar geometric characteristics based on the three principles, which are proximity, similarity and contiguity, from Gestalt psychology [3]. There are different types of header and body that are differentiated from each other by the geometric characteristics.

The method next creates a functional structure tree from the sequence of different header and body based on repetitive characteristics of their labels. Normally, a document contains quite a few sections and each section is composed of lower level sections with hierarchically nested structures. Specifically, each of the section structure is identified by the section title and the title of the sub-section is placed after the title of the section that it is contained in. Therefore, the proposed method creates a functional structure tree in top-down manner by splitting a sequence repeatedly with the repetitive header as the base as shown in Fig. 2(b). If the sequence contains a single header that corresponds to the title of a lower level section, it is split using this as the base.

Secondly, the parsing method applies a document model on a functional structure tree and creates a logical structure tree. By doing depth-first search on a functional structure tree, the method tests whether the hierarchical structure of interior nodes and the geometric characteristics of leaf nodes are acceptable under the grammars of the document model. The method responds appropriately to interior nodes including a root node according to whether the child of the node in question is a leaf node or an interior node. If the child node is a leaf, it is labeled with an element name that satisfies its geometric characteristics. In case of an interior node, one of permissible element names is given and whether the corresponding content model of the element is appropriate or not is tested recursively. If the child node is invalid, the proposed method backtracks to an alternative label for the parent node.

As a result, the proposed parsing method completes a logical structure tree by assigning a label to each node of the functional structure tree. Finally, the method generates an XML document as the result of logical structure analysis by doing depth-first search on a logical structure tree. Particularly, whenever a leaf node is encountered, its corresponding OCR result of the text region is added.

3   Performance Analysis

To evaluate the performance of the proposed methods, we have experimented with 26 journal papers. In terms of geometric structure analysis, experimental results show an accuracy of 99.3% in average. Particularly, to succeed in logical structure analysis, the exact identification of functional components from text lines is very important. In the case of the identification rate of header and body, the proposed method performed in an accuracy of 98.9% in average. Because the parsing method takes a functional structure tree, it is faster than the conventional methods, which the basic units for parsing are either pixels or text lines. Particularly, the proposed method generates XML documents as the result of structural analysis, so that it enhances the reusability of documents and independence of platform.

References

1. Nagy, G.: Twenty Years of Document Image Analysis in PAMI. IEEE Trans. Pattern Analysis and Machine Intelligence. 1 (2000) 38–62
2. Summers, K.M.: Toward a Taxonomy of Logical Document Structures. Proc. Dartmouth Institute for Advanced Graduate Studies (DAGS'95), Boston (1995) 124–133
3. Koffka, K.: Principles of Gestalt Psychology. Harcourt, Brace and World, New York (1935)

Human Interactive Proofs and Document Image Analysis

Henry S. Baird and Kris Popat

Palo Alto Research Center, 3333 Coyote Hill Road, Palo Alto, CA 94304 USA
{baird|popat}@parc.com
www.parc.com/istl/groups/did

Abstract. The recently initiated and rapidly developing research field of 'human interactive proofs' (HIPs) and its implications for the document image analysis (DIA) research field are described. Over the last five years, efforts to defend Web services against abuse by programs ('bots') have led to a new family of security protocols able to distinguish between human and machine users. AltaVista pioneered this technology in 1997 [Bro01, LBBB01]. By the summer of 2000, Yahoo! and PayPal were using similar methods. In the Fall of 2000, Prof. Manuel Blum of Carnegie-Mellon University and his team, stimulated by Udi Manber of Yahoo!, were studying these and related problems [BAL00]. Soon thereafter a collaboration between the University of California at Berkeley and the Palo Alto Research Center (PARC) built a tool based on systematically generated image degradations [CBF01]. In January 2002, Prof. Blum and the present authors ran the first workshop (at PARC) on HIPs, defined broadly as a class of challenge/response protocols which allow a human to authenticate herself as a member of a given group – e.g. human (vs. machine), herself (vs. anyone else), an adult (vs. a child), etc. All commercial uses of HIPs known to us exploit the gap in ability between human and machine vision systems in reading images of machine printed text. Many technical issues that have been systematically studied by the DIA community are relevant to the HIP research program. This paper describes the evolution of HIP R&D, applications of HIPs now and on the horizon, highlights of the first HIP workshop, and proposals for a DIA research agenda to advance the state of the art of HIPs.

Keywords. Human interactive proofs, document image analysis, CAPTCHAs, abuse of web sites and services, the chatroom problem, human/machine discrimination, Turing tests, OCR performance evaluation, document image degradations, legibility of text

1 Introduction

In 1997 Andrei Broder and his colleagues [LBBB01], then at the DEC Systems Research Center, developed a scheme to block the automatic submission of URLs [Bro01] to the AltaVista web-site: their approach was to present a user with an

D. Lopresti, J. Hu, and R. Kashi (Eds.): DAS 2002, LNCS 2423, pp. 507–518, 2002.
© Springer-Verlag Berlin Heidelberg 2002

image of printed text formed specially so that machine vision (OCR) systems could not read it but humans still could. In September 2000, Udi Manber, Chief Scientist at Yahoo!, challenged Prof. Manuel Blum and his students [BAL00] at The School for Computer Science at Carnegie Mellon University (CMU) to design an "easy to use reverse Turing test" that would block 'bots' (computer programs) from registering for services including chat rooms, mail, briefcases, etc. In October of that year, Prof. Blum asked the first author, of the Palo Alto Research Center (PARC),, and Prof. Richard Fateman, of the Computer Science Division of the University of California at Berkeley (UCB), whether systematically applied image degradations could form the basis of such a filter, stimulating the development of PessimalPrint [CBF01].

In January 2002, Prof. Blum and the present authors ran a workshop at PARC on 'human interactive proofs' (HIPs), defined as *a broad class of challenge/response protocols which allow a human to authenticate herself as a member of a given group – e.g. human (vs. machine), herself (vs. anyone else), an adult (vs. a child), etc.* All commercial uses of HIPs known to us exploit the gap in ability between human and machine vision systems in reading images of text.

Many technical issues that have been systematically studied by the document image analysis (DIA) community are relevant to the HIP research program. In an effort to stimulate interest in HIPs within the document image analysis research community, this paper details the evolution of the HIP research field, the range of applications of HIPs appearing on the horizon, highlights of the first HIP workshop, and proposals for a DIA research agenda to advance the state of the art of HIPs.

1.1 An Influential Precursor: Turing Tests

Alan Turing proposed [Tur50] a methodology for testing whether or not a machine can be said to think, by means of an "imitation game" conducted over teletype connections in which a human judge asks questions of two interlocutors – one human and the other a machine – and eventually decides which of them is human. If judges fail sufficiently often to decide correctly, then that fact would be, Turing proposed, strong evidence that the machine possessed artificial intelligence. His proposal has been widely influential in the computer science, cognitive science, and philosophical communities [SCA00] for over fifty years.

However, no machine has "passed the Turing test" in his original sense in spite of perenniel serious attempts. In fact it remains easy for human judges to distinguish machines from humans under Turing-test-like conditions. Graphical user interfaces (GUIs) invite the use of images as well as text in the dialogues.

1.2 Robot Exclusion Conventions

The Robot Exclusion Standard, an informal consensus reached in 1994 by the robots mailing list (robots@nexor.co.uk), specifies the format of a file (the http://.../robots.txt file) which a web site or server may install to instruct all robots visiting the site which paths it should not traverse in search of documents. The Robots META tag allows HTML authors to indicate to visiting robots whether or not a document may be indexed or used to harvest more links (cf. `www.robotstxt.org/wc/meta-user.html`).

Many Web services (Yahoo!, Google, etc) respect these conventions. Some of the problems which HIPs address are caused by deliberate disregard of these conventions.

1.3   Primitive Means

For several years now web-page designers have chosen to render some apparent text as image (e.g. GIF) rather than encoded text (e.g. ASCII), and sometimes in order to impede the legibility of the text to screen scrapers and spammers. One of the earliest published attempts to automate the reading of imaged-text on web pages was by Lopresti and Zhou [DZ00]. Kanungo et al [KLB01]reported that, in a sample of 862 sampled web pages, "42% of images contain text" and, of the images with text, "59% contain at least one word that does not appear in the ... HMTL file."

1.4   First Use: The Add-URL Problem

In 1997 AltaVista sought ways to block or discourage the automatic submission of URLs to their search engine. This free "add-URL" service is important to AltaVista since it broadens its search coverage and ensures that sites important to its most motivated customers are included. However, some users were abusing the service by automating the submission of large numbers of URLs, and certain URLs many times, in an effort to skew AltaVista's importance ranking algorithms.

Andrei Broder, Chief Scientist of AltaVista, and his colleagues developed a filter (now visible at [Bro01]). Their method is to generate an image of printed text randomly (in a "ransom note" style using mixed typefaces) so that machine vision (OCR) systems cannot read it but humans still can (Figure 1). In January 2002 Broder told the present authors that the system had been in use for "over a year" and had reduced the number of "spam add-URL" by "over 95%." A U.S. patent [LABB01] was issued in April 2001.

1.5   The ChatRoom Problem

In September 2000, Udi Manber of Yahoo! described this "chat room problem" to researchers at CMU: 'bots' were joining on–line chat rooms and irritating the people there, e.g. by pointing them to advertising sites. How could all 'bots' be refused entry to chat rooms?

CMU's Prof. Manuel Blum, Luis A. von Ahn, and John Langford articulated [BAL00] some desirable properties of a test, including:

 – the test's challenges can be automatically generated and graded (i.e. the judge is a machine);

Fig. 1. Example of an AltaVista challenge: letters are chosen at random, then each is assigned to a typeface at random, then each letter is rotated and scaled, and finally (optionally, not shown here) background clutter is added.

- the test can be taken quickly and easily by human users (i.e. the dialogue should not go on long);
- the test will accept virtually all human users (even young or naive users) with high reliability while rejecting very few;
- the test will reject virtually all machine users; and
- the test will resist automatic attack for many years even as technology advances and even if the test's algorithms are known (e.g. published and/or released as open source).

They coined the term "CAPTCHA," an acronym for Completely Automated Public Turing Test to Tell Computers and Humans Apart, which seems to have stuck. Theoretical security issues underlying the design of CAPTCHAs were addressed by Nick Hopper and Manuel Blum in [HB01].

They developed 'GIMPY' which picked English words at random and rendered them as images of printed text under a wide variety of shape deformations and image occlusions, the word images sometimes overlapping. The user was challenged to read some number of them correctly. An example is shown in Figure 2.

A simplified version of GIMPY, using only one word-image at a time (Figure 3), is presently in use by Yahoo! (visible at chat.yahoo.com after clicking on 'Sign Up For Yahoo! Chat!'). It is used to restrict access to chat rooms and other services to human users.

1.6   Screening Financial Accounts

PayPal (www.paypal.com) is screening applications for its financial payments accounts using a text-image challenge (Figure 4). We do not know any details about its motivation or its technical basis.

A similar CAPTCHA has recently appeared on the Overture website (click on 'Advertiser Login' at www.overture.com).

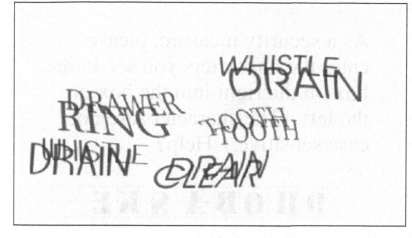

Fig. 2. Example of a GIMPY image.

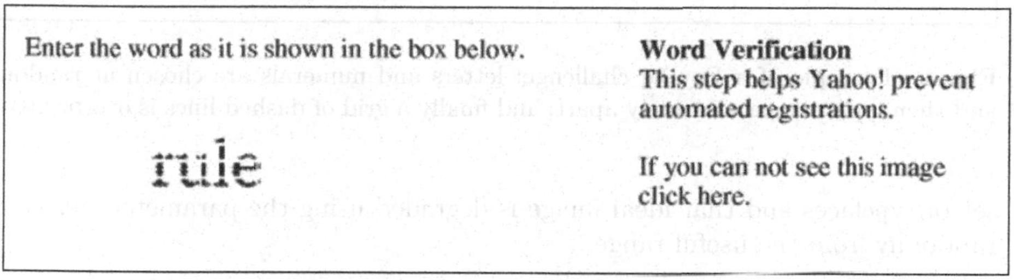

Enter the word as it is shown in the box below.   **Word Verification**
This step helps Yahoo! prevent
automated registrations.

rule

If you can not see this image
click here.

Fig. 3. Example of a simplified Yahoo! challenge: an English word is selected at random, then the word (as a whole) is typeset using a typeface chosen at random, and finally the the word image is altered randomly by a variety of means including image degradations, scoring with white lines (shown here), and non-linear deformations.

1.7 PessimalPrint

The first author, together with Richard Fateman and Allison Coates of UCB, applied a model of document image degradations [Bai92] that approximates ten aspects of the physics of machine–printing and imaging of text, including spatial sampling rate and error, affine spatial deformations, jitter, speckle, blurring, thresholding, and symbol size. Figure 4 shows an example of PessimalPrint challenges that was synthetically degraded according to certain parameter settings of this model.

An experiment assisted by ten UCB graduate-student subjects and three commercial OCR machines located a range of model parameters in which images could be generated pseudorandomly that were always legible to the human subjects and never correctly recognized by the OCR systems. In the current version of PessimalPrint, English words are chosen randomly from a set of 70 words commonly found on the Web; then the word is rendered using one of a small

As a security measure, please
enter the characters you see in the
box on the right into the box on
the left. (The characters are not
case sensitive.) Help?

Fig. 4. Example of a PayPal challenge: letters and numerals are chosen at random and then typeset, spaced widely apart, and finally a grid of dashed lines is overprinted.

set of typefaces and that ideal image is degraded using the parameters selected randomly from the useful range.

2   The First International HIP Workshop

A workshop on Human Interactive Proofs, apparently the first on this topic, was held January 9-11, 2002, at the Palo Alto Research Center.

As a starting point for discussion, HIPs were defined as

> *automatic protocols allowing a person to authenticate him/herself — as being, e.g., human (not a machine), an adult (not a child), himself (no one else) — over a network without the burden of passwords, biometrics, special mechanical aids, or special training.*

The workshop was a two-and-one-half day event that took place mostly in PARC's Weiser Commons (a.k.a. the famous "bean-bag chair room"). It was a one-hundred-percent participation workshop, meaning that whoever attended was expected to contribute an abstract and to speak. There were thirty-eight participants, with particularly strong representations from CMU, UCB, and PARC. The CMU group was led by Prof. Manuel Blum, co-organizer of the workshop with the first author. Profs. Richard Fateman, Doug Tygar, and Jitendra Malik and their students attended from UCB. Robert Sloan, Director of the NSF Theory of Computing Program, attended and expressed warm support for this new research area. Prof. John McCarthy of Stanford University presented an invited

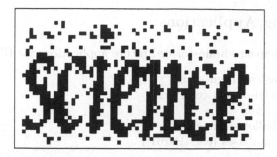

Fig. 5. Example of a PessimalPrint challenge: an English word is chosen at random, then the word (as a whole) is typeset using a randomly chosen typeface, and finally the word-image is degraded according to randomly selected parameters (with certain ranges) of the image degradation model.

plenary talk on "Frontiers of AI". The Chief Scientists of Yahoo! and Altavista were present, along with researchers from IBM Research, Lucent Bell Labs, and Intertrust STAR Labs.

There was considerable breadth of interests represented; topics presented and discussed included:

- Completely Automatic Public Turing tests to tell Computers and Humans Apart (CAPTCHAs): criteria, proofs, and design
- Secure authentication of individuals without using identifying or other devices
- Catalogs of actual exploits and attacks by machines to commercial services intended for human use
- Funding prospects for HIP work
- Design and implementation case study of "Ransom Note" style CAPTCHA
- Audio-based CAPTCHAs
- CAPTCHA design considerations specific to East-Asian languages
- Authentication and forensics of video footage
- Feasibility of text-only CAPTCHAs
- CAPTCHAs based on the human-machine gap text recognition ability
- Images, human visual ability, and computer vision in CAPTCHA technology
- Usability issues in cryptography tools
- Human-fault tolerant approaches to cryptography and authentication
- Robustly non-transferable authentication
- Protocols based on human ability to memorize through association and perform simple mental calculations.

The workshop was single-track except for the convening of four ad-hoc working groups on the afternoon of the second day, on the following topics: theory, performance, computer vision, and applications. The workshop concluded with a panel discussion — and then general discussion — on "the way forward." Abstracts were collected from and distributed to participants, but not published.

For further details of the HIP2002 workshop, including the Program and Participants' list, consult www.parc.com/istl/groups/did/HIP2002.

3   Emerging Applications

Workshop participants brainstormed future applications for HIPs:

- thwarting password guessing
- blocking denial-of-service attacks
- suppressing spam
- preventing ballot stuffing
- protecting databases (e.g. [Bar01])

Some believe that similar problems are likely to arise on Intranets.

4   Implications for DIA Research

The emergence of 'human interactive proofs' as a research field offers a rare opportunity (perhaps unprecedented since Turing's day) for a substantive alliance between the DIA and the theoretical computer science research communities, especially theorists interested in cryptography and security. The implications for DIA research are substantive.

At the heart of CAPTCHAS based on reading–ability gaps is the choice of the family of challenges: that is, the technical conditions under which text–images can be generated that are reliably human–legible but machine–illegible. This triggers many research questions:

- Historically, what do the fields of Computer Vision, Pattern Recognition, and DIA suggest are the most intractable obstacles to machine reading: segmentation? gestalt? image degradation? style consistency?
- What are the conditions under which human reading is peculiarly (even better, inexplicably) robust? What does the literature in cognitive science and the psychophysics of human reading suggest?
- Where, quantitatively and qualitatively, are the margins of good performance located, for machines and for humans?
- Having chosen one or more of these 'ability gaps', how can we reliably generate an inexhaustible supply of challenges that lie on the human-capable side of that gap?

It is well known in the DIA field that low-quality images of printed-text documents pose serious challenges to current image pattern recognition technologies [RJN96,RNN99]. In an attempt to understand the nature and severity of the challenge, models of document image degradations [Bai92,Kan96] have been developed and used to explore the limitations [HB97] of image pattern recognition algorithms. These methods must be extended theoretically and be better characterized in an engineering sense, in order to make progress on the questions above.

In our choice of image degradations for PessimalPrint, we were often guided by the discussion in [RNN99] of cases that defeat modern OCR machines, especially:

- thickened images, so that characters merge together;
- thinned images, so that characters fragment into unconnected components;
- noisy images, causing rough edges and salt–and–pepper noise;
- condensed fonts, with narrower aspect ratios than usual; and
- Italic fonts, whose rectilinear bounding boxes overlap their neighbors'.

Does the rich collection of examples in this book suggest other effective means that we should exploit?

To our knowledge, all DIA research so far has been focused at applications in *non-adversarial environments*. We should look closely at new security-sensitive questions such as:

- how easily can an image degradation be normalized away?
- can machines exploit lexicons more or less effectively than people?

Our familiarity with the state of the art of machine vision leads us to hypothesize that nomodern OCR machine will be able to cope with the image degradations of PessimalPrint: but how can this well-informed intuition be supported with sufficient experimental data?

Blum et al. [BAL00] have experimented, on their website www.captcha.net, with degradations that are not only due to imperfect printing and imaging, but include color, overlapping of words, non-linear distortions, and complex or random backgrounds. The relative ease with which we have been able to generate PessimalPrint, and the diversity of other means of bafflement at hand, suggest to us that the range of effective text–image challenges at our disposal is usefully broad.

There are many results reported in the literature on the psychophysics of human reading which appear to provide useful guidance in the engineering of PessimalPrint and similar reading-based CAPTCHAs. [LPSS85] reports on studies of the optimal reading rate and reading conditions for people with normal vision. In [LKT97] an ideal observer model is compared quantitatively to human performance , shedding light on the advantage provided by lexical context. Human reading ability is calibrated with respect to estimates of the intrinsic difficulty of reading tasks in [PBFM02], under a wide range of experimental conditions including varying image size, white noise, and contrast, simple and complex alphabets, and subjects of different ages and degrees of reading experience. These and other results may suggest which image degradation parameters, linguistic contexts, style (in)consistencies, and so forth provide the greatest advantage to human readers.

How long can a CAPTCHA such as PessimalPrint resist attack, given a serious effort to advance machine–vision technology, and assuming that the principles — perhaps even the source code — defining the test are known to attackers?

It is easy to enumerate potential attacks, but close studies of the history of image pattern recognition technology [Pav00] and of OCR technology [NS96] in particular support the view that the gap in ability between human and machine vision is wide and is only slowly narrowing. We notice that few, if any, machine vision technologies have simultaneously achieved all three of these desirable characteristics: high accuracy, full automation, and versatility. Versatility — by which we mean the ability to cope with a great variety of types of images — is perhaps the most intractable of these, and it is the one that pessimal print, with its wide range of image quality variations, challenges most strongly.

Ability gaps exist for other species of machine vision, of course, and in the recognition of non–text images, such as line–drawings, faces, and various objects in natural scenes. One might reasonably intuit that these would be harder and so decide to use them rather than images of text. This intuition is not supported by the cognitive science literature on human reading of words. There is no consensus on whether recognition occurs letter–by–letter or by a word–template model [Cro82,KWB80]; some theories stress the importance of contextual clues [GKB83] from natural language and pragmatic knowledge. Furthermore, many theories of human reading assume *perfectly formed* images of text. However, we have not found in the literature a theory of human reading which accounts for the robust human ability to read despite extreme segmentation (merging, fragmentation) of images of characters.

The resistance of these problems to technical attack for four decades and the incompleteness of our understanding of human reading abilities suggests that it is premature to decide that the recognition of text under conditions of low quality, occlusion, and clutter, is intrinsically much easier — that is, a significantly weaker challenge to the machine vision state–of–the–art — than recognition of objects in natural scenes. There is another reason to use images of text: the correct answer to the challenge is unambiguously clear and, even more helpful, it maps into a unique sequence of keystrokes. Can we put these arguments more convincingly?

5   Discussion

The HIP2002 Workshop revealed a research community in the early stages of formation. It seems to us to be a promising field, already enjoying a critical mass of hard problems, smart researchers, and commercial value. The academic disciplines that were represented at the workshop included:

- cryptography
- security
- document image analysis
- computer vision
- artificial intelligence

Perhaps this list is too narrow; other disciplines that could make important contributions may include:

- biometrics
- cognitive science
- psychophysics
- psychology

Acknowledgments. Our interest in HIPs was triggered by a question – could character images form the basis of a Turing test? – raised by Manuel Blum of Carnegie–Mellon Univ., which in turn was stimulated by Udi Manber's posing the "chat room problem" at CMU in September 2000. Manuel Blum, Luis A. von Ahn, and John Langford, all of CMU, shared with us much of their early thinking. Manuel proposed the HIP workshop, accepted our offer to hold it at PARC, and promoted it vigorously, inviting key participants. John Langford, Lenore Blum, and Luis A. von Ahn helped with many details of planning and execution. Charles Bennett of IBM Research took the group photo. We are especially grateful to many PARC researchers and staff for helping us run the workshop so smoothly: Prateek Sarkar, Tom Breuel, Tom Berson, Dirk Balfanz, David Goldberg, Jeanette Figueroa, Randy Jenkins, Beej Martinez, Eleanor Alvarido, Dan Novarro, Mimi Gardner, Dayne Peavy, Mike Hornbuckle, Sally Peters, and Kathy Jarvis. Allison Coates provided references and commentary related to the cognitive science literature. Monica Chew provided references and commentary related to the psychophysics of vision literature. This paper has benefited from discussions with Hermann Calabria, Andrei Broder, and Udi Manber and from careful readings by Monica Chew and Victoria Stodden.

References

[Bai92] H. S. Baird, "Document Image Defect Models," in H. S. Baird, H. Bunke, and K. Yamamoto (Eds.), *Structured Document Image Analysis*, Springer–Verlag: New York, 1992, pp. 546–556.

[BAL00] M. Blum, L. A. von Ahn, and J. Langford, *The CAPTCHA Project*, "Completely Automatic Public Turing Test to tell Computers and Humans Apart," www.captcha.net, Dept. of Computer Science, Carnegie–Mellon Univ., and personal communications, November, 2000.

[Bar01] D. P. Baron, "eBay and Database Protection," Case No. P-33, Case Writing Office, Stanford Graduate School of Business, 518 Memorial Way, Stanford Univ., Stanford, CA 94305-5015, 2001.

[Bro01] AltaVista's "Add-URL" site: altavista.com/sites/addurl/newurl, protected by the earliest known CAPTCHA.

[CBF01] A. L. Coates, H. S. Baird, R. Fateman, "Pessimal Print: a Reverse Turing Test," Proc., IAPR 6th Intl. Conf. on Document Analysis and Recognition, Seattle, WA, September 10–13, 2001, pp. 1154–1158.

[Cro82] R. G. Crowder, *The Psychology of Reading*, Oxford University Press, 1982.

[DZ00] D. Lopresti and J. Zhou, "Locating and Recognizing Text in WWW Images," *Information Retrieval*, May, 2000, Vol. 2, No. 2/3, pp. 177–206.

[GKB83] L. M. Gentile, M. L. Kamil, J. S. Blanchard 'Reading Research Revisited , Charles E. Merrill Publishing, 1983.

[HB97] T. K. Ho and H. S. Baird, "Large-Scale Simulation Studies in Image Pattern Recognition," *IEEE Trans. on PAMI*, Vol. 19, No. 10, pp. 1067–1079, October 1997.

[HB01] N. J. Hopper and M. Blum, "Secure Human Identification Protocols," In: C. Boyd (Ed.) Advances in Crypotology, Proceedings of Asiacrypt 2001, LNCS 2248, pp.52 -66, Springer-Verlag Berlin, 2001

[Kan96] T. Kanungo, *Document Degradation Models and Methodology for Degradation Model Validation*, Ph.D. Dissertation, Dept. EE, Univ. Washington, March 1996.

[KLB01] T. Kanungo, C. H. Lee and R. Bradford,"What Fraction of Images on the Web Contain Text?", Proc. of Int. Workshop on Web Document Analysis, Seattle, WA, Sept. 8, 2001, web publication only, at www.csc.liv.ac.uk/~wda2001.

[KWB80] P. A. Kolers, M. E. Wrolstad, H. Bouma, *Processing of Visible Language 2*, Plenum Press, 1980.

[LABB01] M. D. Lillibridge, M. Abadi, K. Bharat, A. Z. Broder, "Method for Selectively Restricting Access to Computer Systems," U.S. Patent No. 6,195,698, Issued February 27, 2001.

[LKT97] G. E. Legge, T. S. Klitz, and B. S. Tjan. "Mr. chips: An ideal-observer model of reading," *Psychological Review* 104(3):524–553, 1997.

[LPSS85] G. E. Legge, D. G. Pelli, G. S. Rubin, and M. M. Schleske, "Psychophysics of reading: I. normal vision," *Vision Research*, 25(2):239–252, 1985.

[NS96] G. Nagy and S. Seth, "Modern optical character recognition." in *The Froehlich / Kent Encyclopaedia of Telecommunications*, Vol. 11, pp. 473–531, Marcel Dekker, NY, 1996.

[Pav00] T. Pavlidis, "Thirty Years at the Pattern Recognition Front," King-Sun Fu Prize Lecture, 11th ICPR, Barcelona, September, 2000.

[PBFM02] D. G. Pelli, C. W. Burns, B. Farell, and D. C. Moore, "Identifying letters," *Vision Research*, [accepted with minor revisions; to appear], 2002.

[RNN99] S. V. Rice, G. Nagy, and T. A. Nartker, *OCR: An Illustrated Guide to the Frontier*, Kluwer Academic Publishers, 1999.

[RJN96] S. V. Rice, F. R. Jenkins, and T. A. Nartker, "The Fifth Annual Test of OCR Accuracy," ISRI TR-96-01, Univ. of Nevada, Las Vegas, 1996.

[SCA00] A. P. Saygin, I. Cicekli, and V. Akman, "Turing Test: 50 Years Later," *Minds and Machines*, 10(4), Kluwer, 2000.

[Tur50] A. Turing, "Computing Machinery and Intelligence," *Mind*, Vol. 59(236), pp. 433–460, 1950.

Data GroundTruth, Complexity, and Evaluation Measures for Color Document Analysis

Leon Todoran, Marcel Worring, and Arnold W.M. Smeulders

Intelligent Sensory Information Systems, University of Amsterdam,
Kruislaan 403, 1098SJ Amsterdam, The Netherlands
{todoran, worring, smeulders }@science.uva.nl
http://www.science.uva.nl/~todoran, worring, smeulders

Abstract. Publications on color document image analysis present results on small, non-publicly available datasets. We propose in this paper a well defined and groundtruthed color dataset existing of over 1000 pages, with associated tools for evaluation. The color data groundtruthing and evaluation tools are based on a well defined document model, complexity measures to assess the inherent difficulty of analyzing a page, and well founded evaluation measures. Together they form a suitable basis for evaluating diverse applications in color document analysis.

1   Introduction

Color is now playing an important role in publishing everything from scientific journals, newspapers, magazines, to advertisements. The nature of documents in current applications is therefore rapidly shifting from simple black-and-white documents to complex color documents. Some tools for color documents as color OCR [3,18], color document compression [1], and color string localization [12, 2,4,6] have been developed. However, whereas document analysis for black-and-white documents is mature, color document analysis is still in its infancy.

Two factors have been instrumental in advancing the field of black-and-white document analysis. Firstly, the existence of public domain data sets like the UW[9] and MTDB [15], freeing researchers from the labor intensive task of creating datasets to work on. Secondly, the availability of standard evaluation tools for OCR and page segmentation [10], [20], [14] allowing knowledge exchange between different researchers.

For color document image analysis, no such data set standardization has taken place. As a consequence, each developer now uses its own dataset for evaluating tools. Typically the data sets used are small as providing a ground truth for color documents is a time consuming task. In this paper we report on the creation of a large dataset with ground truth which could be a first step in standardizing the evaluation of color document analysis.

The dataset consists of over 1000 pages with a ground truth describing the document components, their layout and logical structure. As we focus on aspects specific to color documents, we leave out the document textual content

D. Lopresti, J. Hu, and R. Kashi (Eds.): DAS 2002, LNCS 2423, pp. 519–531, 2002.

in the ground truth. In fact, we make the assumption that whenever a system can reliably decompose a document into its constituent components and their structure, that existing OCR methods can extract the content from a text zone.

The documents in the dataset show a great variety in complexity, ranging from simple one-column pages with one picture, to pages with several layers of document objects with multiple overlapping pictures. It is important to be able to quantify the complexity of a document in the collection prior to evaluation. If the complexity of documents in a dataset is known and well-defined, the complexity measures can be used to weight the evaluation results leading to evaluation independent of page difficulty [5]. It should be noted here that complexity is task dependent. A document can be simple for one task while being very difficult for another. Therefore, there is a need for a set of measures that collectively cover the whole document analysis process.

Such a set of complexity measures would rank the data, but evaluation measures are needed to assess the algorithm's performance on that data.

The existing evaluation methods for layout analysis can be grouped into two main categories: text-based and region-based evaluation. Text-based evaluation [7] uses textual ground truth and the edit distance to measure the errors in layout detection. Region-based evaluation methods [20,9,8,10] compare the outline of the detected zones with the zone description in the ground truth.

For evaluating document analysis algorithms for color documents the region based methods are most suited as they can easily be applied to both text, pictures, and graphics. We do, however, have to extend them first to be able to evaluate color document analysis.

This paper is organized as follows. In Section 2 we describe the dataset and a model for its content. Section 3 defines the complexity of the documents with respect to the different tasks in color document analysis. For each of these tasks an appropriate evaluation measure is derived in Section 4. Finally, Section 5 discusses how the ground truth is generated .

2   Document Dataset

In this section we will describe the documents that comprise the document dataset. We then define models to describe the content of each document.

2.1   Dataset Content

A dataset for evaluation of color document analysis should be created following some guidelines. Firstly, to cover different applications, the dataset must be comprised of document pages of varying style and complexity. Secondly, color must be an essential component of the message the author wants to convey. Otherwise, the document is probably equivalent to a black-and-white document.

We found that commercial color magazines form the most representative category of color documents. Even inside a single issue the document pages show a great variety in style, ranging from simple pages containing text only, to highly complex color advertisements. Especially in the latter category of pages, the color is chosen carefully to attract the readers' attention. A system tested well on such a dataset will perform well on most other applications.

For the UvA Color Document Dataset, we have scanned (300dpi, color-24bits) full issues of the internationally available magazines listed in Table 1. These are representatives of scientific magazines, informative magazines, lifestyle magazines, and weekly news magazines. The issues together form a dataset of more than one thousand scanned pages.

The dataset set is made available via a website[1]. Access to this site is restricted to registered researchers. To use the images in publications each author should individually seek permission from the magazines' publication office.

2.2   The Document Model

For defining the ground truth, which provides the basis for evaluation, a document model is needed that captures all essential information in the document.

The model should be based on two different views of the document: the layout information - encoding the presentation of the document - and the logical information - encoding the meaning of the document.

The basic entities in both views are the n document objects in the document object set $\mathcal{O} = \{o_1, o_2, ..., o_n\}$, which hold the content of the document. Each document object is an entity in which the content has a uniform style expressing some intention of the author. So, an element in $\mathcal{O}$ can for example be a single picture used as illustration or a text line in bold acting as a header.

The two different views of the content of a document objects use different attributes to describe the content. Layout attributes are restricted to the geometric and color properties of the document objects. Logical attributes are functional labels expressing the function of the document object. The object sets $\mathcal{O}_g$ and $\mathcal{O}_l$ denote the set $\mathcal{O}$ with geometric and logical attributes added respectively.

An element in $\mathcal{O}$ does not appear in isolation, but an author adds structure to the set $\mathcal{O}$. A simple tree, often use for black-and-white documents, cannot describe all possible spatial relations between the document objects. Separate graphs are used to describe relations like overlap and inclusion. Thus the layout structure is given by a set of graphs where the vertices are the document objects $\mathcal{O}_g$ and the edges $\mathcal{R}_g$ denote a relation between the objects. The graphs can be directed or undirected and can have weights to encode attributes of the edges. As the vertices are the same for every graph, the layout structure is defined as follows: $\mathcal{G} = \langle \mathcal{O}_g, \mathcal{R}_g^1, \mathcal{R}_g^2, ... \rangle$. Similarly the logical structure is defined as: $\mathcal{L} = \langle \mathcal{O}_l, \mathcal{R}_l^1, \mathcal{R}_l^2, ... \rangle$.

Although logical structure (and sometimes layout) can span different pages, we use, for simplicity, a page based approach where every page receives a layout and logical structure. A full document $\mathcal{D}$ is represented by: $\mathcal{D} = \langle (\mathcal{G}_1, \mathcal{L}_1), (\mathcal{G}_2, \mathcal{L}_2) ... \rangle$. In the following subsections we describe how the generic model defined above is instantiated to describe the ground truth for the dataset.

---

[1] http://www.science.uva.nl/uva-doc

2.3 Geometric Description

For the geometric description of a document we consider three major different categories of documents objects namely text, image, and graphics.

In the description of the outline of these objects we make a distinction between the *shape* and the *region* of a document object. With shape we denote the perceived shape of the object which in a layered document could be partly obscured by another document object. The object region is the true shape of the object. In the following, the object itself will be indicated as o, the shape of the object as $\bar{o}$ and the region of the object as $\hat{o}$. In a similar way $\hat{O}$ where O is a set of objects denotes the regions of all objects in the set.

To describe a geometric document object, the following attributes are used:

- geometric attributes;
  - category: {text, image, graphics};
  - shape: {line, rectangle, polygon, ellipse};
  - object region: set of polygons with possible holes;
  - orientation: horizontal, vertical, other;
- color attributes for text objects;
  - text: {uniform, mixture of uniform colors, texture}
  - background: {uniform, mixture of uniform colors, image, texture }

For later use, let us define notations for the following subsets of geometric document objects based on individual category and one mixed class for pictorial information: $T=\{o \in \mathcal{O}_g | category(o)=text\}$, $G=\{o \in \mathcal{O}_g | category(o)=graphics\}$, $I=\{o \in \mathcal{O}_g | category(o)=image\}$ and $P=\text{GUI}$. With respect to the shape of the document object we have: $\mathcal{O}_g^X = \{o \in \mathcal{O}_g | shape(o)=X\}$. For text document objects we introduce the generic notation T_f^b indicating a textobject with foreground type t and background type b. Choices for f and b are uniform (u), non-uniform ($\neg u$), graphic (g), image (i), or nothing (), the latter indicating that the foreground or background can be any of the given types.

The geometric structure of the document is the structure induced by the layers in the document. Edges in the geometric structure graph are defined by the *on top* relation, indicating that the object is in a higher layer. The relation is formally defined as $\mathcal{R}_g = \{(o_1, o_2) \in \mathcal{O}_g | \bar{o}_1 \cap \bar{o}_2 \cap \hat{o}_1 \neq \emptyset\}$.

2.4 Logical Description

After an analysis of the magazines in the dataset, for each type of document object a set of possible representative logical labels were selected. Object classes which are not frequently appearing in the dataset receive the label *"Other"*. Of course these could be refined later. It leads to the following logical attributes:

- logical label
  - text: {Author, Abstract, Bibliography, Caption, Equation, Header, Footer, Foot Note, List, Table, Title, Quote, Paragraph, Page Number, Advertisement, Note, Other};
  - image: {Advertisement, Image Containing Scene Text, Other};
  - graphics: {Separator, Border, Logo, Map, Barcode, Graph, Other};

All of the above document objects with their logical labels could be part of the logical structure of the document. As reading order is most important, we focus on this particular structure.

The reading order is based on the relation *before in reading* denoted by $<_r$. So the logical structure graph has as vertices the logical document objects $\mathcal{O}_l$ and there is a directed edge between $o_1, o_2 \in \mathcal{O}_l$ whenever $o_1 <_r o_2$. To be a proper reading order graph it should be a-cyclic. Then, any path in the graph is an independent reading order in the document. If there are multiple paths in the graph they are related to groups of document objects which can be read in arbitrary order. So for logical structure we have: $\mathcal{R}_l = \{(o_1, o_2) \in \mathcal{O}_l | o_1 <_r o_2\}$

3 Document Complexity

The performance of an algorithm on a given dataset depends on two things. Namely the quality of the algorithm itself and the complexity of the data. This complexity of the data is task dependent. When a ground truth is available the complexity can be computed beforehand. It can then be used to order the documents in the dataset so that one can choose a certain level of complexity for designing and testing the algorithm.

Before defining such a set of complexity measures we first consider which steps are performed when doing color document analysis.

3.1 Document Analysis Steps

We decompose color document analysis into four major steps:
- *page segmentation*: determination of the set of geometric document objects $\mathcal{O}_g$.
- *layout detection*: determination of the relation $\mathcal{R}_g$.
- *logical object classification*: determination of the logical document objects $\mathcal{O}_l$.
- *reading order detection*: determination of the relation $\mathcal{R}_l$.
For each of the steps a complexity measure will be derived: C_1 - Complexity for page segmentation; C_2 - Complexity for layout detection; C_3 - Complexity for logical object classification; C_4 - Complexity for reading order detection. These measures are all defined for a document page and can be computed from the ground truth graphs corresponding to the page. For a document, the complexity of each task is computed by averaging the complexities of individual pages.

3.2 Document Complexity for Page Segmentation

Analyzing the difficulties of the page segmentation algorithms described in literature [11,13,19], we identified four main factors that influence the quality of the results. These factors are: *non-uniformity in color, shape irregularity, picture/text ratio* and the *amount of pictorial document objects containing text*.

Taking into account the above, we consider a document page containing only uniformly colored text objects, having rectangular shapes, on a uniform background to have complexity zero. An example of a document page of maximum complexity is one containing an image in the background, completely covering the page, with text objects with non-uniform color and irregularly shaped boundaries placed on top of it. For each of the four factors we have designed a complexity measure which is normalized to the range [0,1].

The first measure is based on the textstrings that are either not uniformly colored or have a non-uniform background. Using $|.|$ to denote the cardinality of a set and using the shorthands from section 2.3: $c_1^1 = \frac{|\mathcal{T}_u^g| + |\mathcal{T}_u^i| + |\mathcal{T}_{\neg u}|}{|\mathcal{T}|}$. The second measure considers the percentage of non-regular shapes: $c_1^2 = \frac{|\mathcal{O}_g^P| + |\mathcal{O}_g^E|}{|\mathcal{O}_g|}$. The third complexity measure considers the area of the geometric union of all the shapes corresponding to pictorial document objects, normalized by the width (w) and height (h) of the page: $c_1^3 = \frac{Area(\cup_{o \in P} \delta)}{w * h}$. Finally, the fourth measure considers the subset of graphics and image objects containing text, denoted by P^{ct} : $c_1^4 = \frac{|P^{ct}|}{|P|}$.

The complexity C_1 for page segmentation is defined as a linear combination of the four complexity features defined above.

$$C_1 = \frac{c_1^1 + c_1^2 + c_1^3 + c_2^4}{4} \tag{1}$$

3.3 Document Complexity for Layout Detection

The problem of detecting multiple layers in color documents has, to our knowledge, not been addressed. The DjVu system [1] can be seen as an exception, however, the system is restricted to one foreground and one background layer, and more importantly the goal is compression not analysis.

As defined in section 2.3 the geometric structure is based on the observation that we perceive a regularly shaped objects as the full object even if it is partly occluded. Clearly the larger the occlusion the less clear this observation can be made. Therefore, to measure the complexity of the decision whether two elements overlap we consider the area of the intersection relative to the union of the two objects. Subsequently this is summed over all object pairs.

$$C_2 = \frac{1}{|\mathcal{R}_g|} \sum_{o_1 \neq o_2} \left\{ \frac{Area(\bar{o}_1 \cap \bar{o}_2)}{Area(\bar{o}_1 \cup \bar{o}_2)} \right\} \tag{2}$$

3.4 Document Complexity for Logical Object Classification

In general, logical object classification is based on layout features (visual appearance), content, and possible apriori information about the document class. Here, for deriving a complexity measure we use visual appearance only.

The complexity of the classification problem is determined by the similarity in visual appearance within a logical class and the dissimilarity between different logical classes. However, the variability and separability depend on the geometric features used and the classification method. As we want the complexity measure to be independent of the specific method used, we focus on the number of different classes on the page that have to be distinguished rather.

To be precise, let L_t denote the set of possible text labels for logical objects and let L_i and L_g be defined likewise for image labels and graphics labels. Furthermore, let L' denote the set of labels actually present on the page. Then the complexity measure for logical labeling is given as:

$$C_3 = \frac{1}{3} \left\{ \frac{|L_t'|}{|L_t|} + \frac{|L_i'|}{|L_i|} + \frac{|L_g'|}{|L_g|} \right\}$$

(3)

3.5 Document Complexity for Reading Order Detection

Analyzing existing methods for reading order detection [17,16], it is observed that methods work well if document objects are nicely ordered e.g. in a column. Performance degrades if the reading order "jumps" from one object to the other in a non-regular way. To that end we will derive a complexity measure that measures the irregularity of the reading path when it is visiting the different text objects in the document.

Recall that the reading order is defined through the before in reading order relation $<_r$. Each maximal path in the graph with edges defined through this relation gives an independent reading path. Thus we can write the relation $\mathcal{R} = r_0, r_1, \ldots$ where each $r_i = (o_1, o_2, \ldots, o_{m(i)})$ is such a maximal path in the graph.

We now define a measure of irregularity for a path r_i. We consider the polyline with vertices p_j for $j = 1, m(i)$ that results if one connects the centres of gravity of the subsequent document objects in r_i. Now for analysis of reading order, based on geometric information, the simplest assumption one can make is that for finding p_{j+1} from p_j one continues in the direction of the vector from p_{j-1} to p_j. In general cases the point will be found in a different direction. Therefore, we define the turning angle α_j at p_j as the angle between the expected direction and the actual direction in which p_{j+1} can be found. The turning angle can be computed using the innerproduct as:

$$\alpha(j) = \cos^{-1} \frac{|\overrightarrow{p_{j-1}, p_j} \cdot \overrightarrow{p_j, p_{j+1}}|}{|\overrightarrow{p_{j-1}, p_j}||\overrightarrow{p_j, p_{j+1}}|}$$

(4)

For a page, the average turning angle on any path is computed. Normalizing to $[0,1]$ the complexity measure for reading order detection is given by:

$$C_4 = \sum_{i=1}^{|\mathcal{R}|} \left(\frac{1}{(m(i) - 2)\pi} \sum_{j=2}^{m(i)} \alpha(j) \right)$$

(5)

For the four complexity measures, examples of increasing complexity are presented in Figure 1. To get an insight in the overall distribution of documents in the dataset, Table 1 gives the four complexity values averaged for each document of the UvA Data Set.

4   Evaluation Measures

Complexity measures give an indication of the expected difficulty of a task based on the data, prior to the use of an algorithm. Evaluation measures are needed to compare different algorithms performing the task.

4.1   Precision and Recall

Precision and recall are well known evaluation measures. Let us first consider the general definition. Let S be a set of ground truth elements and let S' be the result of any task aiming at deriving the ground truth elements. Then precision and recall are given by: $p = \frac{|S' \cap S|}{|S'|}$ $r = \frac{|S' \cap S|}{|S|}$

When results are not discrete sets, but correspond to regions in the image, the same definitions can be used by using the area of the regions instead of counting the number of elements in a set.

To identify how elements contributed to the precision and recall measures, we can derive the following sets: $Correct = S \cap S'$, $Misdetection = S \backslash S'$ and $FalseAlarm = S' \backslash S$. In the following, the sets S and S' will be made specific for the evaluation of the different tasks.

4.2   Page Segmentation

For evaluation of page segmentation we are faced with the problem that there is no one-to-one correspondence defined between the areas found by the algorithm and the areas given in the ground truth. The same problem was encountered in evaluation of segmentation of a page into text lines by Liang et al. [9,8]. We base our measures on the method proposed in the reference and extended by Mao and Kanungo in [10]. It is straightforward to use the definitions for the more general objects we consider.

So let us make this more precise. Whereas the ground truth objects are given by $\mathcal{O}_g$ let the result of the page segmentation be given by $\mathcal{O}'_g$. To find the likelihood of a match between elements in the two sets we consider the pairwise

Table 1. The average complexity values for UvA Color Document Dataset.

Magazine	Pages	C_1	C_2	C_3	C_4
Cosmopolitan	362	0.29	0.09	0.11	0.05
Time	94	0.22	0.22	0.24	0.16
NewsWeek	64	0.22	0.20	0.25	0.29
National Geographic	160	0.20	0.04	0.09	0.02
IEEE Spectrum	106	0.10	0.15	0.26	0.27
The NewYorker	96	0.08	0.04	0.07	0.01
IEEE Computer	132	0.02	0.03	0.07	0.01

Fig. 1. Example images of various complexities. On the first row, complexity for page segmentation is ranging from a simple page containing only text, to a page with an image as background and polygonal text zones on top($C_1 = 0.0, 0.07, 0.66, 0.74$). On the second row, one can see documents with increasing complexity for layout detection ($C_2 = 0.0, 0.02, 0.12, 0.42$). The simplest example has document objects fully visible. In the most complex example the occluded area is large. Third row shows documents with increasing complexity ($C_3 = 0.03, 0.17, 0.27, 0.48$.) for logical classification. The first document has 1 logical label only, whereas the last document has 12 different labels. On the fourth row are presented documents with increasing complexity for reading order detection ($C_4 = 0.0, 0.20, 0.54, 0.91$.). Paths clearly range from regular to very irregular.

precision and recall between the object with index i in $\mathcal{O}'_g$ and the object with index j in $\mathcal{O}_g$ as follows:

$$p_1^{ij} = \frac{Area(\hat{o}'_i \cap \hat{o}_j)}{Area(\hat{o}'_i)} \qquad r_1^{ij} = \frac{Area(\hat{o}'_i \cap \hat{o}_j)}{Area(\hat{o}_j)} \tag{6}$$

Based on the analysis of the values for all possible pairs, Liang et.al. introduced six categories to measure the quality of detection. The first three are similar to the ones we encountered, but the imprecision of the match between two objects is taken into account.

To identify the correctly detected elements, let us define the approximate intersection $X \tilde{\cap} Y$ which gives the pairwise area intersection of all elements for which $r_1^{ij} \approx 1$ and $p_1^{ij} \approx 1$. Further categories are *misdetection* if for all $j : r_1^{ij} \approx 0$ and *false alarm* if for all $i : p_1^{ij} \approx 0$. In addition some more sets are identified to give the category of error, similar to [9,8].

Note that the above definition requires two thresholds T_l and T_h to judge whether values are close to 0 or 1 respectively. The actual values for these two thresholds were selected by analyzing the p_1^{ij} and r_1^{ij} matrices, for 7 randomly selected pages from the dataset, groundtruthed twice. We found $T_h = 0.80$ and $T_l = 0.05$ to be the appropriate threshold values for the UvA data set.

The above-described measures give accurate local information. The definitions of global precision and recall for a page are:

$$p_l = \frac{Area(\hat{O}_g \tilde{\cap} \hat{O}'_g)}{Area(\hat{O}'_g)} \qquad r_l = \frac{Area(\hat{O}_g \tilde{\cap} \hat{O}'_g)}{Area(\hat{O}_g)} \qquad (7)$$

After this task we assume that we have found the match between $\mathcal{O}$ and $\mathcal{O}'$ defined by the pairs of elements in the two sets for which $r_1^{ij} \approx 1$ and $p_1^{ij} \approx 1$. The objects in the matched graphs will be denoted by $\tilde{O}$ and $\tilde{O}'$ respectively. Likewise, relations between those objects in the result and the ground truth are indicated by $\tilde{R}_g$ and $\tilde{R}'_g$. Further evaluation is restricted to those two object sets and relations to assure that errors made in the page segmentation do not propagate into further evaluation.

4.3   Evaluation of Layout Detection

In the layout detection for color documents, what needs to be evaluated is whether the geometric relations between document objects are found correctly. In our case this corresponds to evaluating whether the edges corresponding to pairs in the overlap relation $\mathcal{R}_g$ are correct.

Following the notation just introduced, this gives the following precision and recall measures for step 2 of the analysis process:

$$p_2 = \frac{|\tilde{R}'_g \cap \mathcal{R}_g|}{|\tilde{R}'_g|} \qquad r_2 = \frac{|\tilde{R}'_g \cap \mathcal{R}_g|}{|\tilde{R}_g|} \qquad (8)$$

4.4   Evaluation of Logical Objects Classification

To evaluate the classification of objects into logical classes we have to find the objects in both the ground truth and the results with a specific label. We define: $\tilde{O}_l^i = \{o \in \tilde{O} | \text{logical label}(o) = i\}$ and $\tilde{O}_{l'}^i = \{o \in \tilde{O}' | \text{logical label}(o) = i\}$.

Furthermore, we need the intersection m of the objects in the result and the ground truth according to the labels: $m_{ij} = \tilde{O}_l^i \cap \tilde{O}_{l'}^i$.

By considering the cardinality of each m_{ij} we get the well known confusion matrix for classification. To evaluate the performance on the whole page we need to identify the set of objects M which were classified correctly i.e. all elements in m_{ii}. It leads to the following overall measures:

$$p_3 = \frac{|\bigcup_i(\tilde{O}_l^i \cap \tilde{O}_{l'}^i)|}{|\bigcup_i(\tilde{O}_{l'}^i)|} \qquad r_3 = \frac{|\bigcup_i(\tilde{O}_l^i \cap \tilde{O}_{l'}^i)|}{|\bigcup_i(\tilde{O}_l^i)|} \qquad (9)$$

4.5   Evaluation of Reading Order Detection

Evaluation of the final step in the analysis is similar to the layout detection as both are directly computed from the match between the edges of the graph. Again to avoid error propagation only the elements which received the correct label in the previous step are considered when matching the edges in the logical graph. Following the same notation conventions as earlier the relations between those objects in the result and the ground truth are indicated by $\tilde{R}_l$ and $\tilde{R}_{l'}$ respectively. So the final evaluation measures are given by:

$$p_4 = \frac{|\tilde{R}_{l'} \cap \tilde{R}_l|}{|\tilde{R}_{l'}|} \qquad r_4 = \frac{|\tilde{R}_{l'} \cap \tilde{R}_l|}{|\tilde{R}_l|} \qquad (10)$$

5   Implementation

Groundtruthing a complex color document is a difficult task. Firstly, because of the many relations between the different objects. Secondly, some subjective choices have to be made. We have therefore defined a set of rules the groundtruther has to obey. These are included in the dataset distribution. Even when the guidelines are strictly obeyed there will always be a variation between different evaluators as the boundary of an object has to be indicated by hand.

To measure the inherent variability in ground truth definition we performed a variability test. From each magazine we selected 4 document pages for each of the four complexity classes, thus 16 document pages. These were ground truthed 4 times in total by two different evaluators. The 4 ground-truth files obtained by the four evaluation runs are evaluated in pairs, each of them playing the role of ground-truth and result respectively. We use the same evaluation measures used before for each step to compute the variability. The evaluation results for all six possible pairs are averaged to get the variability measure. We concluded from these measures that the groundtruth in UvA-dataset is reproducible up to 97% -99% depending on task.

The ground truth was manually generated using the **GT-UvA** ground-truth editor software, implemented in VisualC++. The user interface allows the user to indicate the perceived shape of document objects by drawing rectangular, circular, elliptical, or polygonal shape around the document objects. The true shape is automatically computed. The layout and logical descriptions are then introduced via a property dialog box. The ground truth can be exported in a plain ASCII or in XML format. The evaluation measures described in Section 4 are implemented in a C++ program, called **Eval**. Eval takes as arguments two text files, one containing the ground truth information, the other the result description of a document page. It prints out the four precision and recall values.

6   Conclusion

To advance the field in color document analyis a well-defined dataset is essential. We have created the UvA color document dataset consisting of over 1000 document pages, ground truthed at the geometric and logical level.

To describe the document pages a graph based model is proposed. Based on the model the process of document analysis has been decomposed into four steps dealing with the vertices or edges of either the geometric graph or the logical graph describing the document.

As the variety of color documents ranges from very simple to complicated structures, we have defined four complexity measures which rank the document complexity for each of the four steps of the document image analysis.

For each of the four steps evaluation measures are defined. All of them are derived from the general evaluation measures precision and recall.

Finally, the documents and associated tools are available on a restricted basis to the research community via a special website.

References

1. L. Bottou, P. Haffner, P.G. Howard, and Y. LeCun. Djvu: Analyzing and compressing scanned documents for internet distribution. In *ICDAR'99, Bangalore, India*, pages 625–628, 1999.
2. W.Y. Chen and S.Y. Chen. Adaptive page segmentation for color technical journals' cover images. *Image and Vision Computing*, 16(3):855–877, 1998.
3. C. Garcia and X. Apostolidis. Text detection and segmentation in complex color images. In *Proceedings of IEEE International Conference on Acoustics, Speech and Signal Processing*, pages 75–78, Istanbul, 2000.
4. H. Hase, T. Shinokawa, M. Yoneda, M. Sakai, and H. Maruyama. Character string extraction from a color document. In *ICDAR'99*, pages 75–78, India, 1999.
5. X.S. Hua, L. Wenyin, and H.J. Zhang. Automatic performance evaluation for video text detection. In *Proc. of the 6th ICDAR'01*, pages 545–550, Seattle, USA, 2001.
6. A.K. Jain and B. Yu. Automatic text location in images and video frames. *Pattern Recognition*, 31(12):2055–2076, 1998.
7. J. Kanai, S.V. Rice, T.A. Nartker, and G. Nagy. Automated evaluation of ocr zoning. *IEEE Transactions on PAMI*, 17(1):86–90, 1995.
8. J. Liang, I.T. Phillips, and R. Haralick. An optimization methodology for document structure extraction on latin character documents. *IEEE Transactions on PAMI*, 23(7):719–734, 2001.
9. J. Liang, R. Rogers, R. Haralick, and I. Phillips. Uw-isl document image analysis toolbox: An experimental environment. In *Proc. of the 4th ICDAR, Ulm, Germany, August 1997.*, pages 984–988, 1997.
10. S. Mao and T. Kanungo. Empirical performance evaluation methodology and its application to page segmentation algorithms. *IEEE Transaction on PAMI*, 23(3):242–256, 2001.
11. G. Nagy. Twenty years of document image analysis in PAMI. *IEEE Trans. Pattern Analysis and Machine Intelligence*, 22(1):38–62, 2000.
12. T. Perroud, K. Sobottka, H. Bunke, and L. Hall. Text extraction from color documents - clustering approaches in three and four dimensions. In *Proceedings of the 6th ICDAR'01*, pages 937–941, Seattle, USA, 2001.

13. D.S. Ryu, S.M. Kang, and S.W. Lee. Parameter-independent geometric document layout analysis. In *Proceedings of the 2000 International Conference on Pattern Recognition ICPR'00.*, pages 397–400, Barcelona, Spain, 2000.

14. J. Sauvola, S. Haapakoski, H. Kauniskangas, T. Seppanen, M. Pietiklainen, and D. Doermann. A distributed management system for testing document image analysis algorithms. In *Proceedings of the 4th ICDAR'97*, pages 989–995, Ulm, Germany, 1997.

15. J. Sauvola and H. Kauniskangas. MediaTeam Document Database II. CD-ROM collection of document images, University of Oulu, Finland. http://www.mediateam.oulu.fi/MTDB/index.html.

16. L. Todoran, M. Aiello, C. Monz, and M. Worring. Logical structure detection for hetrogeneous document classes. In *Proc. SPIE Vol. 3407, Document Recognition and Retrieval VIII.*, pages 99–111, San Jose, California, 2001.

17. S. Tsujimoto and H. Asada. Major Components of a Complete Text Reading System. *Proceedings of the IEEE*, 80(7):1133–1149, 1992.

18. V.Wu, R. Manmatha, and E.M. Riseman. Textfinder: An automatic system to detect and recognize text in images. *IEEE Trans. on PAMI*, 21(11):1224–1229, 1999.

19. T. Watanabe and T. Sobue. Layout analysis of complex documents. In *Proceedings of the 2000 International Conference on Pattern Recognition ICPR'00.*, pages 447–450, Barcelona, Spain, 2000.

20. B. Yanikoglu and L. Vincent. Pink panther: A complete environment for ground-truthing and benchmarking document page segmentation. *Pattern Recognition Letters*, 31(9):1191–1204, 1997.

Exploiting WWW Resources in Experimental Document Analysis Research

Daniel Lopresti

Bell Labs, Lucent Technologies Inc.
600 Mountain Avenue
Murray Hill, NJ 07974 USA
dpl@research.bell-labs.com

Abstract. Many large collections of document images are now becoming available online as part of digital library initiatives, fueled by the explosive growth of the World Wide Web. In this paper, we examine protocols and system-related issues that arise in attempting to make use of these new resources, both as a target application (building better search engines) and as a way of overcoming the problem of acquiring ground-truth to support experimental document analysis research. We also report on our experiences running two simple tests involving data drawn from one such collection. The potential synergies between document analysis and digital libraries could lead to substantial benefits for both communities.

1 Introduction

In the six years that have passed since a paper at an earlier DAS workshop identified potential synergies between the World Wide Web and the field of document analysis [1], the Web has established itself as the largest distributed collection of documents in the history of civilization. Many researchers are now exploring problems that have arisen out of this phenomenon, including, for example, the extraction and recognition of text embedded in color GIF and JPEG images [2,3]. Document analysis is being applied to the conversion process of placing archival material on the WWW (*e.g.*, [4]). Moreover, the pervasive impact of the Web has spawned work in related areas, including the use of XML to represent recognition results [5]. Such opportunities and challenges were the subject of a recent workshop [6].

Despite this flurry of activity centered around the Web, there is an important development that appears to have been largely overlooked: that is, the rapidly growing body of traditional scanned documents now being made available online. In retrospect, this should come as no surprise as: (1) the WWW was always touted as a delivery mechanism for multimedia content, (2) documents serve as a basic "quantum" of information in our society, and (3) most users are generally oblivious to the distinction between a page presented in image format versus one encoded in, say, HTML. Often, collections of scanned documents are

D. Lopresti, J. Hu, and R. Kashi (Eds.): DAS 2002, LNCS 2423, pp. 532–543, 2002.

the product of digital library projects aimed at preserving and disseminating works of historical significance (*e.g.*, [7,8]).

For example, the *Making of America* collection (part of Cornell University's Prototype Digital Library [7]) comprises 267 monographs (books) and 22 journals (equaling 955 serial volumes) for a total of 907,750 pages, making it almost 1,000 times larger than the dataset offered on the UW1 CD-ROM [9]. The procedures used in creating this digital library match standard methodologies employed in experimental document analysis research:

> "The materials in the MOA collection were scanned from the original paper source, with materials disbound locally due to the brittle nature of many of the items ... The images were captured at 600 dpi in TIFF image format and compressed using CCITT Group 4. Minimal document structuring occurred at the point of conversion, primarily linking image numbers to pagination and tagging self-referencing portions of the text ...
>
> Further conversion included both optical character recognition of the page images, and SGML-encoding of the ensuing textual information." [10]

While OCR results are used for full text retrieval purposes, the default view returned to users of the system is an image of a scanned page.

Fig. 1 shows a snapshot of a browser window displaying a page from *Making of America* on the left [11], and another example of an online document image, a card from the catalog for Princeton University's library, on the right [12].

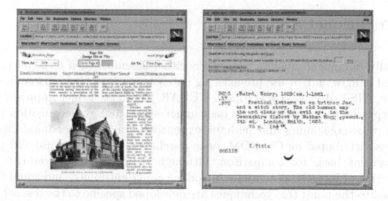

Fig. 1. Examples of documents delivered in image format on the Web

As a result of such efforts at bringing scanned documents online, several intriguing opportunities present themselves to researchers working in document analysis. The most obvious of these would be to apply state-of-the-art techniques to build higher quality and/or more powerful indices for information retrieval and presentation. This notion of crafting a better third-party search engine for digital libraries has an analog on the Web as a whole, where competing search engines vie for users by indexing documents encoded in HTML, PDF, PostScript, and other "easy" formats. It is certainly possible to imagine doing a better job on the MOA collection; for example, a search for the keyword "modem" returns 1,364 hits in documents published between 1815 and 1926, even though the word was first coined in the early 1950's.[1] Two of the librarians in the project write:

> "Our attention to retaining pagination and document structure will allow us to selectively insert improved OCR as it is completed. As we insert the more accurate OCR over time, we expect that the greatly improved OCR will make the searching tools even more effective." [14]

Beyond this relatively straightforward improvement, it seems conceivable that higher-level document analysis methods could provide useful new paradigms for retrieval from digital libraries.

Another thought-provoking possibility would be to use existing online collections of scanned images as a way of overcoming the problem of acquiring sufficient training and testing data to support experimental document analysis research. This matter is regarded as so pressing that it was one of the prime motivations behind the creation of the Open Mind Initiative [15], a project to enlist Web users around the world to assist in the labeling of ground-truth data for algorithm development. But while Open Mind deals with this one aspect of the problem, it does not address where the raw data comes from, or what qualifies it as "relevant." These issues will be a focus of this paper.

2   Traditional Approaches

Typically, document analysis researchers either assemble their own collections of scanned images and/or use pre-existing datasets, such as those disseminated by UW [9], NIST [16], UNLV [17], and CEDAR [18]. The former approach allows the corpus to be targeted to the task under study, but the acquisition process can be time-consuming and perhaps expensive. On the other hand, standard datasets distributed on CD-ROM, once purchased, are easy to use and provide a convenient basis for comparison, although they may not cover the precise application of interest, potentially introduce copyright issues, and could become overused to the point that techniques are developed specific to the test set, which is usually relatively small.

Another methodology designed to replace or supplement the previous two approaches involves synthesizing training or testing data. There are, for example, models for generating noisy page images [19] and for creating random instances of tables [20]. While it is possible to produce an endless stream of data in this way, there is always the question of whether such data is truly representative.

---

[1] This test was inspired by a discussion in Baker's book *Double Fold*, p. 71 [13].

3   Exploiting WWW Resources

As we have noted, there is an enormous quantity of page image data now available on the Web. How might this be used to support document analysis research? Consider the basic steps involved in building datasets for either training or testing purposes: (1) collecting and scanning representative pages, (2) labeling the ground-truth, and (3) distributing the dataset. While the last step might not seem strictly necessary, good scientific practice requires describing experiments in sufficient detail that it is possible to reproduce them. With that in mind, it clearly becomes important that the test data be accessible to other researchers.

With digital libraries, the first and last of these steps are already taken care of. The pages have been scanned and are freely available online. The developer of the library presumably has dealt with any copyright issues connected to the works in question. Furthermore, it is easy to argue that such pages must be representative because they are, in fact, real documents of definite value to some target audience. Still, there remains the question of what to do about labeling the ground-truth. What are the available options?

One solution would be to make use of the existing ground-truth provided by the digital library itself (*e.g.*, the OCR results in the case of the *Making of America* collection). Another would be to develop protocols for using truth produced and/or maintained by a third party (previous researchers who have used the same test documents, or an Open Mind-like entity). A third approach would be to study evaluation techniques that do not depend on having an explicit ground-truth (*e.g.*, comparing retrieval effectiveness relative to what is obtained when using the source library's tools).

4   Proof of Concept: Analysis of a Digital Library

To explore the ideas outlined in this paper, we have performed two simple "proof of concept" exercises: the first using the *pagereader* system developed by Baird at Bell Labs [21] to OCR a set of pages randomly chosen from the *Making of America* digital library [7], and the second examining an algorithm we have proposed with colleagues for table detection [22]. This sort of evaluation is fundamentally different from the kinds typically described in the literature. Because the selection of test images is unbiased and completely automatic, the pages in question are never seen in advance by the researcher(s) involved in running the tests; there can be no attempt, explicit or subconscious, to discard images that do not fit the model or to tune an algorithm to the dataset.[2] As a result, this criterion is almost certainly more demanding than what is normally encountered.

Most research systems for document analysis, including *pagereader* and our table detection code, assume the input image will be in TIF format, however TIF is not a native encoding for current Web browsers. In the case of *Making of America*, the pages are delivered in one of three possible formats: a "50% size"

---

[2] It is, of course, quite acceptable to maintain a record of the test documents that were used for an after-the-fact analysis.

GIF image, a "100% size" GIF image, and a PDF document containing the original scanned TIF. The GIF forms have relatively low spatial resolution, making use of grayscale (image depth) to compensate, and hence would be difficult to use without a significant amount of extra work. Hence, we chose to implement a process pipeline that first converts the PDF version of the page into PostScript and then extracts the image directly from the PostScript. In addition to the various image "flavors" of the page, the OCR output used to create the searchable index for *Making of America* is available. We can use this text for evaluation purposes, but must be careful about making assumptions concerning its quality or the way that it is formatted.[3]

Lacking our own complete index of the digital library, our approach to retrieving a random page image from *Making of America* is to issue a query by choosing a term from the Unix *spell* dictionary, which contains 24,259 words including a number of proper names. From the results of this search, we randomly choose one of the works (book or journal) that is returned, and from that work we select a specific page that contains a match. The implementation of the Web interface is programmed in Tcl/Tk using the Spynergy Toolkit [23].

It takes a total of six HTTP "round-trips" to get the data we need:

1. First, issue a search request using a randomly chosen keyword and retrieve the results.
2. The results are presented in "slices" of 50 works per HTML page. Randomly select a slice and retrieve it.
3. Within the slice, determine one of the works at random and retrieve it.
4. Within the work, randomly choose one of the matches and retrieve it.
5. Based on the HTML for the final target page, retrieve the PDF file that contains the embedded TIF image (which is then extracted locally).
6. In the same way, retrieve the OCR text corresponding to the target page.

The last step is skipped in the table detection experiment as it is unnecessary. We have developed a set of simple "wrappers" to extract the required information from the HTML code returned by the MOA server.

4.1 Optical Character Recognition

For the OCR experiment, we retrieved 250 pages from the digital library. On the occasions when an HTTP fetch timed-out (after 30 seconds for the initial connection, and 5 seconds for each subsequent buffer), the search was attempted again using a different term.[4] This situation seemed to arise most often when the original query generated an extremely large number of hits (tens of thousands); it is likely that the machine serving *Making of America* builds data structures that grow with the size of the result. The 10 most- and least-frequent matches are listed in Table 1. Note that there is a wide distribution and even arcane terms arise occasionally in the collection.

---

[3] Generally, we assume that the text may contain a modest number of OCR errors, but that any severe problems will have been detected and corrected by those responsible for building the digital library.

[4] We also re-ran searches that returned no matches.

Table 1. Most- and least-frequent matches in the OCR experiment

Most-Frequent			Least-Frequent		
Search Term	Matches	Works	Search Term	Matches	Works
enemy	236,021	15,000	psychopathic	4	4
science	103,160	31,956	gumdrop	4	2
edge	46,007	20,291	glamorous	3	3
sold	44,467	18,834	pentagram	3	3
empire	42,054	14,677	uninominal	3	3
taught	39,429	20,574	constructible	2	2
request	35,812	12,803	saddlebag	2	2
guide	35,667	17,192	dressmake	1	1
base	34,123	17,139	godparent	1	1
virtue	31,952	16,175	riverfront	1	1

The times need to retrieve and process the pages are graphed, in order of decreasing total time, in Fig. 2 (note that the y-axis uses a log scale).[5] The four components of the total are the times need to: (1) fetch the data, (2) convert the PDF to TIF, (3) OCR the image, and (4) compare the output from *pagereader* to the ground-truth. The minimum total time was 93 seconds, the maximum was 1,966 seconds, and the average was 376 seconds. These values are dominated by the time it took to perform OCR (minimum 42 seconds, maximum 1,890 seconds, average 323 seconds). In other words, OCR was responsible for 86% of the computation time, on average. On the other hand, processing the HTTP requests and retrieving the page images over the Internet amounted to only about 6% of the total. This ratio is likely to hold true for any kind of sophisticated document analysis, so overhead due to network delay should not be an issue.

Given the output from OCR and a suitable ground-truth, we would ordinarily apply techniques from approximate string matching to classify errors and provide a quantifiable measure of the accuracy of the recognition process. Such an approach will not work here, however. Although we presume the ground-truth contains a reasonably reliable representation of the text on the page (a "bag of words," if you will), we cannot be certain of the precise layout standards used by those who built the digital library. For example, a two-column page could be represented that way in the ground-truth, or it may be de-columnized. Arbitrary conventions might be employed for unrelated articles appearing on the same page. The fact that we have no guarantee there will be a correspondence between the reading orders for the OCR output and the truth, combined with the potential for large numbers of OCR errors and the need for the evaluation to be fully automated, means that string matching methods must be ruled out.

Instead, we have chosen to perform evaluation by applying a well-known measure developed in the context of information retrieval. The vector space model, first proposed by Salton, *et al.* [24], assigns large weights to terms that

---

[5] All tests were performed on an SGI O2 workstation (200 MHz MIPS R5000 CPU, 64 MB RAM).

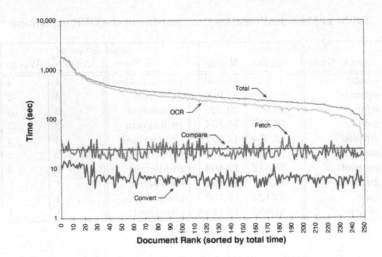

Fig. 2. Times to retrieve and process the 250 test pages used in the OCR experiment

occur frequently in a given document but rarely in others because such terms are able to distinguish the document in question from the rest of the collection. Let tf_{ik} be the frequency of term t_k in document D_i, n_k be the number of documents containing term t_k, T be the total number of terms, and N be the size of the collection. Then a common weighting scheme ($tf \times idf$) defines w_{ik}, the weight of term t_k in document D_i, to be:

$$w_{ik} = \frac{tf_{ik} \cdot log(N/n_k)}{\sqrt{\sum_{j=1}^{T}(tf_{ij})^2 \cdot (log(N/n_j))^2}} \ . \tag{1}$$

The summation in the denominator normalizes the length of the vector so that all documents have an equal chance of being retrieved. Given query vector $Q_i = (w_{i1}, w_{i2}, \ldots, w_{iT})$ and document vector $D_j = (w_{j1}, w_{j2}, \ldots, w_{jT})$, a dot product is computed to quantify the similarity between the two. In our analysis, we apply this measure using word unigram tokens with stopword removal.

The similarity scores for the 250 test documents relative to their ground-truths are graphed in Fig. 3, sorted in order of decreasing similarity. The maximum was 0.916, the minimum 0.030, and the average 0.520. While these values may seem low, one must keep in mind several important mitigating factors: (1) the severity of the test, (2) the "ground-truth" may itself contain OCR errors, and (3) vector space similarity is not identical to OCR accuracy. A more detailed examination of the results for the 5 best and 5 worst documents, as listed in Table 1, provides subjective confirmation that this paradigm makes useful distinctions between "easy" and "hard" pages for the system under study.

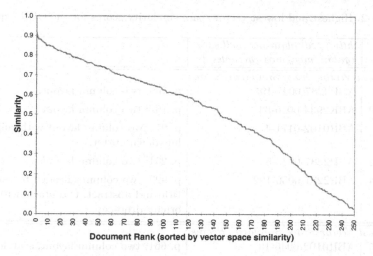

Fig. 3. Vector space similarity scores for the 250 test pages used in the OCR experiment

4.2 Table Detection

Our past work on table detection considered input in both ASCII and image format. In the latter case, we tested our techniques on a relatively small number of pages that we knew in advance contained tables. The focus was on whether the algorithm could correctly delimit the boundaries of a table and its various component regions. Another important aspect of the detection problem, however, is deciding when tables are present in an unknown input. Indeed, for many real applications this must be the first step and hence becomes a key issue.

As reported elsewhere (*e.g.*, [22]), our approach to table detection is to formulate the task of partitioning the input into tables as an optimization problem that can be solved using dynamic programming. Say that $tab[i, j]$ is a measure of our confidence when text lines i through j are interpreted as a single table. Let $merit_{pre}(i, [i+1, j])$ be the merit of prepending line i to the table extending from line $i+1$ to line j, and $merit_{app}([i, j-1], j)$ be the merit of appending line j to the table extending from line i to line $j-1$. Then:

$$tab[i, j] = \max \begin{cases} merit_{pre}(i, [i+1, j]) \; + \; tab[i+1, j] \\ tab[i, j-1] \; + \; merit_{app}([i, j-1], j) \end{cases} \qquad (2)$$

The merit functions are based on white space correlation. This defines an upper triangular matrix with values for all possible table starting and ending positions.

The partitioning of the input into tables can then be expressed as an optimization problem. Let $score[i, j]$ correspond to the best way to interpret lines i through j as some number of (*i.e.*, zero or more) tables. The computation is:

$$score[i, j] = \max \begin{cases} tab[i, j] \\ \max_{i \leq k < j} \{score[i, k] \; + \; score[k+1, j]\} \end{cases} \qquad (3)$$

Table 2. Highest and lowest vector space similarity scores for the OCR experiment

Score	http://cdl.library.cornell.edu/ cgi-bin/moa/moa-cgi?notisid=	Note
Highest Vector Space Similarity Scores:		
0.916	ABP2287-0047-195	p. 766: two column layout.
0.889	ABK2934-0016-34	p. 192: two column layout.
0.883	ABR0102-0171-4	p. 97: two column layout with ruling line down gutter.
0.882	ABP2287-0042-55	p. 251: two column layout.
0.874	ABP2287-0056-192	p. 929: two columns headed by centered title and abstract, text starts with ornate drop-cap.
Lowest Vector Space Similarity Scores:		
0.045	ABR0102-0045-13	p. 661: two column layout, scan looks light, ground-truth also noisy.
0.038	ABS1821-0024-102	p. 46: three columns (newspaper format), page looks slightly skewed, irregular line spacing.
0.036	ABK4014-0008-45	p. 285: two columns, obvious skew, small font, tight spacing.
0.036	ABS1821-0006-20	p. 6: three columns, line drawing in middle of page, scan skewed and light, ground-truth also noisy.
0.030	ANU4519-0130	p. 881: two columns (index page from pension records including many proper names), sparse text, obvious skew.

The precise decomposition can be obtained by backtracking the sequence of decisions made in evaluating Eq. 3. Any region on the optimal path whose *tab* value is higher than a predetermined threshold is considered a table region.

Since our table detection procedure assumes single-column input, we used Nagy and Seth's X-Y cut algorithm [25] to segment the page images recursively, from the level of logical columns down to individual word bounding boxes.

The vast majority of pages in the *Making of America* collection contain no tables. Rather than begin with a completely random document as in the OCR experiment, we chose to search for pages that held a match for the query term "table." This yielded 103,176 hits in 33,595 works. Note that most of these still do not possess what we would call a table, since the term has many other, unrelated meanings (*e.g.*, it is an article of furniture). From this sub-collection, we selected 250 random pages and ran the X-Y cut and table detection algorithms, saving the 100 highest scores. For the steps shared with the first experiment, fetching the PDF file and converting it to TIF, the average times were comparable at

17 and 7 seconds, respectively (recall Fig. 2). The time to segment a page using X-Y cut was 31 seconds, and table detection required a little over 6 seconds.

For evaluations such as this, the familiar concepts of precision and recall are appropriate performance measures. While the former is relatively easy to compute after-the-fact (we simply need to examine each instance where the algorithm claims to have found a table), the latter requires knowing something about every document in the corpus which is not feasible when the collection is large. Hence, for now we must limit ourselves to precision measurements; these results are presented in Fig. 4. Ultimately, however, as knowledge is acquired working with the digital library, it should be possible to accumulate it for use in future tests. This "meta-data" (*e.g.*, which pages in MOA contain tables) could perhaps be published on the WWW as a supplemental index into the collection.

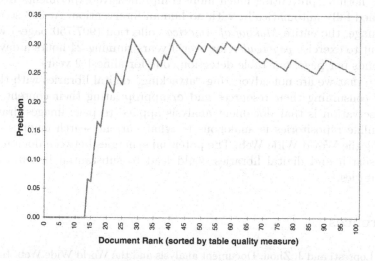

Fig. 4. Precision for the table detection experiment (top 100 hits)

Turning to the results, the 14 pages with the highest table quality measures (the value of $score[i, j]$ in Eq. 3) are false positives. In examining the documents in question (*e.g.*, http://cdl.library.cornell.edu/cgi-bin/moa/moa-cgi?notisid= ABS1821-0013-90, p. 30), we found that this was due to engraved line drawings with fine cross-hatching. While we had tuned our implementations of X-Y cut and table detection to ignore small components as noise, these made it through and generated extremely high white space correlations, thus fooling our system. Other problems were caused by page headings that use table-like spacing but are not really tables. Such scenarios might have been easy to overlook if not for the random page selection process used in the experiment.

5   Conclusions

In this paper, we have suggested that the recent phenomenon of digital libraries serving vast collections of scanned page images can be exploited by document analysis researchers, both as a target application (building better search engines) and as a way of overcoming the problem of acquiring ground-truth to support experimental investigations. We discussed some of the protocols and system-related issues involved, and offered solutions in the specific case of using the *Making of America* collection to exercise Baird's *pagereader* system and an algorithm we have developed for table detection.

It is important to reiterate that these evaluations were performed with no *a priori* knowledge of the test images or their ground-truths. The selection process was completely random, working from a very large collection. In principle, there is nothing preventing much more comprehensive experiments from being performed fully automatically, with no human intervention. At 323 seconds per page image, the entire *Making of America* collection (907,750 pages) would be sufficient to exercise *pagereader* for over 9 years running 24 hours a day and, at 62 seconds per page, our table detection code for almost 2 years.

Note that we are not advocating "attacking" digital libraries with the intention of consuming their resources and/or appropriating their content. Rather, our observation is that document analysis applied to page images drawn from such online repositories is analogous to what current search engines do when indexing the World Wide Web. The potential synergies between document analysis research and digital libraries could lead to substantial benefits for both communities.

References

1. D. Lopresti and J. Zhou. Document analysis and the World Wide Web. In *Proceedings of the Second IAPR Workshop on Document Analysis Systems*, pages 651–669, Malvern, PA, Oct. 1996.
2. D. Lopresti and J. Zhou. Locating and recognizing text in WWW images. *Information Retrieval*, 2(2/3):177–206, May 2000.
3. A. Antonacopoulos and D. Karatzas. An anthropocentric approach to text extraction from WWW images. In *Proceedings of the Fourth IAPR International Workshop on Document Analysis Systems*, pages 515–525, Rio de Janeiro, Brazil, Dec. 2000.
4. A. C. Downton, A. C. Tams, G. J. Wells, A. C. Holmes, S. M. Lucas, G. W. Beccaloni, M. J. Scoble, and G. S. Robinson. Constructing web-based legacy index card archives – architectural design issues and initial data acquisition. In *Proceedings of the Sixth International Conference on Document Analysis and Recognition*, pages 854–858, Seattle, WA, Sept. 2001.
5. O. Hitz, L. Robadey, and R. Ingold. An architecture for editing document recognition results using XML technology. In *Proceedings of the Fourth IAPR International Workshop on Document Analysis Systems*, pages 385–396, Rio de Janeiro, Brazil, Dec. 2000.

6. *International Workshop on Web Document Analysis*, Seattle, WA, Sept. 2001. http://www.csc.liv.ac.uk/~wda2001/.
7. Cornell University Prototype Digital Library. http://moa.cit.cornell.edu/.
8. Library of Congress: Digital Library Initiatives. http://memory.loc.gov/ammem/dli2/index.html.
9. I. Phillips, S. Chen, and R. Haralick. CD-ROM document database standard. In *Proceedings of Second International Conference on Document Analysis and Recognition*, pages 478–483, Tsukuba Science City, Japan, Oct. 1993.
10. About Making of America: The conversion process. http://moa.cit.cornell.edu/moa/moa_conversion.html.
11. Search result for Making of America, page 520 of *The Development of College Architecture in America* by Ashton R. Willard. http://cdl.library.cornell.edu/cgi-bin/moa/moa-cgi?notisid=AFJ3026-0022-73.
12. Search result for Princeton University Electronic Card Catalog, card 60 following the guide card Baird. http://imagecat1.princeton.edu/cgi-bin/ECC/cards.pl/disk9/0367/A4103?d=f&p=Baird&g=2000.500000&n=60&r=1.000000.
13. N. Baker. *Double Fold: Libraries and the Assault on Paper*. Random House, New York, NY, 2001.
14. E. J. Shaw and S. Blumson. Making of America: Online searching and page presentation at the University of Michigan. *D-Lib Magazine*, July/Aug. 1997. http://www.dlib.org/dlib/july97/america/07shaw.html.
15. D. G. Stork. The Open Mind Initiative. http://www.openmind.org/index.shtml.
16. M. D. Garris, S. A. Janet, and W. W. Klein. Federal Register document image database. In *Proceedings of Document Recognition and Retrieval VI (IS&T/SPIE Electronic Imaging)*, volume 3651, pages 97–108, San Jose, CA, Jan. 1999.
17. S. V. Rice, J. Kanai, and T. A. Nartker. Preparing OCR test data. Technical Report TR-93-08, UNLV Information Science Research Institute, Las Vegas, NV, June 1993.
18. CEDAR Databases. http://www.cedar.buffalo.edu/Databases/.
19. H. S. Baird. Document image defect models. In H. S. Baird, H. Bunke, and K. Yamamoto, editors, *Structured Document Image Analysis*, pages 546–556. Springer-Verlag, New York, 1992.
20. Y. Wang, I. T. Phillips, and R. Haralick. Automatic table ground truth generation and a background-analysis-based table structure extraction method. In *Proceedings of the Sixth International Conference on Document Analysis and Recognition*, pages 528–532, Seattle, WA, Sept. 2001.
21. H. S. Baird. Anatomy of a versatile page reader. *Proceedings of the IEEE*, 80(7):1059–1065, 1992.
22. J. Hu, R. Kashi, D. Lopresti, and G. Wilfong. Medium-independent table detection. In *Proceedings of Document Recognition and Retrieval VII (IS&T/SPIE Electronic Imaging)*, volume 3967, pages 291–302, San Jose, CA, Jan. 2000.
23. H. Schroeder and M. Doyle. *Interactive Web Applications with Tcl/Tk*. AP Professional, Chestnut Hill, MA, 1998.
24. G. Salton, A. Wong, and C. Yang. A vector space model for information retrieval. *Communications of the Association for Computing Machinery*, 18(11):613–620, Nov. 1975.
25. G. Nagy and S. Seth. Hierarchical representation of optically scanned documents. In *Proceedings of the Seventh International Conference on Pattern Recognition*, pages 347–349, Montréal, Canada, July 1984.

An Automated Tachograph Chart Analysis System

A. Antonacopoulos and D.P. Kennedy

PRImA Group, Department of Computer Science, University of Liverpool
Peach Street, Liverpool, L69 7ZF, United Kingdom
http://www.csc.liv.ac.uk/~prima

Abstract. This paper describes a new system that analyses tachograph charts. These circular charts are legal records of information on the different types of driver activity (driving, other duty, standby and rest) and vehicle data (speed and distance travelled). As each driver of each passenger and goods vehicle over a certain capacity must use a chart for every 24-hour period, there is a significant need for automated analysis (currently, tachograph charts are analysed manually).

The system starts by determining the shape parameters of the chart (location of the centre and radius). The position of the start of the 24-hour period (radius from centre to 24 hour tick mark) is then estimated. Finally the driver activity trace (recorded in a circular manner) is extracted, converted into a linear representation and recognised. Results from the evaluation of the system against professionally prepared ground truth indicate at least 94% accuracy in reading the driving time even on difficult (with scratches and marks) charts.

1 Introduction

Tachographs are devices that are fitted by law to all goods and passenger vehicles above a certain capacity (3.5t in the EU). These devices record onto circular paper-based charts the speed of the vehicle, different types of driver activity and the distance travelled (and sometimes additional information, such as engine speed and fuel consumption) over a 24-hour period [1].

Tachograph charts are legal documents that can, at any time, be inspected by the police for breach of driving regulations (relating to the supervision of the social welfare conditions for road traffic). Tachograph charts can also be used as evidence in court. Therefore, the accuracy by which the information is extracted from them is crucial.

There is a wealth of information contained on a tachograph chart. Apart from the information that the driver has to enter (start and end location and mileage reading), the other parameters that are recorded automatically can be cross-referenced to reveal inconsistencies. For instance, if the tachograph was tampered with to hide some part of the driving trace, there would be an inconsistency with the distance and speed traces.

It is common practice for transportation companies to gather the charts from their drivers at regular intervals and have them analysed by service bureaus. Given

D. Lopresti, J. Hu, and R. Kashi (Eds.): DAS 2002, LNCS 2423, pp. 544–555, 2002.
© Springer-Verlag Berlin Heidelberg 2002

the multitude of vehicles around the world (most countries have the same tachograph standards) there is a significant market for the analysis of these charts.

Currently, the most widespread tachograph chart analysis method involves the mounting of the chart under a magnifying lens and the visual examination of the information. A semi-automated system using a turntable under a fixed linear CCD has been developed to read relatively coarse information. This approach has the significant disadvantage of being very limited in the information it can extract (does not allow cross-referencing with other information on the chart) and it requires the manual placing of each chart on the turntable.

Ideally, human intervention should be kept to a minimum. The system proposed in this paper uses a commercial scanner to obtain images of the charts. A stack of charts can be placed in a sheet feeder, thus eliminating the need for accurate placement by hand. The scanned image of each chart is then analysed to extract the required information.

The characteristics of the chart and of the scanned image are described in sections 2 and 3, respectively. The system and its processes are detailed in Section 4. The paper concludes with the presentation of results and a discussion in Section 5.

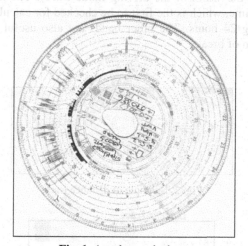

Fig. 1. A tachograph chart.

2   Chart Nature and Characteristics

A tachograph chart is made out of a circular thin card coated with wax. Sandwiched between the card and the wax is a layer of special ink. When the chart is inserted into the tachograph, three styli record different types of information by scratching the wax off the card. Where the ink is exposed to air it darkens to become black. The chart completes a full rotation inside the tachograph in 24 hours. Each driver has to use a new chart for each 24-hour period.

An example of a tachograph chart can be seen in Figure 1. Starting from the centre, four main areas with recorded information are present. At the innermost part of the chart, the handwritten information is completed by the driver. It records their name, starting point, destination, dates of departure and arrival, kilometre recordings before and after the trip, and total distance covered (in kilometres).

The next band of information records the distance travelled in up and down strokes of 5Km each (see Figure 2). This trace is useful in calculating the total distance travelled and in detecting when the vehicle stopped (the stroke becomes horizontal).

The third band of information is the one most often checked first for breach of driving regulations. It records the type of activity (mode) performed by the driver at any given point in time during the 24 hours. The different activities are represented by varying the thickness of the circular trace (see Figure 3). The two thickest trace bands denote driving time and other working time (other tasks at the workplace), respectively. The next trace band (thinner that the two above) denotes stand-by time—co-driver times, sleeping in cabin during the trip, and waiting times. Finally, the thinnest band denotes resting time. It should be noted that this very thin rest band does not always appear at the bottom of the mode trace. Instead it could be placed anywhere within the limits of the width of the duty band (e.g., it could appear starting from the middle of the width of the driving mode trace). The most important band here is the driving time, which is the first to be checked for calculating the total hours spent driving during 24 hours. The other bands are also useful for determining the number and duration of breaks.

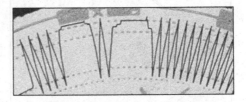

Fig. 2. Example of distance trace.

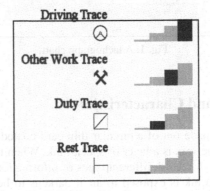

Fig. 3. Explanation of mode trace.

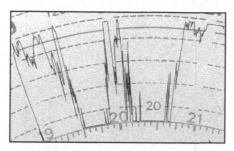

Fig. 4. Example of speed trace.

The area of the chart furthest from the centre (see Figure 4) records the speed at which the vehicle travelled, displaying details of acceleration and deceleration.

Apart from the recorded information, the following characteristics can be observed. First, there is a significant amount of pre-printed information comprising digits and tick marks corresponding to the hours in the day, and various symbols aimed at explaining to the human operator the relative thickness of each of the activities of the mode trace.

Second, the hole in the centre of the chart has a shape that indicates a particular direction. In fact, the longest axis of the hole coincides with the notional axis passing through the tick marks of the 12 hour point on one side and of the 24 hour point on the other. Figure 5 illustrates the landmarks of the tachograph chart. Although different manufacturers will vary the pre-printed information on the chart, the main layout is basically the same (the layout illustrated in the figure is the one used in the vast majority of charts). It can also be seen that there is a semicircle printed running between the 12 and 24 hour points. This line could be useful in establishing the direction of the 12–24 axis.

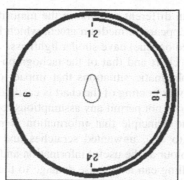

Fig. 5. Chart layout model showing landmarks.

The final physical characteristic to be noted is the colour of the tachograph chart. While the background of the chart (wax) is a very light grey, the pre-printed

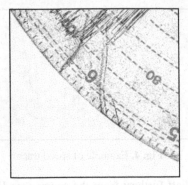

Fig. 6. Example of scratches on a chart.

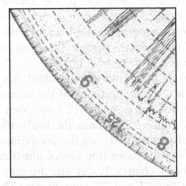

Fig. 7. Example of frayed edge.

information can appear in different colours. In the majority of cases (over 90%) the pre-printed information appears in medium green, which has distinct grey level (see below). Other colours (red or blue) have similar lightness.

The nature of the chart and that of the tachograph apparatus in general, give rise to a number of problematic situations that impact on the performance of the system. First, the fragile wax coating of the chart is easily damaged by rough handling (the nature of the work does not permit any assumptions regarding careful handling of the charts). By the same principle that information is recorded on the chart (ink darkens when exposed to air), unwanted scratches and marks can appear. These scratches are the same colour as the useful information and frequently intersect with it (see Figure 6). Bad handling can also cause damage to the inner (hole) and the outer edge of the chart. Figure 7 illustrates a frayed edge. An indistinct edge can cause difficulties in establishing the correct location of the chart (see below).

Second, a potential problem can be caused by variations in temperature in the vehicle. In cold weather, the wax is harder and the stylus does not remove it completely off the trace. This makes the corresponding trace appear lighter and non-uniform, as the ink has not darkened to the same degree across the trace. Thin gaps in

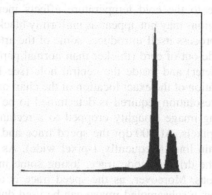

Fig. 8. Examples of mode trace overlapping with pre-printed information.

Fig. 9. A (smoothed) histogram of a typical chart.

Fig. 10. Shadow introduced by scanning

the trace may be confused with standby mode, especially when the vehicle is frequently stopping (e.g., a delivery vehicle in an urban environment).

Finally, either through normal wear or through manipulation, a stylus may become slightly bent. The corresponding trace will not, therefore, be recorded at the intended location on the chart. Instead it may overlap with some of the pre-printed information. This can be a problem when parts of the mode trace overlap with the explanatory symbols for the same trace (see Figure 8).

3 Image Characteristics

From the above description of the nature of the tachograph chart it can be concluded that, in order to preserve potentially differentiating information, the scanned image should be greyscale. As can be seen in Figure 1, the different types of information (and noise) are present in the form of different greylevels.

It is interesting to note that the structure of the greylevel histogram of a chart is very stable. This structure can be seen in Figure 9 (the reader can refer to Figure 1). Starting from the lightest region on the right, the rightmost peak corresponds to the background generated by the scanner cover. The highest peak to its left corresponds to the background of the chart itself (wax), while the low hump to the left of that corresponds to the pre-printed information. The recorded (etched) information appears as the very low peak to the far left (black) of the histogram.

A number of characteristic artefacts are noted in the image. First, it can be observed that although the useful information appears to be well separated in greylevel from the rest of the data, scratches and marks appear in the same greylevels too. Furthermore, due to the cold temperature effects mentioned in the previous section, some trace regions may not appear as uniformly black as expected in general.

The scanning process itself introduces some of the artefacts in the image. Due to the chart being made out of card (thicker than normal paper), a shadow appears at the outer edge (perimeter) and inside the central hole (see Figure 10). This shadow complicates the estimation of the exact location of the chart and its centre (see below).

The scanning resolution required is determined to be at least 400 dpi. At that resolution the resulting image (roughly cropped to a rectangle around the chart) is about 2000 by 2000 pixels. At 400 dpi the speed trace and the rest mode trace are represented as very thin lines (frequently 1-pixel wide). As the primary goal of the system is to extract the driving mode trace, losing some information from the rest trace is not very serious. Moreover, as the speed trace is also not exploited in the current implementation, a subsampled image can be used during some operations for faster processing (see below).

4 The System

The input to the system is a greyscale (8-bit at 400dpi) image, containing a tachograph chart. This image can be the result of batch-scanning a stack of charts using a high-speed scanner with an appropriate sheet-feeder. The chart could land anywhere n the scanner, although scanner software enables the *approximate* cropping of the image to a square containing the chart. In the image, no assumption is made about the orientation of the 12-24 axis of the chart.

In order to extract the driving mode trace (the goal of the current system), the circular chart has to be accurately located in the image and its centre must be established. Following that, the orientation of the 12-24 axis is estimated, in order to determine the time of the day at which each of the driving intervals occurred. The circular band describing the mode trace is read after 'unwinding' the chart, obtaining a linear representation. Each of these stages is explained I more detail in each of the following subsections.

4.1   Chart Localisation

Chart localisation involves three processes: histogram analysis, tracing of the outside edge of the chart and estimation of the parametric form of the chart (circle radius and location of the centre).

From the (smoothed) image histogram, the greylevel range corresponding to the image background (scanner cover) can be determined, as explained in Section 3 above. Having that information, an attempt is made to trace the outside edge of the chart. This is not a straightforward way to recognise the circular shape, as explained above, as the circular shape of the chart is not accurately represented in the image due to edge imperfections and shadow effects.

As the tracing is an image-based operation and the shape of the chart is a basic circle, the image is safely subsampled to a third of its original size. The tracing follows the boundary between what is identified as the image background and what is not [2]. At the end of this process, to adjust for the shadow, an attempt is made to 'push in' each edge point toward the centre of the disk. Each edge point can move inward so long as the next pixel toward the centre is at least as dark as the original edge pixel. As an attempt to maintain the shape of the original circle and avoid spurious 'inlets', each original pixel is not allowed to go in more than a fixed length (usually 1 to 2 pixels) further than its neighbours.

The identified boundary pixels can be used as the basis for estimating the parameters of the circular shape of the chart. The Hough transform is used for this estimation [3]. To improve efficiency, only one every 50 boundary points (experimentally determined) are used as input. In addition, the Hough transform is performed in two stages. In the first stage, a coarse accumulator is used. A smaller fine-resolution accumulator is then used in the second application of the transform, centred around the parameters identified at the end of the first stage.

At the end of the localisation process, the centre and radius of the circular chart are available for the identification of the 12-24 axis and the subsequent reading of the mode trace.

4.2   Location of the 12–24 Axis

Although not essential for calculating the total driving time during a 24-hour period, the location of the 12-24 axis enables the registration of each time interval on the chart with the actual time of day it occurred.

A first approximate location of the 12-24 axis is based on the assumption that it coincides with the orientation of the central hole (see Section 2 and Figure 5). To the best of the authors' knowledge, this assumption always holds (it is not stated as a fact since there is no information on the rules governing the actual manufacturing process of the charts). To achieve this first estimate, the inside edge of the central hole is traced and the edge point that lies further from the centre is noted. The line through that point and the centre should coincide with the required axis. In fact, the error of this process is within the ±7.5° range, which equates to ±30 minutes with the current image parameters.

A more accurate estimate is obtained by starting with the above information and complementing in the following way. A strip is read in a circular manner along the perimeter of the chart (full-size image). This strip is wide enough (10% of the radius) to contain the numerals denoting the hours. The resulting strip is a long narrow rectangle, where the pixel intensities along the columns are summed to produce a 1-dimensional signal. This signal is then averaged and a standard 1-D Sobel filter [-1, 0, 1] is passed twice over it. The resulting signal contains both positive and negative peaks. Peaks whose magnitude is less than a third (experimentally determined) of the maximum magnitude are removed and the remaining positive and negative peaks are concatenated.

A characteristic pattern (a group of successive negative-positive-negative peaks) corresponds to single digit numerals and a different pattern (a group of successive negative-positive-negative-positive-negative peaks) to double digit ones. Other combinations of peaks are considered to be irrelevant. It should be noted that the peak in the centre of each of the two patterns above denotes the presence (location) of the hour tick mark.

The next task is to identify the 24 hour tick mark. For this purpose, any tick mark that gives a well-defined signature in the 1-D signal is identified and the corresponding angular difference between that and the approximate estimate (from the hole alignment is used). As the hole estimate is accurate to within 30 minutes, the true hour of the day can be established for the chosen tick mark. From that established tick mark, the accurate position of the 24 hour tick mark can then be calculated. The resulting axis is the one passing through the resulting tick mark and the identified centre of the chart.

4.3   Reading the Mode Trace

Having established the centre of the chart and its start and end (radius to 24 hour tick mark), the chart is 'unwound' to form a long rectangle. This 'unwinding' is performed in the full-size image by reading pixels along straight lines (Bresenham's algorithm [4] is used) as consecutive radii from the centre of the chart toward the perimeter.

As discussed in Section 3, recorded information appears as the darkest regions the image. In particular, the mode trace lies approximately (it is not certain, as explained in Section 2) in the middle of the chart, i.e. the half radius area. Suitable regions are identified as bounding boxes (parts of the mode trace can be isolated)

Within each of the bounding rectangles identified above, the greylevel values of the pixels are summed along each column. Columns corresponding to driving have a very low count, while columns corresponding to rest (or no activity) have the highest count. Each column is then grouped with its neighbours (if appropriate) to form bands representing the same activity: driving (lowest count), duty (medium count), rest (high count) and nothing (highest count).

As each column corresponds to a 14-second interval, the start time and duration of the different mode bands are then established.

5   Results and Discussion

The performance of the system was evaluated by analysing a representative (leaning toward difficult) data set of 108 charts varying from average difficulty (55%) to difficult (34%) to very difficult (11%). An example of a chart of average difficulty can be seen in Figure 11, whereas an example of a very difficult (mainly due to scratches) chart can be seen in Figure 12. For each of the charts there was corresponding ground truth prepared by bureau professionals. The accuracy of the system was determined by examining the discrepancies between the total duration of an activity during 24 hours as identified by the system and as read by the professionals.

The overall accuracy of the system for reading the *driving* mode is 94%. More specifically, charts of average difficulty were read with 97.9% accuracy, while difficult and very difficult charts were read with 94.4% and 90% accuracy respectively.

With regard to the *duty* mode, the overall accuracy was 97.2%. This can be broken down to 99.3% accuracy for charts of average difficulty, and 95.2% and 97.1% accuracy for difficult and very difficult charts, respectively.

All the above results are regarded as very good by the professionals, as 5 to minute discrepancies are not crucial in everyday circumstances. Some facts that shed light to the reading of charts by a human operator will help put the performance of the system into context. The device used by human operators has a resolution of 1 minute, whereas each mode trace pixel in the automated system (with the current settings) corresponds to 14 seconds. In practice, human operators 'average out' regions of sudden stops and starts, rendering precise estimates of accuracy rather difficult.

The main reason for error can be isolated as the inaccurate location of the centre of the chart. The precise location of the centre is crucial to all the processes that perform circular reading. In some cases, there is clearly room for further improvement, especially in making the initial tracing and centre estimation operations more robust.

Another issue to be raised is the appearance of the rest node trace. As mentioned in Section 3, this appears as 1-2 pixels wide in the 400dpi image. Moreover, as it is so thin, it tends to be represented by lighter greylevels. If the rest trace was deemed to be necessary to read accurately, the image would have to be scanned at a higher resolution (at the cost of memory and efficiency).

While the system is complete, it is still an experimental prototype. Further work will concentrate on two fronts. First, other options for improving accuracy will be investigated and integrated into the existing setup. Second, engineering aspects such as optimising the system for speed and, interfacing with and controlling the high-speed scanner will be pursued.

In conclusion, this paper has presented a system that automates the analysis of tachograph charts. The charts are scanned using a commercially available scanner, as opposed to the proprietary setup of a previous semi-automated method. The information of most interest is that recorded in the work mode trace, and the system concentrates on this. However, there is a wealth of information present on the chart which can be read from the same image, for its own worth or for cross referencing and validating the mode trace.

Acknowledgement. The authors are grateful to Tachograph Analysis Consultants (TAC) Ltd of Liverpool UK, for providing the tachograph charts and ground truth.

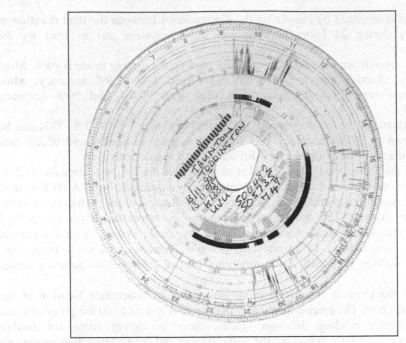

Fig. 11. A chart of average difficulty.

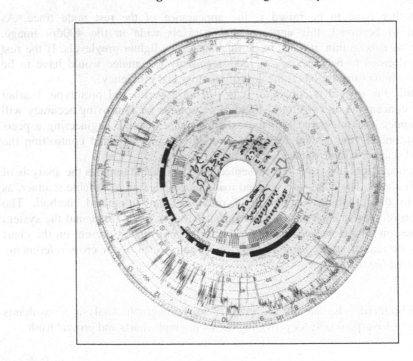

Fig. 12. A 'very difficult' chart to analyse.

References

[1]   VDO Kienzle, *Manual for the Evaluation and Use of the Original Kienzle Tachograph Chart*.
[2]   T. Pavlidis, *Algorithms for Graphics and Image Processing*, Springer, Berlin, 1982.
[3]   M. Sonka, V. Hlavac and R. Boyle, *Image Processing, Analysis and Machine Vision*, 2nd ed, PWS – International Thomson Publishing, 1999.
[4]   D.F. Rogers, *Procedural Elements for Computer Graphics*, McGraw-Hill, 1985.

A Multimodal System for Accessing Driving Directions

Ashutosh Morde[1], Ramanujan S. Kashi[2], Michael K. Brown[3], Deborah Grove[1] and
James L. Flanagan[1]

[1] CAIP, Rutgers – The State University of New Jersey, Piscataway, NJ 08855
{amorde,dgrove,jlf}@caip.rutgers.edu
[2] Avaya Research Labs, Basking Ridge, NJ 07920
ramanuja@avaya.com
[3] Cydyreal Inc, North Plainfield, NJ
mkb@cydyreal.com

Abstract. The focus of this paper is describing a system that repurposes a web
document by a spoken language interface to provide both visual and audio
driving directions. The spoken dialog interface is used to obtain the source and
destination addresses from a user. The web document retrieved by querying the
user on the addresses is parsed to extract the maps and the associated text. Further the system automatically generates two sets of web documents. One of
these sets is used to render the maps on a hand-held device and the other set is
used for the spoken dialog interface through a traditional phone. The system's
user interface allows navigation both through speech and pen stylus input. The
system is built on a PhoneBrowser architecture that allows the user to browse
the web by speech control over an ordinary telephone.

1 Introduction

As the popularity of the web has increased over the past few years, so has the amount
of information available. The conventional method of accessing such information is
using desktop web browsers. Access to online information is crucial for professionals
on the move. Telephone penetration is still greater than that of laptops. Telephone access to on-line data using touch – tone interfaces is already common. These interfaces
have a hierarchical structure; they are essentially menu driven. The user is provided a
list of options and he is required to select a particular option from these. A long list of
options taxes the users memory while a deep menu structure can frustrate the user.
Speech, on the other hand, provides a natural way of capturing spontaneous thoughts
and ideas. Voice as an access mechanism allows additional tasks to be performed
while the hands or eyes are busy [1].

This suggests the use of speech or spoken dialog to access online information as an
alternative to conventional desktop browsers. One of the commonly accessed information is that of driving directions. The user either tries to memorize the driving steps
or take a copy of the directions. Obtaining driving directions and help in navigation is
often required on the road where access to a desktop computer is not available. So it
becomes necessary to have a system that can both query the user using a spoken dia-

D. Lopresti, J. Hu, and R. Kashi (Eds.): DAS 2002, LNCS 2423, pp. 556–567, 2002.
© Springer-Verlag Berlin Heidelberg 2002

log interface and render driving directions through mobile/conventional phones and hand-held devices.

The application developed at the Center for Advanced Information Processing (CAIP)/Avaya allows the user to access driving directions through a regular telephone connection. Visual feedback is provided to the user by displaying the driving maps and the directions onto the users wireless handheld device. In particular Compaq's iPAQ was used for the system development. The speech interface was provided by PhoneBrowser [2].

2 Need for a Multimodal Interface

In a visual environment, the users can immediately see the information available to them; it persists on the screen as long as the user desires. The users have plenty of time to analyze the information available at a given time before they need to make a decision. In a nonvisual environment, however, a system must list the information serially. Audio is slow for the listener to consume large amounts of speech and the user must rely upon short-term memory since audio does not persist like a visual display [3]. The inherent lack of visual feedback in a speech-only interface can lead users to feel less in control and makes it much harder for the user to absorb spoken information [4].

In the current system these shortcomings associated with a speech-only interface were mitigated by providing the user with an additional visual modality of providing driving directions and maps on a wireless handheld device. This visual display of information gives the user more time to assimilate the data and aids navigation. In addition to using a speech interface to move between driving steps the user also gets the flexibility to navigate using the stylus input of the handheld device.

3   Application for Driving Directions

Figure 1 shows the driving directions application setup. The user calls up the Phone-Browser using a regular telephone connection. The exchange of information between the PhoneBrowser and the web server hosting the driving direction application is through the regular HTTP protocol over the web.

The user calls up the PhoneBrowser number and logs into the Rutgers Voice portal by saying the login ID "Rutgers Database Search". Once the user logs into the system he is guided in building the origin and destination street addresses with verification dialog turns to remove any misrecognition error.

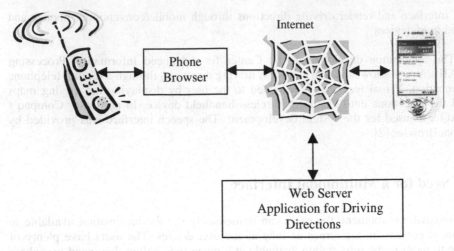

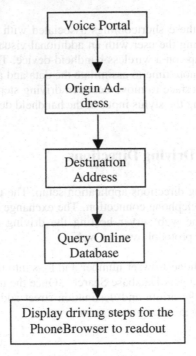

Internet

Phone
Browser

Web Server
Application for Driving
Directions

Fig. 1. Application setup

Figure 2 shows the flowchart for the speech only interface aspect of the application. As the address construction process is similar for both the origin and the destination, its flow is shown separately in Figure 3. This figure represents the two modules of "Origin Address" and "Destination Address" in the main flowchart.

Voice Portal

Origin Address

Destination Address

Query Online Database

Display driving steps for the PhoneBrowser to readout

Fig. 2. Application flowchart with telephone interface only

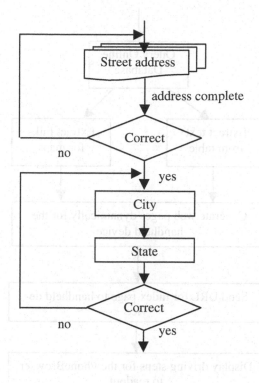

Fig. 3. Address construction

To provide a visual interface web pages are built dynamically, the content being dependent on the driving step requested by the user. Figure 4 indicates the modification required to the application flow for a visual interface. The user has a wireless handheld device connected to the web. The web server sends information to the server running on the handheld device using sockets. Figure 5 shows the user interaction once the online database has been queried and the PhoneBrowser reads out the driving directions. The system can be roughly divided into 4 tasks – dialog for user interaction, information retrieval, information presentation and bootstrapping the grammar.

3.1   Dialog

The user-system interaction consists of dialog for accessing the origin address, which is broken up into following components.
- dialog turns for origin street address, origin city and origin state
- similarly, there is dialog for accessing the destination address from the user
- dialog turns for verifying that the system has understood the user correctly
- dialog for providing the user with context sensitive help
- dialog for the case of no recognition of user input by PhoneBrowser
- dialog to control the way information is provided to the user

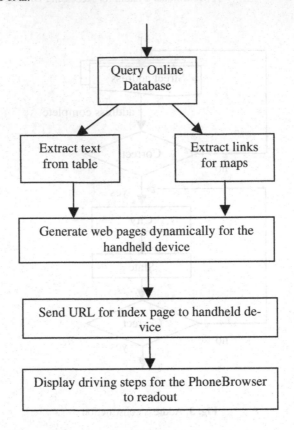

Fig. 4. Modification required to application flow for visual interface

If the users are to be given flexibility as to what they can speak, the appropriate grammar has to be designed for the system. The speech interface is achieved using the PhoneBrowser, which is a tool that allows a user to access web information through a telephone line. The system grammar is embedded in web pages, which are read by the PhoneBrowser. The user input as recognized by the PhoneBrowser is passed onto the system cgi-script, which then takes appropriate action based on user utterances.

The general syntax for embedding the grammar in web pages is

```
<a> href = "URL" special_tags > URL title </a>
```

where the special tag is rule-based grammar written in the Java Speech Grammar Format (JSGF) and URL is the URL to the cgi-script that acts on the user utterances or just a static web page to be read out to the user.

An example of the grammar is

```
<a> href = "URL" JSGF=([can you|could you](go to
the)(previous|next|last)(step))
> URL title </a>
```

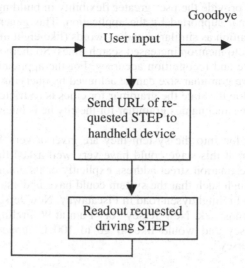

Fig. 5. Driving direction readout control

The finite state representation of this grammar is shown in figure 6. The user can go to the web page pointed to by the URL by saying, "Can you go to the last step", "go to the next step" or any other phrase or sentence defined by the finite state grammar.

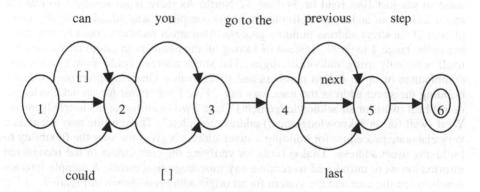

Fig. 6. Finite state grammar

The processing of user input is achieved using the URLINSERT tag with the URL pointing to a cgi-script. Its syntax is

```
<a>href ="http://host/path?userip=%s" URLINSERT
JSGF=((next|previous)(step)) > title </a>
```

When PhoneBrowser sees the URLINSERT tag, instead of just going to the URL location, it replaces the %s with its interpretation of user input. Further details of the various PhoneBrowser tags can be found in [5].

It is tempting to provide the user greater flexibility in building his sentences by increasing the grammar supported by the application. This generally results in an increase in misrecognition as similar sounding words (like eight and ate) are introduced in the grammar, not to mention increased search times. So there are tradeoffs involved in the grammar size and recognition accuracy. For the application at hand, for large databases, restrictive grammar size can be achieved by querying the user for the state. Then depending upon the state the grammar for cities is restricted and finally the user is provided with the street names grammar for the city he is interested in.

When the users log into the system they are given a very brief overview of the system. The system at this stage could have very well asked the user to provide the entire origin and destination street address explicitly or its grammar could have been made complex enough such that the system could have understood a sentence like "I want to go from 96 Frelinghuysen road in Piscataway, New Jersey to 100 Commercial Avenue in New Brunswick, New Jersey" or "I am at 96 Frelinghuysen Road in Piscataway, New Jersey and would like to go to 100 Commercial Avenue in New Brunswick, New Jersey".

The problem with such an approach is that there are no delimiters for street address, city and state as the address can be anything – the user may want to go to Old New Brunswick Road in New Brunswick. So in spite of recognizing what the user has said the system can't process the information provided to it into a meaningful form. As a result a guided approach was chosen in which the entire process is broken up into smaller dialog turns with each turn acting as delimiter for an address component.

Moreover special consideration is required for the street address as the user may want to say just Biel road or 54 East 32 North. As there is no standard format for street address an additional delimiter "address complete" was added to signify completion of the street address building process. Also street numbers could be any number in the range 1 to 9999. Instead of having all the numbers in grammar the number itself was built using individual digits. The street address could now contain any combination of up to 4 digit numbers and street names. On being prompted to begin building the street address the user may say "Five Four (wait for an acknowledgement) East (wait for an acknowledgement) Three Two (wait for an acknowledgement) West (wait for an acknowledgement) address complete". Though this may seem as a very elaborate procedure for building a street address it gives the user the flexibility to build any street address. Dialog turns for verifying the correctness of the recognized information were introduced to remove any misrecognition errors. A sample interaction between the user and the system for an origin address is shown in Figure 7.

A confirmation for each component of the street address is given by the system as it can misrecognize individual digits. If there is an error the user can say "address complete" and then rectify the error. The user can ask for help at any stage by saying "direction help". The user is then provided with help for the pertinent dialog turn. If the user feels that he needs the help for entire application he can say "full help" or he can say, "return to application" and return to the dialog turn through which he initiated help with all his state information intact. The context sensitive help is initiated by the system if the user does not respond for a time period of 20 seconds.

```
...
System: Please start dictating the origin street address. Say address complete
when you are finished dictating.
User: nine six
System: Ninety-six
User: Frelinghuysen Road
System: 96 Frelinghuysen Road
User: address complete
System: You want to start from 96 Frelinghuysen Road. Is it correct?
User: yes
System: Please tell me the name of the city
User: Piscataway
System: Street is 96 Frelinghuysen Road. You are in Piscataway. Now tell me
the name of the state.
User: New Jersey
System: Street address is 96 Frelinghuysen Road. You want to start from Pis-
cataway in New Jersey. If this is correct say start?
User: Start
System: Please start dictating the destination street address. Say address com-
plete when you are finished dictating
...
```

Fig. 7. Usage scenario

3.2   Information Retrieval

Once the origin and destination address have been verified the system queries the
Avis Rental Company site (http://www.avis.com). The result of the query is a regular
web document with maps and table of direction steps. This information can be directly provided to the PhoneBrowser, it will ignore the images and start reading out
the directions. But there will be no control as to how the information is presented to
the user. So after the system grabs the results page from the web it parses the html
document to extract the driving steps text from the tables. This text is formatted to introduce longer pauses between steps. A special control character, which disables the
spelling of capitalized words by the PhoneBrowser, is inserted at the beginning of
each step. This is required as the street names and left and right turns are capitalized.
The formatted text is then presented to the PhoneBrowser. The steps are also stored as
state information so that they can be used later to present the information to the user
in the format he desires. At this step grammar for context sensitive help is also provided to the PhoneBrowser.

3.3   Information Presentation – The Wireless Handheld Device

In an earlier version of this project all the information was presented to the user
through the voice interface only. Usability experiments showed that the users had

trouble memorizing the driving steps [6]. These usability experiments guided us to add the visual modality – the turn-by-turn maps and the driving steps were rendered onto a wireless handheld device.

The spoken dialog interface obtains the origin and destination addresses from the use and is used to retrieve an appropriate web document. The driving steps and the URL's to the turn-by-turn maps was obtained by parsing this web document. The extracted driving steps were used in the creation of web pages dynamically on the fly. This approach avoids the download of images from the web onto the web server. The content of these web pages depends upon the user input and the driving step content. Figure 8 shows a typical driving direction web page as viewed on a handheld device.

Our implementation   includes a server running on the wireless handheld device to synchronize the information displayed with that requested by the user over the phone. It is implemented using two threads – the dialog thread and the worker thread. The dialog thread is responsible for monitoring the user stylus input for starting and stopping the server while the worker thread is responsible for monitoring the socket for URL information from the web server.

The user starts the web server by clicking on the start button of the dialog. This causes the worker thread to be created, which initializes the socket and starts listening for input from the web server. When the PhoneBrowser starts reading out the driving directions the web server sends the URL, of the index page of the set of web pages created for the user, to the server running on the wireless handheld device. The server then launches Internet Explorer. Whenever the user requests to go to any specific step,

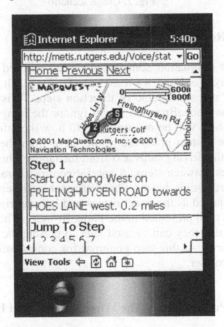

Fig. 8. Driving directions displayed on a handheld device

in addition to reading out the step through PhoneBrowser, the web server sends the URL for that step to the server running on the wireless handheld device. This URL is passed on to the launched pocket Internet Explorer. A sample interaction between the user and the application while the driving directions are being read out is as shown in Figure 9.

The user can jump to the web page of any step either through spoken input to the telephone or using the stylus input on the hand-held. The grammar available to the user is

```
[can | could] [you] [repeat | go to] (step (0 | (1 | 2 | 3
| 4 | 5 | 6 | 7 | 8 | 9) [(0 | (1 | 2 | 3 | 4 | 5 | 6 |
7 | 8 | 9))])) | (next | previous | last) step).
```

So the user can say go to step 3, repeat step 3, go to next step, next step and so on. The other set of grammar available to the user is for finding the total travel time and distance. The user can ask the system for the total travel time or the total travel distance. The user can stop the web server by clicking on the STOP button of the dialog. This causes the worker thread to be terminated and the sockets to be cleaned up. All the web pages visited by the pocket Internet Explorer are stored in a temporary cache on the wireless handheld device. By doing so these pages can be retrieved and viewed later if so desired.

....
User: Go to next step
System: Step 2. Turn RIGHT onto TUNISON ROAD. 0.6 miles
    (Send URL for step 2 to Handheld device)
User: Go to step 5
System: I think you asked me to go to step 51 but there are only 7 steps
User: Go to step 5
System: Step 5. Merge onto NJ-18 north. 0.1 miles
    (Send URL for step 5 to Handheld device)
User: Repeat step 4
System: Take the exit on the left towards US-1 south/NEW BRUNSWICK.
0.2 miles
    (Send URL for step 4 to Handheld device)
User: Jump to last step
....

Fig. 9. Read out control usage scenario

3.4   Bootstrapped Grammar

It may not always be possible to provide all possible street names in the application grammar. In such an instance the application can start off with a few street names in the grammar and then build up its own grammar.

While the HTML document is being parsed to extract direction steps the extracted text is also analyzed for street names. Most of the web sites providing driving directions capitalize the street names and the left or right turns to be taken. The automatic grammar update algorithm first replaces all street name abbreviations with their full forms, e.g., dr by drive and pl by place. It then chooses a sequence of capitalized words ending with one of the predefined street name endings as its initial guess. This eliminates the selection of words for turns to be included in the grammar. The algorithm then determines whether the particular sequence of selected words lie in a single sentence. This check is necessary as it is quite possible that a step ends with a street name while the immediate next step begins with another street name. Requiring that the words belong to a single sentence eliminates the inclusion of such concatenated street names into the grammar. Once it has been decided that the selected sequence of words is a valid street name it is compared with the existing street names in the grammar to avoid duplication and only then inserted in the grammar. The next time the grammar is used; it can be in the same session, e.g., if the user wants a second set of directions, the user can say any new street name that has just been added to the grammar. Thus the application grammar is bootstrapped.

4 Summary

A multimodal system for accessing driving directions, whose user interface allows navigation both through speech and pen stylus input has been implemented. The system is built on a PhoneBrowser architecture that allows the user to browse the web, by speech control over an ordinary telephone. The user-system interaction was tested only for the speech interface. The users showed a marked preference for jumping between driving steps. The usability experiments also confirmed that the user finds it difficult to memorize driving directions without any visual aid.

The future directions for this application involve enhancing the grammar for a more natural user interface and making the call through the users handheld device instead of a telephone. Also to minimize the errors resulting from an increased street name grammar size the application flow can be reversed. The user can be asked to provide the information for the state first followed by city and then the street. This will restrict the amount of grammar loaded onto the PhoneBrowser thereby minimizing the chances of recognition error. Usability studies for the application with both the speech and visual interface need to be conducted to study the user-system interaction.

References

[1]   Martin, G.L. "The utility of speech input in user-computer interfaces." *International Journal of Man-Machine Studies*, 30:355–375, 1989
[2]   Brown, Michael K., Stephen C. Glinski, Bernard P. Goldman, and Brian C. Schmult. "PhoneBrowser: A Web-Content-Programmable Speech Processing Platform." *Position Paper for The W3C Workshop on Voice Browsers*, Cambridge, Massachusetts, October 1998

[3]   C. Schmandt. "Multimedia Nomadic Services on Today's Hardware." *IEEE Network*, September/October 1994.
[4]   Stifelman, Lisa, Barry Arons, Chris Schmandt, and Eric Hulteen, "VoiceNotes: A Speech Interface for a Hand-Held Voice Notetaker." *ACM INTERCHI '93 Conference Proceedings*, Amsterdam, The Nether-lands, April 24–29, 1993
[5]   Brown, Michael K. "PhoneBrowser User's Guide." *Avaya Communication Inc.* October 2000
[6]   Morde, Ashutosh. "An Application for Voice Controlled Driving Directions", *Master of Science Thesis, Rutgers – The State University of New Jersey*, May 2002.

Author Index

Lecture Notes in Computer Science

For information about Vols. 1–2338
please contact your bookseller or Springer-Verlag

Vol. 2381: U. Egly, C.G. Fermüller (Eds.), Automated Reasoning with Analytic Tableaux and Related Methods. Proceedings, 2002. X, 341 pages. 2002 .(Subseries LNAI).

Vol. 2382: A. Halevy, A. Gal (Eds.), Next Generation Information Technologies and Systems. Proceedings, 2002. VIII, 169 pages. 2002.

Vol. 2383: M.S. Lew, N. Sebe, J.P. Eakins (Eds.), Image and Video Retrieval. Proceedings, 2002. XII, 388 pages. 2002.

Vol. 2384: L. Batten, J. Seberry (Eds.), Information Security and Privacy. Proceedings, 2002. XII, 514 pages. 2002.

Vol. 2385: J. Calmet, B. Benhamou, O. Caprotti, L. Henocque, V. Sorge (Eds.), Artificial Intelligence, Automated Reasoning, and Symbolic Computation. Proceedings, 2002. XI, 343 pages. 2002. (Subseries LNAI).

Vol. 2386: E.A. Boiten, B. Möller (Eds.), Mathematics of Program Construction. Proceedings, 2002. X, 263 pages. 2002.

Vol. 2387: O.H. Ibarra, L. Zhang (Eds.), Computing and Combinatorics. Proceedings, 2002. XIII, 606 pages. 2002.

Vol. 2388: S.-W. Lee, A. Verri (Eds.), Pattern Recognition with Support Vector Machines. Proceedings, 2002. XI, 420 pages. 2002.

Vol. 2389: E. Ranchhod, N.J. Mamede (Eds.), Advances in Natural Language Processing. Proceedings, 2002. XII, 275 pages. 2002. (Subseries LNAI).

Vol. 2391: L.-H. Eriksson, P.A. Lindsay (Eds.), FME 2002: Formal Methods – Getting IT Right. Proceedings, 2002. XI, 625 pages. 2002.

Vol. 2392: A. Voronkov (Ed.), Automated Deduction – CADE-18. Proceedings, 2002. XII, 534 pages. 2002. (Subseries LNAI).

Vol. 2393: U. Priss, D. Corbett, G. Angelova (Eds.), Conceptual Structures: Integration and Interfaces. Proceedings, 2002. XI, 397 pages. 2002. (Subseries LNAI).

Vol. 2395: G. Barthe, P. Dybjer, L. Pinto, J. Saraiva (Eds.), Applied Semantics. IX, 537 pages. 2002.

Vol. 2396: T. Caelli, A. Amin, R.P.W. Duin, M. Kamel, D. de Ridder (Eds.), Structural, Syntactic, and Statistical Pattern Recognition. Proceedings, 2002. XVI, 863 pages. 2002.

Vol. 2398: K. Miesenberger, J. Klaus, W. Zagler (Eds.), Computers Helping People with Special Needs. Proceedings, 2002. XXII, 794 pages. 2002.

Vol. 2399: H. Hermanns, R. Segala (Eds.), Process Algebra and Probabilistic Methods. Proceedings, 2002. X, 215 pages. 2002.

Vol. 2401: P.J. Stuckey (Ed.), Logic Programming. Proceedings, 2002. XI, 486 pages. 2002.

Vol. 2402: W. Chang (Ed.), Advanced Internet Services and Applications. Proceedings, 2002. XI, 307 pages. 2002.

Vol. 2403: Mark d'Inverno, M. Luck, M. Fisher, C. Preist (Eds.), Foundations and Applications of Multi-Agent Systems. Proceedings, 1996-2000. X, 261 pages. 2002. (Subseries LNAI).

Vol. 2404: E. Brinksma, K.G. Larsen (Eds.), Computer Aided Verification. Proceedings, 2002. XIII, 626 pages. 2002.

Vol. 2405: B. Eaglestone, S. North, A. Poulovassilis (Eds.), Advances in Databases. Proceedings, 2002. XII, 199 pages. 2002.

Vol. 2406: C. Peters, M. Braschler, J. Gonzalo, M. Kluck (Eds.), Evaluation of Cross-Language Information Retrieval Systems. Proceedings, 2001. X, 601 pages. 2002.

Vol. 2407: A.C. Kakas, F. Sadri (Eds.), Computational Logic: Logic Programming and Beyond. Part I. XII, 678 pages. 2002. (Subseries LNAI).

Vol. 2408: A.C. Kakas, F. Sadri (Eds.), Computational Logic: Logic Programming and Beyond. Part II. XII, 628 pages. 2002. (Subseries LNAI).

Vol. 2409: D.M. Mount, C. Stein (Eds.), Algorithm Engineering and Experiments. Proceedings, 2002. VIII, 207 pages. 2002.

Vol. 2410: V.A. Carreño, C.A. Muñoz, S. Tahar (Eds.), Theorem Proving in Higher Order Logics. Proceedings, 2002. X, 349 pages. 2002.

Vol. 2412: H. Yin, N. Allinson, R. Freeman, J. Keane, S. Hubbard (Eds.), Intelligent Data Engineering and Automated Learning – IDEAL 2002. Proceedings, 2002. XV, 597 pages. 2002.

Vol. 2413: K. Kuwabara, J. Lee (Eds.), Intelligent Agents and Multi-Agent Systems. Proceedings, 2002. X, 221 pages. 2002. (Subseries LNAI).

Vol. 2414: F. Mattern, M. Naghshineh (Eds.), Pervasive Computing. Proceedings, 2002. XI, 298 pages. 2002.

Vol. 2415: J. Dorronsoro (Ed.), Artificial Neural Networks – ICANN 2002. Proceedings, 2002. XXVIII, 1382 pages. 2002.

Vol. 2417: M. Ishizuka, A. Sattar (Eds.), PRICAI 2002: Trends in Artificial Intelligence. Proceedings, 2002. XX, 623 pages. 2002. (Subseries LNAI).

Vol. 2418: D. Wells, L. Williams (Eds.), Extreme Programming and Agile Methods – XP/Agile Universe 2002. Proceedings, 2002. XII, 292 pages. 2002.

Vol. 2419: X. Meng, J. Su, Y. Wang (Eds.), Advances in Web-Age Information Management. Proceedings, 2002. XV, 446 pages. 2002.

Vol. 2420: K. Diks, W. Rytter (Eds.), Mathematical Foundations of Computer Science 2002. Proceedings, 2002. XII, 652 pages. 2002.

Vol. 2421: L. Brim, P. Jancar, M. Krstinsky, A. Kucera (Eds.), CONCUR 2002 – Concurrency Theory. Proceedings, 2002. XII, 611 pages. 2002.

Vol. 2423: D. Lopresti, J. Hu, R. Kashi (Eds.), Document Analysis Systems V. Proceedings, 2002. XIII, 570 pages. 2002.

Vol. 2430: T. Elomaa, H. Mannila, H. Toivonen (Eds.), Machine Learning: ECML 2002. Proceedings, 2002. XIII, 532 pages. 2002. (Subseries LNAI).

Vol. 2431: T. Elomaa, H. Mannila, H. Toivonen (Eds.), Principles of Data Mining and Knowledge Discovery. Proceedings, 2002. XIV, 514 pages. 2002. (Subseries LNAI).

Vol. 2436: J. Fong, R.C.T. Cheung, H.V. Leong, Q. Li (Eds.), Advances in Web-Based Learning. Proceedings, 2002. XIII, 434 pages. 2002.

Vol. 2442: M. Yung (Ed.), Advances in Cryptology – CRYPTO 2002. Proceedings, 2002. XIV, 627 pages. 2002.